Lecture Notes in Computer Science 10283

Commenced Publication in 1973
Founding and Former Series Editors:
Gerhard Goos, Juris Hartmanis, and Jan van Leeuwen

More information about this series at http://www.springer.com/series/7409

Gabriele Meiselwitz (Ed.)

Social Computing and Social Media

Applications and Analytics

9th International Conference, SCSM 2017
Held as Part of HCI International 2017
Vancouver, BC, Canada, July 9–14, 2017
Proceedings, Part II

 Springer

Editor
Gabriele Meiselwitz
Towson University
Towson, MD
USA

ISSN 0302-9743   ISSN 1611-3349   (electronic)
Lecture Notes in Computer Science
ISBN 978-3-319-58561-1   ISBN 978-3-319-58562-8   (eBook)
DOI 10.1007/978-3-319-58562-8

Library of Congress Control Number: 2017939728

LNCS Sublibrary: SL3 – Information Systems and Applications, incl. Internet/Web, and HCI

Printed on acid-free paper

This Springer imprint is published by Springer Nature
The registered company is Springer International Publishing AG
The registered company address is: Gewerbestrasse 11, 6330 Cham, Switzerland

Foreword

The 19th International Conference on Human–Computer Interaction, HCI International 2017, was held in Vancouver, Canada, during July 9–14, 2017. The event incorporated the 15 conferences/thematic areas listed on the following page.

A total of 4,340 individuals from academia, research institutes, industry, and governmental agencies from 70 countries submitted contributions, and 1,228 papers have been included in the proceedings. These papers address the latest research and development efforts and highlight the human aspects of design and use of computing systems. The papers thoroughly cover the entire field of human–computer interaction, addressing major advances in knowledge and effective use of computers in a variety of application areas. The volumes constituting the full set of the conference proceedings are listed on the following pages.

I would like to thank the program board chairs and the members of the program boards of all thematic areas and affiliated conferences for their contribution to the highest scientific quality and the overall success of the HCI International 2017 conference.

This conference would not have been possible without the continuous and unwavering support and advice of the founder, Conference General Chair Emeritus and Conference Scientific Advisor Prof. Gavriel Salvendy. For his outstanding efforts, I would like to express my appreciation to the communications chair and editor of *HCI International News*, Dr. Abbas Moallem.

April 2017   Constantine Stephanidis

HCI International 2017 Thematic Areas and Affiliated Conferences

Thematic areas:

- Human–Computer Interaction (HCI 2017)
- Human Interface and the Management of Information (HIMI 2017)

Affiliated conferences:

- 17th International Conference on Engineering Psychology and Cognitive Ergonomics (EPCE 2017)
- 11th International Conference on Universal Access in Human–Computer Interaction (UAHCI 2017)
- 9th International Conference on Virtual, Augmented and Mixed Reality (VAMR 2017)
- 9th International Conference on Cross-Cultural Design (CCD 2017)
- 9th International Conference on Social Computing and Social Media (SCSM 2017)
- 11th International Conference on Augmented Cognition (AC 2017)
- 8th International Conference on Digital Human Modeling and Applications in Health, Safety, Ergonomics and Risk Management (DHM 2017)
- 6th International Conference on Design, User Experience and Usability (DUXU 2017)
- 5th International Conference on Distributed, Ambient and Pervasive Interactions (DAPI 2017)
- 5th International Conference on Human Aspects of Information Security, Privacy and Trust (HAS 2017)
- 4th International Conference on HCI in Business, Government and Organizations (HCIBGO 2017)
- 4th International Conference on Learning and Collaboration Technologies (LCT 2017)
- Third International Conference on Human Aspects of IT for the Aged Population (ITAP 2017)

Conference Proceedings Volumes Full List

1. LNCS 10271, Human–Computer Interaction: User Interface Design, Development and Multimodality (Part I), edited by Masaaki Kurosu
2. LNCS 10272 Human–Computer Interaction: Interaction Contexts (Part II), edited by Masaaki Kurosu
3. LNCS 10273, Human Interface and the Management of Information: Information, Knowledge and Interaction Design (Part I), edited by Sakae Yamamoto
4. LNCS 10274, Human Interface and the Management of Information: Supporting Learning, Decision-Making and Collaboration (Part II), edited by Sakae Yamamoto
5. LNAI 10275, Engineering Psychology and Cognitive Ergonomics: Performance, Emotion and Situation Awareness (Part I), edited by Don Harris
6. LNAI 10276, Engineering Psychology and Cognitive Ergonomics: Cognition and Design (Part II), edited by Don Harris
7. LNCS 10277, Universal Access in Human–Computer Interaction: Design and Development Approaches and Methods (Part I), edited by Margherita Antona and Constantine Stephanidis
8. LNCS 10278, Universal Access in Human–Computer Interaction: Designing Novel Interactions (Part II), edited by Margherita Antona and Constantine Stephanidis
9. LNCS 10279, Universal Access in Human–Computer Interaction: Human and Technological Environments (Part III), edited by Margherita Antona and Constantine Stephanidis
10. LNCS 10280, Virtual, Augmented and Mixed Reality, edited by Stephanie Lackey and Jessie Y.C. Chen
11. LNCS 10281, Cross-Cultural Design, edited by Pei-Luen Patrick Rau
12. LNCS 10282, Social Computing and Social Media: Human Behavior (Part I), edited by Gabriele Meiselwitz
13. LNCS 10283, Social Computing and Social Media: Applications and Analytics (Part II), edited by Gabriele Meiselwitz
14. LNAI 10284, Augmented Cognition: Neurocognition and Machine Learning (Part I), edited by Dylan D. Schmorrow and Cali M. Fidopiastis
15. LNAI 10285, Augmented Cognition: Enhancing Cognition and Behavior in Complex Human Environments (Part II), edited by Dylan D. Schmorrow and Cali M. Fidopiastis
16. LNCS 10286, Digital Human Modeling and Applications in Health, Safety, Ergonomics and Risk Management: Ergonomics and Design (Part I), edited by Vincent G. Duffy
17. LNCS 10287, Digital Human Modeling and Applications in Health, Safety, Ergonomics and Risk Management: Health and Safety (Part II), edited by Vincent G. Duffy
18. LNCS 10288, Design, User Experience, and Usability: Theory, Methodology and Management (Part I), edited by Aaron Marcus and Wentao Wang

19. LNCS 10289, Design, User Experience, and Usability: Designing Pleasurable Experiences (Part II), edited by Aaron Marcus and Wentao Wang
20. LNCS 10290, Design, User Experience, and Usability: Understanding Users and Contexts (Part III), edited by Aaron Marcus and Wentao Wang
21. LNCS 10291, Distributed, Ambient and Pervasive Interactions, edited by Norbert Streitz and Panos Markopoulos
22. LNCS 10292, Human Aspects of Information Security, Privacy and Trust, edited by Theo Tryfonas
23. LNCS 10293, HCI in Business, Government and Organizations: Interacting with Information Systems (Part I), edited by Fiona Fui-Hoon Nah and Chuan-Hoo Tan
24. LNCS 10294, HCI in Business, Government and Organizations: Supporting Business (Part II), edited by Fiona Fui-Hoon Nah and Chuan-Hoo Tan
25. LNCS 10295, Learning and Collaboration Technologies: Novel Learning Ecosystems (Part I), edited by Panayiotis Zaphiris and Andri Ioannou
26. LNCS 10296, Learning and Collaboration Technologies: Technology in Education (Part II), edited by Panayiotis Zaphiris and Andri Ioannou
27. LNCS 10297, Human Aspects of IT for the Aged Population: Aging, Design and User Experience (Part I), edited by Jia Zhou and Gavriel Salvendy
28. LNCS 10298, Human Aspects of IT for the Aged Population: Applications, Services and Contexts (Part II), edited by Jia Zhou and Gavriel Salvendy
29. CCIS 713, HCI International 2017 Posters Proceedings (Part I), edited by Constantine Stephanidis
30. CCIS 714, HCI International 2017 Posters Proceedings (Part II), edited by Constantine Stephanidis

Social Computing and Social Media

Program Board Chair(s): **Gabriele Meiselwitz, USA**

- Rocio Abascal Mena, Mexico
- Sarah Omar AlHumoud, Saudi Arabia
- Areej Al-Wabil, Saudi Arabia
- James Braman, USA
- Cesar Collazos, Colombia
- Habib Fardoun, Saudi Arabia
- Cristóbal Fernández Robin, Chile
- Panagiotis Germanakos, Cyprus
- Carina S. Gonzalez Gonzales, Spain
- Sara Hook, USA
- Ali Shariq Imran, Norway
- Rushed Kanawati, France
- Tomas Kincl, Czech Republic
- Styliani Kleanthous, Cyprus
- Carsten Kleiner, Germany
- Niki Lambropoulos, Greece
- Soo Ling Lim, UK
- Fernando Loizides, UK
- Hoang Nguyen, Singapore
- Anthony Norcio, USA
- Elaine Raybourn, USA
- Christian Rusu, Chile
- Christian Scheiner, Germany
- Stefan Stieglitz, Germany
- Giovanni Vincenti, USA
- José Viterbo Filho, Brazil
- Evgenios Vlachos, Denmark
- Yuanqiong (Kathy) Wang, USA
- June Wei, USA
- Brian Wentz, USA

The full list with the Program Board Chairs and the members of the Program Boards of all thematic areas and affiliated conferences is available online at:

http://www.hci.international/board-members-2017.php

HCI International 2018

The 20th International Conference on Human–Computer Interaction, HCI International 2018, will be held jointly with the affiliated conferences in Las Vegas, NV, USA, at Caesars Palace, July 15–20, 2018. It will cover a broad spectrum of themes related to human–computer interaction, including theoretical issues, methods, tools, processes, and case studies in HCI design, as well as novel interaction techniques, interfaces, and applications. The proceedings will be published by Springer. More information is available on the conference website: http://2018.hci.international/.

General Chair
Prof. Constantine Stephanidis
University of Crete and ICS-FORTH
Heraklion, Crete, Greece
E-mail: general_chair@hcii2018.org

http://2018.hci.international/

Contents – Part II

Social Media for Communication, Learning and Aging

Strategies for Communicating Reputation Mechanisms
in Crowdsourcing-Based Applications 3
  Orlando Afonso, Luciana Salgado, and José Viterbo

Collaboration Increase Through Monitoring and Evaluation
Mechanisms of the Collaborative Learning Process 20
  Vanessa Agredo Delgado, Cesar A. Collazos, Habib M. Fardoun,
  and Nehme Safa

ADMemento: A Prototype of Activity Reminder and Assessment Tools
for Patients with Alzheimer's Disease 32
  Sarah Alhassan, Wafa Alrajhi, Amal Alhassan, and Alreem Almuhrij

From GreedEx to GreedEx Tab v2.0: Tool for Learning Greedy Algorithms
on iPad Following CIAM Mobile Methodology 44
  Yoel Arroyo, Manuel Ortega Cordovilla, Miguel A. Redondo,
  Ana I. Molina, María del Carmen Lacave, and Manuel Ortega Cantero

Memorializing the Deceased Using Virtual Worlds: A Preliminary Study 55
  James Braman, Alfreda Dudley, and Giovanni Vincenti

Social Media and Elderly People: Research Trends 65
  Mayela Coto, Fulvio Lizano, Sonia Mora, and Jennifer Fuentes

WhatsApp 82
  Cristóbal Fernández Robin, Scott McCoy, and Diego Yáñez

An Analysis of Online Discussion Platforms for Academic
Deliberation Support 91
  Fabrício Matheus Gonçalves, Emanuel Felipe Duarte,
  Julio Cesar dos Reis, and M. Cecília C. Baranauskas

Design of Digital Literacy Environments Based-On Interactive
Learning Services 110
  Jaime Muñoz Arteaga, José Eder Guzmán Mendoza,
  Fco. Javier Álvarez Rodríguez, and René Santaolaya Salgado

Building up a Verified Page on Facebook Using Information
Transparency Guidelines 125
  Alexandre Pinheiro, Claudia Cappelli, and Cristiano Maciel

An MDA Approach to Develop Language-Learning Activities   138
    Gabriel Sebastián, Ricardo Tesoriero, Jose A. Gallud,
    and Habib M. Fardoun

Designing an Electronic Hand Glove for Teaching Vowels
to Deaf Children   148
    Julián Sotelo, Jaime Duque, Andrés Solano, and Sandra Cano

Chat-Based Application to Support CSCL Activities   161
    Ricardo Tesoriero, Habib M. Fardoun, and Hachem Awada

Toward a Supporting System of Communication Skill: The Influence
of Functional Roles of Participants in Group Discussion   178
    Qi Zhang, Hung-Hsuan Huang, Seiya Kimura, Shogo Okada,
    Yuki Hayashi, Yutaka Takase, Yukiko Nakano, Naoki Ohta,
    and Kazuhiro Kuwabara

Opinion Mining and Sentiment Analysis

Sentiment Analysis on Arabic Tweets: Challenges to Dissecting
the Language   191
    Malak Abdullah and Mirsad Hadzikadic

Analyzing User Experience Through Web Opinion Mining   203
    Silvana Aciar and Gabriela Aciar

A Review on Corpus Annotation for Arabic Sentiment Analysis   215
    Latifah Almuqren, Arwa Alzammam, Shahad Alotaibi,
    Alexandra Cristea, and Sarah Alhumoud

AraSenTi-Lexicon: A Different Approach   226
    Hadeel AlNegheimish, Jowharah Alshobaili, Nora AlMansour,
    Rawan Bin Shiha, Nora AlTwairesh, and Sarah Alhumoud

Investigating the Relationship Between Trust and Sentiment Agreement
in Arab Twitter Users   236
    Areeb Alowisheq, Nora Alrajebah, Asma Alrumikhani,
    Ghadeer Al-Shamrani, Maha Shaabi, Muneera Al-Nufaisi,
    Ahad Alnasser, and Sarah Alhumoud

Investigating the Polarity of User Postings in a Social System   246
    Afonso M.S. Lima, Paloma B.S. Silva, Lívia A. Cruz,
    and Marilia S. Mendes

Intent Classification of Social Media Texts with Machine Learning
for Customer Service Improvement   258
    Sebastián Pérez-Vera, Rodrigo Alfaro, and Héctor Allende-Cid

Sentiment Analysis for Micro-blogging Platforms in Arabic 275
  Eshrag Refaee

Automatic Tweets Classification Under an Intelligent Agents Framework. . . . 295
  Sebastián Rodríguez, Rodrigo Alfaro, Héctor Allende-Cid,
  and Claudio Cubillos

User Experiences Around Sentiment Analyses, Facilitating
Workplace Learning 312
  Christian Voigt, Barbara Kieslinger, and Teresa Schäfer

Social Data and Analytics

Visual Exploration of Urban Data: A Study of Riyadh Taxi Data 327
  Aljoharah Alfayez and Salma Aldawood

Understanding Gendered Spaces Using Social Media Data 338
  Aljoharah Alfayez, Zeyad Awwad, Cortni Kerr, Najat Alrashed,
  Sarah Williams, and Areej Al-Wabil

Visual Exploration Patterns in Information Visualizations: Insights
from Eye Tracking 357
  Jumana Almahmoud, Saleh Albeaik, Tarfah Alrashed,
  and Almaha Almalki

The Rise of Hackathon-Led Innovation in the MENA Region: Visualizing
Spatial and Temporal Dynamics of Time-Bounded Events 367
  Sitah Almishari, Nora Salamah, Maram Alwan, Nada Alkhalifa,
  and Areej Al-Wabil

How Visual Analytics Unlock Insights into Traffic Incidents
in Urban Areas 378
  Abdullah Alomar, Najat Alrashed, Isra Alturaiki, and Hotham Altwaijry

SparQs: Visual Analytics for Sparking Creativity in Social
Media Exploration. 394
  Nan-Chen Chen, Michael Brooks, Rafal Kocielnik, Sungsoo (Ray) Hong,
  Jeff Smith, Sanny Lin, Zening Qu, and Cecilia Aragon

Social Networks Serendipity for Educational Learning by Surprise
from Big and Small Data Analysis 406
  Niki Lambropoulos, Habib M. Fardoun, and Daniyal M. Alghazzawi

What People Do on Yik Yak: Analyzing Anonymous Microblogging
User Behaviors 416
  Joon-Suk Lee, Seungwon Yang, Amanda L. Munson, and Lusene Donzo

BLE-Based Children's Social Behavior Analysis System
for Crime Prevention   429
    Shuta Nakamae, Shumpei Kataoka, Can Tang, Yue Pu,
    Simona Vasilache, Satoshi Saga, Buntarou Shizuki, and Shin Takahashi

Unified Structured Framework for mHealth Analytics:
Building an Open and Collaborative Community   440
    Hoang D. Nguyen and Danny Chiang Choon Poo

Discovering Subway Design Opportunities Using Social Network Data:
The Image-Need-Design Opportunity Model   451
    Tianjiao Zhao, Kin Wai Michael Siu, and Han Sun

Author Index   467

Contents – Part I

User Experience and Behavior in Social Media

Investigating Arab DHH Usage of YouTube Videos Using Latent Variables
in an Acceptance Technology Model   3
  Lamia Abdul Aziz Bin Husainan, Hanan Ali AL-Shehri,
  and Muna Al-Razgan

Can the Success of Mobile Games Be Attributed to Following Mobile
Game Heuristics?   13
  Reham Alhaidary and Shatha Altammami

The Collective Impression of Saudis' Perceptions of Entertainment   22
  Noura Alomar and Alaa Alhumaisan

Getting Interrupted? Design Support Strategies for Learning Success
in M-Learning Applications   32
  Upasna Bhandari and Klarissa Chang

World of Streaming. Motivation and Gratification on Twitch   44
  Daniel Gros, Brigitta Wanner, Anna Hackenholt, Piotr Zawadzki,
  and Kathrin Knautz

Do Members Share Knowledge in Facebook Knowledge Groups?   58
  Li-Ting Huang and Ming-Yang Lu

Assessing Symptoms of Excessive SNS Usage Based on User Behavior
and Emotion: Analysis of Data Obtained by SNS APIs   71
  Ploypailin Intapong, Saromporn Charoenpit, Tiranee Achalakul,
  and Michiko Ohkura

Research on the Social Experience of Mobile Internet Products.   84
  Tian Lei and Sijia Zhang

The Impact of Texting Interruptions on Task Performance   94
  Scott McCoy, Eleanor Loiacono, and Shiya Cao

Improving Engagement Metrics in an Open Collaboration Community
Through Notification: An Online Field Experiment   103
  Ana Paula O. Bertholdo, Claudia de O. Melo, and Artur S. Rozestraten

What Happens When Evaluating Social Media's Usability?   117
  Virginica Rusu, Cristian Rusu, Daniela Quiñones, Silvana Roncagliolo,
  and César A. Collazos

On User eXperience in Virtual Museums   127
    Cristian Rusu, Virginia Zaraza Rusu, Patricia Muñoz, Virginica Rusu,
    Silvana Roncagliolo, and Daniela Quiñones

Customer Behavior and Social Media

Why Social Media Is an Achilles Heel? A Multi-dimensional Perspective
on Engaged Consumers and Entrepreneurs   139
    Adela Coman, Ana-Maria Grigore, and Oana Simona Caraman Hudea

The Influence of Privacy, Trust, and National Culture
on Internet Transactions   159
    Jon Heales, Sophie Cockcroft, and Van-Hau Trieu

Analysis of Trade Area for Retail Industry Store Using Consumer
Purchase Record   177
    Sachiko Iwasaki, Ko Hashimoto, Kohei Otake, and Takashi Namatame

From Bowling to Pinball: Understanding How Social Media Changes
the Generation of Value for Consumers and Companies   190
    Marc Oliver Opresnik

Online Travel Agencies as Social Media: Analyzing Customers' Opinions . . .   200
    Virginica Rusu, Cristian Rusu, Daniel Guzmán, Silvana Roncagliolo,
    and Daniela Quiñones

Analysis of Cancellation Factors Based on the Characteristics
of Golf Courses in Reservation Sites   210
    Naoya Saijo, Kohei Otake, and Takashi Namatame

Analysis of the Characteristics of Repeat Customer in a Golf EC Site   223
    Yusuke Sato, Kohei Otake, and Takashi Namatame

Video Blogs: A Qualitative and Quantitative Inquiry of Recall
and Willingness to Share   234
    Purvi Shah, Eleanor T. Loiacono, and Huimin Ren

Valuation of Customer and Purchase Behavior of a Supermarket Chain
Using ID-POS and Store Causal Data   244
    Syun Usami, Kohei Otake, and Takashi Namatame

Promoting Technological Innovations: Towards an Integration
of Traditional and Social Media Communication Channels   256
    Timm F. Wagner

Understanding the Gift-Sending Interaction on Live-Streaming
Video Websites   274
    Zhenhui Zhu, Zhi Yang, and Yafei Dai

Social Issues in Social Media

Creating and Supporting Virtual Communities: A City that Happens
on a Facebook Group   289
   Andre O. Bueno and Junia C. Anacleto

Examining the Legal Consequences of Improper Use of Social Media Sites
in the Workplace.   307
   Alfreda Dudley and Davian Johnson

Inter-country Differences in Breaking News Coverage via Microblogging:
Reporting on Terrorist Attacks in Europe from the USA,
Germany and UK   317
   Kaja J. Fietkiewicz and Aylin Ilhan

e-Voting in America: Current Realities and Future Directions   337
   Nathan Johnson, Brian M. Jones, and Kyle Clendenon

Entrepreneurial Orientation and Open Innovation: Social Media as a Tool . . .   350
   Claudia Linde

For Those About to Rock – Social Media Best Practices from Wacken
Open Air   362
   Christian W. Scheiner and Nick Hüper

Do Social Bots (Still) Act Different to Humans? – Comparing Metrics
of Social Bots with Those of Humans   379
   Stefan Stieglitz, Florian Brachten, Davina Berthelé, Mira Schlaus,
   Chrissoula Venetopoulou, and Daniel Veutgen

A Twitter Analysis of an Integrated E-Activism Campaign:
#FeesMustFall - A South African Case Study   396
   Abraham G. van der Vyver

Author Index   411

Social Media for Communication, Learning and Aging

Strategies for Communicating Reputation Mechanisms in Crowdsourcing-Based Applications

Orlando Afonso[✉], Luciana Salgado[✉], and José Viterbo[✉]

Department of Computer Science, Fluminense Federal University (UFF), Niteroi, Brazil
{oafonso,luciana,viterbo}@ic.uff.br

Abstract. With the emergence of crowdsourcing-based applications – those systems that make intensive use of information provided voluntarily by a crowd of generally unknown users - the participation of end users in digital content generation has been increasing continuously. This scenario, thus, allow users to move from consumers to producers of information, and vice versa. Therefore, some criteria is needed and used (by the application and end-users) to decide and classify whether some content provided by any other user is realiable or not. In the real world, the current or historical people's good reputation usually ensures a high degree of reliability of the information and data received from them. Our work, in turn, aimed at exploring reputation Mechanisms in two Crowdsourcing-Based Applications contexts. Firstly, we studied the strategies used by the applications to identify, ensure and communicate to end users, the degree of reliability of users-generated content. Second, we explored, empirically, how users interpret and understand those strategies. This paper presents the results of the studies and the potential influences to human-computer interaction.

Keywords: Mobile social computing and social media · Crowdsourcing · Semiotic engineering · Human-computer interaction · Reputation

1   Introduction

We live in a connected and information-driven world. The Internet is widely used across the globe on diverse communication devices and in many different forms. Internet users are able to look for news about their favorite sports, the city they live and about other people. In addition, users may see information about weather forecast, traffic conditions, and the best hotel to stay in a trip. Besides all these tasks, ordinary users become more active on Web. Now, users play another role by generating content to the Web applications. Many applications, sites and social networks have as main information source, data from their users, who is not always conscious about that. [3, 18, 21].

The easy access to the user-generated content brings many benefits, but great challenges, as well. One of those refers to digital producers' reputation, because the content produced by them become useful information to the final users of an application. As related by [17], reputation is commonly defined as the quantity of trust inspired by a specific community member in a specific environment. Community members with good

© Springer International Publishing AG 2017
G. Meiselwitz (Ed.): SCSM 2017, Part II, LNCS 10283, pp. 3–19, 2017.
DOI: 10.1007/978-3-319-58562-8_1

reputation are more influent, because their contributions to the community. On the other hand, users with bad reputation are gradually excluded from the community.

The reputation of a person or a group of people is totally linked to the judgment background. For instance, a renowned physician can have a great reputation in relation to treatment methods of a disease; however, he could present a bad reputation in computer science community.

The concept of reputation is common in many areas of activity. When the subject is Science or academic area, e.g., reputation represents an important attribute to evaluate the quality of publications and career of scientists, researchers etc. To contract someone to work in a company, it is very common to look for the past actions and activities of that person. Therefore, reputation can be associated to the decision-making process about something or someone that depends on the actions (or content provided by) of someone in a period.

In Computer Science, reputation is a subject that is present in different areas of knowledge, e.g., Recommender Systems, Collaborative Systems, Human-Computer Interaction, Wireless Sensor Networks etc. Mui and co-authors [19] treats reputation in environments as eBay[1], where reputation is calculated accordingly to the positive or negative classifications about a seller, in a specific period of time (weeks, months, years, etc.). For online auction systems, for example, the reputation of a seller can be considered as a guarantee of product receiving.

Nowadays, there are many applications to solve real-life problems, which have as main characteristic the participation of a group of people congregated to reach a specific goal, namely, crowdsourcing-based applications. From data posted or automatic generated by other users, it is possible to estimate the delay of a bus, to know preferences of people, to help in scientific researches, etc.

However, we must face up to the new challenges arising in this context. For instance, how to attribute/calculate/classify something as reliable? The challenge becomes bigger when there is huge volume of information-generated day-by-day and from a large number of different digital producers. In many cases, the context of use of an app demands a fast response time to make a decision, so, the question around this is: which trust resources are offered to final users to support conscious decisions to reach their objectives?

In crowdsourcing-based apps, a lot of information is provided in a short period of time and in many domains [14]. Crowdsourcing represents an open call to the crowd to solve a problem or to perform some tasks in exchange for payment, social recognition or entertainment. Wexler [25] defines crowdsourcing as a concept related to a group of people who do not necessarily know each other personally and have a weak relationship link, involved in favor of an activity.

Other authors [12] consider an integrated definition of crowdsourcing, based on many works and researches about this topic. So, crowdsourcing refers to a kind of online participatory activity, in which a person, organization or company with sufficient means, proposes to a heterogeneous group, of varied knowledge and experiences, through a

---

[1] http://www.ebay.com/.

flexible open call, the voluntary commitment of a task. With this, the commitment of these tasks always implies mutual benefits.

This paper presents the results of a study to explore and characterize the strategies (adopted by this kind of applications) to communicate reputation mechanisms and how these mechanisms are perceived by users, investigating, thus, their communicability, with the lenses of Semiotic Engineering theory [8]. We present and discuss the results of a qualitative study [5], using a mix of methods: The Semiotic Inspection Method [10] and Observation Method. Our main findings are a common set of strategies to communicate reputation mechanisms and their respective fragilities.

This paper has been divided as follows. In Sect. 2 we present our theoretical foundation. In Sect. 3, we present an overview of some related work in HCI. The Sect. 4 presents more details about our methodology and the Sect. 5 presents the studies and the results founded by them. Finally, we discuss and conclude our results in Sect. 6.

2   Theoretical Foundation

2.1   Semiotic Engineering

In this study, we used Semiotic Engineering [7] as our theoretical framework. Semiotic Engineering is a semiotic theory of HCI, in which the interactive systems and the human-computer interaction are seen as a special case of metacommunication from designers to users. To this theory, the interface represents the main point of communication between designers and users, acting as designer's deputy, since the designer is not present, physically, next to the user at interaction time [23]. The computer-mediated communication between designers and users communicates the designers' understanding of who the users are, what they know the users want or need to do, in which preferred ways, and why.

Semiotic is a discipline dedicated to the study of signs and how they are used in communicative processes [8]. By the studies of Charles Sanders Peirce [20], sign is anything that represents something to someone. Thus, it can be an object, symbol, word, draw, icon etc. that represents and transmits some information to someone. As reported by [10], some of the most frequent signs in computer systems are: images, words, colors, dialog structures, layouts, among others. Each sign used in the application's interface may have different meanings to different users.

In the perspective of Semiotic Engineering, the main quality factor is the communicability, i.e., the property of a system to effectively and efficiently transmit the intentions and principles that guided its design [23]. When the user is not able to comprehend the message intended by the designer, then communication breakdowns may take place at interaction.

2.2   Semiotic Inspection Method

In this research, we used the Semiotic Inspection Method (SIM), a Semiotic Engineering tool for HCI evaluation. With this method, the evaluators can analyze the communicability of the interactive artifacts [10]. The focus is to inspect the designer-to-user metacommunication aiming at identifying the potential communication breakdowns. In the evaluation process, the evaluator examines the interface and classify the signs as metalinguistic, static or dynamic.

Metalinguistic signs are the first one to be analyzed, since they explicitly express and explain other parts of the designer's metacommunication. This class of signs is usually found throughout the interface in instructions, explanations, warnings and error messages, focusing on online help, user manuals and system propagation materials [10].

Static signs are those that communicate their meaning regardless of cause and effect relationships and can be interpreted from snapshot portraits of the screen. Thus, they express the state of the system at a given moment. They are represented by the elements present in the interface screens (or equivalents in non-visual interfaces), such as labels, images, text boxes, buttons, menus, etc., as well as layout, size, color, font and other char-acteristics. Its analysis should consider only the interface elements presented in each screen at an instant of time, without examining the behavior of the system, nor the temporal and causal relations between interface elements [10].

As for the dynamic signs, [10] show that in the analysis, the evaluator must inspect the interaction process that the user can experience through the interface. These signs are perceived through changes in the interface that communicate to the user the behavior of the system as a result of user actions (clicking the mouse, pressing enter, changing the focus from a form field to another, etc.), by external events (receiving an email, Internet connec-tion fails, etc.) or over the time. Dynamic signs are usually represented by animations, opening and closing dialogs, transitions between screens or modifications to the elements of a screen (for example, enabling a button, updating a text or image, modifying the layout of some interface elements, etc.).

In order to inspect the interface, the SIM proposes 5 steps to be followed by the eval-uator [23]. In the first three steps, the main goal is to rebuild the designer's metacommu-nication, by using the following template of the designer's metacommunication [23] for each category of signs (metalinguistic, static and dynamic): *"Here is my understanding, of who you are, what I've learned you want or need to do, in which preferred ways, and why. This is the system that I have therefore designed for you, and this is the way you can or should use it in order to fulfill a range of purposes that fall within this version"*.

Step 1: Metalinguistic signs inspection. At this stage, the evaluator explores the documentation and help system

Step 2: Static signs inspection. At this stage, the evaluator inspects the static signs of the interface

Step 3: Dynamic signs Inspection. At this stage, the evaluator inspects the signs that emerge from the interaction

Step 4: In this stage, the evaluator contrasts and compares the metacommunication messages from steps 1, 2 and 3. In this step, the evaluator must register the inconsis-tencies and potential problematic interpretations that may take place at interaction time by the users

Step 5: Appreciating the quality of the metacommunication, in this step, the evaluator produces a report containing the communicability problems found that might frustrate or prevent the user to understand the intended message by the designer, affecting their productivity

In this method, the evaluator is the user's advocate. Thus, it takes the role of the user and represents it interacting with the system in order to represent it.

The SIM can be applied for technical or scientific purposes. When used for research purposes, a step should be added to its execution: the triangulation of the results [10].

3   Related Works

Tausczik and Pennebaker [24] consider that there are two perspectives on the role of reputation in online collaborative projects. The user's reputation should be minimized to promote engagement by increasing the number of contributions and the reputation of a digital producer can be a good feature for the quality of his contributions and it may become easier to find high quality content. The study examined how users' offline and online reputation affect perceived quality in an online community called MathOver-Flow[2] where members post high-level Math questions. For the research, the authors used the following method: information about registered users combined with registered behavior collected in the community. The users could vote about the quality of a question or an answer posted based on interesting or its innovation. For each author of a question or answer, different reputation measures were collected such as offline reputation and number of points in the online community. The study shows that past activities also represents a good measure of reputation which can be correlated with the quality of a post. In our work, the correlation between offline user's reputation and quality of content was not identified.

De Paoli and co-authors [6] present a design experience to create badges and named levels as mechanisms for representing the reputation in an online community. The badge is a symbol, a representative object of an abstract idea, for example: seals that represent the level of knowledge of a collaborator. Named levels are representations in text format that indicate the level of a participant. In many applications, when the users perform certain tasks, they reach higher levels. The badges and the named levels have been used as reputation mechanisms on various social networks, crowdsourcing-based applications to promote the users' engagement. Another point reported in the study is that, many users bring experiences about the use of such features from other platforms and sites, being necessary to consider this question on design time. The badges were identified in our study, representing a strategy to communicate reputation.

Bente and co-authors [2], in turn, address the issue of reputation, reliability and use of avatars in e-commerce to reduce uncertainty in online buying and selling relationships. However, the study focuses whether these found mechanisms designed for Western culture also apply to other cultures. For this, the authors compared the buying decisions of Arab and German participants in an experimental game of confidence. The study points out that reputation systems based on profile scoring can influence trust by attributing trustworthiness to the sellers, regardless of culture. Our work does not cover questions related to cultural factors, but we also identified photos and avatars as strategies to communicate reputation.

---

[2] http://mathoverflow.net/.

Woodruff [26] presents a qualitative study of how users manage their online reputation. The study is about users who bother with their online information and how they do it to recover from defamation and damage to their reputation. In this case, it involves the concept of offline reputation, that means how the information in the virtual world affects people's lives and how to recover from that situation. In the most of results, the users were not able to repair well the problems that affected their reputation. This last contribution indicates that this topic deserves special attention from HCI area, motivating researches to create technological, social and legal mechanisms to prevent such damage.

Coetzee and colleagues [4] studied how design affects the participation and engagement of students in an online course. For this, they created a reputation system where students who created more useful posts earned a score. The study demonstrates how reputation systems lead to faster response times, increasing the number of comments per post and bring differences in the way of students ask questions, even though they don't have an immediate effect on school performance. The score mechanism is also studied in our paper, being one of the strategies to communicate reputation.

Pinheiro and co-authors [22] address the problem of the huge volume of data generated in social networks, the sharing of unreliable information and the availability of content generated to confuse or deceive users. This study presents a solution to add auditing capacity to social networks, based on a catalog that organizes characteristics, besides suggesting a guide for the engineering of software with the reliability feature. The auditing capacity is a necessary issue to increase the quality of the information available in an environment. Therefore, the reputation systems' communicability is a very important issue.

Luca and Zervas [18] discuss the problem of fraud by companies, creating false comments for themselves or their competitors, identifying some aspects in common and the motivations behind these actions by analyzing the economic or financial view. For this, the authors analyzed reviews of restaurants that were identified by Yelp[3]'s algorithm as suspect or fake. For the accomplishment of the studies the authors made empirical studies creating mathematical models for validation of the results. In the study, the authors identified that 16% of restaurants reviews on Yelp are filtered. With this, tend to be extreme (favorable or unfavorable) and the prevalence of suspicious comments has grown over time. A restaurant is more likely to commit fraud when its reputation is weak, when it receives comments or negative reviews. In which case, such fraud could happen by creating fake profiles to include positive comments about the restaurant or to defame competition. In addition, restaurant chains are less likely to commit fraud, according to the study. Our empirical studies identified strategies to communicate bad reputation and to confirm an information, thus, preventing fraud questions.

Josang and co-authors [17] provide an overview of existing reputation systems and proposals that can be used to generate reliability and reputation measures for Internet transactions. The authors define two types of reputation systems: centralized and distributed. In the centralized system, information about the performance of a particular user is collected as evaluations of other community members who have had direct experience with that participant. So, the central authority collects all the evaluations about a user and derives a reputation score for each participant and makes that score available to the

---

[3] https:www.yelp.com.

community. In the distributed reputation system, there is no central place for submitting reviews or for scoring other users. This may be done indirectly, when the users receive information from other users and evaluate them individually about the digital producer's reputation. The work presents mechanisms of reputation used by some sites too.

4 Methodology

The methodology used in this work follows a non-predictive paradigm and makes use of interpretative and qualitative methods [5, 11]. In order to find out the strategies to communicate reputation mechanisms and how users perceive them, i.e., the communicability, we conducted two empirical studies, which contributed to a broader study (see Fig. 1). We selected the mobile applications Waze[4] and TripAdvisor[5]. Waze addresses traffic-related issues, displaying alerts and other traffic features, reported by its users and TripAdvisor aims to help with travel planning through comments and user reviews on some place, such as hotel, a restaurant etc. Any other application based on crowdsourcing could be used in this study, but it was preferred to adopt smartphone applications, with a context of use where decisions about the information visualized should be taken in a faster way. The versions used in the studies was Waze, 4.7.0.1 version, Android[6] platform and for TripAdvisor application, the 17.8 version and Android.

First, we conduct a study (S1), in Waze app to understand how it communicates reputation mechanisms. In the first step (Step 1), we ran the semiotic inspection, where there is no users' participation. We focused on understanding the *emission* of such mechanisms. In the second step (Step 2), we ran observations tests with users to identify how the message was understood by them. We focused on understanding the *reception* of such mechanisms by the users. After these two steps, we arrived at the results founded by contrasting the two parts (Results S1) [1].

Then, we conducted a second Study (S2), using the same steps of S1, but in a different domain. We arrive at results in this second Study (Results S2), by contrasting the *emission* and *reception* of reputation mechanisms, following the same methodology.

In the Step 3, we compare both studies and identify common and divergent meaning categories, searching the communicative strategies adopted by them (Comparison between S1 and S2 – Step 3 (S3)). We, thus, drew our conclusions based on the set of categorized meanings that guided the interpretation of findings and help us answer the primary research question. The Fig. 1 illustrate the steps used on this research.

Finally, in order to validate our study, scientifically, we ran a triangulation step. To this, we perform an exogenous triangulation (S4) using a different application, in a different domain to achieve this objective. Following, we present more details about the steps of the studies 1 and 2.

---

[4] https://www.waze.com.

[5] https://www.tripadvisor.com.

[6] https://www.android.com.

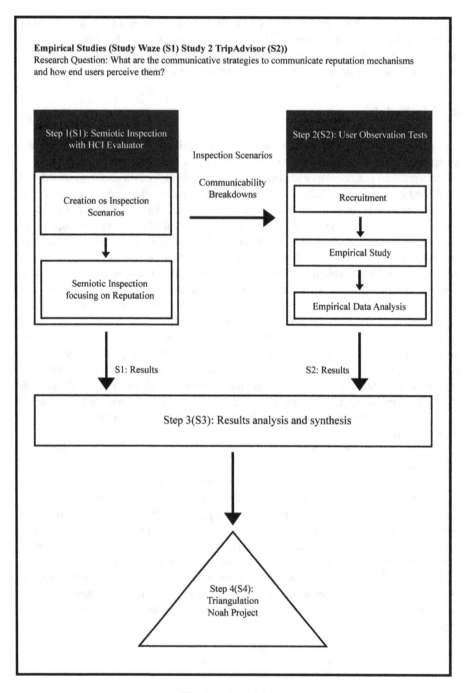

Fig. 1. Methodology

The studies were divided in two main steps. The same methodology was adopted in both studies. In Step 1, an HCI evaluator inspected the selected application using the semiotic inspection method. An inspection scenario guided the tasks.

In Step 2, participants were recruited to evaluate the inspection scenarios. Participants received an invitation by e-mail, as well as a pre-test questionnaire in order to know a little more about their habits and knowledge about their use of technologies. This empirical study was conducted with the following phases:

- **Presentation of the study:** the researcher presented to the participants the basic concepts needed to carry out the study. In addition, it was explained how the study would be conducted and the application used in the test.
- **Evaluation activity:** the researcher started the evaluation activity based on a scenario of use. In the S1, the evaluator accompanied the participants, in a real route, inside a vehicle, using the app Waze. In the S2, the user observation test was conducted in a lab.
- **Post-Test Interview:** the researcher conducted this step to investigate how participants perceived reputation issues and to verify if the reputation mechanisms used by the apps were recognized and signified by them.

The main empirical data collected in this stage came from the participant's discourse through the evaluation activity and the post-test interview. The audio transcript of these empirical data was carried out in order to investigate using the discourse analysis technique.

5   Results

In this section, we present the main strategies founded involving the communication (*emission* and *reception*) of reputation mechanisms.

5.1   Strategies from Step 1 (Inspection Studies)

Shortly, we can summarize the main strategies to help users know more about digital content providers and make decisions well informed: (i) offer ways of connecting (following) known people; (ii) show the users' (digital producers) contributions and/or engagement; (iii) categorize users and show their contributions' levels; (iv) provide alerts about divergent or incongruent information to prevent frauds; (v) provide ways to end users report/collaborate about the information quality.

About strategy (i), we identify that both apps use some *communicative strategies* to allow the users to connect with known people. When the people know each other, the meaning of reputation offline is clearer. Thus, if some end users know the digital producer, it is easier to identify his reputation. Both applications have ways of connecting known people. Waze uses mainly phone book contacts, allowing establishing estimated arrival times in the case of meetings with these contacts via the map. It also offers the possibility to login through a Facebook[7] account. The TripAdvisor, in turn,

---

[7] https://www.facebook.com/.

when connected to Facebook, display ratings and reviews from friends, firstly. This feature enables users to have a criterion for selecting if the information posted is reliable or not, accordingly to the offline reputation of a friend. In the case of Waze, the benefits of this functionality could be perceivable if the application, for example, identify an alert made by a friend on the map. However, this task is not well communicated by the app, because there is no notification about alert issues by known users.

The two applications also present *communicative strategies* (ii) to show the users' contributions (digital producers), for example. Waze uses different colors to identify the traffic situation, as well as having avatar resources to promote the engagement of its users. TripAdvisor brings together in the users' profile the cities already visited and evaluated by them and a seal, that represents the knowledge and participation of a profile. Waze makes use of avatars to promote users' engagement and uses them to demonstrate user's moods and levels of influence and engagement in the application. When interacting with the app, completing some tasks, the digital producers earn points, becoming more influential on posting information. Waze also present specific avatars to communicate to end users who edited maps or corrected some failures. Therefore, there is specific signs to communicate reputation in this environment, showing the users who collaborate more frequently, who are more influent in this context. However, this feature is not well communicated, because only through the analysis of the metalinguistic signs (help system) it was possible to understand it. Therefore, many users may consider this feature only as a way of personalizing the avatar, without perceiving the influence communicated by this mechanism. TripAdvisor does not present the avatar resource, but it uses seals – a kind of badges. Seals communicate to end users who are the digital producers whom are more collaborative, highlighting those who have made more evaluations about a specific topic, such as restaurants. Thus, when trying to establish a comparison, such profiles would take advantage of the comments, because they are considered as specialists. However, we found communicability breakdowns in the observation tests. Some users do not understand the meaning of the seals and could not associate it to the reputation of a digital producer.

About the strategy identified to communicate user's reputation (iii), we found out the profile scoring. In Waze, the scoring is used to rate users who participate more and to promote engagement. Strangely, Waze, for instance, increases user's score when driving with the application open, so, taxi drivers' who transit all day long, will probably have a good score in the app, but it is not necessarily correct to assume that they are digital producers' with a high reputation. So, this resource presents breakdowns in communicating reputation, too. On TripAdvisor, users who include ratings' content, earn points. Thus, the score is a way to evaluate the reputation of a profile. In the observation test studies, users had doubt about how the calculation of these points were made, which was also not clear in the inspection step. However, this communicative strategy is better communicated in this environment than in Waze.

The apps present communicative strategies (iv) to prevent frauds. Waze presents the "No Exists" option where a user reports a false warning that was posted. It also presents as a strategy to limit the number of alerts per day and per hour of each user. An account may be blocked, being stopped to reporting more warnings or lose points in its score, regressing in the evolution of his avatar. Therefore, these features help prevent malicious users from acting, but it is not reported in a user's profile that it has been sanctioned, thus, an end user can not verify if a user has bad historical reputation. On TripAdvisor, there is a place to report false reviews. In this case, the moderators will check the denunciation and if the fraud is confirmed, they assign a bad environment/profile seal to establishment/user and it loses points in the ranking. Moreover, because of the analysis of metalinguistic signs, it is clear the prohibition of employees not being able to make evaluations on their own establishment or concurrent. There is also the option of limiting evaluations about a same place/establishment by user for only once. Preventing hotel owners, for example, from commenting positively over time about their establishment. Another feature founded is to limit the evaluations to recent experiences. Therefore, TripAdvisor has as sign to communicate bad reputation.

To avoid situations like the one previously reported, applications do not allow posting made on behalf of others. However, this ends up constituting only as a site policy, not being presented to users, explicitly, at interaction time. Another feature presented in this sense, is about location. By Waze policy, it is only possible to inform alerts near the user is, however, during the inspection it was verified that alerts can be created anywhere on the map.

Another way to prevent fraud is the presence of moderators, one of the ways to control the information provided in the application, increasing the reliability of what is posted. In the Waze is not clear the presence of moderators, although, in the observation of user's test, the participants believe that all the things posted in the app were its responsibility. On TripAdvisor, the presence of moderators is perceived, however, its presence is more common when denounces are made or about the control of frequency of evaluations policy. The moderators only check to see it the evaluation does not contain offensive content, verifying reputation question only on demand (when a user reports that something is wrong).

Another communicative strategy (v) adopted about reputation is the confirmation of information. The number of "thanks" in Waze keeps the information (alert) longer in the application. However, this feature can be easily confused with the thank function only, without verifying whether it is true, as being difficult to filter useful comments in a context of use of application (in traffic). TripAdvisor presents a sign below the ratings which users have given their opinion informing if the evaluation was useful. However, the problem is that the sign used is very similar to the "Like" sign of Facebook, and can be interpreted only as a way to thank for the information or to enjoy writing.

Those apps also offers mechanisms to digital producers enhance their contributions, such as comments and photos. In Waze, for example, analyzing each comment during the time in which while drives, it becomes a non-viable task. On TripAdvisor, in turn, comments are the main task and objective of the evaluations made.

Photos are also considered as a mechanism. TripAdvisor profiles that showed more photos, whether from places visited or in their own profile were considered in the observation test of users as more reliable, presenting better reputation characteristics than one they do not have. In Waze, alerts that display photos associated with them were considered more reliable too, by end users.

With this two studies, we conclude that the user profile represents the main communicative strategy in terms of reputation. In Waze, the profile displays information such as avatar, name, score, overall rating and the time the user began to use the app. On TripAdvisor, the profile presents information such as score, number of seals and display of the kind of seal, photos, visited and evaluated cities, place of origin of user and the year in which they started to be part of the app.

The recurrent mechanisms used in the applications studied were: integration with social networks or e-mails accounts, use of avatars or user profiles, score and classification features associated with a user profile, use of badges to denote the participation and knowledge of a given profile, number of evaluations or comments made, date that the user became part of application, profile photos and location (can be used as a confirmation of the information) and strategies to prevent fraud. In the case of Waze, in particular, there is still the possibility of emitting alerts by anonymous users, which is a problem in evaluating a user's reputation.

5.2   Strategies from Step 2 (Users' Observation Studies)

In this step, we identify potential breakdowns in designer-to-user communication, in relation to our focus. It is worth to mention that the five communicative strategies listed in Sect. 5.1 were not considered efficient by end-users, during our empirical studies. In both apps, participants do not know and do not worry about (self) reputation and they were not able to recognize the reputation mechanisms described in this section. In Waze, participants do not understand the avatars or any other ranking/score mechanisms to classify user-generated content. Most of them, believe that "the system" is trustable and the information is provided by "the system". Additionally, because the use of Waze is mainly on the road, participants can check the information before make decisions.

With Trip Advisor, in turn, participants recognize the ranking/score mechanisms as important strategies to communicate reputation and they are aware of resources to contribute in reputation, such as comments.

We identified specific signs that potentiate the occurrence of communicability breakdowns. The use of some signs similar to other applications, such as the "Like" sign on Facebook. In Waze, it represents the number of thanks and in TripAdvisor it means the review is "helpful". Users who have been using Facebook for a long time may not understand the meaning of such signs and contribute differently to the way expected, since this sign on the social networks has nothing about reputation issues. For example, the user behaving in front of the sign presented by Waze, "enjoying" what was posted, may end up keeping the information visible for longer in the application. In case the information is a fake alert, this may end up compromising the decisions of users that will avoid selecting the route with this warning. The same can be considered with the "useful" sign, if any user, activate this option because he liked writing only, without verifying that was posted is true, will contribute to the user profile, giving score to him unconsciously. Other users can take account of this information as if it had been validated and choose that hotel based on that mechanism, at risk of having a poor hosting experience. Therefore, the choice of the signs to be used is a point that must be considered when designing crowdsourcing-based applications and its context of use.

The number of comments is also used as a way to validate information on TripAdvisor. Many users reported rejecting places with few reviews and/or comments. However, the minimum number is a subjective concept, as observed in user observation tests.

The use of avatars to demonstrate the users who collaborate more and do the editing of maps also the feelings of the users in the traffic, in the app Waze, also can generate breakdowns in communication. For a beginner user, the feature can be seen just as a profile customization, since it is not communicating the most influent users on the map and contributions. During the observation test with users, they did not recognize this strategy.

As reported during the study, an alert made is evident on the map until other users confirm via thank option. If the alert is not confirmed, it will no longer be displayed in the app. However, it is no clear how long it will remain, the absence of a sign that explain this verification can also cause problems. Given the context of use, in relation to traffic issues, a user could stop going on a route on account of that warning, suddenly choosing a more dangerous route. Therefore, it might be important to exist some element communicating that the warning has not been validated. There is the option of thanks sign, but as we have already, their meaning is implied in some occasions.

The score mechanism, in some cases, such as that of TripAdvisor, is not clear how points are calculated. Thus, many participants were in doubt whether they could actually use this criterion. It is clear that a user, who has more points, participates more and can be more influential, but, it is also necessary to communicate the way to earn those points, to make a more conscious decision.

Seals and badges are widely used as mechanisms to communicate the reputation of users. However, some seals and their quantity can create doubts for users. In our study, participants were beginners to using crowdsourcing-based applications, and some of them do not understand the meaning of the seals. By the inspection of the signs, the function of the signs becomes clear, so, for a better communicability, there should be a greater harmony between the signs used.

The lack of prior knowledge of end users about the subject of our research, has also proved to be a potential cause of breakdowns in communication and also the need for more dynamic metalinguistic signs, since users don't understand the meaning of representations used in the interfaces. In the observed cases, participants give to the applications the responsibility for the information they provided. Therefore, they believe that the alerts and evaluations have already been validated by some moderator. As we know, crowdsourcing-based applications do not necessarily have effective moderation, so, to know more information about who is posting information is a very important step.

5.3 Triangulation

In order to have different perspectives of the same object, explored in different contexts, giving plausibility and consistency to the interpretation process, we performed the triangulation stage, a qualitative research procedure [5, 11].

To do this, we perform an exogenous triangulation to confirm the communicative strategies about reputation in a website, that we found out with the two studies. Thus, triangulation was conducted in a new application, in a different domain and in a desktop environment, completely different from the mobile version. We chose the website version of the Project Noah[8] to search for divergent and convergent categories of the previous studies.

The Project Noah, according to its website, "is a software platform designed to help people to reconnect with the natural world. To do so, it harnesses the power and popularity of new mobile technologies to collect important ecological data and preserve global biodiversity. Through the help of crowdsourcing, organizations around the world are documented, ranked, generating up-to-date information about local and global biodiversity."

In order to keep the same focus on the context situation, when searching for convergences and divergences during the inspection step in this environment, a context of use was created to guide us.

Just as the strategy (i) to offer ways of connecting (following) known people, the Project Noah presents in the user profile, a website associated with the profile, or an e-mail. However, to create an account, it is necessary to have an account with Google+[9], Facebook, Twitter[10], etc. This feature tries to ensure that participants are real, not being fake profiles. In case of this app, a clear strategy for connecting with known people was not identified. There are several types of account, but is unclear if this can be used to select the contacts while browsing the website. However, it is confirmed the need to integrate with another social network, or e-mail, preventing fake profiles to be created.

As in strategy (iii) to categorize users and show their contributions' levels, we have identified the use of user profiles containing information about users and their activities. The profiles also presents a photo, number of contributions, images, location of origin, site or associated e-mail, number of comments made, number of suggestions made, number of favorites, number of followers and contribution seals (called patches by the website). Thus, we see that the strategies used to communicate the reputation and collaboration of the users identified in early studies are also used in this environment, as well the use of user profiles and its information. Users who have a high index of collaboration receive a ranger seal (expert) and influences the community, as seen in other studies. This is possible through the amount of collaboration seen by the moderators or by indication of other users via e-mail. We did not identify in this study the use of score to communicate the reputation in this website.

The photos are strongly used in the studies, being one of the main features of this website and is directly linked to the participation and collaboration activities. In this case, the photos can be used to help users and moderators make decisions about what is posted, as well as the activities of a digital producer.

The website also presents strategies (iv) to provide alerts about divergent or incongruent information to prevent frauds. User may denunciate by sending messages to more expert users and/or by using a flag sign (this option is only visible to users who have an account on this website). It was not clear what are the consequences of the report of a problem. There is no sign to communicate bad reputation in this environment. However, it confirms the strategies of having a sign to communicate something that is incorrect and also confirms the fact that it is not possible to put information on behalf another person.

---

[8] http://www.projectnoah.org/.
[9] https://plus.google.com/.
[10] https://twitter.com/.

As strategies (v) to provide ways to end users report/collaborate/confirm the information quality, the website has a voting scheme. At least 3 votes are required to confirm a post. This information was found in the help of the website, but in practice it did not always appear available. The sign used is similar to Google+, representing the voting validation for what was posted. However, it can also be confused with a thanks icon. Another form is through comments and suggestions placed by other users, which are sorted by date, the most recent being shown first. The amount of comments and suggestions that a profile makes may represent his ability to collaborate on the site, but the same cannot be fully stated as far as reputation is concerned. However, the number of followers is a communicative strategy for the reputation of digital producers. Underneath each post, some signs are shown, communicating that information has already been verified or not. With each post, the location of the post can be added and it can be from anywhere in the world. However, for a particular option, the missions, only may posted near the place it happened.

Finally, it is clear the presence of moderators, being the website organizers or specialist users, that verify all the information posted, in a collaborative way, in order to guarantee the integrity of information.

In conclusion, we can say that the result of this triangulation contributes to the consistency of this research and confirms the scientific validity of the results found in these exploratory studies.

6   Conclusions

In this research, it was possible to identify: (a) five strategies adopted to communicate the reputation of digital producers in examples of applications based on crowdsourcing; and, (b) potential breakdowns in designer-to-user communication, in relation to our focus. This research also indicates that users (end users and digital producers) should be aware of the meaning reputation in order to promote better user use of the applications.

About the communicability, we noticed a huge difference in terms of the application domain. For example, in traffic, reporting of reputational aspects is very fast, being related to making instant decisions, such as selecting a route based on the user who posted the information. In the case of TripAdvisor, it is expected that the information will be available for a long time, in order to give more conditions to decide on the choice of a hotel, for example.

In conclusion, the results reveal the potential risks involved in the use of the application (by users), according to the communicate strategy adopted by the designers, indicating that the design process of such applications should be rethinking for such possibilities of breakdowns and alternative solutions.

The identification of communicative strategies on the reputation of the digital producers and the mapping of resulting problems from the adopted strategies begin to fill a gap in the study of reputation with a focus on HCI.

Additionally, such strategies can serve as the foundation for the study on how to improve the HCI design process for such applications. This work does not provide immediate solutions, but presents challenges and opportunities to improve the design of crowdsourcing-based systems. Thus, some identified strategies may serve as a guide, or may even be avoided. In addition, to emphasizing the importance of reflecting on the context of use in which users will interact with the application created.

In this research, we were faced with the challenge of doing research with innovative systems and profiles of beginner users. For this, we needed a theoretical foundation that would allow the exploration of an innovative environment such as crowdsourcing-based applications and also that would lead to identify possible new problems. For this reason, we adopted Semiotic Engineering and communicability as a criterion of quality, since it allowed us to study the processes of signification and communication, without leaving us limited to heuristics or guidelines, based on concepts prior to the technology studied.

The combination of the SIM with scientific purpose and the observation of the users with a focus on communicability has revealed itself with a good methodology and contributes to the identification of the new problems relation to the reputation and needs of users that we had not even imagined. Therefore, this methodology favors the extension of the knowledge of the problem by the evaluator.

The findings of this research point out to interesting opportunities for future work. In our study, the participants 'profile of our empirical studies was the digital consumer. The same study could be conducted with expert users in these two apps or digital producers.

Acknowledgments. The authors would like to thank all people who participated in empirical studies and thus contributed to the research partly reported in this paper. Luciana Salgado and Jose Viterbo also thanks CNPq and FAPERJ for financial support received.

References

1. Afonso, O., Salgado, L.C.C., Viterbo, J.: User's understanding of reputation issues in a community based mobile app. In: Meiselwitz, G. (ed.) SCSM 2016. LNCS, vol. 9742, pp. 93–103. Springer, Cham (2016). doi:10.1007/978-3-319-39910-2_9
2. Bente, G., Dratsch, T., Rehbach, S., Reyl, M., Lushaj, B.: Do you trust my avatar? Effects of photo-realistic seller avatars and reputation scores on trust in online transactions. In: Nah, F.F.-H. (ed.) HCIB 2014. LNCS, vol. 8527, pp. 461–470. Springer, Cham (2014). doi: 10.1007/978-3-319-07293-7_45
3. Blank, G., Reisdorf, B.C.: The participatory web: a user perspective on Web 2.0. Inf. Commun. Soc. **15**(4), 537–554 (2012)
4. Coetzee, D., Fox, A., Hearts, M.A., Hartmann, B.: Should your MOOC forum use a reputation system? In: Proceedings of the 17th ACM Conference on Computer Supported Cooperative Work and Social Computing, pp. 1176–1187. ACM (2014)
5. Creswell, J.W.: Qualitative Inquiry and Research Design: Choosing Among Five Approaches, 2nd edn. Sage, Thousand Oaks (2007)
6. De Paoli, S., De Uffici, N., D'andrea, V.: Designing badges for a civic media platform: reputation and named levels. In: Proceedings of the 26th Annual BCS Interaction Specialist Group Conference on People and Computers, pp. 59–68. British Computer Society (2012)
7. De Souza, C.S.: The Semiotic Engineering of Human-Computer Interaction. MIT Press, Cambridge (2005)
8. De Souza, C.S., Leitão, C.F.: Semiotic engineering methods for scientific research in HCI. Synth. Lect. Hum. Cent. Inform. **2**(1), 1–122 (2009)

9. De Souza, C.S., Leitão, C.F., Prates, R.O., Bim, S.A., Da Silva, E.J.: Can inspection methods generate valid new knowledge in HCI? The case of semiotic inspection. Int. J. Hum. Comput. Stud. **68**(1), 22–40 (2010)

10. De Souza, C.S., Leitão, C.F., Prates, R.O., Da Silva, E.J.: The semiotic inspection method. In: Proceedings of VII Brazilian Symposium on Human Factors in Computing Systems, pp. 148–157. ACM (2006)

11. Denzin, N.K., Lincoln, Y.S.: Collecting and Interpreting Qualitative Materials, vol. 3. Sage, London (2008)

12. Estellés-Arolas, E., González-Ladrón-de-Guevara, F.: Towards an integrated crowdsourcing definition. J. Inf. Sci. **38**(2), 189–200 (2012)

13. Josang, A., Ismail, R., Boyd, C.: A survey of trust and reputation systems for on-line service provision. Decis. Support Syst. **43**(2), 618–644 (2007)

14. Kazai, G.: In search of quality in crowdsourcing for search engine evaluation. In: Clough, P., Foley, C., Gurrin, C., Jones, G.J.F., Kraaij, W., Lee, H., Mudoch, V. (eds.) ECIR 2011. LNCS, vol. 6611, pp. 165–176. Springer, Heidelberg (2011). doi:10.1007/978-3-642-20161-5_17

15. Luca, M., Zervas, G.: Fake it till you make it: reputation, competition, and Yelp review fraud. Harvard Business School NOM Unit Working Paper No. 14-006 Management Science (2016)

16. Nicolaci-da-Costa, A.M., Leitão, C.F., Romão-Dias, D.: Gerando conhecimento sobre homens, mulheres e crianças que usam computadores: algumas contribuições da psicologia clínica. In: IV Workshop sobre Fatores Humanos em Sistemas Computacionais, IHC 2001, pp. 120–131. Anais SBC, Florianópolis (2001)

17. Michiardi, P., Molva, R.: Core: a collaborative reputation mechanism to enforce node cooperation in mobile ad hoc networks. In: Jerman-Blažič, B., Klobučar, T. (eds.) Advanced Communications and Multimedia Security. ITIFIP, vol. 100, pp. 107–121. Springer, Boston (2002). doi: 10.1007/978-0-387-35612-9_9

18. Mika, P., Greaves, M.: Editorial: semantic Web & Web 2.0. Web Semant. Sci. Serv. Agents World Wide Web **6**(1) (2012)

19. Mui, L., Mohtashemi, M., Halberstadt, A.: A computational model of trust and reputation. In: Proceedings of the 35th Annual Hawaii International Conference on System Sciences, HICSS 2002, pp. 2431–2439. IEEE (2002)

20. Peirce, C.S., Houser, N.: The Essential Peirce: Selected Philosophical Writings, vol. 2. Indiana University Press, Bloomington (1998)

21. Petz, G., Karpowicz, M., Fürschuß, H., Auinger, A., Stříteský, V., Holzinger, A.: Opinion mining on the Web 2.0 – characteristics of user generated content and their impacts. In: Holzinger, A., Pasi, G. (eds.) HCI-KDD 2013. LNCS, vol. 7947, pp. 35–46. Springer, Heidelberg (2013). doi: 10.1007/978-3-642-39146-0_4

22. Pinheiro, A., Cappelli, C., Maciel, C.: Checking information reliability in social networks regarding user behavior and developers' effort to avoid misinformation. In: Meiselwitz, G. (ed.) SCSM 2016. LNCS, vol. 9742, pp. 151–161. Springer, Cham (2016). doi:10.1007/978-3-319-39910-2_15

23. Prates, R.O., De Souza, C.S., Barbosa, S.D.: Methods and tools: a method for evaluating the communicability of user interfaces. Interactions **7**(1), 31–38 (2000)

24. Tausczik, Y.R., Pennebaker, J.W.: Predicting the perceived quality of online mathematics contributions from users' reputations. In: Proceedings of the SIGCHI Conference on Human Factors in Computing Systems, pp. 1885–1888. ACM (2011)

25. Wexler, M.N.: Reconfiguring the sociology of the crowd: exploring crowdsourcing. Int. J. Sociol. Soc. Policy **31**(1/2), 6–20 (2011)

26. Woodruff, A.: Necessary, unpleasant, and disempowering: reputation management in the internet age. In: Proceedings of the SIGCHI Conference on Human Factors in Computing Systems, pp. 149–158. ACM (2014)

Collaboration Increase Through Monitoring and Evaluation Mechanisms of the Collaborative Learning Process

Vanessa Agredo Delgado[4(✉)], Cesar A. Collazos[1],
Habib M. Fardoun[2], and Nehme Safa[3]

[1] Department of Computing, Universidad del Cauca,
Street 5 Number 4–70, Popayan, Colombia
ccollazo@unicauca.edu.co
[2] Information Systems, Faculty of Computing and Information Technology,
King Abdulaziz University, Jeddah, Saudi Arabia
hfardoun@kau.edu.sa
[3] Educational Technology, Faculty of Education,
Lebanese University, Beirut, Lebanon
nsafa@ul.edu.lb
[4] Corporacion Universitaria Comfacauca - Unicomfacauca,
Street 4 Number 8–30, Popayan, Colombia
vagredo@unicomfacauca.edu.co

Abstract. Computer supported collaborative learning is a research area that is concerned with collaborative activities that generate learning, through the use of software for interaction between its participants. This area focuses mainly on how people can learn together with the help of computers, being one of the most promising innovations to improve teaching and learning with the help of modern information and communication technologies. In many situations, it has been believed that the availability of the technological infrastructure guarantees an effective collaboration, but for this, it is necessary to go beyond providing a set of class practices, laboratories and the respective technological tools. For there to be collaboration in the execution of an activity is necessary to learn how to do it, not everything is a matter of putting in the same place a group of people, provide them with a software tool and advise them to collaborate. This is why, it is important to define strategies to increase collaboration and it is necessary to analyze some external factors such as group of people, activities and technological infrastructure, besides taking into account the monitoring and evaluation of the learning process by the teacher, who must be in continuous attention that the collaboration is carried out. In this paper shows a project that was carried out through the monitoring of general phases of improvement of software processes, where the collaborative learning process was analyzed, finding some improvement opportunities that were applied and later validated in different case studies. Finally, a strategy was developed to increase collaboration through a set of monitoring and evaluation mechanisms of the collaborative learning process that were consolidated into a formal specification. From this research it was concluded that the definition of the different monitoring and evaluation mechanisms of the collaborative learning process is useful and helps to increase the collaboration although its application is moderately complex, for which we analyze

© Springer International Publishing AG 2017
G. Meiselwitz (Ed.): SCSM 2017, Part II, LNCS 10283, pp. 20–31, 2017.
DOI: 10.1007/978-3-319-58562-8_2

some other strategies that can be taken into account for subsequent projects and how they can help in the increase of the collaboration in these processes.

Keywords: Education · Collaborative learning · Modelling · Mechanisms · Collaborative process improvement

1   Introduction

Several researches have shown that students that work collaboratively develop better attitudes towards the learning process, dedicate more time to learning tasks, are more tolerant, listen more the opinion of the others and have better abilities to negotiate [1, 2]. Computer supported collaborative learning –CSCL– brings together the same characteristics and qualities of traditional collaborative learning, but includes a motivational element associated with technology, the computer. Besides, its uses allow carry out a more detailed follow up the process [3].

The most relevant and necessary to work cooperatively or collaboratively is to learn how to do it. It is not a matter of putting a group of people in the same place face to face and instructs them to cooperate or collaborate in the carrying out of an activity [3]. Here is where the main problem appears, many times it has been believed that having the technological infrastructure guarantees an effective collaboration. However, to achieve this proper collaboration, it is necessary to organize and analyze additional aspects, since, in order to have a collaborative activity that generates learning among its participants, it is necessary to go further than accepting and organizing class practices set, laboratories, and their tools. It is necessary to take into account a deeper approach to guarantee the cooperation among the work teams and a common and equal learning by means of the analysis of all the external factors that must be involved in this process [4].

For the reason explained above, in this work, these three aspects are taken into account in an integrated manner: the analysis of the characteristics of the groups of people, the way in which the activities should be designed, and the technology that will be used for the interaction, considering the elements defined in [5], also adding the necessary mechanisms that allow the evaluation, monitoring and improvement of the collaborative process. From this point of view, it is important to figure out what degree of collaboration has there been during the learning process of the group. For this reason, comes out the idea of evaluating, monitoring and improving the collaborative learning process, when a group of people works around in a common activity, with a collaborative learning environment, using several interaction devices for communication. Because of the need to collaborative learning process improve with the support of monitoring and evaluation mechanisms, is necessary to use tools to guide the improvement in this context.

Based on the above, it is proposed to generate a strategy to increase collaboration through the use of mechanisms that allow monitoring and evaluation of the collaborative learning process, mechanisms that can be used both by the participants and by the coordinator of the group activity and finally a greater collaboration between the participants.

This paper is organized as follows: an introduction, where the idea of the work and the research problem is presented, later a summary of the related works, presents the phases of the collaborative learning process improvement application and finally the conclusions drawn from the work.

2 Related Works

In recent years it has led to a large increase in the use of virtual environments (or mediated by technology) in different contexts of education. The literature has long recognized the role of Information and Communication Technology (ICT) as mediators and facilitators of the teaching and learning processes. Specifically, the communication processes that take place in virtual learning environments have been the subject of numerous investigations developed from different perspectives. Often the interaction analysis has been framed in the collaborative context and joint construction of knowledge among students who are part of this process. This analysis of the interaction is not framed in these situations because the social communication should systematically involve collaborative processes, but by the boom that have acquired the collaborative methodologies in training contexts, also by the interest shown, observation of interactive processes within these dynamics, especially measured by the possibilities of the use of such technology to support teaching and learning [6].

Due to the importance that has managed collaborative learning, it is necessary to define what makes reference and how to correct application for greater efficiency and effectiveness in activities that wish to develop in a collaborative environment and towards a common learning [7].

During the development of this paper is especially used the concepts of Learn and Collaborate and is necessary to have a general meaning for these, in order to contextualize the reader and facilitate their interpretation. The Royal Academy of the Spanish Language defines Learning as "acquire knowledge of something through study or experience" and Collaborate as "work with another or others persons in the accomplishment of a work" [8].

The computer supported collaborative learning is an emerging area of science learning responsible of how people can learn together with the help of computers. The inclusion of collaboration, computer-mediated and distance education has problematized the notion of learning and has led to new questions about how to study it. The concept of collaborative learning is in constant discussion. Different researchers continue to investigate what are its main distinctive features and possible differences with the cooperation because they are terms of constant confusion in understanding the collaborative activities. Some believe that there is such a clear distinction between the two concepts and their common characteristics are more important than their differences [9]. In this sense, Kreijns et al. [10], explain that both collaboration and cooperation, develop the possibility of an active learning, the teacher's facilitator role, education, learning from shared experiences and responsibilities of students in the own learning.

Other researchers, however, point out differences between the two types of learning and are interested in defining cross-collaborative learning. For example, Stahl et al. [11], determined that since computer-assisted collaborative learning, two forms of group work are distinguished: cooperation and collaboration. At working cooperatively, students solve tasks individually and then combine the partial results to obtain a final product; while as in collaborative work, each member of the group is committed to a common task, which is built around the group, this task is performed by the group negotiation and only then knowledge is constructed collaboratively. Dillenbourg [12] similarly explains that cooperation and collaboration are differentiated by the degree of division of labor. In cooperation, partners divide and resolve individual subtasks and then link the partial results into a final result. While in collaboration, peers perform the task "together", and although some division of activities is presented horizontally, there is a division in which the roles are continually exchanged, also Dillenbourg in [5], believes that the chances of collaborative interactions generated increase when appropriate initial conditions are set (set groups, establish appropriate problems, use the appropriate software, etc.) and when the teacher takes the role of facilitator making minimum educational interventions to redirect teamwork in a productive way. Thus, collaboration can be promoted in a complementary manner, either by structuring the collaborative process or retroactively regulating interactions.

2.1 Evaluation and Monitoring of the Collaborative Learning Process

In [13] studies have been made regarding how evaluation and monitoring the collaborative learning process should be done, where it is proposed that for this process to be effective, certain guidelines should be followed and some roles defined. But, the simple definition of these guidelines and roles does not guarantee that learning is performed in the most efficient way.

Hurtado [14], designs a collaborative learning activity for the Chemistry teaching, through a computational tool that allows the creation of work groups in classrooms in order to work in this activity.

Barros et al. [15] built a platform (DEGREE) for the analysis of the collaboration that is given in the groups from the analysis of the interactions. Allowing the study of the different stages that occur in an argumentative discussion. In addition to these, platforms have been built to assess the content of interactions as well as attitudes towards collaboration.

In relation to the content of the interactions, Martínez et al. [16] presents a way of evaluating interactions by capturing events and processing them to model the state of the interaction. Based on these studies, it can be determined that there are mechanisms that allow the evaluation and monitoring of a collaborative process, which only focuses on having people, activities and technological tools, without taking into account the improvement of the process and the analysis of external factors that affect the process.

Lovos [17] creates a customized environment that integrates teaching paradigms: Problem-Based Learning (PBL) and computer supported collaborative learning, which has a collaborative learning environment in virtual teaching situations, through tools that provide synchronous and asynchronous services that are very useful in teaching.

Based on these studies, it can be determined that there are mechanisms that allow the evaluation and monitoring of a collaborative process, which only focuses on having people, activities and technological tools, without taking into account the improvement of the process and the analysis of factors that affect the process and the form for increasing the collaboration in these activities.

3 Research Methodology

In order to increase collaboration in the Collaborative Learning Process, a methodology focused on the execution of an improvement plan was used to validate and refine the application of a set of phases applied to the collaborative learning context, allowing the creation of monitoring and evaluation mechanisms of the process.

3.1 Phase 1: Installation

The objective of this phase was to launch and detailed project planning (schedule, budget, and activities diagrams, among others).

Coordination, assignment of tasks and responsibilities were carried out for this purpose. This allowed the areas, the people that were the subject of research, the scope of the project and its objective to be delimited, as well as the improvement objectives, which were established from the needs of the collaborative learning process, in search of the increase of the collaboration through the use of mechanisms of monitoring and evaluation of this process.

3.2 Phase 2: Definition

The objective of this phase was to analyze the characteristics at the level of the group of people, activities, and technology, in order to make a diagnosis of how the collaborative learning process is currently being carried out.

Support activities were also carried out to achieve the objectives of the project, including conducting a theoretical research, defining sources of information and selecting the group on which the collaborative activity would be carried out, a list of the characteristics to evaluate in the selected group, a collaborative activity was designed, based on the work of Pre – Process, Process, and Post – Process activities carried out in [18], the first version of monitoring and evaluation mechanisms was defined for each activity of these stages, in addition to design of the case studies that were carried out, in such a way that it gets the data to be evaluated, the group on which the research was to be carried out and the purposes of those case studies were obtained.

3.3 Phase 3: Formulation

The objective of this phase was to develop conceptual models of how collaborative processes are currently performed, analyzing the activities, groups and tools, as well as obtaining the main diagnosis of the current collaborative learning process, which allowed to detect opportunities for improvement, roles, activities, steps and tools of monitoring and evaluation for the Process stage, based on the analysis carried out in the previous phase. For this, a case study was developed that was modeled through the use of SPEM 2.0 [19], modeling the processes that were diagnosed in an academic environment without the use of tools to support the monitoring and evaluation of the collaborative learning process. Another case study was carried out where a Moodle to monitor and evaluate through the guide in [18], in a Software development undergraduate course, adding in this tool the implementation of the first version of the proposal of monitoring and evaluation mechanisms, in each of the stages of the collaborative process. In this case study was obtained results that are found in the article Agredo et al. [20].

Taking into account the results of these case studies, improvement opportunities were defined, which were assigned a candidate support tool to solve said deficiency, and subsequently, these improvement opportunities were prioritized to implement those with higher priority and greater positive effect on the collaborative learning process.

3.4   Phase 4: Metrics

The objective of this phase was to define the use of a set of indicators and collaboration metrics through the improvement opportunities found, in such a way that the new process is appreciable and verifiable. The metrics that were taken from Collazos et al. [13], which served to analyze the results and to define the increase of the collaboration were: number of errors, solution to the problem, strategies use, keep the strategy, communicate the strategy, messages of strategy, strategy work messages, strategy coordination messages, total messages. In addition, five indicators were taken: four of them are based on Johnson & Johnson's proposed activities [21]: strategy use, intra-group cooperation, performance, monitoring and review of success criteria.

3.5   Phase 5: Mechanisms

The objective of this phase was to develop mechanisms that allow the evaluation and monitoring of the collaborative process taking into account all aspects analyzed previously.

At this stage, other activities were also taken into account, among which are:

- Analysis of existing mechanisms that serve as the base for the given definition.
- Apply the mechanisms of opportunities for improvement.
- Update implementation plan for the next iteration.
- Perform and update implementation report.

In this project developed mechanisms that allowed the evaluation and monitoring of the collaborative process, determining that the stage where the work will do, would be the Process stage with each of its activities, stage where is centered all the existing collaborative moment between the students and executed the monitoring and evaluation of the process by the teacher, it is for this reason that after consulting experts on the activities propose of this phase and the suggested monitoring and evaluation mechanisms, doing a quantitative analysis of their opinions obtained the final activities defined for this Process phase, with their respective mechanisms and each of the necessary elements for their accomplishment, as they are: guides, documents, tools, inputs, outputs, among others.

Like a strategy to increase the collaboration, a definition about the monitoring and evaluation mechanisms, was initially made and a guide to its correct use was then generated to guide the students towards learning and provide the necessary collaboration among the participants of a collaborative activity, the mechanisms that were defined after the activities previously analyzed are: forums use, chats use, wikis use, electronic mail use, activities management use, groups and roles management use, evaluation management use. The definition of each of these mechanisms is found in the paper by Agredo et al. [22].

The set of these mechanisms they were: guides, selection of tools that facilitated tasks in the process of collaborative learning, documents that specified the importance of each of these tools, in addition to the recommendations for their correct use in favor of collaboration, Are the defined mechanisms that later allowed to be applied through a software tool and delivered to both teachers and students to be used in the development of a collaborative learning activity.

3.6   Phase 6: Improvement

In this phase, the improvement opportunities identified above were materialized through the creation of a model, is a proposal for a collaborative process improved model that would solve the shortcomings found in each of the activities, roles and tools that are part of the collaborative learning, model conformed to a Process phase activities model (See Fig. 1 where show the diagram) and a model a process with the application of the improvements found.

From these activities designed, for each one was generated a list of inputs, outputs, and roles. In addition to these activities, sub-tasks were generated with which a detailed specification was made that contained the description of the activity and their respective monitoring and evaluation mechanisms to achieve increased collaboration.

3.7   Phase 7: Test

Having the formal process with each of its specifications, field tests were developed in different classrooms with different groups of students and teachers in order to evaluate, validate and modify the conceptual infrastructure and the proposed improved model with the objective to compare the results obtained in the diagnosis and the current results.

This stage also involved the creation of a software application called MEPAC (Monitoring and Evaluation of the Collaborative Learning Process) that contained the strategy for increasing collaboration through the compendium of tools that allowed all these mechanisms to monitor and evaluate the process collaborative formalized previously, which served as support for the accomplishment of a collaborative activity in a group of people. These mechanisms defined guidelines for the teacher and the student to use them in order to generate greater collaboration between groups. MEPAC

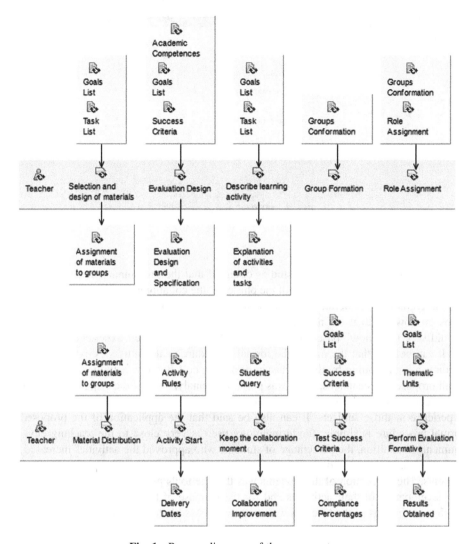

Fig. 1. Process diagrams of the process stage

(See Fig. 2) also had a space for the design, management, and execution of the activity, for the deliveries administration and execution of the activity requested.

After the improvement, a process feedback was made, evaluating the state of the academic course before and after the improvement, based on the metrics and indicators that were used to determine the collaboration between the students and thus guaranteeing the improvement of the collaborative learning process, obtaining results that were compared before the improvement vs the results obtained in the indicators and metrics after the improvement, from them it was observed that the values increased on the premise that this type of metrics and indicators measure us the collaboration improvement executed in the activities that the teacher has carried out.

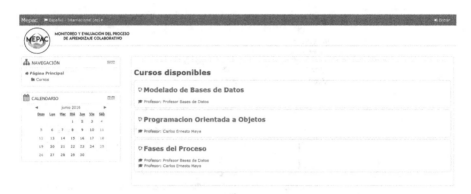

Fig. 2. MEPAC software tool

3.8 Result Analysis

As results of the diagnostic case studies obtained that the preliminary mechanisms of monitoring and evaluation in each of the phases of the collaborative process adapted for the undergraduate academic field, is useful and moderately applicable. However, the steps on how to do it are not clearly defined, therefore, the teacher and the student should seek this "how" based on other methodologies or in their experience.

It can be said that the use of the formal procedure in its entirety is extensive and requires a high training by the teacher in designing collaborative activities, correct use of all proposed mechanisms, but it was possible to analyze that if the design is repeated and execution of the phases, the time recorded would be lower, due to the gaining of experience in those subjects. It can also be said that the application of the proposed formal procedure is simple; the terminology used is very close to the teaching environment. In addition, the percentage of students who approved the activities increased, consolidating the proposed mechanisms as useful to increase the good performance of students. The perception of the students was that the tools provided were a support for the development of their activities and for the increase of the collaboration. The perception on the part of the teachers was that it was possible to classify the improvement as useful taking into account the positive impact that was generated.

From the results obtained after the analysis of the metrics and indicators, it can be said that the implementation of a set of mechanisms that allow the monitoring and evaluation of the processes of collaborative learning allow achieving the increase of the collaboration, to the extent that they are used correctly according to the strategy proposed.

There are also other ways to increase this collaboration, for example strategies where the teacher can intervene through synchronous and asynchronous mechanisms that were not taken into account in this formal specification, mechanisms that can be used by the teacher and by the student at the time that the teacher thinks fit to look for the increase of the collaboration. Another strategy that can be taken into account is the customization of content, which analyzes and interprets the student's actions and dynamically adapts content. Some common methods used, for example, to determine the level of knowledge or personal preferences, are the preliminary test or the definition of profiles. Depending on the results, the contents and functions of each student are configured to design a personalized training offer always looking for better learning depending on their own characteristics and in this way collaboration will increase. The basic requirements for this are a wide variety of modules in terms of contents and functions, and a high level of interactivity [23]. In addition to these strategies can be included the gamification, which is a learning technique that moves the mechanics of the games to the professional educational field in order to achieve better results, either to absorb some knowledge better, improve some skill, or reward concrete actions, among many other objectives. A series of mechanical and dynamic techniques extrapolated from games are used [24].

These strategies can be included as ways to increase collaboration, and many others that can be studied in future work, thus remaining a broad path to pursue in order to increase collaboration, taking into account that it is not an easy task, requiring the Analysis of many characteristics, technologies and people in charge of this work. In addition to being able to use this work as a basis to include in this formal specification and in the software tool MEPAC, new mechanisms and new strategies that achieve a cohesion of ways to increase collaboration.

4 Conclusions

To increase collaboration, it is not enough to deliver an activity and a software tool. To achieve true collaborative processes, it is necessary to structure the activities, analyze the type of people that make up the groups, the external factors that can affect the collaborative work and have a tool designed for the use of control, monitoring and evaluation mechanisms activity; so that collaboration is promoted and is not simply an individual work activity.

Having a software tool that contains a compendium of mechanisms that allow to evaluate and monitor collaborative learning by the teacher, is of great help so that it can generate better results of collaboration between the students who participate in the same, so that are of great benefit and allowing an active collaboration and a common and egalitarian learning.

From the final case studies, the values obtained in the surveys carried out to the students, teachers and the results after the execution of the improvement, it was possible to determine that the strategy to increase the collaboration enriched with monitoring and evaluation mechanisms in the Process phase is useful and that its application is not easy for an execution of a collaborative activity. Useful because it provides the necessary activities to improve the processes and is not easy to apply because, although it exposes a guide of its application, it requires a high level of effort evaluated in the number of hours necessary for its implementation.

Based on what has been done, it is possible to have as future work the inclusion of new functionalities in MEPAC tool that facilitate collaborative activities, which will allow a simpler degree of monitoring and evaluation of the process to take corrective actions of the process at time, besides performing an analysis of all external factors that influence the process of collaboration, so that they can be used in favor of it.

References

1. Webb, N., Palincsar, A.: Group processes in the classroom. In: Berliner, D.C., Calfee, R.C. (eds.) Handbook of Educational Psychology, pp. 841–873. MacMillan, New York (1996)
2. Jonhson, D., Jonhson, R.: Cooperative learning and social interdependence theory. In: Tindale, R., Heath, L., Edwards, J., Posavac, E., Bryant, F., Suarez-Balcazar, Y., Henderson-King, E., Myers, J. (eds.) Theory and Research on Small Groups, pp. 9–36. Plenum Press, New York (1998)
3. Collazos, C., Guerrero, L., Pino, J., Renzi, S., Klobas, J., Ortega, M., Redondo, M., Bravo, C.: Evaluating collaborative learning processes using system-based measurement. Educ. Technol. Soc. **10**(3), 257–274 (2007)
4. Scagnoli, N., Stephens, M.: Collaborative learning strategies in online education. In: Illinois Online Conference for Teaching and Learning (IOC2005) (2005)
5. Dillenbourg, P.: What do you mean by collaborative learning? In: Dillenbourg, P. (ed.) Collaborative-Learning: Cognitive and Computational Approaches, pp. 1–19. Elsevier, Oxford (1999)
6. Centro interuniversitario de desarrollo-CINDA: Las Nuevas Demandas del Desempeño Profesional Y sus Implicancias Para la Docencia Universitaria, Centro Interuniversitario de Desarrollo CINDA, Santiago, Chile (2000)
7. Sthal, G.: Global Introduction to CSCL, 4th edn. Gerry Stahl at Lulu, Philadelphia (2010)
8. Real academia de la lengua Española (2015). http://lema.rae.es/drae/srv/search?id=Wbqr6R3D7DXX2VCMXWE7
9. Johnson, J., Johnson, R.: Learning Together and Alone: Cooperative. Allyn and Bacon, Needham Heights (1987)
10. Kreijns, K., Kirschner, P., Jochems, W.: Identifying the pitfalls for social interaction in computer-supported collaborative learning environments: a review of the research. Comput. Hum. Behav. **19**(3), 335–353 (2003)
11. Stahl, G., Koschmann, T., Suthers, D.: Computer-supported collaborative learning: an historical perspective. In: Sawyer, R.K. (ed.) de Cambridge Handbook of the Learning Sciences, pp. 409–426. Cambridge University Press, Cambridge (2006)
12. Dillenbourg, P.: Over-scripting CSCL: the risks of blending collaborative learning with instructional design. In: Kirschner, P.A. (ed.) Three Worlds of CSCL: Can We Support CSCL?, pp. 61–92. Herleen Open Universiteit, Netherland (2002)
13. Collazos, C., Muñoz, J., Hernández, Y.: Aprendizaje Colaborativo apoyado por computador, 1era, Ed. (2014)
14. Hurtado, C., Guerrero, L.: ColaboQuim: Una Aplicación para Apoyar el Aprendizaje Colaborativo en Química (2010)
15. Barros, B., Mizoguchi, R., Verdejo, F.: A platform for collaboration analysis in CSCL. An ontological approach. In: Proceedings Artificial Intelligence in Education AIIED 2001 (2001)
16. Martinez, A., Dimitriadis, Y., Rubia, B., Gomez, E., Garachon, I., Marcos, J.: Studying social aspects of computer-supported collaboration with a mixed evaluation approach. In: Proceedings of Computer Support for Collaborative Learning Conference, CSCL 2002, Boulder, CO, USA (2002)
17. Lovos, E.: El Uso de Herramientas Colaborativas en los Cursos de Introducción a la Programación. Universidad Nacional de La Plata (2012)
18. Ramirez, D., Bolaños, J., Collazos, C.: Guía para el diseño de actividades de aprendizaje colaborativo asistida por computador (CSCoLAD), Monografía de Trabajo de Grado. Universidad del Cauca (2013)

19. Ruiz, F., Verdugo, J.: Guía de Uso de SPEM 2 con EPF Composer, Universidad de Castilla-La Mancha Escuela Superior de Informática Departamento de Tecnologías y Sistemas de Información Grupo Alarcos, vol. 3, p. 93 (2008)
20. Agredo, V., Collazos, C., Paderewski, P., Estudio de caso sobre mecanismos para evaluar, monitorear y mejorar el proceso de aprendizaje colaborativo, Campus Virtuales, vol. 5, no. 1. (2016)
21. Johnson, D., Johnson, R., Holubec, R.: Circles of Learning, 4th edn. Interaction Book Company, Edina (1993)
22. Agredo, V., Collazos, C., Paderewski, P.: Definición de mecanismos para evaluar, monitorear y mejorar el proceso de aprendizaje colaborativo, Tencologia educativa Revista CONAIC, vol. 3, no. 3 (2016)
23. Leris, D., Sein-Echaluce, M.: la personalización del aprendizaje: un objetivo del paradigma educativocentrado en el aprendizaje, ARBOR Ciencia, Pensamiento y Cultura, vol. 187, no. 3 (2011)
24. Díaz, J., Troyano, Y.: el potencial de la gamificación aplicado al Ámbito educativo, Universidad de Sevilla Ciencias de la educación, vol. 3, no. 1 (2016)

ADMemento: A Prototype of Activity Reminder and Assessment Tools for Patients with Alzheimer's Disease

Sarah Alhassan[1]([⊠]), Wafa Alrajhi[1], Amal Alhassan[2], and Alreem Almuhrij[1]

[1] Computer Science Department, Al Imam Muhammad Ibn Saud Islamic University,
Riyadh, Saudi Arabia
salhassan.ccis@gmail.com, wafa7d@gmail.com, alreem.almuhrij@gmail.com
[2] Information Technology Department, King Saud University, Riyadh, Saudi Arabia
amalhassanx@gmail.com

Abstract. Due to the need to restore the life balance of mild-stage Alzheimer's disease (AD) patients and their caregivers, prototype of the system presented in this paper, ADMemento, enhances the independency of AD patients and reduces the caregivers' burden. The proposed mobile application includes an activity reminder that sends notifications regarding daily activities and events to patients with their preferred prompts. By observing AD symptoms, the system utilizes some assessment tools as an aid to determine AD progress and early intervention treatment. These assessments, which include recall rates determined by the activity reminder, pronunciation, common knowledge and family-related information loss indications, are presented to caregivers and therapists. A wearable wristband sensor is used to derive the patient's stress levels that are triggered due to the life-changing and cognitive impairment that patient is facing. ADMemento applies interface design guidelines that are suitable for aging.

Keywords: Social computing · Dementia · Alzheimer's disease · Activity reminder · AD assessment · AD aid

1 Introduction

Due to the recent increase in research pertaining to medicine and health that helps people to live longer, statistics expected that the number of people over the age of 60 will be doubled by 2050 [1]. Elderly people have a significant impact on society, and since the previous study [1] emphasizes increasing their numbers in the upcoming years, a great deal of research and investments should be designed to facilitate their lives. Moreover, different technologies should be developed to suit their needs and to adopt with the disabilities that are related to aging.

Unfortunately, longer life does not indicate a healthier life. One of caregivers' biggest concerns is how to coexist with elderly people who are suffering from Alzheimer's Disease (AD). AD is considered to be the most common type of

© Springer International Publishing AG 2017
G. Meiselwitz (Ed.): SCSM 2017, Part II, LNCS 10283, pp. 32–43, 2017.
DOI: 10.1007/978-3-319-58562-8_3

dementia and age is the best-known risk factor for it [2,3]. Recent statistics from 2016 showed that of 5.4 million Americans with AD, 5.2 million are above the age of 65 [4,5]. Despite scientific advancements, no cure has been found for AD. The currently existing treatments are used to reduce the symptoms' impact and enhance the life quality of the patients and caregivers [4,6]. AD affects the brain cells and results in major problems in memory and cognitive decline. It can be classified in three main stages—mild, moderate, and severe—and, in the advanced stages of the disease, the patient's condition worsens and he\she will rely more on the caregiver [7,8]. In the early stage of AD (mild stage), the patient suffers from several symptoms such as short-term memory loss and forgetting places or common words [9,10]. However, the patient can rely on himself at this stage.

Since an AD patient in the mild stage suffers from memory loss, some form of assistance should be provided in order for him or her to independently complete daily activities [10]. Thus, in this paper we propose a prototype of a mobile application that targets mild-stage AD patients to assist them in performing their daily activities and routines independently and also to support their caregivers and reduce their cumbersome burden. The proposed system (ADMemento) includes activity reminders for patients with preferred prompts from pictorial, auditory and text categories. It also allows the caregiver and the therapist to track the proportion of activities that have not been recalled and visualize the data that is gathered to show the AD progress. Moreover, ADMemento provides some assessment tools, such as pronunciation, memory loss assessments. It also uses a wearable sensor in order to detect the stress levels of the patients as an indication of emotional deficits and need for support.

The next section defines AD, its symptoms and stages, followed by a description of extant related work. Then, the system prototype, which includes a description of the system architecture, functionalities and prototype interface, is presented.

2   Alzheimer's Disease (AD)

AD is considered to be a type of dementia that is marked by deterioration in the memory and in the brain's abilities. It causes a disruption in the functions performed by the patient and the inability for him or her to be self-reliant [2,3]. According to the National Institute on Aging, AD is defined as "an irreversible, progressive brain disorder that slowly destroys memory and thinking skills and, eventually, the ability to carry out the simplest tasks." In the following subsections, the symptoms for each stage of AD are presented. Then, the deficits of AD are described.

2.1   AD Stages and Symptoms

Through symptoms, as mentioned in the introduction, AD can be classified in three main stages: mild (early stage), moderate (middle stage) and severe (late stage) [9,10]. The condition of an AD patient deteriorates over time and the symptoms gradually worsen while the patient progresses from one stage to another [6].

Each of these stages has symptoms. For example, in the mild stage, the patient may experience some difficulties in performing ordinary tasks and have memory lapses in general knowledge or with recent events. In addition, the patient may experience some difficulties in planning and problem solving and suffer from personal and behavior changes (e.g., irritability, anxiety and depression). Non-drug approaches can be used in order to reduce and manage the behavior of AD patients by considering their emotions [4].

In the moderate stage, the patient becomes more forgetful than the mild stage. Consequently, the patient may need assistance with daily activities, such as dressing, showering, etc. Upon reaching the severe stage, the patient requires personal assistance. The patient may lose the ability to communicate or speak and might also suffer from a decline in basic physical activities, such as walking, sitting, etc. [6,8].

2.2 AD Deficits

One of the main symptoms and deficits caused by AD is memory loss. Such loss can affect semantic memory, which is related to the general knowledge of the patient, or episodic memory, which is related to events [6,11]. In addition, AD can damage a part of the brain that is responsible for language, causing problems in reading and writing, as well as the recognition of spoken and written words (i.e., aphasia). Moreover, AD can cause agnosia disorder, which affects the recognition of the objects, people, smells, shapes and sounds. This disorder causes the inability to process sensory information. AD might also cause the inability to remember the sequence of movements that are required to perform a specific task, such as the sequence of movements needed to change clothes. This disorder causes the inability to perform voluntary movements, but the physical health of the patient is intact [11].

3 Related Work

A review of previous studies on assistive technologies used with Dementia, AD included, from 1992 to 2007 is presented in [12]. It shows the lack of studies that support the patients and their caregivers. Moreover, it presents the strengths and gaps of the previous research to insist upon the needs of the patients and their caregivers [12]. In addition, AD research in particular still has limitations despite the increased prevalence of AD [13]. While the burden of caregivers is still ongoing and requires external assistance, [14] illustrated the efficiency of home therapy with assistive technology to diminish the burden and reduce the depression levels of 94 caregivers within a six-month time period. Another study presented in [15] investigated a 12-month computer-mediated automated interactive voice response (IVR) intervention designed for AD caregivers. It proves how the caregivers' depression, anxiety and bothersome should be considered [15]. Furthermore, home health care systems have proved effective, especially while using current technologies such as wearable sensors [16]. Light-based wearable sensors can be used in the data acquisition process for monitoring patients in a continuous and unobtrusive manner. For example, a stress sensor can be used for stress diagnosis and early intervention treatment [16,17]. Moreover, studies in [18] illustrated how assistive technologies reduce stress levels, enhance medical intervention at the right time and increase the independency of people who suffer from dementia and live alone.

In 2003, a pilot study presented the electronic memory aid (EMA), which can be used to support people with mild AD in increasing their independence and improving the quality of their lives [19]. Moreover, the study showed the possibility for mild-AD patients to be trained to use the EMA and how it is superior to using written lists or free recalls [19]. Another study showed that patients can transact with automated prompts without caregiver intervention by using automated verbal- and audio-prompt systems [20]. The system presented in [21] has used the Assisted Living Hub (ALH), which is an intelligent device with wireless interface cards that communicates with the Assisted Living Service Provider (ALSP) server. The ALH receives a patient's prescription and appointments from the ALSP server and sends them as reminders to active wireless-enabled devices, such as television sets (TVs) [21]. Further, MEM-X, which is a vocal memory aid with alerts of specific times and dates using caregivers' recorded voices, can be used to help an AD patient [22]. Another memory aid system developed at Dundee University introduces Memojog [23], which prompts reminders for memory-impaired people. It transfers text-based prompts to voices that users can easily recognize [23].

4   ADMemento System Prototype

ADMemento is mainly designed for people with mild AD, who still have the ability to use mobile applications. The system aims to provide new insight into a new way of reminding patients about their activities with some assessments through the use of mobile phone applications (mobile app). A description of the system architecture and its main functionalities is presented in the following.

4.1   System Architecture

Figure 1 demonstrates the overall components of the ADMemento system. It consists of a wristband wearable device, database, cloud server, and mobile app that the patient and caregiver/therapist could use. Two views are provided for the mobile app, where the first view is to aim to serve the AD patient, and the other view is to serve the caregiver and therapist. Using the caregiver view, the caregiver can adjust the patient's daily activities along with time to help the patient to recall these activities later. Subsequently, via the patient view, the patient will receive the activity reminders. Additionally, the application will be able to

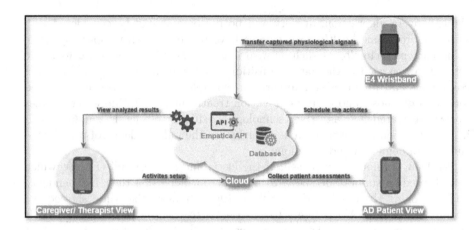

Fig. 1. System architecture

capture the patient's assessments, where the physiological signals will be captured from a wristband wearable device. The captured data will be accessed via Application Programming Interface (API) to be analyzed where a cloud server is used to reduce the burden of analyzing the data in the mobile application. To accomplish all of the system features, the cloud will analyze the patient entries and the captured physiological signals to estimate the patient's stress level. Ultimately, the caregiver and the therapist will be able to view the patient's records in graphical charts. All of the data will be stored into a database for further use.

4.2   System Functionalities and Features

The system has multiple functions that can be used to assist patients and caregivers and to provide assessments of the disease progress for caregivers and therapists. A description of the system functionalities is as follows.

Activity Reminder for AD Patient. Maintaining daily living routines is highly recommended for AD patients, as it helps with increasing their confidence and with raising their morale. The primary function of the system's prototype is to deliver the activities in a manner that the patient prefers, where the activities should be easy to interpret when considering the AD deficits.

The activity reminder allows the caregivers to add and customize a sequence of activities, where each activity should be assigned to a specific time and day (e.g., family gatherings on Mondays at 4 PM), and it can also be a daily reminder, such as for lunch time at 12 PM. Furthermore, the priority levels of activities can be increased for critical activities, such as taking medications. Accordingly, if a patient has missed a high-priority activity, the caregiver will receive a notification. Moreover, an optional feature that can be used is a location tag that might be used for outdoor activities. In case an outdoor reminder is triggered, the system retrieves by Global Positioning System (GPS) the patient location and matches it with the tagged location; if not, the caregiver is aware of that by notification.

Due to the variation of deficits that the AD patient might suffer—as mentioned in Sect. 2—different types of reminder prompts are used, depending on the patient deficit to enable the user to interpret the prompt correctly. Subsequently using written-language reminders will not be effective with a patient who suffers from aphasia. Thus, the system prototype provides for the caregiver three types of reminders—pictorial, auditory, and text reminders—allowing the caregiver to select the best way of giving a reminder to the AD patient.

Moreover, because stress is a common condition of an AD patient [24], the auditory prompts will be recorded with a voice that is familiar to the patient so that the patient will feel reassured. The system considers other problems that are related to aging, such as difficulties with hearing and vision, which will play an important role in the reminders as well [25]. Finally, the application had to be carefully approached from design perspectives; Sect. 4.3 provides further details.

Activities Recall Assessment. Tracking the activities that the patient can recall without assistance plays a critical role in estimating the patient's cognitive health [14]. Activity assessment aims to replace the self-report questionnaires of daily activity functioning with the direct observation of the patient. Thus, the system prototype provides the patient with two buttons for every reminder ("I remember" and "I forget") in text-based or voice-based format. Depending on the patient's selection, the system will save the selection on the database server and the data will be used to assess the patient's recall ability.

Pronunciation Assessment. The AD patient frequently exhibits verbal issues as the disease progresses [26], which, in turn, will influence his or her ability to communicate negatively. Communication can have a huge impact on people's lives, significantly influencing social relationships. Thus, attention has been devoted to helping patients to exercise and measure their ability to pronounce words correctly. Moreover, the deterioration of the patient's ability to pronounce might indicate the patient's transmission to the moderate stage. Some patients struggle with the pronunciation of words, and others falter while speaking. In the system prototype, pronunciation assessment detects the patient's verbal issues by presenting two modes: a random written sentence and random recorded audio. In the first mode, the patient attempts to read the sentence, whereas the patient repeats the recorded audio in the second mode. In both modes, the system is going to record the patient's pronunciation and convert it to text using Google Cloud Speech API [27]. Then, the system is going to compare the words collected from the patient with the original text that is already saved on the database server.

Stress Assessment. Balancing patients' daily stress can have a major benefit on their collective health [28]. Managing stress is very crucial for people who

Fig. 2. E4 wristband

suffer from AD, and it can be reflected negatively in their behavior; thus, we have provided an approach for monitoring patients' daily stress. Stress is reflected in a number of physiological parameters, such as the heart rate and sweat rate. Therefore, stress levels can be estimated based on analyzing these physiological signals [29].

The E4 wristband–which is a non-invasive wearable sensor–is used in the system. The E4–as shown in Fig. 2–is a sensing device used for measuring the physiological signals that are strongly related to stress. It consists of a pho-toplethysmography (PPG) sensor, galvanic skin response (GSR) sensor, and infrared thermopile [30]. The PPG sensor captures the heart rate (HR) and heart rate variability (HRV) from the blood volume pulse (BVP), which is the rate of blood flow over a period of time. The BVP can be used to interpret stress because blood flow is decreased during stress [31]. Many clinical studies have shown that HRV, the variation of time between two heart beats [32], is one of the most reliable signals in addressing stress [33]. GSR has also been wildly used for stress assessment [34]. GSR, known as electrodermal response (EDR) or electrodermal activity (EDA), is defined as a change in the electrical conduc-tance of the skin [35]. Infrared thermopile reads skin temperature (ST), where changes in ST can indicate the occurrence of stress [34]. A high stress level is estimated with a higher HR, GSR, and ST; a lower BPV; and changes in the HRV and ST [31,35].

To measure the stress level, data will be collected directly from the sensor via Empatica API for analysis. Indeed, it will help both clinicians and caregivers to find patterns such as the most stressful time on a daily, weekly, or monthly basis. Likewise, it will help with figuring out the changes of the stress levels for the patient, which will indicate the evolution of the disease.

Common Knowledge and Family-Related Recall Assessment. As men-tioned in Sect. 2, one of the main symptoms of Alzheimer's disease is the progres-sive loss of memory that gets worse with time, where the patient may not be able to remember some personal information and common knowledge, such as family members' names. Therefore, in the setup phase of this assessment, the system collects some personal information about the patient from the caregiver, such as the date of birth and the number of siblings, etc. Then, periodically, the system will ask the patient multiple questions randomly chosen from the content previously collected from the caregiver or some common knowledge. Subsequently, the system will assess the patient's memory condition based on the accuracy of response. The caregiver is the one who evaluates the response's accuracy, giving the answer a score (correct or incorrect).

Eventually, the system will visualize the previous assessments' results as dynamic charts that the therapist and caregiver can view in daily or monthly aggregations. As a result of observing these charts, the caregiver can derive information regarding the patient's ability to remember the activities and the patient's stress levels remotely without the need for the caregiver's presence. Moreover, the therapist and caregiver can keep track of the AD progress.

4.3   User Interface Prototyping

While designing the system prototype, the age of the end users was considered along with the disabilities that accompany the elderly. Thus, the system was designed to reduce the challenges of using the mobile phone where the elderly might find difficulties with coping with the current technologies. The system prototype focuses on presenting short familiar text that the elderly easily recognize to achieve a better understanding [36]. Furthermore, the text in the system prototype does not consist of abbreviations or technical terms. Accordingly, the system limits the size of the text that the caregiver can enter, and it provides a prompt message alerting him to avoid abbreviations and to write the text in a meaningful sentence. Additionally, the system will limit the recording length in audio reminders as well.

Another challenge that was considered is the visual deficits that the elderly may suffer [37], which make it difficult for them to read small texts. Thus, the texts in the system prototype are written in a large and easy-to-read font to fulfill the elderly's needs.

Additionally, the buttons need to be clearly identifiable; there should be a visual indication that an item or word is clickable to reduce the confusion that causes the elderly to make an incorrect selection and to avoid causing any stress.

The AD elderly might require a longer response time to accomplish a task because of their cognitive changes. In fact, most time will be spent on the decision process [38]. Considering this issue, the system prototype provides the AD elderly with sufficient time to respond. Additionally, it is hard for the elderly to distinguish between similar objects, especially when they have low contrast [39]. Thus, the most appropriate colors to use in designing the prototype was black text on a white background [38]. Furthermore, voices could help in improving the use of the application [40]; thus, the buttons will provide sound feedback to indicate to the elderly that they have been pressed—as in a real world situation—and they will change their colors as well. These guidelines are applied in the proposed system interfaces as shown in Figs. 3, 4, 5, and 6.

Fig. 3. Activity reminder (Picture Source: www.apartmentguide.com)

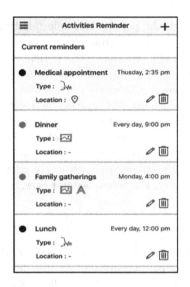

Fig. 4. Reminders list

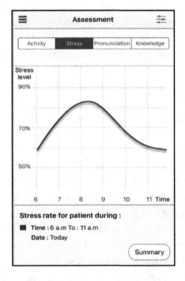

Fig. 5. Stress assessment

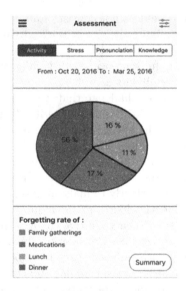

Fig. 6. Activity recall assessment

5   Conclusion

AD is considered life changing for patients and their caregivers. Patients' adaptation to the disease progress is tremendously needed. That can be achieved by raising the patients' independence in their activities and routines, and, as a consequence, their self-esteem. The proposed system presents an activity reminder with some assessment tools that are helpful for caregivers and therapists to observe the disease progress. For future work, this system will be tested on patients; thus, the results of using the system will be validated to check the evolution of patients' quality of life. Also, monitoring the stress level requires experimental parameters and levels to be more accurate. Moreover, some functionalities might be added to make the caregiver more involved with and aware of their patients' progress.

References

1. Lindmeier, C., Brunier, A.: WHO: number of people over 60 years set to double by 2050; major societal changes required. World Health Organization (2015). goo.gl/qIW8dv. Accessed 13 Oct 2016
2. Thies, W., Bleiler, L.: 2011 Alzheimer's disease facts and figures. Alzheimer's Dement. **7**, 208–244 (2011). doi:10.1016/j.jalz.2011.02.004
3. Rosenblatt, A.: The art of managing dementia in the elderly. Clevel. Clin. J. Med. (2005). doi:10.3949/ccjm.72.suppl_3.s3
4. Alzheimer's Disease Education and Referral Center: National Institute on Aging. www.nia.nih.gov/alzheimers. Accessed 15 Oct 2016
5. Centers for Disease Control and Prevention. www.cdc.gov. Accessed 15 Oct 2016
6. Alzheimer's Association. www.alz.org. Accessed 20 Oct 2016
7. American Psychological Association: Diagnostic and Statistical Manual of Mental Disorders, 4th edn. American Psychological Association, Arlington (2000)
8. Wherton, J., Monk, A.: Technological opportunities for supporting people with dementia who are living at home. Int. J. Hum.-Comput. Stud. **66**, 571–586 (2008). doi:10.1016/j.ijhcs.2008.03.001
9. Alzheimer's Society. www.alzheimers.org.uk. Accessed 20 Oct 2016
10. Hong Kong Hospital Authority: Dementia. In: Smart Patient Websie (2014). goo.gl/ZTqbWP. Accessed 23 Oct 2016
11. Bergman, H., Arcand, M., Bureau, C., et al.: Relever le défi de la maladie d'Alzheimer et des maladies apparentées Une vision centrée sur la personne, l'humanisme et l'excellence. Gouvernement du Québec (2009)
12. Topo, P.: Technology studies to meet the needs of people with dementia and their caregivers: a literature review. J. Appl. Gerontol. **28**, 5–37 (2009). doi:10.1177/0733464808324019
13. Gogia, P., Rastogi, N.: Clinical Alzheimer Rehabilitation. Springer, New York (2009)
14. Eisdorfer, C., Czaja, S., Loewenstein, D., et al.: The effect of a family therapy and technology-based intervention on caregiver depression. The Gerontologist **43**, 521–531 (2003). doi:10.1093/geront/43.4.521
15. Mahoney, D., Tarlow, B., Jones, R.: Effects of an automated telephone support system on caregiver burden and anxiety: findings from the REACH for TLC intervention study. The Gerontologist **43**, 556–567 (2003). doi:10.1093/geront/43.4.556
16. Warren, S., Yao, J., Barnes, G.: Wearable sensors and component-based design for home health care. In: Proceedings of the Second Joint of 24th Annual Conference and the Annual Fall Meeting of the Biomedical Engineering Society EMBS/BMES Conference on Engineering in Medicine and Biology, pp. 1871–1872. IEEE (2002)

17. Choi, J., Ahmed, B., Gutierrez-Osuna, R.: Development and evaluation of an ambulatory stress monitor based on wearable sensors. IEEE Trans. Inf. Technol. Biomed. **16**, 279–286 (2012). doi:10.1109/titb.2011.2169804
18. Taylor, F.: Care managers' views on assistive technology. J. Dement. Care **13**, 32–35 (2016)
19. Oriani, M., Moniz-Cook, E., Binetti, G., et al.: An electronic memory aid to support prospective memory in patients in the early stages of Alzheimer's disease: a pilot study. Aging Ment. Health **7**, 22–27 (2003). doi:10.1080/1360786021000045863
20. Labelle, K., Mihailidis, A.: The use of automated prompting to facilitate handwashing in persons with dementia. Am. J. Occup. Ther. **60**, 442–450 (2006). doi:10.5014/ajot.60.4.442
21. Wang, Q., Shin, W., Liu, X., et al.: An open system architecture for assisted living. In: IEEE International Conference on Systems, Man and Cybernetics, SMC 2006 (2006)
22. How the Mem-x Voice Reminder Works. Pivotell. goo.gl/Gcu0XH. Accessed 27 Sept 2016
23. Morrison, K., Szymkowiak, A., Gregor, P.: Memojog – an interactive memory aid incorporating mobile based technologies. In: Brewster, S., Dunlop, M. (eds.) Mobile HCI 2004. LNCS, vol. 3160, pp. 481–485. Springer, Heidelberg (2004). doi:10.1007/978-3-540-28637-0_61
24. Bieber, T., Leung, D. (eds.): Atopic Dermatitis, 1st edn. Marcel Dekker, New York (2002)
25. Lapointe, J., Bouchard, B., Bouchard, J., et al.: Smart homes for people with Alzheimer's disease: adapting prompting strategies to the patient's cognitive profile. In: The 5th International Conference on PErvasive Technologies Related to Assistive Environments, PETRA 2012 (2012)
26. Fraser, K., Meltzer, J., Rudzicz, F.: Linguistic features identify Alzheimer's disease in narrative speech. J. Alzheimer's Dis. **49**, 407–422 (2015). doi:10.3233/jad-150520
27. Speech API - Speech Recognition. Google Cloud Platform. cloud.google.com/speech/. Accessed 5 Nov 2016
28. Endler, N.: Hassles, health, and happiness. In: Janisse, M. (ed.) Individual Differences, Stress, and Health Psychology, pp. 24–56. Springer, New York (1988)
29. Pozo, G., Vázquez, I., Ávila, C., et al.: State of the Art-Wearable Sensors (2014)
30. E4 wristband: Empatica. www.empatica.com/e4-wristband. Accessed 24 Nov 2016
31. Gross, T., Gulliksen, J., Kotzé, P. (eds.): INTERACT 2009. HCI, vol. 5727. Springer, Heidelberg (2009)
32. Simola, A.: The Roving Mind: A Modern Approach to Cognitive Enhancement. ST Press, New York (2015)
33. Filippini, D. (ed.): Autonomous Sensor Networks. Springer, Berlin (2013)
34. Palanisamy, K., Murugappan, M., Yaacob, S.: Multiple physiological signal-based human stress identification using non-linear classifiers. Elektronika IR Elektrotechnika (2013). doi:10.5755/j01.eee.19.7.2232
35. Sharma, N., Gedeon, T.: Artificial neural network classification models for stress in reading. In: Huang, T., Zeng, Z., Li, C., et al. (eds.) Neural Information Processing, pp. 388–395. Springer, Heidelberg (2012)
36. Haug, C., Kvam, F.: Tablets and elderly users: designing a guidebook. Master's thesis, University of OSLO Department of informatics
37. Thakur, T., Sethi, D.: A descriptive study to assess the impact of low vision on activities of daily living among elderly people living in selected residential areas of Kurali (Punjab). Imperial J. Interdiscip. Res. **2**, 711–717 (2016)

38. Slavíček, T.: Touch screen mobile user interface for seniors. Master's thesis, Czech Technical University (2014)
39. Echt, K.: Designing web-based health information for older adults: visual consideration and design directives. In: Morrell, R. (ed.) Older Adults, Health Information, and the World Wide Web, pp. 59–86. Lawrence Erlbaum Associates, Mahwah (2002)
40. Galitz, W.: The Essential Guide to User Interface Design, 3rd edn. Wiley, Indianapolis (2007)

From GreedEx to GreedEx Tab v2.0: Tool for Learning Greedy Algorithms on iPad Following CIAM Mobile Methodology

Yoel Arroyo, Manuel Ortega Cordovilla, Miguel A. Redondo, Ana I. Molina,
María del Carmen Lacave, and Manuel Ortega Cantero[✉]

Escuela Superior de Informática, Universidad de Castilla-La Mancha,
Paseo de la Universidad, 4., 13071 Ciudad Real, Spain
{Yoel.Arroyo,Manuel.Ortega1,Miguel.Redondo,AnaIsabel.Molina,
Carmen.Lacave,Manuel.Ortega}@uclm.es

Abstract. The growth in the use of mobile devices have allowed for the development of new educational modalities within e-Learning. Because of this, we have shown the evolution experienced by GreedEx, a desktop application that facilitates the learning of greedy algorithms. Two iPad versions were developed (GreedEx Tab v1.0 and v2.0). The first iPad version adapted many functionalities to mobile devices, whilst the latest one adds several pedagogical usability characteristics. For that, we followed the CIAM Mobile methodology, improving the educational and collaborative aspects. Our main aim is to verify that this methodology is useful for the production of new methodological approaches aligned with the principles of MDE (Model-Driven Engineering) that gives support to learning activities within a group. Therefore, this work can be considered a preliminary m-CIAM test case .

Keywords: Mobile usability · Mobile learning · Methodology · Greedy algorithms learning · Knapsack problem · iOS · iPad · Model-driven development

1 Introduction

The growth in the use of mobile devices have allowed for the development of new educational modalities within e-Learning. Because of this, we have shown the evolution experienced by GreedEx, a desktop application that facilitates the learning of greedy algorithms. Two iPad versions were developed (GreedEx Tab v1.0 and v.2.0).

GreedEx Tab is an application for iPad developed by the CHICO (Computer-Human Interaction and Collaboration)[1] research group to facilitate the learning of greedy algorithms [1]. In the latest version, we wanted to solve the usability problems found in its predecessor [2] and add several pedagogical characteristics. Furthermore, the application presents groupware characteristics, allowing both students and teachers to work collaboratively on a learning task thanks to iCloud.

---

[1] http://chico.esi.uclm.es/cms/.

© Springer International Publishing AG 2017
G. Meiselwitz (Ed.): SCSM 2017, Part II, LNCS 10283, pp. 44–54, 2017.
DOI: 10.1007/978-3-319-58562-8_4

Thus, GreedEx Tab v2.0 has been developed by following the CIAM Mobile (m-CIAM) methodology [3]. This new methodology assumes a quality leap over the CIAM (Collaborative Interactive Applications Methodology) methodology [4] by integrating it with the MoLEF (Mobile Evaluation Framework) usability framework [5], providing evaluation and design mechanisms to facilitate the development of collaborative mobile learning systems.

Our main aim is to verify if this methodology is useful for the production of a new methodological approach aligned with the principles of MDE (Model-Driven Engineering) that gives support to learning activities within a group. Therefore, this work can be considered a preliminary m-CIAM test case.

The structure of the paper is as follows: Section two introduces similar programming and algorithm tutoring systems that already exists and the current state of the methodologies and frameworks implied. In the next section, the evolution GreedEx experienced and the obtaining of the different versions is explained. Then, we talk about some current and future work, with m-CIAM methodology and MDE as a starting point. Finally, we close this paper with some conclusions related to this work.

2 Previous and Related Work

It is important to teach novice programmers how to analyze a given problem, identify the computing requirements, and develop an algorithm appropriate for its solution. The main problem is they are not aware of designing an algorithm before writing code. They believe that developing an algorithm will increase the time necessary to do an assignment. However, many students struggle through the programming process, and end up spending a considerable amount of time debugging numerous logical or design errors.

Nowadays, there exist similar algorithm tutoring systems such as GreedEx. For example, AlgoTutor (The Algorithm Tutor) [6] is an online, graphical and interactive tool which provides automatic assessment of student designed algorithms. In addition to the student algorithm design interface, there is an instructor interface that allows the teacher to create/edit problems and their solutions, manage student accounts, and analyze student grades as well as student activities. As far as disadvantages are concerned, it is just for novice programmers.

Another tool of this kind is ANIMAL (A New Interactive Modeler for Animations in Lectures) [7]. It offers a selection of powerful features that can easily be combined to create and display animations of algorithms, data structures and many other topics. Animations can be generated using a visual editor, by scripting or via API calls. The main advantage is that it has a good collection of algorithms of different categories, including backtracking, graph, searching and sorting, trees, hashing, etc. So, it is usually used by intermediate level programmers.

Similar systems such as JHavé [8] or AlgoViz [9] can serve the same purpose. However, if we focus on greedy algorithms visualization and experimentation, we should talk about GATutor (Greedy Algorithms Tutor) [10] and GreedEx (Greedy Experimentation) [11]. GATutor is a rule based framework for teaching greedy algorithms. It allows the user to develop an algorithm providing them stimulating questions and timely hints to real life scenarios. Later, all this data could be analyzed by the system providing insights to the teacher. GATutor is a good choice, but the learning process is relatively more complex than GreedEx. The main difference is that GATutor could be considered a visualization system program, usually designed to aid in analyzing program behavior, whilst GreedEx objective is less general, designed to aid students in understanding algorithm behavior. In Sect. 3 more details about GreedEx and its different versions are described.

The second and latest GreedEx Tab version was developed following the m-CIAM methodology. It is a methodology used in the development and modeling of m-Learning applications. It integrates the CIAM methodology [4] with MoLEF [5] usability framework factors and dimensions. CIAM provides support in the modeling of collaborative and interactive aspects of e-learning systems, while MoLEF incorporates evaluation or analysis techniques for mobile learning applications. In other words, MoLEF adds support for mobile learning applications evaluation and implementation where CIAM does not have.

Currently, we are validating the m-CIAM methodology in other scopes such as MDE (Model-Driven Engineering). As we said in section before, our main aim is to verify if this methodology is useful for the production of new methods like these. Therefore, the design and implementation of GreedEx Tab v2.0 may be considered further proof of this methodology, apart from getting an improved version of the original application.

3   From GreedEx to GreedEx Tab v2.0

GreedEx (Greedy Experimentation) [11] is a desktop application developed by LITE (Laboratory of Information Technologies in Education)[2] research group for discovery learning and experimentation of greedy algorithms. Their original intention was to develop an educational system to support any greedy algorithm. However, due to the huge difference in the visualization of the different greedy algorithms this goal should have been abandoned by designing a system that supports a fixed but extensible set of problems.

Currently, GreedEx supports six optimization problems, the activity selection problem [1] and five knapsack problems: The fractional and the 0/1 knapsack problems, as well as three variations with different maximization measures (number of objects introduced into the knapsack, weight of these objects, and number of objects introduced into two knapsacks).

The main goal is to state a selection function for one of these problems and prove its optimality. Which means, the student must figure out all the selection functions that could characterize an optimal greedy algorithm for a given problem. To accomplish this, GreedEx provides several selection functions for each problem. A selection function is defined on the set of available candidates, returning to each step the most promising candidate with respect to some measure. For example, in the knapsack problem users may select among the *increasing order of index, decreasing order of index, increasing order of weight,*

---

[2]   http://www.lite.etsii.urjc.es/.

decreasing order of weight, increasing order of profit or *decreasing order of profit* between other selection functions. They must interact with them and seek the maximum size subset of objects to be included in the knapsack, discarding the non-optimal ones.

For that, GreedEx provides a user interface with three different areas clearly distinguishable. Figure 1 shows an interactive session with the knapsack problem. The top area is the visualization panel, which shows the graphical representation of the problem. The lower left area is the theory panel, with two tabs: one to show the problem statement written in natural language, and the other tab shows the solution to the greedy algorithm written in pseudocode. The lower right area is the table panel, with four tabs containing the input data table, the results table, the history table, and the summary table. This user interface is possible in desktop devices due to the huge size of the screen. In mobile devices, such as a smartphone or iPad as it is the case, it must be analyzed for new design and development, adapting its functionality and interface taking advantage of interaction, visualization and animation of these kinds of devices.

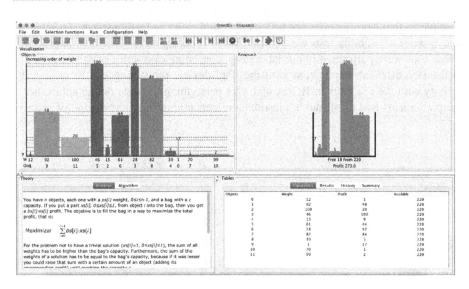

Fig. 1.   GreedEx session with knapsack problem

With this purpose, our research group evaluated GreedEx in collaboration with the LITE research group through an eye tracking tool (the Eye-Tracker Tobii ×60) available in our laboratory in the Computer Science Engineering College of Ciudad Real. The results of this evaluation [12, 13] identified some shortcomings in its user interface and learning methods that suggested that a more interactive tool could improve this learning. One of the main complaints between students were that the graphical representations was lacking in an interactive nature and were difficult to understand, so they preferred the tabular data representation to consult the results and interact with the problem. For that reason, what we considered interesting was to build up GreedEx Tab [2], an application where graphical representations takes on greater role by improving the interaction within the representation of the results, amongst other things.

GreedEx Tab [2] was developed in our laboratory for this purpose. The selected device was an iPad. The larger size of the screen was one of the motives for choosing this mobile device, in comparison with others such as an iPhone, where graphical representations could be difficult to understand and to develop.

This version was obtained following SCRUM [14] as management methodology along with OpenUP [15] and CIAM [4] as development methodologies. SCRUM and OpenUP are agile methods to work with based on the *Manifesto for Agile Software Development* [16]. For that, we considered them ideal for small projects like GreedEx Tab. More details about these methodologies and how to follow them could be reviewed [2], where the application obtained was explained.

While SCRUM and OpenUP guides the project via sprints and the typical phases such as initiation, elaboration, construction and transition, CIAM gives support to modeling the collaborative and interactive aspects. It is really useful for applications such as GreedEx Tab whose main premise is to reach a healthier computer-human interaction.

We tried to make it intuitive and fast, allowing users to interact in the simplest way possible so that learning does not become a complicated and tedious task. To achieve that, a series of usability tests were carried out [17] during its implementation process. These tests were performed in our laboratory, consisting of a series of activities to do in the GreedEx Tab application with the iPad device, registering and recording all activity with the eye tracker. Before and after performing the tests on the application, the participants had to fill out a questionnaire concerning their knowledge of greedy

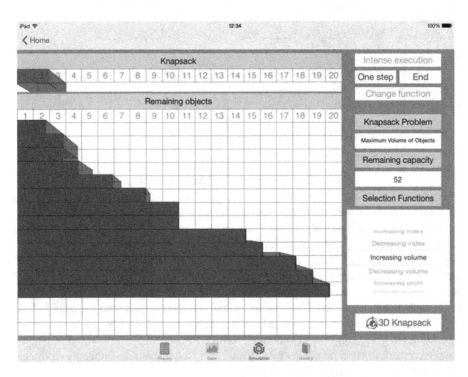

Fig. 2. GreedEx Tab session with knapsack problem

algorithms and their experience with the application respectively. All the information collected was finally analyzed, determining that the initial shortcomings in the graphical user interface and in the learning methods detected were resolved. In this version, the graphical representations as shown in Fig. 2 are the most representative and consulted, instead of the tabular representations of GreedEx.

However, the results obtained were not satisfactory at all. We could appreciate that these representations increased the use of the graphical representations but continue to be difficult to understand, obtaining only acceptable values in this area. For example, users complained about the 3D visualization of the knapsack because they considered it not intuitive, making the learning process difficult. For that reason, we decided to enhance the user interface again, trying to solve these problems using other methods that could help us obtain improved pedagogical and technological values.

Moreover, looking at [2], some usability principles were taken into account in the design and development process, such as the golden rules of Ben Shneiderman [18], the established for Apple for its applications [19] and the usability patterns for mobile devices defined by Jacob Nielsen [20]. Nevertheless, these were not enough to achieve our objectives.

Thus, we must mention the addition of MoLEF [5] in the implementation of GreedEx Tab in its second version. MoLEF is a design and evaluation framework for collaborative m-Learning systems. It provides some guidelines that developers must take into account to obtain improved pedagogical and user interface usability values. In contrast with CIAM, MoLEF is focused on the development of mobile learning applications. That is the way m-CIAM arose, with their integration, providing an updated and more powerful methodology.

The results were satisfactory in general, solving several of the complaints about GreedEx Tab. For example, the knapsack of the problem was replaced by a barrel metaphor (see Fig. 3). It is not only more attractive and comfortable, but more interactive, providing information of its state whenever the user wants just by touching it. It also provides a more detailed legend. Furthermore, the screen space is well exploited. As shown in Fig. 3, the state of the problem is always known because of the objects implied and the knapsack are in the same place, facilitating the learning process.

To achieve that we followed the m-CIAM steps as described [3]. To verify that this methodology is useful in obtaining better pedagogical and user interface usability values, an exploratory evaluation with real users was performed in our laboratory. Sixteen undergraduate students from our school took part in it. In this case, the students had to compare the first GreedEx Tab version with the latest one. For that, they accomplished a series of scheduled tasks with both applications while recording and registering all data with our eye-tracking tool. After that, they had to fill out the CECAM (Questionnaire for the Evaluation of the Quality of m-Learning Applications) questionnaire [21], which is part of m-CIAM and provided by MoLEF. This questionnaire is made up of 56 items, 29 of them corresponding to pedagogical usability and the rest in the user interface usability. It is really useful as an evaluation checklist for usability of m-Learning systems, but it can also be used as an heuristics checklist for its design, previously explained [3].

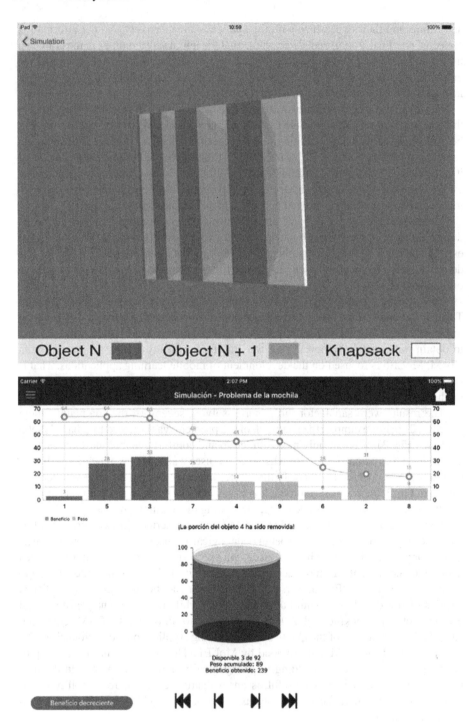

Fig. 3. The representation of a knapsack on GreedEx Tab v1.0 and GreedEx Tab v2.0

The results obtained were positive. The new version received better pedagogical and user interface values, fulfilling the stated objective, making it more comfortable and usable in both pedagogical and technological aspects. In a comparative way, as shown in Table 1, the evolution experienced on some characteristics by the applications involved. In this table, we can see thanks to the follow up of m-CIAM, most of them were updated and improved in the latest version. Whilst, for example, the multilingual support on GreedEx Tab v2.0 is scheduled as future work.

Table 1. Comparative table between versions and its characteristics

Characteristic	GreedEx	Gx Tab	Gx Tab 2
Concepts explained and presented in a clear manner	X	X	X
Activities reflects practices relevant to professional life	X	X	X
Intuitive and consistent icons for actions	X	X	X
Appropriate feedback information	-	-	X
Navigation simple, familiar and intuitive	-	-	X
Adjusted and adapted information for screen size	X	X	X
Pleasant and attractive aesthetics	-	-	X
Interactive charts selected to facilitate learning	-	-	X
Collaborative functions for students and mentors	-	X	X
Interactive knapsack provided	-	X	X
Multilingual support	X	X	-

Thus, after joining all collected data and verifying the results, we can conclude that the stating students were more comfortable and satisfied with the latest version. The first iPad version introduced several updates and enhancements in the user interface, whilst the latest version also improved the learning methods. For that, we considered this methodology interesting for the development of applications of this kind.

4   Applying MDE for Generalizing Our Approach

In recent years, we are also working to provide a new methodological approach aligned with the principles of MDE (Model-Driven Engineering) that gives support to learning activities within a group. It is focused in the CSCL (Computer Supported Collaborative Learning) [22] paradigm, which exploits the advantages provided by groupware systems in the field of e-Learning.

The development of such systems is not a simple task. There are aspects such as the support to model collaborative processes, the roles supported by the system or the existence of spaces for sharing information, which has become key in design and implementation requirements [21].

That is the reason why CIAM methodology was firstly developed. It covers some groupware usability requirements (i.e., incorporating coordination and communication tools, a design-based on models of users and tasks, role modeling, etc.), providing a series of notations and stages to design collaborative systems. Nevertheless, it only supports the analysis and design phases, and other important aspects such as the implementation of communication mechanism, the access control to shared resources, the support to coordination, the management of sessions or the inclusion of awareness elements are not technologically supported.

For that reason, the SpacEclipse framework [23] was also developed. The main advantage is that, integrating it with CIAM, allows designers to generate a collaborative modeling tool adapted to any domain. More simply put, we could obtain collaborative synchronous modeling tools specialized for the domain of application previously modeled.

However, as we are focused in the CSCL paradigm it is necessary to consider its educational and pedagogical aspects during the different phases of the method. To achieve that, we used MoLEF as a reference, which provides these necessary criteria and guidelines. For instance, by integrating CIAM Mobile (giving support to the analysis and design phases) with the SpacEclipse framework (giving support to the implementation phase), full support for the development of CSCL tools may be obtained.

Currently, groupware engineers use these methodologies and frameworks in a 'manual' way. Thus, our further objective is to facilitate their work by providing a systematic technological support that takes into account pedagogical usability aspects. To achieve that, we are carrying out more exhaustive studies, with evaluations that include comparisons between tools developed using the method and without using it, and comparisons between tools generated using different characteristics of the method to achieve that. However, the results of these studies are outside the scope of this paper.

5   Conclusions and Future Work

In this paper, we have shown the evolution experienced by GreedEx, a desktop application that facilitates the learning of greedy algorithms. Two iPad versions were developed (GreedEx Tab v1.0 and v.2.0). The first version adapted many functionalities to mobile devices whilst the latest one improves user interface by adding several pedagogical usability characteristics, thus enriching the educational and collaborative aspects.

To achieve that, the latest version has been developed by following the CIAM Mobile (m-CIAM) methodology. This methodology assumes a quality leap on the CIAM methodology by integrating it with the MoLEF usability framework, which provides some evaluation and design guidelines to facilitate the development of collaborative mobile learning systems.

The results obtained were positive, obtaining better pedagogical and user interface usability values in general. The students were more comfortable with it. Moreover, the CECAM questionnaire and data collected with our eye-tracking tool verifies those results. Thus, we consider this methodology interesting for developing applications of these kinds.

Nevertheless, we are working to provide a new methodological approach aligned with the principles of MDE (Model-Driven Engineering) that gives support to learning activities within a group. This method is focused in the CSCL paradigm so it is necessary to consider its pedagogical usability dimension. Thus, we also must take as reference

MoLEF, and for instance, the m-CIAM methodology, which provides these necessary criteria and guidelines.

To reach our goal, we are carrying out more exhaustive studies, with further evaluations that includes comparisons between tools developed using the method and without using it, and comparisons between tools generated using different characteristics of the method.

Acknowledgments. This research has been partially funded by the Ministry of Science and Innovation through the project TIN2015-66731-C2-2-R and the JCCM Project PPII11-0013-1219.

References

1. Cormen, T.H.: Introduction to Algorithms. MIT Press, Cambridge (2009)
2. Ortega Cordovilla, M., et al.: GreedEx Tab: tool for learning Greedy algorithms on mobile devices. In: IARIA 2016, pp. 28–35 (2016)
3. Arroyo, Y., Navarro, C.X., Molina, A.I., Redondo, M.A.: CIAM mobile: methodology supporting mobile application design and evaluation applied on GreedEx Tab. In: Luo, Y. (ed.) CDVE 2016. LNCS, vol. 9929, pp. 102–109. Springer, Cham (2016). doi: 10.1007/978-3-319-46771-9_14
4. Molina, A.I., et al.: CIAM: a methodology for the development of groupware user interfaces. J. UCS **14**(9), 1435–1446 (2008)
5. Navarro, C.X., et al.: Framework to evaluate M-learning systems: a technological and pedagogical approach. IEEE Revista Iberoamericana de Tecnologias del Aprendizaje **11**(1), 33–40 (2016)
6. Pettey, C., et al.: A tool for promoting algorithm development in introductory CS classes. In: Proceedings of ED-MEDIA (2009)
7. Rößling, G., Schüer, M., Freisleben, B.: The ANIMAL algorithm animation tool. ACM SIGCSE Bull. (2000). ACM
8. Naps, T.L.: JHAVÉ: supporting algorithm visualization. IEEE Comput. Graph. Appl. **25**(5), 49–55 (2005)
9. Ullrich, T., Fellner, D.: AlgoViz-a computer graphics algorithm visualization toolkit. In: World Conference on Educational Multimedia, Hypermedia and Telecommunications (2004)
10. Lahoti, M.: GATutor: Intelligent Tutoring System for Greedy Algorithms. Indian Institute of Technology Bombay, Mumbai (2014)
11. Velazquez-Iturbide, J.A., et al.: GreedEx: a visualization tool for experimentation and discovery learning of greedy algorithms. IEEE Trans. Learn. Technol. **6**(2), 130–143 (2013)
12. Molina, A.I., et al.: Evaluación basada en eye tracking de las técnicas de visualización de programas soportadas por el sistema GreedEx
13. Molina, A.I., et al.: Assessing representation techniques of programs supported by GreedEx. In: 2014 International Symposium on Computers in Education (SIIE). IEEE (2014)
14. Schwaber, K.: SCRUM development process. In: Sutherland, J., Casanave, C., Miller, J., Patel, P., Hollowell, G. (eds.) Business Object Design and Implementation, pp. 117–134. Springer, London (1997)
15. Kroll, P., MacIsaac, B.: Agility and Discipline Made Easy: Practices from OpenUP and RUP. Pearson Education, Boston (2006)
16. Beck, K., et al.: Manifesto for agile software development (2001)

17. Ortega Cordovilla, M.: Usability Tests of GreedEx Tab. CHICO Wiki. http://chico.inf-cr.uclm.es/greedextab/wiki/index.php/Pruebas_de_usabilidad. Accessed 29 Dec 2016
18. Shneiderman, B., Plaisant, C.: Designing the User Interface: Strategies for Effective Human-Computer Interaction, vol. 5. Addison-Wesley Publishing Co., Boston (2010)
19. Apple Inc.: iOS Human Interface Guidelines. Apple Developer Website. https://developer.apple.com/ios/human-interface-guidelines/overview/design-principles/. Accessed 10 Jan 2017
20. Nielsen, J., Budiu, R.: Mobile Usability. MITP-Verlags GmbH & Co. KG (2013)
21. Molina, A.I., et al.: A Model-Driven Approach for the Development of CSCL Tools that Considers Pedagogical Usability
22. Koschmann, T.D.: CSCL, Theory and Practice of an Emerging Paradigm. Routledge, New York (1996)
23. Gallardo, J., Bravo, C., Redondo, M.A.: A model-driven development method for collaborative modeling tools. J. Netw. Comput. Appl. 35(3), 1086–1105 (2012)

Memorializing the Deceased Using Virtual Worlds: A Preliminary Study

James Braman[1](✉), Alfreda Dudley[2](✉), and Giovanni Vincenti[3](✉)

[1] School of Technology, Art and Design, Computer Science/Information Technology, Community College of Baltimore County, 7201 Rossville Boulevard, Rosedale, MD, USA
jbraman@ccbcmd.edu
[2] Department of Computer and Information Sciences, Towson University, 8000 York Rd., Towson, MD, USA
adudley@towson.edu
[3] Division of Science, Information Arts and Technologies, University of Baltimore, 1420 N. Charles St, Baltimore, MD, USA
gvincenti@ubalt.edu

Abstract. Virtual worlds, for many users represent a very real space that intersects with aspects of real life. Time spent in these online environments represent extensions to everyday life, including our expressions and connections to other users. As these spaces become even more entwined into our way of life, there will be an increase of expressions being played-out in these environments. The focus of this paper addresses how memorials used for expression and remembrance of the deceased are represented in cyberspace. Several questions are posed concerning how virtual worlds can be used in this way along with a presentation of information collected from a preliminary survey. Our survey concentrates on user perceptions of various aspects of virtual world memorials.

Keywords: Memorials · Virtual worlds · Online legacy · Social networks

1 Introduction

Virtual worlds and social networking sites play an increasing role in our everyday interaction. These environments are becoming important venues for the expression of grief and for gaining support to cope with loss. Not only can these online spaces allow us to connect to other people in various ways; but, also to represent and memorialize loved ones that have died. Technology has influenced how we deal with and interact with death in many new and profound ways. In this project, we are in the beginning stages of investigating the application of virtual worlds in memorialization, for both in-world (virtual) and real-world deaths. In addition, exploring this technology can be used throughout the grieving process. This paper follows our previous research examining the education of users on the implications of social networking sites and virtual worlds regarding their own death [1–4]. Moreover, we discuss the results of data collected from a preliminary survey, which provides insights on user perceptions of various aspects of virtual world memorials.

© Springer International Publishing AG 2017
G. Meiselwitz (Ed.): SCSM 2017, Part II, LNCS 10283, pp. 55–64, 2017.
DOI: 10.1007/978-3-319-58562-8_5

Two main purposes of a memorial artifact are: (1) to serve as a reminder or representation of someone who is deceased; or, (2) to serve as a reminder or representation of an important event or accomplishment. In the context of the deceased, memorials can take many forms (i.e., gravestones, statues, elaborate monuments, etc.). While most memorials are constructed for long term use, they can exist in more temporary forms (i.e., arrangements of flowers, letters, items or candles on the road side). Variations of memorials are defined across cultures and religions purposes to fit many types of needs. Some memorials are well planned, while others are created more spontaneously depending on the circumstances (i.e., unanticipated or violent deaths) [5]. Similarly, online memorials can have several formats and exist over varying time frames. The construction of an online memorial can include a digital artifact in a 3D space; such as, a virtual world or in a virtual reality, or that of a website or other memorization through a social networking site.

As the prevalence of online memorials grow, so too does the ability to interact with these forms of remembrances of the deceased. Technological advancements allow for various types of interaction with digital memorials. There has been an increasing number of funeral homes not only using the web to advertise their services, but to also provide information on funeral arrangements, and, to serve as online memorials for the deceased. For example, websites like legacy.com offer an array of services and information ranging from assistance in searching for funeral homes, sending flowers, and, the ability to search obituaries and online memorials. There have been other technological influences like Quick Response (QR) codes that add features on some headstones [6]. Many users are also turning to social media sites (i.e., Facebook) to express grief [7] as well as other online technologies. For some, online technology is becoming a familiar mechanism to use in the grieving process. More precisely, we can say that thanatechnology is any technology that "Include[s] all types of communication technology that can be used in the provision of death education, grief counseling, and thanatology research" [8, p. 33]. It can be said that tools like social media and virtual worlds fall into that category when used for memorialization.

Another related issue is the use of these tools during our life time and how that can contribute to the data we leave behind when we die. Posts on social media inevitably construct a narrative of our life events [9], particularly if such use is over prolonged periods of our life. Posts across social networking sites, blogs, and other social media become (intentionally or unintentionally) become part of the online legacy one leaves behind. This is also true for interactions and created content in online virtual worlds. Previous research has proposed several key questions that one can use to assess content as they are posting or storing content online or on a social networking site, or even in the context of virtual worlds which include [3]: (1) Is this content something I'm alright with if it becomes part of my digital legacy? (2) Is this content something that should be protected if something were to happen to me? And, (3) If this content should be protected, how can it be protected? Posts on social media can have negative effects as well and cause feeling of regret after certain content has been posted, particularly if the content is very personal [10]. This could be particularly troublesome if content becomes part of someone's digital legacy and content is taken out of context. Also, one should consider posts that may be viewed by unintended audiences [10].

2   Toward Virtual Memorials

"Funerals, memorial services, and other post-death ceremonies can serve as meaningful times of coming together of family members to acknowledge and share the loss of a loved one" [11, p. 173]. This is also true in the context of virtual worlds or through the technologies afforded by such technologies. Virtual worlds can be defined as "an electronic environment that visually mimics complex physical spaces, where people can interact with each other and with virtual objects, and where people are represented by animated characters" [12, p. 472]. As technologies improve and as users gain more mainstream access, the prevalence and usage of virtual worlds and other social networking tools will continue to grow. Since virtual worlds mimic many aspects of real life, but without many of its limitations, it is not surprising that death and mourning and related elements find its way in. However, there are many questions related to virtual memorials, particularly with perception, how to interact with them and how they should be designed.

How should we represent memorials in a virtual world? How should we interact with these digital artifacts? As virtual worlds often represent a malleable but persistent environment, the possibilities of configuration and design could vary widely. However, the long-term sustainment of online memorials could raise concerns about costs depending on the virtual world, amount of space and length of time the artifact remain. Both the design and existence of a memorial within in a particular world dictates some of the interaction potential of the memorial as bound by the limitations of the environment. For instance, some virtual worlds allow for more possibilities and functionality for the user through the user's avatar. There are many questions to be answered such as how a memorial should be designed, its function, location, timeliness, and its appropriateness for the deceased.

We are also interested in knowing more about how the manner of death may affect the virtual memorial design and desire for such an artifact. Using the NASH categories (Natural, Accidental, Suicide, Homicide) used for the classification of death on death certificates, we can begin to analyze and compare with memorial designs. Although the NASH categories can be obscure in some cases [13], they would lead to some preliminary insights. In addition to considering aspects of a user's physical death, aspects of their virtual presence while alive is also important to consider. Did the user have a strong in-world virtual presence within a particular virtual world? Were they a prolific content creator or a designer for a virtual world? The users from that environment may be more prone to create a virtual memorial in remembrance.

Additionally, there are factors influencing comfort with the use of social media for grieving, including public versus private grieving styles [14]. Those not familiar with virtual worlds, virtual reality, social media or online gaming may have a very different view of the idea of virtual memorials and using technology during the grieving process. One's level of comfort with technology is an additional factor. There also are cultural, social and other expectations during grieving that may influence the use of technology following a loss [14]. Comfort with using technology in this context can also be influenced by one's resilience in coping or when dealing with complicated grief.

3 Preliminary Survey Results

To begin to answer some of these questions raised in this paper, we have adapted a previous survey that was used in a similar study aimed at examining the impact of social networks and virtual worlds related to preparation and education about one's death and digital legacy [2, 3]. This survey was more specific about perceptions and proposed design of virtual memorials. The survey was distributed electronically to students at a large community college at the end of the fall 2016 academic semester. Participants were selected from a limited number of technology courses such as introductory courses and various levels of computer programming courses. One main limitation of the survey used in the preliminary study is the limited number of respondents and high level of technology use of those participating.

Thirty-two participants responded to the survey which consisted of students primarily majoring in computer science, information technology and general studies. The average age of the participants was 23.06 years old and consisted of 68.75% male, 25% female and 6.25% that preferred not to answer. Participants reported spending a significant amount of time online each day actively using the internet with 10 (31.25%) reporting an average of 1 to 3 h, 9 (28.13%) 4 to 6 h, 9 (28.13%) 7 to 9 h and 4 reporting more than 9 h online each day. The survey did not specify how participants were connecting to the internet or what was considered as being online or connected (e.g. cell phones, wearable devices, laptops, tablets). Additionally, the survey asked participants if they currently had a profile on any social networking site and if so, to list website. Twenty-eight (87.5%) responded "Yes" and the remaining 4 (12.5%) responded "No". Those that reported which sites in which they are active included: Facebook (85.7%) Instagram (35.71%), Twitter (25%), Tumblr (10.71%), Snapchat (10.71%) and LinkedIn (3.57%). Participants could list multiple responses for this question.

Through the survey, we wanted to capture information regarding the type of content that was posted on the participant's social networks to gain insight into usage. Table 1 illustrates the responses to the survey question asking about the types of content posted. Participants could select more than one response. Those choosing "E. None" commented that they primarily chat and read other user's posts. Following the question regarding content, the survey asked participants to rate the importance of the personal content that was contained on their social networking sites. The results of that question are summarized in Table 2.

Table 1. Type of posted content

Choice	Total (n = 30)
A. Pictures	26
B. Text based posts	23
C. Video	14
D. Music or other audio	7
E. None	3

Table 2. Content ratings

Rating	Total (n = 32)
A. Not at all important	4
B. A Little important	9
C. Somewhat important	11
D. Very important	3
E. Extremely important	5

Additionally, participants were asked if they knew anyone that had died but still had a present/active profile on a social networking site. From the responses, 22 (68.75%) reported "Yes" and the remaining 10 (12.25%) reported "No". Next, the participants were asked if they would want their social networking page to remain active after their death. Interestingly, 20 (62.50%) responded "No" and 12 (37.50%) responded "Yes". They were also asked "What types of digital assets do you currently have online that need to be protected after your death?". This was a multiple choice question, where more than one answer could be selected. A summary of the responses can be found in Table 3.

Table 3. Digital assets that need protecting

Category	Total (n = 32)
A. Photos	11
B. Documents	5
C. Music	5
D. Video	4
E. Intellectual property (i.e. things that you or others have created)	9
F. Personal information (i.e. tax documents, addresses, financial data etc.)	21
G. No response	3

Following the question about the general protection of content, participants were asked "After your death would you want your digital content to be deleted, preserved with restrictions or remain the same (as it is currently)". All 32 participants responded and 8 (25%) reported "deleted", 17 (53.13%) reported "preserved with restrictions" and 7 (21.8%) reported that their final wishes would be for their site to remain the same as it currently is. Eight participants noted additional comments in regards to the restrictions they wanted to be in place. This primarily included wishes that only friends and family would continue to have access or someone specifically designated to facilitate the account of whom was designed prior to their death. One participant noted a time frame for friends and family to have access, but only to save pictures that they would want before the account and content would be removed. They were also asked if there were files or other content that they would want erased so no one would know about. Eighteen (56.25%) reported "Yes" there is content they would want erased, and the remaining 14 (43.75%) reported "No".

More specific questions were then asked in the survey regarding virtual worlds and online games as related to virtual memorialization. When asked "Do you play online games or use virtual worlds?", 23 (71.88%) responded "Yes" and 9 (28.13%) responded "No". Next, the survey asked "Would you want a virtual memorial when you pass away? (For example a permanent 3D memorial in an online world or game?)". Fourteen (43.75%) of the participants said "Yes", while 18 (56.25%) responded "No" to this question. There were some interesting comments from those expressing that they would be interested in a 3D memorial. In this case they were asked to comment in a few words, what their idea of a virtual 3D memorial would look like.

The majority expressed interest in having a small permanent space or object that would represent aspects of their real life that other users or players of the world could visit. This majority noted including having interactive components that would allow for the viewing of picture slideshows or text that described their life. Other comments included having a 3D avatar that would look like either their real life self or a replica of their in-game avatar where others could visit. Three comments noted to recreate a virtual graveyard that is similar to how it would exist in real life. One interesting comment was to create an in-game quest that would lead players in the "ghost at the gravestone" of the person that was deceased. Additionally, one other comment asked for the creation of a world that would contain everything that the person had wanted, loved or valued in their real life as a representation.

Following was a very similar question that asked participants to comment on their idea of what an "online" memorial would be or look like. The majority of the comments are summarized in Table 4 from 16 participants. The remaining 16 participants had no comment or left the question blank.

Table 4. Summary of comments for online memorials

Comment summary
Having a website that contains the majority of one's social media and general information
Website similar to "online memories" and comments from a funereal message board
A photo stream or video that would show positive moments and life events.
A digitized version of a guestbook
Online obituary
Art or other works memorialized in an online format

The survey also asked: "Have you ever seen or encountered an online or virtual memorial?". From the 28 participants responding, 18 (64.29%) said "No", while 10 (35.71%) said "Yes". Next, the participants were asked "Do you currently have any documentation dictating your final wishes for your online content". From this question: 31 participants responded, where one (3.23%) person reported "Yes" and the remaining 30 (96.77%) reported "No".

Participants were asked to rank categories using a Likert scale based to 1 (low) to 7 (high), their feelings in three categories related to virtual memorials or social networking sites. Table 5 describes the results from 31 participants.

Table 5. Rating for virtual memorials

Rating	Freq.	Rating	Freq.	Rating	Freq.
Disrespectful		*Not important*		*Useful*	
1	3	1	5	1	7
2	1	2	7	2	2
3	3	3	4	3	6
4	4	4	5	4	4
5	6	5	3	5	6
6	6	6	4	6	3
7	8	7	3	7	3
Respectful		*Important*		*Not useful*	

Twenty-eight participants responded to the next questions which asked: "Do you think the idea of having a virtual memorial in an online game or virtual world would be beneficial?" From the respondents, 11 (39.29%) reported "No", 10 (35.71%) reported "Yes" and the remaining 7 (25%) responded as "Maybe" or "Unsure". The survey asked: "Would you feel better about your own death if you know there would be an online memorial dedicated to you?" From this question, Twenty-nine participants responded, where 17 (58.62%) responded "No", 10 (34.38%) "Yes" and 2 (6.90%) as "Undecided". We also asked "If you had an online memorial, what would you want it to represent about you?". Table 6 summarizes the responses. Participants could list more than one response.

Table 6. Summary of comments for representation

Comments (n = 27)	Frequency
Information about me/my past/my interests/my life	18
Accomplishments	9
Pictures	8
Family information	3
People's lives that I have impacted	1

Interestingly, in regards to pictures, all participants noted that they either wanted positive pictures that illustrated them with someone they loved or doing something they loved or something that represented something about their lives. The survey also asked the participants: "Would you want to setup your own virtual memorial before your death so that you can control the content or after your death, where someone else controls the content?" From the responses: 19 (59.4%) responded "before their death" and 12 (37.5%) responded "after" and 1 (3.1%) did not respond. Lastly, the participants were asked: "Would having a virtual memorial (in a 3D world/game or social net-working site) help you cope with the death of loved one?" The majority of the participants 12 (37.5%) responded "No", 10 (31.3%) responded "Yes", 6 (18.7%) were undecided, 1 (3.1%) could not make an informed decision due to not experiencing a loss of a loved one, and 3 (9.4%) did not respond.

4 Discussion

Even though the survey was preliminary, the data is useful in providing some insights. Most of the participants noted that they knew someone that had died, but there still exists a present or active profile on some social network representing that person. It was unknown if it was a social networking page that remained active after the person's death or if it was created purposefully as a memorial. When asked if they wished to have a virtual memorial when they themselves died it was relatively divided with fourteen (43.75%) stating "Yes", while 18 (56.25%) responding "No". Investigating deeper into this question could reveal interesting results as the view and understanding of virtual memorials at the time of the question was unknown. Although the survey asked participants to self-identify as "gamers", there was not a clear distinction between gamers and virtual world users or how this could influence the results of this question. Additionally, different types of online games could affect the perception of online "death" and the perception of the legitimate use of a virtual memorial in the grieving process.

Since we were interested in how the participants viewed virtual memorials and their construction, the responses to several questions were helpful. Several respondents seemed to view a virtual memorial within the same physical limitations in design as one would in real life (e.g. 3D avatar "statue", having a permanent space or object). While others noted using the technology in ways to interact with users, display photos and video streams etc. Much of the comments on the perception of a virtual memorial was based on web based designed. Likewise, the summary of comments revealed that the majority of the respondents would want their memorial to contain information about themselves such as general information, past, interests and their life overall. This was followed by lists of accomplishments, pictures, family information, and impacts. Interestingly when asked "Would you want to setup your own virtual memorial before your death so that you can control the content or after your death, where someone else controls the content?" The majority, 59.4% responded "before their death" and 37.5% responded "after" with 1 (3.1%) not responding. As the importance of digital legacy grows (either through virtual worlds or social networking sites) users may want or need to have more control and input on the digital artifacts that represent them after their death. However, respondents viewed having a virtual memorial was respectful and useful, but not generally important. When asked "Would you feel better about your own death if you know there would be an online memorial dedicated to you?" 58.62% responded "No", 34.38% "Yes" and 6.90% as "Undecided". This seems to coincide with the view on memorials and the general misgivings on death overall.

The results of the survey provided interesting insights on the view of virtual memorials, but much more research is needed to begin to answer some of the questions raised in this paper. We are only beginning to understand how a virtual world based memorial should be designed, represented and interacted with. Previously [1] noted that there are four types of users as related to death as viewed in Fig. 1. Type A represents users who are physically alive and maintain an active presence in an online environment (such as a virtual world or social network). Type B includes users who are also alive, but who do not have a presence in any virtual or online space. Thirdly, type C users are those

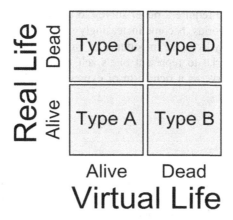

Fig. 1. Four states of being [1]

who have physically died, but have an active virtual memorial or social networking site. Type C users would include those who have died, and someone else created a memorial on their behalf, hence still having an active online presence. Type D users represent users that have died, and have no online presence or memorial. The online persona of a type D user could have been erased or taken down after their death.

Type B users may have either never had a presence in a virtual world or social network, or may have chosen to delete their account at some point. There is also a growing trend for users to have online "funerals" to commemorate the deactivation of an account or avatar.

5 Summary and Future Work

In summary, we have discussed how memorials are viewed and can be used for the remembrance of the deceased in cyberspace. Several questions were posed concerning how virtual worlds can be used for memorialization and presented information collected from a preliminary survey. Our survey focused on user perceptions and design issues in a preliminary fashion, to help guide future work and additional surveys. There is a great deal of research that still needs to be conducted to answer many of these questions. We are planning several additional studies to address this in future research. In addition, we plan to conduct field work in virtual worlds such as Second Life to gain further insight into these questions, particularly related to interaction and design. There are still many questions that need to be explored such as the role of attachment to one's online persona, time spent online, avid gamers and more distinction between online versus virtual memorials. Do gamers or heavy computer users feel differently about online memorials?

Two major limitations to this study were the low number of questions covered in the survey and a small sample size and participant selection. To gain a much deeper insight, a much larger and diverse sample population needs to be evaluated. One of our main questions is to understand the design and interaction potential for virtual memorials, which would require a richer survey to be administered to a much larger population. As virtual worlds, become increasingly mainstream, realistic and used for many aspects of our daily lives, the importance of virtual memorials will also increase. Having a virtual memorial to represent one's self or a loved one has far reaching implications and can serve as a rich form of expression and representation of one's digital legacy.

References

1. Braman, J., Dudley, A., Vincenti, G.: Death, social networks and virtual worlds: a look into the digital afterlife. In: Proceedings of the 9th International Conference on Software Engineering Research, Management and Applications (SERA 2011), Baltimore, MD, USA (2011)
2. Braman, J., Vincenti, G., Dudley, A., Wang, Y., Rodgers, K., Thomas, U.: Teaching about the impacts of social networks: an end of life perspective. In: Ozok, A.A., Zaphiris, P. (eds.) OCSC 2013. LNCS, vol. 8029, pp. 240–249. Springer, Heidelberg (2013). doi:10.1007/978-3-642-39371-6_28
3. Braman, J., Thomas, U., Vincenti, G., Dudley, A., Rodgers, K.: Preparing your digital legacy: assessing awareness of digital natives. In: Mallia, G. (Ed.) The Social Classroom: Integrating Social Network Use in Education, pp. 208–223. IGI Global, Hershey, PA (2013). doi:10.4018/978-1-4666-4904-0.ch011
4. Braman, J., Dudley, A., Vincenti, G.: Thana-technology education: the importance of considering social networks and virtual worlds. In: The Quarterly Publication of the Association for Death Education and Counseling, vol. 41, no. 1. The Thanatology Association, January–February 2015
5. Haney, C.A., Leimer, C., Lowery, J.: Spontaneous memorialization: violent death and emerging mourning ritual. OMEGA J. Death Dying 35(2), 159–171 (1997)
6. Living headstones (2017). https://www.monuments.com/living-headstones
7. Brubaker, J.R., Hayes, G.R., Dourish, P.: Beyond the grave: Facebook as a site for the expansion of death and mourning. Inf. Soc. 29(3), 152–163 (2013)
8. Sofka, C., Cupit, I., Gilbert, K.: Dying, Death, and Grief in an Online Universe: For Counselors and Educators. Springer, New York (2012)
9. Mitra, A.: Creating a presence on social networks via narbs. Glob. Media J. 9, 16 (2010)
10. Wang, Y., Norcie, G., Komanduri, S., Acquisti, A., Leon, P.G., Cranor, L.F.: I regretted the minute I pressed share: a qualitative study of regrets on Facebook. In: Proceedings of the Seventh Symposium on Usable Privacy and Security, p. 10. ACM (2011)
11. Cook, A.: The family, larger systems, and loss, grief, and mourning. In: Meagher, D.K., Balk, D.E. (eds.) Handbook of Thanatology: The Essential Body of Knowledge for the Study of Death, Dying, and Bereavement, 2nd edn. Routledge, New York (2013)
12. Bainbridge, W.: The scientific research potential of virtual worlds. Science 317(5837), 472–476 (2007)
13. Shneidman, E.: A Commonsense Book of Death, Reflections at Ninety of a Lifelong Thanatologist. Rowman & Littlefield, Lanham (2008)
14. Solfka, C.: Using digital and social media in your work with the dying and bereaved. In: Webinar. Association for Death Education and Counseling (2015). http://www.adec.org/ADEC/Main/Continuing_Education/My_Online_Learning/

Social Media and Elderly People:
Research Trends

Mayela Coto[(⊠)], Fulvio Lizano, Sonia Mora, and Jennifer Fuentes

Universidad Nacional, Heredia, Costa Rica
{mcoto,flizano,smora,jennifer.fuentes.bustos}@una.cr

Abstract. Population aging is now a global reality a global reality, and interaction with social media as well. The older adult population is increasing significantly and their mental and physical health will be a worldwide priority.
Social networks have been seen as an important ally to support older people. It is
therefore important to know how the elderly population interacts with social
media and the potential benefits and dangers in this interaction. This paper
reports the results of a systematic literature review in the field of social media
and the elderly. The analysis of the research papers focused on their research
approach, methods of data collection, research domains, objectives and results.
Our findings indicate that currently there is no predominant research approach
for this field of study, samples are generally very small, research efforts are
focused on specific domains, and there is a lacking of rigor in the reporting
process. This work is important because it identifies the current state of research
in this field and guides new potential research.

Keywords: Elderly · Social media · Literature review

1 Introduction

The world's population is aging. According to the United Nations [1], it is estimated
that the number of older people will more than double between 2013 and 2050, from
841 million to more than 2,000 million. For 2047, it is expected that for the first time,
older people will exceed the number of children. In turn, the older population is
growing older. In 2013 the proportion of people over 80 years within the older population was 14% and it is projected to reach 19% by 2050. If so, by that year, there will
be 392 million people over 80 years worldwide, which means more than three times the
present amount.

As people age, their physical capacities begin to degenerate, they have limited
mobility and their response time is much slower. Such a limitation in their mobility often
results in less participation in social activities, which may tend to increase feelings of
loneliness, and decrease morale and satisfaction with life [2, 3]. It is also well known
that for the elder population, their health and well-being depends, to a greater extent, on
the emotional and social relationships they have with their family members and friends
[2, 4, 5]. Technology can play an important role helping the elderly to keep these social
connections. It can improve their quality of life by reducing their sense of isolation,

© Springer International Publishing AG 2017
G. Meiselwitz (Ed.): SCSM 2017, Part II, LNCS 10283, pp. 65–81, 2017.
DOI: 10.1007/978-3-319-58562-8_6

contributing to their psychological well-being and sense of empowerment, and supporting their relationships regardless of time and location [2, 6–12].

As Hawkley and Cacioppo [13] argue, that finding ways to support older people in establishing and maintaining social connections should be a priority for public health. Older adults represent the fastest growing portion of the world's population [14], and their social needs can be satisfied through participation in social networks [7, 15]. Social networking has become a vital part of everyday life for many people. In recent years more and more older adults have begun to use social media [16–19]. According to Madden [20], from 2000 to 2009, there was a 70% increase in Internet use by people aged 50–64 years, and a 38% increase by those over 65 years; and during 2010 there was an increase of 88% in the use of social media by people aged 50–64 years, and a 26% increase by those over 65 years. However, in comparison to young people, the use of social media by older adults is still low [21, 22].

In the last decade there has been an increasing number of scientific publications presenting new ideas and methodologies on how social media can improve the quality of life of older adults [4, 9, 15, 23–35]. This paper presents a systematic review of studies on social media and older adults published between 2005 and 2016. We were interested in studying these papers from the research point of view, i.e. what kind of research approaches are been used with this population?, what kind of data collection methods?, what are the more prevalent research domains?, what are the main research goals and obtained results?, what do researchers point out as future work?

The remainder of this paper will proceed as follows: Sect. 2 will review the main theoretical concepts, while Sect. 3 will provide an overview of our study methodology. Section 4 presents the results, and Sect. 5 discusses the findings. The paper closes with concluding remarks in Sect. 6.

2   Related Concepts

2.1   Elderly People

Defining "old" is difficult and age classification may vary in different world regions and over time. The United Nations adopted the definition of older person as those aged 60 years or older [36]. Some organizations have separated the elderly population into three groups: the "young old" aged between 60 and 75; the "old old" aged between 75 and 85; and the "very old" with ages over 85 years [9]. There are also differences among the research community, some researchers consider older people those persons over 65 [2, 6], while others regards people over 60 years as elders [19, 37, 38]; for [30, 39, 40] the elderly is people who are over 55 years old, and [41, 42] consider as elderly people those aged over 50.

A growing concern related to the growth of the elderly population is social isolation [8, 13, 34, 35, 43–45]. According to Couture [43], 43% of people over 65 feel lonely on a regular basis and this feeling is related to a decrease in health or even premature death. Social isolation can be understood as a low quantity and poor quality of contact with other people. This includes the number of contacts a person has, his feelings of belonging, and how satisfactory his relationships and his engagements with others are [34].

2.2 Social Media

Even, when there is no agreed definition for social media, Obar and Wildman [46] identify four commonalities of current social media services: (1) They are Web 2.0 Internet-based applications; (2) Its lifeblood is user-generated content; (3) Individuals and groups create user-specific profiles; and (4) They facilitated the development of social networks online by connecting a profile with those of other individuals and/or groups. In sum, social media can be understood as internet-based applications that create links among users and user-generated content in online environments [46]. Social media applications can be used to interact with other people via blogs, web forums, social bookmarking sites, photo and video sharing communities, content communities, social networking sites, and virtual games with the goal to consume, co-create, share, and modify content generated by the same users [9, 31, 32, 47–50]. Some of the more popular social media nowadays are: Facebook, WhatsApp, LinkedIn, Skype, Google+, Instagram, Twitter and Snapchat [46].

2.3 Social Media and Elder People

Preventing and alleviating social isolation and loneliness is a key element in improving the quality of life of older adults. Information and communication technology (ICT), together with initiatives led by local communities or government agencies, can be used as a tool to help reduce feelings of loneliness and increase the mental well-being of older adults. The wide availability of mobile communications networks, smart phones and tablets, combined with social media applications, make it easier for elders to contact and share information with family and friends through text, voice and images [2, 9, 34, 51] with the potential to decrease loneliness and increase perceived social support, sense of belonging and feelings of connectedness [42, 45, 52, 53].

Social media can be even more useful for elders with limited mobility and for those who are no longer geographically close to family and friends because it may help, regardless of time and place, to maintain social connections that would otherwise be difficult to conserve [2, 50]. Besides this, the elderly population have recently shown a special enthusiasm for the adoption of new network tools that allow them to share, with a growing network of contacts, links, photos, videos, news and status updates [3, 7, 20, 54], and consequently improve their skills and opportunities for communication, information searching, knowledge sharing, and relationship building [9, 14].

In general, social media allows older adults to express themselves, participate in discussions and stay in contact with society [3]. Participating in social networks can empower older people and provide them with a sense of connectedness and greater control and self-efficacy [31]. An interesting trend in the use of social media by elders is health care. It can be a good source of health support. Patients can locate and obtain health-related information and services [34, 41]; they can give and receive information to manage specific diseases [17]; and establish relationships with health professionals for medical assistance [32].

On the other hand, the research community have also identified a number of educational, cognitive, physiological and experiential factors that may hinder the use of social media by the elder population [3, 15, 17, 19, 29, 34, 53, 55–57]. Lee et al. [57] found four dimensions of constraints that elders experience while dealing with technology: intrapersonal barriers, structural barriers, interpersonal barriers, and functional barriers. They also found that these limitations were less restrictive for people with higher incomes and higher education, but perceived to be more restrictive as the age of users increased.

3 Methodology

To identify relevant studies, we searched relevant databases such as EBSCO, ACM, Scopus, Springer, Science Direct, JSTOR, Academic Search Complete, Emerald, ERIC, and Web of Science. We used the keyword social media with combinations of the following keywords: old people, elderly, seniors and older adults. This initial search returned a total of 88 articles. Then we repeat the same search in Google Scholar obtaining 78 articles. In overall the searching process returned 166 articles. To be included in the present review, an article needed to contain the selected keywords, and meet three inclusion criteria which are (A) include experiments, scientific studies, literature reviews or experiences with seniors in the use of social media tools; (B) explain the study methodology; (C) explain how social media was used, for example what kind of interaction they analyzed with Facebook, Twitter and so on.

In a first round the screening of the articles with respect to the inclusion criteria was performed independently by two authors. As a result, 28 articles were accepted for inclusion by both authors and 32 additional articles were accepted by only one of the authors. In a second round, a third author examined these 32 articles and accepted the inclusion of 14 of them. Subsequently, three articles were eliminated because the full-text version could not be obtained, (only the abstract), two for being posters (and no full papers) and one for being duplicated. In sum, 36 articles were included in the study for a full-text review (Appendix). After inclusion, the articles were analyzed with the following criteria: (1) article "demography": publication channel (journal or conference), authors' affiliation, and target audience; (2) aim of the study/research questions; (3) research approaches; (4) data collection methods; (5) main domains of research; (6) participants' demography: number, gender, age, educational level; (7) main results and (8) future work.

4 Results

Unless otherwise noted, all the results presented in the following sections are based on 36 research papers (N = 36). To document the results, the numbers of the articles are shown as #paper Number, for example #5 refers to research paper #5 which in turn is the reference [30], according to the list in Appendix. In addition, in order to illustrate some of the categories or findings, we decided to use as examples the research papers which have a high number of citations, according to Google Scholar.

4.1   Publication Channel

Of the total of 36 articles analyzed, 26 articles (72%) were published in journals, and the remaining 10 articles (28%) were presented in conferences. The most cited journal articles (#55, #51, #129, #5), according to Google Scholar, were published in journals such as: Journal of Medical Internet Research, Educational Gerontology, Gerontology, and Decision Support Systems. On the other hand, the most cited conferences articles (#127, #112, #131) were presented in conferences such as: ACM Conference on Hypertext and Social Media, AMCIS (Association for Information Systems), and the International Conference on Universal Access in Human-Computer Interaction.

4.2   Geographical Distribution

Considering the author's affiliation indicated in the research papers, researchers from four of the six continents show an interest in investigating the relationship between social media and the elderly. The continent with the majority of studies in this research is Europe with fifteen papers, followed by the American continent with thirteen papers and finally Asia with eleven. On the other hand, continents like Oceania present only one article and there were no articles representing Africa and Antarctica.

The leading country on the American continent is United States with ten papers; other countries such as Mexico, Canada and Chile also contribute but with less strength. A different situation can be seen on the European continent, where a greater number of countries are represented, including: Norway, Italy, Scotland, Northern Ireland (United Kingdom), Switzerland, Sweden, France, Netherlands, Ireland, Spain, Finland, and Germany.

4.3   Disciplinary Areas

The disciplinary area was determined by the academic affiliation of the researchers. As it is expected due to the interrelation between social media and elders, the two disciplines with more representation are Computer Science (47%) and Health (25%); followed by Computational Design and Art and Design (14%). There are also some researchers coming from disciplines like Journalism, Economics, Education, Management and Human Resources. Only 4 out of 36 studies were interdisciplinary, for example, paper #131 was written by researchers in Industrial Design, Computer Science, and Physical Medicine and Rehabilitation.

4.4   Domain and Audience

Domain and audience are other interesting dimensions present in the literature of social media and the elderly. The domain dimension, obtained from the analysis of the keywords, allowed us to classify the research papers in three types of domains. The first type is related to elderly matters including keywords such as elderly, aging, adults, wisdom, privacy-preserving, communication, participation, peer influence and information sharing. The second type of domain focuses on technology, software development and design. This is a technological domain that includes keywords such as social media, social network sites (SNS), Web 2.0, socio-technical systems, ICT, user experience, and requirements. The last type of domain is related to quality of life. Here, it is possible to find research papers with keywords such as social isolation, social inclusion, mental health, and elderly care assistance.

On the other hand, the audience dimension includes designers, researchers, policymakers, elderly care assistants, and elderly people itself. Table 1 contains the classification of the studies included in this research based on domain and audience. In each dimension we add an "Other" classification to locate those papers that do not include keywords to determinate their domain or for those cases where the analysis of the paper failed to figure out a specific audience.

Table 1. Domain and audience. N = 36

Audience	Domain			
	Elderly matters	Software dev. & design	Quality of life	Other
Designers	6–9–85–96–106–109–112–131–133–153	2–3–6–9–55–85–96–106–109–112–131–133–153	2–55–95–153	60–147–148–156
Researchers	5–6–98–106–153	5–6–37–55–98–95–106	55–98–95–153	156
Policymakers	90–98–115–118	90–98–99–115–118	98–99–115–118	15
Elderly care assistance	18–59–93–127–129–132–133	18–59–93–127–129–132–133	18–59–93–95–127–129	
Other	43–54–117	43–117	54	

Source: Author's own work

Several research papers can be classified in several domains and audiences as well. Considering this, totals and percentages must be contrasted, exclusively, in relation to the total number of studies analyzed in this research. In the domain dimension, the technological domain contains the largest number of studies (29 out of 36, 80%), followed by the elderly matters domain (24 out of 36, 67%) and the quality of life domain (14 out of 36, 39%); 5 research papers out of 36 (14%) do not specified domain at all.

When it comes to the audience dimension, the analysis of the research papers included in this study allows to recognize that designers are the major audience identified (18 of 36, 50%), followed by researchers (10 out of 36, 28%), elderly care assistance (8 out of 36, 22%) and policy makers (6 out of 36, 17%). Finally, 3 out of 36 papers (8%) do not provide enough information to define an audience.

4.5   Age Segmentation

As we mentioned before there is not a global agreement about the age that defines an "older person" or how to segment this population. 12 papers out of 36 (33%) did not define the age of the population they considered. For the remaining 24 papers (67%) the age segmentation was diverse. Table 2 shows the age inferior limit the authors considered in their studies. These results confirm that there are is clear criteria to establish a minimum age to consider a person an older adult, and this lack of agreement among researchers may make it difficult to study this population and compare the research findings. In addition, few documents clearly define other characteristics of the sample, such as gender or educational level, the papers that do are papers #3, #5, #9, #106 and #105.

Table 2. Age segmentation. N = 36

Minimum age	40	45	50	55	60	65	70	85
Paper #	99	95	15–85–117–127–153	5–96–106–132–148	51–60–93–98–115	37–54–59–112–131	109	6

Source: Author's own work

4.6   Defining Social Media

Only seven papers (19%) define the term "social media", four of them were published in journals (#2, #51, #133, #147), and the other three (#95, #96, #156) were published in conferences. The general omission to define the term "social media", presupposes, to some extent, that the authors assume that their audience is familiar with it, however in a subject where so many disciplines converge, the non-definition of the term can lead to different interpretations of the research findings.

4.7   Research Questions and Results

The classification of the research papers by using the research questions can be made based on two different dimensions. The first dimension is focused on the elderly people itself and consider three main research areas: influence and impact of social media on elderly people; use of social media technology to facilitate interaction between elderly people and other persons; and research related to the characteristics of elderly people that use, or potentially can use, social media artifacts. The second dimension is related to research focused on social media from a technological point of view. In this dimension it is also possible to identify three main perspectives: research oriented to design or assess social media technology; research dealing with the use of social media artifacts and, studies which are oriented to characterize social media technology.

Table 3 shows the classification of the 36 research papers on these two dimensions. Considering that results are connected to the research questions, this classification

Table 3. Research question and results. N = 36

Technological dimension	Elderly dimension		
	Influence and impact of social media on elderly people	Interaction between elderly people and others by social media	Characteristics of elderly people using social media
Design or assessment of social media artifacts	2–37–55–60	3–9–37–90	106–156–109
Use of social media artifacts	2–15–59–95–117–127	5–6–40–53–93–99–115–127–131–132	5–18–43–51–54–85–98–109–118–127–133–153–156
Characteristics of social media artifacts	129	112–147	51–96–109–153

Source: Author's own work

allows us to synthesize in a clear and easy way both, the research questions and the corresponding results of the articles included in this literature study.

According to the data, the largest number of research papers belongs to the intersection of characteristics of elderly people using social media (elderly dimension), and use of social media artifacts (technological dimension). These 13 papers represent the 36% of the literature included in this review. As an example, the most cited article in this list is paper #51 which proposes two research questions. The first research question is related to the exploration of older adults' perceptions about social media. The second research question is focused on the educational strategies that facilitate older adults' learning of social media. The main results of this research indicate that, there is a clear concern of this population on privacy (characterizing the elderly users of social media), also, privacy was identified as the primary barrier to the adoption of social media applications.

It is clear from the results that the major concern of the researchers is the characterization of both the elderly and the applications of social media suitable for them. It is an emerging topic that requires further research.

4.8   Research Approaches and Data Collection Methods

Similar to the research questions and results, it is possible to classify the research papers included in this study by using two different dimensions. The first dimension is focused on their research approach. The second dimension is related to specific data collection methods or techniques used by the researchers. Considering this classification, some of the research approaches used in research on elderly and social media are user-centered participatory approach, case studies, exploratory studies, ethnographic studies, grounded theory approach, and literature reviews. On the other hand, the data collection methods, usually considered in research on elderly and social media are: observation, focus group, questionnaires, and interviews. Table 4 shows the results. In the "not explicit" category we locate the papers that do not explicitly declare the research method or data collection method used.

Table 4. Research approaches and data collection methods. N = 36

Research approach	Data collection methods					
	Observation	Focus group	Questionnaire	Interview	Systematic review	Not explicit
User-centered participatory approach	3	3	3–131	3–106		
Formative study				9		
Case study	37			37		
Exploratory study		51	153	112–132		
Ethnographic study	93–99			99		
Grounded theory approach				96		
Literature review					18–55–129–133	43–147
Training and other approaches	2	2	2			117–156
Not explicit	5–6–15–118	6–15–60–95–109–148	15–54–60–85–95–98–115–118–127–148	6–59–109–90		

Source: Author's own work

One of the predominant research approaches, explicitly declared by the authors, is literature review (6 out of 36, 17%) followed by exploratory studies (4 out of 36, 11%). However, the greater number of papers published on elderly and social media do not declare an explicit research approach. In the case of data collection methods, questionnaires are the instrument more used, followed by interviews, focus groups and observations.

From the data, we can see that elderly and social media research usually combine several techniques in order to triangulate results, for example papers #2, #3 and #15 use observation, focus groups and questionnaires.

In the research papers included in this study, there are six literature reviews (17%). Some of these literature reviews focus on the elderly and their typical problems of isolation and health (#18, #55), the use of social media by elderly people (#129) and economic or social context in elderly and social media (#43, #133).

4.9   Sample Sizes and Data Collection Methods

Another relevant issue to explore in the research papers is the sample size or number of participants. For our purposes, we only considered the elder participants, several papers mention the participation of other types of participants (e.g. young people, elderly care assistants, etc.), and these participants were not included in these results. In addition, papers related to literature review studies were excluded in this section due to their nature. Considering this, the total number of papers included in this section are 30 (N = 30).

We defined two dimensions to present the results. The first dimension corresponds to the number of participants included in the studies. Here, we defined several ranges of number of participants in order to facilitate the analysis. The second dimension corresponds to the data collection methods that were presented in Table 4.

Table 5 shows the final results. Again, in the "not explicit" category we locate the papers that do not explicitly declare the number of participants or the data collection method used.

Table 5. Number of elderly participants and data collection methods. N = 30

Number of participants	Data collection methods				
	Observation	Focus group	Questionnaire	Interview	Not explicit
1–10	2–3–6–37–93–99	2–3–6–51–95–109	2–95	3–6–9–37–96–99–106–109–112	
11–100	15	15	3–15–85–98–127–131–153	132	
101–1000	5		54–148	59	
>1000			115		
Not explicit	118	60–148	60–118	90	117–156

Source: Author's own work

In general, the sample sizes of the studies were small, the majority of them (13 out of 30, 43%) had between 1 to 10 participants and consistent with this sample size and the qualitative nature of these studies, the primary research methods used in these studies were interviews, focus groups and observation.

Questionnaires were more often used in the range of 11 to 100 participants. In general, 14 out of 30 studies (47%) use questionnaires. Two research papers (#3, #148) used different number of participants with different instruments, for example in paper #3, the authors considered 5 participants in experimental interviews and 60 participants in questionnaires.

4.10   Limitations in Research on Social Media and Elderly

As part of the analysis of the limitations found by the researchers on this area, it is interesting to mention that only in 20 out of 36 papers (56%), the authors reflected on the main limitations they faced in their studies. The largest number of papers (16 out of 20, 80%) established as their main limitation that the results make impossible the generalization and establishment of cause-and-effect relations due to the sample, either because it was very homogeneous, very small or biased. For example, in paper #51, the authors mentioned that in their study, the sample was very small, the participants were predominantly African American females who had some computer experience, thus they suggest to do additional research addressing other groups to determine whether the results could be or not generalized.

4.11 Future Work

A very important aspect in a literature review is the analysis of the future work identified by the researchers. Of the total of 36 papers, 24 of them (67%) mentioned some ideas for future work. These ideas have been classified in three groups: (1) The largest number of research papers (17 out of 24, 71%) proposed the need to extend the present study in terms of the sample, the time of the study, the data collection methods or an analysis of another social media. For instance, in paper #5, the authors proposed to study the distrust of older adults to share information on social networks. The authors of paper #59 mentioned as future work, to extend the study to other mobile devices and in article #112, the authors proposed to analyze more deeply if the concerns of the elderly about privacy affects or not their online interaction; (2) Five articles (20%) propose the development of new social media applications geared to better meet the needs of older adults; and (3) Two studies (9%) propose new training strategies to get older adults to overcome their fears about privacy and security in social media applications.

5 Discussion

As it was established at the beginning of our paper, we were interested in studying the research papers in social media and elderly from the research point of view. Several questions were defined previous to initiate our research. In the same vein, we will use these questions to guide our analysis.

What kind of research approaches are been used with the elderly population? Social media and the elderly are a relatively recent field of study, and knowing the current orientation of research, will provide guidance to future researchers interested in this topic. From our data it is possible to see that the predominant research approach among our sample is literature review. This type of research approach offers interesting research lines in emerging fields such as social media research and elders. Similar to our research, in general there is a clear interest in identifying future research lines on this field; the literature review research is a suitable method to establish what is already known and where new research is needed [58, 59]. In our study, we identified several research approaches. The results reveal that currently there is not a predominant research approach to address this subject. In reality, 15 papers out of 36 (42%) do not declare, explicitly, their research approach. This fact also may reveal certain lack of writing technical rigor by avoiding to explain something as fundamental as the research approach used. Additionally, there is a low number of articles that defined the term "social media" something that can be risky, because it leaves the audience with the responsibility of interpreting central concepts.

What kind of data collection methods are currently used in social media and elderly research? Questionnaires are the most frequently used method, followed by interviews, focus group and observation. The characteristics of the elderly, explain to some extent the methods of data collection used. Methods such as observation, focus groups and interviews use a small number of participants (from 1 to 10 participants). Probably, the own limitations of older people explain this sample limitation. Questionnaires allow for greater participation and are used more frequently in the range of 11 to 100 participants. The low number of participants in the studies analyzed can also be explained by the age segmentation. The identification of who belongs or does not belong to the group of older adults seems to depend on many cultural and social variables. On the other hand, 6 studies (out of 30) did not indicate the number of participants, which supports our previous finding about the lack of rigorous communication of results. Documenting the characteristics of the sample, especially the number of participants, is one of the central methodological aspects of any research.

What are the more prevalent research domains? The literature on social and elderly media extends among the three domains defined in our research. Most of the work (81%) contributes in the technological domain followed by the elderly matters domain (67%) and the domain of quality of life (39%). We can conclude that current research efforts in this field are of a very diverse nature which is consistent with our initial appreciation of how incipient research is in this field. Contrasting this matter with the audiences, the data reveals that designers are the main audience (50%), who are typically located in the technological domain cited above. This fact evidence a clear researchers' interest in proposing more suitable social media artifacts for the elderly. Other identified audiences were researchers, elderly care assistance and policymakers. These kinds of audiences were more focused on the elderly matters domain.

What are the main research goals and obtained results? In the technological dimension, a relevant number of research papers have research questions and results related to the use of social media artifacts. In the elderly dimension, the studies were mainly classified into the category of characteristics of elderly people using social media. This relation is understandable, use of social media artifacts drives characterization of their users, or viewed from the other angle, the elderly people characteristics need to be studied in order to research on their use of social media artifacts. In addition, it is possible to see that the technological domain and the elderly matters domain were primarily where researchers concentrated their efforts. Therefore, it is not surprising the relevant number of research papers belonging to the intersection of the characteristics of older people using social media (elderly dimension) and the use of social media artifacts (technological dimension). However, there is an incongruity between the number of studies related to "design or assessment of social media artifacts" in Table 3 and the number of articles oriented to designers as audience in Table 1.

What researchers point out as future trends? The analysis of future trends should first consider the limitations. A significant number of researchers have established as their main limitation that the results obtained are not generalizable because the sample used was very homogeneous, very small or biased. Thus, the main considerations on future work, as stated by the researchers, refer to do further research in terms of improve sampling, research approaches, and data collection methods. These expectations clearly reflect a goal of increasing rigor in their research. In addition, from our point of view, there are some relevant research lines needed in order to understand better the impact of social media in the elderly population. We noticed that the quality of life domain has the lowest attention of researchers. Elderly population have special characteristics, as we cited before, these persons have limited mobility that results in less participation in social activities increasing feelings of loneliness and decreasing satisfaction with life [2, 3]. They also need to strengthen the emotional and social relationships with family members and friends [2, 4, 5]. Research oriented to increase elderly quality of life, should focus in understand the positive or negative impact of social media tools on elders and also guide social media designers in such way. In this regard, it is also important to consider design strategies based on approaches such as human-computer interaction and participatory design that will allow designers to propose social media tools more suitable for older people, taking into account their life situations, habits and attitudes, and physical and mental conditions. Future research efforts should also lead to greater integration between different disciplinary areas.

6 Conclusion

This paper reports the result of a systematic literature review in the field of social media and the elderly. Our study included 36 research papers, selected after an iterative process. Elders are the fastest growing population around the world and any effort oriented to improve their quality of life is important. Our findings show that there is currently no predominant research approach to address this field of study. Samples were generally small and questionnaires were the most common method of data collection. Many of the research efforts are focused on aspects of design, the interaction of the elderly with social media and how it affects their lives.

An interesting aspect we found was an informal approach to report results. Many papers do not define social media and an important number do not indicate the research approach nor the number of participants. Another difficulty is to clearly define who is an older adult.

Future work should be aimed at increasing the experience of researchers in the field, fostering interdisciplinary research processes, and a deeper understanding of the benefits of social media in older adults, and of aspects that complicate for them the use of these tools.

Appendix: Research Papers in the Study

In the following list we cross reference the paper number that we use in the tables and in the text with their correspondent number in the list of references (in square brackets), for example paper #2 corresponds to reference [32]: Spagnoletti, P., Resca, A., Sæbø, Ø.:

Design for social media engagement: Insights from elderly care assistance. Journal of Strategic Information System, vol. 24, no. 2, pp. 128–145 (2015). https://doi.org/10.1016/j.jsis.2015.04.002s.

2 [32]	51 [19]	96 [24]	127 [14]
3 [39]	54 [54]	98 [37]	129 [31]
5 [30]	55 [17]	99 [48]	131 [27]
6 [4]	59 [41]	106 [3]	132 [28]
9 [53]	60 [40]	109 [25]	133 [18]
15 [51]	85 [55]	112 [2]	147 [7]
18 [35]	90 [48]	115 [10]	148 [6]
37 [29]	93 [9]	117 [22]	153 [42]
43 [54]	95 [23]	118 [26]	156 [34]

References

1. United Nations: World Population Ageing: 2013. United Nations, New York (2013)
2. Erickson, L.B.: Social media, social capital, and seniors: the impact of Facebook on bonding and bridging social capital of individuals over 65. In: Presented at the AMCIS (2011)
3. Lin, S.-H., Chou, W.H.: Developing a social media system for the Taiwanese elderly by participatory design. Bull. Jpn. Soc. Sci. Des. **60**(3), 39–48 (2013). https://doi.org/10.11247/jssdj.60.3_39
4. Cornejo, R., Tentori, M., Favela, J.: Enriching in-person encounters through social media: a study on family connectedness for the elderly. Int. J. Hum Comput Stud. **71**(9), 889–899 (2013). https://doi.org/10.1016/j.ijhcs.2013.04.001
5. Gilbert, E., Karahalios, K.: Predicting tie strength with social media. In: Proceedings of the SIGCHI Conference on Human Factors in Computing Systems, pp. 211–220. ACM, New York (2009). https://doi.org/10.1145/1518701.1518736
6. Dumbrell, D., Steele, R.: Privacy perceptions of older adults when using social media technologies. In: Healthcare Informatics and Analytics: Emerging Issues and Trends: Emerging Issues and Trends, p. 67 (2014)
7. Finn, K.: Social media use by Older Adults (2010). http://wiserusability.com/wpfs/wp-content/uploads/2015/07/Social-Media-Use-by-Older-Adults.pdf
8. Fokkema, T., Knipscheer, K.: Escape loneliness by going digital: a quantitative and qualitative evaluation of a Dutch experiment in using ECT to overcome loneliness among older adults. Aging Ment Health **11**(5), 496–504 (2007)
9. Haris, N., Majid, R.A., Abdullah, N., Osman, R.: The role of social media in supporting elderly quality daily life. In: 2014 3rd International Conference on IEEE Presented at the User Science and Engineering (i-USEr), pp. 253–257 (2014)
10. Richter, D., Bannier, S., Glott, R., Marquard, M., Schwarze, T.: Are internet and social network usage associated with wellbeing and social inclusion of seniors? – The third age online survey on digital media use in three european countries. In: Presented at the International Conference on Universal Access in Human-Computer Interaction, pp. 211–220 (2013)
11. Russell, C., Campbell, A., Hughes, I.: Research: ageing, social capital and the internet: findings from an exploratory study of Australian "silver surfers". Australas. J. Ageing **27**(2), 78–82 (2008). https://doi.org/10.1111/j.1741-6612.2008.00284.x

12. Shapira, N., Barak, A., Gal, I.: Promoting older adults' well-being through Internet training and use. Aging Ment Health **11**(5), 477–484 (2007)
13. Hawkley, L.C., Cacioppo, J.T.: Aging and loneliness: downhill quickly? Curr. Dir. Psychol. Sci. **16**(4), 187–191 (2007). https://doi.org/10.1111/j.1467-8721.2007.00501.x
14. Bell, C., Fausset, C., Farmer, S., Nguyen, J., Harley, L., Fain, W.B.: Examining social media use among older adults. In: Presented at the Proceedings of the 24th ACM Conference on Hypertext and Social Media, pp. 158–163 (2013)
15. Coelho, J., Duarte, C.: A literature survey on older adults' use of social network services and social applications. Comput. Hum. Behav. **58**, 187–205 (2016). https://doi.org/10.1016/j.chb.2015.12.053
16. Perrin, A.: Social Networking Usage: 2005–2015. Pew Research Center (2015)
17. Stellefson, M., Chaney, B., Barry, A.E., Chavarria, E., Tennant, B., Walsh-Childers, K., Sriram, P.S., Zagora, J.: Web 2.0 chronic disease self-management for older adults: a systematic review. J. Med. Internet Res. **15**(2), e35 (2013). https://doi.org/10.2196/jmir.2439
18. Xie, B., Huang, M., Watkins, I.: Technology and Retirement Life: A Systematic Review of the Literature on Older Adults and Social Media. The Oxford Handbook of Retirement. Oxford University Press, New York (2012)
19. Xie, B., Watkins, I., Golbeck, J., Huang, M.: Understanding and changing older adults' perceptions and learning of social media. Educ. Gerontol. **15**(2), e35 (2013). https://doi.org/10.2196/jmir.2439y
20. Madden, M.: Older adults and social media: social networking use among those ages 50 and older nearly doubled over the past year. Pew Research Center (2010)
21. Maier, C., Laumer, S., Eckhardt, A.: Technology adoption by elderly people – an empirical analysis of adopters and non-adopters of social networking sites. In: Heinzl, A., Buxmann, P., Wendt, O., Weitzel, T. (eds.) Theory-Guided Modeling and Empiricism in Information Systems Research, pp. 85–110. Physica-Verlag HD, Heidelberg (2011)
22. Meiler-Rodríguez, C., Freire-Obregón, D., Rubio-Royo, E.: SEVENTI: new approach for teaching seniors basic skills through social media. In: INTED2012 Proceedings, pp. 3503–3510 (2012)
23. Boyd, K., Nugent, C., Donnelly, M., Bond, R., Sterritt, R., Gibson, L.: Investigating methods for increasing the adoption of social media amongst carers for the elderly. In: Presented at the XIII Mediterranean Conference on Medical and Biological Engineering and Computing 2013 (2014)
24. Lin, S.-H., Chou, W.H.: Bridging the social media usage gap from old to new: an elderly media interpersonal and social research in Taiwan. In: Presented at the International Conference on Human Centered Design (2011)
25. Alakärppä, I., Jaakkola, E., Päykkönen, K., Väntänen, J.: Experiences of the elderly, their relatives, and volunteers of a social media application in monitoring of wellbeing. In: Presented at the eTELEMED 2014 : The Sixth International Conference on eHealth, Telemedicine, and Social Medicine (2014)
26. Grigoryeva, I., Vidiasova, L., Zhuk, D.: Seniors' inclusion into e-governance: social media, e-services, e-petitions usage. In: Presented at the Proceedings of the 9th International Conference on Theory and Practice of Electronic Governance (2016)
27. Tsai, T.-H., Chang, H.-T., Wong, A.M.-K., Wu, T.-F.: Connecting communities: designing a social media platform for older adults living in a senior village. In: Presented at the International Conference on Universal Access in Human-Computer Interaction (2011)
28. Karimi, A., Neustaedter, C.: My Grandma Uses Facebook: Communication Practices of Older Adults in an Age of Social Media. School of Interactive Arts & Technology, Simon Fraser University, Surrey (2011)

29. Larsson, E., Nilsson, I., Larsson Lund, M.: Participation in social internet-based activities: five seniors' intervention processes. Scand. J. Occup. Ther. **20**, 471–480 (2013). https://doi.org/10.3109/11038128.2013.839001

30. Chakraborty, R., Vishik, C., Rao, H.R.: Privacy preserving actions of older adults on social media: exploring the behavior of opting out of information sharing. Decis. Support Syst. **55** (4), 948–956 (2013). https://doi.org/10.1016/j.dss.2013.01.004

31. Leist, A.K.: Social media use of older adults: a mini-review. Gerontology **59**(4), 378–384 (2013). http://www.karger.com/DOI/10.1159/000346818

32. Spagnoletti, P., Resca, A., Sæbø, Ø.: Design for social media engagement: insights from elderly care assistance. J. Strateg. Inform. Syst. **24**(2), 128–145 (2015). https://doi.org/10.1016/j.jsis.2015.04.002s

33. Wu, J., Koon, L.C.: Tangible social-media application for the elderly. In: Proceedings of the 6th International Conference on Rehabilitation Engineering & Assistive Technology, pp. 37:1–37:4. Singapore Therapeutic, Assistive & Rehabilitative Technologies (START) Centre, Kaki Bukit TechPark II, Singapore (2012)

34. Yang, Y., Yuan, Y., Archer, N., Ryan, E.: Adoption of social media and the quality of life of older adults. In: Presented at the 2016 49th Hawaii International Conference on System Sciences (HICSS), pp. 3133–3142 (2016)

35. Chen, Y.-R.R., Schulz, P.J.: The effect of information communication technology interventions on reducing social isolation in the elderly: a systematic review. J. Med. Internet Res. **18**(1), e18 (2016). https://doi.org/10.2196/jmir.4596

36. United Nations: The World Aging Situation: Strategies and Policies. Department of International Economic and Social Affairs, New York (1985)

37. Chandrakar, R., Joglekar, A.: Role of media on social health of elderly in Durg Bhilai City. Int. J. Sci. Res. **5**(6), 740–742 (2016). http://dx.doi.org/10.21275/v5i6.30051601

38. Selwyn, N., Gorard, S., Furlong, J., Madden, L.: Older adults' use of information and communications technology in everyday life. Ageing Soc. **23**(5), 561–582 (2003). https://doi.org/10.1017/S0144686X03001302

39. Chou, W.H., Lai, Y.-T., Liu, K.-H.: User requirements of social media for the elderly: a case study in Taiwan. Behav. Inf. Technol. **32**(9), 920–937 (2013). https://doi.org/10.1080/0144929X.2012.681068

40. Norval, C.: Understanding the incentives of older adults' participation on social networking sites. ACM SIGACCESS Accessibility Comput. (102), 25–29 (2012). https://doi.org/10.1145/2140446.2140452

41. Tennant, B., Stellefson, M., Dodd, V., Chaney, B., Chaney, D., Paige, S., Alber, J.: eHealth literacy and web 2.0 health information seeking behaviors among baby boomers and older adults. J. Med. Internet Res. **17**(3) (2015). https://doi.org/10.2196/jmir.3992

42. Hutto, C., Bell, C., Farmer, S., Fausset, C., Harley, L., Nguyen, J., Fain, B.: Social media gerontology: understanding social media usage among older adults. Presented Web Intell. **13**, 69–87 (2015)

43. Couture, L.: Loneliness linked to serious health problems and death among elderly. Activities Adapt. Aging **36**(3), 266–268 (2012). https://doi.org/10.1080/01924788.2012.708846

44. Drennan, J., Treacy, M., Butler, M., Byrne, A., Fealy, G., Frazer, K., Irving, K.: The experience of social and emotional loneliness among older people in Ireland. Ageing Soc. **28** (8), 1113–1132 (2008). https://doi.org/10.1017/S0144686X08007526

45. Shaw, L.H., Gant, L.M.: In defense of the internet: the relationship between internet communication and depression, loneliness, self-esteem, and perceived social support. CyberPsychology Behav. **5**(2), 157–171 (2002). https://doi.org/10.1089/109493102753770552

46. Obar, J., Wildman, S.: Social media definition and the governance challenge: an introduction to the special issue. Telecommun. Policy **39**(9), 745–750 (2015). http://dx.doi.org/10.2139/ssrn.2647377
47. Bandyopadhyay, S., Shaw, V., Banerjee, A., Nag, D.: Social knowledge management: use of social media for disseminating informal wisdom of elderly to the youth. Int. J. Knowl. Innov. Entrepreneurship **1**(1–2), 107–115 (2013)
48. Beneito-Montagut, R.: Encounters on the social web everyday life and emotions online. Sociol. Perspect. **58**(4), 537–553 (2015)
49. Kaplan, A.M., Haenlein, M.: Users of the world, unite! The challenges and opportunities of social media. Bus. Horiz. **53**(1), 59–68 (2010). https://doi.org/10.1016/j.bushor.2009.09.003
50. Nef, T., Ganea, R.L., Müri, R.M., Mosimann, U.P.: Social networking sites and older users – a systematic review. Int. Psychogeriatr. **25**(7), 1041–1053 (2013). 007/001, https://doi.org/10.1017/S1041610213000355
51. Li, Q.: Characteristics and social impact of the use of social media by Chinese Dama. Telematics Inform. **34**(3), 797–810 (2016). http://dx.doi.org/10.1016/j.tele.2016.05.020
52. Aarts, S., Peek, S.T.M., Wouters, E.J.M.: The relation between social network site usage and loneliness and mental health in community-dwelling older adults. Int. J. Geriatr. Psychiatry **30**(9), 942 (2015). https://doi.org/10.1002/gps.4241
53. Muñoz, D., Cornejo, R., Gutierrez, F.J., Favela, J., Ochoa, S.F., Tentori, M.: A social cloud-based tool to deal with time and media mismatch of intergenerational family communication. Future Gener. Comput. Syst. **53**(C), 140–151 (2015). https://doi.org/10.1016/j.future.2014.07.003
54. Moss, G., Wulf, C., Mullen, H.: Internet marketing to 50+ generations in the UK and France. J. Int. Consum. Mark. **25**(1), 45–58 (2013). https://doi.org/10.1080/08961530.2013.751799
55. Baker, P.M.A., Bricout, J.C., Moon, N.W., Coughlan, B., Pater, J.: Communities of participation: a comparison of disability and aging identified groups on Facebook and LinkedIn. Telematics Inform. **30**(1), 22–34 (2013). https://doi.org/10.1016/j.tele.2012.03.004
56. Jaeger, P.T., Xie, B.: Developing online community accessibility guidelines for persons with disabilities and older adults. J. Disabil. Policy Stud. (2008)
57. Lee, B., Chen, Y., Hewitt, L.: Age differences in constraints encountered by seniors in their use of computers and the internet. Comput. Hum. Behav. **27**(3), 1231–1237 (2011)
58. Levy, Y., Ellis, T.J.: A systems approach to conduct an effective literature review in support of information systems research. Informing Sci. Int. J. Emerg. Transdiscipline **9**(1), 181–212 (2006)
59. Webster, J., Watson, R.T.: Analyzing the past to prepare for the future: writing a literature review. MIS Q. **26**, xiii–xxiii (2002)

WhatsApp

Cristóbal Fernández Robin[1(✉)], Scott McCoy[2], and Diego Yáñez[1]

[1] Universidad Técnica Federico Santa María, Valparaíso, Chile
{cristobal.fernandez,diego.yanez}@usm.cl
[2] Mason School of Business, Williamsburg, Virginia, USA
scott.mccoy@mason.wm.edu

Abstract. More than one billion people use WhatsApp nowadays, out of which 70% uses it daily. In this scenario, this study seeks modelling the variables that influence the intention to use WhatsApp. To this end, 579 surveys based on the Unified Theory of Acceptance and Use of Technology are conducted. The descriptive results show that individuals use WhatsApp mainly motivated by leisure. In this sense, according to the SEM, the variable with greatest influence on behavioral Intention is hedonic motivation, followed by social influence, performance expectancy and effort expectancy. These results indicate that people use WhatsApp principally because it is fun, enjoyable, very entertaining, something more inherent to an entertainment application than to a messaging application.

Keywords: WhatsApp · Social computing · Leisure

1 Introduction

More than a billion people in more than 109 countries use WhatsApp to keep in touch with their friends and family, at any time and place. WhatsApp is free, and offers messaging and calls in a simple, safe and reliable way that is available in smartphones around the world. In fact, currently more than 42 billion messages are sent, and more than 100 million voice calls are made through this application. Furthermore, 70% of the WhatsApp users report using it daily, and on average 1 million of new users register per day [16]. In this context, some questions arise with respect to the motivators that affect the use of WhatsApp, in other words, why are people using WhatsApp? In that sense, this work intends to determine what factors influence the intention to use this popular application and how the relationship of these factors is articulated.

2 Literature Review

One of the first successful attempts to model the intention to use technological systems was the Technology Acceptance Model [6]—created as link to the world of the technologies of the Theory of Reasoned Action [7]—which explains the intention to use a technology based on the perceived ease of use defined as the degree to which a person believes that using a particular system would be free of effort [6] and the

© Springer International Publishing AG 2017
G. Meiselwitz (Ed.): SCSM 2017, Part II, LNCS 10283, pp. 82–90, 2017.
DOI: 10.1007/978-3-319-58562-8_7

perceived usefulness defined as the degree to which a person believes that using a particular system would enhance his or her job performance [6]. Subsequently, various efforts were made to enhance this model, including the addition of social influence named subjective norm and cognitive processes variables such as image, job relevance, output quality, result demonstrability, and experience and voluntariness [19]. Later on, this was also attempted by means of the Unified Theory of Acceptance and Use of Technology [20]. This theory aims at predicting the intention to use using variables such as performance expectancy, effort expectancy and social influence, which have a definition similar to that of perceived usefulness, perceived ease of use and subjective norm, respectively. Other variable added was facilitating conditions, defined as the extent to which an individual believes that some organizational and technical infrastructures exist to support the use of a system [20]. However, the original TAM model was created to examine IT/IS adoption in business organizations. Then, Venkatesh, Thong and Xin Xu [21] proposed extending the Unified Theory of Acceptance and Use of Technology, to study the acceptance and use of technologies in a consumption setting, incorporating three new variables: hedonic motivation, price value and habit. As can be seen, the motivations to use ICT's are varied. According to Brandtzaeg and Heim [4], people use social networks to get in contact with new people, to keep in touch with their friends and general socializing, which might be closely related to the subjective norm. On the other hand, Quan-Haase and Young [13] support that people use instant messaging to maintain and develop their relationships, as well as to kill time [11]. Furthermore, Xu et al. [22] suggest that user utilitarian gratifications of immediate access and coordination, hedonic gratifications of affection and leisure—which might be related to perceived usefulness and to perceived ease of use, accordingly—and website social presence are three positive predictors of usage.

In the case of WhatsApp, there are certain motivators linked to cost, sense of community and immediacy [5], as well as to unlock new opportunities for intimate communication [8]. Moreover, even addictive behaviors have been detected towards this application [18]. In this sense, several studies have been carried out on the use of Whatsapp [12], the importance of family groups [1], the use of status within the application [15], interactions in educational settings [3, 17], and concerns about privacy [14], among others. This article intends to model the intention to use WhatsApp, based on the Unified Theory of Acceptance and Use of Technology [21].

3 Methodology

To model the intention to use WhatsApp and understand the variables explaining the attitudes towards this application, a study with an initial exploratory stage is conducted to review the background details of the use of this application at a global level. Subsequently, a concluding second stage consisting in the application of an online questionnaire to 579 people is conducted. To this end, a questionnaire was elaborated based on the variables of the UTAUT2 model [21]. The sample is composed mostly by young people, university students and graduates, due to the high degree of penetration that WhatsApp has in their daily lives.

The model proposed considers the following variables: hedonic motivation, performance expectancy, effort expectancy, social influence, and behavioral intention. First, hedonic motivation is defined as the pleasure an individual feels when behaving in a particular way or carrying out a specific activity [10]. Second, performance expectancy points to the extent to which using a technology benefits consumers when performing certain activities [21]. Third, effort expectancy is the degree of ease associated with consumers' use of technology [21]. Fourth, social Influence is the extent to which consumers perceive it is important that others think they should use a particular technology [21]. The latter social influence or subjective norm is closely related to the intention to use a social network [9]. Lastly, behavioral intention refers to the set of motivational factors that indicate to what extent people is willing to try or how much effort they plan to make in order to develop certain behavior [2]. The structural model, together with its latent variables and the proposed relationships, are shown in Fig. 1.

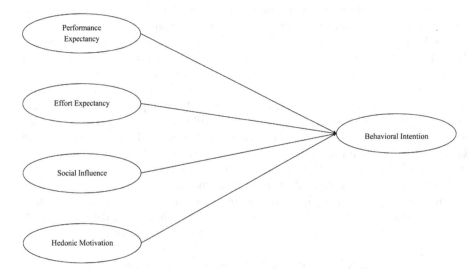

Fig. 1. Proposed model

As can be seen in the Fig. 1 a simplified model is proposed, it allows to measure the intention to use WhatsApp based on the direct influence of the variables Performance Expectancy, Effort Expectancy, Social Influence, and Hedonic Motivation.

In that sense and regarding the latent variables included in the structural model, Table 1 shows the observable variables, which were assessed using a Likert-type scale ranging from 1 to 5 in the survey that was applied to a total of 579 individuals. Thus, the first four variables refer to Performance Expectancy, the following four questions refer to Effort Expectancy. Then, the following three variables refer to Hedonic Motivation, and the next three variables to Social Influence. Finally, the last three questions refer to the Behavioral Intention of using WhatsApp. The questionnaire also contains variables to measure demographic variables such as sex, age and their last level of education completed, as well as questions to measure behavioral variables such

Table 1. Observed variables

I find WhatsApp useful in my daily life
Using WhatsApp increases my chances of achieving things that are important to me
Using WhatsApp helps me accomplish things more quickly
Using WhatsApp increases my productivity
Learning how to use WhatsApp is easy for me
My interaction with WhatsApp is clear and understandable
I find WhatsApp easy to use
It is easy for me to become skillful at using WhatsApp
Using WhatsApp is fun
Using WhatsApp is enjoyable
Using WhatsApp is very entertaining
People who are important to me think that I should use WhatsApp
People who influence my behavior think that I should use WhatsApp
People whose opinions that I value prefer that I use WhatsApp
I intend to continue using WhatsApp in the future
I will always try to use WhatsApp in my daily life
I plan to continue to use WhatsApp frequently

as the number of hours per day devoted to the use of WhatsApp and the number of times per day that respondents use this application.

4   Analysis and Results

As aforementioned, a total of 579 valid surveys were obtained, that is, eliminating incomplete or biased answers. Out of the respondents, 57% are women while the others 249 respondents are men. In terms of educational level, 60% were still university students, followed by 25% people with complete higher education.

Regarding the motives to use the application, 62.3% reported mainly using WhatsApp for leisure, while the following 23.4% used this application for informational purposes. The remaining respondents manifested that they use WhatsApp primarily in their jobs, more precisely, as a working tool. While it is clear that WhatsApp usage is explained by a combination of work, leisure, information and other motivators, the purpose of the question is to understand what is the primary use with which consumers perceive WhatsApp to be related, in that sense, it is interesting to rescue the close relationship with leisure and fun.

Afterwards, a descriptive analysis of the observable variables of the questionnaire is made, Table 2 shows the mean and standard deviation obtained for each one of the questions applied to measure the proposed model.

Table 2 shows that most of the observed variables get a mode of 5, it should be remembered that the scale used for the survey corresponds to a Likert scale five points, where 1 means strongly disagree, 2 means disagree, 3 means neither agree nor disagree, 4 means agree and 5 means strongly agree. In fact, it is remarkable the case of the four

Table 2. Descriptive statistics of observed variables

Observable variable	Mode	Mean	SD
I find WhatsApp useful in my daily life	5	4.42	.97
Using WhatsApp increases my chances of achieving things that are important to me	4	3.67	1.28
Using WhatsApp helps me accomplish things more quickly	5	3.97	1.21
Using WhatsApp increases my productivity	4	3.01	1.41
Learning how to use WhatsApp is easy for me	5	4.61	.89
My interaction with WhatsApp is clear and understandable	5	4.47	.95
I find WhatsApp easy to use	5	4.63	.85
It is easy for me to become skillful at using WhatsApp	5	4.53	.92
Using WhatsApp is fun	5	4.31	.98
Using WhatsApp is enjoyable	5	4.22	1.03
Using WhatsApp is very entertaining	5	4.22	.97
People who are important to me think that I should use WhatsApp	5	3.75	1.23
People who influence my behavior think that I should use WhatsApp	3	3.42	1.28
People whose opinions that I value prefer that I use WhatsApp	5	3.73	1.25
I intend to continue using WhatsApp in the future	5	4.40	.96
I will always try to use WhatsApp in my daily life	5	3.81	1.27
I plan to continue to use WhatsApp frequently	5	4.21	1.04

questions that point to measure the Effort Expectancy as they reach a mode of 5 with standard deviations less than 1, Learning how to use WhatsApp is easy for me (4.61), My interaction with WhatsApp is clear and understandable (4.47), I find WhatsApp easy to use (4.63), and, It is easy for me to become skillful at using WhatsApp (4.53).

On the other hand, there is a variable that reach a mode of 3, this implies that the majority of the respondents states not to agree or disagree with the assertion, this is the case of the variable People who influence my behavior think that I should use WhatsApp (3.42). This could mean that the opinion of people who influence my behavior is not transcendental when deciding whether or not I should use WhatsApp, then the intention to use this mobile application does not respond to the influence of people close to me. However, when the standard deviation is found to be among the highest between the observed variables (1.28), a second look at this question suggests that there might be people who influence my behavior who thinks I should use WhatsApp while there are other people which also influence my behavior but think I should not use WhatsApp. For example, my friends think I should use WhatsApp and keep sending those funny memes, while my boss and my doctor think I should not use WhatsApp, focus on my work and do more exercise to stay healthy. This second explanation for the low valuation achieved by this observed variable makes more sense when it is found that the observable variable with the highest standard deviation is using WhatsApp increases my productivity (1.41), following our example above, maybe my boss is right and I should stop using WhatsApp to focus on doing my job. Maybe not.

Finally, the interesting thing about this first approximation to the data is that it seems that the most important variables are Effort Expectancy and Hedonic Motivation. So, it can be assumed that people intend to use WhatsApp motivated by the fun they find when using it and the ease of use that shows this popular mobile app.

After the descriptive analysis, a scales reliability analysis is performed using Cronbach's alpha test in IBM SPSS Statistics. Regarding this analysis, it may be seen that the five independent structural variables of the model (Performance expectancy, Effort expectancy, Social influence and Hedonic motivation) have satisfactory results in terms of the reliability of the constructs used, they all are higher than 0.7, this is also repeated for the dependent variable in the structural model, where Behavioral Intention achieves a Cronbach's alpha of .812. It should be noted that none of the structural model variables obtained a higher Chronbach's alpha by eliminating some of the observable variables in each case. The results are shown in Table 3.

Table 3. Cronbach's alpha reliability analysis

Performance expectancy	.736
Effort expectancy	.801
Social influence	.867
Hedonic motivation	.725
Behavioral intention	.812

Then, the structural model was tested using IBM SPSS Amos, thereby obtaining an adequate absolute, incremental, and parsimony model fit. Figure 2 shows the structural equation model, with the observable variables and errors in each case. It is important to mention first that all the proposed relationships between latent variables are significant (p-value < .001).

As described in Fig. 2, the model reaches a coefficient of determination of .52 to model behavioral intention of use WhatsApp. In this sense, it can be assumed that this simple model is able to explain 52% of the variability in the intention to use this popular application for smartphones. Then, the influence of the latent variables proposed as independent variables of the model is analyzed, for this the standardized regression weights of latent variables are analyzed.

The most influencing variable is hedonic motivation, with a standardized regression weight of .499, which indicates that people use WhatsApp motivated mainly by pleasure, entertainment and fun. This is also related to the 62.3% of users that reported using WhatsApp for leisure, as noted above. The other variables that explain the behavioral intention to use this instant messaging application are social influence, with a .333 standardized estimate, followed by performance expectancy (.305), and effort expectancy (.256). After reviewing some of the observable variables, it should be first noted that, for the hedonic motivation factor, the variable "Using WhatsApp is fun" obtains a very high mean of 4.37 and a mode corresponding to 5, what it means that respondents are tally agree with the fact that using WhatsApp is fun. On the other hand, it is interesting to remark the social influence factor, where the variable "People who are important to me think that I should use WhatsApp" achieves a mean of 3.57, with its

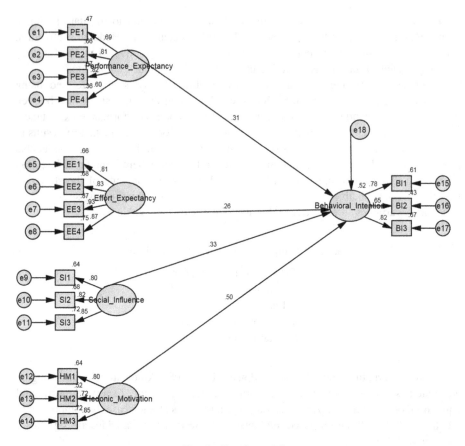

Fig. 2. Result model

mode in 3, thus indicating a certain degree of indifference regarding social influence as staded before. In fact, if considering the three observable variables of social influence, a mean of 3.75 is obtained with highest standard deviation. Finally, the variable "Using WhatsApp increases my productivity" also stands out due to its high dispersion, with a standard deviation of 1.41 and a mean of 3.01. Therefore, some questions arise about whether this observed variable is applicable to a technology of this kind, anyway, if this variable is removed from the study the Cronbach's alpha of the performance expectancy remains at .783.

5 Discussion

Based on the results of the study, it is observed that the variable that influences the most the intention to use WhatsApp is hedonic motivation, that is, people use What-sApp because it is fun, enjoyable, and very entertaining. This, coupled with the fact that respondents express that their main motivation to use WhatsApp is leisure, lead us to think that this application is perceived more as a form of entertainment than as a means of communication or, in other words, it is used to communicate with close people and to seek entertainment through that interaction, thereby unlocking new opportunities for intimate communication [8] while sending memes, videos and links to entertaining things.

Although all the variables are significant in the proposed model, it should be noted the low impact of social influence, for which a greater influence was expected, since WhatsApp is an instant messaging application that does not work if people important to us are not using it, moreover, a high valuation was expected (between 4 to 5) for the variables contained in the social influence factor, owing to the fact that WhatsApp is an application that allows people to communicate with family and friends. The descriptive statistical analysis previously shown suggests that the low impact of Social Influence on Behavioral Intention of using WhatsApp can be explained to a great extent because there are people who influence my behavior who thinks I should use WhatsApp while there are other people which also influence my behavior but think I should not use WhatsApp. As exemplified above, my friends could widely agree that I use whatsapp while my doctor might recommend not using whatsapp and do more exercise to stay healthy. In that sense, it could also be that people who influence my behavior may think that I should use WhatsApp in some contexts, for example to warn that I am coming late to a meeting, but at other times they could say that I should not use WhatsApp, for example when I am having dinner with them in a restaurant. Then, measuring Social Influence as a predetermining factor of Behavioral Intention turns difficult in the case of WhatsApp.

Even though the influence of Performance Expectancy on Behavioral Intention is positive and significant, it is also worth mentioning the high degree of variability of the observable variables that make up Performance Expectancy. This could be explained by the fact that there is more than one type of WhatsApp user, thus, if people admit to using WhatsApp because it is entertaining, fun and enjoyable, the use of WhatsApp could be detrimental to their work performance. On the other hand there are those who also find it entertaining, fun and enjoyable, but they are able to use it as a communication tool that supports their productivity and performance in things important to them.

Finally, this study achieves to explain the intention to use in 52% of the cases with the most important variable being hedonic motivation, then, the positioning that this type of applications should seek in the minds of consumers might not only appeal to be a tool of communication, but an entertaining funny and enjoyable communication.

References

1. Aharony, N., Gazit, T.: The importance of the WhatsApp family group: an exploratory analysis. Aslib J. Inf. Manage. **68**(2), 174–192 (2016)
2. Ajzen, I.: The theory of planned behavior. Organ. Behav. Hum. Decis. Process. **50**(2), 179–211 (1991)
3. Bouhnik, D., Deshen, M.: WhatsApp goes to school: mobile instant messaging between teachers and students. J. Inf. Technol. Educ. Res. **13**, 217–231 (2014)

4. Brandtzæg, P.B., Heim, J.: Why people use social networking sites. In: Ozok, A.A., Zaphiris, P. (eds.) Online Communities and Social Computing, OCSC 2009. LNCS, vol. 5621, pp. 143–152. Springer, Heidelberg (2009). doi:10.1007/978-3-642-02774-1_16

5. Church, K., de Oliveira, R.: What's up with WhatsApp?: comparing mobile instant messaging behaviors with traditional SMS. In: Proceedings of the 15th International Conference on Human-Computer Interaction with Mobile Devices and Services, pp. 352–361. ACM (2013)

6. Davis, F.D.: Perceived usefulness, perceived ease of use, and user acceptance of information technology. MIS Q. 13(3), 319–340 (1989)

7. Fishbein, M., Ajzen, I.: Belief, attitude, intention, and behavior: an introduction to theory and research. Philos. Rhetoric 10(2), 130–132 (1977)

8. Karapanos, E., Teixeira, P., Gouveia, R.: Need fulfillment and experiences on social media: a case on Facebook and WhatsApp. Comput. Hum. Behav. 55, 888–897 (2016)

9. Ku, Y.C., Chu, T.H., Tseng, C.H.: Gratifications for using CMC technologies: a comparison among SNS, IM, and e-mail. Comput. Hum. Behav. 29(1), 226–234 (2013)

10. Moon, J.W., Kim, Y.G.: Extending the TAM for a World-Wide-Web context. Inf. Manag. 38(4), 217–230 (2001)

11. Pelling, E.L., White, K.M.: The theory of planned behavior applied to young people's use of social networking web sites. CyberPsychology Behav. 12(6), 755–759 (2009)

12. Pielot, M., de Oliveira, R., Kwak, H., Oliver, N.: Didn't you see my message?: predicting attentiveness to mobile instant messages. In: Proceedings of the 32nd Annual ACM Conference on Human Factors in Computing Systems, pp. 3319–3328. ACM (2014)

13. Quan-Haase, A., Young, A.L.: Uses and gratifications of social media: a comparison of Facebook and instant messaging. Bull. Sci. Technol. Soc. 30(5), 350–361 (2010)

14. Rashidi, Y., Vaniea, K., Camp, L.J.: Understanding Saudis' Privacy Concerns when Using WhatsApp (2016)

15. Sánchez-Moya, A., Cruz-Moya, O.: "Hey there! I am using WhatsApp": a preliminary study of recurrent discursive realisations in a corpus of WhatsApp statuses. Procedia-Social Behav. Sci. 212, 52–60 (2015)

16. Smith, C.: DMR (n.d.). http://expandedramblings.com. Accessed 11 Nov 2016

17. So, S.: Mobile instant messaging support for teaching and learning in higher education. Internet High. Educ. 31, 32–42 (2016)

18. Sultan, A.J.: Addiction to mobile text messaging applications is nothing to "lol" about. Soc. Sci. J. 51(1), 57–69 (2014)

19. Venkatesh, V., Davis, F.D.: A theoretical extension of the technology acceptance model: four longitudinal field studies. Manage. Sci. 46(2), 186–204 (2000)

20. Venkatesh, V., Morris, M.G., Davis, G.B., Davis, F.D.: User acceptance of information technology: Toward a unified view. MIS Q. 27(3), 425–478 (2003)

21. Venkatesh, V., Thong, J.Y., Xu, X.: Consumer acceptance and use of information technology: extending the unified theory of acceptance and use of technology. MIS Q. 36(1), 157–178 (2012)

22. Xu, C., Ryan, S., Prybutok, V., Wen, C.: It is not for fun: an examination of social network site usage. Inf. Manag. 49(5), 210–217 (2012)

An Analysis of Online Discussion Platforms for Academic Deliberation Support

Fabrício Matheus Gonçalves[✉], Emanuel Felipe Duarte, Julio Cesar dos Reis, and M. Cecília C. Baranauskas

Institute of Computing, University of Campinas (UNICAMP), Campinas, Brazil
{fmatheus,emanuel.duarte,julio.dosreis,cecilia}@ic.unicamp.br

Abstract. Asynchronous online discussions are relevant for supporting and promoting debates among people. Nevertheless, achieving beneficial discussion requires adequate software applications with specific features to support people's participation, *e.g.*, mechanisms for structured pros and cons arguments. Although literature is vast in discussing online forums usage, requirements for the design of platforms for academic deliberation has not been addressed in the same proportion. In this paper, we analyze three online discussion platforms for deliberation. We conduct a structural analysis regarding their interaction concepts and, based on activities of graduate students attending a Human-Computer Interaction discipline, this study conducts a usage analysis of the platforms. Results reveal the level of participants' engagement in academic discussions and the effects on their learning perception. Moreover, results expose the impact of software design choices in the deliberation outcome.

Keywords: Academic deliberation · Collaboration · Social computing · Interaction design · HCI · ConsiderIt · Debate Hub · Trello

1 Introduction

Nowadays, people use online software applications to support sharing of thoughts regardless of space and time constraints. Platforms for online forums can play an important role in supporting debates, but existing software environments sometimes fail in providing features and design choices to promote more informed discussions. In this context, participants may invest a high amount of effort without achieving a mutually acceptable outcome. This problem is aggravated in free-for-all forums such as those from major newspapers websites or social networks, where individual self-expression prevails, leading to monologues and flaming [7,8]. These problems may lead to people avoiding to participate in discussions, even when the outcome may affect their lives. Although recent literature proposes methods and tools for online deliberation [14], there is still a need to further study their effects and how they may foster better discussions in which people are willing to participate.

© Springer International Publishing AG 2017
G. Meiselwitz (Ed.): SCSM 2017, Part II, LNCS 10283, pp. 91–109, 2017.
DOI: 10.1007/978-3-319-58562-8_8

Deliberation is a central skill to exercise respect for different perspectives and still be able to collaborate towards a common objective. Practice on deliberation in an academic context may prepare future researchers to an active and democratic behavior in their research communities and general society [11]. The challenge is to obtain the adequate software features for academic deliberation support. While a rigid software structure promotes a more focused discussion at the expense of limiting the variety of ideas; a flexible structure may promote unexpected and creative participations at the expense of blurring the discussion focus and avoiding proper deliberation [10].

In this article, we investigate three different deliberation-based platforms by assessing their different characteristics in a specific scenario of a graduate course in Human-Computer Interaction (HCI). The goal is to understand the interaction features that may influence people's engagement. In our research methodology, we first selected the platforms based on a literature review. We explored *Considerit* [7], *Debate Hub* [15] and *Trello* [1]. The selection of these platforms was guided by their key features. Their choice is justified by the fact that they provide different styles and structures for discussion. First, we conducted a structural analysis to understand the design structure and interaction flow in the platforms.

We then set up their use in the context of a HCI graduate course during a whole semester by involving 17 graduate students and 1 facilitator. The platforms were used as a discussion space for pre-chosen HCI and Philosophy of Science scientific papers. During the semester the students had 9 reading assignments. After the finalization of the course, we collected quantitative usage data obtained by server logs, which provides hints concerning the participants' engagement and prefered collaboration patterns. This data was an important asset towards understanding which design features might influence engagement, be it in a negative or positive manner.

Furthermore, participants provided qualitative feedback concerning how the platforms influenced their perception of the topics being discussed, as well as their preparation for the *a posteriori* face-to-face discussion. Participants' opinions were thoroughly examined to obtain insights that might be useful to inform the design of online discussion platforms. Results indicate that most of the participants were positively affected by the platforms regarding their understanding of the papers. Our findings provide central elements to guide the design of online deliberation software platform to be explored in academic settings.

This paper is organized as follows: Sect. 2 describes the background to the study, Sect. 3 presents the investigation context and the methods used in the analyses; Sect. 4 reports on the results with respect to the structural analysis, quantitative analysis and qualitative analysis regarding the use of the platforms, followed by a discussion on our main findings. Finally, Sect. 5 presents conclusions and suggests further work.

2 Background on Platforms For Discussion

In online discussion forums, participants can either start a new discussion thread by creating a new post or continue an existing thread by replying to others' posts. Posts in a given thread are linked to each other in a chronological order. Literature has acknowledged the benefits of threaded forum for supporting online discussions and learning. The participants potentially have time to thoroughly thinking before responding and have access to the whole discussion to examine and reflect on the ideas presented. Nevertheless, the threaded online forums might not be the best choice for supporting collaborative processes important in learning situations [6].

Gao *et al.* [6] synthesized among the constraints of threaded forums: (a) the difficulties of maintaining focus; (b) of promoting interactive dialogues; (c) of synthesizing ideas; and (d) lack of emotional cues. The authors point out other relevant literature mentioning digressions, for example, students posting their own ideas without paying attention or responding to the others' ideas. They remain in the surface of discussion, seldom going deeper through negotiation of meaning. Furthermore, some researchers acknowledge the problems due to the structure and design features of those software systems, demanding efforts into their design to increase the likelihood of effective discussions. Relying on this fact, we have investigated deliberation platforms, to serve a similar purpose in the context of this study.

Other models of online discussion involve deliberation and debate among people. Online deliberation is defined by Towne and Herbsleb [12] as "a Web-based form of reasoning that gathers and carefully considers options for action and possible consequences of each". Through the Internet, platforms for online deliberation go beyond gathering information, allowing the exploration, synthesis and critical examination of new knowledge. While a debate is usually an oppositional process where ideas are put forward and defended, or proved wrong, a deliberation assumes that participants propose pieces of an answer to a problem. Thus, it is a collaborative process seeking common understanding and common ground for action. Other authors, as for example, Davies and Chandler [3], explain both deliberation and debate as parts of the same process. They take "deliberation" to denote "thoughtful, careful, or lengthy consideration" by individuals, and "formal discussion and debate" in groups, *i.e.*, as a type of communication among people that is reasoned, purposeful, and interactive.

As shown by Towne and Herbsleb [12], most online deliberation platforms have roots in the Information-Based Information Systems (IBIS), developed in the 70's. They were transformed into a graphical version in the late 80's for recording the design rationale of small groups of designers, the graphical IBIS (gIBIS) system, which evolved to the current *Compendium* open-source software. The knowledge structure graphically represents the topics, issues, questions of fact, positions, arguments, and possible relationship among these. Besides *Compendium*, several other systems extended the IBIS concepts. Towne and Herbsleb [12] elaborated five design requirements for a deliberation platform to be useful: (a) it must attract contributions, (b) make the deliberation content navigable, (c) have conformance to usability standards, (d) focus on quality content, and (e) promote wide-scale adoption.

Early research has proposed *ConsiderIt*, a platform where people can publicly deliberate and reflect on others' thoughts without emphasizing direct discussions. This platform showed its utility to general public measuring the discretionary use in a real web deployment in the context of an election [5,7]. The probable deliberative disposition of the self-selected users highlighted opportunity for a controlled experiment that revealed how *ConsiderIt* led to significant changes in standpoint, perceived knowledge, and perceived understanding [11]. In addition, participants' willingness to include counter-arguments in their statements and to change a standpoint on the basis of new information supports the platform's potential to increase people's deliberative skills and attitudes. Our study takes the next step by applying deliberative platforms in a real academic context to facilitate students' understanding and critical analysis of academic literature.

In this work, we define "academic deliberation" as an exercise of people's exposure to and processing of diverse information from others; willingness to argue with argument quality, and to participate in the debate of ideas. In this task, participants are challenged or exposed to new and contradicting information or ideas of others. Instead of reaching a common understanding, the aim is to develop critical thought based on their own as well as on the others position regarding the ideas being discussed. As Gao *et al.* [6], in the concept of "academic deliberation", we acknowledge the dispositions to: (a) discuss to comprehend and vice-versa, (b) discuss to critique, (c) discuss to construct knowledge, and (d) discuss to share, which address different and interrelated perspectives to learning.

Based on the above discussion, we raised some questions regarding the design and use of deliberation platforms to support academic discussion: How can we better understand online deliberation in certain academic contexts? Do existing platforms address specificities of academic deliberation? How can we better inform the design of online deliberative platforms aimed at involving people in a meaningful, consequential and inclusive way?

This study addressed the three following platforms:

1. *ConsiderIt* [7] supports public deliberation where users are encouraged to reflect upon the issue by considering trade-offs, as the discussion is framed by arguments featured as pros or cons. People can position themselves in a free scale with extremes in "agree" and "disagree" and contribute with pro or con arguments.
2. *Debate Hub* [15] supports communities in raising issues; sharing ideas, debating pros and cons, and voting in contributions with a metaphor of thumbs up or down. It allows the community to collectively organize ideas based on their acceptance by its members.
3. *Trello* [1] graphically organizes information in boards. The boards, in turn, can be divided in lanes containing cards as a unit of information. Even though *Trello* is mostly used for project management, it has a flexible representation of information, which allowed us to appropriate the platform with specific conventions and color codes to use it as a platform for group deliberation.

3   Study Design

In this section, we present the study context and the involved participants. Afterwards, we report on the methods conducted to collect and analyze data within quantitative and qualitative perspectives.

3.1   Context and Participants

This study was conducted during a semester in an Human-Computer Interaction (HCI) discipline of a Computer Science graduate program at the Institute of Computing, University of Campinas, Brazil. The discipline had 60 h in the semester, organized in 2 classes per week, with 2 h each. It was conducted by a professor with support of an facilitator.

Each week, students were assigned to read and discuss a selected peer-reviewed academic paper about a hot topic in HCI and Philosophy of Science research (*e.g.*, [2,4,9,13]), summing 9 papers in total. They were invited to use one of the platforms to discuss the paper, a week long online activity denominated "warm up". They were invited to formulate propositions regarding important and/or controversial aspects of the papers; and arguing by means of pro or con arguments. Depending on the platform used, they could provide different forms of feedback to classmates by including: comments (*ConsiderIt* and *Trello*); thumbs up/down (*Debate Hub*); or even reuse classmates' arguments to compose their stance (*ConsiderIt*). After a week of the online "warm up" through a platform, the paper was discussed in class in the form of the professor guided debate.

Students used *ConsiderIt* during 6 weeks, *Debate Hub* during 4 weeks and *Trello* during 2 weeks, summing 12 weeks in total. The last week using each platform was dedicated to discuss the platform itself in the light of the previous discussions (platform's meta-analysis). The participants discussed the way the platform's design helped or disturbed the deliberations as well as their understanding of the papers. The participants' feedbacks constituted the main data for our qualitative analysis.

The participants involved 17 graduate students (11 male and 6 female). Most of them (11 in total) were already used to read at least one academic paper per week. Regarding reading strategies, participants are well divided among those who: (a) do not summarize; (b) only highlight the relevant points; and (c) those who make summaries. Only one participant reported to use concept maps. Around half of them do not use online discussion tools, the other half cited discussion forums like those present in *Stackoverflow*[1], *Slack*[2], and *Moodle*[3].

The platforms were briefly presented in class by the facilitator before the first time of their use. The facilitator posted in the Learning Management System the link to the platform and presented brief instructions including deadlines

---

[1] https://stackoverflow.com/.
[2] https://slack.com/.
[3] https://moodle.org/.

of the activities. From time to time, some additional feedback was included by the facilitator to make clear some of the academic expectations. For example, clarifying that students should include citations and references to substantiate their arguments, and incentivizing them to engage in more difficult tasks, like to elaborate proposals or to use less obvious platform's features. The participation in online discussion was rewarded with up to 5% of the final mark in the course, depending on the quality and quantity of tasks performed. The use of the platforms during the whole semester produced the interaction data for our different types of analyses.

3.2   Methods

The first step involved to analyze the interaction structure of the platform's interfaces. To this end, we studied the terms used to denote the different interaction concepts in the three platforms. Our goal was to understand how the interaction is organized in each platform.

The next step involved to examine the usage of the platforms. We explored quantitative and qualitative analyses to comprehend distinct aspects regarding the platforms. This study assumes that by exploring these types of analyses may reveal thorough aspects relevant for deliberation platforms' design. Our study intended to quantify the interaction among the students in each different platform and specific content discussion. For this purpose, we devised a metric of participants' engagement by counting all activities (proposals, arguments, comments, endorsements) done by them during each reading assignment, which was obtained through usage logs of each platform.

The endorsement data were slightly different in each platform. In *ConsiderIt*, we considered an action of endorsement when a participant appropriated (*i.e*, got behind) another participant's argument. In *Debate Hub*, endorsement was counted by means of "thumbs up" or "thumbs down" given by participants on arguments, which means that an argument is flagged as convincing or unconvincing respectively. Lastly, in *Trello*, we considered the action of adding yourself as a member of a card as an action of endorsement, similar to *ConsiderIt*'s appropriation concept. We focused on participant's engagement because we consider it a central aspect in deliberation platforms, and participants' endorsement behavior, in turn, remains an important aspect of the engagement. We analyzed the activities regarding the reading assignment separately from the platforms meta-analysis.

For qualitative data, we focused on participants' feedbacks regarding the platforms from the meta-analysis activity. Unlike the normal reading "warm-up", in the meta-analysis, the proposals were provided by instructors to access students' theoretical understanding of the previous readings. In this case, the platforms were used as a practical context to exercise students' design and evaluation skills with regard to aspects that appeared from the papers reading. The following aspects were considered:

- **Human vs. User:** As discussed by Bannon [2], a piece of mediating technology can be designed to simply improve productivity, as in the perspective of classical HCI, the "user" perspective. However, the author argues for a new approach that "encompasses a much more challenging territory that includes the goals and activities of people, their values, and the tools and environments that help shape their everyday lives", the "human" perspective. In our study, for each platform, the participants were provoked with the proposal "This tool is for users instead of humans".

- **Neutrality:** According to Fallman [4], technologies always transform experiences in predicted and unpredicted ways; hence it is not possible for them to actually be neutral: "for every revealing transformation there is a simultaneously concealing transformation of the world, which is given through a technological mediation". For this reason, "the user needs to care for the mediating technology, which might come to affect both how people behave in certain situations as well as how others perceive them". For each platform, the participants were asked to position themselves in relation to the following statement: "This tool is not neutral with regard to the discussion".
- **Change of Perception:** Inspired by Traunmueller's research [13], which investigated visual factors that promote a change of safety perception in urban places, participants were asked to discuss upon the following statement: "This tool alters the perception of understanding of the assigned reading". The participants were asked to highlight examples and/or design features from each platform to illustrate if and how its use affected his/her perception of the reading.
- **Bugs and Features:** In response to the proposals: (a) "This tool can help me" and (b) "This tool is better than the previous one", the participants were invited to provide feedbacks regarding the platforms' features, report bugs, in addition to issues they experienced by using the platforms. For instance, by starting from the second platform, the participants answered to proposals in the form *"Debate Hub vs. ConsiderIt"*. They could compare platforms' features they had used so far.

We considered these aspects relevant for the design of deliberation platforms, and to the best of our knowledge, they were never analyzed in the literature in the context of deliberation platforms. We manually synthesized the participants' main arguments based on these aspects looking for understanding the way platforms' design choices affect their usage and perceptions. When appropriated, we summarized the syntheses of the arguments according to categories that emerged from the participants' opinions.

4   Results

In this section, we present our findings in the three distinct analyses. We start by analyzing the deliberation platforms, their characteristics, structure and interaction flow. Afterwards, we report on the results regarding usage analyses, which emcompasses a quantitative and a qualitative analysis.

4.1   Structural Analysis

ConsiderIt main user interface (Fig. 1) includes the main interaction elements involved in the socially enhanced personal deliberation. The deliberation category (1 in Fig. 1) groups related proposals. It allows to navigate through proposals in the same group. The proposal and opinion slider (2 in Fig. 1) consist in a statement, its author and details. The slider allows the user to choose in a continuum between "disagree" and "agree". The user may move a blue "face" icon which varies from unhappy to happy depending on the agreement level. Over the slider there is a pictorial histogram that represents the stance of other users. In another view, this histogram can be used to explore others' opinions by segments, highlighting the arguments of groups of users with similar opinions.

Fig. 1. *ConsiderIt* main interface: (1) proposal category; (2) proposal statement and opinion slider with others' opinion pictorial histogram; (3) new arguments entry in the center and draggable arguments of others in the interface borders; (4) comments to the argument.

A opinion may be supported by arguments (3 in Fig. 1). Others' arguments are presented on the interface borders and can be dragged into a personal argument list in the center. In this list, the platform enables the users to write new pros and cons composed by a succinct summary, and details of the argument that might include evidences backing the argument. Once published, new arguments become available to others. Authors are represented by avatars on the side of the argument balloon. When someone else appropriate the argument, *i.e.*, get behind it, this person's avatar appears behind the author's avatar. By clicking on this supporters' avatar cluster, the platform presents their different stances in the histogram. Users can also post comments (4 in Fig. 1) to an argument. They are displayed within the arguments details when the summary balloon is clicked.

Debate Hub main screen (Fig. 2) shows the main discussion elements. There is an issue or debate title (1 in Fig. 2). It presents a description and a summary of how many views, ideas, participants and votes were posted. At this place, the platform indicates the remaining time to end the discussion. The votes are used to rank the ideas in terms of community acceptance. There is a feature designed to enable users to submit a new idea, as well as to view previous ideas status (2 in Fig. 2). It includes the title, description of an idea and author's avatar. The thumbs up/down are used to cast a vote claiming the idea as strong or weak. The vote bar indicates the current support for the idea including arguments and votes.

The "for" and "against" arguments are divided in two lists under each idea (3 in Fig. 2). They are represented with a title, its description and the author avatar. Thumbs up/down display the number of "convincing"/"unconvincing"

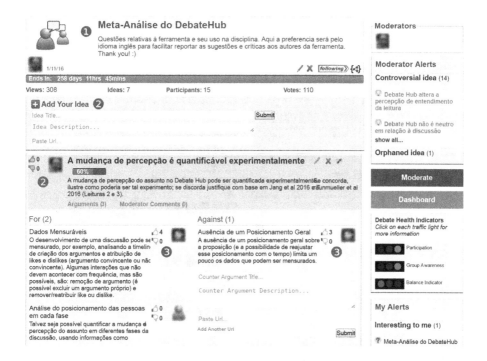

Fig. 2. *Debate Hub* main screen: (1) issue; (2) submission of a new idea or votation of others' ideas; (3) addition and vote for/against arguments. Dashbord of computer supported analytics with debate health indicators and alerts (right).

votes received by the argument based on clicks on it. The interface affords the addition of new arguments at the bottom of each list. Unlike *ConsiderIt,* there is no support to propose comments on arguments and the interface do not reveal the voters.

The *Debate Hub* features computer-supported debate analytics in the form of a debate healthy semaphore (Fig. 2, dashbord on the right) and alerts including hints to moderators. The healthy semaphores indicate key aspects of discussion flow. For instance, if there is balance between types of posts and community participation; it has links to advanced graphic visualisations of debate progress and other usage analysis.

Trello (Fig. 3) organizes information in a visually hierarchical structure. The board (1 in Fig. 3) as the top level element is used to group related proposals. New boards can be created to hold debate on other issues. Inside a board, the lists (2 in Fig. 3) divide the board in subgroups used to represent each proposal in discussion. The list title holds the proposal statement. A new proposal is introduced by creating a new list.

The user interface element named "card" (3 in Fig. 3) refers to the unit of information inside the list used mainly to hold arguments. Besides its title, a card displays (when the card is opened) details of its description and activity log. The

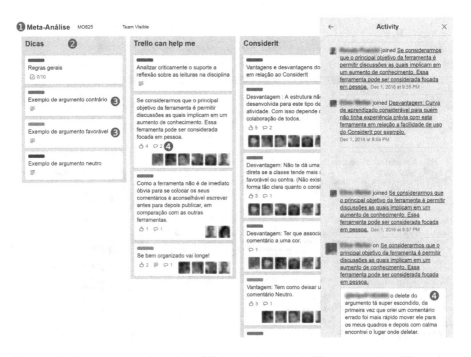

Fig. 3. *Trello* main screen interface: (1) discussion board; (2) proposal list; (3) con/pro cards; and (4) comments indicator in the card and comment in the activity log (on the bottom right).

card can be marked with a colored label; the used color convention was: blue colored card to hold the description of the proposal; green or red card to hold pro and con arguments, respectively. Users can become card members to show support for a card. The members are displayed as avatar below card's title.

Trello affords the posting of comments (4 in Fig. 3) as another type of direct interaction with others' card. The user interface indicates, in front of the card, the number of comments a card received. All the actions performed by users are logged into activity indicator (right) and are notified to all those interested in a card. *Trello* has also a plugin that supports vote for a card, indicated by the number of thumbs up on the card, but lacks a way of computing total votes by labels or lists.

To configure this platform for deliberative usage in a way more aligned with the previous platforms, the first list of proposal was used to hold extra usage conventions. The first card (blue) defined 10 textual rules to attribute deliberative semantics and meaning to UI elements and actions, *e.g.* "A card with con argument must be labeled red", "Agreement with the argument in a card is expressed by becoming member of it". Also a card with each color label was given as example.

The platforms use a similar hierarchical approach to organize discussion by employing different terms to designate the involved concepts. In the first level, different terms are used to group the issues to be discussed. In the second level, while *ConsiderIt* collects "opinions" instead of "proposals", *Debate Hub* counts "votes" for "ideas" and *Trello* has abstract "list" and computes "votes" only in the third level, for "cards". Table 1 presents our mapping of these interaction concepts in each platform.

Table 1. Terms that designate the interaction concepts in each hierarchy level of the platforms.

Level	ConsiderIt	Debate Hub	Trello
1	Category	Debate/Issue	Board
2	Proposal (opinion)	Idea (vote)	List
3	Pro/Con point	For/Against argument	Green/Red card (vote)
4	Comment	–	Comment

In addition to the levels treated, and less visible in the user interfaces, each platform defines and manages the working group and website address. *ConsiderIt* provides a subdomain with specific *URL* for each community; the *Debate Hub* allows the creation of "Discussion Group" for each community/project; and *Trello* employs a similar approach, but name it as a "Team".

4.2   Usage Analysis

In this section, we present the results for the quantitative analysis followed by the qualitative analysis.

Quantitative Analysis. We examine the participants' engagement for the three distinct platforms. First, we computed the sum of average contributions from all reading assignments (*cf.* Fig. 4). The contributions refer to messages related to proposals, pros and cons arguments, comments and endorsements.

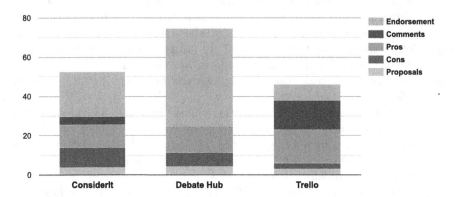

Fig. 4. Engagement as the sum of average contributions (proposals, cons, pros, comments and endorsements) using the platforms for paper discussion.

Results reveal that the number of proposals remains similar to all platforms. *Considerit* presents a higher number of cons arguments while *Trello* presents a higher number of pros arguments, which are represented by green cards. *Debate Hub* does not have the feature of comments, and we observed a higher number of participants' comments in *Trello*. With regard to the Endorsement activity, the results show that participants explored *Debate Hub* much further than the other platforms, possibly to compensate the lack of comment support. Other way used to workaround this limitation was by citing previous argument's authors in the new argument text.

We further computed the contributions in the meta-analysis activity for the three platforms (*cf.* Fig. 5). First, the number of contributions remains higher than for the reading assignments. This may be explained by the fact that, in these activities, the proposals were provided by instructors based on already discussed papers and experienced platform usage. *Debate Hub* presents the highest number of contributions mostly due to the Endorsement. In this platform, the number of cons arguments increased with respect to the results presented in Fig. 4. *Trello* presents an increased number of Endorsements compared with Fig. 4. This may be explained by the learning effect, since not all participants understood how to use this feature in the only paper discussed in this platform, but received additional instruction before using it again in the meta-analysis.

Qualitative Analysis. The qualitative data shed light on design principles and practices that converge or diverge among the platforms. In this section, we present the results for each of the aspects investigated in our study.

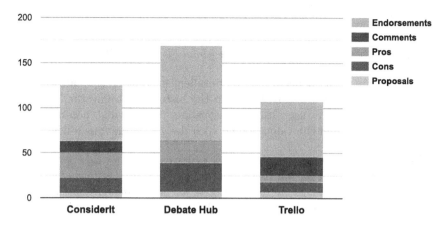

Fig. 5. Engagement as the sum of average number of contributions (proposals, cons, pros, comments and endorsements) for the meta-analysis activity by using the platforms.

Humans vs. Users. The majority of participants disagree with the statement "This platform is for users instead of humans" for all platforms. Among the collected feedbacks, we highlighted the design features that may have led them to perceive it as "for humans":

> *"The non binary 'opinion slider' reflects human beings [subjectivity], even allowing one person in complete agreement incorporate opposing arguments in his/her opinion".* (Participant 8, regarding *ConsiderIt)*

> *"Focus on the 'health' of the community [...] as can be seen by the healthy semaphore indicating participation, group awareness and balance" [in the discussion]* (Participant 2, regarding *Debate Hub)*

> *"It is interesting to think about different types of discussion and the open possibilities" [in reorganizing discussion flow and card meaning]* (Participant 3, with respect to *Trello)*

Participants reported that the *ConsiderIt* has an "educative design" to promote better discussions by teaching users to develop refined communicational habits. Furthermore, it allows breaking a complex discussion into simpler pieces of argument with a practical and guided interface with examples and hints. *Trello,* on the other hand, had usage rules that were harder to learn, but participants could collectively review and redefine these rules.

Neutrality. The majority of participants recognized that a deliberation platform cannot be neutral. Most of the feedbacks were applied for all studied platforms. The non-neutrality concerns mostly discussions framed by pro vs. con assertive arguments, and the platforms lack the use of non-verbal communication, as highlighted by a participant.

"Non-neutrality comes from how the platforms mediate the discussion. For instance, by sacrificing non-verbal aspects of a discussion such as body language, voice intonation, and interpersonal distance". (Participant 4)

Other non-neutrality aspects were more salient in some of the platforms. For instance, in *ConsiderIt,* the positioning in the histogram, by avatars' adjusted position, to indicate the user stance. Regardless the inherent non-neutrality, participants understand the value behind such design decision, as follows:

"The exercise of expressing a discussion in terms of propositions is a useful practice to reflect on the topic addressed. The polarized format of the responses, in turn, makes the tool attractive for more pragmatic uses, such as popular consultations". (Participant 2)

Furthermore, the automated ranking of provided information affects the neutrality since the order of others' arguments are presented using a custom ranking algorithm. Such aspects were less perceived in *Debate Hub* debate analytics. Some students also felt the "Disagree" position as less comfortable, and this could marginally favor the "Agree" side. This is reinforced by design hints, which includes the use of red for disagreement and green for agreement. *Trello* received some appreciation for the more flexible structure allowing more neutral considerations.

As a counterpoint, the neutrality goes further than the platforms design choice. For instance, one participant highlighted that the nature and quality of the content affect the discussion flow, in particular, the phrasing of the propositions.

Change of perception mediated by the platform. Most of the participants agree that by using the platforms after individual reading positively affected their understanding of the papers. Some of them, however, remained indifferent. Among the collected feedbacks, we highlighted arguments that explain how the platforms lead to a change in perception:

"ConsiderIt is very effective in showing the grouping of opinions according to their point of view. [. . .] We feel encouraged to rethink, reflect and better support [our point of view]." (Participant 10, endorsed by 5 colleagues)

"As we have to present two positions [. . .] sometimes I felt induced to manifest both for and against [reflecting on trade-offs]." (Participant 17, endorsed by 1 colleague)

After a complete semester of weekly deliberations, participants perceived: (1) arguments based on personal experience or citation induce more reflection; (2) different people may highlight different aspects of the text, and collectively they construct the discussion flow; (3) participants must develop capabilities to craft insights as proposal or evidence grounded arguments to better influence the discussion flow; and (4) the routine use of the platforms may lead to the need of review some points that seemed clear before the online discussion.

Table 2. Summary of participants' feedback comparing the platforms regarding learning curve, transparency, engagement and bugs. Each aspect was considered among participants as (▲) positive, (▼) negative or (♦) controversial.

	ConsiderIt	Debate Hub	Trello
Learning curve	▲ Easy to learn, visually appealing ♦ Resembles a personal pros/cons list	♦ Resembles traditional online discussion forum	▼ Demands learning the basic use of the platform besides extra usage conventions
Transparency	▲ Graphical overview of each participant positioning ▲ Explicit visual endorsement	▲ Thumbs up/down ideas and arguments ▼ It does not show who endorsed the ideas	▼ Lack of positioning summary ▲ Endorsement visible by becoming a card member
Engagement	▲ Graphics of positioning overview and of endorsement ▲ Direct argument feedback through comments ▲ Daily easy to read e-mail report (customizable)	▼ Not easy to see the others' participation ▼ Lack of direct reply, cross references and argument reuse ▼ Unreliable notification ▲ Dashboard with graphics and statistics ▲ Optional timed debate with stages deadline	▲ Comments with cross references and notification ▲ Direct notifications and activity summary ▲ Flexibility to redefine interaction rules and UI meanings ▼ Needs commitment to usage conventions not enforced by the UI
Bugs	▼ Some arguments were lost ♦ At least 2 bugs reported and fixed during use ▲ Mobile responsive layout	▼ Some interface issues (*e.g.*, font size, character encoding) ▼ No mobile responsive layout ▼ E-mail report with broken links	▲ Stable and consolidated platform ▲ Mobile responsive layout and dedicated app

Features and Bugs. We compiled the main aspects to compare the platforms into four dimensions. The dimensions emerged from the manual examination of the participants' contributions in the meta-analysis activities, which are: learning curve, transparency, engagement and bugs (*cf.* Table 2). The aspects summarized in Table 2 are marked according to the perceived outcome of the discussion: as (▲) positive or (▼) negative, when there was no objections among participants or the majority agreed on it; or as (♦) controversial, when discussions did not reach a clear consensus.

The results regarding **learning curve** tended towards *ConsiderIt*. It showed a clean visual, and was judged as a relatively simpler interaction structure. *Debate Hub* appeared mostly as traditional online forums structure, which was appraised by some participants as easier to read the entire discussion thread without extra clicks. *Trello* was considered more complex, since it demanded extra work to learn the UI usage conventions.

With respect to the **transparency,** *ConsiderIt* received positive feedback due to its graphical overview of the group positioning and the explicit visual endorsement. The *Debate Hub* thumb up and down interface feature for arguments was welcomed, but the participants expected to visualize who cast the votes. *Trello* presented an endorsement feature as visible as the feature implemented in *ConsiderIt*. However, the instructor needed to present to the participants how to use the "card member" feature to express endorsement. In this context, the participants judged negative the lack of visual or numerical summary on the proposal. This occurs because votes in *Trello* are summarized by cards (third level), but not by lists (second level) as the other platforms.

The **engagement** dimension attracted most of the students' attention indicating that they perceived its importance for group collaboration. According to the participants, the engagement appeared more natural with *ConsiderIt*. It supports direct feedbacks through comments in arguments. The *Debate Hub* enforced deliberation (without comments or references to other's arguments) appeared more difficult for participants. Direct notification and activity summary of *Trello* was very appreciated and may explain part of the increase in the number of comments (*cf.* Fig. 4)

The **bugs** considered mainly whether the platform presents a mobile responsive layout. *Trello* as a commercial platform was the most stable. *ConsiderIt* and *Debate Hub* presented some interface issues during their use. In *ConsiderIt*, some participants claimed to lose the text of some arguments, and even reported some bugs that were fixed by developers. In *Debate Hub*, one participant claimed to be unable to create an user account.

4.3   Discussion

This study proposed to investigate online deliberation in academic contexts by analysing the interaction structure of distinct software platforms, their utilization via analyses that inquired and measured engagement, endorsement and aspects of neutrality and change of perception. Our findings showed a trade-off between rigid and flexible interaction structures provided by the platforms. We found that some features seemed not helpful for academic deliberation. For example, the identification of the most acceptable proposal from the discussion, via direct opposition of ideas, as featured by votes in *Debate Hub*. On the other hand, the ranking feature in *ConsiderIt* by using avatar histogram was capable of contributing for the transparency as a Graphical overview of each participant positioning.

Although the engagement was more prominent in the *Debate Hub* (Figs. 4 and 5), this was mostly attributed to endorsement. In this case, we thoroughly examined how endorsement differs among the platforms. The anonymous vote in *Debate Hub* remains the only kind of direct argument feedback using interface features in this platform. It was probably a lesser commitment when compared to getting behind others' arguments as occurs in *ConsiderIt* and *Trello* endorsements, through personal avatars. We can assume that comments and endorsements complement each other as forms of direct feedback among users. For instance, we observed a significant reduction in comments after the participants have learnt how to endorse using the feature of adding membership to card in *Trello*.

Besides the effects of interaction design on the engagement metrics (Fig. 4), we found that the activity design and the nature of concepts under discussion naturally influence engagement. For example, the engagement level doubles in meta-analysis activities for all platforms (Fig. 5). This is partly because more proposals were provided by instructors, the readings were already discussed in class, and the necessary experience using the platforms were already acquired.

The qualitative analysis highlighted some essential aspects shared by the studied platforms. While all platforms contemplated human valued aspects, each platform manifested it in a different manner. For instance, *ConsiderIt* presented its continuum opinion slider enriched with others' opinion histogram; *Debate Hub* presented its healthy debate semaphore indicator that contributes for the community; and *Trello* presented its flexibility to accommodate group personalized discussion flow. Although no mediating platform can be neutral, the platforms' non-neutrality targets the human necessity of collaboration and knowledge sharing.

This research elucidated that the deliberation platforms were capable of mediating a change of perception regarding the understanding of the selected papers, and promoted reflection on the complex concepts involved. Although it occurred in the proposed activities at some degree, the platforms lack aspects relevant to structure the discussions. The most prominent aspects were specific features to deal with the difficulties faced by participants to formulate instigating proposals.

The features reported by the participants' opinions reveal salient elements behind the design choices that differentiate the platforms and their outcome. We detected that specific features, such as graphical representations, can help users perceiving and understanding the positioning of their peers. This influenced further reflections and the way the participants prepared themselves to participate in the face-to-face discussion. Nevertheless, it required a slightly modification in the activities setup to enable the participants to identify relevant and/or controversial material to formulate proposal for discussion.

This study enabled to detect to which extent the existing platforms address specificities of academic deliberation, but it presents some limitations. To further support online deliberation in this context requires more situated design to elucidate relevant interaction features. We need to help participants to clarify the addressed issues and identify the affected stakeholders. This may reduce difficulties faced by people to formulate good proposals in academic deliberation. In further work, we plan to design, develop and evaluate a platform for academic deliberation, with prospective interested parties.

5   Conclusion

Online discussions require adequate Web-based software application to support people in proposing ideas for action and argumenting regarding the consequences of these options, for a deliberation. Although literature has proposed platforms to this end and studied human behaviour in this context, the design features of software platforms to support argumentation and debate of ideas in academic deliberations remains hardly investigated. In this paper, we conducted a comparative analysis of three online discussion platforms, based on a real academic context of use. Results revealed central aspects and limitations to guide the design of online deliberation software systems. We found that the discussion quality is highly dependent on the design choices the participants encounter for elaboration of well directed propositions. Further research involves a thorough characterization of the nature and values of academic discussion and the co-design and development of a situated-interaction platform.

Acknowledgments. We thank the National Council for Scientific and Technological Development (CNPq) (grants #136239/2013-7 and #308618/2014-9), the Coordination for the Improvement of Higher Education Personnel (CAPES), and the São Paulo Research Foundation (FAPESP) (grants #2014/14890-0 and #2015/165280) for funding. We are in debt to the students for their indirect contribution to this work. The opinions expressed in this work does not necessarily reflect the view of the grant agencies.

References

1. Trello web site (2016). https://trello.com
2. Bannon, L.: Reimagining HCI: toward a more human-centered perspective. Interactions **18**(4), 50–57 (2011)
3. Davies, T., Chandler, R.: Online deilberation design: Choices, criteria, and evidence (2011)
4. Fallman, D.: The new good: exploring the potential of philosophy of technology to contribute to human-computer interaction. In: Proceedings of the SIGCHI Conference on Human Factors in Computing Systems, pp. 1051–1060. ACM (2011)
5. Freelon, D.G., Kriplean, T., Morgan, J., Bennett, W.L., Borning, A.: Facilitating diverse political engagement with the living voters guide. J. Inf. Technol. Polit. **9**(3), 279–297 (2012)
6. Gao, F., Zhang, T., Franklin, T.: Designing asynchronous online discussion environments: recent progress and possible future directions. Br. J. Educ. Technol. **44**(3), 469–483 (2013)
7. Kriplean, T., Morgan, J., Freelon, D., Borning, A., Bennett, L.: Supporting reflective public thought with considerIt. In: Proceedings of the ACM 2012 Conference on Computer Supported Cooperative Work, pp. 265–274. ACM (2012)
8. Kriplean, T., Toomim, M., Morgan, J., Borning, A., Ko, A.: Reflect: supporting active listening and grounding on the web through restatement. In: Proceedings of the Conference on Computer Supported Cooperative Work, Hangzhou, China (2011)
9. Lincoln, Y.S., Lynham, S.A., Guba, E.G.: Paradigmatic controversies, contradictions, and emerging confluences, revisited. In: The Sage Handbook of Qualitative Research, vol. 4, pp. 97–128 (2011)
10. Shipman, F.M., Marshall, C.C.: Formality considered harmful: experiences, emerging themes, and directions on the use of formal representations in interactive systems. Comput. Support. Coop. Work (CSCW) **8**(4), 333–352 (1999)
11. Stiegler, H., de Jong, M.D.: Facilitating personal deliberation online: immediate effects of two considerIt variations. Comput. Hum. Behav. **51**, 461–469 (2015)

12. Towne, W.B., Herbsleb, J.D.: Design considerations for online deliberation systems. J. Inf. Technol. Polit. **9**(1), 97–115 (2012)
13. Traunmueller, M., Marshall, P., Capra, L.: ...when you're a stranger: evaluating safety perceptions of (un)familiar urban places. In: Proceedings of the Second International Conference on IoT in Urban Space, pp. 71–77. ACM (2016)
14. Verdiesen, I., Cligge, M., Timmermans, J., Segers, L., Dignum, V., van den Hoven, J.: Mood: massive open online deliberation platform a practical application. In: 1st Workshop on Ethics in the Design of Intelligent Agents, pp. 6–11 (2016)
15. Xiao, L., Zhang, W., Przybylska, A., De Liddo, A., Convertino, G., Davies, T., Klein, M.: Design for online deliberative processes and technologies: towards a multidisciplinary research agenda. In: Proceedings of the 33rd Annual ACM Conference Extended Abstracts on Human Factors in Computing Systems, pp. 865–868. ACM (2015)

Design of Digital Literacy Environments Based-On Interactive Learning Services

Jaime Muñoz Arteaga[1]([⊠]), José Eder Guzmán Mendoza[2],
Fco. Javier Álvarez Rodríguez[1], and René Santaolaya Salgado[3]

[1] Universidad Autónoma de Aguascalientes (UAA), Aguascalientes, Mexico
jmauaa@gmail.com, fjalvar.uaa@gmail.com
[2] Universidad Politécnica de Aguascalientes (UPA), Aguascalientes, Mexico
jose.guzman@upa.edu.mx
[3] Centro Nacional de Investigación y Desarrollo Tecnológico (CENIDET),
Cuernavaca, Mexico
rene@cenidet.edu.mx

Abstract. The differences in terms of access and ICT skills between different groups in society have created a problem of digital divide. To overcome this problem, informal learning models and strategies are required to achieve a greater impact on the population and that population can develop skills that enhance inclusion in the society knowledge. This work proposes the design of a digital literacy informal environment that aims to set a new educational paradigm approach to encourage different learning communities to uses new ICT that allows them to be more competitive in today's world and thus shorten the digital divide. Finally, a case study is presented. The case study was implemented in the Aguascalientes State, Mexico, in a learning community composed by librarians.

Keywords: Digital literacy · Informal learning · Learning environments · Learning services · Interactive systems

1 Introduction

The influence of ICT in the knowledge society has changed economic, political, cultural and social concepts allowing access to other levels of welfare and progress. To develop a knowledge society, it is necessary to define new approaches and models of knowledge acquisition. The inclusion in the knowledge society will enable individuals to access other levels of welfare and progress (Orrego and Velásquez 2011). However, the 21st century citizen must first acquire new personal, professional and social digital skills that are required by the knowledge society for inclusion in a digital world based-on ICT. The process of acquiring digital skills is known as digital literacy. This term refers to an individual's ability to use technologies appropriately, as well as to understand and be able to express themselves in different languages and digital media, as well as to develop knowledge related to information through ICT, and to develop social and political values and attitudes in relation to technologies.

© Springer International Publishing AG 2017
G. Meiselwitz (Ed.): SCSM 2017, Part II, LNCS 10283, pp. 110–124, 2017.
DOI: 10.1007/978-3-319-58562-8_9

In this sense, education as an individual process to be inserted into society throughout life is done through public or private institutions and also in the daily coexistence that seeks to integrate the individual in a specific cultural time and context. As Marciales Vivas (2012) and Sánchez (2013) point out, "in the course of our lives we move in three educational spaces: (a) formal, given by the institutions and that obeys to a curriculum certified by public and/or private governmental institutions and whose purpose is to qualify us for work; (b) non-formal, which refers to complementary formations without curricular value, and whose purpose is to keep us updated in our professions or to acquire skills, knowledge, etc., useful for daily life; (c) the informal, which is the education that is received every day in the social ambit and is what gives meaning to our socio-cultural integration in the particular society in which we live".

Although education is a universal right, there are still social segments throughout the world that by their economic resources, geographical location, gender, age, beliefs, language, race, disability, schooling, etc. (Block 2004), cannot access to an education that is based on a closed system. Formal and non-formal education creates a closed space where only a few have access, creating even a gap in accessibility to education. On the other hand, informal education represents an alternative to break the old educational paradigms and create new educational models that are capable of creating real and virtual environments where citizens of diverse social segments grouped in learning communities can receive digital literacy. Ann et al. (2009) claim that most learning takes place in communities. Formal education cannot prepare people for a world that changes rapidly and continually. So, we need to live in learning communities.

Based on these limitations, in our study, a multicontext-aware resource recommendation model and strategy for service-oriented ubiquitous learning environment is proposed with taking into consideration not only the services and learners' dynamic context information Finally, by presenting our prototype system and illuminating a typical scenario, we could show that our proposal can help learners obtain the proper resources to enhance the learning efficiency.

As it is very difficult for learners to find the most proper contents according to their preferences from massive resources in E-learning environment (Luo et al. 2008), the learning services compositions mechanism as a core component must be introduced.

This paper proposes the design of a digital literacy environment based-on interactive learning services that aims to encourage different learning communities into the knowledge society and thus able to decrease the digital divide.

The model is composed by different levels of layers, and its main element is a process of knowledge acquisition for transferring dynamic and gradually the digital skills that allow an individual become into a digital citizen certificated. Finally, a case study is presented.

The case study was implemented in the Aguascalientes State, Mexico, in a learning community composed by librarians.

1.1 Digital Literacy

In the twenty-first century, the progress and development of a country no depends solely on its material resources or on the investment of capital, but increasingly, it is necessary to have human resources (citizens) qualified or literate in the use of ICT (Area Moreira 2002), in such a way that through these human resources innovation and development can be fostered, thus advancing towards a knowledge society. Therefore, to overcome the obstacles to closing the digital divide, it is necessary to provide the population with a series of digital skills. This digital skills are known as "Digital Literacy".

The term digital literacy refers to the ability of an individual to properly use the technologies, as well as to understand and be able to express themselves with different languages and digital media. In addition, being digitally literate involves developing knowledge and skills in relation to information through ICT, as well as developing values and attitudes of a social and political nature in relation to technologies. Digital literacy is a learning process that involves providing people with concepts and methods, as well as practices that allow them to appropriate of the ICT.

1.2   Informal Learning

Generally the basic learning in life is learned informally. Education, as an individual process to be inserted into society throughout life, is carried out through public or private institutions and also in the daily coexistence that seeks to integrate the individual in a specific time and cultural context. Marciales Vivas (2012) and Sánchez (2013) claim *"in the course of our lives we move into three educational spaces: (A) formal, given by institutions and following a curriculum certified by public and/or private governmental institutions and which is intended to qualify for work; (B) non-formal, which refers to complementary formations with no curricular value, and whose purpose is to keep us updated in our professions or to acquire skills, knowledge, etc., useful for everyday life; (C) the informal, which is the education that is received every day in the social field and is what gives meaning to our socio-cultural integration in the particular society in which we live"*.

2   Related Works

In Pinto and Sales (2007) work the public libraries represent the vehicle of knowledge, they are an essential support for lifelong education, the cultural progress of an individual and the social groups that make up a given environment. They argue that public libraries face the new challenges of the digital divide that the information society and knowledge provoke in today's society. Public libraries, in their proactive role, can play a decisive role in integrating minority groups into society through the promotion of cultural exchange and training programs in information literacy. Thus, public libraries can serve as forums for informal learning for all groups in society.

Villa Orrego and Moncada Velásquez (2011) implemented a government program oriented at digital literacy in a rural community. The research aimed to identify and analyze the communication processes derived from the participation of a rural community in the Medellín Digital project. It was evidenced that the participation of people in this process of digital literacy promotes the renewal of some communicative practices, the configuration of new roles within the family, and the social appropriation of the project. This particular experience to approach Information and Communication Technologies (ICT) modified the lifestyle of participants, their beliefs and future education expectations, their self-esteem and their social cohesion level.

3 Digital Literacy Environments Based-On Interactive Learning Services

The new knowledge society has transformed the way we work, live and learn. This situation implies the development of new skills for the management and usage of emerging technologies that facilitate adaptation to the new economic, political, social, lifestyle, and lifelong training requirements. Online learning environments have contributed to the transformation of teaching methods, giving priority to the creation of communities with common learning objectives.

The online learning environments are designed based on the needs of the users, the learning objectives as well as the technology available. Online learning environments can be used to complement the learning process in formal and non-formal education systems, through the exchange of experiences and knowledge, collaboration and creation of working groups, interaction with other community members and the possibilities of self-evaluation. In this context, learning communities find support services oriented to their learning needs, their competencies and their collective behavior (Sloep and Berlanga 2011).

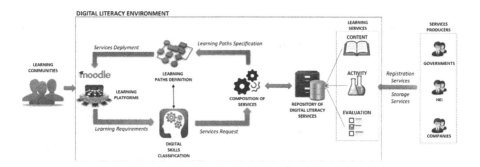

Fig. 1. Design of digital literacy environments based-on interactive learning services.

Each segment of the population perceives in different ways the use of ICT according to their cultural characteristics (Kyriakidou et al. 2011). Under this premise, a digital literacy environment should be designed based on cultural, geographic, political, economic, and even age and gender characteristics of a particular learning community. In this sense, if we consider these characteristics for the design of digital literacy environments, a population of individuals can be segmented into several more homogeneous communities, and thus learning services can be more efficient to attend the digital literacy needs of each learning community. In the following subsections, the main elements of Fig. 1 are described.

3.1 Learning Communities

A population of individuals can be segmented into learning communities, grouped according to the similarity of their characteristics as age, gender, economic, social, geographical, political or cultural circumstances, thus, it is possible to define more homogenous learning communities. The formation of Learning Communities -as homogeneous as possible- allows obtaining more detailed specification requirements for the development of digital literacy services. The step of obtaining the requirements specification based on the context of the learning community allows defining the classification of digital skills that must be acquired by that community (Fig. 2).

Fig. 2. Example of learning communities classification

Through the services approach, different learning scenarios can be created for the different profiles of learning communities.

3.2 Service Producers

It is ambitious to bring digital literacy to a large number of learning communities and that they can move to the knowledge society. However, it is not impossible if we consider actors that can create collaborative ecosystems that allow us to take advantage of the use of installed infrastructure, technological, human and economic resources and social interaction.

Taking advantage of this collaboration, it is possible to design collaborative strategies that are transformed into processes of knowledge transfer and appropriation of ICT in each of the different learning communities. After the study and analysis of different models of digital literacy, it was possible to identify and classify the main actors that can be the producers of services.

Governments: Through their digital agendas integrate public policies necessary to boost the innovation and competitiveness of their nations. This implies to offer better services in infrastructure and accessibility, and to ensure equal access by promoting rights and obligations for digital citizenship, as well as being the main promoter of digital inclusion campaigns.

Higher Education Institutions (HEI): The development of a knowledge society is a complex and multivariate challenge, which requires a multidisciplinary vision for its decrease. The HEI can offer this panoramic vision, as well as contributing with pedagogical and knowledge transfer models, with digital contents, educational platforms, etc., in such a way that they are relevant mediators to achieve the digital inclusion in the citizenship.

Companies: The companies are an important factor as agents promoting innovation and competitiveness. Thus, they promote the development of the most competitive human capital. They also have the function of generating digital services according to the demands and needs of citizens.

3.3 Digital Skills Classification

Digital Skills refer to good understanding and broad knowledge about the nature, function and opportunities of ICT in everyday situations of private, social and professional life. Also, people must understand the possibilities offered by ICT as tools to support creativity and innovation (Revuelta-Domínguez 2011).

If a citizen wants to get in the knowledge society, first, it is necessary to acquire a series of digital competences classified at basic, intermediate and advanced levels. These digital competencies can be acquired through formal, non-formal and informal educational processes (Fig. 3). In such a way, when the individual appropriates ICT, he or she becomes a digital individual, and thus, he or she can into a certification process that accredits his or her digital skills, so, become a digital citizen.

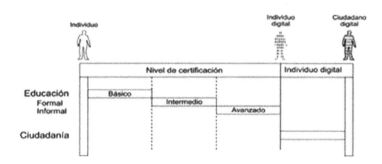

Fig. 3. Transition from Individual to digital citizen (Muñoz Arteaga et al. 2015)

The longer an individual spends more time using ICT, is gaining more experience and digital skills that allow him to move to higher levels, which involves performing more complex tasks with the use of ICT, to achieve inclusion in the knowledge economy.

As already mentioned, ICTs have a sense of utility for a learning community, when they are used to solve problems of daily life and work. Based on this idea, a classification of digital skills defined for a learning community is not necessarily useful for another learning community. Therefore, each learning community has associated a classification of digital skills that are useful for its context.

3.4   Learning Paths

Learning paths in education have emerged as an important advantage in planning, organizing, and controlling learning processes. The adaptability of learning paths includes changes to the user interfaces that are used to control the learning process. According to Yang et al. (2014) a learning path defines the steps that should guide a student in effectively building of their knowledge and skills.

Learning paths add a logical approach to model the task for a user interface, necessary to provide a cognitive function for the adaptation of the context, in this case, the context is represented by each learning community. Therefore, a learning path defines the interactive processes for the learning of the digital skills based-on the learning services.

3.5   Repository of Digital Literacy Services

The repositories are used by the institutions as a place for the organization, access, preservation and diffusion of digital objects in a specific subject, or digital files of different topologies (Texier et al. s/f; Álvarez Terrazas et al. 2011). The learning services repository is the space where service producers can publish, classify, disseminate and improve learning services.

Accessibility is the main feature of the learning services repository. Open access to learning services helps design learning environments to serve a wide variety of learning communities. A service producer can also evaluate other services created by other producers, with the aim of improving them if necessary, so that, they can adapt them to other learning communities.

The service repository is classified into three types of learning services:

– *Learning services* are organized and structured as a set of knowledge and skills.
– *Content services* are all those actions and tasks performed by an individual to strengthen skills and knowledge.
– *Evaluation services* that are used as instruments to measure the level of domain of the skills and knowledge of an individual, as well as to detect their failures and to make the necessary adjustments within the learning paths.

4   Case Study: Learning Community of Librarians

The following case study presents the design and implementation of a digital literacy environment for a community of librarians in the state of Aguascalientes, Mexico.

4.1   Context of Public Libraries in Aguascalientes State, México

The Government of Aguascalientes State, within its sexennial plan 2010–2016, considers as one of the main activities to close the digital divide for the improvement of the quality of life in Aguascalientes. Based on this need, the Fomix Aguascalientes

2011-01 project was created as an intervention strategy that contributes to the social appropriation of ICT in an effective and efficient way in urban and rural areas mainly.

In January 2012, the Government of Aguascalientes State announced that it would be the first entity in the Mexican Republic and Latin America to be connected by a digital network called: State Network of Education, Health, Government and Security (in Spanish Red Estatal de Educación, Salud, Gobierno y Seguridad: REESGS) (Prensa 2012). The purpose of REESGS is to encourage the exchange of information between the departments that provide services to their community, in this way, and with a project of such magnitude, the called "digital divide" would be shortened, and thus, the society of Aguascalientes would have significant resources to acquire digital citizenship.

The impact of this news involved the Cultural Institute of Aguascalientes (in Spanish Instituto Cultural de Aguascalientes: ICA), which is the agency responsible for administering 66 public libraries that are distributed in each of the 11 municipalities of the state of Aguascalientes (Fig. 4).

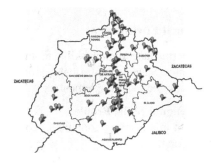

Fig. 4. Geographical distribution of 66 public libraries in the state of Aguascalientes.

Table 1 presents the relationship between the number of libraries and the number of inhabitants of each municipality.

Table 1. Total of libraries distributed in each Municipality and population that it attends

Municipality	No. of libraries	Population served
Aguascalientes	21	797,010
Asientos	6	45,492
Calvillo	7	54,136
Cosió	5	15,042
El Llano	2	18,828
JesúsMaría	5	99,590
Pabellón de Arteaga	4	41,862
Rincón de Romos	6	49,156
San Francisco de los Romos	4	35,769
San José de Gracia	3	8,443
Tepezalá	3	19,668
Total general	**66**	**1,184 996**

Thus, through the Public Libraries of the Aguascalientes State seeks to implement an informal learning model aimed at the entire population with the purpose that they can acquire the skills and competences that allow them to use computers and any kind of electronic devices that through which they can connect to the digital network and they can access to the information that is of priority for their daily needs.

4.2 Problematic

A diagnosis applied in the librarians of the state of Aguascalientes allowed to identify the level of digital competences that they possess. Most librarians have a basic level of digital skills. In order to be able to successfully implement the informal digital literacy model through public libraries, first, it is necessary that librarians can achieve higher levels of digital skills so that they will later be responsible for bringing digital literacy services into the population of Aguascalientes.

4.3 Digital Literacy Informal Environment

To strengthen basic and intermediate digital skills in the learning community of librarians in the Aguascalientes State, an informal learning environment based-on digital literacy services was designed and implemented.

Learning Community and Digital Skills Profile
The case study was carried out in a learning community composed of 47 librarians in the Aguascalientes State, Mexico.

In order to know the profile of librarians that working in the library system, a diagnostic tool was designed and divided into five blocks. In each block, the experience gained, the competences assimilated, the search skills, as well as their didactic-pedagogical skills, and their training needs were investigated.

From the obtained results, it was possible to identify two important aspects:

(1) The current level of digital skills that the librarians possess corresponds to a basic level, which allowed to establish an initial parameter and thus to be able to establish the digital literacy environment for that learning community.
(2) A librarian profile that associates the digital skills and the tasks that it performs in a public library (Fig. 5).

Service Producers
The problem of the digital divide extends to an entire society, and even can affect organizations of all sizes, including governments. The digital divide is a multivariate challenge, so an interdisciplinary and interinstitutional group is needed that can provide an extended perspective to generate integral strategies to reduce it. Table 2 describes the service producers who through their collaboration it was possible to design the digital literacy environment as an integrated intervention solution that covered mainly the points of installed infrastructure, connectivity, digital literacy, certification and learning services.

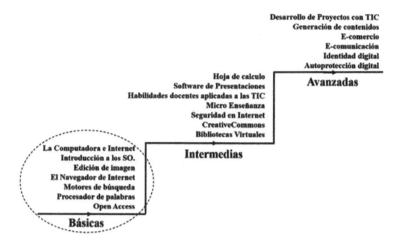

Fig. 5. Profile of librarian associated to the classification of digital skills.

Table 2. Description of service producers

Producer	Kind	Actors
UAA (Autonomous University of Aguascalientes)	Higher education institutions	• Researchers • Students • Librarians experts staff
ICA (Cultural Institute of Aguascalientes)	Government	• Staff • Coordinator
IDSCEA (Institute for the Development of the knowledge society of the Aguascalientes State)	Government/company	• Authorities

Design and Implementation

The design of the digital literacy environment for the case of the learning community of Aguascalientes librarians can be observed in Fig. 6. For digital literacy, two courses were defined that covered the digital skills in basic and intermediate level. Each course was structured by a series of modules, where each module corresponds to a digital competence. This way of structuring the courses by modules facilitated the decomposition of the digital competence, in sub-skills associated to a series of topics. With the decomposition of sub-skills it was possible to define more specific and precise learning paths that were the guides for the development of the user interfaces of the learning services.

After defining the logical model of the informal learning environment, the activities corresponding to the curricular design were performed, as described in Fig. 7. The classification of the digital skills was defined by the experts staff of the UAA library and the Coordinator of the ICA. The ICA staff was in charge of designing the study

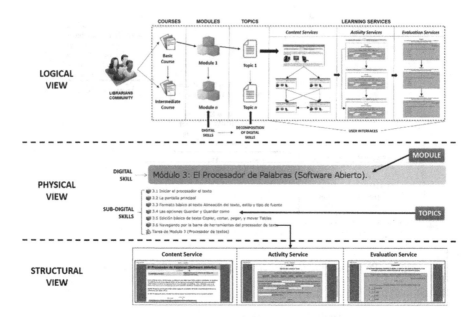

Fig. 6. Design of digital literacy environment for librarians of Aguascalientes State based-on learning services.

programs for the basic and intermediate course, according to the classification of digital skills. The ICA coordinator and the UAA Library expert staff validated the final study programs. After defining the study programs, the UAA library experts staff did the process of decomposing the digital skills and then, they designed the learning paths for each sub-skill. At this stage a validation of learning paths was also made. ICA staff along with some students of the UAA were responsible for the development of learning services. Content services were developed using HTML templates, while activity and evaluation services were developed using authoring tools.

The learning services were deployed on a Moodle platform managed by UAA researchers. The composition of the learning services was done manually, because the repository of learning services was not yet available. The implementation of the courses and the follow-up of the learning activities were managed and evaluated by ICA staff and the UAA library experts staff. The implementation of the informal digital literacy environment lasted 12 weeks. Before the implementation, a diagnosis of the available infrastructure of the 66 public libraries was made. It was found that xx public libraries did not have an Internet connection, in addition to having obsolete PCs. For this reason, through the administrative managements of the IDSCEA it was possible to obtain economic resources to equip some of the libraries with wireless internet service, as well as the renovation of computer equipment.

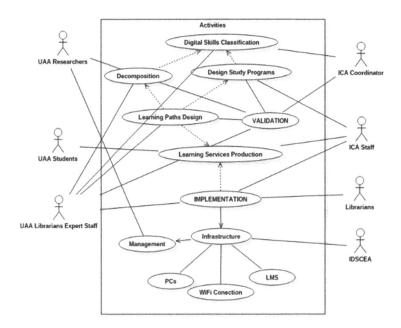

Fig. 7. Use case diagram to describe collaborative activities

Description of Learning Path interacting with Learning Services

Learning paths were specified using flowchart notation. From the specification of the learning paths, the service producers began to development of all digital literacy services to cover each learning path. It should be noted that the repository of services that mechanize the composition of learning services is not yet available (the repository is under construction). For this reason, the services were composed manually and implemented in a Moodle platform.

Next, the implementation of the learning path for the basic competence "Word Processor" is described (Fig. 8). First, the digital skill was decomposed into five word processor skills. After the decomposition of skill, the learning path was composed of five learning activities. Then, each learning activity was associated with a learning service. The resulting learning path is a logical representation that served as a guide for instructional design -in e-learning modalities- for the implementation of digital literacy services within the Moodle platform.

As can be seen at Fig. 8, the learning services have levels of granularity and composition. Granularity is determined based on the range of functions that services need to develop a digital skill, or how services need to be organized into compositions. The service composition refers to the situation in which an individual's service request is not satisfied by a single pre-existing service but can be satisfied by the appropriate combination of some pre-existing services available.

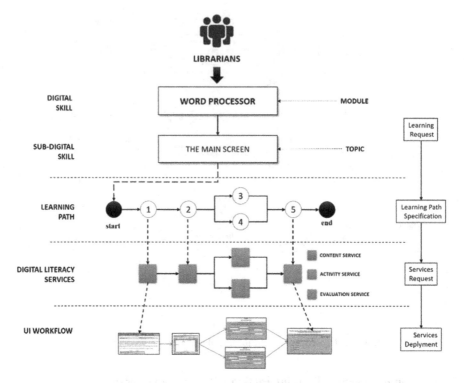

Fig. 8. Architectural view of the interaction between learning and services.

4.4 Results

The implementation of the learning environment was oriented to the training of basic and intermediate levels of digital literacy for the learning community. The 47 librarians acquired knowledge not only in relation to digital skills, but in different areas of the domain of their profession that are related to improving the services offered by public libraries, as follow:

- The librarian understands the cycle of information that includes its generation, treatment, organization and dissemination.
- Ability to manifest and solve an informational need and acquire the skills to transmit it to an automated data system.
- Define strategies for seeking information.
- Define information retrieval strategies in the context of the information being developed.
- Ability to acquire the knowledge that allow the librarian to analyze and evaluate the retrieved information.
- Integrate the information obtained and incorporate it into the knowledge already acquired.

- Develop the capacity to understand the information received and to express it in logical way.
- Knowledge to respect the authorship of the works used by other people and apply the various ways of citing the sources consulted.
- Pedagogical skills that allow you to interact with the community.
- Skills and abilities for the use of computer resources.
- Develop knowledge needed to implement learning and knowledge technologies (LKT).

However, transforming the community of librarians in the state of Aguascalientes into prosumers has been the most important result of the implementation of the informal digital literacy environment. Thus, Aguascalientes librarians, in addition to consuming learning services, have the capacity to create learning services in a creative, critical and responsible way, and adapt them to the specific needs of the end users of public libraries in the state of Aguascalientes.

5 Conclusions

This paper proposes a way of designing learning environments oriented to digital literacy based on learning services. The main objective of the development of learning environments of this type is to be able to bring ad-hoc processes of digital literacy to a diversity of learning communities in a dynamic way so that they can achieve their inclusion in the knowledge society.

In a society, each individual, according to his or her economic, political, geographical and cultural situation, perceives the use of ICT in different ways. Therefore, starting from this premise, transforming a society into a knowledge-based society can be a complex task. On the other hand, the learning community approach allows working with more homogenous groups, and so, it is easier to identify digital literacy needs and establish the digital competences that can be as useful as possible to the context of the learning community.

Currently, there is a wide variety of learning communities (eg, older adults and housewives) who are excluded from formal learning systems, and this situation does not allow them to receive digital literacy. It is therefore necessary to design new informal learning environments where all learning communities can be included in digital literacy processes, and these communities can get into the knowledge society, and thus, improve their quality of life.

On the other hand, the services approach was a key element in getting librarians to acquire digital skills in a gradual and systematic way. The ability to granularity and composition of services helped to create a dynamic and flexible learning environment that adapted to the different learning styles presented by librarians.

References

Álvarez Terrazas, J.A., Álvarez Terrazas, M.M., Gallegos Cereceres, V., Polanco Rodríguez, I.: La importancia de los Repositorios Institucionales para la Educación y la Investigación. Synthesis, vol. 57 (2011). Recuperado a partir de http://www.uach.mx/extension_y_difusion/synthesis/2011/08/18/la_importancia_de_los_repositorios_institucionales_para_la_educacion_y_la_investigacion.pdf

Ann, P.B., Bertram, C.B., Cameron Jones, M.: Community inquity and informatics: collaborative learning through ICT, Chap. 1. In: Carroll, J.M. (ed.) Learning in Communities. Springer, London (2009)

Area Moreira, M.: Igualdad de oportunidades y nuevas tecnologías. Un modelo educativo para la alfabetización tecnológica. Educar **29**, 55–65 (2002)

Block, W.: The "Digital Divide" is not a problem in need of rectifying. J. Bus. Ethics **53**, 393–406 (2004)

Luo, J., Dong, F., Cao, J., Song, A., Liu, B.: A multicontext-aware resource recommendation mechanism for service-oriented ubiquitous learning environment, vol 2, pp. 792–797. IEEE (2008). https://doi.org/10.1109/ICPCA.2008.4783717

Kyriakidou, V., Michalakelis, C., Sphicopoulos, T.: Digital divide gap convergence in Europe. Technol. Soc. **33**, 265–270 (2011). Elsevier

Marciales Vivas, G.P.: Competencia informacional y brecha digital: Preguntas y problemas emergentes derivados de investigación. Educación y competencias informacionales **36**, 127–143 (2012)

Muñoz Arteaga, J., Guzmán Mendoza, J.E., Álvarez Rodríguez, F.J.: Modelo de alfabetización digital para disminuir la brecha digital por estratos sociales. En Disminución de la brecha digital, Primera, pp. 13–27. Pearson, México (2015)

Pinto, M., Sales, D.: Alfabetización informacional para una sociedad intercultural: Algunas iniciativas desde las bibliotecas públicas. Anales de Documentación **10**, 317–333 (2007)

Prensa: Aguascalientes será la 1era. entidad conectada por red digital en toda Latinoamérica. Organización Editorial Mexicana (2012). Recuperado a partir de http://www.oem.com.mx/laprensa/estaticas/quienessomos.aspx

Revuelta-Domínguez, F.I.: Digital competence: learning develop with virtual worlds in "Escuela 2.0". Edutec-e. Revista Electrónica de Tecnología Educativa, vol. 37 (2011)

Sánchez Arias, V.G.: Integración de la formación informal a la formal: Una propuesta conceptual para una plataforma basada en espacios educativos a partir de una reflexión y una experiencia. Tecnologias y Aprendizaje. Avances en Iberoamerica **1**, 113–120 (2013)

Sloep, P., Berlanga, A.: Redes de aprendizaje, aprender en red. Comunicar **19**(37), 55–64 (2011)

Texier, J., De Giusti, M., Oviedo, N., Villarreal, G.L., Lira, A.: El Uso de Repositorios y su Importancia para la Educación en Ingeniería. E-prints in library & information science (s/f). Recuperado a partir de http://eprints.rclis.org/17862/1/Texier2012.pdf

Villa Orrego, N.H., Moncada Velásquez, Y.M.: Efectos de la Implementación de un programa gubernamental orientado a la Alfabetización Digital en una Comunidad Rural. Investigación y Desarrollo **19**(1), 26–41 (2011)

Yang, F., Li, F.W.B., Lau, R.W.H.: A fine-grained outcome-based learning path model. IEEE Trans. Syst. Man Cybern. Syst. **44**(2) (2014)

Building up a Verified Page on Facebook Using Information Transparency Guidelines

Alexandre Pinheiro[1(✉)], Claudia Cappelli[1], and Cristiano Maciel[2]

[1] Universidade Federal do Estado do Rio de Janeiro - UNIRIO,
Rio de Janeiro, Brazil
{alexandre.pinheiro,claudia.cappelli}@uniriotec.br
[2] Universidade Federal de Mato Grosso - UFMT, Cuiabá, Mato Grosso, Brazil
cmaciel@ufmt.br

Abstract. Online credibility is a quality pursued by users, business and brands on Internet. Having a verified page on Facebook means improvement of the social web presence, reliability and reinforcement of security against impersonations of identity, unwanted fake pages and spams. Since the Facebook's page verification request has become more complex and the requirements to receive a verified page badge are uncertain, this paper describes the use of foundations of transparency on information systems to fulfill the data on the forms of the application for verification to improve the success in receiving the verified page status.

Keywords: Transparency · Facebook · Social networks · Verifiability · Pages

1 Introduction

The Online Social Networks (OSNs) expect transparency and integrity from users about their names, informations and the interweaving of personal, professional and social life. Although the OSNs looks forward for characteristics of data previously stated, the process of building an identity as a mechanism of individualization is under a subjective approach in this kind of system. This subjectivity is associated with the identity appropriation of a person, company or institution and it happens when people behind fake accounts take advantage of information verification weaknesses in systems with a huge amount of active users such as OSNs.

Among the actions of fake accounts users operators are: the audience manipulation, creation of biased information about an individual or organization, and duplication of identity for fraudulent intention. As an example of the number of people exploiting this information verification gap, we can cite the social network Facebook has approximately 83 million of fake profiles (disregarding users involved with tests and those who have more than one account for content segmentation purposes) [1]. The frenzied speed of information and misinformation spreaded in OSNs and it's tendency to generate mass behavior increase the focus on researches about users and pages information disclosure and the content that they publish. Under transparency foundations, the characteristic of Verifiability becomes essential for systems that are intended to be a reliable source of information for their users. Trying to minimize problems caused by

© Springer International Publishing AG 2017
G. Meiselwitz (Ed.): SCSM 2017, Part II, LNCS 10283, pp. 125–137, 2017.
DOI: 10.1007/978-3-319-58562-8_10

fake accounts and consequently avoid the spread of misinformation by operators of those accounts, the developers of the most prominent social networks such as Facebook, implemented the verified pages and the verified user profiles.

Through a methodology based on design science research, this paper presents the use of characteristics included in a catalog of information auditability in social networks [2] in guidance to fulfill the necessary data to create a page on Facebook with more chances to receive the status of verified page. Strengthen the knowledge base about the process thats allow users, companies or institutions to have verified pages is important to make possible solutions in a scenario where obtaining a verified page is a way to be recognized in OSNs avoiding the creation of fake pages and identity theft.

2   Online Identities

In the past, people behind anonymous profiles on Internet used to spread unreliable content through forums, chats and other online communication tools. The online anonymity covered up malicious practices, but today with the predominance of OSNs, any published content on these systems is associated with a well-defined identity of a page or user profile [3]. Even with the premise of the personification of the offline identity (use of the real name of a person, company or institution) this aspect is not enough to determine the credibility of the content published by users or pages in the social networks. People with bad intentions have noticed the inability of some users to distinguish between real and fake profiles, especially pages of public figures and companies. In this scenario it's possible to manipulate users through attractive content share from a fake profile or page [4]. An example of this type of action are scams from fake Apple's pages on Facebook publishing advertisements of free iphones and ipads [5], these publications were clickbaits and directed the user to malicious external websites.

The option of page creation was available from the early years of Facebook and the purpose of pages is to create presence of business, organizations, public figures and brands on that social network [6], but in May 2013 the company launched verified pages to help people find the authentic accounts of public figures, celebrities, organizations, governments and highly sought users in areas like journalism, sports, music and others [7]. Twitter [8] and Google+ [9] had already such a practice by identifying the authenticity of well-know user accounts and organizations. From this perspective, when the operators of verified page publish information or interact in OSNs they will be heavily observed, leading the spreaded content for a central position of surveillance from other users.

2.1   Research About Fake Pages and Profiles in OSNs

Close to reach the mark of 2 billion active users monthly [10], problems with fake pages or profiles are recurring on Facebook. The researchers watchful about this scenario studies the increase of false accounts and the use of these accounts for scams, frauds and social engineering on social networks.

Mawere and Mpofu [11] analyze attempts of scams made by people with malicious behavior that use fake pages to deceive users. The main method applied in these scams is to gain the trust of users who access a particular page, extracting as much information about these users. The users believe they are accessing official pages because the impostors copies real pages in all aspects such as images, published multimedia and general information. The fake pages related to business and organizations are also used for defraud users, collecting their information through scams and using it to spread spam and theft of financial data. Public figures, organizations and companies can protect their identities by requesting the verification of their accounts in OSNs. In the research cited above solutions are discussed such as report of fake pages through the Facebook Help Center.

According to De Cristofaro et al. [12] fake pages are built on Facebook primarily to attract attention and users 'likes'. After earning the expected audience, these pages can be used to influence more users and make money from advertising and promotions using their false reputation. The method of attracting user audience through attractive offers is known in social engineering as *honeypot*. In addition to promoting content that attracts users these fake pages increase their numbers of followers using underground Internet services like 'user farms'. Behind the user farms are companies that offer services of creation of fake user accounts to endorse pages, creating a false audience. Users usually trust in pages with a huge amount of followers and likes, but in the case of pages used as honeypots this number was manipulated through the services of user farms. As a suggestion to solve the problem the researchers demonstrate actions to perform the elimination of fake pages by analyzing the user profiles that support them. The fake users have a behavior of system usage that allows to differentiate them from the legitimate users and when these fake users are removed from Facebook the audience that they give for fake pages is also suppressed.

The research of Fire et al. [13] discuss the use of data from pages and profiles by Facebook Applications. Due to the inexperience of users with privacy settings setup, their sensitive information is accessed by applications and can be used to create fakes on Facebook or external websites. With access to sensitive information malicious users can create fake pages with real data, assuming the identity of people or companies to deceive others. The presence and reputation of a user or company on Facebook can be used to apply scams outside the context of the OSNs, since several websites accept logins through accounts of that social network. The work of Fire et al. describes the use of softwares of *Social Privacy Protection* (SPP) as a solution to keep safe important user data from being used for fraudulent purposes.

3   Information Transparency on Social Networks

The popularity of OSNs has boosted the distribution of information globally and for an individual or brand to stand out in this digital ecosystem it is necessary to be transparent and be prepared to explain their conduct [14]. Due the overwhelming amount of content published on Facebook, if a hoax is created and spreaded by a fake account impersonating people or companies, the owners of these real identities will have not the control without a strong presence in this social network. The lack of attention of some individuals when dealing with uncertain sources of the information is worrying, especially in the moment that the malicious users of social networks started to create fake pages of celebrities and companies to attract and scam people.

To perform a transparent communication for users and strengthen the presence of a public figure, brand or institution, the social network should have auditability, in other words, the capability to examine the information carefully and accuracy with the intent of verification [15]. The OSNs with the ability to audit information and provide verification mechanisms allow the analysis of publications that can unmask fake pages and also protect the real pages already marked as verified. The auditability of information in social networks can be promoted by the use of guidelines that follows a catalog with the proposal of designing transparency of information in this kind of system [2]. This catalog of information auditability in social networks is a conceptual model generated from the elicitation of software's non-functional requirements related to aspects of information transparency [16].

The catalog was made by setting objectives that the software should meet (softgoal) until the operationalization and implementation of these objectives [17]. The representation of the objectives cited above is supported by Softgoal Interdependency Graphs (SIG) and the SIG of catalog of information transparency in social networks is shown in Fig. 1. Among the characteristics present in the catalog of auditability of information in social networks we have the following: Accountability, Adaptability, Clarity, Completeness, Composability, Correctness, Extensibility, Traceability, Uniformity, Validity and Verifiability. These characteristics have operationalizations that, when used, will contribute to system auditability either in the implementation of a feature by a developer or in a user action in a particular section in the OSNs. We detailed below only the characteristics contextualized to this article.

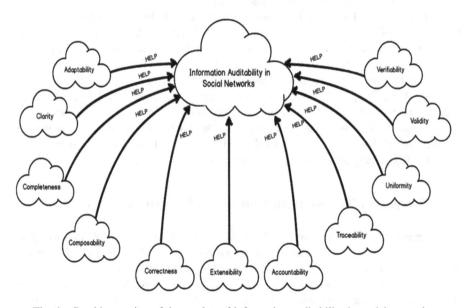

Fig. 1. Graphic notation of the catalog of information auditability in social networks.

The Facebook page verification mechanism is an example of Verifiability implementation because it helps the user to evaluate information and make decisions about content generated by a particular page. Users behavior is different when the information they access comes from a verified page. The users can identify verified pages because a visual element is displayed on the page and helping to understanding that it is authentic and passed through a previous check of the social network. This visual element that alerts users about the authenticity of a page should be present in the system as a whole. For example, if some user searches for a page on the social network the verified page one will be highlighted among the others. Due to these definitions the characteristic of verifiability is the one that best represents the objective of this work.

When a page is created some information is requested about the identity that this page will represent on the social network. For example, to built a business page on Facebook details such as business phones and opening hours can be informed. The availability of these data agrees with characteristic of Composability, which uses information from different sources to reinforce the content supply. A business page presents reliability when it shows a contact phone, so users can call and check the legitimacy of a business. Celebrities (public figures) can make available on their Facebook page a link to a website with information complementary to those one on social network or a bundle of multimedia items like videos and photos. Any initiative that stand up the use of trustful external information that helps to validate the information already present in OSNs will count as use of composability characteristic.

Along with the composability also applies to this research the characteristic of Traceability. In the evaluation process made by OSNs, the data entered or publish by the owner of candidate page for verification will be tracked. The page's owner needs to prove that the page represents a public figure or brand it claims to be, so the data is tracked and analyzed. The tracking to give a page the verified status can include in the process requests for real evidence of page ownership like presentation of ID card or other official documents to evaluation teams of the social networks.

3.1   The Power of a Verified Icon

To increase security and transparency, several systems uses visual aids to alert or inform their users about their actions or status. An example is the lock icon displayed by browsers when a page that handles security certificates is accessed. When the lock icon is displayed, users have greater perception of security in their online access [18]. Following the initiative to increase their safety, the OSNS adopted a verification icon as a way to identify verified pages and accounts. On Facebook, verified pages have an icon with a check mark (blue badge) along their names and this icon also appear in related search results, timelines and other sections in the system. For pages of business or organizations categories a gray badge is displayed. Twitter, Instagram, Google+, Sina Weiboand other social networks uses an icon to indicate the verified account, following a pattern using the mark sign or a letter V for verified. This visual feature reinforces for users the special condition of those accounts (Table 1).

The struggle of OSNs administrators is to avoid scams and impersonations made by people using fake pages or profiles and these were some of the reasons that led to the

Table 1. List of icons displayed on verified accounts or pages in some OSNs

Icon	Online Social Network
✔	Facebook (For public figures, media companies and brands)
✔	Facebook (For business and organizations)
✔	Twitter
✔	Instagram
✔	Google+
V	Sina Weibo (For people)
V	Sina Weibo (For business)

creation of accounts verification mechanisms [19]. Even pages created by public figures fans can compromise the reputation of the original identities. An opinion issued by a public figure can influence people in different contexts [20] and held a verified status protects its owner against hoaxes or unwanted impersonations. Being verified also represents a way to reclaim lost impressions, disqualifying suspicious pages or profiles. For companies and brands the verified status the verification status represents to be highlighted in their segments, improve their credibility and social search presence in addition to increasing protection against spam involving their identities. Some OSNs give privileges to verified account holders such as: earlier access to new features, more elaborate statistical data and unique applications. These benefits emphasize the importance of verified accounts and increase the credibility of the information spreaded by them.

4 Projecting a Page with Transparent Information

To unfold the possibilities and features of a popular social network like the Facebook, it is necessary to detail the steps taken during development of the work, opening the research topic for discussions and verification. To reach the definition above, we use the methodology of *Design Science Research* (DSR) in this article considering the importance of delivering content that should be assimilated by both: academia and society [21]. The DSR approach laying at the need of general people understand a research topic is also related to the systems transparency foundations and the concernment of user understanding in issues about the features that an information system offers, the purpose of these features, how they work and how to use them [22].

To begin creating a page with the intention of submitting it to the verifications procedures and avoid the fake ones, some observations about the scenario of operation of this mechanism in other OSNs besides Facebook is important. The openness of application for users with less notoriety to the process of verifiability of their accounts in social networks made the rules less strict for an account be verified. Although the rules to be followed from users to receive verified status on their accounts are not transparent, due to the fewer requirements for application, the number of verified accounts began to increase in some OSNs. The Facebook does not provide public data on the number of verified users but the trend of more users getting verified account status can be seen on Twitter in the account that groups only verified users [23]. At this point the goal of this article is analyzed, considering the possibility that a user with less notoriety but who has some influence in a particular area (public figure) can use transparency guidelines for social networks to increase their chances of having it's page approved in the application for verification on Facebook. With the "verified status" and establishment of the presence in the social network consequently the protection against fake pages and unallowed impersonations is reinforced.

4.1   Fill up the Forms to Build a Traceable Page

To create the page with information filled following the transparency guidelines for social networks, the first step was access the Facebook[1] and at the bottom of the website, to click on the link "Create a Page". After click the link, we went introduced to different categories of pages that can be created as shown in the Fig. 2. In this work we used as an example a page from the category *Public Figure*. The idea is to explain characteristics and operationalizations from a guideline of transparency in social networks used in the submission for verification of a page created to establish the social presence of a teacher in his area of research. Despite the existence of a subcategory called teacher we did not select it, since only profiles of the category public figure can be verified.

With the category filled in and a given name to set the identity (in this case the teacher name's) we clicked the button "Get Started" that bringed us to the page setup. At the setup the actions were the definition of the page identification image and the page background image. The display of these images is mandatory and the visual appeal is very important for the page exposure.

Afterwards, to ensure the traceability of the page, the system offered the creation of a unique friendly link for direct access to the page created. The URL is created from the username given to the page (not the page name) and can be used for quotes within Facebook when preceded by the @ symbol. Another relevant information that must be provided is the URL of a website outside the social network containing important data, complementing and ensuring the reliability of the information on the page. The availability of a contact email is also relevant in this context.

The exposure and the number of page followers can help in the verification process and the concept of a public figure concerns to be popular and to have followers in the social network. The Facebook provides a page promotion tool that enhances the display (like advertisements) of the page across the system and also on Instagram, but the tool is a paid feature. People and brands interested in reach a larger audience, as quickly as possible, use the promotion tool to boost the exposure of their pages. The page

---

[1] https://www.facebook.com.

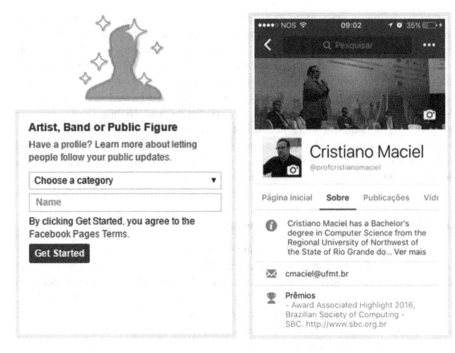

Fig. 2. Selection of the page category and example of the page displayed on a mobile device.

promotion option ends up reinforcing the credibility and traceability, since the financial data of people that use the tool will be informed to the social network.

4.2   Using the Composability Characteristic in the Biography

The data informed about a person's identity can be analyzed in their source, some of these sources are external to the Facebook and the need to take advantage of information from external sources to reinforce the credibility of the content is related to the composability characteristic in the transparency guidelines for social networks. Any knowledge that adds value to information about a person can help in a assessment for verified status even this data is stored or supplied by other systems [2].

Following the composability feature explained above, we filled some fields on the form option "About" located at the page setup as shown in Fig. 3. Formerly, in the Story field, a long biographical description with relevant information about the candidate page for verification was provided. This information describes the qualities, lifestyle and works that promote the identity of a page as a public figure category. Following the category of a public figure used at our example page, relevant biographical data are: important publications, general projects in progress, promotions and recognition of the community. The field story should contain links to news, events and publications highlighting the person's notoriety as a public figure to reinforce the success in the application for page verification.

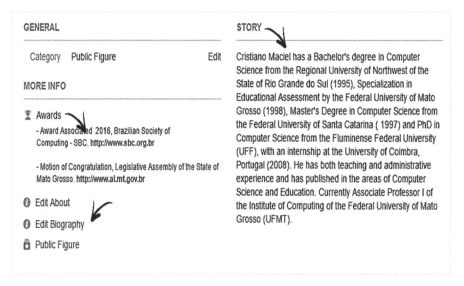

Fig. 3. Example of information filled in the form option "About" at page setup menu.

Fig. 4. Exploring the multimedia capability of the page with videos and notes.

Unlike the story field, in the Biography field the description should be shorter without including the links. The data in this field is usually displayed in smaller panels to follow some visual design patterns in the social network. The About field, that has a 255 characters limit, should receive objective description as a brief summary of the page, it is not biographical and should not have links.

There is an exclusive field to inform the awards received by the individual represented on the page. Usually award winning ceremonies have records that can be referenced in this field, links with news and multimedia of these awards are important to be informed.

Multimedia content is not only important on the page setup, but also in the updates of the page and in the menu options videos or notes. As shown in the Fig. 4, we take advantage of all the tools to include information that proves the notoriety of the identity portrayed on the page such as videos imported from Youtube and notes from blogs or websites.

4.3 Public Figure Page Verification

Until the launch of the Facebook Mentions mobile application in 2014 July [24], Facebook maintained a form page where users could submit their pages for verification. The application form has been discontinued and only submissions for verification of business and organizations pages are directly available from Facebook nowadays. Since then, Facebook Mentions has become the application where the page verification request can be made besides having exclusive. The Facebook claims that the Mentions application is a better way to for verified pages owners to interact with their followers [25]. The application allows live broadcasting, simultaneous sharing of updates to various social networks, improvements in communication with followers, summary of trending stories and other features.

To submit our example page for verification we downloaded the Facebook Mentions on a mobile device and after starting the application we clicked on the "Get started" button. After the start, we entered our page name at login but the application only allows the login of pages already verified, so we used the option "My page or verified profile isn't here…". When choosed, the option for unverified pages redirects to a form containing a list of pages candidates for verification that were created by the user logged in as show in Fig. 5.

We selected the page used as an example for verification and after submitting the form the system directed us to a Facebook support page with the notice that the request will be evaluated by the responsible team of the social network. At this point the requester need to wait the response to get the page verified.

The step of page evaluation to earn the verified status is not transparent, just as the process for requesting the verification that became more complicated after the closure of the form allowing this action to be made directly by Facebook without relying on the Mentions application. Since this process is not clearly explained in the user support pages of Facebook, the guidelines in this article can help those who wish to verify their pages and have characteristics that distinguish their identity as a public figure.

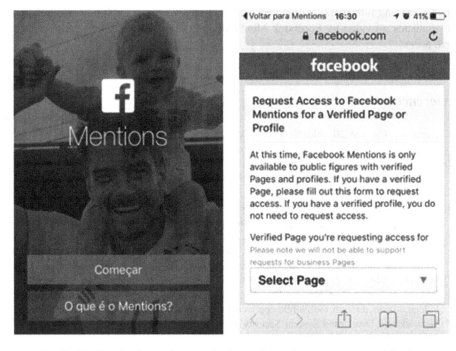

Fig. 5. The Facebook mentions application and form to request page verification.

5   Discussions and Future Works

The proliferation of fake pages and attempts of impersonation in social networks became a problem since many users do not realize that these pages do not produce reliable content and are source of misinformation. Some OSNs like Facebook have created mechanisms that help legitimize pages of businesses and public figures. This mechanism highlights the pages that have passed through the analysis of a team of social network experts to check the veracity of the information about the ownership. After it is analyzed successfully a visual element identifies the verified pages.

Seeing the page verification as a guarantee of greater protection against fake pages, public figures and brands have started to request the verified status to the social networks administration teams also as a way of reinforce their presence. The verification application process is not transparent and Facebook changed making this request more difficult by public figures interested in verify their pages.

After exposed the problem, we showed a way to create a Facebook page on guidance of characteristics of audibility of information in social networks so that people recognized as public figures can have their chances improved. The explanation was made using DSR methodology. As opportunities to future works about the subject we can highlight the submission to verification of Facebook pages following the guidance of this article to analyze success in achieving verified page status. Another research extension of this article addresses issues related to the power of verified profile when spreading information compared with fake pages and the exploration of features and statistics provided by Facebook Mentions that only those who own verified page have access.

References

1. Zephoria: The top 20 valuable Facebook statistics. Zephoria Digital Marketing (2016). https://zephoria.com/top-15-valuable-facebook-statistics/. Accessed 28 Oct 2016
2. Pinheiro, A.H.: Projetando Auditabilidade de Informações em Softwares de Redes Sociais. Master's thesis, Universidade Federal do Estado do Rio de Janeiro (UNIRIO), Rio de Janeiro, Brazil (2015)
3. Correa, D., Silva, L.A., Mondal, M., Benevenuto, F., Gummad, K.P.: The many shades of anonymity: characterizing anonymous social media content. In: ICWSM, pp. 71–80 (2015)
4. Köse, D.B., Veijalainen, J., Semenov, A.: Identity use and misuse of public persona on Twitter. In: Majchrzak, T.A., Traverso, P., Monfort, V, Krempels, K.-H. (eds.) Proceedings of the 12th International Conference on Web Information Systems and Technologies, WEBIST 2016, vol. 1, pp. 164–175 (2016)
5. Rastogi, V., Shao, R., Chen, Y., Pan, X., Zou, S., Riley, R.: Are these ads safe: detecting hidden attacks through the mobile app-web interfaces. In: Proceedings of the 23rd Annual Network and Distributed System Security Symposium (NDSS 2016). The Internet Society (2016)
6. Facebook: About pages. Facebook help center – using Facebook (2016). https://www.facebook.com/help/282489752085908/?helpref=hc_fnav. Accessed 13 Dec 2016
7. Facebook: Verified pages and profile – Facebook news room (2013). http://newsroom.fb.com/news/2013/05/verifiedpages-and-profiles/. Accessed 28 Oct 2016
8. Siegler, M.G.: Twitter starts verifying accounts without actually verifying them. Techcrunch (2009). https://techcrunch.com/2009/06/11/twitter-starts-verifying-accounts-without-verifying-them/. Accessed 21 Dec 2016
9. Yu, W.: Google+ update: verification badges for profiles – Google+ (2011). https://plus.google.com/+Wen-AiYu/posts/ZiXUSJQ3fGA. Accessed 17 Jan 2017
10. Fiegerman, S.: Facebook is closing in on 2 billion users. CNN technology (2017). http://money.cnn.com/2017/02/01/technology/facebook-earnings. Accessed 4 Feb 2017
11. Mawere, C., Mpofu, T.P.: Profile impostoring: a use case on the rising social engineering attack on Facebook users. Int. J. Sci. Res. 3(6) (2014)
12. De Cristofaro, E., Friedman, A., Jourjon, G., Kaafar, M.A., Shafiq, M.Z.: Paying for likes?: understanding facebook like fraud using honeypots. In: Proceedings of the 2014 Conference on Internet Measurement Conference, pp. 129–136. ACM (2014)
13. Fire, M., Kagan, D., Elyashar, A., Elovici, Y.: Friend or foe? Fake profile identification in online social networks. Soc. Netw. Anal. Min. 4(1), 1–23 (2014)
14. Kim, B., Hong, S., Cameron, G.T.: What corporations say matters more than what they say they do? A test of a truth claim and transparency in press releases on corporate websites and Facebook pages. J. Mass Commun. Q. 91(4), 811–829 (2014)
15. Leite, J.C., Cappelli, C.: Software transparency. Bus. Inf. Syst. Eng. 2(3), 127–139 (2010)
16. Cappelli, C.: Uma abordagem para transparência em processos organizacionais utilizando aspectos. Ph.D. thesis, Pontifícia Universidade Católica do Rio de Janeiro (PUC-Rio) (2009)

17. Cruz, S.M.S., Castro Leal, A.L.: Enhancing provenance representation with knowledge based on NFR conceptual modeling: a softgoal catalog approach. In: Ludäscher, B., Plale, B. (eds.) IPAW 2014. LNCS, vol. 8628, pp. 235–238. Springer, Cham (2015). doi:10.1007/978-3-319-16462-5_23

18. Dong, Z., Kapadia, A., Blythe, J., Camp, L.J.: Beyond the lock icon: real-time detection of phishing websites using public key certificates. In: 2015 APWG Symposium Electronic Crime Research (eCrime), pp. 1–12. IEEE (2015)

19. Digital Media Law Project: La Russa vs. Twitter, Inc., DMLP (2009). http://www.dmlp.org/threats/la-russa-v-twitter-inc. Accessed 26 Dec 2016

20. Cacciatore, M.A., Yeo, S.K., Scheufele, D.A., Xenos, M.A., Choi, D.H., Brossard, D., Corley, E.A.: Misperceptions in polarized politics: the role of knowledge, religiosity, and media. PS Polit. Sci. Polit. **47**(03), 654–661 (2014)

21. Dresch, A., Lacerda, D.P., Júnior, J.: Design science research: método de pesquisa para avanço da ciência e tecnologia. Bookman Editora (2015)

22. Matei, S.A., Russell, M.G., Bertino, E.: Transparency in Social Media: Tools, Methods and Algorithms for Mediating Online Interactions. Springer, Cham (2015)

23. TwitterCounter (2017) Twitter verified status statistics – number of Twitter followers.http://twittercounter.com/verified#public-profile-following Accessed 5 Jan 2017

24. Etherington, D.: Facebook launches 'Mentions' the exclusive FB app for playing the fame game – Techcrunch (2014). https://techcrunch.com/2014/07/17/facebook-launches-mentions-the-exclusive-fb-app-for-playing-the-fame-game/. Accessed 5 Jan 2017

25. Facebook: About Facebook mentions (2017). https://www.facebook.com/about/mentions. Accessed 10 Feb 2017

An MDA Approach to Develop Language-Learning Activities

Gabriel Sebastián[1(✉)], Ricardo Tesoriero[1], Jose A. Gallud[1],
and Habib M. Fardoun[2]

[1] ESII, University of Castilla-La Mancha (UCLM), Albacete, Spain
{gabriel.sebastian, ricardo.tesoriero,
jose.gallud}@uclm.es
[2] King Abdulaziz University (KAU), Jeddah, Saudi Arabia
hfardoun@kau.edu.sa

Abstract. Nowadays, more and more people are interested in learning a second and even a third foreign language due to the globalization phenomenon and the extensive use of Internet. The process of learning a foreign language is defined by methodologies and supported by technology. The development of these kind of applications is complex, so that this article proposes a model-driven approach to develop software to support different language learning processes. The article describes a metamodel that defines the entities and its relationships. This metamodel allows us to support different methods to learn a foreign language.

Keywords: Model-driven development · Languages learning methodologies and app

1 Introduction

The interest in studying a foreign language is increasing in the last few years. The globalization process and the general access to Internet can be pointed out as the main factors that explain this tendency.

The number of students that are enrolled in languages academies and schools is increasing each year. Moreover, the number of bilingual studies is also increasing at all levels: Primary, Secondary school and universities.

At the same time, the number of different methodologies to learn a foreign language is increasing in the same proportion.

Technology has taken part in this process as it does in many other fields. So, there are many applications and tools offered to users that are related to this learning process. The rapid growing of smartphone usage has provoked that mobile apps be, together with the Web, one of the favourite environments to learn a foreign language.

The development of this kind of application is something complex due to the diversity of learning language methodologies, the variety of execution environments (Web, mobile and desktop) and the number of different technologies that can be used. This why the proposal presented in this article, make use of Model Driven Development and Model-Driven Architecture approaches, as a mean to develop complex solutions maximizing the savings in time and cost.

© Springer International Publishing AG 2017
G. Meiselwitz (Ed.): SCSM 2017, Part II, LNCS 10283, pp. 138–147, 2017.
DOI: 10.1007/978-3-319-58562-8_11

This article presents a first result in this direction. It consists in a metamodel that models the main features that are present in most of the learning language methodologies. The solution is illustrated by modelling two similar activities from two language learning methodologies, using almost the same model.

The paper is organized as follows: Sect. 2 describes the research context together with the related work. Section 3 presents the metamodel proposed, including a description of the main blocks with which is composed. Section 4 shows an example that illustrates the concepts. Section 5 includes an analysis of additional modelling capabilities derived from our proposal. Finally, the conclusions and future work are presented in Sect. 6.

2 Research Context

This section contains the research context, which includes two main elements. First, essential concepts and general features extracted from different learning methodologies are presented. Secondly, selected related work in the field of Model Driven Development is presented.

Learning a foreign language is a process that involves different methods, techniques and tools, each one appearing more effective than the others. In this paper, we have focused in those methodologies that offer some kind of technological support (Web site, mobile app or similar).

Among the methodologies object of study are Lexiway [1], Duolingo [2] Lexiway is a newer methodology that emphasizes the pronunciation, both in vocabulary and the sentence composition rather than in grammar. Lexiway offers a variety of tools: a virtual classroom and an iOS app. Duolingo is a method to learn English that takes advantage of the generalization of mobile apps. This method emphasizes the student motivation and it is based on gamification [6].

Although these methodologies offer different viewpoints, it is possible to identify some common elements. The Model Driven Development approach will be responsible to abstract all the elements that are present in the different methodologies. However, before we can perform this abstraction process, we first must study some of the most relevant methodologies to learn a foreign language.

The Model-Driven Architecture approach is proposed by the OMG (Object Management Group) in 2011. In the MDA Guide [5], MDA is defined as a solution to use models in the software development. This solution gives a main role to the models in the systems under development. As the name indicates, it is said model driven since it runs all the phases from inception, design, building, development, maintenance and modification.

In the MDA core, there are a number of important OMG standards: the Unified Modeling Language (UML), the Meta Object Facility (MOF), XML Metadata Interchange (XMI) and the Common Warehouse Metamodel (CWM). These standards define the central MDA infrastructure, which has been successfully used in the modelling and development of modern systems.

In the field of Human-Computer Interaction it can be found an approach that makes use of models to obtain the user interface (Model Based User Interface Development or

MB-UID) [3]. In this way, since this work is focused in the development of interactive systems, MB-UID can provides us some interesting aspects.

The general opinion is that MDD is going to play an important role in the near future of software development, if only more power MDD tools be delivered. Maybe this is the reason there are so few related works that formalize by means a metamodel to support a foreign language learning methodology.

Nevertheless, there are a number of related works that use a MDD or MDA approach in the development of Web applications [8–10]. In [4], MDA is used to develop a music learning application.

A methodology to model e-learning applications can be found in [7], although this methodology is not focused in developing foreign language learning applications. Moreover, our approach presents a set of models at different abstraction levels (architecture), which show different application viewpoints depending on the abstraction level.

3 The Proposed Metamodel

After the study and analysis of the different foreign language learning methodologies, we are going to get, through an abstraction or generalization process, the common elements to all of them. In this section, these common elements and its formalization by means an ECORE metamodel with OCL (Object Constraint Language) constraints, are presented.

First, we are going to describe the common elements of the language learning applications used by the different methodologies.

All the analyzed applications manage concepts (it can be words and sentences). These concepts are organized hierarchically (for example lesson, units and so on). Each concept is associated to a set of resources, for instance, the concept "house" can have associated one or more images, audios, videos.

Secondly, all the language learning applications have exercises. There a great variety of exercises like multiple choice, filling the gaps, sentence composition and so on.

The third pillar in all methodologies is the established order by which the concepts are studied. For instance, in a particular methodology, a student only can begin a determined level if only she/he has passed the previous level. This established order defines the workflow.

In summary, the common elements are:

- Concept and Concepts hierarchy
- Resources
- Exercises
- Workflow

The next step is to model, by an abstraction process, all the common elements considering these general MDA principles:

- Abstraction
- Reuse

As a summary of the abstraction process, we can say that a methodology model (instance of Methodology) defines four different concerns: workflow (Workflow package), content (Content package), media (Media package) and presentation (Activity and Presentation package).

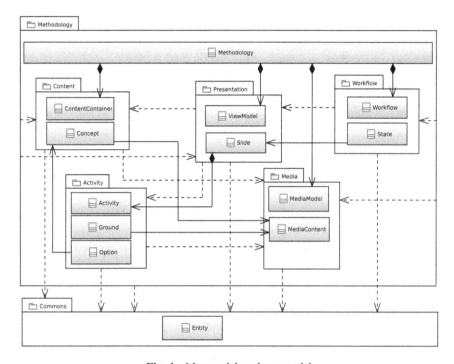

Fig. 1. Metamodel package model

Figure 1 shows different packages representing the common elements. The central package of this model architecture has been called Methodology and it is divided into 5 packages: Workflow, Content, Media, Activity and Presentation. A sixth package called commons contain utilities that will be explained later.

The next paragraphs describe the mapping among the common elements and the packages.

The first common elements are the "concepts" managed by the methodology, which are modeled by the different elements of the package Content (it contains the meta-classes Concept and ContentContainer). The hierarchy is also modeled by these same package (specifically by the metaclass ContentContainer).

The resources are modeled by the elements defined in the Media package.

The exercises are organized into two packages (Presentation and Activity). The Presentation package represents the particular kind of exercise as, for example, multiple choice or filling the gap. The Activity package represents the content of the exercise as, for instance, the different options of the multiple exercise or the statement.

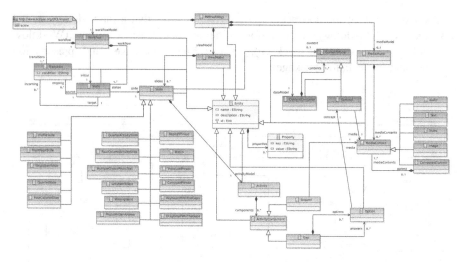

Fig. 2. Metamodel that models language learning methodologies (Color figure online)

The last common element, the workflow is modeled by the elements defined in the *Workflow* package.

A detailed view of the metamodel is shown in Fig. 2, which presents the defined metaclasses.

The *Content* package (see purple metaclasses in Fig. 2) is used to represent the organization of the conceptual content that will presented to the student. This content has a tree structure that allows designers to establish relationships among concepts depending on the strategy defined by the methodology. For example, in a given methodology, a level can be composed by units and, a unit can be composed by lessons. The metaclasses *Content, ContentContainer and Concept* are defined following a composite design pattern.

The *Media* package (see turquoise metaclasses in Fig. 2) is used to represent the resources that will be used in the presentation. It defines four kinds of media: audio, text, video and image (*Audio, Text, Video* and *Image* metaclasses), which can be combined to represent complex media (for instance, text and speech).

The concepts of the *Content* package are associated to elements of the *Media* package.

The *Presentation* package (see green metaclasses in Fig. 2) is used to represent the graphical interface of the different exercises offered to the students in the learning process. This package defines the concept of slide (*Slide* metaclass), which is associated to a particular activity (*Activity* metaclass, from the *Activity* package). This feature allows the reutilization of a slide's view (*Slide* metaclass) in different activities (*Activity* metaclass) and vice versa.

The package *Activity* (see orange metaclasses in Fig. 2) provides the capability to parametrize the functionality of the activities that are carried out in the learning process. Every *Activity* metaclass provides information to the user (*Ground* metaclass), which is used to define an exercise or activity through elements of the *MediaContent* (the text of the statement). Additionally, an Activity metaclass defines information provided by the user through the *Gap* metaclass in order to complete the exercise. A *Gap* metaclass defines set of options and answers using the *Option* metaclass. Option metaclass is associated to a concept (*Concept* metaclass), which is associated to a MediaContent.

Let us to illustrate this with an example based on multiple choice exercise. In this case, the exercise consists in playing a speech and showing different images where one of them corresponds with the speech. This exercise is represented by the *MultipleChoicePhotoText* metaclass, which defines the mechanism (playing the speech and the possibility to select different options). Both the speech (*Ground* metaclass) and the options (*Gap*) is parametrized by an instance of *Activity*.

The Workflow package (see grease metaclasses in Fig. 2) allows us to represent the application presentation's flow (*Workflow* metaclass). In order to represent this information flow, we adopt the classical graph notation, where the nodes represent the states (*State* metaclass) associated to a representation (*Slide* metaclass in the *Presentation* package), and the edges represent the different transitions (*Transition* metaclass) among states or slides.

Finally, the *Methodology* package (see light grease metaclasses in Fig. 2) defines the metaclass *Methodology*, which represents the whole methodology.

All the metaclasses in this metamodel descend from the *Entity* metaclass, which is defined in a package called *Commons* (see yellow metaclasses in Fig. 2). This package provides other metaclasses with the identification (*Entity* metaclass) and extension (*Property* metaclass) capabilities.

Additionally, an editor has been developed to manage (create, edit and verify) the models according to the metamodel. This editor has been developed as an Eclipse plugin, by using the Eclipse Modeling Framework (EMF). This plugin has been defined by using OclInEcore, which is a dialect of the OMG Essential Meta-Object Facility (EMOF). OclInEcore allows us to define OCL constraints that are used to define the model invariants and queries.

4   Case Study

The main goal of this case study is to illustrate the flexibility and adaptability of the proposed metamodel to model different learning language methodologies. Therefore, we will show an example of model that includes an activity based on a multiple-choice exercise. During the activity, the student hears a word and she/he must select one option among four pair image-text.

This case study will show the common elements of two similar activities taken from two different methodologies (Duolingo and Lexiway).

Figure 3 shows how to model the presentation of the activity in the case of Lexiway. In that figure, we can appreciate two parts. First, the exercise (GUI) as is presented to the student and, secondly, the model is shown (particularly, the workflow).

The example is based in Lexiway Junior (a version of the method specially adapted to young people), and it has only two slides: the first one contains only information on the exercise; the second one includes the multiple choices exercise.

Let us review the metamodel concepts explained using this example.

As it has been mentioned in the previous section, a methodology model (instance of Methodology) defines four different concerns: workflow, content, media and presentation (see Figs. 3 and 4).

Fig. 3. Two slides presentation and workflow in Lexiway (Color figure online).

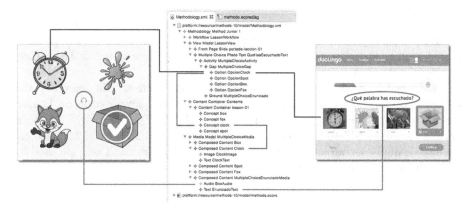

Fig. 4. Presentation in Lexiway and Duolingo of a multiple-choice activity using the same elements.

With the Content package we can represent any conceptual organization. In the case of Duolingo (a method to learn English using Spanish as a original language), the organization is based on 59 units (ContentContainers). Each unit has a variable number of lessons (ContentContainers). Each lesson contains a set of new and related words (Concepts). Once the user has studied these words, she/he has the possibility to reinforce them in later lessons. In the case of the Lexiway Junior, the method is organized in 6 blocks (ContentContainers). Each block is organized in 4 units (ContentContainers), which contains 2 lessons each. A lesson contains 16 words grouped in 4 quarters (ContentContainers).

In this example, we define a lesson that contains four concepts.

From the media model viewpoint (MediaModel metaclass), each of the four concepts has associated a set of multimedia resources (ComposedContent metaclass), which are composed with different image (Image) and text (Text) resources. This model also defines the media elements that are related to the exercise statement: audio (Audio) and text (Text). In this exercise, the statement text is defined as "¿Qué palabra has escuchado?" ("What word have you heard?" in Spanish) and the speech is "Box". This requires the definition of another composed multimedia content resource (ComposedComponent).

The Activity package is used to define the needed information to carry out the exercise. This information is contained in an instance of Activity (Activity MultipleChoiceActivity) that includes, both the statement (Ground MultipleChoiceEnunciado) and the user's answer (Gap MultipleChoiceGap). In this case, the Gap has 4 possible options (Option) and only one established as the right answer.

The Presentation package is used to model the activities views (Slides) of the methodology. The views in this example are the following: an activity with the introduction to the lesson and a multiple choice activity. The modeling of the introduction to the lesson, a presentation view is instantiated (FrontPageSlide portada-lección-01) that defines a null activity (Activity NullActivity), which contains the information of the introduction. To define the view of the multiple choice activity, a multiple choice view is instantiated (MultipleChoicePhotoText QueHasEscuchado-Text), linked to the MultipleChoiceActivity.

The package Workflow is used to define the workflow model, where two states (States) and one transition (Transition) with the precondition established to true, are defined. Each of the states is associated to a view (see the blue lines in Fig. 3). So, the transitions among them define a change of views. Graphically, this transition is showed as a button (always enabled due to the precondition) on the user interface (see green line in Fig. 3).

The Fig. 4 shows the correspondence among the different elements of the model of the case study, the multiple-choice activity from both methodologies Lexiway and Duolingo. Figure 4 illustrates the expressiveness power of this technology, since it shows how the same model is used to represent two similar activities from two different learning methodologies.

5   Analysis of the Proposal

In this section the different modeling alternatives are analyzed. The different options will depend on the concerns that are defined in the learning processing methodology.

Considering the modeling of the learning methodology content (ContentModel), it allows define different kinds of structures. Let us see an example. In the case of Lexiway, a structure is modeled in 5 levels (level, block, unit, lesson and item); and in the case of Duolingo, the structure is modeled in 3 levels (units, lessons and words).

The resources can be organized using a tree structure through the MediaModel definition, allowing the reutilization of resources from different methodologies. The independence between the content and resource models (ContenModel and Media-Model) allows that a resource can be associated to different concepts (Concept) and vice-versa. Additionally, the independence between the resources (MediaModel) and activity (ActivityModel) models allows the reutilization or interchange of resources among different components (ActivityComponent) of an activity (Activity).

The modeling of the exercises is carried out by defining two models: the presentation model (instance of Slide metaclass) and the activity model (instance of Activity metaclass). This separation allows us to reuse different activities taken as invariant the same presentation behavior (see Fig. 4). So, it is possible to define different activities such as the following:

- Filling the gaps (either drag and dropping or by writing)
- Sentence composition
- Sentence translation
- Associate elements from two sets
- Sentence repetition
- Write the lacking word
- Speech to text
- Multiple choices (with different options)

Likewise, it is possible to represent different kinds of exercise. For instance, the introduction of a unit or lesson, different concept layouts distribution, and so on.

In the case of modeling the learning methodology workflow, it is possible to define any workflow by using a conditional graph as, for example, to establish an order for the lessons or to decide what lessons are enabled to be studied. In the case of Lexiway, for instance, the student must pass all the lessons in a unit before she/he can start the next lesson. Inside a lesson, the "presentation" is mandatory before accessing to the "practice", "variations" or "spelling" lessons. Moving to Duolingo, there are lessons or tests that, once the student did pass them, she/he can avoid some lessons.

Finally, it is important to note that by using the Commons package, we can model class instances, with the capability to identify (Entity) and to extend (Property) them.

6 Conclusions and Future Work

In this article, a metamodel that allows us to collect and represent the main features that can be considered common to most of the learning language methodologies, is presented.

This metamodel is the first and fundamental piece in the Model-Driven Architecture, which will allow us to develop learning language applications.

Our MDA proposal consists in defining four models: Content, Media, Workflow, and Presentation. Each one represents a different view that allows us to get the projection of the modeled methodology.

To illustrate the flexibility of the proposed metamodel, an example has been presented. This example is used to compare the modeling a similar activity taken from two different methodologies. Therefore, it has been proved that the resultant models do not vary significantly and they have a high degree of reuse.

All the defined models follow the OMG standards, which guarantee the interoperability among them and other external models that follow the OMG. This interoperability is implemented using reflexive editors based on the Eclipse Modeling Framework, which allow us to create Eclipse plugins.

Future work includes to develop a GMF based tool to get and verify models obtained with our metamodel. After that, the convenient transformations will be developed to generate code from the models.

Finally, a customized tracking system for the users is being developed, which it will allow us to analyze their profiles and experience when using the language learning applications.

References

1. LEXIWAY. http://academialexiway.com/metodo-academia-ingles. Accessed 15 Jan 2017
2. DUOLINGO. https://es.duolingo.com/. Accessed 15 Jan 2017
3. Puerta, A.R.: A model-based interface development environment. IEEE Soft. **14**(4), 40–47 (1997)
4. Tian, Y., Yang, H., Landy, L.: MDA-based development of music-learning system. In: Proceedings of the 14th Chinese Automation and Computing Society Conference in the UK, Brunel University, West London, 6 September 2008
5. Object Management Group: Model-Driven Architectures. http://www.omg.org/mda/
6. Vesselinov, R., Grego, J.: Duolingo effectiveness study. Final report, December 2012
7. Fardoun, H., Montero, F., Jaquero, V.L.: eLearniXML: Towards a model-based approach for the development of e-Learning systems considering quality. Adv. Eng. Soft. **40**, 1297–1305 (2009)
8. Koch, N., Kraus, A.: Towards a common metamodel for the development of web applications. In: Lovelle, J.M.C., Rodríguez, B.M.G., Gayo, J.E.L., Puerto Paule Ruiz, M., Aguilar, L.J. (eds.) ICWE 2003. LNCS, vol. 2722, pp. 497–506. Springer, Heidelberg (2003). doi:10.1007/3-540-45068-8_92
9. Retalis, S., Papasalouros, A., Skordalakis, M.: Towards a generic conceptual design metamodel for web-based educational applications. In: Proceedings of IWWWOST 2002, CYTED (2002)
10. Blumschein, P., Hung, W., Jonassen, D., Strobel, J. (eds.): Model-Based Approaches to Learning: Using Systems Models and Simulations to Improve Understanding and Problem Solving in Complex Domains. Sense Publishers, Rotterdam (2009). ISBN 978-90-8790-710-5 (hardback)

Designing an Electronic Hand Glove for Teaching Vowels to Deaf Children

Julián Sotelo[1], Jaime Duque[1(✉)], Andrés Solano[1], and Sandra Cano[2]

[1] Universidad Autónoma de Occidente, Santiago de Cali, Colombia
{julian_and.sotelo,jaime_and.duque,afsolano}@uao.edu.co
[2] Universidad de San Buenaventura, Santiago de Cali, Colombia
sandra.cano@usbcali.edu.co

Abstract. Children with hearing impairment at birth face a variety of barriers related to development of language and communication skills. They have difficulties in the learning process in specialized and regular institutes; in addition they have difficulties to relate with the society. Nowadays, interactive systems as videogames are being used not only for entertainment purposes, but also in the educational context to promote the construction of knowledge in a didactic and interactive way, this as a support to the teaching/learning process. For this reason, this paper proposes an interactive system that tries to support the teaching process of vowels to deaf children, which is composed of a videogame and an electronic glove. This paper presents a tangible object, such as the electronic hand glove, for the child to achieve a multisensory interaction with the videogame. The child provides input data to the videogame by using the glove. He must represent each vowel of a word by the dactylology alphabet. The glove was built using flex sensors, which detect the movements of the children's fingers. Considering the potential of an electronic glove to support the process of teaching literacy and reinforcing the dactylology alphabet, it could be used to acquire and consolidate knowledge in a non-traditional way, generating a better learning experience and a greater motivation for the child.

Keywords: Deaf children · Videogame · Electronic glove · Vowels · Dactylology

1 Introduction

The learning of literacy is one of the most important tasks that the deaf child has to face. Although reading and writing have the potential to provide the deaf child with an alternative mode of communication, which allows them to access a lot of information, a large proportion of deaf children never reach competent reading and writing levels [1]. This is due to unfavorable conditions for learning and communication, causing them to be in a marginal situation.

Deaf children of birth face various barriers in developing language and communication skills; they not only present difficulties in the learning process in specialized and regular institutes, but also they have difficulties in relating to society. Literacy is a means that allows people to integrate and communicate with society. For deaf people,

G. Meiselwitz (Ed.): SCSM 2017, Part II, LNCS 10283, pp. 148–160, 2017.
DOI: 10.1007/978-3-319-58562-8_12

communication is addressed through the use of different mechanisms, such as: sign language and the dactylology alphabet. The last one allows to represent the spelling of a word, which means, the letters that make up the alphabet by the hands [2]; this mechanism is used to support the teaching of literacy to deaf children.

A deaf child who has no hearing aid has the sign language as the first language, and uses the spelling of each word through the dactylology alphabet as a way of knowing the writing of a word. In addition, the non-appropriation of the dactylology alphabet (which is necessary to establish a link between sign language and spelling relations) [3] by the rest of the citizens causes a communicative barrier, bringing effects such as partial or total marginalization or exclusion of the social, labor and educational life of the children.

Nowadays, interactive systems as videogames are being used not only for entertainment purposes, but also in the educational context to promote the construction of knowledge in a didactic and interactive way, this as a support to the teaching/learning process. For this reason, this research proposes an interactive system that tries to support the teaching process of vowels to deaf children, which is composed of a videogame and an electronic hand glove. The glove allows the child a multi-sensory interaction with the videogame. thanks to being a tangible objects the electronic glove, take advantage of this benefits of constructivist learning through the use of practical experimentation with integrated computer technologies [4]. In addition, the glove (tangible object) takes advantage of the senses and the multi-modality of human interactions with the physical world, providing a multi-sensory experience, fundamental for deaf children [5].

Considering the above, this paper presents the design of the electronic hand glove that allows the child a multi-sensory interaction with the videogame. The glove was made using flex sensors. These detect the movements of children's fingers and generate a range of values that varies depending on the flexion performed on them. Additionally, this paper presents the preliminary evaluation of the glove through a set of tests with deaf children. During these tests were considered the metrics: time taken to complete a task and number of errors. This in order to performing a quantitative analysis.

This paper is structured as follows: Sect. 2 presents a set of related works. Section 3 describes the proposed interactive system emphasizing the electronic glove. Section 4 presents the activities carried out as part of the evaluative process of the electronic glove. Finally, Sect. 5 presents a series of conclusions and future work.

2 Related Works

In [6] was proposed the development of a haptic glove with vibratory feedback, called Virtual Touch. This glove uses bending sensors to capture at all times the movement performed by the hand. Also, this uses small vibration motors that indicate to the user the contact with a virtual object. This research aims to develop a flexible glove using flex sensors that allow to capture in real time the position of each finger and provide vibrational feedback to the user. This type of sensors was selected as object of study in the present work due to the ease of implementation, the reduced cost and the accuracy that they deliver.

In [7] is presented a system that allows the interpretation of Colombian sign language, this consists of a hardware divided into three components. The first one is a glove made in cloth with five deflection sensors, one for each finger of the hand, an electronic sensor composed by a gyroscope that determines the movement of the hand in each one of the axes and three accelerometers to detect the acceleration of moving objects. The second component is a data acquisition card, in this case implemented with the Arduino Mega 2560, which is responsible for converting the analog signals into digital. Finally, the third component is the algorithm implemented for the recognition of the signals.

In [8] is presented a prototype that is based on a translator of movements of the hand through a glove, which allows to translate the dactylology alphabet, so that in this way, the deaf children can communicate with the rest of the people. The glove consists of eight flexible sensors, which vary their ohmic value when folded. These are located as follows: one in the little finger, one in the thumb and two in the remaining fingers (index, middle and ring). Each data obtained by the glove will be interpreted by a data acquisition card with USB communication. This consists of a microcontroller which will process the data for later sending them to the computer and decrypt them as a symbol representing a certain letter. The letter will be displayed in a graphical interface developed in Matlab.

In [9] is presented a project whose objective is the development of a glove composed of the following elements: (a) five flexibility sensors located in the bottom of the glove to calculate with more precision the resistance exerted by the fingers in each of the sensors, (b) an accelerometer located on the top of the wrist to avoid discomfort to the user, (c) Zigbee as a wireless data communicator; and (d) an Arduino FIO as a microcontroller located also in the upper part of the wrist. The glove elements are use to quantify the rehabilitation process of sports injuries and the sample of advances in therapeutic gymnastics therapies. For the preparation of the electronic glove [9] the standard measure of flexibility sensors on the market was taken into account, which prevented the possibility of scaling the glove size. Therefore, flexibility sensors were manually-constructed.

3   Proposed Interactive System

Proposed Solution. In education deaf children face a complex process of teaching literacy, since it involves the sound-word relationship. But in this case, by omitting the sound, they must learn to extract information visually by relating the concepts to the vocabulary [10, 11].

Based on the above, an interactive system is proposed that supports the process of teaching vowels to deaf children. This system is oriented to interact with unconventional input mechanisms using an electronic hand glove, so the system involves a hardware and software component. In this way, the system will allow the child to interact in a digital as well as a real environment.

The software component refers to a videogame, which is supported in Tablet's and presents a narrative story that takes place in a kingdom called *Las Vocales* (The Vowels). This kingdom is ruled by the princess *Lectra* and remains under the protection of five magicians. Each magician is represented by a vowel. The villain *Analfabet* steals the powers of the magicians. Then comes a hero who will be incarnated by the child and he will have the mission to travel to different worlds to overcome a series of challenges, and thus to recover the powers of the magicians and save the kingdom.

The hardware component refers to an electronic hand glove (see Fig. 1). The child provides input data to the videogame by using the glove. In this interaction, the child must represent each vowel of a word by the dactylology alphabet to complete the levels proposed in the videogame. This helps the child to memorize both gestural and visually the writing of the vowels in a series of words.

Fig. 1. Hardware and software components of the interactive system.

Design of the electronic hand glove. The User-Centered Design (UCD) was the approach followed for the design and development of the interactive system [12], this in order to knowing and understanding the user's needs. Among the identified needs, it is important for the child to interact with real objects in a real environment. Therefore, an electronic glove was defined as a hardware device.

For the design of the electronic glove were used average measures of the hands of the children, this decision obeys the following reasons: first, the group of children under study has a different age range, so that the body morphology, especially the hands, varies considerably. Second, the UCD suggests that designing gloves for different user profiles (and not for an average profile) is a good practice [13], however, it was complex because of economic constraints and lack of expertise regarding the use of segmented sensors. Thus, it is considered as future work the design of a glove that fits the size of each child's hand.

The work intends that the proposed interactive system be used in the Institute of Special Therapy of Senses (ITES) in the city of Santiago de Cali (Colombia). For this reason, the cost of implementing the hardware component should be minimal because most of its Students come from low-income backgrounds. In addition, the economic support that the institute receives from other Colombian organizations is scarce.

The measurements (length and thickness of the fingers) were obtained by an activity conducted with the children, in which each of them shaped the figure of his hand on a sheet of paper. After having the average measures, we then looked for a dressmaker who would make the glove. The glove fabric was selected considering the following criteria:

- Flexible and adaptable to children's hand shape.
- Softness and comfort.
- Avoid skin irritation due to factors such as humidity and heat.

Related works were an important input for the selection of the sensors and elements necessary in the glove elaboration. For the development of the electronic glove, hardware elements (plates, sensors) of Adafruit Industries were used, which have an adequate quality-price ratio and these meet the needs and requirements raised in the project. The programming was done using the Arduino IDE, which is compatible with the Adafruit plates. Table 1 describes the elements used in the glove specifying its name and a brief description.

Table 1. Electronic glove elements.

Name	Description
Short Flex Sensor	These sensors detect flexing in one direction; they are easy to use, because they are basically resistors that change their value depending on the amount of flexion exerted on them
Flora V3	Microcontroller created by Adafruit and compatible with Arduino, designed mainly to power wearable projects
Sewable Snaps – 5 mm Diameter	Brooches 5 mm diameter, used mainly to sew the microcontroller Flora V3 to the glove
Lithium Ion Polymer Battery – 3.7 V 2500 mAh	Lithium-ion polymer battery, with a capacity of 2500 mAh used to give autonomy to the electronic glove
Adafruit Micro Lipo – USB LiIon/ LiPoly charger – V1	Charger for rechargeable batteries of 3.7 V–4.2 V
Módulo Bluetooth HC-06	This module allows sending the data obtained from the electronic glove to the video game wirelessly

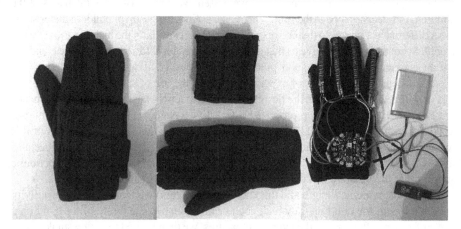

Fig. 2. Electronic glove – hardware component.

At the end of the assembly process of all the mentioned elements, the design of the electronic glove was obtained as hardware component of the interactive system. Figure 2 shows the result obtained.

Interaction videogame–electronic glove. First, when the child uses the interactive system the challenge screen is displayed (on the Tablet). This screen shows the doors where the vowels are enclosed. Once the child selects a door, a brief introduction will appear on the screen where he will observe the instructions to interact with the video-game. Then, an image associated with the word is presented, and in that word the vowels involved are highlighted (with a green tone). This in order to the child begins to under-stand the image-word relationship and identifies the vowels. Subsequently, the video-game begins and appears different words to which the vowels are missing (see Fig. 3). Each word is associated with an image so that the child understands the meaning of it. To complete the word the child must represent the gesture of the corresponding vowel using the dactylology alphabet. Then the gesture is captured by the electronic glove and sent wirelessly to the videogame.

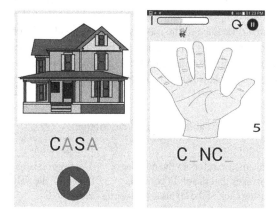

Fig. 3. Instruction interface and interaction with videogame.

For each word the child completes correctly, the system gives a certain number of stars (from one to three), which are related to the time the child took to complete the word. The stars will allow the child to advance to a new word to complete. Star assignment is the scoring system selected due to the field observation conducted in the classroom of the children, where the stars are awarded for good behavior or for successfully achieving the objectives proposed by the teacher during the class.

The electronic glove allows the child a multi-sensory interaction with the videogame. For the one hand, the use of the proposed videogame stimulates the visual sense due to the use of images and icons, seeking to reinforce the child's comprehension, integrate new knowledge (organizing, processing and prioritizing new or known information) and iden-tify misconceptions through the representation of words and images. For other hand, the sense of touch is stimulated directly and indirectly. In a direct way, when the child inter-acts only with the videogame because child must press the vowels that are presented in the screen of the Tablet to complete the different levels. In a indirect way, through the use of the electronic glove because the child reacts to stimuli that mainly include the contact. The proposed interactive system tries to reinforce the gestural abilities of the child, since in order to complete the levels he must use the dactylology alphabet to represent the vowels. This stimulates the appropriation of the dactylology alphabet.

4   Evaluation of the Proposal

This section presents information related to the evaluation process of the electronic glove. For this, we analyzed the results obtained from the interactions of the children with the interactive system considering a set of metrics.

4.1   Definition and Selection of Metrics

To carry out the analysis of results, a set of metrics were defined to objectively measure the results obtained from the conducted evaluations. Thus, the selected metrics are: *number of errors and time taken to complete a task*. These metrics were selected because they are the measures with the most relevance to the moment that the children interact with the video-game. These metrics provide vital information for the validation of the interactive system. Thus, less time taken to complete a task and fewer errors may indicate an effective under-standing of the image-word relationship by the child. Table 2 presents the description of the selected metrics.

Table 2.   Metrics description.

Metric	Description	Interpretation
Number of errors (E)	This metric refers to the number of mistakes that the child commits during each of the levels that make up a word when selecting/representing the vowels	The fewer mistakes are committed by the child, the value of the metric is closer to 0
Time taken to complete a tasks (T)	This metric refers to the time it takes a child to successfully complete each of the levels that make up a word	The less time a child takes to complete a level, the better

The selected metrics correspond to basic measures according to the theory of measure-ment, this indicates that they do not depend on any other measure and whose form of measurement is a method of measurement [14]. On the other hand, the number of metric errors is associated with an absolute scale type [15] since there is only one possible way to measure: counting; while the metric time used to complete the activity is associated with a type of ratio scale, which has a fixed reference point: zero.

At the time of the measurement process, the values of the metrics are not between 0 and 1 (exceed 1), so a standardization table must be used to scale them to values between 0 and 1. After normalizing the values, the metrics generate a real number that is comprised in the interval [0, 1]. Thus, the metrics provide positive evidence if the values are close to 0 and negative evidence if they are close to 1.

4.2   Users Evaluations

Conditions for the evaluation. The evaluation of the interactive system was subject to the following conditions.

- The tests were done in the classroom. During the tests with the children it was suggested to them to be at rest in order to avoid distractions and difficulties when interacting with the system.
- Test sessions were recorded using two mobile devices.
- In tests the devices used are two 7-inch tablets, a Nexus 7 second generation and a Samsung Galaxy Tab 4.

The tests were carried out with the first grade children of the Cali San Fernando ITES Lions Club (Cali, Colombia) and with the accompaniment of the teacher. In each test with the children were taken measures associated with the metrics; Also, as part of the observation process during the tests, annotations were made regarding the children's comprehension capacity when interacting with the system.

Based on the aforementioned process, once the measurements were made, the normalization of the measures associated with the metrics **E** and **T**. The following section presents the results obtained from the evaluation of the interactive system. The following sections present the analysis of the vowel A world due to document extension constraints.

Evaluation of the interactive system.   In the evaluation process a series of abbreviations are defined for the normalization of the metrics. The abbreviations used are: word 1 level 3 (**P1 N3**), word 2 level 3 (**P2 N3**), word 3 level 3 (**P3 N3**). In addition, **Tn** represents the normalized value of the metric **T**, **En** represents the normalized value of the metric **E** and **Ev**, represents each of the evaluations performed. Three children in the first grade participated in this evaluation.

The tests performed with the electronic glove reveal that the child works two channels of input to capture the information through the senses, visual and gestural. This serves as a support for memorizing the respective vowels more quickly, as a visual recognition is performed to complete the word accompanied by the sign, which makes use of the dactylology alphabet. Next, Tables 3 and 4 present the values of the metrics **T** and **E** for the evaluations of the interactive system.

Table 3. Measures of T metrics.

World	Child	P1N3							P2N3							P3N3						
		Ev. 1		Ev. 2		Ev. 3			Ev. 1		Ev. 2		Ev. 3			Ev. 1		Ev. 2		Ev. 3		
		T	Tn	T	Tn	T	Tn	P	T	Tn	T	Tn	T	Tn	P	T	Tn	T	Tn	T	Tn	P
A	1	48	1	28	0,44	12	0,00	0,48	31	0,53	18	0,17	23	0,31	0,33	15	0,08	34	0,61	21	0,25	0,31
	2	39	0,95	23	0,11	26	0,26	0,44	40	1	29	0,42	35	0,74	0,72	24	0,16	28	0,37	21	0	0,18
	3	14	0,08	25	0,5	12	0	0,19	37	0,96	30	0,69	24	0,46	0,71	38	1	33	0,81	27	0,58	0,79

Table 4. Measures of E metrics.

World	Child	P1N3							P2N3							P3N3						
		Ev. 1		Ev. 2		Ev. 3			Ev. 1		Ev. 2		Ev. 3			Ev. 1		Ev. 2		Ev. 3		
		E	En	E	En	E	En	P	E	En	E	En	E	En	P	E	En	E	En	E	En	P
A	1	0	0	0	0	0	0	0	0	0	0	0	0	0	0	0	0	0	0	0	0	0
	2	0	0	1	1	0	0	0.33	1	1	0	0	0	0	0.33	1	1	1	1	0	0	0,67
	3	1	1	0	0	1	1	0,67	0	0	1	1	1	1	0,67	1	1	0	0	0	1	0,67

Based on Tables 3 and 4, despite the small size of the user sample, the results obtained show a considerable decrease in the metrics **T** and **E**. The results obtained are a consequence of the previous interaction of the children directly with the video game. Thus, completing the words through the electronic glove makes it easier for the children, because being familiar with the dactylology alphabet, the time of action to represent the vowel and the number of errors are significantly reduced.

Tables 3 and 4 highlight at each level the highest (red) and lowest (green) registers in the three evaluations performed, based on Table 2, the values that are close to 1 and register Under values close to 0. According to the above, it is observed that child 2 presented the lowest register (0.18), indicating that he understood the contents present in the video game and also how to interact with the electronic glove. On the other hand, it is observed that child 3 presented the highest register (0.79), which indicates that it is best to better out the present information in the video game and adjust the response times obtained by each of the Flex sensors in the Electronic glove, since all children do not have the same agility or the same size of hand to make the representation of each of the vowels in the dactylology alphabet.

One factor that predominates in the difference of averages is the learning process, which is unique in each child and varies from one to another. In the case of child 1, his/her learning process has been constant during the three years he/she has been in the institution, being present from the first school level (pre-school, according to article 11, of the General Law of Colombian Education) until First grade of elementary school, while child 3 only takes one year in the institution and its learning process is beginning. In this sense, it is important to generate stimuli at a young age, since children establish the bases for cognitive, emotional and social development [16]. In addition, it rapidly increases the frequency with which children use signs to refer to objects and actions [17].

In the development of tests, the electronic glove influenced the achievement of high values regarding the metric **T**, this because the children had no previous experience with a physical device similar to this. For this reason, in the initial stage of the tests the children focused their attention on observing the glove, and not performing the activities suggested in the video game. However, it should be mentioned that aesthetics and ergonomics play an important role since the glove should be pleasing to the sight of the child, comfortable and soft for the child's hand. It should be avoided so much that the fingers touch the sensors as to leave elements (sensors, cables) in sight, because the children think that the glove could cause them damage.

In the course of the evaluations, it was possible to observe the excellent manipulation of the glove on the part of the children, with which the interaction with the video game and completing the tasks was satisfactory with respect to the metric **E**. The children had no major complications at the time of Represent the vowels through the glove. However, in some cases confusion occurred regarding the representation of vowels A and E. This confusion is estimated to correspond to the image - word relationship and not to the representation of vowels through the dactylology alphabet. Finally, Fig. 4 indicates that the values of the metric **T** decrease as the evaluations pass. These results suggest that children, based on the use of the proposed interactive system, achieve an adequate interpretation of the relationship: vocal (represented in dactylology alphabet) - image.

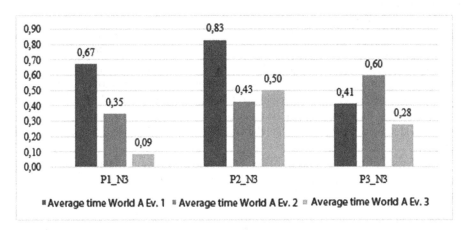

Fig. 4. Average of the metric T referring to the world of vowel A, hardware - software component.

On the other hand, based on Table 4 and Fig. 5, it can be seen that the values for the metric E present in 8 of the 9 evaluations the same value, since an average of approximately 0.33 was obtained with a minimum amount of 0 errors and a maximum of 2. This indicates that the previous interaction of the child with the software allowed him/her to understand the image-word relationship, in addition, the use of the alphabet as a tool to

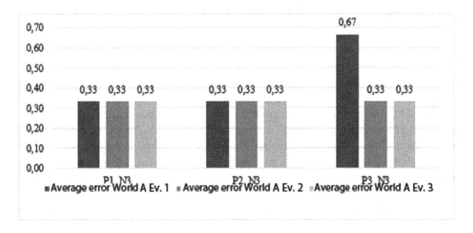

Fig. 5. Average of the metric E referring to the world of vowel A, hardware - software component.

complete the activities, the results, due to the excellent mastery that the children have of the dactylology alphabet. For this gives children not only the communication with the environment, but themselves, this being, from a Vygotsky perspective, an indicator of the internalization of the social environment, conducive to constitute the internal language and the child's thinking [18]. Finally, the correct functioning of each of the components of the electronic glove results in a better experience between the child and the electronic glove, which encourages the children's motivation for learning and continue to explore this element.

However, the average value of the metric **E** for each of the evaluated words presents an invariable behavior (0.33), which indicates that the evaluated children were able to correctly interpret the vocal relation (represented in the dactylology alphabet) - image, for each one of the words presented regardless of whether they changed and also managed to interpret the mentioned vowels through the electronic glove. On the other hand, the obtained results can be associated to the proximity that the children have with the words used, since previous to the evaluation with the electronic glove, direct tests with the videogame were realized; so, the children had prior knowledge of the words to complete.

Finally, about the ergonomics of the electronic glove, the evaluations allowed to detect some problems during its use. On the one hand, the position of the Flex sensors and their cables at certain times did not adapt to the constant manipulation of the children and yielded to sudden movements of the hand. On the other hand, the position in the upper part of the battery glove, the microcontroller and the Bluetooth module, did not give an adequate freedom for the representation of the vowels, mainly due to the weight that these objects generate in the children's hands.

5   Conclusions and Future Work

Conclusions. Through the present work it was possible to obtain an interactive system conformed by a software component and a hardware component. The software component refers to a videogame in which its basic mechanics consists of completing words associated with images by using the vowels. The hardware component is an electronic hand glove for the child to interact with the videogame representing the vowels using the dactylology alphabet to complete a series of words.

This work tries to positively impact society, generating greater inclusion to deaf children. Considering the potential that can be obtained by using an electronic glove as a support for the process of teaching literacy and reinforcing the dactylology alphabet, it could be used to acquire and consolidate knowledge in a non-traditional way generating a better experience and greater motivation for the child. The use of the electronic glove allows children constantly practice the representation of the vowels of the dactylology alphabet. Also, children can reinforce the style of visual learning as they must relate an image to a word.

With the present project an interactive system was developed that contributed to satisfy the needs identified in the tarjet audience. The project allowed the children to interact with the videogame in a non-traditional way (using the electronic glove). It is important to mention that several incidents occurred while the children were using the glove. Although it caught the attention and curiosity of children, it presented drawbacks when it was used, specifically with the Flex sensors and the cables used in the connections. The cables yielded repeatedly due to the manipulation of the children, causing interruptions in the accomplishment of the activities of completing the words. The cause of the problem relates to the selected cables because they did not provide the required resistance.

Regarding to the development of the electronic glove, the activity with greater complexity was to connect and calibrate the installed sensors, because when the sensors were tested as a whole the values obtained presented a high number of variations compared to the individual tests. This complicated the process of representation of the vowels using the dactylology alphabet.

Future Work. It is desirable to refine elements of the videogame. We hope to improve the designs of the characters, scenarios, images associated with the words used, as well as increase the number of words that make up each world of a vowel.

Regarding to electronic glove, we hope to include improvements in glove making materials for greater ease of use, strength and ergonomics. It is convenient to incorporate a system that allows to adjust the glove to different sizes of hands so that it can be used by a wider group of users. In addition, we will review other technological elements such as: more advanced sensors, accelerometers or gyroscopes, among others, that can be added to the glove. This in order to detect a greater number of characters of the dactylology alphabet and to achieve a greater accuracy in the representation of them.

References

1. Augusto, J.M., Adrián, J.A., Alegría, J., De Antoñana, R.M.: Dificultades lectoras en niños con sordera. Psicothema **14**, 746–753 (2002)
2. Herrera, V., Puente, A., Alvarado, J., Ardila, A.: Códigos de lectura en sordos: La dactilología y otras estrategias visuales y kinestésicas. Revista Latinoamericana de Psicología **39**, 269–286 (2007)
3. Treiman, R., Hirsh-Pasek, K.: Silent reading: insights from second-generation deaf readers. Cogn. Psychol. **15**, 39–65 (1983)
4. Piaget, J., Inhelder, B.: Psicología del niño. Ediciones Morata (1997)
5. Falcão, T.P.: Fostering exploratory learning in students with intellectual disabilities: how can tangibles help? In: Proceedings of the Sixth International Conference on Tangible, Embedded and Embodied Interaction, pp. 397–398. ACM (2012)
6. Albán, O.A.V., Tribaldos, M.R.D., Ocampo, J.M.E.: Interfaz háptica tipo guante con retroalimentación vibratoria. Revista EIA **12** (2016)
7. Benjumea Herrera, J.S., Gil Arboleda, S.: Sistema Mecatrónico para la Interpretación de la Lengua de Señas Colombiana (2012)
8. Espinosa Aguilar, P.A., Pogo León, H.A.: Diseño y construcción de un guante prototipo electrónico capaz de traducir el lenguaje de señas de una persona sordomuda al lenguaje de letras, p. 182. Facultad de Ingeniería, Ingeniero Electrónico, Universidad Politécnica Salesiana, Cuenca (2013)

9. Arenas, M.A., Palomares, J.M., Girard, L., Olivares, J., Castillo-Secilla, J.M.: Diseño y construcción de un guante de datos mediante sensores de flexibilidad y acelerómetro, vol. 1, pp. 3–4 (2011)
10. Sotelo, J., Solano, A., Duque, J., Cano, S.: Design of an interactive system for teaching deaf children vowels. In: Proceedings of the XVII International Conference on Human Computer Interaction, pp. 1–2. ACM, Salamanca (2016)
11. Cano, S., Peñeñory, V., Collazos, C.A., Fardoun, H.M., Alghazzawi, D.M.: Training with Phonak: Serious game as support in auditory–verbal therapy for children with cochlear implants. In: Proceedings of the 3rd Workshop on ICTs for Improving Patients Rehabilitation Research Techniques, pp. 22–25. ACM (2015)
12. Dix, A.: Human-Computer Interaction. Springer, Heidelberg (2009)
13. Granollers i Saltiveri, T.: MPIu+a. Una metodología que integra la Ingeniería del Software, la Interacción Persona-Ordenador y la Accesibilidad en el contexto de equipos de desarrollo multidisciplinares (2004)
14. Albert, W., Tullis, T.: Measuring the User Experience: Collecting, Analyzing, and Presenting Usability Metrics. Newnes, Oxford (2013)
15. Velthuis, P., Rubio, M.G.G., Parra, F.G., Bocco, J.G., Velthuis, M.P.: Medición y estimación del software: técnicas y métodos para mejorar la calidad y la productividad. Alfaomega (2008)
16. Piaget, J.: La teoría de Piaget. Infancia y Aprendizaje 4, 13–54 (1981)
17. Castro, P.: Aprendizaje del lenguaje en niños sordos: Fundamentos para la adquisición temprana de lenguaje de señas. Universidad de Chile, Santiago (2003)
18. Kelman, C.A.: Egocentric language in deaf children. Am. Ann. Deaf 146, 276–279 (2001)

Chat-Based Application to Support CSCL Activities

Ricardo Tesoriero[1](✉), Habib M. Fardoun[2], and Hachem Awada[3]

[1] University of Castilla-La Mancha, Av. España S/N, 02001 Albacete, Spain
ricardo.tesoriero@uclm.es
[2] Information Systems, King Abdulaziz University, Jeddah, Saudi Arabia
hfardoun@kau.edu.sa
[3] Information Systems, Faculty of Education, Lebanese University, Beirut, Lebanon
awadahachem@hotmail.com

Abstract. The evolution of the actual labor market requires people to perform long life learning activities. As people leave the formal education system, the time and place to perform these activities varies according to their private life. Therefore, traditional learning scenarios where students are located in the same classroom as professors at the same time are not the most suitable for people that have left the formal education system. Distance learning programs enable students to carry out learning activities anytime anywhere. This article presents a chat tool that enables users to center the discussion on an artifact; where the artifact can be a report, a map, an image, a slide or any electronic document. During the discussion, users exchange messages and documents. Messages are contextualized using references to: previous messages, documents or document fragments of text and images. These graphical references linking chat messages to observations in the document improve the understanding of messages, reduce the message composition time, enable participants to focus on different threads of information at the same time and introduce 3 different types of context information into the message: temporal, conceptual and observational; which are not available on traditional chats.

1 Introduction

The evolution of the actual labor market requires people to perform long life learning activities. As people leave the formal education system, the time and place to perform these activities varies according to their private life. Therefore, traditional learning scenarios where students are located in the same classroom as professors at the same time are not the most suitable for people that have left the formal education system. Distance learning programs enable students to carry out learning activities anytime anywhere.

Computer Supported Collaborative Learning (CSCL) fosters the collaboration among teachers and students to improve the learning experience. These activities are traditionally carried out using Learning Management Systems (LMS) [6], such as Moodle [14]. These systems provide many tools to carry out

© Springer International Publishing AG 2017
G. Meiselwitz (Ed.): SCSM 2017, Part II, LNCS 10283, pp. 161–177, 2017.
DOI: 10.1007/978-3-319-58562-8_13

collaborative activities such as email, chats, forums, workshops, surveys, questionnaires, wiki, blogs, peer evaluation, slide presentations, videos, documents, etc. These tools are an excellent option to carry out simple activities such as getting answers to questions using forums and chats, making simple decisions using surveys, presenting results in blogs, building a wiki to show findings, presenting a subject of study using slides or videos, etc.

However, there is a gap between the formulation of the problem to solve and the presentation of the conclusions of the work. This gap in the process is filled with the analyses and discussions that leaded to the conclusions. These tight-coupled activities are not well-supported by traditional LMS.

These activities involve students as well as teachers. For instance, suppose a hypothetic scenario where teachers provide students with a video, or a set of slides, containing the subject to learn. Then, students have a slot of time to ask questions that are answered by teachers, or other students in a forum. Once questions are answered, teachers ask students to write in groups research reports to evaluate the knowledge acquired by students.

From the Computer Supported Collaborative Work (CSCW) perspective, the presentation, question and answer, and writing report activities, are carried out asynchronously. However, the process involving each of them can be performed synchronously.

The presentation and question and answer sessions can be performed using audio or video conference systems. They enable students to ask questions to teachers during the presentation session instead of using a forum. Students have the opportunity to ask questions, and teachers to answer them, in the context in which the part of the subject requires extra explanation.

The writing research report group activities involve 3 phases: the learning material review (slides, electronic books, notes, annotations, etc.), the selection of findings to introduce into the reports, and the report authoring activities.

During the learning material review, students share questions and answers that use the slides as the center of the discussion. Then, students discuss about the findings to select them. Again, the discussion is centered on the documents (HTML pages, notes, spreadsheets, slides, docs, book chapters, etc.) students have found during the research process. During the learning material review and the selection of findings phases, students employ different tools to exchange information (i.e. chats, audio and video conferences, desktop sharing applications, online document sharing tools, etc.) Finally, students compose the research report based on the discussion carried out during the selection of findings phase using on-line document editing tools or file sharing utilities.

This article presents a tool to improve the communication between teacher and students where text documents, spreadsheets, slides and images, play an important role during the conversation. This tool enriches messages with information related to the context in which they were posted enabling users to recover the context afterwards.

This article is organized as follows. Next section presents the motivation for this work. Then, it defines the contextual chat conference tool functionality in terms of the user interface and the system architecture characteristics. Afterwards, it discusses the benefits of using this tool, and how this proposal improves learning activities. Finally, it presents conclusions and future work.

2   Motivation

In face-to-face scenarios, students and teachers share information during learning activity sessions. During these sessions, teachers share comments with students using slides, geographical maps, mathematical function graphs, equations, block diagrams, conceptual maps, etc. to expose subject contents. Besides, share comments with their colleges using practice spreadsheet reports, annotations, book chapters, etc. to fulfill teacher assignments The result of these activities usually consists only of summaries of the discussion and the conclusions.

Therefore, a large amount of information is lost during the transition between the discussion and the conclusion of the learning activity. This information could be critical in future activities where they have to answer questions such as Why did we discard this alternative? Why did we choose this one? Who proposed this alternative? Who suggested this solution? As only the summary of the discussion and conclusions where stored, it is difficult to backtrack in the discussion to answer these questions.

In distance learning scenarios, discussions are carried out in different ways; for instance, using conference phone calls, video conferences, and lately, personal computer assisted conferences (i.e. Skype) where users do not have to be grouped into a video conference room. The way teachers and students share information varies according to the media they use to communicate.

2.1   Conference Phone Calls and Audio Conferences

In conference phone calls and audio conferences, documents are printed on paper before the session.

The main problem regarding printed documents is setting the right document in the conversation context because participants have to synchronize these documents "by hand". For example, suppose that medical students are discussing about the evolution of a patient by analyzing 3 clinical analyses. To comment a set of values that are out of the normal range in a section of a report, they have to explicitly include in the comment the context information about the section of the report the comment is about.

This overhead of information may lead to misunderstandings. Suppose that a student comments to a section of an analysis without mentioning to the analysis. As the same section is present all reports, the rest of the students may link the comment to sections of different analysis.

This situation becomes worst if students talk about different versions of images, where the section (or region) to contextualize the comment is difficult to describe.

2.2   Video and Personal Computer Assisted Conferences

In video conferences and personal computer assisted conferences, the software usually provides sharing mechanisms such as desktop sharing applications (i.e. Microsoft NetMeeting [24]) or document sharing capabilities (i.e. Google Docs [23]).

They provide participants with a synchronized view of the document that is the subject of the conversation because all participants share the view of the same artifact. However, participants dealing with different documents sharing the same view have to deal with the "document overlapping" problem where participant hide some documents to see other documents.

A compromise solution is achieved when combining document and desktop sharing applications. Participants use the document sharing application to manipulate documents, and the desktop sharing application to show their contributions to the rest of the participants. Although the "document overlapping" problem is solved, and the information overhead decreases, this approach does not provide participants with any mechanism to link document to comments. For instance, following the clinical analyses example, the information about the evolution of the levels located in different analyses cannot be explicitly linked to a comment without introducing explicit contextual information.

Sometimes conclusions cannot be obtained in a single session; therefore, it is important to record all the information during to continue with the discussion. If the media to record the information is audio or video, the analysis and review process of a conversation is not easy.

From a technological perspective, searching information on this type of media is difficult. From a semantic point of view, it is not easy to discern between information that is part of the focus of the conversation, from the information that is part of the comment context.

Although it is possible to link video and audio resources to text comments at specific times using voice recognition technologies, it is not easy to link videos to external resources such as documents, images, graphs, etc. due to the separation between the communication tool and the resource manipulation application.

2.3   Document Comment Tool

A potential solution to this problem lays on the use of comments provided by the most of document sharing applications. Comments are an interesting alternative to support the exchange of information among session participants. The main problem behind this approach is the lack of temporal context provided by conversation.

Comments are attached to the structure of the document, instead of the temporal development of the conversation. It is difficult to follow a conversation from document comments, because the order in which comments are located is defined by the structure of the document, instead of the time the comment was created. This situation becomes worst when participants are dealing with more than one document at the same time. Each document have its own structure.

Another issue to take into account is the relationship between comments. In forums, participants are able to link posts to other posts to represent a relationship between them. For instance, a participant posting a question usually finds the answer to the question in a nested post. Therefore, during a meeting, participants are able to refer comments that are related to other comments that are not the actual subject of the conversation.

For instance, suppose that a group of medical students are discussing about the set of symptoms affecting a patient that are linked to clinical analysis results. At the beginning of the conversation, a student suggests a medical diagnostic assay to diagnose the potential disease causing of these symptoms. To keep in mind which symptoms the student is referring, the comment about the medical diagnostic assay is linked the comment related to the symptoms. As the conversation goes on, the patient exhibit new symptoms, and new alternatives about the disease are taken into account. At the end of the discussion, students can easily relate the assay to diagnose assay to the symptoms and then, relate the assay to the clinical analysis results. Thus, comments have temporal and subject contexts at the same time.

We summarize the analysis of the meeting scenarios as:

1. Lack of information regarding the learning activity process
2. Overhead of information related to the need to introduce context information into comments
3. Difficulty in the analysis and review of conversations using audio and video conferences
4. Lack of relationship on communication channels. While resources are managed by document sharing applications; conversations are carried out using conference systems
5. Lack of temporal awareness when using "the comment tool" on document sharing applications during a conversation, due to the comment dependency on the document structure
6. Observations cannot be easily related to other observations due to the lack of a mechanism to support temporal and semantic linking at the same time.

This article presents a contextual chat conference tool that enables participants to create references to different parts of meeting documents to cope with the problems mentioned in the previous paragraphs.

3   The Contextual Chat Conference Tool

The Contextual Chat Conference Tool (CCCT) is inspired by chat conference applications that enable a set of participants to exchange text messages and anchored conversations [4]. This proposal links messages to documents, fragments of text, regions of images, mixed parts of a document including regions of images and fragments of texts, and other messages.

The remaining of this section exposes the most relevant characteristics of the CCCT user interface supporting the reference mechanism that links documents to messages. Besides, it describes the architectural characteristics of the system used as a platform to support the exchange of messages as well as documents.

The CCCT employs a multi-user communication channel where all the information is shared by all the chat participants that are connected to a channel or chat room.

The information density of a channel of information defines the unit of information (i.e. character, line, or message) chat participants exchange. The density of the information that flows through a CCCT channel is the message. Therefore, the message composition process is private, and no one, except for the author, is able to see any message until it is posted through the communication channel.

As, The CCCT is a Groupware application that can be classified using to the space/time classification matrix proposed in [10]. From the temporal perspective, this application support both, synchronous and asynchronous work sessions. It supports synchronous work sessions because it enables participants to exchange messages in real-time. Besides, it supports asynchronous work sessions because conversations are persistent to enable the analysis, review or continuation of work sessions. From the space perspective, as the most of chat systems, CCCT enables in-situ as well as geographical distributed conversations.

The extension to the classification proposed in [17] adds 3 new characteristics to classify CSCW systems: Information sharing, Communication and Coordination. This application is a *communication* tool that supports the *information sharing* by enabling participants to exchange documents and messages linked to portions of these documents. Although it could be used as a *coordination* tool (you can use this tool to schedule the next steps of a rehabilitation process); it was not intended to play this role.

According to [20], there are two types of elements that are part of a computer supported communication: the artifact and the prose. While the prose expresses an observation textually, the artifact is the center, or the focus, of the conversation. In CCCT, the role of the artifact is played by documents (such as presentations, reports, images, etc.), and comments linked to document regions play the role of the prose (i.e. messages).

3.1   The Contextual Chat Conference Tool User Interface

The Fig. 1 depicts the 5 interaction areas the CCCT user interface: the Artifact Interaction Area (AIA), the Prose Review Area (PRA), the Prose Arte fact Connection Area (PACA), the Prose Composition Area (PCA) and the Presence Awareness Area (PAA).

The PAA provides participants with 2 interaction components: the user presence list, where participants see the rest of the participants' state (Away, Busy, On line, Free to chat, etc.), and the participant state selector where they set their own state.

The PCA enables participants to compose the prose to be sent to the chat conference channel. It also enables them to change the message font family, size and color as well as set the bold and italic font attributes.

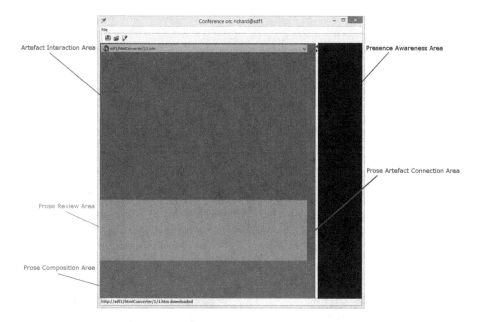

Fig. 1. Contextual Chat Conference Tool user interface interaction areas

The PRA shows the messages sent by chat participants. When participants click on a message, the reference to a message, or a document region, is displayed accordingly.

The AIA displays the artifact of the conversation related to message observations. It consists of two parts: the document view area showing a document, and the document selection area that enables participants to select the document to be displayed on the document view area. This area renders documents and marks, where a mark is mechanism to identify fragments of documents. The type of mark depends on the media to be referred (i.e. text or image).

The application supports different types of media resources included in the artifacts (i.e. documents); for instance, plain text and compositions of texts and images. These resources are embedded into documents of different formats (ANSI Plain Text [19], Graphics Interchange Format [5], Joint Photographic Experts Group [8], Portable Network Graphic [26], Rich Text Format [3], Microsoft Word format [13], Microsoft Excel [11], Microsoft PowerPoint [12] and references to static HTML [25]).

Regarding messages, the CCCT enables chat participants to improve the message expressiveness by setting the message text attributes, such as the font family, size, colors, bold and italics styles.

Messages can be linked to a document, a region of a document or another message. These links consist of 3 parts: the source, the reference link and the target. While the source is always a chat message, which is defined when the message is composed by the author, the target could be another message, a document or a region of a document. The link reference is represented by a line that binds both, the source and target elements.

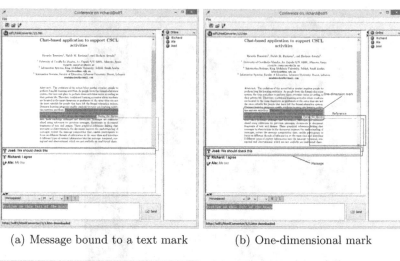

(a) Message bound to a text mark   (b) One-dimensional mark

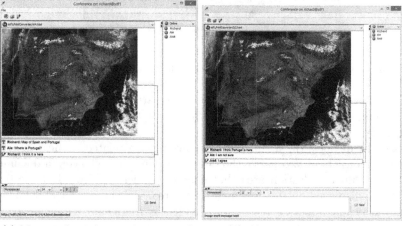

(c) Message bound to an image mark   (d) Chain of linked messages

Fig. 2. Contextualized chat message samples

Some examples of marks on documents are exposed in Fig. 2. The Fig. 2(a) shows a message bound to a text mark. If the target is a fragment of a document, we employ a mark to set the limits of the region. Thus, we define 2 types of marks: one-dimensional marks and two-dimensional marks.

One-dimensional marks enable chat participants to create lineal marks to enclose parts or sets of lines. This type of mark is the most suitable to mark paragraphs of text or parts of them (see Fig. 2(b). On the other hand, two-dimensional marks enable participants to mark sections of documents as rectangles. This type of mark is the most suitable to mark images (see Fig. 2(c)). Finally, the Fig. 2(d) shows a message to message reference link, where the chain of linked messages shows message marks.

3.2   The Contextual Chat Conference Tool System Architecture

A client-server architecture is employed to implement the system. Clients enable participants to exchange documents and messages linked to fragments of these documents through 2 servers: the Document Converter Server (DCS) and the Message Delivering Server (MDS).

While the MDS is in charge of delivering chat information among participants (messages, presence awareness, etc.), the DCS is in charge of delivering documents to chat participants. Besides, as the client supports different document formats, the DCS is in charge of converting all document formats to HTML to allow the client to treat all documents homogeneously.

Before linking a message to a fragment of a document, participants have to share a document. To share a document, the system executes 2 steps: the document conversion step and the document dissemination step.

Document Conversion. The document conversion step is carried out by the DCS. The Fig. 3 shows the document conversion process which starts when a participant selects a document to share. Then, this document is sent to the conversion service as the body of an HTTP [15] POST request.

The request is received by a Web service implemented using the Java Servlet Technology [9], and it is stored to be processed in an Apache Tomcat [2] Web server running on a Microsoft Windows Server 2003 [21]) operating system.

Once the document is stored, it is converted into HTML according to the document format. Simple documents, such as ANSI text, PNG, GIF and JPG files, are embedded into an HTML file. However, complex documents such as Microsoft Word, Excel and PowerPoint are converted to HTML files using the COM API of native applications [22]. To use the COM API from the Java

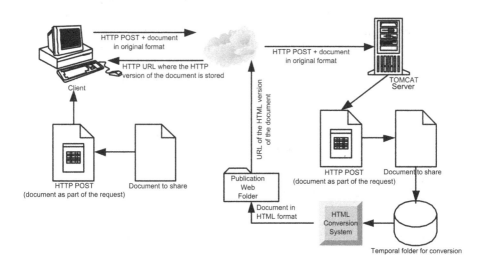

Fig. 3. The document conversion and dissemination processes

programming language, we have employed the JACOB (JAva COM Bridge) API [1] which is based on the JNI [16] (Java Native Interface) technology.

Once the conversion process is finished, HTML files are published on the HTTP server. The response to the request sent from the client contains the URL of the HTML version of the document.

Document Dissemination. Once the document conversion process is finished, the document dissemination process wraps the URL referring to the HTML version of the document within a message, and it is delivered to the rest of the participants through the MDS.

Although the document information is delivered as a message, this information is not shown on the PRA. Instead, it is shown on the combo box that is part of the AIA, where participants choose the document to manipulate in the AIA canvas. Thus, participants are able to select the document from the combo box, and any fragment of the selected document, from the AIA canvas.

The MDS is a Jabber server based on the eXtensible Messaging and Presence Protocol (XMPP) [18]. This protocol allows the bi-directional communication between the server and all clients using XML. The implementation employed to deploy the CCCT is the Openfire [7].

To support the exchange of documents and message references, we have implemented an extension of the XMPP.

The main advantage of the XMPP protocol is the capability to define message extensions to enrich the information sent and received by chat participants.

The Fig. 4 shows the XML document sent by sender@server.com to the room@server.com channel. The Fig. 5 shows the XML that is received by receiver@server.com from the room@server.com. To extend the message contents with extra information we employ the 'x' tag. In order to process the 'x' tag, it defines the xmlns attribute which identifies the type of information that is contained with the tag. The Fig. 6 shows an example of a message received by receiver@server.com that uses a message extension to include information about the time the message was sent because it was not delivered on time.

Therefore, we have defined message extensions using 'x' tags to exchange messages including links to documents, fragments of documents and messages.

```
<message from='sender@server.com/home' id='hfsd76fds'
 to='room@server.com' type='groupchat'>
<body>This is a message</body>
<html>
 <body>
  <p>This is a <b>message</b></p>
 </body>
</html>
</message>
```

Fig. 4. XML content of an XMPP message to be sent

```
<message to='receiver@server.com/work' id='hfsd76fds'
 from='room@server.com/sender'>
<body>This is a message</body>
<html>
 <body>
  <p>This is a <b>message</b></p>
 </body>
</html>
</message>
```

Fig. 5. XML content of an XMPP message received

```
<message id='xmkos2yh' from='room@server.com/sender'
 to='receiver@server.com/work'>
<subject>Welcome!</subject>
<body>Welcome to Jabber!</body>
<x xmlns='jabber:x:delay' from='source@server.com/home'
 stamp='20011206T18:22:09'>
Offline Storage</x>
</message>
```

Fig. 6. XML content of an XMPP message with extensions

The Fig. 7 shows a sample of a message extension that delivers the location of the Testing.doc document that was converted to HTML and stored at the http://localhost:8080/ConverterWEB/files/3/3/3.html. This extension is identified by the http://www.richard.org/docMessage XML namespace. It defines the url, description and action nested tags.

```
<x xmlns='http://www.richard.org/docMessage'>
 <url xmlns='http://www.richard.org/docMessage'>
  http://localhost:8080/ConverterWEB/files/3/3/3.html
 </url>
 <description xmlns='http://www.richard.org/docMessage'>
  Testing.doc (1/1)
 </description>
 <action xmlns='http://www.richard.org/docMessage'>add</
     action>
</x>
```

Fig. 7. XML content of an XMPP message with a document extension

The url tag defines the location of the HTML version of the document.

The description tag contains information about the original version of the document; for instance, it contains the document file name and the page number of the document. This information is useful because most documents

(PNG, JPG, GIF, Microsoft Word, etc.) are stored in single files; however, presentations in Microsoft PowerPoint and spreadsheets in Microsoft Excel are stored in multiple files (one file for each slide/sheet). Therefore, as the message format supports only one page for each message, the converter delivers as many messages as HTML pages were the result of the conversion. As we have mentioned before, the page number is part of the description of the message.

Finally, the action tag identifies the action of the message (i.e. add document, remove document, update document). The only action that was implemented is the add action. Conceptually speaking, the remove action is a dangerous action to implement because if documents are removed, some messages could lose the context of the document. Another alternative is removing documents jointly with messages that are linked to these documents; however, if we remove messages from the conversation, we lose the temporal context of the conversation messages generating "holes" in the story. The situation regarding the update action is similar to the remove action.

There are different types of message references. The Fig. 8 shows a sample of a message extension to represent an image mark linked to a message. The message that points to the mark is implicitly defined because the 'x' tag is a nested tag of the message tag that contains the message information.

The type of the mark is defined by the xmlns attribute which is set to 'jabber:x:imageMark'. The reference tag defines the document in which the mark is embedded by defining the url attribute that points to the URL of the document being referred.

```
<x xmlns='jabber:x:imageMark'>
 <reference
  url='http://localhost:8080/ConverterWEB/files/1/1/1.html'
     xmlns='jabber:x:imageMark'/>
 <anchor xmlns='jabber:x:imageMark'>
  <color b='0' r='255' g='0' xmlns='jabber:x:imageMark'/>
 </anchor>
 <selection xmlns='jabber:x:imageMark'>
  <background b='0' r='255' g='0'xmlns='jabber:x:imageMark'/>
  <foreground b='0' r='255' g='0'xmlns='jabber:x:imageMark'/>
  <offset xmlns='jabber:x:imageMark'>23207</offset>
  <rectangle xmlns='jabber:x:imageMark'>
   <x xmlns='jabber:x:imageMark'>25</x>
   <y xmlns='jabber:x:imageMark'>159</y>
   <width xmlns='jabber:x:imageMark'>287</width>
   <height xmlns='jabber:x:imageMark'>34</height>
  </rectangle>
 </selection>
</x>
```

Fig. 8. XML content of an XMPP message with an image mark extension

The anchor tag defines the color of the link between the mark on the document and the message which is drawn on the PACA. In the example, the color tag defines the red color by defining the r, g and b attributes to 0, 255 and 0 respectively.

The selection tag defines the image mark on the document. It requires four nested tags to define the image mark characteristics. The background and foreground tags define the background and foreground colors of the image mark using the color nested tag in the same way as the anchor tag does.

As the application supports documents that have text interleaved with images, the offset tag contains the information about the relative image position within the text to identify the image.

Finally, the rectangle tag contains the information of the mark dimension and position using the x, y, width and height inner tags.

The Fig. 9 shows an example of the message extension to represent text marks. As in the image mark, the type is defined by the xmlns attribute, which is set to 'jabber:x:textMark'.

The reference and anchor tags are defined as in the image mark. However, the selection tag defines the start and end tags, instead of the rectangle and offset tags to represent the beginning and the end of the text fragment that represents the mark.

```
<x xmlns='jabber:x:textMark'>
<reference url='http://localhost:8080/ConverterWEB/files
    /1/1/1.html'
  xmlns='jabber:x:textMark'/>
<anchor xmlns='jabber:x:textMark'>
  <color b='0' r='255' g='0' xmlns='jabber:x:textMark'/>
</anchor>
<selection xmlns='jabber:x:textMark'>
  <background b='0' r='255' g='0' xmlns='jabber:x:textMark'/>
  <foreground b='0' r='255' g='0' xmlns='jabber:x:textMark'/>
  <start xmlns='jabber:x:textMark'>9932</start>
  <end xmlns='jabber:x:textMark'>9954</end>
</selection>
</x>
```

Fig. 9. XML content of an XMPP message with a text mark extension

4   Discussion

This section presents how the problems that motivated this work are tackled by this proposal. Besides, it highlights the benefits of employing the CTTT application instead of traditional systems/procedures in the development of eLearning activities.

The discussion is presented from two different perspectives. On the one hand, the user perspective describes the solution conceptually. On the other hand, the technological perspective presents the arguments that leaded the architectural and technological decisions.

4.1 The User Perspective

From the user perspective, the lack of information regarding the learning activity process (1) is a key issue to board when conversations are carried out using audio and video conference systems. To cope with this situation, the system is based on a chat conference system. The benefits of this approach are not only the capability of searching or analyzing specific information in a text-based form, CCCT is also capable of identifying the author of the information being shared. Besides, as observations can be linked, a semantic network could be easily derived from stored information to recreate the learning process.

The overhead of information (2) derived from the description of the artifact in the observation to put it in context is an important issue to deal with in traditional chat conferences because the extra information increases the message composition time, and it makes the observation more difficult to discern from the context information.

The integration of the document sharing and marking capabilities into the chat conference tool enables participants to easily put messages in context. This approach goes further and provides different marking capabilities according to the media (text or image) to improve the expressiveness of the context. Thus, this system reduces the message composition time and increases the precision of the context description reducing the risk of misunderstandings.

Due the media nature in which the audio and video is manipulated, apart from the problems (1) and (2), these communication medias do not allow chat participants to focus their attention on 2 audios or videos at the same time (3). However, the situation becomes more manageable when participants are dealing with simultaneous chats.

There are some studies showing that the late-coming of participants occurs very often depending on the participants' culture. Therefore, it is important to support the possibility of following two threads of conversation at the same time as well as reviewing information that was already shared during the same or different conversation sessions.

Chats seem to be the most suitable communication medium when participants join into a conference that is already in progress because they can follow the actual thread of the conversation while reviewing previous messages and documents in real-time. Another consequence of this approach, is the reduction of information access time which makes the conversation smoother.

The use of different applications which are not coupled to manage observations and artifacts (4) leads to problems, such as the overhead of information (2) and analysis difficulties (3). This approach integrates and relates observations and artifacts into the same user interface to overcome this situation.

Modern document processors support comments on documents. Although most of these comments do not distinguish between comments linked to texts from those linked to graphics, they provide a good mechanism to attach observations to artifacts. However, there is a lack of temporal awareness among observations (5) because comments are linked to the document structure instead of the conversation structure. Consequently, the benefits of the improvement regarding the overhead of information (2) and the difficulty to analyze conversations (3) is diminished by an increment of the loss of information regarding the record of the learning activity process (1) because the importance of what is being said is as important as when it was said, particularly during a review process.

As this approach integrates both views, the temporal as well as the artifact context, they are synchronized to provide a complete view of the conversation. As word processors enable participants to "reply" comments with new comments, observations can be easily related (6) improving the decision making process analysis (1). This feature is also included in our proposal as links to other messages. Thus, message contexts are enriched with information from three different sources: time, observation and artifact context information.

4.2   The Technological Perspective

From a technological perspective, our approach presents some advantages over other alternatives. The first advantage is the low communication bandwidth that is required by the system to work, compared to the amount of resources required to process audio or video conference systems. This feature makes the system more suitable in extreme situations where this resource is poor (i.e. mountains, isles, forests, etc.)

The system deals with two types of processes: the document sharing and the message exchange. As the document sharing process does not support the document edition, the information to be provided does not change over the time; therefore, a simple and worldwide-known stateless communication protocol, such as HTTP, provides the most flexible solution to implement the DCS where Web services are in charge of converting and publishing documents in HTML format on the Internet.

The message exchange process requires extra information involving message and participant states. To implement this requirement, we have chosen the XMPP protocol to fulfill MDS requirements. As XMPP is an open standard, there are many implementations and public servers, and the most of them, are capable of playing the role of the MDS.

Finally, the XMPP requires a full duplex communication channel to keep clients up to date. Although HTML 5 [28] provides messaging capabilities, they are not are fully supported by some browsers. Therefore, we have employed Java to develop the client application to implement a multi-platform solution.

5   Conclusions and Future Work

This paper presents a chat-based application to support CSCL activities in order to improve the communication and the analysis of collaborative conversations when the focus of these conversations are artefacts such as reposts, images, etc.

The proposed solution is based on a chat conference system that integrates observations with artefacts. It enables chat participants to link observations to an artefact in a graphic way. As result of this action, users obtain: an improvement of message understandings, a reduction of the message composition time, the capability to focus on different threads of information at the same time, and the introduction of 3 different types of context information into a message: temporal, conceptual and observational. The temporal context information defined by the chat message sequence, the conceptual context information defined by links between messages and the observational context information defined by the links between messages, and the artefact which is the focus of the observation.

A usability evaluation based on heuristics was performed on this tool by usability professionals which concurred in the good performance of the application.

Regarding future works, we are actually working on a new version of the tool clients based on the HTML 5 [27] standard introducing the Web Messaging (or cross-document messaging) API [28] to support message delivering. Besides, we are working on supporting PDF documents which are becoming a standard on the field. Finally, we are also working on the implementation of a mobile version of the tool client in HTML 5 [27].

References

1. Adler, D.: The JACOB Project: A JAva-COM Bridge (2014). http://danadler.com/jacob/. Accessed 12 May 2014
2. Apache Software Foundation: Apache Tomcat Web site (2014). http://tomcat.apache.org/index.html. Accessed 12 May 2014
3. Biblioscape 9: Rich Text Format (RTF) Version 1.5 Specification (2014). http://www.biblioscape.com/rtf15_spec.htm. Accessed 12 May 2014
4. Churchill, E.F., Trevor, J., Bly, S., Nelson, L., Cubranic, D.: Anchored conversations: chatting in the context of a document. In: Proceedings of the SIGCHI Conference on Human Factors in Computing Systems, CHI 2000, NY, USA, pp. 454–461 (2000). http://doi.acm.org/10.1145/332040.332475
5. CompuServe Incorporated, World Wide Web Consortium (W3C): Graphics Interchange Format (2014). http://www.w3.org/Graphics/GIF/. Accessed 12 May 2014
6. Ellis, R.K.: Field Guide to Learning Management Systems (2009)
7. Ignite Realtime: Openfire. Jive Software (2014). http://www.igniterealtime.org/projects/openfire/. Accessed 12 May 2014
8. Independent JPEG Group (IJG): JPEG Homepage ISO/IEC IS 10918-1. ITU-T Recommendation T.81. (2014). http://www.jpeg.org/jpeg/. Accessed 12 May 2014
9. Java Community Process: SR-000340 Java TM Servlet 3.1. Java Community Process Web site (2014). https://jcp.org/aboutJava/communityprocess/final/jsr340/. Accessed 12 May 2014
10. Johansen, R.: Groupware: Computer Support for Business Teams. The Free Press, Macmillan Inc., New York (1988)
11. Microsoft Corporation: Microsoft Excel. Microsoft Web site (2014). http://office.microsoft.com/es-es/microsoft-excel-software-de-hoja-de-calculo-FX010048762.aspx. Accessed 12 May 2014

12. Microsoft Corporation: Microsoft Power Point. Microsoft Web site (2014). http://office.microsoft.com/es-es/microsoft-powerpoint-software-de-presentacion-de-diapositivas-FX010048776.aspx. Accessed 12 May 2014
13. Microsoft Corporation: Microsoft Word. Microsoft Web site (2014). http://office.microsoft.com/es-es/microsoft-word-software-de-procesamiento-de-texto-y-documentos-FX010048798.aspx. Accessed 12 May 2014
14. Moodle: Moodle web site (2017). https://moodle.org/. Accessed 12 Jan 2017
15. Network Working Group: Hypertext Transfer Protocol - HTTP/1.1. RFC 2616 (1999). http://www.w3.org/Protocols/rfc2616/rfc2616.html. Accessed 12 May 2014
16. Oracle: Java Native Interface (2014). http://docs.oracle.com/javase/7/docs/technotes/guides/jni/. Accessed 12 May 2014
17. Penichet, V.M.R., Marin, I., Gallud, J.A., Lozano, M.D., Tesoriero, R.: A classification method for CSCW systems. Electron. Notes Theoret. Comput. Sci. **168**, 237–247 (2007). http://dx.doi.org/10.1016/j.entcs.2006.12.007
18. Shigeoka, I.: Instant Messaging in Java: The Jabber Protocols. Manning Publications, San Diego (2002)
19. The Unicode Consortium: The Unicode Consortium Web site (2014). http://www.unicode.org/. Accessed 12 May 2014
20. Whittaker, S., Brennan, S.E., Clark, H.H.: Co-ordinating activity: an analysis of interaction in computer-supported co-operative work. In: Proceedings of the SIGCHI Conference on Human Factors in Computing Systems, CHI 1991, NY, USA, pp. 361–367 (1991). http://doi.acm.org/10.1145/108844.108944
21. Wikipedia: Microsoft Windows Server 2003 (2003). http://es.wikipedia.org/wiki/Windows_Server_2003. Accessed 12 May 2014
22. Wikipedia: Component Object Model (2014). http://es.wikipedia.org/wiki/Component_Object_Model. Accessed 12 May 2014
23. Wikipedia: Microsoft Docs (2014). http://en.wikipedia.org/wiki/Google_Docs. Accessed 11 May 2014
24. Wikipedia: Microsoft Net Meeting (2014). http://en.wikipedia.org/wiki/Microsoft_NetMeeting. Accessed 11 May 2014
25. World Wide Web Consortium (W3C): HTML 4.01 Specification (1999). http://www.w3.org/TR/html401/. Accessed 12 May 2014
26. World Wide Web Consortium (W3C): Portable Network Graphics (PNG): Functional specification. ISO/IEC 15948: 2003 (E) (2003). http://www.w3.org/TR/PNG/. Accessed 12 May 2014
27. World Wide Web Consortium (W3C): HTML 5.1 Nightly. a vocabulary and associated APIs for HTML and XHTML (2014). http://www.w3.org/html/wg/drafts/html/master/. Accessed 12 May 2014
28. World Wide Web Consortium (W3C): HTML5 web messaging (2014). http://www.w3.org/TR/webmessaging/. Accessed 12 May 2014

Toward a Supporting System of Communication Skill: The Influence of Functional Roles of Participants in Group Discussion

Qi Zhang[1], Hung-Hsuan Huang[1(✉)], Seiya Kimura[1], Shogo Okada[2],
Yuki Hayashi[3], Yutaka Takase[4], Yukiko Nakano[4], Naoki Ohta[1],
and Kazuhiro Kuwabara[1]

[1] College of Information Science and Engineering, Ritsumeikan University,
Noji-higashi 1-1-1, Kusatsu City, Shiga 525-8577, Japan
hhhuang@acm.org
[2] School of Computing, Department of Computer Science,
Tokyo Institute of Technology, 4259 Nagatsuta-cho, Midori-ku,
Yokohama, Kanagawa 226-8502, Japan
[3] College of Sustainable System Sciences, Osaka Prefecture University,
1-1, Naka-ku, Sakai-shi, Osaka 599-8531, Japan
[4] Department of Computer of Information Science, Seikei University,
3-3-1 Kichijoji Kita-cho, Musashino-shi, Tokyo 180-8633, Japan

Abstract. More and more companies are putting emphasis on communication skill in the recruitment of their employees and are adopting group discussion as part of recruitment interview. In our project, we aim to develop a system that can provide advices to its users in improving the impression of their communication skill during group discussion. In this paper, we focus on the functional roles of the participants in group discussion and report the results of the analysis of the relationship between communication skill impression and functional roles. This work is based on a group discussion corpus of 40 participants. The participants' communication skill of the corpus was evaluated by 21 external experts who had experience of recruitment. In addition, seven functional roles: *Follower, Gatekeeper, Information giver, Objector, Opinion provider, Passive participant,* and *Summarizer* were defined and annotated. Furthermore, we analyzed the conversational situations of corpus and the difference of between participants with high-score and low-score communication skill in these situations.

Keywords: Group discussion analysis · Communication skills · Social interaction · Conversational mode

1 Introduction

When working in a company as a project member, the communication skill that connects the team is important. In recent years, there has been a growing number of companies that adopted group discussion in the recruitment of employers.

© Springer International Publishing AG 2017
G. Meiselwitz (Ed.): SCSM 2017, Part II, LNCS 10283, pp. 178–188, 2017.
DOI: 10.1007/978-3-319-58562-8_14

In group discussion task, job applicants have to collaborate with each other on an assigned topic, where their communication skill and personality can be observed by the investigators of the companies. Therefore, giving the impression of a high communication skills to the recruiters, may increase one's chance of success while job hunting.

In our ongoing project, we aim to develop a system that can provide advices to its users in improving the impression of their communication skill can be estimated from the verbal and nonverbal signals of the participants [1]. However, the estimation is based on the data of the whole period of the experiment session. There is only one result, that is, a judgment (high/low or a score) of the communication skill of each participant at the end of the discussion session. It could be difficult to utilize the results for developing a support system for the participants: the participants cannot know when and how to improve their behaviors.

In order to develop a support system, a finer unit at appropriate size of the behaviors of the participant is required. It is known from social science that people's roles in group interaction structure nonverbal behavior in important ways [2]. In this paper, we propose the use of functional roles of the participants as the unit to trace the dynamics of the interaction among the participants. We considered that the functional roles can be treated as a template or a style of actual behaviors. By exploring the temporal transitions of the roles of an individual participant and the situation (the roles of other participants) were the participant was in, we expect that it is possible to derive the relationship between functional roles and impression of communication skill. The results are then supposed to be able be used in conducting the strategy in improving the impression of communication skill.

The analysis of the functional roles is based on a data corpus collected in actual group discussion experiments. It is composed of video and audio data of 10 groups by three sessions of group discussion conversation as well as sensor data like head motion and eye tracking. The participants' communication skill on the whole corpus was evaluated by 21 experts who had the experience in personnel management or recruitment. After the definition of functional roles, firstly we analyzed the relationship between functional roles and communication skill impression to confirm whether the distribution of roles played by an individual participant has influence on the impression of his/her communication skill. Second, we analyzed the characteristics of the group evaluated as high communication skill comparing to the group evaluated as low in the sense of how they responded to the situation where they are in.

2   Related Works

Researchers in organizational psychology have studied the communication skill or the individual personality in group meetings for decades, uncovering statistical relationships between nonverbal behaviors, personality, hire ability, and professional performance. In the context of group meeting, based on the nonverbal features, including features like speaking turn, voice prosody, visual activity, and visual focus of attention feature and so on. Aran and Gatica-Perez [3] presented an analysis on the participants' personality prediction in small group. Similarity, Okada et al. [1] developed a regression model to infer the score for communication skill using multi modal features including linguistic and non-verbal features: voice prosody, speaking turn, and head activity. Similar to our goal, Schiavo et al. [4] presented a system that monitors the group members' non-verbal behaviors and acts for an automatic facilitator. It supports the follow of communication in a group conversation activity. Furthermore, job interviews also have been studied in the research field of multi modal interaction, too. Raducanu et al. [5] made use of "The Apprentice" reality TV shows, which features a competition for a real, highly paid corporate jobs. The study was carried out using non-verbal audio cues to predict the person with highest status and to predict the candidates going to be fired. Muralidhar et al. [6] implemented a behavioral training framework for students with the goal of improving the impressions their hospitality perceived by others. They also evaluated the relationship between automatically extracted non-verbal cues and various social signals in a correlation analysis.

Taken together, these studies show that high-prediction models could be achieved by using multi modal nonverbal information (speaking turn, voice prosody, visual activity, and visual focus of attention). Which can be used for predicting communication skills or personalities.

In the present study, we aim to develop a system that can provide advices to its users in improving the impression of their communication skill during group discussion. Our work therefore selected functional roles of participants by incorporating multi modal non-verbal and verbal features, to analyzed the relationship with the impression of communication skill. In order to be able to timely feedback on the performance of the participants, we also analyzed the relationships with the impression of communication skill and conversational situations in shorter interval compared with the former studies. And found the difference of performance between participants with high-score and low-score communication skill.

3 Group Discussion Corpus

In this section, in order to analyze the relationships between the functional roles and the impression of communication skill, it is necessary to achieve the communication skill models by using the group discussion corpus as training dataset. And the assessment of communication skills and the roles' annotation of participants were also executed in this corpus.

3.1 Data Collection Environment

We therefore used a multi-modal corpus in which groups of four people discussed three different topics [7]. The experiment was to collect the verbal information and non-verbal information of the participants in the group discussion. Then, recruited 40 Japanese university students who did not know each other

Fig. 1. Setup of the experiment environment.

before to participant in the experiment, and divided them into 10 groups of four people.

Each group had three discussion sessions in Japanese. In order to simulate the actual job interviews, they reviewed the group discussion tasks which were used frequently in recruiting in Japanese companies. And three kinds of discussion themes were designed as following: Celebrity guest selection, Booth planning for school festival, and Travel planning for foreigner friends. And the state of the discussion has been recorded and measured using a variety of sensors (Fig. 1).

3.2 Assessment of Communication Skills

The corpus also includes the communication skills of each participant, which was assessed by 21 external observers with the experience of human resource management. In this paper, we presented a brief overview of the assessment of communication skills [1]. The communication skills were defined according to the paper [8,9], including four categories [*smooth interaction, aggregation of opinions, communicating one's own claim, logical and clear presentation*] and total communication skill to assess the communication skills of the participants. The scores of four traits were evaluated between one and five, and the total communication skill was evaluated between one and ten. The observers assessed the skills by watching the video of the group discussion. The procedure applied to the assessment was as follows. The video of a session was segmented into three portions (five to seven minutes). Of the 21 observers, seven assessed the skill score by watching one of three partitions in a session. This means that the session is assessed by all of the observers (seven observers * three partitions). The agreement between the observers for each skill index was confirmed in terms of Cornbach's alpha (α), and all of α the values of are greater than 0.85.

3.3 Annotations of Roles

In terms of roles, the paper [10,11] indicated that the participant plays one of three type of roles, including group-task role, maintenance role, and individual role in group discussion. According to the previous works and the observation on our data corpus, we also added non-verbal description into the definition of roles. And finally defined seven types of roles, including *follower, gatekeeper, information giver, objector, opinion provider, passive participant,* and *summarizer* (Table 1).

In the part of roles annotation, three annotators watched the videos and annotated the roles of participants according to the definition above. Each annotator was assigned with the data of four groups. One group was randomly selected for the measurement of inter-annotator reliability. The pair-wise Kappa Coefficients were 0.41, 0.51, and 0.63.

Table 1. The overview of roles' definition

Role	Definition
Follower	Go along with the activity of the group, praises, agrees with, and accepts the contributions of others. Often look at the person who is speaking and nod or say some words to chime in
Gatekeeper	Facilitate the flow of the discussion. Encourage the participants who are not so willing to engage. Often look around the other members
Information giver	Provide objective information which is supplementary to the discussion
Objector	Take an opposing or negative attitude toward the topic being discussed at this moment. Often with head aslant and don't nod
Opinion provider	State the participant's own opinion which might be subjective. Convince others to agree with it
Passive participant	Does not join the discussion actively. Almost does not provide the participant's own opinion to the topic being discussed. Often stay silent and low the head.
Summarizer	Make a brief summary or conclude the discussion or current topic

4 Communication Skill Models

4.1 Guidelines for Creating Models

In order to identify whether there has relationships between roles and communication skills, we used the duration ratio of each type of role as feature at both regression and classification problems. Due to a part of audio files cannot be used for roles' annotation, the 110 data points are used for the experiments. Evaluation is done with a cross validation testing, we used data samples observed from participants in one group for test data and remaining samples from groups for training.

4.2 Regression Model and Results

In the regression experiments, we assessed the models on predicting the actual communication skill impression scores for five traits. We used R^2 (coefficient determination) as a criteria of performance of the regression model, and the results are shown in Fig. 2 From this figure, the R^2 of the regression model of total communication ability is 0.55, while aggregation of opinions is 0.56.

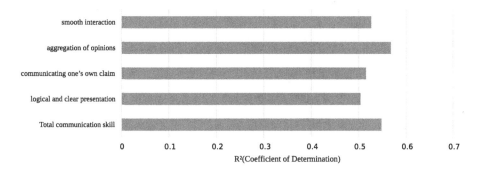

Fig. 2. Result of support vector machine regression model

4.3 Classification Model and Results

For the classification experiments, we converted the problem to a classification problem by defining two classes for each trait as high and low, based on the scores. More specifically, to calculate the mean m and the standard deviation σ of all evaluation value in five traits in first. Then, classify the evaluation values which were over $m + \beta\sigma$ into the label of high, while below $m - \beta\sigma$ were classified into the label of low. Considering the balance of the size of two classes, we decided to set β as 0.5. We chose to use logistic in the classification analysis, and estimated the model with the values of precision, recall and F-Measure. And Table 2 showed the estimation results of five traits.

From Table 2 we can indicate that the precisions and F-Measure of the classification model of aggregation of opinions is 0.903, while total communication skill is 0.892. That is to say that we can confirm the communication skill impression of participant is high or low from the duration ratios of roles in a high precision by using our classification model.

Table 3 showed the significance probability of each role that influence the classification between the label of high and low in independent T-tests.

Table 2. Results of logistic classification model

	Precision	Recall	F-Measure
Total communication skill	0.839	0.837	0.838
Smooth interaction	0.797	0.795	0.796
Aggregation of opinions	0.839	0.833	0.832
Communicating one's own claim	0.843	0.843	0.843
Logical and clear presentation	0.765	0.756	0.757

Table 3. Significance test result of each role. $+$: $p < .1$, $*$: $p < .05$, $**$: $p < .01$, n.s.: not significant

	Total communication skill	Smooth interaction	Aggregation of opinions	Communicating one's own claim	Logical and clear presentation
Follower	n.s	n.s	n.s	n.s	n.s
Gatekeeper	**	**	**	**	**
Information giver	**	**	*	**	**
Objector	+	n.s	n.s	n.s	+
Opinion provider	**	**	**	**	**
Passive participant	**	**	**	**	**
Summarizer	**	+	+	+	**

According to the result that illustrated by Table 3, we confirmed that the roles of gatekeeper and opinion provider are strongly correlated with classification between two classes, and those who are whether trying to maintain or improve the social relationships within group would have great difference in the communication skill impression. While follower and objector are weakly compared with other roles.

5   Analysis of Conversational Situations

We can confirm there is a certain relationship between roles and communication skill impression of the participants according to the result in last section. Moreover, these analyses were overlooked by a long time which about 15 min to 20 min in one session, and lead to cannot provide current advice for users in time. Therefore, in order to be suitable for real-time processing, we considered that if extracting the roles of participants in more details, and analyzing the conversational situations from participants' individual point of view that would get some useful information that can be added into our supporting system. For example, which kind of situation often appear, and high-communication-skill people would to play which type of roles in this situation. On the other hand, we also tried to find what the difference between high-skill-score and low-skill-score' performance in same situation, and analyzed which kind of mode impacts the communication skill impression.

5.1 Analysis Method

Although there were four participants in each group, the layout was symmetric from the view point view of each participant. In this section, we call the participant who is being analyzed as the *center participant*. The conversational situation is then modeled as the combination of the role of the center participant and a set of roles of the other participants. Each participant group conducted group discussion in three topics and therefore 30 experiment sessions were recorded. Due to partial data failures, 26 of them were annotated. Each session was divided to three segments with length from five to seven minutes. Since there are four participants in one group, this leads to 312 data. According to the Nyquist-Shannon sampling theorem, perfect reconstruction is guaranteed possible for a band limit $B < fs/2$. Considering that the minimum interval of role annotation in whole dataset is about 300 ms, in order to explore the temporal dynamics of group discussion, all 312 data points were sliced into 100 ms intervals.

5.2 Overall Distribution of Situations

There were 1,084,206 intervals in total. The occurrence frequency of the conversational situations is shown in Fig. 2. From the whole data corpus, 63 kinds of situations were found in total. The 36 situations which had occurrences less than 1% were combined in category, "Others." Overall, there were no dominating situations, the distribution of situations was relatively averaged. However, if we look into the role distribution of more frequent situations, it could be found that the activity of the participants was not high while they were often playing passive or follower roles. With relatively fewer occurrences, one of the participants provided objective information or tried to facilitate the discussion, but few of them tried to express their opinions.

5.3 Analysis of Situations Difference

Next, we analyzed how different the participants with high scores responded to the situations than the participants with low scores. We selected the participants evaluated with scores at least 0.4 times of standard deviation σ higher than the mean m of all participants as high group and the ones with scores at least 0.4σ lower than m as low group.

Figure 3 shows the results of the comparison between high and low groups. Then, we conducted an independent t test to verify which situation differed between high-score and low-score. From which we understand the followings (Fig. 4):

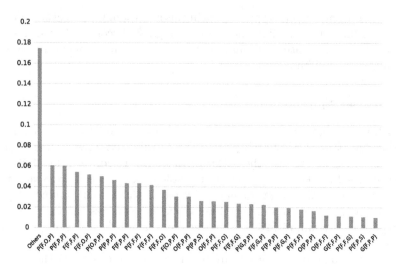

Fig. 3. Occurrence frequency of conversational situations. The letter outside of "{}" is role of center participant, and the roles of the other three participants were shown in "{}" 's. Here, the abbreviations of functional roles are shown as the follows: F: Follower; G: Gatekeeper; I: Information giver; B: Objector; O: Opinion provider; P: Passive participant; S: Summarizer

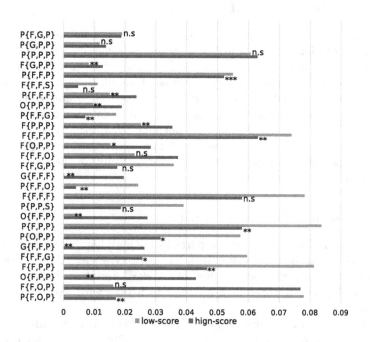

Fig. 4. Comparison between the participants with high scores and low scores. The results of two-tailed t test: +: $p < .1$, *: $p < .05$, **: $p < .01$, n.s.: not significant

- The conversational situations that have a significantly high frequency of high-score communication skill at the time of F{G,P,P}, P{F,F,F}, O{P,P,P}, F{P,P,P}, F{O,P,P}, G{F,F,F}, O{F,F,P}, G{F,F,P}, and O{F,P,P}. That is to say, the participants with high-score communication skill preferred to state their own opinions when the others had lower activity. The high group participants also played the gatekeeper role more frequently in similar situations. Apart from P{F,F,F}, they almost to show a positive attitude even the other participants had no feedback to the problem being discussed.
- Oppositely, the participants evaluated with low scores had significantly higher frequency in the situations: P{F,F,P}, P{F,F,G}, F{F,F,P}, P{F,F,O}, P{F,P,P}, P{O,P,P}, F{F,F,G}, F{F,P,P}, and P{F,O,P}. Compared with high-score participants, low-score participants tended to be "Follower" or "Passive participant" no matter whether anyone was expressing their opinion or not. To summarize, the high-score participants more actively joined the discussion, express their opinions more, and lead the discussion. On the other hand, the low-score participants were passive to the discussion and showed negative attitude.

6   Conclusion and Future Direction

In this study, seven functional roles of the participants were defined. We firstly proposed regression and classification model for analyzing the relationship between functional roles and communication skill of participants in group discussion, which were based on a previous collected database. The performance of the proposed classification model was 0.838 in its F-Measure. We also calculated the significance probability of the duration ration of each role, and confirmed four types of roles influenced the communication skill impression of a participant most. On the basis of these results, we analyzed the relationship between conversational situations and the total communication skill score. The conversational situation was modeled as the combination of the roles of the participants. From the analysis results, it was found that the participant with high scored of communication skill did show clearly different behaviors (playing the roles) than the ones evaluated as low. They were more active, tended to express their own opinions, and facilitate the discussion.

In terms of future direction, we note that only use the duration ratio of roles as feature is not sufficient, so we will pay attention to the characteristic of runtime, to add some more detailed features in the next step. For example, the verbal features, the interaction with other participants, the role change patterns of the participants. Finally, to establish the supporting system of communication skill that teach the users to play what kind of role will have high communication skill impression, based on the types of roles which participants play.

References

1. Okada, S., Ohtake, Y., Nakano, Y., Hayashi, Y., Huang, H.H., Takase, Y., Nitta, K. Estimating communication skills using dialogue acts and nonverbal features in multiple discussion datasets. In: 18th ACM International Conference on Multimodal Interaction, pp. 169–176 (2016)
2. Hall, J.A., Coats, E.J., LeBeau, L.S.: Nonverbal behavior and the vertical dimension of social relations: a meta-analysis. Psychol. Bull. **131**(6), 898 (2005)
3. Aran, O., Gatica-Perez, D.: One of a kind: inferring personality impressions in meetings. In: 15th ACM on International Conference on Multimodal Interaction, pp. 11–18 (2013)
4. Schiavo, G., Cappelletti, A., Mencarini, E., et al.: Overt or subtle? Supporting group conversations with automatically targeted directives. In: 19th International Conference on Intelligent User Interfaces, pp. 225–234 (2014)
5. Raducanu, B., Vitria, J., Gatica-Perez, D.: You are fired! nonverbal role analysis in competitive meetings. In: 2009 IEEE International Conference on Acoustics, Speech and Signal Processing, pp. 1949–1952 (2009)
6. Muralidhar, S., Nguyen, L.S., Frauendorfer, D., et al.: Training on the job: behavioral analysis of job interviews in hospitality. In: 18th ACM International Conference on Multimodal Interaction, pp. 84–91 (2016)
7. Nihei, F., Nakano, Y.I., Hayashi, Y., et al.: Predicting influential statements in group discussions using speech and head motion information. In: 16th International Conference on Multimodal Interaction, pp. 136–143 (2014)
8. Core, M.G., Allen, J.: Coding dialogs with the DAMSL annotation scheme. In: AAAI Fall Symposium on Communicative Action in Humans and Machines, p. 56 (1997)
9. Greene, J.O., Burleson, B.R.: Handbook of Communication and Social Interaction Skills. Psychology Press, Hove (2003)
10. Benne, K.D., Sheats, P.: Functional roles of group members. J. Soc. Issues **4**(2), 41–49 (1948)
11. Hare, A.P.: Types of roles in small groups a bit of history and a current perspective. Small Group Res. **25**(3), 433–448 (1994)
12. Ishii, R., Kumano, S., Otsuka, K.: Analyzing mouth-opening transition mode for predicting next speaker in multi-party meetings. In: 18th ACM International Conference on Multimodal Interaction, pp. 209–216 (2016)

Opinion Mining and Sentiment Analysis

Sentiment Analysis on Arabic Tweets: Challenges to Dissecting the Language

Malak Abdullah[(✉)] and Mirsad Hadzikadic

College of Computing and Informatics, University of North Carolina at Charlotte, Charlotte, NC, USA
{mabdull5,mirsad}@uncc.edu

Abstract. Sentiment analysis and opinion mining are designed to detect peoples' emotions and opinions. Many public and private sectors are interested in extracting information regarding opinions that consist of subjective expressions across a variety of products or political decisions. Recently, the Arab region has had a significant role in international politics and the global economy that has grasped the attention of political and social scientists. Detecting Arabic tweets will be helpful for politicians in predicting global events based on the popular news and people's comments. Still, the Arabic language has not received a proper attention from modern computational linguists. This literature review provides a comprehensive study of sentiment analysis on Twitter data and analyzes the existing work that has been done in order to detect and analyze Arabic tweets.

Keywords: Twitter · Sentiment analysis · Opinion mining · Natural language processing · Machine learning · Classification · Arabic language

1 Introduction

Sentiment analysis and opinion mining are considered hot topics where researchers are extracting information regarding emotions and viewpoints. It is believed that these concepts consist of subjective expressions across a variety of products or political decisions [6,42]. The terms sentiment analysis and opinion mining are not exactly the same. The meaning of the term "opinion" is broader than the term "sentiment". Prior researchers have used these two terms interchangeably. In this literature review, the term sentiment analysis has been used to refer to both of them. Sentiment analysis is used to track attitudes and opinions on the web and determines if the audience positively or negatively receives these ideas. This helps companies determine strategies for improving the quality of their products or to assist decision makers. Sentiment analysis of data involves building a system by using natural language processing, statistics, and machine learning methods to examine opinions or sentiments in a text unit [6].

Microblogging services, such as Twitter and Facebook, are considered important communication tools for people to share their opinions or spread information. The nature of these microblogs encourages people in their daily lives to post

© Springer International Publishing AG 2017
G. Meiselwitz (Ed.): SCSM 2017, Part II, LNCS 10283, pp. 191–202, 2017.
DOI: 10.1007/978-3-319-58562-8_15

real-time messages about their opinions on current events. People are sharing their daily life activities on these microblogging tools [30].

The Twitter microblog was launched in July 2006, and since then it has gained worldwide popularity. Many scholars hold the view that the use of Twitter is playing a vital role in spreading information and influencing people's opinions in a specific direction. Statistics from Statista website show that the Twitter in 2016 has more than 317 million active users. Many users tweet their opinions on a variety of subjects, discuss many political topics or marketing issues, and express their views on many aspects of their lives. Every tweet has a maximum length of 140 characters. Due to the shortness of the messages, people convey their opinions and thoughts openly most of the time. Therefore, Twitter is considered a rich data bank and one of the largest platforms that is full of sentiments [32].

According to recent reports, the fastest growing language on Twitter between 2010 and 2011 was Arabic [24]. While there is a great need for natural language analysis of large amounts of Arabic language text, the reality shows little work has been done in this area. Most of the sentiment analysis resources and systems built so far are tailored to English and other Indo-European languages. Reasons for the lack of research in this area include the complexity and the variety of dialects of the Arabic language that make it harder to build one system that is applicable to all of its dialects [10,45].

The Arabic language belongs to the Semitic language family. It is recognized as the fifth most widely spoken language in the world and is considered the official or native language for 22 countries (approximately more than 300 million people) [25,29]. The Arab region has a large, growing population and has become an important player in international politics and the global economy. Furthermore, the Arabic language is in the top ten of the most used languages to create Internet content [45].

This study primarily aims to review the efforts of building sentiment analysis systems for the Arabic language and lists some applications and systems that have been built to analyze Arabic Twitter data. This research also presents a general study of sentiment analysis and explores some of the machine learning algorithms and natural language processing classification techniques.

The remainder of this literature review is organized as follows. Section 2 gives the reader general background material on Twitter sentiment analysis by describing techniques and vital features that have been used in this area. Section 3 examines the techniques that have been used to analyze Arabic tweets and to summarize the key findings of recent research in this field. This literature review concludes with future directions of research in Sect. 4.

2   Background on Sentiment Analysis

In general, tweets generated by users can be categorized as objective or subjective tweets. Objective tweets contain facts that refer to the nature of entities, events, and attributes [46]. An example of an objective tweet is: *Election Day in the United States of America is the Tuesday following the first Monday in November.*

While subjective tweets express users' opinions regarding entities, events, and attributes. Subjectivity classification seeks tweets that contain users opinions. Some examples of subjective tweets include:

- *I'm happy election day is almost here.* (positive tweet)
- *I hate this election. Everything about it makes me miserable.* (negative tweet)
- *I don't care who wins the upcoming presidential election.* (neutral tweet)

Sentiment analysis is considered a part of the Natural Language Processing (NLP) field. It was first explored in 2003 by Nasukawa and Yi [35]. In sentiment analysis of Twitter data, the researchers focus their studies on subjective, not objective, tweets. They are interested mainly in classifying tweets as positive and negative [27]. The researchers studied sentiment analysis through three levels. The first level is the document level that classify and analyze sentiments for the whole document [36,49]. Analyzing sentences is considered a second level. And finally, the phrase level is when the researchers are analyzing sentiments in phrases [5,50]. They also investigated the utility of linguistic features for detecting the sentiment of Twitter posts.

2.1 Sentiment Analysis Work-Flow

The process of performing sentiment analysis for a micro-blogging tool usually goes through multiple phases [10,12]:

- Phase 1: Data-gathering (crawling data). In this phase, the required amount of tweets that are related to a specific topic are retrieved. This data is filtered according to a particular time frame and keywords/users.
- Phase 2: Data-preprocessing (text normalization). This is an important step in the data mining field. The retrieved data from the first phase will be tokenized by converting the sentences into words. These words will be cleaned to remove any irrelevant and redundant information.
- Phase 3: Building-a-classifier. In this phase, a classifier model will be selected. Subsect. 3.2 discusses the classification techniques that can be used to analyze peoples' sentiments more deeply.
- Phase 4: Visualization. This phase focuses on visualizing the results of sentiments attached to a particular topic and follows opinion changes over time. This can be performed by a graphical representation in several forms.

2.2 Sentiments Classification Algorithms

There are many techniques that perform sentiment analysis on Twitter data. According to Boiy [14], Symbolic techniques and Machine Learning techniques are the two basic methodologies used in sentiment analysis for text [45]. Symbolic technique, which is also called Semantic Orientation, uses sentiment lexicons which are lists of words or phrases associated with positive and negative sentiments. Some of these lexicons add other features and provide a score to specify the strength of its class. This approach works to extract the score of its words and sum them up to show an overall positive or negative sentiment. Turney [49] used bag-of-words approach in which the document is treated as a collection of words regardless of the relationship between the words. Turney gave every word a value and combined all the values by using aggregation functions. Turney's technique is used to figure out the overall value for the whole document. On the other hand, Kamps [26] developed a distance metric on wordNet which is a database consisting of words and their relative synonyms. Another simple classifier model is the k-nearest neighbor algorithm that uses distance measure to assign a class label y to x if y is the nearest label to x [47].

Many classifier models have been built to classify tweets as positive, negative, or neutral according to their training data sets. These are grouped under the machine learning umbrella. The term machine learning was first coined by Samuel in the 1950s and was meant to encompass many intelligent activities that could be transferred from human to machine. The research in this field focuses on finding relationships in data [20]. Machine learning modeling methods can be supervised or unsupervised. In the supervised learning classification model, a training labeled set of data are used to predict the class of a search query. While in the unsupervised learning classification models, there is no labeled training data and the model will classify the corpus to specific classes based on some clustering computations. Labeling data in many applications is an expensive process and sometimes it may be labeled with errors and that may reflect the classification results. The unsupervised learning model is used frequently to predict the topic for a page or a text. Out of the sentiment analysis models that are using the supervised modeling in this survey, most of them have been built by using one of three standard algorithms: Naive Bayes classification, Maximum Entropy classification, and Support Vector Machines classification [6].

The efficiency of a classifier depends on the type of engineering feature associated with it. Feature extraction is the process of creating a representation for, or a transformation from, the original data. Numerous feature extraction algorithms have been proposed and successfully applied in many classifier models. Features can be binary, categorical, or continuous. Some of these powerful features are [6,12]:

1. Term Presence vs. Term Frequency: It has been proven experimentally that the presence of a term is more important than counting the term frequencies.
2. Term Position: The term position can determine the sentiment for a tweet which plays an important role in sentiment analysis.
3. Part-of-Speech: Many articles show that this feature plays an important role in all Natural Language Processing tasks. This feature concentrates on the adjective and adverb words in the text.
4. Unigram: In this feature, a single word can be considered as a feature by itself. The results showed that unigram presence taken as feature turns out to be the most efficient.

Results show that n-grams features are the most widely used features for Twitter sentiments analysis [6].

The performance of sentiment classification system can be evaluated by using a well-known table called (Error Matrix) or (Confusion Matrix) [48]. Each column of the matrix represents predicted classifications and each row represents actual defined classifications. Based on the Confusion Matrix, four indexes can be computed to reflect the performance. These are Accuracy, Precision, Recall and F1-score.

3 Arabic Sentiment Analysis

3.1 Arabic Language Aspects and Challenges

Arabic is the mother tongue of 22 countries with more than 300 million people speaking that language [25]. It is also the language of more than 1.4 billion Muslims around the world. It has been used for more than 2000 years [28]. The Arabic alphabet consists of 28 letters with no upper or lower cases and the orientation of writing is from right to left. Its letters can be written with different shapes according to their position in the word. According to [22,25], the Arabic language is classified into two main categories: Standard Arabic (SA) and Dialectical Arabic (DA). SA consists of two forms: Classical Arabic (CA), and Modern Standard Arabic (MSA). CA is the standard poetic language and the language of the Qur'an (Holy Islamic Book). While MSA language, which is a simplified form of CA, is used in most current printed Arabic publications such as books, newspapers, and also used in news broadcasts or formal speeches [44]. Although MSA is the primary language of the media and education in Arab countries, it is not spoken as a native language in people's informal daily communication. In contrast to MSA, DA is spoken but not written in books or taught in schools. DA has a strong presence in texting SMS on cellular phones, commenting on microblogging networks or in emails, blogs, discussion forums, and chats. Each dialect is spoken by a specified geographical area for daily verbal communication. Therefore, there is only one MSA language for all Arabic speakers but several dialects with no formal written form [18]. According to [28], the dialects are affected by many factors such as: which Arab tribe has lived in this geographical area and which foreign language was the source of loanwords. Also, if the geographical area is a village or countryside, or if the people are bedouin or sedentary. Arabic Dialects are greatly varied, and are classified into five main groups according to [51]: Egyptian, Levantine, Iraqi, Gulf, and Maghribi.

3.2 Classification Techniques for Arabic Tweets

Minimal work has been done in Arabic sentiment analysis area. Several reasons may have explained the lack of studies in this area. Assiri in [12] mentioned two main reasons: 1- limited research funding in this area, 2- Arabic has a very complex morphology relative to the morphology of other languages. The complexity and variety of Arabic dialects require advanced pre-processing and lexicon-building procedures [10,12,45].

Working in this area needs a full understanding of Arabic standard layer-based structure of linguistic phenomena such as phonology, morphology, syntax and semantics [43]. Arabic is a highly inflectional and derivational language with many word forms and diacritics. Several suffixes, affixes, and prefixes in Arabic words make it harder for lexicon or morphological analyzers to extract the root of words correctly [19].

MSA has more studies and analysis as compared to DA. Numerous tools for detecting sentiments on short or long texts in MSA have been built. Knowing that applying NLP tools designed for MSA directly to DA yields significantly lower performance. This led a group of researchers to build other resources and tools for analyzing DA [15,39,45].

Many researchers have applied Machine Translation (MT) in their studies by translating Arabic statements into English and then applying sentiment analysis tools on the translated materials [33,40]. This approach has been explored widely for other foreign languages by performing sentiment analysis on the English translation [9,13]. The problem of this approach was the loss of nuance after translating the source to English. It is shown in [11] that finding an Arabic MT that meets human requirements is a difficult task. This field still needs more efforts to be improved. Most of the previous work focused on the translation of news and official texts. Much work has been done on MSA; however, research on DA is still lacking in MT [41].

A prior important step for analyzing sentiments in any language is Building Resources (BR). This step aims at creating lexica, corpora with annotated expressions or opinions. There is a need for large scale of annotated resources for the Arabic language in order to do sentiment analysis. Some efforts have been paid to build Arabic Treebanks that contain collections of manually-annotated syntactic analyses of sentences [21,23,31]. Researchers focus mainly on building corpus/corpora that contain annotated data for MSA and less attention is paid towards DA. Most of these resources are either of limited size or not available for public. Recently, a study [17] addressed this problem and generated a large multi-domain dataset for sentiment analysis in Arabic. The study scraped 33K annotated reviews for movies, hotels, restaurants and products. Then, the researchers built multi-domain lexicons from the generated datasets and tested the classifier models on this data. Another research published in 2014 [37] with a dataset of 8,868 multi-dialectal Arabic annotated tweets. They employed morphological features, simple syntactic features, such as n-grams, as well as semantic features. Other research studies can be found in Table 1 which summarizes the recent work on building resources for Arabic language.

Most of the sentiment analysis tools perform three main data pre-processing steps before applying the classification techniques in order to prepare the Arabic texts, which are: 1- Normalization, 2- Stemming, and 3- Stop word removal. Once data pre-processing has been applied to the text, it will be ready for the feature extraction step. Several text features are considered for the Arabic sentiment analysis: n-grams, term presence or its frequency, part-of-speech, or emoticon symbols. The goal of feature extraction step is to select which text features are

Table 1. Building resources for Arabic

Ref.	Name	Year	Description
[38]	OCA	2011	Arabic corpus contains 500 movie reviews collected from different web pages and blogs in Arabic with 250 positive reviews and 250 negative reviews. It has limited size and for specific domain (movies)
[1]	AWATIF	2012	Multi-genre corpus of Modern Standard Arabic labeled for subjectivity and Sentiment Analysis. It is only dedicated for MSA and not available for public
[34]	LABR	2014	Over 63,000 book reviews rated on a scale of 1 to 5 stars. It is only for specific domain (books)
[2]	SANA	2014	A large scale multi-genre sentiment lexicon (more than 200K) of MSA and some Arab dialects. It is also not public
[37]	NA	2014	A dataset of 8,868 multi-dialectal Arabic annotated tweets
[17]	NA	2015	A large multi-domain dataset (33K annotated reviews for movies, hotels, restaurants and products) for sentiment analysis in Arabic

best to be applied in sentiment analysis tool. Most of the features in Arabic sentiment analysis are classified into three types [7]: (1) Syntactic, which includes: word/POS tag n-grams, phrase patterns, punctuation, (2) Semantic, this type includes: polarity tags, appraisal groups, semantic orientation, and (3) Stylistic, which is concerned with lexical and structural measures of style.

A considerable amount of previous work has been published on Arabic sentiment analysis. This literature review is focused on the studies that categorized the Arabic tweets into specific domains using different classification techniques. Table 2 presents and summarizes the latest work in this area according to the classification techniques and extracted features. It also states whether the study has been applied to MSA or DA.

In 2012, a study [45] proposed a model that used two machine learning approaches, NB and SVM. The researchers used a list of stop words from Egyptian dialect in the preprocessing step. They selected 1000 tweets that hold only one opinion, not sarcastic, subjective and from different topics. SAMAR, is another proposed tool in the same year [3]. It is also a machine learning system for Arabic social media texts. The researchers tested their tool in four different genres: chat, Twitter, Web forums, and Wikipedia talk pages. For Twitter, a corpus of 3015 Arabic tweets has been collected that has a mixture of MSA and DA.

Next year, 2013, a new study [7] annotated 4000 tweets from different popular topics: technology, politics, religion, and sports, respectively. The study found that it is better to use unigrams with tweets. Another study has also been presented in 2013 [33] that built a baseline system for performing subjectivity and sentiment analysis for Arabic news and tweets. MT has been employed to translate an existing English subjectivity lexicon to build large coverage lexicons

Table 2. Analysis of previous work on Arabic sentiment analysis for Twitter data.

Ref.	Year	Tweets	Features	Classification techniques	Performance	MSA or DA
[45]	2012	1000	Unigrams and bigrams	NB and SVM	SVM Acc 72.6%	Egyptian DA
[3]	2012	3015	Morphological, POS tags, and adjective polarity lexicon	SVM-light	Acc of 71.85%	MSA and DA
[7]	2013	4000	N-Grams and unigrams	SVM, NB, MaxEnt, Bayes Net, and J48 D-tree	SVM Acc 86.38%	-
[33]	2013	2300	Stem-level, sentence-level, and tweet specific	NB	Acc 80.6%	MSA and DA
[4]	2013	2000	Unigram	Supervised (SVM, NB, KNN, and D-tree) and unsupervised ML	Acc 87.5%	MSA and Jordanian DA
[16]	2013	500	POS tag with weight	Unsupervised approach	Acc 83.8%	Egyptian DA
[15]	2014	25000	-	NB, k-NN, SVM	NB (76.78%)	MSA and Jordanian DA
[39]	2014	340,000	Opinions-oriented words extraction	D-tree and SVM	Prec 76%, recall 61%	Kuwaiti DA
[8]	2015	900	Giving weights to words	Unsupervised	Acc 86.89%	MSA
[25]	2015	1000	Linguistically and syntactically motivated	Semi-supervised with SVM	Acc 95%	MSA and DA

in Arabic. Another study in 2013 [4] addressed both approaches; supervised and unsupervised, for sentiment analysis for Arabic twitter data. The researchers in this study collected and labeled 2000 tweets in both MSA and Jordanian dialect. One of the key finding of this study was that the unsupervised approach gives much lower accuracy compared to the supervised approach. A group of researchers constructed a lexicon-based tool to analyze sentiments of egyptian dialectical tweets in 2013 [16]. Every word in the lexicon has been assigned weights that determined semantic orientation based on the sentiment lexicon.

In 2014, an Arabic sentiment analysis tool was presented in [15] which contains a lexicon that maps Jordanian Dialect to MSA, a lexicon that maps Arabizi words to MSA, and a lexicon of emoticons. In the same year, SVM classifier has also been tested on a corpus of 340,000 tweets in Kuwait [39]. This system handeled Kuwaiti dialect which used Opinions-Oriented words extraction features to extract the opinion-oriented words through language resources that they have been developed for the Kuwaiti dialect.

Recently in 2015, another tool that used an unsupervised (lexicon-based) approach has been introduced [8]. This tool has access to a sentiment lexicon that contains a set of words along with their sentiment values. A sentiment lexicon of about 120,000 Arabic terms has been constructed through three steps: collect Arabic stems, translate them into English, and use online English sentiment lexicons to determine the sentiment value of each word. They stated that the proposed tool performed better than the keyword-based approach.

Finally, a research [25] studied an Arabic idioms/saying phrases lexicon to improve the sentiment polarity in Arabic sentences has gained a high accuracy around 95%. This study used semi-supervised approach with using SVM classifier to analyze MSA and Egyptian dialectal Arabic tweets and microblogs, such as hotel reservation, and product reviews.

4   Conclusion

This paper has presented the challenging task of sentiment analysis and opinion mining on Twitter data in the domain of the Arabic language. We reviewed numerous studies that analyzed people's opinions in English and other Indo-European languages. However, we found few studies that analyzed people's opinions in the Arabic language.

This current investigation examined the prior studies to determine how the sentiment analysis was applied to a high volume of Arabic tweets. This study aimed to help newcomers to this field understand the different aspects posed by the research within the past few years. A sophisticated categorization of a large number of recent articles has been reviewed in this study to cover a wide variety of sentiment analysis in the Arabic language.

One of the main findings of this review shows that there is still a great need for extensive research to gain a better understanding of Arabic dialects in addition to further MSA studies. Up to the time of writing this literature review, no single system existed that could handle all Arabic dialects and MSA with high accuracy. This has created a wide gap in this field for researchers to address in subsequent investigations.

This study demonstrated a need for building and publishing additional lexicon Arabic resources with different genres and various dialects for both the public and research community. Assembling all lexicons for Arabic dialects from different geographical areas in the Middle East in one lexicon repository is a worthy goal.

Recently, growing Internet usage has produced a new written form called Arabizi. This type of the Arabic language is derived from the spoken Arabic dialects and is written using Latin letters and numbers. Detecting and analyzing tweets written in Arabizi has not been thoroughly studied. Knowing that Arabizi has been used widely by teen-agers, it is important to conduct future studies on this type of language and to include young researchers and annotators to bridge the gap.

References

1. Abdul-Mageed, M., Diab, M.T.: AWATIF: a multi-genre corpus for modern standard Arabic subjectivity and sentiment analysis. In: LREC, pp. 3907–3914. Citeseer (2012)
2. Abdul-Mageed, M., Diab, M.T.: SANA: a large scale multi-genre, multi-dialect lexicon for Arabic subjectivity and sentiment analysis. In: LREC, pp. 1162–1169 (2014)
3. Abdul-Mageed, M., Kübler, S., Diab, M.: SAMAR: a system for subjectivity and sentiment analysis of Arabic social media. In: Proceedings of the 3rd Workshop in Computational Approaches to Subjectivity and Sentiment Analysis, pp. 19–28. Association for Computational Linguistics (2012)
4. Abdulla, N.A., Ahmed, N.A., Shehab, M.A., Al-Ayyoub, M.: Arabic sentiment analysis: lexicon-based and corpus-based. In: 2013 IEEE Jordan Conference on Applied Electrical Engineering and Computing Technologies (AEECT), pp. 1–6. IEEE (2013)
5. Agarwal, A., Biadsy, F., Mckeown, K.R.: Contextual phrase-level polarity analysis using lexical affect scoring and syntactic n-grams. In: Proceedings of the 12th Conference of the European Chapter of the Association for Computational Linguistics, pp. 24–32. Association for Computational Linguistics (2009)
6. Agarwal, A., Xie, B., Vovsha, I., Rambow, O., Passonneau, R.: Sentiment analysis of Twitter data. In: Proceedings of the Workshop on Languages in Social Media, pp. 30–38. Association for Computational Linguistics (2011)
7. Ahmed, S., Pasquier, M., Qadah, G.: Key issues in conducting sentiment analysis on Arabic social media text. In: 2013 9th International Conference on Innovations in Information Technology (IIT), pp. 72–77. IEEE (2013)
8. Al-Ayyoub, M., Essa, S.B., Alsmadi, I.: Lexicon-based sentiment analysis of Arabic tweets. Int. J. Soc. Netw. Min. **2**(2), 101–114 (2015)
9. Alexandra, B., Marco, T.: Multilingual sentiment analysis using machine translation. In: Proceedings of the 3rd Workshop in Computational Approaches to Subjectivity and Sentiment Analysis, pp. 52–60 (2012)
10. Alhumoud, S.O., Altuwaijri, M.I., Albuhairi, T.M., Alohaideb, W.M.: Survey on Arabic sentiment analysis in Twitter. Int. Sci. Index **9**(1), 364–368 (2015)
11. Alqudsi, A., Omar, N., Shaker, K.: Arabic machine translation: a survey. Artif. Intell. Rev. **42**(4), 549–572 (2014)
12. Assiri, A., Emam, A., Aldossari, H.: Arabic sentiment analysis: a survey. Int. J. Adv. Comput. Sci. Appl. **1**(6), 75–85 (2015)
13. Bautin, M., Vijayarenu, L., Skiena, S.: International sentiment analysis for news and blogs. In: ICWSM (2008)
14. Boiy, E., Hens, P., Deschacht, K., Moens, M.F.: Automatic sentiment analysis in on-line text. In: ELPUB, pp. 349–360 (2007)
15. Duwairi, R., Marji, R., Sha'ban, N., Rushaidat, S.: Sentiment analysis in Arabic tweets. In: 2014 5th International Conference on Information and Communication Systems (ICICS), pp. 1–6. IEEE (2014)
16. El-Beltagy, S.R., Ali, A.: Open issues in the sentiment analysis of Arabic social media: a case study. In: 2013 9th International Conference on Innovations in Information Technology (IIT), pp. 215–220. IEEE (2013)
17. ElSahar, H., El-Beltagy, S.R.: Building large arabic multi-domain resources for sentiment analysis. In: Gelbukh, A. (ed.) CICLing 2015. LNCS, vol. 9042, pp. 23–34. Springer, Cham (2015). doi:10.1007/978-3-319-18117-2_2

18. Eviatar, Z., Ibrahim, R.: Why is it hard to read Arabic? In: Saiegh-Haddad, E., Joshi, R.M. (eds.) Handbook of Arabic literacy, pp. 77–96. Springer, Netherlands (2014)
19. Farra, N., Challita, E., Assi, R.A., Hajj, H.: Sentence-level and document-level sentiment mining for Arabic texts. In: 2010 IEEE International Conference on Data Mining Workshops, pp. 1114–1119. IEEE (2010)
20. Guyon, I., Elisseeff, A.: An introduction to feature extraction. In: Guyon, I., Nikravesh, M., Gunn, S., Zadeh, L.A. (eds.) Feature Extraction, pp. 1–25. Springer, Heidelberg (2006)
21. Habash, N., Roth, R.M.: CATiB: The Columbia Arabic treebank. In: Proceedings of the ACL-IJCNLP 2009 Conference Short Papers, pp. 221–224. Association for Computational Linguistics (2009)
22. Habash, N.Y.: Introduction to Arabic natural language processing. Synth. Lect. Hum. Lang. Technol. **3**(1), 1–187 (2010)
23. Hajic, J., Smrz, O., Zemánek, P., Šnaidauf, J., Beška, E.: Prague Arabic dependency treebank: development in data and tools. In: Proceedings of the NEMLAR International Conference on Arabic Language Resources and Tools, pp. 110–117 (2004)
24. Harrag, F.: Estimating the sentiment of Arabic social media contents: a survey. In: 5th International Conference on Arabic Language Processing (2014)
25. Ibrahim, H.S., Abdou, S.M., Gheith, M.: Sentiment analysis for modern standard Arabic and colloquial. arXiv preprint, arXiv:1505.03105 (2015)
26. Kamps, J., Marx, M., Mokken, R.J., De Rijke, M.: Using wordnet to measure semantic orientations of adjectives. In: LREC, vol. 4, pp. 1115–1118. Citeseer (2004)
27. Khairnar, J., Kinikar, M.: Machine learning algorithms for opinion mining and sentiment classification. Int. J. Sci. Res. Publ. **3**(6), 1–6 (2013)
28. Khrisat, A.A., Alharthy, Z.A.: Arabic dialects and classical Arabic language. Adv. Soc. Sci. Res. J. **2**(3), 254–260 (2015)
29. Korayem, M., Crandall, D., Abdul-Mageed, M.: Subjectivity and sentiment analysis of Arabic: a survey. In: Hassanien, A.E., Salem, A.-B.M., Ramadan, R., Kim, T. (eds.) AMLTA 2012. CCIS, vol. 322, pp. 128–139. Springer, Heidelberg (2012). doi:10.1007/978-3-642-35326-0_14
30. Kouloumpis, E., Wilson, T., Moore, J.: Twitter sentiment analysis: the good the bad and the OMG!. ICWSM **11**, 538–541 (2011)
31. Maamouri, M., Bies, A., Buckwalter, T., Mekki, W.: The penn Arabic treebank: building a large-scale annotated Arabic corpus. NEMLAR Conf. Arabic Lang. Res. Tools **27**, 466–467 (2004)
32. Mohammad, S.M., Kiritchenko, S., Zhu, X.: NRC-Canada: building the state-of-the-art in sentiment analysis of tweets. In: Second Joint Conference on Lexical and Computational Semantics (*SEM), vol. 2, pp. 321–327 (2013)
33. Mourad, A., Darwish, K.: Subjectivity and sentiment analysis of modern standard Arabic and Arabic microblogs. In: Proceedings of the 4th Workshop on Computational Approaches to Subjectivity, Sentiment and Social Media Analysis, pp. 55–64 (2013)
34. Nabil, M., Aly, M.A., Atiya, A.F.: LABR: a large scale Arabic book reviews dataset. CoRR, abs/1411.6718 (2014)
35. Nasukawa, T., Yi, J.: Sentiment analysis: capturing favorability using natural language processing. In: Proceedings of the 2nd International Conference on Knowledge Capture, pp. 70–77. ACM (2003)

36. Pang, B., Lee, L.: A sentimental education: sentiment analysis using subjectivity summarization based on minimum cuts. In: Proceedings of the 42nd Annual Meeting on Association for Computational Linguistics, p. 271. Association for Computational Linguistics (2004)
37. Refaee, E., Rieser, V.: An Arabic Twitter corpus for subjectivity and sentiment analysis. In: LREC, pp. 2268–2273 (2014)
38. Rushdi-Saleh, M., Martín-Valdivia, M.T., Ureña-López, L.A., Perea-Ortega, J.M.: OCA: Opinion corpus for Arabic. J. Am. Soc. Inf. Sci. Technol. 62(10), 2045–2054 (2011)
39. Salamah, J.B., Elkhlifi, A.: Microblogging opinion mining approach for Kuwaiti dialect. In: The International Conference on Computing Technology and Information Management (ICCTIM2014), The Society of Digital Information and Wireless Communication, pp. 388–396 (2014)
40. Salameh, M., Mohammad, S.M., Kiritchenko, S.: Sentiment after translation: a case-study on Arabic social media posts. In: Proceedings of the 2015 Conference of the North American Chapter of the Association for Computational Linguistics: Human Language Technologies, pp. 767–777 (2015)
41. Salloum, W., Habash, N.: Dialectal Arabic to English machine translation: pivoting through modern standard Arabic (2013)
42. Selmer, O., Brevik, M.: Classification and visualisation of Twitter sentiment data (2013)
43. Shaalan, K., Habash, N.Y.: Introduction to Arabic natural language processing (synthesis lectures on human language technologies). Mach. Transl. 24(3), 285–289 (2010)
44. Shaalan, K.: Rule-based approach in Arabic natural language processing. Int. J. Inf. Commun. Technol. (IJICT) 3(3), 11–19 (2010)
45. Shoukry, A., Rafea, A.: Sentence-level Arabic sentiment analysis. In: 2012 International Conference on Collaboration Technologies and Systems (CTS), pp. 546–550. IEEE (2012)
46. Singh, S.K., Paul, D.S., Kumar, D.: Sentiment analysis approaches on different data set domain: survey. Int. J. Database Theor. Appl. 7(5), 39–50 (2014)
47. Smola, A., Vishwanathan, S.: Introduction to Machine Learning, vol. 32. Cambridge University, Cambridge (2008)
48. Stehman, S.V.: Selecting and interpreting measures of thematic classification accuracy. Remote Sens. Environ. 62(1), 77–89 (1997)
49. Turney, P.D.: Thumbs up or thumbs down?: semantic orientation applied to unsupervised classification of reviews. In: Proceedings of the 40th Annual Meeting on Association for Computational Linguistics, pp. 417–424. Association for Computational Linguistics (2002)
50. Wilson, T., Hoffmann, P., Somasundaran, S., Kessler, J., Wiebe, J., Choi, Y., Cardie, C., Riloff, E., Patwardhan, S.: Opinionfinder: a system for subjectivity analysis. In: Proceedings of HLT/EMNLP on Interactive Demonstrations, pp. 34–35. Association for Computational Linguistics (2005)
51. Zaidan, O.F., Callison-Burch, C.: Arabic dialect identification. Comput. Linguist. 40(1), 171–202 (2014)

Analyzing User Experience Through Web Opinion Mining

Silvana Aciar[✉] and Gabriela Aciar

Instituto de Informática (IdeI) – FCEFyN, Universidad Nacional de San Juan,
San Juan, Argentina
saciar@unsj-cuim.edu.ar, gaby_aciar@yahoo.com.ar

Abstract. Opinion Mining is related to the analysis of the subjective components that are implicit in the contents generated by the users. Obtaining polarity and sentiment analysis based on characteristics are fundamental objectives in the mining of opinions. Words such as good, bad, broken, not working, no, yes, etc. are taken into account. These words represent the state or condition of the product/service or parts of the product/service.

The user experience is composed of factors and elements related to the perception of the user in the interaction with the product/service. It is important to identify in the text written in the opinions words that help infer factors of perception.

In this work we propose a method to evaluate the user experience and not only the positive or negative opinion from the text written by the user.

Keywords: User experience · Opinion Mining · Ontology

1 Introduction

In recent years there has been a growing use of the Internet, especially Internet Mobil, generating a large amount of data produced by users. Users are overwhelmed with lots of information. A person can spend a lot of time searching for what they need and finishing the search with an option that is not the most appropriate for them.

On the other hand, the growth in the use of the Internet has increased the participation of the consumers in the sites of electronic commerce. Consumers generate comments or product reviews, which helps other buyers in the buying process. User feedback on a product is very important and can have a positive or negative impact on other visitors [1, 2]. Users read carefully the opinions and experiences of other users before making the purchases. There is growing evidence that such forums inform and influence consumers' purchase decisions [3, 4]. Information from user reviews is useful for knowing your preferences and predicting recommendations of new product.

In this paper we propose a method to acquire the user experience from the opinions written on the web. Text mining techniques and ontology are used to process user comments about a product.

© Springer International Publishing AG 2017
G. Meiselwitz (Ed.): SCSM 2017, Part II, LNCS 10283, pp. 203–214, 2017.
DOI: 10.1007/978-3-319-58562-8_16

2 Evaluating User Experience (UX)

The user experience is the process that is developed while the user interacts with a product/service. Often the concept of user experience is confused with usability. Usability is the ease of using a product/service/computer tool in order to achieve a specific goal [5, 6]. In contrast, the user experience is composed of a set of factors and elements related to the perception of the user in the interaction with the product/service. The total benefit to a user is achieved when the product/service is usable and generates a positive experience. The user's experience involves social, cultural, contextual factors, expectations and previous user experiences.

The result is the generation of a positive or negative perception of the product/service. To be successful in accepting a product, not only must know the end users, but also the opinions and perceptions that are having users who are using or used the product/service. The success of a product depends on corrective measures and new versions made based on experience. If they had a good experience, they are happy and continue to consume the product or using the service. If you had a bad experience, do not use the product/service and tell your friends.

The evaluation of the user experience is a basic part of a user-centered design; it allows to know the degree of fulfillment of the expectations of the users. One of the most used methods to evaluate the user experience is by testing the product by the user and then performing a questionnaire to obtain the perceptions in the interaction with the product/service.

Table 1. Scale questionnaire from [8]

Scales	Definition	Items
Attractiveness	General impression towards the product. Do users like or dislike the product? This scale is a pure valence dimension	*annoying/enjoyable, good/bad, unlikable/pleasing, unpleasant/pleasant, attractive/unattractive, friendly/unfriendly*
Efficiency	Is it possible to use the product fast and efficient? Does the user interface looks organized?	*fast/slow, inefficient/efficient, impractical/practical, organized/cluttered*
Perspicuity	Is it easy to understand how to use the product? Is it easy to get familiar with the product?	*not understandable/understandable, easy to learn/difficult to learn, complicated/easy, clear/confusing*
Dependability	Does the user feel in control of the interaction? Is the interaction with the product secure and predicable?	*unpredictable/predictable, obstructive/supportive, secure/not secure, meets expectations/does not meet expectations*
Stimulation	Is it interesting and exciting to use the product? Does the user feel motivated to further use the product?	*valuable/inferior, boring/exiting, not interesting/interesting, motivating/demotivating*
Novelty	Is the design of the product innovative and creative? Does the product grab user's attention?	*creative/dull, inventive/conventional, usual/leading edge, conservative/innovative*

Numerous questionnaires have been developed to obtain information about the experience of users in different domains [7, 8, 9, 10, 11]. For the purpose of this paper, we are interested in the questionnaire developed by María Rauschenberger et al. [8], this questionnaire allows to obtain feelings, impressions and attitudes that arise when a user uses the product/service. The user responds 30 questions after using the product/service. The questionnaire consists of 6 categories to evaluate and 26 items. The categories are: Attractiveness, Efficiency, Perspicuity, Dependability, Stimulation, Novelty.

Table 1 shows the scale, definition and items that make up each scale to be evaluated.

Users should answer the questions by selecting one of the items. Figure 1 shows some values of answers that users should select.

	1 ... 7		
annoying	O ... O	enjoyable	1
not understandable	O ... O	understandable	2
creative	O ... O	dull	3
easy to learn	O ... O	difficult to learn	4
valuable	O ... O	inferior	5
boring	O ... O	exciting	6
not interesting	O ... O	interesting	7
unpredictable	O ... O	predictable	8
fast	O ... O	slow	9
inventive	O ... O	conventional	10
obstructive	O ... O	supportive	11
good	O ... O	bad	12
complicated	O ... O	easy	13
unlikable	O ... O	pleasing	14
usual	O ... O	leading edge	15
unpleasant	O ... O	pleasant	16
secure	O ... O	not secure	17
motivating	O ... O	demotivating	18
meets expectations	O ... O	does not meet expectations	19
inefficient	O ... O	efficient	20
clear	O ... O	confusing	21
impractical	O ... O	practical	22
organized	O ... O	cluttered	23
attractive	O ... O	unattractive	24
friendly	O ... O	unfriendly	25
conservative	O ... O	innovative	26

Fig. 1. Values of answers that users should select for questionnaire of User Experience from [8]

3 Opinion Mining

Obtaining information from the user experience through a questionnaire requires that the product/service be used by them and then answer the questions. There is another source containing the experiences of users with products/services. Those sources are social networks, forums and blog of opinions [12, 13, 14].

Extracting the user experience from these sources allows you to make correct decisions, improve versions of products/services, correct and modify the product/service when they detect a problem based on the customer experience. The essential difference of the information sent in the networks compared to the one obtained by surveys is the immediacy. This information is spontaneous and unstructured, companies and communication agencies understand the value of this information for their business strategies, customer service and trend detection.

However, analyzing all these opinions manually would consume a lot of time, by volume, variety and speed.

Mining of feelings or mining of opinions emerged with the purpose of automating the analysis of information of the opinions of users. Automatic analysis of this information provides the ability to process high volumes of data with minimal delay, high accuracy and consistency, and low cost, which allows human analysis to be complemented in a multitude of scenarios [15, 16].

In the Sentiment Analysis aspects like the opinion, intention and emotion of the users of the social networks are measured. The automatic analysis of the contents in these networks has as main objective to know the opinion of the users about products, services, brands, people and institutions.

Research work in Mining Opinions focuses on three main tasks:

- Polarity detection: allows determining if an opinion is positive or negative. Beyond a basic polarity, you may also want to get a numerical value within a given range.
- Analysis of the feeling based on characteristics: allows determining the different characteristics of the product treated in the opinion or review written by the user, and for each of those characteristics mentioned in the opinion, be able to extract a polarity. This type of approach is much more complex than the detection of polarity.
- Emotion analysis: The analysis of emotions tries to detect in an automatic way the emotions involved in the opinion expressed by the users.

4 Mining User Experience (UX)

Opinion Mining is related to the analysis of the subjective components that are implicit in the contents generated by the users. As mentioned in the previous section, obtaining polarity and analyzing feelings based on characteristics are fundamental objectives in the mining of opinions. In [17] the opinions of users of digital cameras are analyzed. The objective of this work is to obtain a numerical value (positive or negative) for each one of the characteristics of the product from the opinions of the users. For example if in the opinion mentioned "… the battery is bad …" is obtained for the characteristic battery of the camera the value −1.

An ontology is used to structure the information of the opinions. The concepts of ontology are the characteristics of the digital camera. Text mining techniques are used to obtain a set of rules that allow to classify each setence of the opinion in positive and negative. The ontology and a list of related words and synonyms are used to identify which concepts of the ontology are involved in sentences classified as positive and negative (Fig. 2).

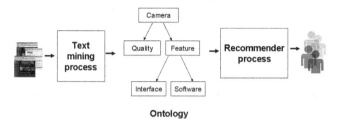

Fig. 2. Sentiment analysis process from [17]

In this work we obtain a positive or negative value for each of the characteristics (Sentiment Analysis) and from these values a unique numerical value of the opinion (Polarity) is inferred. In the whole process, only words such as good, bad, broken, not working, no, yes, etc. are taken into account. These words represent the state or condition of the product or parts of the product.

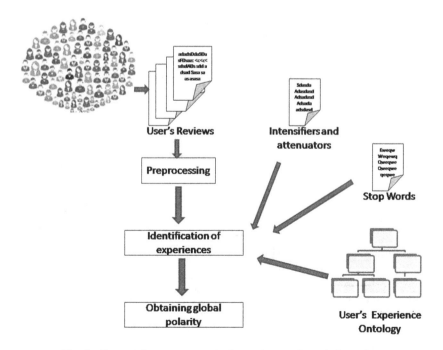

Fig. 3. Text mining process to obtain user's experience information

As mentioned in previous sections, the user experience is composed of factors and elements related to the perception of the user in the interaction with the product/service.

It is important to identify in the text written in the opinions words that help infer factors of perception.

In this work we use the scales of [8] to evaluate the user experience and not only the positive or negative opinion from the text written by the user. Figure 3 shows the process created to obtain user's experiences from text.

The first phase consists in determining those irrelevant words for the analysis in order to debug the text eliminating words and nonsense signs. The elimination was not only based on frequency and length, but on the importance of the word evaluated in the text, for example articles and punctuation marks. It also determines the length of the unit of analysis, the size of the sentences to be analyzed.

The second phase consists in analyzing the polarity of the sentence using an ontology. The ontology represents the categorization of the user experience of [8]. At this stage a syntactic analysis of the sentences is performed to establish a relationship between its components, and the ontology. Each text is segmented into sentences and these into words (tokens). Then words related to the user experience are identified.

4.1 Ontology Construction

The ontology was built based on the user experience questionnaire presented in Sect. 2. It is composed of three parts. The first contains information about the user such as identifier and demographic data. The second part contains information about the product/service that

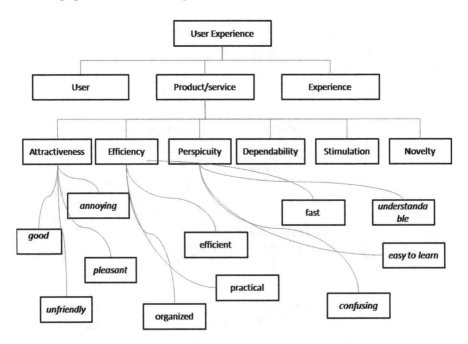

Fig. 4. Ontology representing the user's experience information

is being discussed. This information represents the characteristics of the product/service as described in [17]. The third part represents information about the experience in the interaction with the product/service. In this paper, we will focus on explaining the third part of the ontology. As can be seen in Fig. 4, the concepts involved in ontology are the classification scales of the user experience of [8]. These are Attractiveness, Efficiency, Perspicuity, Dependability, Stimulation and Novelty. These categories represent concepts in the ontology, the concepts are composed of attributes which are the words and related words of the Table 1.

For example the attributes of the Atractiveness concept are annoying, enjoyable, good, bad, unlikable, pleasing, unpleasant, pleasant, attractive, unattractive, friendly, and unfriendly.

The values of these attributes can be positive or negative, representing the polarity of these words.

To expand the text analysis, each attribute contains a list of related words and synonyms created from WordNet [18].

4.2 Prepocessing

In the first step, the pre-processing of the text is performed, where the texts are loaded and the process of eliminating the empty words (stopwords) is applied. This procedure consists of deleting from the text those words that do not contribute relevant information such as articles, auxiliary verbs and words dependent on the context.

In a second step, the text is segmented into sentences, which consists of dividing the text into independent sentences.

In the third step, segmented sentences are fragmented into tokens. In this step you get the most basic elements of a sentence structure, where a token is nothing more than a block of text that is characterized by the function it performs within a sentence.

4.3 Identification of Experiences

Starting from the pre-processed corpus of opinions:

1- Each token is identified in noun, adjective or verbal form, and then look for its occurrence in the ontology developed for this purpose. Each word identified in the ontology has its value of semantic polarity (represented in the value of the attribute in the ontology). In this way, we will obtain the semantic orientation (positive or negative) for each token.
2- Then, all the intensifiers or attenuators of the sentence are identified and the semantic orientation and the token they modify are also calculated. A dictionary of terms identified as intensifiers/attenuators is used for this purpose. There are structures that in themselves contain an enhanced value. Among the most frequent can be mentioned: Up/even/even/not even. You can also find intensifying comparative structures such as "It is easier to use than ...", and the exclamations "How problematic!". For the identification and processing of these structures, dictionaries have been created that contain these grammatical structures.

3- Finally, when the two previous procedures are completed, an ontology instance is obtained for each user's opinion. The instance contains the user experience categories, the terms belonging to each category, the polarity and the intensifiers identified therein.

An example of the instance of the ontology can be seen in the Table 2.

Table 2. Ontology instance

User	Anonymous#2345		
Product	#672839h		
Date	October 15 2015		
Concept	Ontology word	Intensifier	Polarity
Attractiveness	Comfortable	Very (+)	Positive
	Friendly		Positive
Efficiency	Fast		positive
	Timely		
Perspicuity			
Dependability	Secure	Even (+)	positive
Stimulation	Promote		positive
Novelty	Older	Is other than (−)	Negative
	Traditional		Negative

4.4 Obtaining the Polarity of User Experience

This last step consists of the calculation of the polarity of the sentences that summarizes the empirical interpretation that the user wrote in the opinion. We obtain a general value, a numerical quantification that, framed in numerical ranges, aims to give an approximation to the experience contained in the analyzed information. In other words, the goal of calculating the polarity of sentences is to bring interpretation to numerical estimates.

For each category the polarity value is obtained as:

$$PC_i = \begin{cases} .0 \text{ if there is opinions en } c_i \\ \dfrac{\sum\limits_{1}^{n} a_n + \text{int}_n}{n} \end{cases} \tag{1}$$

Where PC_i is the numerical value and its polarity of each category C_i, with $i = 1 \dots 6$. a are the attributes of the category identified in the opinion. a has a value of 1 (positive polarity) or -1 (negative polarity). n is the number of attributes identified in the opinion. Int_n is the intensifier associated with attribute n. In this work int_n can take values 0.5 if it is a positive enhancer or -0.5 if it is a negative enhancer.

For the example the polarity values of the opinion are (see Table 3):

Table 3. Polarity values of the user's experience categories

User	Anonymous#2345			
Product	#672839h			
Date	October 15 2015			
Concept	**Ontology word**	a_n	int_n	PC_i
Attractiveness	Comfortable	*1*	*0,5*	**1,66**
	Friendly	*1*	*0*	
Efficiency	Fast	*1*	*0*	*1*
	Timely	*1*	*0*	
Perspicuity				**0**
Dependability	Secure	*1*	*0,5*	**1,5**
Stimulation	Promote	*1*	*0*	**1**
Novelty	Older	*–1*	*–0,5*	**–1,5**
	Traditional	*–1*	*–0,5*	

5 Case Study

A case study was developed in the tourism domain. The same consisted of obtaining information of the user experience for each category presented in Table 1. The data set available in [19, 20] was used. This consists of more than 100,000 hotel reviews retrieved from TripAdvisor in the period February 2009 to March 2009. These data contain information such as the author, date, content and rating for certain features of the hotel.

From this data set, we only took the opinions of 50 hotels and 1000 reviews for those 100 hotels. From this dataset the process described in Sect. 4 was implemented. Stage 1 is responsible for reading the opinions that were specified in an input xml file and selecting terms that provide useful information, eliminating irrelevant words. Tokens were obtained. We identified the words using dictionaries created for this purpose. Finally, the words representing the user experience were identified and the polarity value was calculated for each category.

	#100	#101	#102	#103	#104	#105	#106	#107	#108	#109	#110	#111	#112	#113	#114	#115	#116	#117	#118	#119	#120	#121	#122	#123	#124
Attractiveness	1,5	-2,5	1,5	1,66	0	-1,25	1	1	1	1,28	0	0	1,2	1	1,2	1,5	2,5	0	1	1,5	0	1,5	0	0	1,28
Efficiency	0	-1,5	1,25	1,28	0	0	-1,5	0	0	1,25	-1,5	2,5	0	0	2,5	0	0	0	1	0	0	1,5	0	0	-1,5
Perspicuity	2,5	1	1	1,25	0	1,5	1	1,28	2,5	1,66	0	2,5	1	1,5	0	1	1	2,5	2,5	1,5	0	1	-1	1	1
Dependability	1	0	1,28	2,5	-1,25	0	0	-1,25	0	0	0	0	-1,5	-1,5	0	0	1	1,25	1,5	1	1,28	1,28	1,5	1,28	-1,5
Stimulation	1	0	1,25	0	0	-1,5	0	0	-1,5	0	1,25	-1,5	0	0	0	1	-1	1	0	1,25	-1	0	-1	0	1
Novelty	2,5	0	1,5	1,28	1,66	1,2	1,66	1,28	0	0	1,28	0	0	1	2,5	0	-1	1	0	1	1	0	1,2	0	0

	#125	#126	#127	#128	#129	#130	#131	#132	#133	#134	#135	#136	#137	#138	#139	#140	#141	#142	#143	#144	#145	#146	#147	#148	#149
Attractiveness	0	0	0	1	1	1	1,5	1,5	-1	1,5	-1,5	0	-1	0	-1	0	-1	-1	2,5	1,5	-1	2,5	1,28	-1,5	-1,5
Efficiency	1	0	1,66	0	-1,5	0	-1,5	0	1,66	0	1,5		1,66	-1,5	0	0	-1,5	-1,5	-1,5	-1,4	2,5	1,25	1,66	1,66	0
Perspicuity	0	0	1,28	1,2	0	0	-1	1,5	-1,3	0	1,28	1,5	-1,5	1,66	1,28	1,66	0	1,5	0	1,5	0	1,5	1,25	0	-1,5
Dependability	0	-1,5	-1,5	0	0	-1,5	0	1	0	1,66	-1,5	1,25	-1,5	-1,4	0	1,25	1,66	1,28	-1,5	1,28	1,28	1,28	1,28	-1,4	0
Stimulation	1	-1	1	-1	1,28	-1,5	1,2	1,66	-1	1,2	1	1	1	0	0	1	0	2,5	-1,5	2,5	-1,5	2,5	0	0	2,5
Novelty	1	-1	1	-1	1	0	1,66	1,5	-1	1,66	1	1,28	1,2	0	-1,5	-1,5	-1,4	0	0	0	0	0	-1,3	0	0

Fig. 5. polarity values obtained for each of the user experience categories of the 50 hotels.

Figure 5 shows the polarity values obtained for each of the user experience categories of the 50 hotels. These values summarize the experience of the users regarding the use of the hotel. Instead of conducting a questionnaire for hotel users, which are not answered many times, the value obtained through this method may indicate to decision makers what to improve based on the experience of previous users.

6   Validation

Below we will present the main measures to evaluate the quality of the classification of the opinions regarding the user experience using the proposed method. For the validation of the results, the same 1000 opinions of the 50 hotels were taken and the opinions were manually tagged.

Each sentence was classified into one of the categories of user experience: Attractiveness, Efficiency, Perspicuity, Dependability, Stimulation and Novelty. Within each category, the sentence was classified according to its polarity (positive or negative) and the intensifiers and attenuators involved in the sentence were identified.

A Accuracy measurement was used to perform the automatic classification validation with the manual (Eq. 2). Accuracy represents the proportion of the total number of predictions that were correct.

$$A = \frac{v}{f + v} \tag{2}$$

Where v is the number of cases where the classification was correct (coincide between manual and automatic classification). f is the number of incorrect cases (mismatch between manual and automatic sorting).

Applying this formula at the level of sentence classification, we obtain the following result:

$$A = \frac{7526}{2594 + 7526} = 0,74$$

The correct classification of 7526 sentence from a set of 10120 indicate the good performance of the proposed method to acquire the user experience automatically.

7   Conclusion

The user experience is composed of factors and elements related to the perception of the user in the interaction with the product/service. Usually, questionnaires are used to obtain information about the experience in the interaction with the product/service.

The use of questionnaires is sometimes frustrating for people. In this work a method was proposed to obtain the same information that would be obtained by questionnaire, but from the opinions voluntarily generated by the users on the web. It is important to identify words written in the text that help infer perceptions. In this work we use the scales of [8] to evaluate the user experience and not only the positive or negative opinion from the text written by the user.

An ontology and dictionaries were created with intensifying and attenuating words and grammatical structures that allow to identify, in addition to the words representing the user experience, the intensity of the perception and orientation of the opinion.

The experiments carried out reflect the importance of the processing of the syntactic analysis of texts taking into account the processing of intensifiers, which significantly increases the classification of the polarity of opinions.

As future work, it is proposed to link the information of the user experience with the information about the sentiment analysis based on characteristics proposed in [17]. We also propose the processing of adversative sentences, which are understood by contradictory sentences. The same sentence can be classified as positive or negative. These cases were detected as common errors in the validation of the results obtained. The proposed method does not know how to handle cases where there is contradiction in the sentence.

References

1. Ambika, P., Rajan, M.B.: Survey on diverse facets and research issues in social media mining. In: International Conference on Research Advances in Integrated Navigation Systems (RAINS), pp. 1–6. IEEE, May 2016
2. Kinholkar, S.A., Waghmare, K.C.: Enhance Digital Marketing Using Sentiment Analysis and End User Behavior (2016)
3. Morris, J.D., Choi, Y., Ju, I.: Are social marketing and advertising communications (SMACs) meaningful? A survey of Facebook user emotional responses, source credibility, personal relevance, and perceived intrusiveness. J. Curr. Issues Res. Advertising 37(2), 165–182 (2016)
4. Valencia-García, R., Colomo-Palacios, R., Alor-Hernández, G.: New trends in opinion mining technologies in the industry. J. Univers. Comput. Sci. 22(5), 605–607 (2016). Journal of UCS Special Issue
5. Nascimento, I., Silva, W., Lopes, A., Rivero, L., Gadelha, B., Oliveira, E., Conte, T.: An empirical study to evaluate the feasibility of a UX and usability inspection technique for mobile applications. In: 28th International Conference on Software Engineering and Knowledge Engineering, California, USA (2016)
6. Nascimento, I., Silva, W., Gadelha, B., Conte, T.: Userbility: a technique for the evaluation of user experience and usability on mobile applications. In: Kurosu, M. (ed.) HCI 2016. LNCS, vol. 9731, pp. 372–383. Springer, Cham (2016). doi:10.1007/978-3-319-39510-4_35
7. Rauschenberger, M., Olschner, S., Cota, M.P., Schrepp, M., Thomaschewski, J.: Measurement of user experience: a Spanish language version of the user experience questionnaire (UEQ). In: 2012 7th Iberian Conference on Information Systems and Technologies (CISTI), pp. 1–6. IEEE, June 2012
8. Cota, M.P., Thomaschewski, J., Schrepp, M., Gonçalves, R.: Efficient measurement of the user experience. Procedia Comput. Sci. 27, 491–498 (2014). A Portuguese version
9. Sauro, J., Lewis, J.R.: Quantifying the User Experience: Practical Statistics for User Research. Morgan Kaufmann, Burlington (2016)
10. Law, E.L.C., van Schaik, P., Roto, V.: Attitudes towards user experience (UX) measurement. Int. J. Hum Comput Stud. 72(6), 526–541 (2014)

11. Park, J., Han, S.H., Kim, H.K., Cho, Y., Park, W.: Developing elements of user experience for mobile phones and services: survey, interview, and observation approaches. Hum. Factors Ergon. Manuf. Serv. Ind. **23**(4), 279–293 (2013)
12. Santosh, D.T., Babu, K.S., Prasad, S.D.V., Vivekananda, A.: Opinion Mining of Online Product Reviews from Traditional LDA Topic Clusters using Feature Ontology Tree and Sentiwordnet (2016)
13. Balazs, J.A., Velásquez, J.D.: Opinion mining and information fusion: a survey. Inform. Fusion **27**, 95–110 (2016)
14. Clavel, C., Callejas, Z.: Sentiment analysis: from opinion mining to human-agent interaction. IEEE Trans. Affect. Comput. **7**(1), 74–93 (2016)
15. Nakov, P., Ritter, A., Rosenthal, S., Sebastiani, F., Stoyanov, V.: SemEval-2016 task 4: sentiment analysis in Twitter. In: Proceedings of SemEval, pp. 1–18 (2016)
16. Cambria, E.: Affective computing and sentiment analysis. IEEE Intell. Syst. **31**(2), 102–107 (2016)
17. Aciar, S., Aciar, G., Zhang, D.: Comparing product specifications to solve the cold start problem in a recommender system. In: Computing Conference (CLEI), 2016 XLII Latin American, pp. 1–8. IEEE, October 2016
18. Jayakody, J.R.K.C.: Natural language processing framework: WordNet based sentimental analyzer (2016)
19. Wang, H., Lu, Y., Zhai, C.X.: Latent aspect rating analysis without aspect keyword supervision. In: The 17th ACM SIGKDD Conference on Knowledge Discovery and Data Mining (KDD 2011), pp. 618–626 (2011)
20. Wang, H., Lu, Y., Zhai, C.X.: Latent aspect rating analysis on review text data: a rating regression approach. In: The 16th ACM SIGKDD Conference on Knowledge Discovery and Data Mining (KDD 2010), pp. 783–792 (2010)

A Review on Corpus Annotation for Arabic Sentiment Analysis

Latifah Almuqren[2,3], Arwa Alzammam[1(✉)], Shahad Alotaibi[2], Alexandra Cristea[3], and Sarah Alhumoud[1]

[1] Computer Science Department, Al-Imam Muhammad ibn Saud Islamic University,
Riyadh, Saudi Arabia
asalzammam@sm.imamu.edu.sa,sohumoud@imamu.edu.sa
[2] Computer Science Department, Princess Nourah University, Riyadh, Saudi Arabia
shahdtaleb92@gmail.com
[3] Computer Science Department, Warwick University, Coventry, UK
almuqren@wawick.ac.uk,a.i.cristea@warwick.ac.uk

Abstract. Mining publicly available data for meaning and value is an important research direction within social media analysis. Even for automatically analyzing collected textual data, a manual effort is needed for a successful machine learning algorithm to effectively classify text. Corpus annotation is labeling datasets with appropriate classes. There is a lack in the Arabic annotated corpus although Arabic is one of the languages that shows a fast uptake of sentiment analysis research, despite limited resources and scarce annotated corpora. In this paper, we review the most recent work on annotation carried out for papers focusing on Arabic sentiment analysis, between the years of 2010 and 2016.

Keywords: Sentiment analysis · Arabic corpus · Social media analysis

1 Introduction

Today, social media has become a key part of many people's life. Social media provides means of communication that allow people to share their sentiments, opinions, and thoughts. By mining the content of social media, targeting opinions, valuable trends and feedback about topics or products could be inferred. One of the known techniques for mining and analyzing social media is *Sentiment Analysis* (SA). SA involves a number of areas, such as natural language processing and text analytics. Its goal is to capture the user sentiment about many aspects, for instance, to detect product preferences and guide company strategies [1].

Whilst sentiment analysis is a current hot topic, especially in the English language, SA for Arabic text remains an inadequately researched area, due to the unique nature and structure of the Arabic language [2]. For instance, whilst Modern Standard Arabic (MSA) is the formal Arabic language that is used in news and media, people in social media rarely use MSA in their daily interaction. Instead, they use dialectal Arabic, which is different from a region to another even in the same country. This variety of forms of the Arabic dialectal written language adds to the challenges of the Arabic SA [3].

© Springer International Publishing AG 2017
G. Meiselwitz (Ed.): SCSM 2017, Part II, LNCS 10283, pp. 215–225, 2017.
DOI: 10.1007/978-3-319-58562-8_17

For the same reason, there is a lack of resources and corpora for Arabic SA [3, 4], and this is the area this paper targets. In order to perform sentiment analysis, a crucial and potentially expensive (in that it is mostly manual) step is needed, which is *corpus annotation*. Leech [5] defined this step as assigning interpretative information to a document collection for mining use. Leech [5] coined the interpretative information as *linguistic information* and he distinguished between the corpus and *interpretative information*. The importance of the annotation process results from making a machine-readable version of the meta-data, by annotating the corpus, for training a machine learning classifier [4].

There are dissimilar levels of corpus annotation, e.g. *syntactic annotation*, which is the process of parsing every sentence in the corpus and labeling it with its structure grammar, *POS tagging* - that is, labeling every word in the corpus with its appropriate part-of-speech label. At the semantic level, several labels are used in the annotation process (positive, negative and neutral). Semantic annotation is used for sentiment mining purpose [6]. Positive and negative sentiments can occur within the same tweet, which is considered a challenge to the annotation process [6].

The three main approaches used to annotate a corpus are first, *manual annotation by individuals* where the annotation is done by a small number of individuals ranging between 2 and 5 annotators. Second, *crowdsourcing* approach which depends on a large number of people as annotators with the assistance of annotation tools. Third, an *Automatic approach* which is annotation inferred from the dataset itself like reviews star-rating. To assure high quality of the first approach, selected annotators should show some linguistic proficiency in the dataset language under consideration. Also, precision and speed, are important factors when assigning annotators [5]. In addition, to ensure consistency between annotators minimizing bias and ambiguity, clear labeling guidelines need to be provided and reinforced.

This paper provides a comprehensive review of the recent work on annotation and its related processes and procedures for Arabic corpora, highlighting the gaps and similarities in the annotation process in the considered research. The report starts by reviewing the methodology that was used in this research. Following, it provides the annotation procedures elicited. Finally, a conclusion is drawn.

2 Methodology

In this paper, we reviewed papers on the topic of Arabic corpora annotation following the methodology in [7], focusing on several angles, such as the *research corpora type, annotation process*, and *verification methodology*. The aim of this review is to highlight the gaps and similarities in the annotation process in the recent research. Starting with comprehensive searches in different electronic databases, such as Google Scholar, ERIC, Science Direct, Sage, and Springer Link, a total of 56 papers in annotation and sentiment analysis were collected, published between the years of 2010 and 2016. The search terms used in the search process were: "Annotation", "Arabic annotation", "sentiment analysis", "Twitter annotation", "Arabic sentiment analysis". The results were then filtered to papers focusing on Arabic Sentiment Analysis, including conference proceedings, peer-reviewed articles and conference workshops. Several papers concentrating on annotating for different languages other than Arabic were eliminated, and thus 27 papers remained. This result highlights the scarcity challenge affecting Arabic sentiment analysis work and points to the need for renewed efforts of the research community in this area.

3   Arabic Corpora Annotation for Sentiment Analysis

This section explains the different stages in the annotation process as encountered in the considered literature. The first subsection explains the different corpus types that are annotated by the authors. The second subsection explains the annotation processes and procedures with regards to the number of annotators' specialty and annotation type. The third subsection is focused on the verification process that follows the annotation, to ensure the quality of annotation.

3.1   Corpus Type

Resources in the Arabic language like corpora, lexicons and datasets are still scarce, compared to other languages that have a high user-generated content on the web [8, 9]. Creating an annotated corpus is a crucial step for sentiment analysis [10], as the quality of the annotation has a direct relation to the accuracy of the classifier. Several attempts have been made to accomplishing Arabic corpora annotation using different types of data during recent research in the period under consideration, between 2010 and 2016. The majority of papers (16 papers, see Table 1) focused on Twitter as a corpus. This result conforms to the body of work in other languages - mainly English - on the social web, and especially Twitter annotation and sentiment analysis [11].

Table 1. Reviewed corpora types

Corpora	Paper count	Paper
Twitter	16	[2, 10, 14, 18–30]
Facebook	1	[19]
News	3	[13, 16, 17]
Penn Arabic Treebank	1	[16]
Reviews and comments	7	[8–10, 12–15]
Chat website	1	[18]
Web forum	2	[8, 18]

Other studies (7 of them) annotated *reviews and comments*. Reviews were mainly from restaurants, movies, books, and products as in [8–10, 12–15]. Comments are scraped from hotel reservation or TV programs' websites [8, 10, 14, 15]. It is interesting to see that reviews and comments are, whilst still popular as a research area, being of lesser interest than Twitter. Again, this conforms with trends for languages such as English [11]. The rest of the literature used other kinds of websites: news [13, 16, 17]; chat websites [18], web forum [8, 18], the Penn Arabic Treebank [16] and Facebook [19].

Another characteristic of the collected corpora that should be mentioned is the different varieties of the Arabic language used in each corpus, such as MSA and dialectal Arabic [3]. As mentioned earlier, MSA is used in books, magazines articles, and news, while in social media people use spoken dialects that are rarely written or addressed formally before [30]. Dialects used are different from country to country and within the same country. This difference affects the collected corpora since a corpus built from one dialect is not necessarily useful for analyzing datasets in other dialects. The same can be applied on MSA and dialects. Also, we can see a pattern where there is a clear relationship between the type of corpus being annotated and the variety of Arabic language used. A corpus built from the news is mainly written in MSA, such as [13, 16]. While a corpus collected from Social media, for example, Twitter, is written in dialect [28]. Yet, there is not a definite rule about a person having to use one form or the other for the Arabic language on the web. While some people prefer to write in MSA, others like to write in dialects. Therefore, there are some cases where a corpus built from one source can have both MSA as well as dialectal Arabic texts inside [10].

Figure 1 shows the varieties of Arabic language used to build the collected corpora. They comprise MSA, MSA and Dialectal Arabic, Dialectal Arabic, Saudi Dialect and Egyptian Dialect.

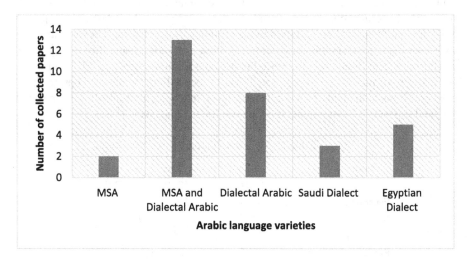

Fig. 1. Varieties of Arabic language used in collected corpora

As shown in the figure, we can see that the researchers conducted their research mainly on corpora that contain MSA and dialectal Arabic, within 13 research papers out of the total retrieved papers. Moreover, out of these 13 papers, eight of them specified using a specific dialect, as in Saudi or Egyptian dialect, for a total number of 3 and 5 papers, respectively.

There are only two papers depending on a corpus that is written mainly in MSA, which are the papers that used the news as their corpus. However, there are around eight papers which annotated a corpus without specification of the dialects of Arabic language used, they either used the term "dialectal Arabic" or "Arabic" in their description of the annotated corpus. Therefore, they are categorized under "Dialectal Arabic" in the figure. Table 2 shows the research papers and the different varieties of Arabic language being annotated in their corpus.

Table 2. The different varieties of Arabic language used in each corpus of the collected papers

Arabic language form	Paper count	Paper
MSA	2	[13, 16]
MSA and Dialectal Arabic	13	[2, 10, 14, 15, 17, 18, 20, 21, 23, 24, 26, 29, 31]
Saudi Dialect	3	[17, 21, 29]
Egyptian Dialect	5	[10, 18, 25, 26, 28]
Dialectal Arabic	8	[8, 9, 12, 19, 22, 27, 30, 32]

3.2 Annotation Process

In the collection of papers on Arabic corpus annotation we have studied, each research adopts a different way to annotate the dataset they are processing. In this section, we summarize these methods, including defining data, such as the *number of annotators* needed and the *labels* used in each research.

Annotation can be done on different levels, such as *sentence level*, *word level* or both. Also, there are different ways that can be adopted for annotating a dataset; for example, the annotation can be done *manually* by a number of native speakers. This means that they are asked to read through the dataset and annotate each sentence or word (depending on the level of annotation). Then they have to assign a label for each sentence or word, based on their perceived sentiment, such as positive, negative, neutral, objective, mixed or other different labels. These labels are normally given to them beforehand. Another way to annotate a dataset is to use the human resources that are available on the Internet, through what is called *crowdsourcing*. Among the papers we covered in this survey, 82% annotated their dataset manually, and the remaining 18% used crowdsourcing tools.

Out of the 22 papers that used the manual annotation method, 20 papers annotated the corpora on *a sentence level*. That is 91% of the total number of the manually annotated corpora. Only two papers, [21, 29], conducted their annotation manually on a *word level*. The preference towards sentence level annotation is possibly due to it being simpler to perform, and annotators are potentially able to deal with issues such as sarcasm and a mixture of different and opposite sentimental words in the same sentence. Moreover, it is a faster method, easier to process by human annotators.

Another research [10] used the manual method involving five Arabic native speakers. Three of them were linguistic specialists. Since in this research they built a lexicon for Arabic idioms and proverbs, linguistic specialists were hence needed to provide accurate annotations for tweets that contained these idioms.

The annotation method using crowdsourcing tools on a sentence level was implemented by researchers in [8, 19, 23, 24, 28]. Thus, the annotation was carried out by volunteers on the web. Annotators were asked to register their usernames and passwords.

Then they annotated the set of tweets that were shown to them, one by one. This method, clearly gaining popularity with Arabic SA researchers as well as researchers for other languages, is a relatively easy method, involving the power of the crowds, and safety in numbers. However, this method can suffer in accuracy, as the knowledge or even interest and dedication of such annotators is not guaranteed [33].

An interesting different way to annotate the dataset involves using *games*, as implemented in [8]. In this research, the players of the game were asked to annotate a set of sentences which was given to them, as they advanced through the levels of the game. Such game-based methods, whilst interesting, are more difficult and expensive to implement, potentially more time-consuming for the annotators, and as a result, are not very frequently encountered, in Arabic SA or elsewhere. The paper [28] can be considered as a special case where the researchers used crowdsourcing tool with a small number of annotators, three in particular. They used the Amazon Mechanical Turk service crowdsourcing tool using an API called Boto [34]. The tool was used to facilitate the annotation process and to reduce time and workload for the annotators. Table 3 summarizes the number of papers and the type and level of annotation process it uses.

Table 3. Annotation types and levels

Annotation process type	Paper count	Paper
Manually by individuals on a sentence level	19	[2, 9, 10, 13–18, 20, 22, 25–27, 30–32, 35, 36]
Manually by individuals on a word level	2	[21, 29]
Crowdsourcing tools on a sentence level	5	[8, 19, 23, 24, 28]
Automatic annotation	1	[12]

The number of annotators also differ between the covered papers. Out of the 27 papers under consideration, nine depended on a total of three native Arabic speakers to annotate their dataset [14, 19, 22, 24, 26–28, 32, 36]. Authors in [10] annotated their dataset with the help of five people. Moreover, six papers did the annotation with only two annotators as in [2, 16, 18, 20, 23, 30]. Authors in [12] which is under the "Automatic Annotation" section in Fig. 2 used a site for reviewing books, called "Goodreads" [37]. To help them with the annotation process, where they collected 16486 user reviews and decided the polarity of the comment based on the number of stars given for a review. That is, no actual annotation is done here, instead, each review label is inferred directly from the star count associated with it. The percentage of annotators is summarized in Fig. 2 which shows the number of annotators for the papers discussed previously, and the percentage for each category.

The rest of the 10 research papers under the "Crowdsourcing" section in Fig. 2 depended on reviews corpora to rate movies, books or hotels or used crowdsourcing tools. This could be a reason why the papers did not mention the number of users helping with the annotation process. Another factor that may have resulted in the omission of the number of annotators in those research papers, is the fact that the annotation process was done by random users on the web, with potentially unknown characteristics, and it

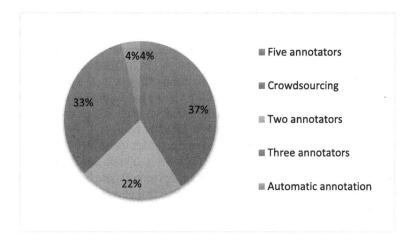

Fig. 2. Number of annotators in the body or research papers retrieved.

is even possible that their number was unknown in some cases. As mentioned, in [8] the authors developed a game, in which the players were annotating the data by playing. Specifically, the players could not move to the next level, until all team members agreed on the same result of annotation. This approach could potentially enforce the agreement and hinder the game experience, by motivating the players to quickly select whatever makes them agree with the other players, just to move onto the next level.

3.3 Verification

The accuracy of the annotation results has a great impact on the sentiment analysis quality. The labels have to be verified manually or by calculating a coefficient. Different kinds of verification methods are used with the annotation methods, ranging from computing a simple *similarity index*, by counting the number of agreements, to more elaborate and accurate methods that eliminate agreements that occur by chance only. For instance, the *Kappa coefficient* is used with categorical data, to measure reliability between two observers assigning cases to a set of k categories [38].

In this subsection, we discuss the verification measures that have been adopted by the authors under consideration in this survey. Some studies implemented the Kappa coefficient and others used manual ways, like deleting any data that has contradicting opinions, moderating the opinions with the help of another annotator, or promoting discussions between the annotators. That is, in the case of a disagreement between two annotators, a third one is brought in, and the *majority-voting principle* is used to finalize the decision, as in [22, 26, 27]. The majority-voting was also used to choose the final label in [19, 23, 24].

In [24] there are two groups of annotators: supervisor annotators, which are three, with one of them the paper author; and non-supervisor annotators, which are the users of their tool. The observation was considered rated correctly if there was a match between the labels assigned by the supervisor annotators and the labels assigned by then on-supervisor annotator.

In papers [14, 16, 18, 20, 32, 36], the authors used the Kappa coefficient to measure the inter-annotators agreements. The results of the Kappa coefficient in [36] is 0.454, in [32] the average is 0.45, in [16] the generic set had an agreement of 0.321, while on the topic-specific set it was 0.397. In [14] it is about 0.96, in [20] the average is 0.51 and in [18] there are four data sets that are listed sequentially with their agreement results: DARDASHA has 0.89, TAGREED has 0.85, TAHRIR has 0.85, and MONTADA has 0.88. Whilst there is no clear agreement on the semantics of the Kappa coefficient range, many researchers agree that a coefficient below 0.2 is poor, and one above 0.75 as excellent [30, 39], showing thus that the analyzed research varies significantly in inter-annotator agreement, and thus inaccuracy. For conflict resolution, in [2, 10], if the annotators disagreed initially, they would discuss it and agree to choose between their labels. If they could not choose one, then they would discard that observation. This procedure, of course, affects the size of the corpus.

In a similar vein, the authors in [17] deleted any review that had no specific orientation towards positive or negative. In the research carried out by [19], the verification process was not mentioned. However, data had to be annotated by at least three users of their annotation tool and users were able to delete any empty data, duplicated data or any data written using English letters. In [28], they used a public tool for sets of three annotators, but if there was a conflict between them in annotating an observation, the respective observation was also ignored. All papers that annotated their corpora based on the review rating, as in number or stars or points, like [9, 12, 31] did not mention the method of verification - and it is not clear if they had any at all.

As can be seen from the methods of verification involved, there is a variety in their approach, but, more worryingly, there is a variety in the level of accuracy that is resulting, including potentially labeled corpora with no verification.

4 Conclusion

Arabic is a rich morphology language with scarce resources and corpora. This research provides a review on the recent annotation approaches carried out in the process of Arabic Sentiment Analysis that encompassed the creation of Arabic-language corpora. The review covered recent studies, published between the years 2010 and 2016, which resulted in only 27 papers. This highlights the need of renewing the efforts towards producing more good quality research in the SA area in general, and for Arabic corpora in particular. In the reviewed papers, the annotation process is carried out via three main approaches: manually by individuals, crowdsourcing, and automatic annotation. In this review, 85% of the literature under consideration performed manual annotation, the remaining using crowdsourcing tools. Moreover, for the sentiment analysis study, we found that the highest annotated corpus was the micro-blogging platform Twitter 56%, other platforms 18% covering Facebook, Newspapers and the Penn Arabic Treebank. The rest of the corpora considered were reviews and comments 26%. The methodology applied in the various papers we reviewed showed a marked lack of consistency. Reviewing the papers, we noted that data was reported unsystematically, with some data missing in some papers e.g., the data on the important verification methods. Our study shows thus very clearly the urgency in supporting more systematic research in the SA area. In particular, there is a clear need to build and provide good quality Arabic benchmark annotated corpora that researchers can use directly, without the burden of going through the stage of annotation for each individual research, separately. This will provide more space to focus on other important research areas, like building better classifiers, stemmers, and lexicons for the Arabic language, and tackling problems like dialectal Arabic language processing.

Acknowledgements. This work was partially funded by Deanship of Scientific Research at Imam Muhammad ibn Saud Islamic University, Riyadh, Saudi Arabia on 2015 with grant number 360911.

References

1. Kaur, A., Gupta, V.: A survey on sentiment analysis and opinion mining techniques. J. Emerg. Technol. Web Intell. **5**, 367–371 (2013)
2. Mourad, A., Darwish, K.: Subjectivity and sentiment analysis of modern standard Arabic and Arabic microblogs. In: Proceedings of the 4th Workshop on Computational Approaches to Subjectivity, Sentiment and Social Media Analysis, pp. 55–64 (2013)
3. Habash, N.Y.: Introduction to Arabic natural language processing. Synth. Lect. Hum. Lang. Technol. **3**, 1–187 (2010)
4. Al-Twairesh, N., Al-Khalifa, H., Al-Salman, A.: Subjectivity and sentiment analysis of Arabic: trends and challenges. In: 2014 IEEE/ACS 11th International Conference on Computer Systems and Applications (AICCSA), pp. 148–155. IEEE (2014)
5. Leech, G.: Corpus annotation schemes. Literary Linguist. Comput. **8**, 275–281 (1993)
6. Aggarwal, C.C., Zhai, C.: Mining Text Data. Springer Science & Business Media, New York (2012)
7. alOwisheq, A., alHumoud, S., alTwairesh, N., alBuhairi, T.: Arabic sentiment analysis resources: a survey. In: Meiselwitz, G. (ed.) SCSM 2016. LNCS, vol. 9742, pp. 267–278. Springer, Cham (2016). doi:10.1007/978-3-319-39910-2_25
8. Al-Subaihin, A.A., Al-Khalifa, H.S., Al-Salman, A.S.: A proposed sentiment analysis tool for modern Arabic using human-based computing. In: Proceedings of the 13th International Conference on Information Integration and Web-Based Applications and Services, pp. 543–546. ACM (2011)
9. Saleh, M., Martín-Valdivia, M.T., Ureña-López, L.A., Perea-Ortega, M.J.: OCA: Opinion Corpus for Arabic. J. Am. Soc. Inf. Sci. Technol. **62**, 2045–2054 (2011)
10. Ibrahim, H., Abdou, S., Gheith, M.: Idioms-proverbs Lexicon for modern standard Arabic and colloquial sentiment analysis. Int. J. Comput. Appl. **118**, 26–31 (2015)
11. Pak, A., Paroubek, P.: Twitter as a corpus for sentiment analysis and opinion mining. In: LREC (2010)
12. Aly, M.A., Atiya, A.F.: LABR: A Large Scale Arabic Book Reviews dataset. In: ACL, vol. 2, pp. 494–498 (2013)
13. Mountassir, A., Benbrahim, H., Berrada, I.: Sentiment classification on Arabic corpora: a preliminary cross-study. Lavoisier **16**, 121 (2013)
14. Ibrahim, H., Abdou, S., Gheith, M.: Sentiment analysis for modern standard Arabic and colloquial. Int. J. Nat. Lang. Comput. (IJNLC) **4** (2015)

15. Al-Kabi, M., Gigieh, A., Alsmadi, I., Wahsheh, H., Haidar, M.: An opinion analysis tool for colloquial and standard Arabic. In: The Fourth International Conference on Information and Communication Systems (ICICS) (2013)

16. Abdul-Mageed, M., Diab, M.T.: Subjectivity and sentiment annotation of modern standard Arabic newswire. In: Proceedings of the 5th Linguistic Annotation Workshop, pp. 110–118. Association for Computational Linguistics (2011)

17. Azmi, A.M., Alzanin, S.M.: Aara'– a system for mining the polarity of Saudi public opinion through e-newspaper comments. J. Inf. Sci. **40**, 398–410 (2014)

18. Abdul-Mageed, M., Kübler, S., Diab, M.: SAMAR: a system for subjectivity and sentiment analysis of Arabic social media. In: Proceedings of the 3rd Workshop in Computational Approaches to Subjectivity and Sentiment Analysis, pp. 19–28. Association for Computational Linguistics (2012)

19. Duwairi, R.M., Qarqaz, I.: Arabic sentiment analysis using supervised classification. In: 2014 International Conference on Future Internet of Things and Cloud (FiCloud), pp. 579–583. IEEE (2014)

20. Abdul-Mageed, M., AlHuzli, H., Abu Elhija, D., Diab, M.: DINA: a multi-dialect dataset for Arabic emotion analysis. In: The 2nd Workshop on Arabic Corpora and Processing Tools 2016 Theme: Social Media (2016)

21. Alhumoud, S., Albuhairi, T., Altuwaijri, M.: Arabic sentiment analysis using WEKA a hybrid learning approach (2015)

22. Al-Osaimi, S., Badruddin., K.: Role of emotion icons in sentiment classification of Arabic tweets. In: Proceedings of the 6th International Conference on Management of Emergent Digital EcoSystems, pp. 167–171 (2014)

23. Duwairi, R.: Sentiment analysis for dialectical Arabic. In: ICICS (2015)

24. Duwairi, R.M., Marji, R., Sha'ban, N., Rushaidat, S.: Sentiment analysis in Arabic tweets. In: 2014 5th International Conference on Information and Communication Systems (ICICS), pp. 1–6. IEEE (2014)

25. El-Makky, K.N.N., Alaa El-Ebshihy, E.A., Omneya Hafez, S.M., Ibrahim, S.: Sentiment analysis of colloquial Arabic tweets. In: Presented at the 3rd ASE International Conference on Social Informatics (SocialInformatics 2014). Harvard University, Cambridge, December 2014

26. Shoukry, A., Rafea, A.: Preprocessing Egyptian dialect tweets for sentiment mining. In: AMTA (2012)

27. Shoukry, A., Rafea, A.: Sentence-level Arabic sentiment analysis. In: 2012 International Conference on Collaboration Technologies and Systems (CTS), pp. 546–550. IEEE (2012)

28. Nabil, M., Aly, M., Atiya, A.: ASTD: Arabic sentiment tweets dataset. In: Proceedings of the 2015 Conference on Empirical Methods in Natural Language Processing, pp. 2515–2519 (2015)

29. Alhumoud, S., Albuhairi, T., Alohaideb, W.: Hybrid sentiment analyser for Arabic tweets using R. (2015). Conference Paper

30. Refaee, E., Rieser, V.: An Arabic twitter corpus for subjectivity and sentiment analysis. In: LREC, pp. 2268–2273 (2014)

31. ElSahar, H., El-Beltagy, S.R.: Building large Arabic multi-domain resources for sentiment analysis. In: Gelbukh, A. (ed.) CICLing 2015. LNCS, vol. 9042, pp. 23–34. Springer, Cham (2015). doi:10.1007/978-3-319-18117-2_2

32. Alhazmi, S., Black, W., McNaught, J.: Arabic SentiWordNet in relation to SentiWordNet 3.0. 2180. 1266, 1 (2013)

33. Hsueh, P.-Y., Melville, P., Sindhwani, V.: Data quality from crowdsourcing: a study of annotation selection criteria. In: Proceedings of the NAACL HLT 2009 Workshop on Active Learning for Natural Language Processing, pp. 27–35. Association for Computational Linguistics (2009)
34. Boto API. https://github.com/boto/boto
35. Tesconi, M., Ronzano, F., Minutoli, S., Marchetti, A., Aliprandi, C.: KAFnotator: a multilingual semantic text annotation tool. In: 5th Joint ISO-ACL/SIGSEM Workshop on Interoperable Semantic Annotation, Hong Kong (2010)
36. Abdul-Mageed, M., Diab, M.: SANA: a large scale multi-genre, multi-dialect Lexicon for Arabic subjectivity and sentiment analysis. In: LREC (2014)
37. Goodreads. https://www.goodreads.com/
38. Cohen, J.: A coefficient of agreement for nominal scales. Educ. Psychol. Measur. **20**, 37–46 (1960)
39. Carletta, J.: Assessing agreement on classification tasks: the kappa statistic. Comput. Linguist. **22**, 249–254 (1996)

AraSenTi-Lexicon: A Different Approach

Hadeel AlNegheimish[1](✉), Jowharah Alshobaili[2], Nora AlMansour[1],
Rawan Bin Shiha[1], Nora AlTwairesh[1], and Sarah Alhumoud[3]

[1] College of Computer and Information Sciences, King Saud University,
Riyadh, Saudi Arabia
{halnegheimish, twairesh}@ksu.edu.sa,
nora.al-mansour@hotmail.com, rawan.binshiha@gmail.com
[2] College of Computer, Qassim University, Buraydah, Saudi Arabia
j.alshobaili@qu.edu.sa
[3] Computer Science Department,
Al-Imam Muhammad Ibn Saud Islamic University, Riyadh, Saudi Arabia
sohumoud@imamu.edu.sa

Abstract. With the spread of social media, the demand for automated systems
that analyze these massive amounts of data on the Web is increasing. One
domain for these systems is sentiment analysis(SA). SA is designed to extract
sentiment from text; this is often accomplished by using lexicons that indicate
the sentiment polarity of words. While there are many English lexicons that are
available, there is a lack of Arabic lexicons. In previous work, an attempt was
made to generate an Arabic sentiment lexicon extracted from Twitter using the
Pointwise Mutual Information (PMI) statistical method. In this paper, we extend
the work by using two different statistical approaches: Chi-Square and Entropy
to generate the lexicons. Intrinsic and extrinsic evaluation was conducted to
compare the three lexicons. The results showed the superiority of PMI.

Keywords: Sentiment analysis · Arabic sentiment lexicon · Lexicon
generation · Dialectal arabic · Twitter

1 Introduction

Since the creation of Web 2.0 technology, information exchange through the internet
has increased rapidly. This new technology gave the power of sharing information not
only to the data manager as its predecessor did, but also to the normal user of the web,
which in turn led to the social media revolution. Social media gives people the
opportunity to interact with each other directly and freely;allowing them to share news
or information, express their feelings or opinions, make comments on events or articles,
or even make new relationships both personal and professional. This flood of data in
social media requires time and effort to read, evaluate, and analyze manually, pressing
the need to have an automated system that could extract valuable insight efficiently.
Accordingly, this has led to the emergence of the new research field of Sentiment
Analysis (SA).

SA is concerned with classifying text into the sentiment polarity that it holds i.e.
(positive, negative, neutral). SA has many beneficial aspects. For example, companies

© Springer International Publishing AG 2017
G. Meiselwitz (Ed.): SCSM 2017, Part II, LNCS 10283, pp. 226–235, 2017.
DOI: 10.1007/978-3-319-58562-8_18

can use it to analyze customer comments and evaluate their satisfaction with the company's products. This feedback provides valuable information that could help them when making their marketing strategies [1]. SA can also be used to determine the user's desires and thus determine the appropriate advertisements based on the type of product the user has commented upon.

One approach to SA is based on using sentiment lexicons. Sentiment lexicons are compiled lists of words with their polarity (positive, negative) [2]. Sentiment intensity could also be provided; it indicates the strength in which the sentiment is being conveyed. In previous work, AlTwairesh et al. [3] generated tweet-specific Arabic sentiment lexicons using two approaches. One of these approaches utilizes the statistical measure Pointwise Mutual Information (PMI). In this paper, we use the same datasets used in [3], but propose two new statistical approaches that exploit the Entropy and Chi-Square measures. We then test and evaluate these lexiconsand compare their results with the results of PMI lexicons published in [3].

This paper is organized as follows: Sect. 2 reviews the related work on sentiment lexicon generation. Section 3 presents the details of the datasets used to generate the lexicons. Section 4 describes the new approaches used to generate the new lexicons. Section 5 details the conducted intrinsic and extrinsic evaluationof the new lexicons while Sect. 6 presents and discusses the results. Finally, we conclude the paper in Sect. 7.

2 Related Work

A sentiment lexicon contains words that are classified as positive, negative and sometimes neutral. The lexicon could contain in addition to the polarity of the word, a score that indicates the sentiment intensity. There are three approaches to generating sentiment lexicons [2]: manual approach, dictionary-based approach, and corpus-based approach. The manual approach as the name implies is done manually, but is usually done in conjunction with automated approaches as a correction step. The dictionary-based approach exploits relations found in a dictionary such as synonyms and antonyms to derive the polarity of words. Most of the works under this approach utilize WordNet e.g. [4–7]. Arabic sentiment lexicons generated using this approach e.g. [8, 9].

The corpus-based approach utilizes a corpus and a set of sentiment bearing words. Words are extracted from the corpus and compared to the set of sentiment words using different statistical methods that measure semantic similarity. Statistical approaches that are commonly used include PMI, and Chi-Square [2]. The PMI is a measure for the strength of association between two words in a corpus, i.e. the probability of the two words to co-occur in the corpus [10]. It has been adapted in sentiment analysis as a measure of the frequency of a word occurring in positive text to the frequency of the same word occurring in negative text. Turney [11]; Turney and Littman [12], was the first work that proposed to use this measurement in sentiment analysis. Other works that used this statistical measure are [13] for English and [14] for Arabic. As for the Chi-Square measure [15] used it for building a sentiment lexicon and their work was adopted in this paper also.

3 Dataset

Since we continue on the work of [3] we will use the same dataset and present here an overview of the dataset and how it was collected. Using the Twitter API, a large dataset of Arabic tweets was collected. The dataset collection was done in two phases. In the first phase, tweets that contained the emoticons ":)" (to be considered positive) and ":(" (to be considered negative) and their "lang" field was set to Arabic were collected during two months. In the second phase, a seed list of 10 Arabic positive words and 10 Arabic negative words were used as search keywords to collect tweets. Accordingly, tweets that contained the positive emoticon or positive keywords were grouped into a set that designated positive tweets and tweets that contained the negative emoticon or negative keywords were grouped into a set that designated negative tweets.

The number of collected tweets was around 6.3 million. However, due to the informal nature of Twitter data; preprocessing and cleaning was conducted on the tweets and the result after filtering and cleaning was 2.2 million Arabic tweets. Statistics of the dataset are shown in Table 1.

Table 1. Dataset statistics

	Positive tweets	Negative tweets	Total
Number of tweets collected	4068571	2272564	6341135
After cleaning and filtering	1480563	745363	2225926
Number of Tokens	21797720	12217401	34015121

4 Lexicon Generation

In this paper, we build on the previous work [3], to explore other approaches in scoring Arabic sentiment lexicons, utilizing entropy and chi-square methods.

These approaches are used to determine the intensity of the polarity of each word in the lexicon, using the frequencies of each word in positive and negative datasets, and are further detailed in the following subsections. However, they do not tell us whether the word is positive or negative. The sign of each, or direction of polarity, is determined in a uniform way, by comparing the conditional probability of the lexicon given its polarity. Concretely:

$$Sign = \begin{cases} 1 & if\ P(c|neg) < P(c|pos) \\ -1 & otherwise \end{cases} \tag{1}$$

where;

$$P(c|i) = \frac{freq(c, i)}{freq(c)} \tag{2}$$

where

c: is the word,
i: is the polarity (positive or negative).
freq(c,i) is the frequency of word c in dataset i:the (positive or negative).
freq(c) is the frequency of word c in the whole dataset.

Next, the sign is multiplied by the word score found by each of the following formula (3, 5), to determine the word's intensity.

4.1   AraSenTi-Entropy

Entropy [16] is often used in Information Theory to measure expected information content; in the case of two labels, entropy is highest when the data is evenly distributed, and lowest when all of the data is under one label. In our context, a word can either be positive or negative, so entropy can be used to measure the intensity of a word's polarity. If the entropy is high, it means that the word occurs in comparable frequency in both positive and negative text, which means that the word has weak polarity. On the other hand, if the entropy is low, it means that the word has a strong polarity, as it occurs in some sentiment significantly more than the other.

Knowing that entropy has an inverse relationship with a word's polarity, given the frequencies of words in positive and negative datasets, we find AraSenTi-Entropy lexicon scores based on the following equation:

$$Score(c) = sign * \frac{1}{-\sum_{i \in \{pos,neg\}} p_i \, log_2 \, p_i} \tag{3}$$

where:

$$p_i = \frac{freq(c,i)}{freq(c)} \tag{4}$$

In the case where the word appears in one polarity only, the score is set to sign $\times$ 1, as Eq. 3 ill be undefined with the denominator being zero.

4.2   AraSenTi-ChiSq

A chi-square test is used to check the validity of some null-hypothesis by evaluating the statistical significance of the difference between observed and expected values.

In the context of sentiment analysis, the intensity of polarity of the word is determined by evaluating the null-hypothesis: "The frequency of the occurrences of a word is the same in positive and negative text". As in AraSenTi-Entropy, frequencies of words in positive and negative text are the sole determinants of scores.

The exact formula for AraSenTi-ChiSq lexicon, was based on the work of [15], and is detailed below:

$$Score(c) = X^2(c) = sign * \sum_{y \in (pos,neg)} \frac{\{freq(c,y) - \overline{freq}(c,y)\}^2}{\overline{freq}(c,y)} \tag{5}$$

where:

$$\overline{freq}(c,y) \text{ is the expected freq and } X^2(c) \geq 0$$

Basically, the score will be the sum of square differences of frequencies normalized by the frequency under each polarity. If the null hypothesis holds, the expected value of frequency (or the frequency under the other polarity), will be equivalent to the original one, and the score will be zero (the intensity of polarity is low). In the case where a word appears under one polarity only, the denominator is set to 1 instead of 0, and the score would be most extreme.

5   Evaluation

To evaluate the performance of the generated lexicons, two evaluation methods were performed; intrinsic and extrinsic. In the intrinsic evaluation, AraSenTi-Entropy, AraSenTi-ChiSq and AraSenTi-PMI [3] lexicons were compared with each other. However, in the extrinsic evaluation, the lexicons were evaluated for their utility in classifying sentiment of three different datasets of Arabic tweets.

5.1   Intrinsic Evaluation

In this evaluation method, the three lexicons were compared to each other to determine the percentage of agreement, i.e. how many words did the lexicons agree on their polarity. Table 2 shows the number of positive and negative words used in this evaluation for each lexicon with a total of 93,295 words.

Table 2. The number of positive and negative words in the lexicons

Lexicon	Positive	Negative
AraSenTi-PMI	56434	36861
AraSenTi-ChiSq	58697	34598
AraSenTi-Entropy	56304	36991

In Table 3, the result of this evaluation is illustrated, and from it, you can notice that the highest agreement percentage was between AraSenTi-PMI [3] and AraSenTi-Entropy. In general, the agreements between the lexicons were very high.

Table 3. The percentage of agreement for the lexicons

Lexicons	Agreement
AraSenTi-PMI & AraSenTi-ChiSq	97.30%
AraSenTi-PMI & AraSenTi-Entropy	99.86%
AraSenTi-Entropy & AraSenTi-ChiSq	97.44%

5.2   Extrinsic Evaluation

We conducted an extrinsic evaluation for the three lexicons to observe the performance of the lexicons on different datasets. We evaluated the lexicons using the same datasets from the previous work which are AraSenTi-Tweet dataset [3] and two external datasets ASTD [17] and RR [18]. Information of these datasets is illustrated in Table 4.

Table 4. Datasets used in the extrinsic evaluation.

Dataset	Positive	Negative	Total
AraSenTi-Tweet	4329	5804	10133
ASTD	797	1682	2479
RR	876	1941	2817

In addition, we computed the balanced F-score (Favg), precision (P) and recall (R) to measure the performance of the lexicons for the positive and negative categories by the following formulas:

$$P = \frac{TP}{TP + FP} \tag{6}$$

$$R = \frac{TP}{TP + FN} \tag{7}$$

$$F = \frac{2 \times P \times R}{P + R} \tag{8}$$

Where TP is the number of true positives, FP is the number of false positives, TN is the number of true negatives and FN is the number of false negatives. Then we calculated the F-score as follow:

$$F_{avg} = \frac{F_{pos} + F_{neg}}{2} \tag{9}$$

For AraSenTi-Entropy and AraSenTi-ChiSq lexicons we followed the same approach used with AraSenTi-PMI [3] lexicon in the previous work. We classified the tweets into positive or negative according to the sum of the sentiment score of the words in each tweet. The threshold we used to classify the data into positive or negative was initially zero. As such, if the sum of the sentiment score of the words in a tweet is greater than zero then the tweet is considered to be a positive tweet. Otherwise the tweet is considered to be a negative tweet. Additionally, we experimented with other values of the threshold to get the best results, we used 0, 0.5 and 1.

6   Results and Discussion

First, it is worth mentioning that the scores for AraSenTi-ChiSq lexicons were clipped to remain between −10 and 10, as there were a few outliers too great in magnitude, affecting its performance. Figure 1 shows the distribution of scores for the different lexicons before and after clipping. In Fig. 1(a), we observe that outliers in ChiSq are great in magnitude, reaching a max of around $1.8 \times e7$. In Fig. 1(b), after clipping the AraSenTi-ChiSq to a min −10 and max 10. Note the similarities between the plots for PMI and Entropy.

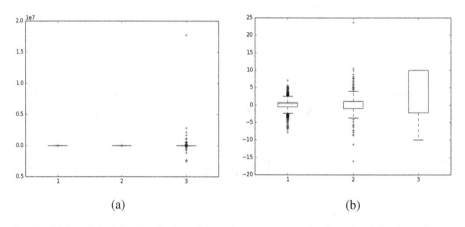

(a)   (b)

Fig. 1. (a) Boxplot of the distribution of the raw scores, as per the formulas defined previously. (b) Shows the distribution of scores after clipping ChiSq, where 1,2,3 is PMI, Entropy, and ChiSq lexicons, respectively.

The results of classifying the datasets using this simple approach with varying levels of threshold, $\theta = [0, 0.5, 1]$, are displayed in Tables 5, 6 and 7 respectively. It is evident that AraSenTi-PMI lexicon performs best regardless of the chosen threshold (with max $F_{avg} = 85.22\%$) for the AraSenTi dataset, and AraSenTi-Entropy close behind it in all experiments. AraSenTi-ChiSq has little variation across experiments, indicating that the differences in thresholds chosen are negligble to the sum of chi-square scores which determines the class. AraSenTi-ChiSq hasworse performance overall, but it is most drastic in the AraSenTi dataset (with max $F_{avg} = 71.82\%$).

Table 5. Results with theta 0.

Lexicon	Dataset	Positive			Negative			F_{avg}
		P	R	F	P	R	F	
AraSenTi-PMI	AraSenTi	86.45	80.07	83.14	84.85	89.89	87.3	**85.22**
	ASTD	38.64	73.4	50.63	78.03	44.77	56.9	**53.77**
	RR	50.26	66.89	57.39	82.43	70.12	75.78	**66.59**
AraSenTi-Entropy	AraSenTi	83.17	78.86	80.96	83.66	87.15	85.37	83.17
	ASTD	37.76	71.64	49.45	76.63	44.05	55.94	52.7
	RR	46.86	63.93	54.08	80.52	67.28	73.31	63.7
AraSenTi-ChiSq	AraSenTi	74.81	59.19	66.09	71.86	83.95	77.44	71.77
	ASTD	36.2	67.63	47.16	73.94	43.52	54.79	50.98
	RR	45.11	56.85	50.3	77.93	68.78	73.07	61.69

Table 6. Results with theta 0.5.

Lexicon	Dataset	Positive			Negative			F_{avg}
		P	R	F	P	R	F	
AraSenTi-PMI	AraSenTi	88.92	75.29	81.54	82.28	92.45	87.07	84.31
	ASTD	39.21	64.99	48.91	75.91	52.26	61.9	55.41
	RR	53.7	57.19	55.39	80.1	77.74	78.9	67.15
AraSenTi-Entropy	AraSenTi	86.08	74.7	79.99	81.59	90.27	85.71	82.85
	ASTD	37.7	63.61	47.34	74.43	50.18	59.95	53.65
	RR	49.38	54.57	51.85	78.47	74.76	76.57	64.21
AraSenTi-ChiSq	AraSenTi	74.98	59.13	66.12	71.87	84.11	77.51	71.82
	ASTD	36.14	67.25	47.01	73.8	43.7	54.89	50.95
	RR	45.15	56.85	50.33	77.95	68.83	73.11	61.72

Table 7. Results with theta 1.

Lexicon	Dataset	Positive			Negative			F_{avg}
		P	R	F	P	R	F	
AraSenTi-PMI	AraSenTi	70.61	79.66	79.99	94.62	86.69	83.18	70.61
	ASTD	57.72	47.32	74.7	59.16	66.03	56.68	57.72
	RR	49.43	53.13	78.53	83.46	80.92	67.03	49.43
AraSenTi-Entropy	AraSenTi	87.03	73.13	79.48	80.83	91.23	85.72	82.6
	ASTD	39.09	61.61	47.83	74.98	54.52	63.13	55.48
	RR	49.89	50.8	50.34	77.61	76.97	77.29	63.82
AraSenTi-ChiSq	AraSenTi	75.13	58.95	66.06	71.83	84.29	77.56	71.81
	ASTD	36.22	67.25	47.08	73.87	43.88	55.06	51.07
	RR	45.13	56.62	50.23	77.88	68.93	73.13	61.68

Table 8. Performance of ChiSq before clipping, it was invariant across experiments

	AraSenTi-ChiSquare (Before Clipping)						
	Positive			Negative			F_{avg}
	P	R	F	P	R	F	
AraSenTi	70.67	79.95	75.02	81.94	73.27	77.36	76.19
ASTD	32.88	57.21	41.76	68.77	44.65	54.15	47.96
RR	38.09	49.09	42.9	73.58	63.99	68.45	55.68

Table 8 shows the performance of ChiSq before clipping, which was static across experiments. We can see that aside from AraSenTiFavg, clipping the scores improved its performance. The degradation in AraSenTi dataset can be attributed to the loss of relative polarity for words with scores greater than the limits.

All lexicons perform best on AraSenTi dataset, with a difference of 20 points or more in Favg. AraSenTi lexicons capture the idiosyncrasies of Twitter data, which apparently does not map well to other benchmark datasets, which may contain modern standard Arabic or other dialects.

For AraSenTi-PMI and AraSenTi-Entropy, the effect of varying threshold decreases the F_{avg} of AraSenTi dataset, but improves it for the other datasets: ASTD and RR. This is expected since the lexicons, which had been extracted from the AraSenTi dataset, have zero-median scores (as can be seen from box plots above). Furthermore, raising the threshold decreases the number of false positives, which increases the true negatives. The amount of negative data in both ASTD and RR far exceeds the amount of positive data, so such an effect is desirable

7   Conclusion

In this paper, we attempted to address a gap of the lack of Arabic sentiment lexicons that are generated from Twitter data. A previous attempt was achieved by exploiting the PMI statistical measure in [3]. New statistical approaches were investigated, these are: ChiSquare and Entropy. Intrinsic and extrinsic evaluations were conducted on the three lexicons. The results show that the performance of the lexicon that was generated using PMI outperforms other lexicons. However, the accuracy achieved from the other lexicons on the experimental datasets was very satisfying.

Acknowledgments. This work was partially funded by Deanship of Scientific Research at Al-Imam Muhammad Ibn Saud Islamic University, Riyadh, Saudi Arabia on 2015 with grant number 360911.

References

1. Heerschop, B., Hogenboom, A., Frasincar, F.: Sentiment lexicon creation from lexical resources. In: Abramowicz, W. (ed.) BIS 2011. LNBIP, vol. 87, pp. 185–196. Springer, Heidelberg (2011). doi:10.1007/978-3-642-21863-7_16
2. Liu, B.: Sentiment Analysis: Mining Opinions, Sentiments, and Emotions. Cambridge University Press, Cambridge (2015)
3. Al-Twairesh, N., Al-Khalifa, H., Al-Salman, A.: AraSenTi: large-scale twitter-specific arabic sentiment lexicons. In: Proceedings of the 54th Annual Meeting on Association for Computational Linguistics. Association for Computational Linguistics, Berlin, Germany (2016)
4. Kamps, J.: Using wordnet to measure semantic orientations of adjectives. In: Proceedings of the 4th International Conference on Language Resources and Evaluation (LREC 2004) (2004)
5. Williams, G.K., Anand, S.S.: Predicting the polarity strength of adjectives using WordNet. In: Third International AAAI Conference on Weblogs and Social Media (2009)
6. Rao, D., Ravichandran, D.: Semi-supervised polarity lexicon induction. In: Proceedings of the 12th Conference of the European Chapter of the Association for Computational Linguistics, pp. 675–682. Association for Computational Linguistics (2009)
7. Baccianella, S., Esuli, A., Sebastiani, F.: SentiWordNet 3.0: an enhanced lexical resource for sentiment analysis and opinion mining. In: LREC, pp. 2200–2204 (2010)
8. Badaro, G., Baly, R., Hajj, H., Habash, N., El-Hajj, W.: A large scale Arabic sentiment lexicon for Arabic opinion mining. ANLP 2014. 165 (2014)
9. Eskander, R., Rambow, O.: SLSA: a sentiment lexicon for standard Arabic. In: Proceedings of the 2015 Conference on Empirical Methods in Natural Language Processing, pp. 2545–2550. ACL, Lisbon, Purtogal (2015)
10. Church, K.W., Hanks, P.: Word association norms, mutual information, and lexicography. Comput. Linguistics. **16**, 22–29 (1990)
11. Turney, P.D.: Thumbs up or thumbs down?: Semantic orientation applied to unsupervised classification of reviews. In: Proceedings of the 40th Annual Meeting on Association for Computational Linguistics, pp. 417–424. Association for Computational Linguistics (2002)
12. Turney, P., Littman, M.L.: Unsupervised learning of semantic orientation from a hundred-billion-word corpus. National Research Council Canada, NRC Institute for Information Technology; National Research Council Canada (2002)
13. Kiritchenko, S., Zhu, X., Mohammad, S.M.: Sentiment analysis of short informal texts. J. Artif. Intell. Res. **50**, 723–762 (2014)
14. Mohammad, S.M., Salameh, M., Kiritchenko, S.: How translation alters sentiment. J. Artif. Intell. Res. **54**, 1–20 (2015)
15. Kaji, N., Kitsuregawa, M.: Building lexicon for sentiment analysis from massive collection of HTML documents. In: EMNLP-CoNLL, pp. 1075–1083 (2007)
16. Han, J., Pei, J., Kamber, M.: Data mining: concepts and techniques. Elsevier, New York (2011)
17. Nabil, M., Aly, M., Atiya, A.F.: ASTD: Arabic sentiment tweets dataset. In: Proceedings of the 2015 Conference on Empirical Methods in Natural Language Processing, pp. 2515–2519 (2015)
18. Refaee, E., Rieser, V.: An Arabic twitter corpus for subjectivity and sentiment analysis. In: Proceedings of the 9th International Conference on Language Resources and Evaluation, LREC 2014, European Language Resources Association (ELRA), Reykjavik, Iceland (2014)

Investigating the Relationship Between Trust and Sentiment Agreement in Arab Twitter Users

Areeb Alowisheq[1(✉)], Nora Alrajebah[2,3], Asma Alrumikhani[1],
Ghadeer Al-Shamrani[4], Maha Shaabi[5], Muneera Al-Nufaisi[6],
Ahad Alnasser[2], and Sarah Alhumoud[1]

[1] Computer Science Department,
Al-Imam Muhammad Ibn Saud Islamic University, Riyadh, Saudi Arabia
{aaalowisheq,sohumoud}@imamu.edu.sa,
asmaalrumi@gmail.com
[2] Information Technology Department,
King Saud University, Riyadh, Saudi Arabia
nrajebah@ksu.edu.sa, ahadfahad75@gmail.com
[3] ECS, University of Southampton, Southampton, UK
[4] Computer Science Department, King Abdulaziz University,
Jeddah, Saudi Arabia
ghadeer.alshamrani@gmail.com
[5] Computer Science Department, Jazan University, Jazan, Saudi Arabia
mishaabi@jazanu.edu.sa
[6] Information Management Department,
Al-Imam Muhammad Ibn Saud Islamic University, Riyadh, Saudi Arabia
Muneera.salah@gmail.com

Abstract. Arab twitter users are rapidly increasing, at the same time the social and political landscape of the Arab world is rapidly changing. Twitter has been used as a lens to examine relationships between society members which is assumed to reflect the real world. There exist several methods to estimate Trust between users on twitter, however only a few have taken the context and sentiment into consideration. We propose a research methodology framework for investigating the relationship between trust and sentiment agreement on twitter, and explain the framework by applying it to a use case from Saudi Arabia.

Keywords: Sentiment analysis · Arabic sentiment analysis · Trust · SNA

1 Introduction

Measuring trust in social networks is an extensively studied topic. Several factors drive the research interest in understanding and measuring Trust. These include social, political, commercial, economical and for security and safety. Moreover, the advances in social network analysis have facilitated quantified research on trust. Nevertheless, the ceaseless expansion of social media content continues to present new challenges for providing scalable solutions.

© Springer International Publishing AG 2017
G. Meiselwitz (Ed.): SCSM 2017, Part II, LNCS 10283, pp. 236–245, 2017.
DOI: 10.1007/978-3-319-58562-8_19

In recent times, the Arab world has gone through political, social and cultural shifts. It is a historically difficult and interesting period where trust ties and alliances have been strained, broken and reformed. Arabs form a significant portion of social media users on Twitter, and it is estimated that by March 2017 there will be over 11 million Arab users [1].

Most of the research about trust on Twitter has not considered the content of the tweets, it was mostly based on the structure of the social network and the users' interaction. Sherchan et al. have emphasized the importance of context to modelling trust [2], meaning that trusting a person in one context, does not mean they will be trusted in another context. We take this notion a step further and hypothesize that not only the context is important, but having similar judgments about context affects trust. In this paper, we introduce a framework to investigate the relationship between trust and agreement on sentiment among twitter users. Sentiment analysis uses natural language processing to identify a user's attitude towards a given topic.

The paper is structured as follows, Sect. 2 provides a literature review of trust metrics on twitter, Sect. 3 introduces our proposed framework. In Sect. 4 a use case demonstrates how we intend the framework to be used. Section 5 concludes the paper and discusses future work.

2 Related Work

Our proposed methodology requires measuring trust and sentiment agreement; in this section, we review approaches for modelling trust on twitter. Then provide a brief overview of sentiment analysis in Arabic, and cite several surveys which explain the current research efforts.

2.1 Measuring Trust on Twitter

There are several existing approaches to model trust on Twitter. In this section, we review seven approaches. These approaches differ in terms of their aims, and the factors they included to represent trust. There are three types of factors: structural, behavioral or interaction-based, and content or semantic based.

Adali et al. [7] developed statistical measures based on the timing and sequence of communications on twitter (interaction information), they did not base the measures on the textual content (semantic information) nor the existing social network structure. Two trust metrics were introduced: conversational trust, and propagation trust. Conversational trust is computed based on the length, frequency and balance of conversations between two users. Propagation trust on the other hand is the measure of the frequency of message propagation between two users. It is based on the assumption that a user A will propagate messages from a user B, if A trusts B, and since the approach is based solely on interaction information, they measured potential propagations, instead of actual propagations, where a message was considered a propagation of another message if the difference in their times was less than threshold. The twitter dataset used for testing had more than 2 million users, containing 15,563,120 public directed messages and 34,178,314 broadcast messages. They also assumed that retweets are indicators of trust, meaning if user A retweets a tweet from user B, then A trusts B. They built a retweet graph accordingly. They then validated their proposed approaches by measuring their coverage of the retweet graph. For the conversational trust the coverage was 11.6% and for the propagation trust it was 14.4%, and both were significantly higher than the random coverage.

MarkovTrust [8] is an adaptation of the EigenTrust algorithm [9] for modelling trust and trust propagation on Twitter, the authors aim was to use their approach to improve tweet recommendations. MarkovTrust is calculated based on users' interactions by retweets and mentions. In addition, it calculates the trust propagation or transitive trust. They developed a system composed of a crawler and a recommender. The crawler calculates trust values for a node's neighbors and updates a ranked list of trusted users using the MarkovTrust while retrieving their tweets. Evaluation of the model was a challenge, since there are no trust scores assigned explicitly on Twitter, there is no straightforward way to achieve this. Therefore, they evaluated its effectiveness using an approach in which they calculated the difference between a node's ranking of trusted nodes, and its neighbors ranking of the same nodes. A dataset was collected that contained 20 users, and after preprocessing they resulted in 314 balanced tweets, 50% where retweets, and 50% where non-retweet. If their model was valid, the differences in ranking would increase as the rank decreased, meaning the users would agree on the ranking of common neighbors. However, in the experiment this was not the case, meaning either the model was wrong or the dataset was too small to verify the model. The recommender part of the system recommends tweets to the user periodically, using machine learning. To create the dataset the authors regarded retweeting as an endorsement, and accordingly checked the origin of the retweet, if it was from the top trusted neighbors they labelled that tweet as positive, and the previous tweet from the same origin as negative this is the same dataset used for evaluating the crawler above. The features they used were the trust score, the words contained in the tweet, and whether the tweet contained a URL. The trust score was calculated by the crawler, the words were labelled negative or positive based on a dictionary. The dictionary was created using words in the labelled tweets in the dataset, a word was labelled positive or negative based on their frequency of occurrence in labelled tweets. They trained two classifiers an SVM and a Naïve Bayes one. To evaluate their recommender, they used 75% of the dataset as a training set, and 25% as test set, and ran the experiment with and without the trust features, although the performance in both settings was low, a slight improvement was exhibited when including trust as a feature, however this result is weakened due to the small size of the dataset.

Unlike the approaches above, the authors' aim in [10] was to develop a model of consumers' trust in new technologies not trust between users. It is still related to our research for two reasons, the first is their model for trust uses twitter as medium, the second is their utilization of tweet sentiment in modelling trust. Their model takes into account the authority of users tweeting about the technology and their sentiment towards it. It incorporates what they call situational trust and behavioral trust and is calculated at a certain point in time. Situational trust is based on the tweets' sentiment and the degree of their senders' authority which measured by the number of followers. Behavioral trust is based on the sentiment of tweets regardless of the senders' authority.

The model also includes several parameters as weights that regulate it in terms of the degree of past trust to include, the balance between situational trust and behavioral trust and others. The sentiment of tweets and their topic were determined using SVM classifiers. The parameters for the model itself were learnt by sampling data from targeted users through questionnaires and tuning the parameters according to the results using regression. They experimented by modelling users' trust in Apple's "iCloud', the resulting mean squared error (MSE) was 0.0439. Moreover, they used the model for building a dynamic visualization tool to monitor trust in ICT services.

In [11], the author introduces a tool for analyzing opinion, influence and trust in twitter. The author introduced three sentiment analysis algorithms, named surface, deep and shallow, for coloring tweets according to their sentiment. For the surface analysis algorithm, negative and positive word lexica were created. To create them, the author used clustering to select tweets in the political domain, then the sense-bearing words are labelled as positive and negative, and supervised classification is applied to the tweets using the lexica as bag of words. In the shallow analysis, instead of using the bag of words, a feature vector was used containing not only words but also phrases. The deep analysis involves relating words to concepts in WordNet to find related concepts, and building what the author called AffectiveSpace. To measure the propagation of opinion, influence and trust, three edge-coloring algorithms were introduced, that utilized the tweet coloring algorithms mentioned above and maximum-flow minimum-cut traditional graph algorithms. These algorithms were demonstrated by implementing them on top of NodeXL [12] as MS Excel macros, which produced several graph illustrations and a dashboard.

The authors objectives in [13] were to study the usage of twitter after the Chilean earthquake in 2010 and to examine the differences between the propagation of false rumors and confirmed news on twitter. They collected 4,727,424 tweets, from 716,344 users and calculated several metrics to analyze the network. They then identified 7 confirmed news and 7 false rumors, and collected tweets about them and categorized those tweets into retweets, affirms, denies and questions, meaning was the tweet about those topics a retweet, a confirmation, a denial, or a question about it. Their results show that the propagation patterns differ between false rumors and confirmed news, as false rumors tend to be denied and questioned more.

In this work [14], the authors focus on inferring trust among twitter users, the inferred trust network is based on interactions and relationships among users. The authors' model includes two stages: inferring (filtering) and propagation (discovery). In the first stage, which is inferring relationships, the authors utilized two twitter indicators to decide whether user A trusted user B, these are retweets, and favorite lists. This resulted in two graphs. To propagate the calculated trust, they used the following methods: simple-transitivity, weighted-transitivity, golbeck-transitivity [15], and structural similarity. Structural similarity, unlike the three transitivity propagation methods, is based on whether two users share similar structures in who they trust, and who they are trusted by. Thus, they resulted in two graphs: retweet and favorite, with four propagation methods. To evaluate the models, they collected data from more than 20,000 users. Because there are no existing trust values for comparison, they assumed that the methods that correctly predict the existing relationships in the Retweet and Favorite graphs, will be able to predict relationships in the rest of the network.

Then they measured the coverage of the method in the two graphs, and the mean absolute error (MAE). They found that the structural similarity method gave the best results.

The aim of the work in [16] is to rate the topic-focused trustworthiness of twitter users and tweets. Their trust model is assumed to be context-dependent. It has two main components: topic-focused similarity-based trust evaluation, and trust propagation. The topic-focused similarity-based trust evaluation focuses on the tweets credibility, which is rated according to their similarity to authentic news articles. The similarity is calculated by integrating three metrics: textual similarity, spatial similarity, and temporal similarity. As for the trust propagation, it is calculated by iteratively propagating the trust evaluation based on four rules, the first and second are related to similarity in semantic and conversational features, and the third and fourth propagate the trust from author of a trusted tweet to the author and their other tweets, and to a user from their friends. They evaluated the model by first evaluating the topic-focused similarity-based trust measure. They collected tweets with the highest score about a specific topic, then they trained an SVM classifier, then used the classifier on new data. They compared the results of the classifier to two classifiers as baselines, one trained on manually ranked tweets and the other on tweets collected by keyword matching. Their classifier achieved better performance than the baseline method. In terms of user trustworthiness, they assumed it depends on the trustworthiness of their tweets. To validate this, they used some twitter measures as trust indicators such as: account time length, favorite count, follower count, friends count, list count, and whether the account was verified or not. They then checked that the correlation between their measure of trustworthiness and the twitter trust indicators was positive and statistically significant. The results show that the positive correlation is significant in most of the indicators.

As many of the proposed trust models for Twitter are adapted from P2P network trust models, Sherchan et al. have stressed the importance of developing trust models that utilize the social network indicators, because the notion of trust and the purpose for the model differs between the two types of networks [2].

2.2 Arabic Sentiment Analysis

Sentiment analysis is concerned with automatically identifying the sentiment of a certain expression or text, the sentiment polarity could be either positive or negative (binary score) or it could have scores representing different degrees of sentiment. Liu [3] provides an extensive background and survey of recent research. Approaches to sentiment analysis can be either supervised, unsupervised or combination of both. Sentiment Analysis in Arabic introduces several challenges such as use of dialectical Arabic, lack of resources, spam detection, co-reference resolution and several others [4]. Alhumoud et al. [5] reviewed several Arabic sentiment analysis approaches. Also, existing resources for Arabic Sentiment Analysis, such as preprocessing tools, sentiment lexica and datasets have been surveyed in [6].

3 Framework

In this section, we introduce a framework that illustrates how we can conceptualize the relationship between trust and sentiment analysis on social networks. Since the research in this field is still in its early stages it would be beneficial to have a general framework that will assist in designing a proper research methodology for this field. This framework can be adapted based on the intended research purposes and the data available for researchers. This framework consists of five stages:

Stage One: Selecting the Basis of Trust
As we have seen in Sect. 2 there are many trust models. Therefore, researchers derive trust measures by utilizing the different functionalities available from social network platforms. In this stage, we will define the meaning of trust, hence; decide what measures are we going to use to measure it. This selection stage will affect how we calculate trust scores in the stage three and what information we need to gather during the data collection phase.

Stage Two: Selecting a User Group to Study
In this stage, we will select users whom we want to measure the extent to which they trust each other according to our definition of trust. We suggest using one of two approaches in this stage, either selecting a group of users manually who we assume have elements of trust between them, or selecting a group of users randomly without a prior assumption. In the first approach, we would select users based on the fact that they collaborate with each other, they explicitly express their belonging to the same movement or that they care about similar issues. This assumption will be our hypothesis that these users trust each other, thus, we want to measure to what extent they statistically or empirically trust each other. For the second approach, we will neglect this assumption and randomly pick users who for example participate in the same hashtags or who follow each other. This stage and the one before it will decide how the data collection will be carried out.

Stage Three: Calculating Trust Scores
In stage one, we define and select the metrics we will use to measure trust between two users. In this stage one or more trust metrics will be calculated, for each pair of users selected in the second stage we will compute the trust between them using all of the selected trust metrics. Each metric yields a score and the scores resulted from all the metrics will be summed so there will be one trust score for each pair of users. Figure 1 shows a matrix of pairwise trust scores among all users in the dataset.

	A	B	C	D
A		t_{ab}	t_{ac}	t_{ad}
B	t_{ba}		t_{bc}	t_{bd}
C	t_{ca}	t_{cb}		t_{cd}
D	t_{da}	t_{db}	t_{dc}	

Fig. 1. Trust metric matrix

The symbols A, B, C, D represent the users in the dataset, and the values t_{xy} represents the trust score of user X trusting user Y, which naturally differs from t_{yx} which represents the opposite. As we have seen in Sect. 2, trust metrics differ in the measures obtained from the social network, which determines the data collection approach.

Stage Four: Calculating Sentiment Agreement
Since our approach aims to study the relationship between the trust metric and the sentiment agreement among users, it is important to state how the sentiment agreement is calculated. To do so we will select a topic which the group of users are interested in, and measure their sentiment towards it. The ideal type of topics would be a hashtag, but it can also be any keyword that the users are posting or tweeting about. A user's sentiment towards a topic would be calculated as a score $SA \in [-1,1]$, where -1 means negative sentiment and 1 means positive sentiment and 0 means that the user's tweets sentiment is neutral towards that topic. Sentiment agreement calculation will take into account all the tweets that contain that particular topic. Two users' agreement on a sentiment would be calculated as the Euclidian distance between their sentiment scores, for example the sentiment agreement between user A, and user B on topic t_1 would be S_{t1ab}. Users' agreement scores will also be stored in a matrix as shown in Fig. 2. As users might be interested in several topics, we can have several matrices, each matrix represents the sentiment agreement of users towards one topic as illustrated in Fig. 3.

Topic 1	A	B	C	D
A	-	$S_{t_1}ab$	$S_{t_1}ac$	$S_{t_1}ad$
B	$S_{t_1}ab$	-	$S_{t_1}bc$	$S_{t_1}db$
C	$S_{t_1}ac$	$S_{t_1}cb$	-	$S_{t_1}cd$
D	$S_{t_1}ad$	$S_{t_1}db$	$S_{t_1}cd$	-

Fig. 2. Sentiment agreement matrix

Topic x {x:1..n}	A	B	C	D
A	-	$S_{t_x}ab$	$S_{t_x}ac$	$S_{t_x}ad$
B	$S_{t_x}ab$	-	$S_{t_x}bc$	$S_{t_x}db$
C	$S_{t_x}ac$	$S_{t_x}cb$	-	$S_{t_x}cd$
D	$S_{t_x}ad$	$S_{t_x}db$	$S_{t_x}cd$	-

Fig. 3. Sentiment agreement matrices for several topics

Stage Five: Comparing Sentiment Agreement and Trust
After computing both the sentiment agreement and the trust between users' pairs, which yield two (or more) matrices one for users' trust and several matrices for their sentiment agreement on one topic. In this stage, we will compare the users' pair trust score and sentiment agreement scores. This will help us to precisely assess the relation

between the users, and to go beyond measuring their numerical trust to actually assess whether they agree on the different topics they are interested in. This stage is also beneficial to assess the relation between trust and sentiment agreement and will give us a deep insight to understand the relation between the two. This will allow us to understand whether trust entails agreement, or not and to what extent trust entails sentiment agreement.

4   Use Case

In this section, we will explain with a practical example how this framework can be applied. During the last quarter of 2016, a huge Saudi feminist movement became very popular among the Saudi community on Twitter. It raises controversial issues about women's rights in Saudi Arabia and gathered people's attention both locally and globally. Many users become involved in this movement and participated by tweeting heavily using the chosen hashtags which are: #الولايه_اسقاط_نطلب_سعوديات187 and #StopEnslavingSaudiWomen. In order to apply the framework in this use case, we will explain the process by which the methodology will be carried out stage by stage.

Stage One
We assume that the conversational trust [7] is selected for measuring trust, then we will need to collect for each user the following: mentions, and tweets, especially the tweets' timings.

Stage Two
We will select the users from Twitter who support this movement, after manually checking that they support the movement and heavily involved in it by tweeting using the hashtags.

Stage Three
Using the metrics chosen in stage one, we will compute the trust metrics and generate the trust pairwise scores matrix.

Stage Four
Since we are only concerned with one topic (regardless of the several hashtags used for it) we will measure users' sentiment agreement and compute the sentiment agreement matrix.

Stage Five
Using both matrices computed in stages three and four, we will compare the trust and sentiment agreement between the selected users and first assess the extent to which users who are involved in this topic trust each other and the extent to which these users actually agree on their sentiment and compare the two scores.

5 Conclusion

In this paper, we have presented a research methodology framework for investigating the relationship between trust and sentiment agreement for Arab Twitter users. The framework was demonstrated by means of a use case from Saudi Arabia. As for future work we will implement a system based on the framework to measure the trust and compare it to sentiment agreement. Our intention is that our work will provide useful insight into the effect of the social and political changes on social capital as signified by trust. However, we must bear in mind that although social network analysis is a powerful lens in understanding societies it can amplify and distort reality and extra measures need to be taken to ensure a reliable representation.

Acknowledgments. This work was partially funded by Deanship of Scientific Research at Al-Imam Muhammad Ibn Saud Islamic University, Riyadh, Saudi Arabia on 2015 with grant number 360911.

References

1. Salem, F.: The Arab Social Media Report 2017: Social Media and the Internet of Things: Towards Data-Driven Policymaking in the Arab World, vol. 7. MBR School of Government, Dubai (2017)
2. Sherchan, W., Nepal, S., Paris, C.: A survey of trust in social networks. ACM Comput. Surv. (CSUR) 45(4), 1–33 (2013)
3. Liu, B.: Sentiment analysis and opinion mining. Synth. Lect. Hum. Lang. Technol. 5(1), 1–167 (2012)
4. Al-Twairesh, N., Al-Khalifa, H., Al-Salman, A.: Subjectivity and sentiment analysis of Arabic: trends and challenges. In: 2014 IEEE/ACS 11th International Conference on Computer Systems and Applications (AICCSA). IEEE (2014)
5. Alhumoud, S., Altuwaijri, M., Albuhairi, T., Alohaideb, W.: Survey on Arabic Sentiment Analysis in Twitter. Int. Sci. Index 9(1), 364–368 (2015)
6. AlOwisheq, A., AlHumoud, S., AlTwairesh, N., AlBuhairi, T.: Arabic sentiment analysis resources: a survey. In: Meiselwitz, G. (ed.) SCSM 2016. LNCS, vol. 9742, pp. 267–278. Springer, Cham (2016). doi:10.1007/978-3-319-39910-2_25
7. Adali, S., Escriva, R., Goldberg, M.K., Hayvanovych, M., Magdon-Ismail, M., Szymanski, B.K., Wallace, W.A., Williams, G.: Measuring behavioral trust in social networks. In: 2010 IEEE International Conference on Intelligence and Security Informatics (ISI), pp. 150–152. IEEE (2010)
8. Lumbreras, A., Gavalda, R.: Applying trust metrics based on user interactions to recommendation in social networks. In: Proceedings of the 2012 International Conference on Advances in Social Networks Analysis and Mining, ASONAM 2012, pp. 1159–1164. IEEE Computer Society (2012)
9. Kamvar, S.D., Schlosser, M.T., Garcia-Molina, H.: The eigentrust algorithm for reputation management in p2p networks. In: Proceedings of the 12th International Conference on World Wide Web, pp. 640–651. ACM (2003)

10. Boertjes, E., Gerrits, B., Kooij, R., Maanen, P.-P., Raaijmakers, S., Wit, J.: Towards a social media-based model of trust and its application. In: Hercheui, M.D., Whitehouse, D., McIver, W., Phahlamohlaka, J. (eds.) HCC 2012. IAICT, vol. 386, pp. 250–263. Springer, Heidelberg (2012). doi:10.1007/978-3-642-33332-3_23

11. Sameh, A.: A Twitter analytic tool to measure opinion, influence and trust. J. Industr. Intell. Inf. **1**(1), 37–45 (2013)

12. Smith, M.A., Shneiderman, B., Milic-Frayling, N., Rodrigues, E.M., Barash, V., Dunne, C., Capone, T., Perer, A., Gleave, E.: Analyzing (social media) networks with NodeXL. In: Proceedings of the Fourth International Conference on Communities and Technologies, pp. 255–264. ACM (2009)

13. Mendoza, M., Poblete, B., Castillo, C.: Twitter under crisis: can we trust what we RT? In: Proceedings of the First Workshop on Social Media Analytics, pp. 71–79. ACM (2010)

14. Tavakolifard, M., Almeroth, K.C., Gulla, J.A.: Does social contact matter? Modelling the hidden web of trust underlying twitter. In: Proceedings of the 22nd International Conference on World Wide Web, pp. 981–988. ACM (2013)

15. Golbeck, J.: Combining provenance with trust in social networks for semantic web content filtering. In: Moreau, L., Foster, I. (eds.) IPAW 2006. LNCS, vol. 4145, pp. 101–108. Springer, Heidelberg (2006). doi:10.1007/11890850_12

16. Zhao, L., Hua, T., Li, C.-T., Chen, R.: A topic-focused trust model for Twitter. Comput. Commun. **76**, 1–11 (2016)

Investigating the Polarity of User Postings in a Social System

Afonso M.S. Lima[1], Paloma B.S. Silva[1], Lívia A. Cruz[2], and Marilia S. Mendes[1(✉)]

[1] Federal University of Ceará (UFC), Russas, CE, Brazil
{afonso.matheus,palomabispo}@alu.ufc.br,
marilia.mendes@ufc.br
[2] Federal University of Ceará (UFC), Quixadá, CE, Brazil
livia.almada@ufc.br

Abstract. Evaluation of Human–Computer Interaction (HCI) in a textual way is a recent type of evaluation, demanding studies of techniques to improve it. This work aims to investigate the automatic classification of the polarity of opinion in postings related to the use of the system. We analyzed 1,345 postings of an academic system with social characteristics and performed two investigations: one uses an automatic classifier and the other applies Data Mining algorithms. As results, we present the most relevant words of each polarity, their characteristics and a discussion about the investigations carried out.

Keywords: Textual evaluation · Polarity · Postings Related to the Use (PRUs)

1 Introduction

Recently, some researchers [8, 9, 11, 17, 19, 22, 25, 31] have focused on user narratives in order to study the usability or the User eXperience (UX). In addition to detailed UX descriptions of users' daily lives, the study of user narratives has provided the identification of usability problems [31]. Thus, some initiatives [7, 9, 11, 17, 19, 21] have arisen in order to evaluate systems in a textual way. From those, some papers [7, 15–19, 21] have focused on the analysis of Postings Related to the Use (PRUs). PRUs are public postings from users who discuss about the system while using it. These postings are characterized by spontaneity, since users are not required to make a report of their use. While using it, they mention facts about the system spontaneously, such as: their doubts, compliments, difficulties, reviews, suggestions or even experience reports. The authors [17] affirm that the spontaneity of the report is important, since the questioning by evaluators can influence the responses provided and the UX itself during use of the system [9, 15, 19], through interviews or questionnaires, or by the system itself, as in the method Experience sampling triggered by events [20].

In previous papers, the authors [15] did an investigation about Twitter PRUs in order to investigate the presence and absence of sentiment in them (Table 1) and they observed that both postings with sentiment and with no sentiment (neutral) are important for obtaining some perception of the system. This way, the identification of the polarity of the PRUs would be relevant to evaluate the satisfaction or dissatisfaction

© Springer International Publishing AG 2017
G. Meiselwitz (Ed.): SCSM 2017, Part II, LNCS 10283, pp. 246–257, 2017.
DOI: 10.1007/978-3-319-58562-8_20

Table 1. Classification of postings with and without sentiment in Twitter.

With sentiment	Without sentiment
"I loooooove it when I feel like making my postings, and then I get a server error!"	*"My Twitter has a problem. It doesn't let me put a gif into the icon"*
"HATE the new Twitter feel!!!"	*"I always type everything with errors and only see them after posted"*

(frustration) of the user in the system, whereas the neutral postings would be relevant to identify doubts in system functionalities.

However, the automatic detection of polarity in sentences is a complex scientific challenge due to the subjectivity present in the natural language. Sentiment Analysis is an area of research that aims to define automated techniques for extracting subjective information from texts in natural language, such as opinions and sentiments, in order to create structured knowledge that can be used by a support or decision-making system [6].

In addition to the existing problematic in automatic detection of polarity in sentences, this work has as differential the study of polarity in spontaneous PRUs. The users can have several ways to show their opinion about the system during its use. They can show it to another user, to a system administrator or even to the system itself, such as some reports of PRUs [17]: *"Dear Twitter, it is {dirty word} to have to delete the tweet when I misspell a word, so put the 'edit tweet' option"*; *"Twitter, remove the line break, please, it's much better without it!"*.

Another differential consists in the texts analysis to evaluate a system. Such as [15], we also believe that the user posture in a website for products evaluation is different from that when they are using a system and then face a problem and decide to report it to vent or even to suggest a solution. Similar to [15] have found PRUs relating exactly specific information about the use, such as: *"Folks, sorry, but I've just had a problem here on Twitter and since then I cannot use punctuation once it opens the Twitter menu whenever I try to"*, which also characterizes the fact that the user may report the error in the own system in use.

This way, the objective of this work is to investigate the automatic classification of the polarity of opinion in spontaneous PRUs, specifically: (a) what words are most relevant to each polarity?; (b) what are the characteristics of these words?; and (c) are the investigated classifiers sufficient for use in an automatic textual evaluation?

In this work, we analyzed 1,345 postings of an academic system with social characteristics (e.g., communities, forums, chats, etc.). Two investigations with the PRUs were performed: (1) using the automatic sentistrength classifier [28] and (2) applying Data Mining (DM) algorithms.

This article is organized as follows: in the next section, we present a background on textual evaluation of systems and on sentiment analysis. In the third section, we present some researches related to ours. In the fourth section, we describe the investigative studies, followed by results, discussion, conclusion and future works.

2 Background

2.1 Textual Evaluation of Systems

The textual evaluation of systems consists of using user narratives in order to evaluate or obtain some perception about the system to be evaluated [17]. It is possible to evaluate one or more criteria of quality of use with textual evaluation, such as usability, UX and/or its facets (satisfaction, memorability, learnability, efficiency, effectiveness, comfort, support, etc.) [9, 11, 17, 19, 25]. Other criteria can be evaluated, such as privacy [13], credibility [4, 13] and security [27]. Evaluation forms vary from identifying the context of use to identifying the facets of Usability or UX. Some papers have analyzed specifically the most satisfactory and unsatisfactory user experiences with interactive systems [8, 22, 25, 31].

The textual evaluation can be manual, through questionnaires with questions about the use of the system or experience reports, in which the users are requested to describe their perceptions or sentiments about the use of the system. The other way is automatic: evaluators can collect product evaluations on rating sites [9] or extract PRUs from Social Systems (SS) [15, 17, 19]. The automatic form allows more spontaneous reports, including doubts when using the system, but, on the other hand, may also contain many texts that are not related to the use of the system, and these must be discarded.

Textual evaluation has its advantages and disadvantages, similar to other types of HCI assessment, such as user testing, heuristic evaluation, among others. The main advantage is to consider users' spontaneous opinions about the system, including their doubts. The main disadvantage is the long time of texts analysis. However, there are few initiatives of automatic textual evaluations, since it is an new evaluation type.

2.2 Sentiment Analysis

The sentiment analysis is the field of study that analyses people's opinions, such as their feelings, evaluations, attitudes and sentiments related to products, services, organizations, people, problems, events, expressed in texts (reviews, blogs, discussions, news, comments, feedback, or any other document) [12]. According to [39], sentiment analysis is a type of evaluation of subjectivity that focuses on identifying positive and negative opinions, sentiments and evaluation expressed in natural language.

According to [14], the techniques of sentiment analysis can still be classified according to the approach they use based on: lexicon, which use a lexicon of sentiments (collection of precompiled sentiment items, such as dictionaries); machine learning, which make use of the already known algorithms of machine learning for text classification; or hybrid, which combine both approaches already mentioned.

There are works in this area that seek to discover neutral terms of phrases or sentences [10, 24], others that focus on the recognition of polarity in order to classify sentences into positive or negative ones [5, 24, 32] and, there are still those that try to identify different degrees of positivity and negativity, as strongly negative, weakly negative, neutral, weakly positive and strongly positive [1, 3, 5, 33]. However, these studies did not investigate spontaneous SS PRUs.

In this work, the sentiment analysis is applied to the classification of sentiment in positive, negative and neutral in PRUs. We compared two techniques, one of them based on lexicon and the other based on machine learning to classify sentiments in order to identify the one that best suits the domain of systems evaluation from PRUs.

3 Related Works

Some papers that have focused on user narratives, in order to study the polarity in them, are [8, 22, 31]. In [8], the authors collected 500 texts written by users of interactive products (mobile phones, computers, etc.), with the purpose of studying UX from their positive experiences. The narratives were collected from the reports in which the users were asked to describe them. They analyzed the structure of satisfaction, the links between needs, affect and product, and differences between categories of experience. The authors presented measures of classification of a UX target in positive. In [22], the authors collected 90 reports of the most satisfactory and most unsatisfactory experiences of the users, in order to evaluate the UX of beginner users of augmented reality mobile applications. The narratives were extracted through online questionnaires and were analyzed with the objective of identifying the UX goal, the activity in which the user was involved, characteristics of the reported experience and application resources that helped or disrupted the experiment. As a main contribution, this study had the understanding of measures adopted in order to improve these applications, analyzing user satisfaction.

In [31], the authors studied 691 user-generated narratives with positive and negative experiences in technologies in order to study UX with them. The narratives were also obtained through online questionnaires and were analyzed with the objective of identifying the main themes portrayed in the texts. The authors proposed a technique similar to an affinity diagram, which consisted of grouping a large number of ideas, opinions and information into groups, according to their affinities. This study showed the importance of narrative content from positive and negative classifications.

Although such works have contributed to studies and to positive and negative textual analysis, the texts collected were not spontaneous and a study of the polarity in the sentences was not performed.

4 Investigations

The investigations were carried out in PRUs written in Brazillian Portuguese, collected from the database of an academic system with social characteristics (communities, discussion forums, chats, etc.) called SIGAA, which is the academic control system of the Federal Universities in Brazil. In this system, students can have access to several functionalities, such as: proof of enrollment, academic report, enrollment process, etc. The system allows the exchange of messages from a discussion forum. Its users are students and employees from the university. For this work, 408 PRUs were selected from a part of the database coming from a previous work [17]. The database contained 1,345 postings. The selection criteria was to collect postings in which users were talking about the system. An example of a PRUs collected was: *"I cannot stand this SIGAA anymore!"*. Postings from students asking questions about their graduation courses, grades, location, etc. were not selected, for example: *"Will the coordination work during vacation?"* and *"Professors did not post the grades yet"*.

The PRUs contained between one and six sentences each. That is why many times the post starts praising the system and ends up criticizing it, for example: *"I think this new system has a lot to improve"* (Negative Feeling)…*"However, it is already much better than the previous one"* (Positive Feeling). In this way, we divided the PRUs into 1,100 sentences. After this division, we performed another analysis in order to verify the related and unrelated sentences to the use of the system, because there were sentences such as: *"Good morning"*, *"Thank you"*, *"Sincerely…"*, *"Coordination is on strike"*, which were not related to the use of the system. In this way, we discarded such sentences, resulting in 832 sentences related to the use. After this step, two of the authors of this article categorized the sentences, resulting in 99 positive, 229 negative and 504 neutral ones.

We carried out two investigations. The first one aimed to identify the quality of the classification based on lexical in PRUs. The lexical classification requires the use of a set of terms, in which each term is associated with a sentiment (positive, negative and neutral). For this experiment, we used the DM tool, SentiStrength [30]. SentiStrength combines supervised and unsupervised classification methods. In this work, we used the version 2.2 of the tool, which is available in [28]. In the second investigation, we used version 7.1 of the RapidMiner tool [26]. RapidMiner is an open-source tool widely used in DM for use of learning algorithms (supervised or not). In this experiment, the Naive Bayes algorithm [29] was used. Then we performed a comparison of the results of the experiments by calculating the following evaluation metrics: (a) coverage; (b) agreement; (c) accuracy; (d) precision; (e) recall; and (f) F-measure.

4.1   First Investigation

In this investigation, we used Sentistrength tool [30]. This tool works through a dictionary that contains several words in a given language and there are 3 possible values for each word: a positive, whose strength varies from 1 (Non positive) to 5 (Extremely positive), or a negative, whose strength varies from -1 (Non negative) to -5 (Extremely negative), or 0 if the word is not contained in the dictionary, thus being classified as neutral [5]. By using this dictionary, each word of each sentence in the text document provided as input will receive its respective positive or negative or neutral score. Then, the values of the positive and negative polarity strength for each sentence will be resumed. For instance, in the sentence *"I like and approve the changes"* the tool ranks each word as follows *"I |0| like |3| and |0| approve |2| the |0| Changes |0|"*. Then, both the positive and negative marks of the sentence are calculated. In this case, we would have the scores 3 (highest strength of the positive valuations present in the sentence) and -1 (since there is no negative strength to be considered. The valuation -1 indicates the absence of any negative feelings). Therefore, this sentence will have the two values $(3, -1)$ thus implying in a sentence with predominantly positive strength.

It was necessary to adapt the database to a format that is accepted by the tool, to perform DM in textual collections using the SentiStrength tool. Then, we applied data pre-processing techniques, such as data cleaning, which consisted in removing accentuations and cedillas, because these special characters are not recognized by the tool. After that, we performed the transformation of the file to be used as input to the tool. After these steps, the tool generates a new document with the following results: the sentence, the sentence rewritten with the scores for each word and the final result of the sentence strength.

4.2   Second Investigation

In the second investigation, we used the RapidMiner tool [26] and the Naïve Bayes algorithm [29], to classify the polarity of the PRUs. The Naïve Bayes algorithm was used in this work because it is one of the Bayesian learning techniques most used in texts classification problems [6]. Naïve Bayes is a probabilistic classifier based on the application of Bayes' theorem. It allows the calculation of probabilities of a new document belonging to each of the categories and assign it to categories with higher probability values [6].

In order to apply the algorithm in the tool, it was also necessary to adapt the database using the following data pre-processing techniques: tokenization (sectioning of sentences into minimal units called tokens, for instance, a word is a token); removal of stopwords (stopwords are tokens without semantic value, for example: articles, pronouns); text cleanup (removal of accentuation, normalization of characters to lowercase); stemming (reduction of tokens to the original radical [23]). The main objective of applying these techniques was to reduce the size of the lexicon and also the computational effort, thus increasing the accuracy of results.

Then, it was necessary to format appropriately the data for the tool input. The technique used was the Vector Space Model. In this model, each sentence is represented by a vector of terms and each term has an associated value that indicates its degree of importance in the document. The weight of a term in a document can be calculated in several ways. For this experiment, the weight was the frequency of terms.

The technique used to test the Naïve Bayes algorithm was Cross Validation, with 10 folds. The sample is divided into k (10) parts of equal size, and preferably the parts (or folds) must have the same amount of patterns, thus guaranteeing the same proportion of classes for each subset. The algorithm is trained under k-1 folds (subsets) generating the rules and it is subsequently validated under the fold (subset) that remains. The training set is formed by the 9 (nine) parts and tested by calculating the hit rate under the data of the unused part, the part that is left over. In the end, the hit rate is an average of the hit rates in the k iterations performed.

4.3   Results

Table 2 presents the confusion matrices for both investigations. The confusion matrix shows how the test set instances were sorted. The class under analysis appears on the

Table 2. Post confusion matrix.

	True negative	True neutral	True positive
First investigation			
Pred. negative	46	69	04
Pred. neutral	115	316	34
Pred. positive	68	119	61
Second investigation			
Pred. negative	206	42	0
Pred. neutral	0	399	0
Pred. positive	23	63	99

row, the classifications found appear in the columns and the diagonal of the matrix matches the correct classifications. For example, the confusion matrix shows that, for the negative class, 46 sentences were correctly classified, while 183 (115 + 68) were classified incorrectly.

A comparison of the results of both investigations will be presented in the next items. We performed the comparison between the results with the calculation of the following model evaluation metrics: (a) coverage; (b) concordance; (c) accuracy; (d) precision; (e) recall; and (f) F-measure.

(a) Coverage: The coverage of the methods used for each class was computed for the two investigations. In Fig. 1, we can compare the coverage of each polarity, which consists of the percentage of flows in an application class that is correctly identified [2]. With these results, we can verify whether both investigations resemble as for correctly detecting the feelings. However, the Naïve Bayes classification algorithm obtained a better result in all classes, mainly in the negative one, with a difference of approximately 70%.

(b) Concordance: In Table 3, we can compare the percentage at which the two classification methods agreed on the polarity of a content. The result indicates that there is little concordance between the classification made by the SentiStrength tool and the Naïve Bayes algorithm.

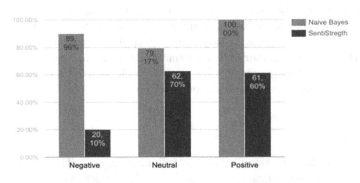

Fig. 1. Coverage of the methods

Table 3. Percentage of agreement between methods.

	SentiStrength
Naïve Bayes	45.91%

(c) Accuracy, (d) Precision, (e) Recall and (f) F-measure: Table 4 illustrates the prediction performance results for each investigation. Accuracy is the most basic measure of efficiency, in which the fraction of instances are correctly classified. Precision determines how many instances of an X class were correctly predicted given all predicted instances of that class. Recall calculation provides how many instances of an X class were correctly predicted given all the instances that truly belong to this class. The F-measure, finally, is the harmonic average between precision and recall.

Table 4. Post confusion matrix.

	Precision	Recall	F-measure
First investigation			
Negative	38.7%	20.1%	26.45%
Neutral	67.9%	62.7%	65.19%
Positive	42.6%	61.6%	50.36%
Second investigation			
Negative	83.06%	89.96%	86.37%
Neutral	100%	79.17%	88.37%
Positive	53.51%	100%	69.71%
Accuracy			
First investigation		50.8%	
Second investigation		84.62%	

5   Discussion

This section intends to discuss the investigations carried out regarding: (a) what words are most relevant to each polarity?; (b) what are the characteristics of these words?; and (c) are the investigated classifiers enough for use in an automatic textual evaluation?

Table 5 presents the most relevant words found (the ones with the highest frequency for each polarity) in Brazillian Portuguese (tokens with stemming) and translated to English.

The characteristics we observed from this result were: (a) the most frequent words refer to system functionalities, such as the name that the user uses to refer to the system: "*system*", "*SIGAA*", "*module*", "*academic*" and its functionalities: "*grade*" and "*enrollment*"; (b) the adjective of intensity "*more*" was found in expressive polarities (positive and negative), indicating the vehemence that users demonstrate their approval or not for the system; (c) the word "*new*" found in the negative polarity indicates a

Table 5. Words with higher frequency.

Language	Positive polarity	Negative polarity	Neutral polarity
Brazillian Portuguese	sistem, mais, bem, melhor, parec, nov, gost, academ, siga, legal	sistem, siga, mais, modul, matricul, academ, not, nov, complic, problem.	sistem, not, matricul, siga, disciplin, turn, alun, ser, professor, histor.
English	system, more, well, better, looks, new, like, academic, SIGAA, cool.	system, SIGAA, more, module, enrollment, academic, grade, new, complicated, problem.	System, note, enrollment, SIGAA, discipline, student, to be (verb), teacher, historical

rejection of the users by the new system, after all, the postings were collected from the beginning of the use of a new one; (d) the names of functionalities found in the negative polarity are those that the users criticized the most, whereas the functionalities present in the positive class would be the most praised - information that would be interesting to know in a system evaluation.

The third point is to discuss whether the classifiers investigated are sufficient for use in an automatic textual evaluation. This point is divided into the following paragraphs between the two approaches used.

By evaluating the results obtained in the first investigation, we noticed that the accuracy, precision and recall measures presented low results for the hit rates. We can attribute this result to the fact that the dictionary provided for the Portuguese language is not adapted to recognize precisely the polarity in PRUs. They need different treatment to recognize what the user wants to say about a given system, since many words can represent different feelings based on the context in which they are used. We can cite as an example the sentence *"Thanks for the help"*, which although the tool treats as a positive feeling, is not one regarding the use of the system. That is, the word *"Thank you"* could not be used as a positive valuation, but as a neutral one. Another example that shows the need to insert a context in the dictionary would be the sentence *"Google Chrome is much better"*. In this example, by the system context, which works only in the Firefox browser, this sentence should be classified as a negative sentiment, since it is criticizing the system limitation of not being supported by other browsers. However, the tool would rank as a positive sentiment, for lack of information.

We also must consider other problems that are recurrent when we work with natural language processing, which requires treatment for particular cases, such as irony, slang and language peculiarities that are regularly used by users of SS. These problems become even more serious when we take into account the number of languages that need a particular study to improve the classification of the tool. In other words, it is necessary to build a method adapted to the domain of PRUs, aiming to obtain more accurate and reliable results in the analysis based on the postings semantics.

From the results obtained in the second investigation, we can observe that the Naïve Bayes classifier obtained a better result for all the metrics evaluated when compared to the ones acquired by the SentiStrength's classifier. It is worth mentioning that it was necessary to use a database for training, in which each sentence was previously labeled with its respective class. Thus, some problems related to the use of Naïve Bayes arose:

(1) manual lettering is onerous, so it is not a viable method for real scenarios; (2) in the systems evaluation, we would like to capture the spontaneity of the user's report [17] and as the extraction of PRUs is done automatically, it is not possible to allow the own user to label their sentiment at the moment of the posting.

6 Final Considerations and Future Work

In this work, we investigated the polarity in PRUs of a university system. The results we presented with the two investigations performed were: more relevant words for each polarity, characteristics of these words and a discussion about the investigations carried out.

The results point to the development of methods for automatic classification of sentiment in PRUs, as well as other investigations in PRUs of other types of systems and with other algorithms.

We carried out some initiatives on textual evaluation, such as: (1) a methodology for evaluating Usability and UX in PRUs [17] and (2) the development of a tool for extracting and classifying PRUs called UUX-Post. The methodology, called MALTU, aims to guide an HCI professional in the evaluation of a system from a set of PRUs. The methodology uses five stages for evaluation: (i) definition of the evaluation context; (ii) extraction of PRUs; (iii) classification of PRUs; (iv) interpretation of results; and (v) reporting the results. In step 1, we define: which system will be evaluated, who the users are and what the objective of the evaluation is. In step 2, the extraction of PRUs is performed, which can be either manually or automatically. In step 3, a classification process of PRUs is performed, which involves classifying them into up to six different categories: (a) type (criticism, doubt, praise, suggestion, comparison); (b) intention (visceral, behavioral, reflexive) [17]; (c) analysis of sentiments (positive, negative, neutral); (d) functionality (what is the functionality of the system the user refers to?); (e) quality of use criteria (usability, UX and its facets); and (f) platform (mobile, desktop). In this step, the sentences are analyzed by experts in order to be classified. The results are then interpreted (step 4) and reported (step 5). Most of these classifications are manual. The UUX-Post tool classifies automatically only the categories: type and quality of use criteria. The research carried out in this work motivates new studies in order to define a context for automatic evaluation of polarity in PRUs.

This experiment must be redone with databases of other systems, with other algorithms and other classification tools, in order to compare, discuss and improve the result to be applied in the UUX-Post tool.

References

1. Albornoz, J.C., Plaza, L., Gervás, P., Díaz, A.: A joint model of feature mining and sentiment analysis for product review rating. In: Clough, P., Foley, C., Gurrin, C., Jones, G. J.F., Kraaij, W., Lee, H., Mudoch, V. (eds.) ECIR 2011. LNCS, vol. 6611, pp. 55–66. Springer, Heidelberg (2011). doi:10.1007/978-3-642-20161-5_8

2. Barros, M.T., Gomes, R.C.M., Alencar, M.S., Ribeiro, P.L.J., Costa, A.: Avaliação de Classificação de Tráfego IP baseado em Aprendizagem de Máquina Restrita à Arquitetura de Serviços Diferenciados. Revista de Tecnologia da Informação e Comunicação (2012)
3. Brooke, J.: A semantic approach to automated text sentiment analysis. Ph.D. thesis, Simon Fraser University (2009)
4. Castillo, C., Mendoza, M., Poblete, B.: Information credibility on Twitter. In: Proceedings of the 20th International Conference on World Wide Web, Hyderabad, India, pp. 675–684 (2011)
5. Esuli, A., Sebastiane, F.: Determining term subjectivity and term orientation for opinion mining. In Proceedings of EACL 2006, Trento, IT, pp. 193–200 (2006)
6. da Silva, C.F.: Grupos gramaticais e sintáticos em categorização automática com Support Vector Machines. Dissertação. Universidade Rio dos Sinos, São Leopoldo (2004)
7. Freitas, L., Silva, T., Mendes, M.: Avaliação do Spotify – uma experiência de avaliação textual utilizando a metodologia MALTU. In: IHC 2016, São Paulo, Brazil (2016)
8. Hassenzahl, M., Diefenbach, S., Goritz, A.: Needs, affect, and interactive products. J. Interact. Comput. 22(5), 353–362 (2010)
9. Hedegaard, S., Simonsen, J.G.: Extracting usability and user experience information from online user reviews. In: Proceedings of CHI 2013, Paris, France, pp. 2089–2098 (2013)
10. Kim, S., Hovy, E.: Determining the sentiment of opinions. In: Proceedings of the COLING Conference, Geneva, pp. 1367–1373 (2004)
11. Korhonen, H., Arrasvuori, J., Väänänen-vainio-mattila, K.: Let users tell the story. Proc. CHI 2010, 4051–4056 (2010)
12. Liu, B.: Sentiment Analysis and Opinion Mining. Morgan & Claypool Publishers, New York (2012)
13. Mao, H., Shuai, X., Kapadia, A.: Loose tweets: an analysis of privacy leaks on Twitter. In: Proceedings of WPES 2011, Chicago, IL, USA, pp. 1–12 (2011)
14. Medhat, W., Hassan, A., Korashy, H.: Sentiment analysis algorithms and applications: a survey. Ain Shams Eng. J. 5(4), 1093–1113 (2014)
15. Mendes, M., Furtado, E., Furtado, V., Castro, M.: How do users express their emotions regarding the social system in use? A classification of their postings by using the emotional analysis of Norman. HCI Int. 2014, 229–241 (2014)
16. Mendes, M.S., Furtado, E.S., Militao, G., Castro, M.F.: Hey, I have a problem in the system. Who can help me? An investigation of Facebook users interaction when facing privacy problems. In: HCI International (2015)
17. Mendes, M.S.: MALTU - model for evaluation of interaction in social systems from the users textual language. 200 f. thesis (Ph.D. in computer science) – Federal University of Ceará (UFC), Fortaleza, CE – Brazil (2015)
18. Mendes, M.S., Furtado, E., Castro, M.F.: Do users write about the system in use? An investigation from messages in natural language on Twitter. In: 7th Euro American Association on Telematics and Information Systems, Valparaiso, Chile (2014)
19. Mendes, M.S., Furtado, E.S., Furtado, V., Castro, M.F.: Investigating usability and user experience from the user postings in social systems. In: HCI International (2015)
20. Obrist, M., Roto, V., Väänänen-vainio-mattila, K.: user experience evaluation – do you know which method to use? Proc. CHI 2009, 2763–2766 (2009)
21. Oliveira, D., Furtado, E., Mendes, M.: Do users express values during use of social systems? A classification of their postings in personal, social and technical values. In: HCI International, Los Angeles, CA, USA (2016)
22. Olsson, T., Salo, M.: Narratives of satisfying and unsatisfying experiences of current mobile augmented reality applications. Proc. CHI 2012, 2779–2788 (2012)

23. Orengo, V., Huyck, C.: A stemming algorithm for the Portuguese language. Published in String Processing and Information Retrieval (2001)
24. Pang, B., Lee, L., Vaithyanathan, S.: Thumbs up? Sentiment classification using machine learning techniques. In: Proceedings of EMNLP, pp. 79–86 (2002)
25. Partala, T., Kallinen, A.: Understanding the most satisfying and unsatisfying user experiences: emotions, psychological needs, and context. In: Proceedings of Interacting with Computers (2012)
26. RapidMiner (2017). <https://rapidminer.com/>
27. Reynolds, B., Venkatanathan, J., Gonçalves, J., Kostakos, V.: Sharing ephemeral information in online social networks: privacy perceptions and behaviours. In: Campos, P., Graham, N., Jorge, J., Nunes, N., Palanque, P., Winckler, M. (eds.) INTERACT 2011. LNCS, vol. 6948, pp. 204–215. Springer, Heidelberg (2011). doi:10.1007/978-3-642-23765-2_14
28. Sentistrength (2017). <http://sentistrength.wlv.ac.uk/#Download>
29. Soelistio, Y.E., Surendra, M.R.S.: Simple text mining for sentiment analysis of political figure using Naive Bayes classifier method. In: Proceedings of 7th ICTS (2015)
30. Thelwall, M., Buckley, K., Paltoglou, G.: Sentiment strength detection for the social web. J. Am. Soc. Inf. Sci. Technol. **63**(1), 163–173 (2012)
31. Tuch, A.N., Trusell, R.N., Hornbæk, K.: Analyzing users' narratives to understand experience with interactive products. Proc. CHI **2013**, 2079–2088 (2013)
32. Turney, P.D.: Thumbs up or thumbs down? Semantic orientation applied to unsupervised classification of reviews. In: Proceedings of ACL, pp. 417–424 (2002)
33. Wilson, T., Wiebe, J., Hoffmann, P.: Recognizing contextual polarity: an exploration of features for phrase-level sentiment analysis. In: Proceedings of ACL (2009)

Intent Classification of Social Media Texts with Machine Learning for Customer Service Improvement

Sebastián Pérez-Vera[1], Rodrigo Alfaro[1,2], and Héctor Allende-Cid[1(✉)]

[1] Pontificia Universidad Católica de Valparaíso, Avda. Brasil 2241, Valparaíso, Chile
sebastian.perez.v@mail.pucv.cl, {rodrigo.alfaro,hector.allende}@pucv.cl
[2] Universidad Técnica Federico Santa María, Avda. España 1680, Valparaíso, Chile

Abstract. Social media platforms in the last few years have facilitated the development of communities that discuss real-world events, and have shaped the way users interact. The content generated in these platforms reflect a variety of intentions, ranging from social interaction to commercial interest, among many others. The present study aims at the implementation of an automatic intent classification system for a Chilean electricity company social media account.

The dataset was created from 5000 tweets that were manually classified by 5 people. If discrepancies were detected, a majority voting scheme was used in order to tag the tweets' intentions. In order to perform the experimental validation of the automatic classification with the machine learning algorithms, several text representations were used (tf-idf, tf-rfl and bin-rfl). The results obtained from the various tests that were conducted yielded satisfactory results. We also analyzed how to assign automatic responses to frequently asked questions, and obtained promising results.

Keywords: Social media · Machine learning · Intent classification

1 Introduction

Intent mining from social data can help filter social media to support organizations in various tasks. However, effective intent mining is an inherently challenging task due to the ambiguity of interpretation, and heterogeneity of the user behaviors in social platforms. Initially considered a sub-discipline of the document classification task, in recent years the classification of documents based on intent, has become a subject of growing interest on its own in the natural language processing community.

The growing interest in automatic processing of intentions contained in text documents is partly a consequence of the exponential growth of user-generated content on the Web, and the increasing concern of companies and governments to analyze, filter or automatically detect the opinions or intentions expressed by their customers or users.

© Springer International Publishing AG 2017
G. Meiselwitz (Ed.): SCSM 2017, Part II, LNCS 10283, pp. 258–274, 2017.
DOI: 10.1007/978-3-319-58562-8_21

Moreover, in the last few years there has been an increasing interest in companies to change the way they interact with their customers. Social media platforms have played a key role in this aspect. Nowadays, most customers interact with their companies through social media instead of using more traditional approaches, and companies have dedicated staff that interacts with customers in these platforms.

Nowadays, frequent use of the Internet and social networks such as Facebook or Twitter has led to the overwhelming growth of this information; since people express their opinions, comments, feelings, yearnings and frustrations of themselves or their environment on these social platforms. With this in mind, a difficult question is born: "What do people think?". This question can be answered with different methods, by extracting, classifying and analyzing what people write in the digital world. For this reason, companies have pointed to this research as a key process in decision making; to be able to know what people think and "feel" about a particular product or campaign is indispensable to take the corresponding measures.

In this study, automatic classification of tweets of a Chilean electricity company into designated categories is discussed and performed. With those classifications, an automatic question answering is implemented for certain tweets that are of common content, in order to facilitate decision-making and management of large volumes of information currently received by the company.

The paper is structured as follows: The next section states the problem. Section 3 presents the State of the Art. The following section presents the proposed methodology. Section 5 presents the experimental results and the last section is devoted to the concluding remarks and future work.

2   Problem

Customer service has evolved in recent years allowing companies and brands to be more connected with their customers in a close, transparent, and immediate way. Customer service through social networks allows organizations to attest to their promise to be close to the customer, to resolve doubts and generate value, in a quick and efficient way.

Assisting the client through social networks is not only an issue of finding the technological tool that will solve the customer's queries as soon as possible. The challenge is to fully comprehend what the customers want and how they want to be assisted through all the channels that this implies.

The study presented in "J.D. power" site [1], tells us that 67% of consumers visit the company's social network profiles to obtain information about services, and about 43% of young people between 18 and 29 would rather interact with brands through social networks than other communication channels. For this reason, the issue of how to interpret this enormous amount of opinions that customers and users have of different brands and companies in social networks takes a prominent role.

With this in mind, it is extremely important to find tools to handle large volumes of information, allowing it to be processed and analyzed in such a way as to find the appropriate answers to the proper functioning of the entities that use social networks as sources of attention.

3 State of the Art

A large part of the user generated content is in the form of texts written in natural language: reviews of products or services, entries of blogs or comments made by other users, threads in public forums (about politics, culture, economy or any other topic), messages written on micro-blogging services like Twitter, or social networks like Facebook; all have a subjective character. On the one hand, these are texts in which Internet users can express their opinions, mood and their points of views; on the other, the practical implications of this type of content are evident for companies or public administrations. For example, many companies nowadays have staff that monitors the opinions on the Internet about the products and services offered by the entities, so that they can actively inter-fere avoiding propagation of negative opinions and their possible consequences in terms of sales; or influencing the image of the company or brand. But regardless of the intended purpose, the number of individual contents that should be con-sidered is of such magnitude, that certain mechanisms of automatic processing has become indispensable. This opens a new sub-discipline known as sentiment analysis or opinion mining, that is to deal with the computational processing of this type of subjective content [9,10]. Thus, sentiment analysis encompasses tasks related to the computational treatment of opinions, feelings and other sub-jective phenomena of natural language. Some of these tasks are the classification of documents according to the positive or negative nature of opinions, the extrac-tion of structured representations of opinions, or the summary of opinion texts, among others [2].

Automatic text classification is usually a supervised process. This means that it requires a set of documents previously classified by human experts, which serve as training input for the system. Thus, a set of documents classified by a human in a certain category, serve for the automatic classifier to generate a classification of its own, given an unknown document. The performance of the automatic classifier will depend on how closely it matches with the human classification, which is evaluated with confusion matrices and other metrics [3].

3.1 Twitter and Its Features

Before discussing how you can infer the intent of comments on Twitter, it is important to understand its structure and main features.

With the appearance of blogs, and responding to the need of users to be able to send messages quickly and easily, Microblogging is born with its leading actor,

Twitter. In this new form of communication, users can write a status or "Tweet" in a short message via Internet, cell phones or emails. This social network was launched in October 2006 and by April 2007 it had 94,000 users. With steady growth, Twitter already had 200 million active users worldwide and 400 million comments per day as of December 2013 [4].

On Twitter, users interact and communicate with each other via tweets. These correspond to short messages with a maximum of strictly 140 characters long. Many of them refer other users of the social network, another Tweet, or a Web page according to the following conventions:

- Mentions (@): If we want to mention other Twitter users, we will do it with the @ code (@username). So even if they do not follow us, they will see in their Twitter feed that we have written to them. This is a way to make those users read us and, if they are interested in what we write, follow us.
- Retweet (RT): A Retweet is a forwarded Tweet, as it has arrived originally or with additional comments. It is usually recognized by the RT code, although it is not mandatory. Twitter official management software, as well as many others available, can identify Retweets.
- **Direct Messages (DM):** A DM to a user, is a message who will only see this user. It is completely confidential and this communication can only be achieved between users that are following each other.
- **Hash tagging (#):** A tag represents a topic, it identifies the subject on which any user can comment simply by typing a tweet with this tag to the message, for example: "#Theme".

4   Proposal

The proposal of this study, is to compare the performances of different automatic classifiers which are trained with inputs that are different representations of Twitter messages. For this aim, a cross-validation process was used, which allows to test the accuracy of the different models in different training and testing scenarios.

The representations that were used in this study are:

1. **Binary:** At each position of the vector the presence (1) or absence (0) of a word corresponding to that position is indicated.
2. **TF-IDF:** This representation is the most frequently used for the classification of texts, where the first section (TF) corresponds to the frequency value of the normalized term, multiplied by (IDf) value, which corresponds to the inverse frequency of the term in the complete collection of documents (N).

$$w(D_i, t_i) = \frac{f_{ij}}{D_i} * \log(\frac{n_j}{N})$$

where n_j is the number of documents containing the term t [5].

3. **TF-RFL:** Corresponds to the relevance of the frequency of a category (label), which is a representation proposed by [6], which constitutes a new representation for the problem of multiple categories.

$$tf - rfl_{tdl} = f_{t_d} * \log(2 + \frac{a_{t,l}}{max(1, mean(a_t, \lambda_{j/l}))}$$

where $mean(a_t, \lambda_{j/l})$ is the average number of documents containing the term t for each document classified into categories other than l.

For the classification stage, the following techniques were be used:

Probabilistic Algorithms (Naïve Bayes). This model is based on probabilistic theory, particularly in the Bayes theorem, which allows us to estimate the probability of an event out of the probability that another event will occur, on which the first depends. The most well-known algorithm, and also the simplest one, is the Naïve Bayes algorithm [6].

Nearest Neighbor Algorithm and Variants. The Nearest Neighbor (NN) algorithm is one of the easiest to implement. The basic idea is as follows: if you calculate the similarity between the document to be classified and each of the training documents, the one that is more similar will be indicating to which class or category the document to be classified should be assigned. One of the most well-known variants of this algorithm is that of the k-nearest neighbor or KNN, which consists in taking the k most similar documents, instead of only the first one. As in those documents there will be, presumably, several categories, the coefficients of each one of them are added together. The one that accumulates more points, will be the suitable candidate.

Decision Trees. Decision Trees are of the most commonly used non-parametric supervised inductive learning methods [6]. As a form of knowledge representation, classification trees stand out for their simplicity. Although they lack the expressiveness of semantic networks or first order logic, their application domain is not restricted to a specific field but can be used in several areas: medical diagnosis, games, meteorological forecasting, quality control, etc.

A classification tree is a way of representing the knowledge obtained in the process of inductive learning. It can be seen as the resulting structure of the recursive partition of the representation space out of the set of prototypes (documents). This recursive partition results in a hierarchical organization of the rendering space that can be modeled by a tree-like structure. Each inner node contains a question about a particular attribute (with a child for each possible answer) and each leaf node refers to a decision (classification).

Support Vector Machines. Support Vector Machines are a set of supervised learning algorithms. These methods are closely related to classification and regression problems. Given a set of training examples, we can label the classes and train an SVM to construct a model that predicts the class of a new sample. Intuitively, an SVM is a model that represents the sample points in space, separating the classes by a space as wide as possible. When the new samples are placed in correspondence with this model, they can be classified to one or another class depending on their proximity. More formally, an SVM constructs a hyperplane or set of hyperplanes in a space of very high dimensionality that can be used in classification or regression problems. An adequate separation between the classes will allow a correct classification.

5   Experimentation

5.1   Dataset

The data set used for the training of the techniques mentioned above is composed of 5,000 Tweets which were obtained by the Company Analitic S.A. The Tweets are fully in Spanish and belong to an emergency account of a chilean electricity company taken between January and April of 2016. As mentioned, the classification techniques require a set of manually classified data to be able to infer to which class not labeled data is assigned. It is for this reason that a system was created that allowed different people to specify to which class a Tweet belongs, in order to obtain an initial data set as objective as possible.

5.2   Category Definition

For the process of data classification, five major categories were established. These categories correspond to:

- **Question:** In this category all the Tweets that contain some interrogative statement were grouped. Their purpose is to know something or obtain some information from the company.
- **Suggestions:** In this category, the Tweets that propose some idea to improve the service or some process of the company were gathered.
- **User Information:** In this category, the Tweets that are delivering some information related to some event or process of the company were grouped.
- **Another:** The Tweets that do not fit in the previous categories or it is unclear to which category they belong, were assembled in this category.
- **Company Information:** In this category, the Tweets that were published by the company and re-twitted by some user were gathered.

5.3   Document Classification

The degree of precision and accuracy that an automatic classifier will be able to provide when sorting a set of unlabeled data will greatly depend on how well it has been trained. In principle then, it is extremely important to have a set of data well classified according to the categories defined above. It is for this reason that a Web site was implemented, in which a group of five people manually classified the dataset.

Five people were considered for the classification to be as objective as possible. For one document to be classified in only one of the categories mentioned, a majority voting system was used. Namely, if a tweet is classified by 3 people in a category, the Tweet will belong to that category; however if there is a tie in the classification of the Tweet, it will be assigned to the Others category prior review. Table 1 shows the voting done by the five users.

Table 1. User voting.

Category/Users	User-1	User-2	User-3	User-4	User-5
Question	2293	2290	2270	2285	2300
Suggestion	85	96	90	92	76
User information	6000	6100	6054	5929	6016
Others	1142	1026	1109	1219	1126
Company information	480	488	477	475	482

The result of the manual classification of documents yielded the following results (Table 2).

Table 2. Manual classification of tweets.

Category	Total	Percentage
Question	2279	22.79%
Suggestion	86	0.86%
User information	5992	59.92%
Others	1173	11.73%
Company information	470	4.70%

5.4   Text Representation

To conduct automatic text classification, each document must be represented in the training examples so that the representation can be applied to the classification algorithm. The most commonly used representation is the vector model, which is largely managed by information retrieval systems.

This model consists on the representation of the collection of documents as an matrix (by terms and by documents) [7]. That is, each text or document is represented as a vector Dj of W terms and a set of vocabulary T. W_{ij} represents a numerical value that expresses to what degree the document D_j possesses the term T_i.

5.5   Dimensionality Reduction

To perform the classification, it is not only necessary to obtain the vector of terms mentioned above, but it is also essential that said vector contains those terms that are more representative, in order to be able to perform the classification with the maximum efficiency possible. Consequently, it is necessary to select those keywords that contribute meaning and to discard those that do not contribute to the distinction between documents. Therefore, it is very convenient to carry out a process of size reduction, thus obtaining a set of reduced terms. This step is essential to determine the quality of the classifier. Thanks to this, it is possible to avoid over training in learning and increase the efficiency and efficacy of the classifier.

Stop Words. Words without meaning such as articles, pronouns, prepositions, etc., are called Stop Words. These were filtered prior to the data processing. A dictionary was generated with the words that have been categorized as empty because they do not add value when classifying a Tweet in any of the categories. Those words that are present in several categories are also included here.

Lemmatization. Lemmatization is a linguistic process that consists of finding the corresponding lemma, given an inflected form of a word (i.e. plural, feminine, conjugated, etc.). The lemma is the form that by agreement is accepted as representative of all the inflected forms of the same word. That is, the lemma of a word is the word that we would find as an entry in a traditional dictionary: singular for nouns, singular masculine for adjectives, and infinitive for verbs.

Element Reduction of a Tweet. Another way to reduce the number of features is based on the analysis of the body of each message. Any reference to a URL was changed to the following "URL_DATA" format, since this text does not add any value to the representation. It is worth noting that when performing the classification manually the contents of these were not visualized, so it did not influence the classification of the Tweet. Also each reference to a topic of interest represented by a # sign, will be changed to the following word "TAG_DATA".

A Tweet can have mentions to several users, and so we would have many names that may not represent any significant importance in the classification of that Tweet. Therefore it has been decided to leave only the mention character

"(@)", which can contribute to the classification of that Tweet. However, a group of users that may have importance at the time of classifying have been detected; these users are the accounts of the companies. Consequently, it has been decided in these cases to leave the complete mention. Some of these users are: @cged_sos, @conafe, @conafe_sos and @elecda_sos among others.

Context Reduction of a Tweet. With the analysis of the context of the Tweets which correspond to messages between the customers of an electric company and vice versa, it has been identified that in many occasions to better perform the assistance, the users indicate their names, which do not contribute by themselves a degree of importance that would allow to predict some category; nevertheless the act of giving their personal data can contribute to predict the category to which the Tweet belongs. Thus, the following rule has been created: a dictionary was created which consists of names and surnames, and each time a name or surname that is registered in the dictionary is found, it will replace that name or surname with the word "CLIENT_NAME". In this way we achieve the aforementioned classification. The same applies to the numeric data, whether RUT, Telephone or customer number (User Identification in the company's system), which have been replaced by the following word: "INFO_NUMERO".

5.6 Training and Classification

In order to carry out this process, a method called Cross-Validation was used. This method is started by splitting a set of data into a K number of partitions, called folds. Cross-validation then iterates between evaluation and training data K times. At each iteration of cross-validation, a different fold is selected as the testing data. In this iteration, the other folds $K - 1$ are combined to form the training data. Therefore, at each iteration we have $(K - 1)/K$ of the data used for the training and $1/K$ used for the testing. Each iteration produces a model, and therefore an estimate of the performance of the generalization; for example, an estimate of the precision. Once cross-validation is complete, all examples have been used only once to evaluate but $K - 1$ times to train. At this point we have yield estimates of all the folds and we can calculate the mean and standard deviation of the accuracy of the model.

The StratifiedKFold iterator provided by Scikit-learn [8] was used. This iterator is an improved version of cross-validation, since each fold is stratified to maintain the proportions between the classes of the original dataset, which usually gives better estimates of bias and variance of the model. A $K = 5$ has been used with 10 iterations in which the methods described below have been evaluated.

5.7 Results of the Classification

The corpus generated after all the processes described above is comprised by 2845 words with which the representation vector of each Tweet was constructed.

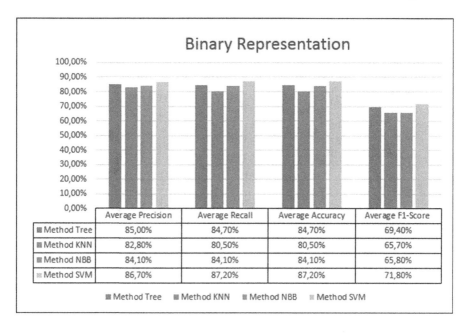

Fig. 1. Binary representation results

Method Tree					
S	Iteration	Classified			
5	Fold	Question	Suggestion	Information	Others	Company
	Question	373	1	65	16	0
R	Suggestion	2	2	7	6	0
e	Information	63	7	1017	106	5
a	Others	8	1	42	183	0
l	Company	3	2	13	1	75

Method KNN					
S	Iteration	Classified			
5	Fold	Question	Suggestion	Information	Others	Company
	Question	288	3	137	27	0
R	Suggestion	0	0	13	4	0
e	Information	21	1	1019	155	2
a	Others	3	1	40	190	0
l	Company	3	0	18	5	68

Method NBB					
S	Iteration	Classified			
5	Fold	Question	Suggestion	Information	Others	Company
	Question	380	0	50	25	0
R	Suggestion	6	0	2	9	0
e	Information	81	0	1044	72	1
a	Others	11	0	51	172	0
l	Company	8	0	7	3	76

Method SVM					
S	Iteration	Classified			
5	Fold	Question	Suggestion	Information	Others	Company
	Question	385	3	55	11	1
R	Suggestion	1	1	7	8	0
e	Information	22	2	1102	35	4
a	Others	7	1	64	162	0
l	Company	3	1	10	0	80

Fig. 2. Confusion matrix binary representation results

Once the vector creation process was generated, three weight assignments were performed to carry out the experiments individually.

As mentioned in the previous section, the Cross-Validation method was used to perform the tests on the different representations used, which consist of the following ones:

- Binary Representation Results (Fig. 1)
  A comparison of the confusion matrices generated in one of the iterations of the cross-validation process, using the techniques applied in the classification

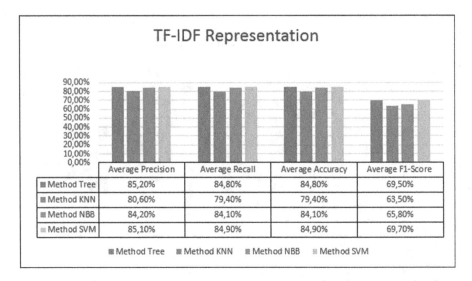

Fig. 3. TF-IDF representation results

Method Tree						
5	Iteration	Classified				
5	Fold	Question	Suggestion	Information	Others	Company
R	Question	404	1	45	5	0
e	Suggestion	0	2	13	2	0
a	Information	57	5	1058	71	7
l	Others	5	5	52	172	0
	Company	5	0	2	3	84

Method KNN						
5	Iteration	Classified				
5	Fold	Question	Suggestion	Information	Others	Company
R	Question	268	0	168	19	0
e	Suggestion	0	2	12	3	0
a	Information	24	1	1095	76	2
l	Others	6	0	75	153	0
	Company	1	0	15	0	78

Method NBB						
5	Iteration	Classified				
5	Fold	Question	Suggestion	Information	Others	Company
R	Question	376	0	64	15	0
e	Suggestion	2	0	12	3	0
a	Information	61	0	1062	72	3
l	Others	13	0	65	156	0
	Company	3	0	5	0	86

Method SVM						
5	Iteration	Classified				
5	Fold	Question	Suggestion	Information	Others	Company
R	Question	394	5	42	10	4
e	Suggestion	5	3	7	2	0
a	Information	64	13	1065	47	9
l	Others	12	2	67	151	2
	Company	1	0	4	0	89

Fig. 4. Confusion matrix of TF-IDF representation results

process, using Binary representation, are shown in Fig. 2. As can be observed the SVM model outperformed all the other State of the Art models in every performance measure.

- TF-IDF Representation Results
  As can be observed in Figs. 3 and 4, using the TF-IDF representation, got similar results as in the previous case. The model that obtained the best results was the SVM model.

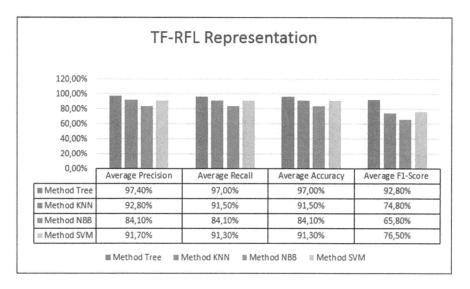

Fig. 5. TF-RFL representation results

	TF-RFL Representation			
	Average Precision	Average Recall	Average Accuracy	Average F1-Score
■ Method Tree	97,40%	97,00%	97,00%	92,80%
■ Method KNN	92,80%	91,50%	91,50%	74,80%
■ Method NBB	84,10%	84,10%	84,10%	65,80%
▦ Method SVM	91,70%	91,30%	91,30%	76,50%

■ Method Tree   ■ Method KNN   ■ Method NBB   ▦ Method SVM

Method Tree

	Iteration	Classified				
5	Fold	Question	Suggestion	Information	Others	Company
	Question	453	0	3	0	0
R	Suggestion	1	13	0	4	0
e	Information	4	0	1168	27	0
a	Others	0	0	3	23	0
l	Company	0	1	0	1	92

Method KNN

	Iteration	Classified				
5	Fold	Question	Suggestion	Information	Others	Company
	Question	422	3	18	13	0
R	Suggestion	0	1	5	12	0
e	Information	7	3	1109	77	3
a	Others	5	4	5	221	0
l	Company	0	1	4	13	76

Method NBB

	Iteration	Classified				
5	Fold	Question	Suggestion	Information	Others	Company
	Question	377	0	64	15	0
R	Suggestion	6	0	8	4	0
e	Information	73	0	1035	91	0
a	Others	19	0	32	184	0
l	Company	4	0	7	2	81

Method SVM

	Iteration	Classified				
5	Fold	Question	Suggestion	Information	Others	Company
	Question	429	2	21	4	0
R	Suggestion	1	2	8	7	0
e	Information	23	11	1113	47	5
a	Others	5	2	31	196	1
l	Company	1	1	5	2	84

Fig. 6. Confusion matrix of TF-RFL representation results

- TF-RFL Representation Results
  In Figs. 5 and 6, we observe the results obtained using the TF-RFL representation. In comparison with the other 2 representations, this one obtained the best results in every performance measure using the Decision Tree algorithm.

  In Figs. 7 and 8 we observe a comparison of the precision and accuracy of the four methods applied with the different representations implemented.

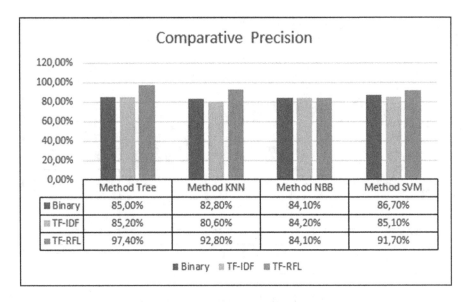

Fig. 7. Precision comparison

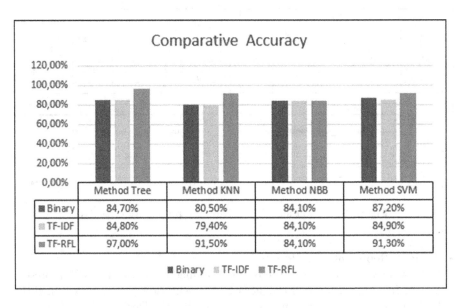

Fig. 8. Accuracy comparison

5.8 Automatic Responses

Automatic responses are messages created in an automated way, which seek to answer common requests that users may have regarding services delivered by a company or platform. The most common use of this measure is the creation of a section in the digital systems called Frequently Asked Questions, where it is sought to give answers to those concerns.

Currently, messaging systems like Twitter, Facebook, WhatsApp and other services are creating automatic responses to messages sent by users. The purpose of these automatic responses, especially for businesses, freelancers and companies, is to warn a client or potential client that you will not be able to answer their query in a certain time. Thus, this mechanism can prevent the client from feeling abandoned and it can be the difference between retaining them or losing them to the competition.

Once the Tweet was classified, it was analyzed whether there were general queries that the users delivered to the company's account and had been answered by the organization. After analysis, three categories were identified; these have common responses to the different messages received. These categories are the following:

Category Others: In this category a group of Tweets was identified, in which the users appreciated the management of the company, which have been answered in a similar way by the organization. Therefore, a default response has been created to reply to such messages. The response created was called "Thanks" Response.

Category Information Users: In this category a particular element has been identified, which refers to the URL of either an image, webpage or file, among others. This URL has been verified by the staff in charge of checking the Tweets, and will not be visualized, either because of the danger that entails opening an unknown URL or because of the time they have to respond to each message. Consequently, a response has been created to reply to these types of messages when it only presents an URL. The response created was called "URL" Response.

Category Question: In this category five questions have been identified which require similar answers. Therefore, five responses have been created to respond to these queries. These are detailed as follows:

- **Answer Public Lighting:** This answer answers the queries made about who is in charge of making maintenance or arrangements to public lighting.
- **Answer Question What is DM?:** This answer responds to the queries made, in which it is asked what a DM is.
- **Answer to General Queries:** This answer is linked to the context of the analyzed accounts which refers, as mentioned above, to an emergency account of an electric company. So general queries such as: what are the opening hours of certain branch or what is the value of kWh, among others, fall outside the scope of the analyzed account.
- **Question Number Emergencies:** This answer is related to inquiries asking for an emergency number.
- **Operability Question:** This answer is related to queries that ask if the company is operational.

5.9   Rules for the Answers

To carry out the automated response process, the following steps were executed: a corpus was obtained for each of the identified responses. Once the corpus was generated, its content was analyzed, yielding a weight factor for each term.

Once each factor was assigned to each element of the corpus a basic rule was generated that allowed to identify if a Tweet belonging to each corresponding category, was possible to answer it in an automated way using the answers created previously.

Evaluation Metrics. Once each factor was assigned to each element of the corpus, a basic rule was generated allowing to identify if it was possible to answer a Tweet belonging to each category in an automated way using the answers created previously.

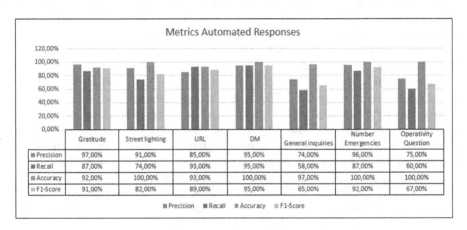

Fig. 9. Automatic replies metrics results

As can be observed in Fig. 9, the best results were obtained in the Street Lighting, DM, Number Emergencies and Operability Question categories obtaining an accuracy of 100%. In terms of accuracy the worst results were obtained in the Gratitude category obtaining 92%. In terms of other performance measures the results were similar. Overall we can say that the results were satisfactory.

6   Conclusions

In the present study three representations were used, which correspond to the representation TF-IDF, Binary and TF-RFL; in addition, the method of Cross Validation was implemented, which served to discern which method of the aforementioned had a better performance at the automatic classifying task. The method with the best performance was the Decision Tree method with the

TF-RFL representation, allowing a good percentage of the Tweets to be classified correctly. Moreover, the Vector Support Machines method also achieved good results using the Binary representation.

It is worth noting the good behavior that has been achieved through the general rules to correctly classify the automatic responses. This gave satisfactory results in some cases such as the response to thank-you Tweets, which achieved an accuracy of 97%. However, there are some answers that did not obtain good results. This can be due to the great variety of cases that the answer covers. This can cause annoyance, since Tweets that should not be answered receive a reply. Thus, this will cause discomfort for the users that will feel abandoned, resulting in a bad image for the company. This result gives rise to the initiative to polish the general rules and look for better results.

It is also important to point out the importance of the feature reduction process, since it has greatly reduced the corpus generated; for in a first instance, a corpus of 7860 words had been generated, of which a large amount did not provide useful information to classify a Tweet in some of the categories. After the feature reduction process, the corpus obtained was of a size of 2845 words, which in view of the obtained results, can be said that it is quite representative.

The overall results are promising. They indicate that in the future it will be possible to fully automatize the process of answering the inquires of the users in a very efficient and quick way. Future work will be focused in obtaining even better results, by exploring different representations and algorithms.

Acknowledgments. This work was supported by the following research grants: Fondecyt Initiation into Research 11150248 and VREIA-PUCV.

References

1. Power, J.D.: Social media benchmark study 2013. http://www.jdpower.com/press-releases/2013-social-media-benchmark-study
2. Baeza-Yates, R., Ribeiro-Neto, B.: Modern Information Retrieval: The Concepts and Technology Behind Search. Addison-Wesley, Reading (1996)
3. Sebastiani, F.: Machine learning in automated text categorization. ACM Comput. Surv. **34**(1), 1–47 (2002). doi:10.1145/505282.505283
4. Pang, B., Lee, L., Vaithyanathan, S.: Thumbs up?: sentiment classification using machine learning techniques. In: Proceedings of the ACL-02 Conference on Empirical Methods in Natural Language Processing, Association for Computational Linguistics, vol. 10, pp. 79–86 (2002)
5. Bacan, H., Pandzic, I.S., Gulija, D.: Automated news item categorization. In: Proceedings of the 19th Annual Conference of The Japanese Society for Artificial Intelligence, pp. 251–256. Springer, Kitakyushu, Japan (2005)
6. Figuerola, C.G., Alonso Berrocal, J.L., Zazo Rodríguez, A.F., Rodríguez, E.: Algunas Técnicas de Clasificación Automática de documentos (2002)
7. Aas, K., Eikvil, L.: Text categorization: a survey. Technical report, Norwegian Computing Center (1999)

8. Pedregosa, F., et al.: Scikit-learn: machine learning in Python. JMLR **12**, 2825–2830 (2011)
9. Pak, A., Paroubek, P.: Twitter as a corpus for sentiment analysis and opinion mining. In: Proceedings of the Seventh Conference on International Language Resources and Evaluation (LREC 2010) (2010)
10. Giachanou, A., Crestani, F.: Like it or not: a survey of twitter sentiment analysis methods. ACM Comput. Surv. **49**(2), 1–41 (2016)

Sentiment Analysis for Micro-blogging Platforms in Arabic

Eshrag Refaee[1,2]([✉])

[1] Department of Computer Sciences and Information Systems,
Jazan University, Jazan 45 142, Kingdom of Saudi Arabia
erefaie@jazanu.edu.sa
[2] School of Mathematical and Computer Sciences, Heriot-Watt University,
Edinburgh EH11 4AS, UK

Abstract. Most previous Sentiment Analysis (SA) work has focused on English with considerable success. In this work, we focus on studying SA in Arabic, as a less-resourced language. SA in Arabic has been previously addressed in the literature, but has targeted text genres of more formal/edited domains (e.g. news-wire) and domains containing longer text instances, i.e. with more contextual information (e.g. reviews). That is, less work has focused on SA in Arabic for a noisy and short-length text genre, like micro-blogs. In addition, the time-changing nature of streaming data (e.g. the Twitter stream) has not been considered in previous work, as SA systems were mainly developed and evaluated on small test-sets that are sub-sets of the original data-set used for training.

This work reports on a wide set of investigations for SA in Arabic tweets, systematically comparing two existing approaches that have been shown to be successful in English. Unlike previous work, we benchmark the trained models against an independent test-set of >3.5k instances collected at different points in time to account for topic-shifts issues in the Twitter stream. Despite the challenging noisy medium of Twitter and the mixed use of Dialectal and Standard forms of Arabic, we show that our SA systems are able to attain performance scores on Arabic tweets that are comparable to the state-of-the-art SA systems for English tweets.

Keywords: Sentiment analysis · Machine learning · Arabic NLP · Twitter

1 Introduction

Over the past decade, there has been a growing interest in collecting, processing and analysing user-generated text from social media. As a sub-task of Affective Computing, Sentiment Analysis (SA) provides the means to mine the web automatically and summarise vast amounts of user-generated text into the sentiments they convey. The growth of research in automatic analysis of people's attitudes and sentiments has coincided with the increasing popularity of social

© Springer International Publishing AG 2017
G. Meiselwitz (Ed.): SCSM 2017, Part II, LNCS 10283, pp. 275–294, 2017.
DOI: 10.1007/978-3-319-58562-8_22

media [22]. This is where the research area of SA plays a major role in capturing and analysing the subjective content from text produced by the general public on social media.

SA research on micro-blogging platforms (e.g. Twitter) is not only motivated by the vast amount of freely available data to crawl [30], but also by their popularity. The selection of Twitter and other sources of big data is motivated by the growing interest in studying content of social networks due to their influence both at social and individual levels [11]. In this context, research has pointed out the significance of Twitter in particular as a valuable resource with regard to the recent unstable political and social circumstances in the Middle East [37].

This work reports on a wide set of investigations for SA in Arabic tweets, systematically comparing two existing approaches that have been shown successful in English. Specifically, we report experiments evaluating fully-supervised-based (SL) and distant-supervision-based (DS) approaches for SA. The investigations cover training SA models on manually-labelled (i.e. in SL methods) and automatically-labelled (i.e. in DS methods) data-sets. Unlike previous work, we benchmark the trained models against an independent test-set of >3.5k instances collected at different points in time to account for topic-shifts issues in the Twitter stream. Despite the challenging noisy medium of Twitter and the mixed use of Dialectal and Standard forms of Arabic, we show that our SA systems are able to attain performance scores on Arabic tweets that are comparable to the state-of-the-art SA systems for English tweets.

The work also investigates the role of a wide set of features, including syntactic, semantic, morphological, language-style and Twitter-specific features. We introduce a set of affective-cues/social-signals features that capture information about the presence of contextual cues (e.g. prayers, laughter, etc.) to correlate them with the sentiment conveyed in an instance. Our investigations reveal a generally positive impact for utilising these features for SA in Arabic. Specifically, we show that a rich set of morphological features, which has not been previously used, extracted using a publicly-available morphological analyser for Arabic can significantly improve the performance of SA classifiers. We also demonstrate the usefulness of language-independent features (e.g. Twitter-specific) for SA. Our feature-sets outperform results reported in previous work on a previously built data-set.

2   Background

The growth of research in automatic analysis of people' s attitudes and sentiments has coincided with the increasing popularity of social media [22]. The ability to classify sentiments is important to understand attitudes, opinions, evaluations and emotions communicated among users across the world about current issues - answering the question of 'what is going on'.

SA has been an active research area recently with a major focus on English, as a well-resourced languages. The most prominent effort for SA on English tweets has been made by a series of well-known international competition, namely SemEval. Between 2013 and 2016, four editions of this competition have been successfully launched [25,33,34]. SemEval includes a number of sub-tasks, e.g. determining overall polarity. Our work is closely related to sub-task B, which aims to classify a given tweet instance into positive, negative or neutral (from its author's perspective). For this task, a benchmark data-set of nearly 10k tweets is created and manually annotated for positive, negative and neutral. The test-sets used were collected at different points in time than that of the training data, allowing for different topics to be covered in training and test data [33]. Results reported in this task ranged between 0.248–0.648 F-score on English tweets. It is interesting to mention that SemEval-2017 will include Arabic for the first time in the task of determining the overall polarity of a tweet.

As for SA in Arabic, less effort has been reflected in the literature. A major cause for this is the limited availability of SA-related resources, including anno-tated data-sets and subjectivity lexica. The limited availability of such resources can be partially attributed to the complexity of Arabic, as a morphologically-rich language. In addition, Arabic has two major language varieties: Modern Stan-dard Arabic (MSA) and Dialectal Arabic (DA), which differs significantly [17]. The formal variety of the language, namely MSA, has been the subject of con-siderable efforts in developing NLP tools spanning various aspects. In contrast, NLP research on DA has only recently flourished to cope with the increasing prevalence of DAs on the web.

Most previous SA work on Arabic has targeted longer and more formal text instances like newswire, reviews and forums with accuracy rates of up to 95% [1,3]. Few recent attempts have addressed the problem of SA in social media platforms like Twitter (Table 1). However, studies on SA of Arabic tweets suffer from a number of shortcomings. For instance, some studies have only targeted a particular dialect, as in [20]. Others have considered only word-based n-gram features, e.g. [5] or use small sizes of data-sets (up to 3k tweets). In this work, we further expand previous work for SA on Arabic tweets by investigating the impact of: (1) expanded and more variant feature-sets, and (2) experimenting on larger and multi-dialectal training data. In addition, we test our models on

Table 1. Prominent previous work on SA for Arabic.

Paper	Data (size)	ML scheme	Results
Abdul-Mageed et al. [4]	Newswire (2.8k sentences)	SVM	95.52% acc.
Farra et al. [15]	Reviews (44 instances)	SVM	89.3% acc.
Abdul-Mageed et al. [3]	Tweets (3k instances)	SVM (held-out)	65.87% acc. and 61.83% F-score
Abbasi et al. [1]	Forums (1k instances)	SVM (CV)	93.60% acc.
Mourad and Darwish [23]	Tweets (<2k instances)	SVM and NB (CV)	71.9% acc. and 70.35% F-score
Duwairi et al. [12]	Tweets (1k Jordanian and MSA)	NB (CV)	76.78% acc.
Nabil et al. [24]	Tweets (10k Egyptian)	SVM (held-out)	69.10% acc. and 62.60% F-score

an independent test-set, collected at different points in time to explore the performance of our models for a dynamic medium like Twitter. In contrast, Mourad and Darwish [23] and Duwairi et al. [12] only use Cross-Validation (CV) to evaluate their classifiers, while Abdul-Mageed et al. [3] and Nabil et al. [24] use a held-out test-set, which is a sub-set of the original data set used for training. This can be less effective for real-world applications wherein the task is to use trained models for classifying a sample of Twitter feeds over a period of time.

3   Data Collection and Annotation

The Twitter API[1] allows Twitter data to be retrieved by external developers using some search criteria (i.e. keywords, user-names, locations, etc.). Following previous work [16], we search the Twitter API with a pre-prepared list of queries (see Table 2). For instance, in SemEval-2015 developers collected tweets that express sentiment about popular topics. Note that for training a classifier, query terms are replaced by place-holders to avoid bias.

Accessing Twitter API is rate limited (180 queries in a 15 min period), and so we set a delay/waiting time between requests of 2–3 min, as suggested by Go et al. [16]. Similar to the work of Purver and Battersby [30] and to avoid bias (i.e. weekends or active users), we collect data at random times of the day and on different days of week. In addition, we calculate the distribution of the number of tweets from individual users (using the unique IDs of authors). The recorded rate we observe in our data-sets is between 1.76 to 2.59 tweets per user showing no skew towards a group of users. To restrict the retrieved tweets to Arabic only, we set the language parameter of the API to *lang:ar*.

For training, we collected two data-sets: the gold-standard manually-annotated data-set and the distant-supervised automatically-labelled data-set.

3.1   Gold-Standard Manually Annotated Data-Set (GS)

This data-set contains a set of 9k tweets randomly sampled out of 57k tweets collected between January 2013 and February 2014. The 9k tweets were manually annotated by two native speakers of Arabic, using the guidelines displayed

Table 2. Examples of query-terms used for collecting the Arabic Twitter Corpus.

Products/brands	iPhone, channel
Social and religious Issues	Divorce, education, early/child marriage, Sheia
Public figures	Obama, Mandilla, Khamenei, Erdogan
Sport	Chelsea, Al-Ahli FC
Internet and technology	YouTube, Instagram, Google
Controversial topics	Isis

---

[1] https://dev.twitter.com/.

Table 3. Sentiment labelling criteria for Arabic Twitter Corpus

Label	Definition	Example	English
positive	Clear positive indicator	كم انت عظيم يا بشّار الأسد	*How great you are, Bashar Al-Asad.*
negative	Clear negative indicator	حنّا للآسف نستخدم ايفون	*Unfortunately, we use the iPhone.*
neutral	• Simple factual statements / news	حالة وفَاة جديده باتش بان٩ بالصين	*A new reported death case with H7N9 in China.*
	• Questions with no emotions indicated	بكم سعر الآيفون ٥ حاليًا؟	*What is the price of the iPhone 5 these days?*
mixed	Mixed positive and negative indicators (i.e. difficult to decide on the strongest)	فوضيّ الأخوَان المسلمين التي تريد تدمير حريّاتنَا	*We love democracy, but hate the mess that Muslim Brotherhood is making to destroy our freedom*
uncertain	Undeterminable indicators/neither positive or negative/ lack subjective cues	احيَانًا فهمنَا الأمورِ بطريقه خطا يكُون هو الصح	*Sometimes, the wrong understanding of things leads to the right thing.*
skip	Redundant or advertising tweets	-	-

in Table 3. Table 5 shows the sentiment distribution of the resultant GS data-set. In order to measure the reliability of the annotations, we conducted an inter-annotator agreement study on the annotated tweets. We use Cohen's Kappa metric [9], which measures the degree of agreement among the assigned labels, correcting for agreement by chance. The resulting weighted Kappa reached $\kappa = 0.786$, which indicates reliable annotations.

What Happens with the Examples Where Both Annotators Disagree? A third annotator is employed to decide the selection of the final annotation, if the 3rd annotator disagrees with both annotators, the tweet will be assigned *uncertain* label. Data instances in this category are also excluded from the data-set [7].[2] This procedure is important for the quality of the gold-standard data-set. As provision of annotated data is a goal of this work, the GS data-set has already been made freely available to the research community via an ELRA repository and at the time of writing this work, the data-set has been accessed more than 162 times and downloaded more than 110 times [31].[3]

3.2 Distant-Supervised (DS) Automatically-Annotated Data-Set

Two DS-based data-sets were created using two popular conventional markers of Twitter, i.e. emoticons and hashtags, to collect and automatically label Twitter instances as positive or negative.

---

[2] The 9k tweets in this data-set represent the final number after all tweets labelled as uncertain were excluded. A total of 3,106 tweets were excluded from the Gold-Standard data-sets.

[3] Further information about how to access/download the corpus can be found at: goo.gl/qNLIZ2.

Table 4. Emoticons and hashtags used to automatically label the DS-based training data-sets.

Emoticon	Sentiment label	Hashtag	Sentiment label
:) , :-) , :)), (: , (-: , ((:	positive	(happy, سعَاده) (joy, بهجة) (hope, أمل)	positive
:(, :-(, :((, :((,): ,)):)-:	negative	(sad, حزن) (bane, مصيبه) (despair, يأس)	negative

Table 5. Sentiment label distribution of the training data-sets: gold standard manually annotated and distant supervision data-sets.

Data-set	Neutral	Polar[a]	Positive	Negative	Mixed	Total
Gold standard (GS)	4,854	4,327	1,346	2,408	573	9,181
Emoticon-based (Emo)	55,076	1,118,356	660,393	457,963	-	1,173,432
Hashtag-based (Hash)	55,076	130,160	59,990	70,170	-	185,236

[a]Polar = positive + negative + mixed

Following [8,16,30], we use a set of emoticons with pre-defined polarity and sentiment-bearing-hashtags (Table 4) to automatically label DS training sets. Conventional markers are merely used to assign the sentiment labels and removed from tweets to avoid any bias, following Go et al. [16].

The number of tweets collected varied in accordance with the popularity of conventional markers (i.e. emoticons and hashtags) that we used to query Twitter. That is, although Emo and Hash data-sets were collected over the same period of time, the total number of tweets retrieved using emoticons is 1,511,621 tweets, while the number of tweets collected using hashtag queries is 926,640 tweets. A similar behaviour was also observed by Purver and Battersby [30] on English tweets. Furthermore, we observe that removing duplicated instances from the emoticon-based and hashtag-based data-sets reveals a very high rate of noisy/repeated tweets in the hashtag-based data-set, resulting in reducing the hashtag-based data-set from 926,640 to 130,160 instances (see Table 5). To illustrate, the discarded content represents 85.9% of the originally collected hashtag-based data-set, as compared to 24.1% of the emoticon-based data-set. A closer look at a random sample of the Hash data-set reveals an extensive use of popular hashtags, e.g. happy, to post advertising content to a wider audience.

Test Data-Set. In order to compare SA systems trained on different training sets, we use an independent test-set to evaluate their performance. That is, considering the evolving nature of the Twitter stream [13], we built a test-set that is a collection of random samples retrieved over different periods of time (Table 6). In addition, the size of the data-set (as shown in the Table 6) is comparable to that created and used in SemEval on English tweets (sizes for Twitter test-sets are 4,435 tweets in 2013 and 2,473 tweets in 2014). Previous studies on Arabic tweets, in contrast, have considered test-sets that are subsets of the original data-set (e.g. [3]) or used cross-validation (e.g. [23]). Both settings are problematic for Twitter due to its evolving nature and topic-shift issues that are likely to influence the predictive ability of a trained model over different points in time.

The test-set is manually annotated by two native speakers of Arabic, following the criteria presented in Table 3 (p. 5). The inter-annotator score for the test-set is at $\kappa = 0.69$. Our test-set is designed to provide a common ground to build and evaluate SA systems, as it (1) is built with a coverage that spans an extended period of time (see Table 6); (2) contains less bias to active users (observed distribution of the number of tweets from individual users is 1.16 tweet per user); (3) is annotated with a rich set of morphological, semantic, and stylistic features; and more importantly, (4) is publicly available.[4]

The class distribution in the test-set indicates the negative class as the majority class. This is in line with our previous manual annotations of the gold-standard training data. Following SemEval [33,34], the instances were randomly selected for manual annotation, which is likely to obtain a representative sample of the Twitter stream [8].

Table 6. Sentiment label distribution of the test data-set.

Data-set	Collection time	Neutral	Polar	Positive	Negative	Total
Test-sample1	Spring 2013	324	377	69	308	701
Test-sample2	Autumn 2013	480	621	285	336	1,101
Test-sample3	Winter 2014	333	518	169	349	851
Test-sample4	Summer 2014	218	667	208	459	885
Total	-	1,355	2,183	731	1,452	**3,538**

3.3   Data Pre-processing

We adapt pre-processing techniques to tackle informality and alleviate the noise typically encountered in social media. We use pre-processing techniques that have been previously employed and shown to be useful for improving performances of SA systems [16,23,32,34]. In particular, the extracted data is cleaned up in a computationally-motivated (i.e. reducing feature space) pre-processing step by:

– **Normalising conventional symbols of Twitter:** this involves detecting entities like: #hash-tags, @user-names, re-tweet (RT), and URLs; and replacing them with place-holders.

---

[4] http://www.macs.hw.ac.uk/~eaar1/Eshrag%20Refaee/myResearch1.html.

- **Normalising exchangeable Arabic letters**: mapping letters with various forms (i.e. *alef* and *yaa*) to their representative character.
- **Eliminating non-Arabic characters.**
- **Removing punctuation and normalising digits.**
- **Removing stop words:** this involves eliminating some frequent word tokens that are less likely to have a role in class prediction (e.g. prepositions).
- **Reducing emphasised words/expressive lengthening**: this involves normalising word-lengthening effects. In particular, a word that has a letter repeated subsequently more than two times will be reduced to two (e.g. *sadddd* is reduced to *sadd*).

Other text pre-processing steps involve:

Text Segmentation: This step is performed to separate tokens based on spaces and punctuation marks. For this, we use the publicly available tokeniser called TOKAN integrated into MADAMIRA [28].

Text Stemming: This is one step further in text pre-processing that aims to alleviate the high dimensionality of the text data by using reduced forms of words (e.g. stems). Abdul-Mageed et al. [3] argue about the importance of employing such a technique, in particular, when dealing with a morphologically rich and highly derivative language like Arabic, as the problem of high dimensionality becomes more pronounced. In this context, Abdul-Mageed [2] highlights the significance of this text pre-processing step and argues that SA on Arabic can be problematic without using the compressed forms of words, as it will result in the sentiment classifiers being exposed to a large number of previously unseen features (words), although they might be present in training and testing but in different forms. For instance, the words:

وبتَالقهَا *and+with+her+brilliance,* وبتَالقه *and+with+his+brilliance,* بتَالقه *with+his+brilliance* and بتَالقهَا *with+her+brilliance* can be reduced to the stem بتَالق meaning *brilliantly/brightly.*

In sum, stemming has shown to be beneficial for SA on Arabic newswire, reviews and social media posts [4–6].

4 Features Extraction

This section presents a number of feature-sets that we extract and employ to examine their utility for SA on Arabic tweets (Table 7). The categorisation and design of feature-sets is inspired by the work of Abbasi et al. [1].

Word-Token-Based Features: This set involves word-stem unigrams and bigrams, as they were found to perform better than other combinations of n-grams in our preliminary experiment.

Table 7. Summary of feature-sets used.

Feature-set	Features	Feature type
Syntactic	Word-stem n-grams	String
Morphological	Aspect	String
	Gender	String
	Mood	String
	Number	String
	Person	String
	POS:word	String
	State	String
	Voice	String
	Diacritics	String
	Has-morph-analysis	Binary
Semantic	Has-positive-lex	Binary
	Positive-lex-count	Numerical
	Has-negative-lex.	Binary
	Negative-lex-count	Numerical
	Has-neutral-lex.	Binary
	Neutral-lex-count	Numerical
	Has-negator	Binary
Affective-cues	Has-consent	Binary
	Has-dazzle	Binary
	Has-laughs	Binary
	Has-regret	Binary
	Has-prayer	Binary
	Has-sigh	Binary
Language-style	Tweet-length (char)	Numerical
	Word-length (char)	Numerical
	Word-offset (char)	Numerical
	Has-exclamation-mark	Binary
	Exclamation-mark-count	Numerical
	Has-question-mark	Binary
	Question-mark-count	Numerical
	Has-dots	Binary
	Dots-count	Numerical
	Has-lengthening	Binary
	Has-positive-emoticon	Binary
	Has-negative-emoticon	Binary
	MSA-or-DA	Binary
	Degree of dialectness	Numerical
Twitter-specific	is-Favourite	Binary
	Favourite-count	Numerical
	is-Retweet	Binary
	Retweet-count	Numerical
	Has-hashtag	Binary
	Has-URL	Binary
	Has-user-name	Binary

Morphological Features: The use of this feature-set is motivated by the rich morphology of Arabic, thus aiming to exploit this aspect by extracting a rich set of morphological features. For that, we employ a state-of-the-art morphological analyser for Arabic, namely MADAMIRA [28]. MADAMIRA on a gold annotated blind test data by Pasha et al. [28] has achieved an accuracy of up to 95.9% for POS tagging and 84.1% for word-level morphological analysis on MSA.

Semantic Features: This feature-set includes a number of binary and numeric features that check the presence and number of occurrences of sentiment-bearing words in each given tweet (Table 7). To extract this feature-set, we utilise a combined sentiment lexicon. Our merged sentiment lexicon exhibits a reasonable degree of coverage/variation as ArabSenti and the Arabic translation of MPQA represent more formal language (both are in Standard Arabic), while our in-house Twitter-based lexicon[5] includes informal and dialectal entries, contributing words like:

طز *go to hell* and بلطجي *bully.*

Affective-Cues/Social-Signals: This feature-set comprises six binary features, indicating whether a tweet has any of these social signals: consent, dazzle, laughs, regret, prayer, and sigh. To obtain these features, we use six manually created dictionaries.[6] To avoid bias, the extracted dictionaries are based on an independent data-set that does not overlap with any of our data-sets. The use of this feature-set is motivated by the idea of finding a set of simple features that can correlate to users' culture and, at the same time, can be used as a means of conveying sentiments. For instance, Ptaszynski et al. [29] employ a manually collected lexicon of emotive expression, i.e. culturally-specific Japanese emotional expressions, and note that these features are useful for SA on Japanese blogs.

Twitter-Specific Features: This set utilises seven features characterising the way Twitter is being used (Table 7). Twitter can be used in various ways: for information sharing (via inclusion of URLs and hashtags) and/or for social networking (via inclusion of user-mentions and re-tweets), as such uses vary across languages [18]. For instance, Hong et al. [18] investigated behaviour differences among users of different languages and observed that communities like Korean and Indonesian tend to exhibit more for social networking, whereas English and German users tend to use Twitter more for information sharing. We are not aware of a similar study on Arabic. Thus, we explored one of our own data-sets comprising 1.2M Arabic tweets and observed a higher tendency for social networking (e.g. up to 36.80% of tweets included user-mentions), while only an average of 16.64% of tweets included hashtags/URLs, i.e. less use of tweets for information sharing.

Language Style Features: This set involves a number of features that characterise the language typically used in social media, including:

(A) **Stylistic features:** This set of features is also referred to as language independent. It captures information about the informal language used in social media and may convey sentiment. That is, stylistic features aim to unveil

---

[5] The lexicon is freely available at: goo.gl/qNLIZ2.
[6] The lists are freely available at: goo.gl/qNLIZ2.

latent patterns that can improve classification performance of sentiments [1]. This set comprises features checking for stylistic variation, i.e. presence of: emoticons, expressive lengthening (e.g. *sadddd*).

(B) **MSA-or-DA feature:** This is a binary feature to investigate the usefulness of employing an explicit feature that identifies the language variety of a tweet instance (MSA or DA). To automatically extract this feature, we use AIDA [14]. In addition to identifying the language variety of a tweet as MSA or DA, AIDA can provide a numerical value between [0,1] reflecting the degree of dialectness for the corresponding tweet, which we also exploit as a feature.

MSA-or-DA feature can be particularly useful for investigations on Arabic tweets to assess the impact of DA presence on the overall performance of SA. The use of this feature is also motivated by the fact that MSA is often referred to as *"the language of the mind"* while the DAs as *"the language of the heart"*.[7]

5   Experimental Setup

In this section, we present the experimental setup we utilised in our empirical investigations.

Machine Learning Scheme: In this work, we use Support Vector Machines (SVMs) [21] as a machine learning scheme that is found to be particularly successful for text classification problems, including SA [7,27,33,34]. Since there are several implementations available for SVM, we follow guidelines by Hsu et al. [19] who show that LIBLINEAR is more efficient in tackling document/text classification problems – wherein both the number of instances and features are large – than LIBSVM, in terms of the time required to obtain a model with a comparable accuracy and memory consumption. Therefore, we use LIBLINEAR for all experiments reported in this work.[8]

Classification Levels: We experiment with two-level binary classification problem formulation (Fig. 1). The choice is based on the results of our preliminary experiments that showed steady better performance for two-level binary classification over single-level three-way classification.

Baselines: We compare our results against several baselines, including a majority baseline (B-Mjr) and a stem n-gram baseline (B-stem).

---

[7] For instance, we find that Dialectal tweets represent 34.12% of the negative tweets, 37.39% of the positive tweets, and only 13.52% of neutral tweets in the GS data-sets, suggesting subjective instances to be more dialectal as compared to neutral ones. In addition, Cotterell and Callison-Burch [10] reported 40% of their Arabic Twitter data-set comprising >40k tweets were manually annotated as highly dialectal.

[8] https://www.csie.ntu.edu.tw/~cjlin/liblinear/.

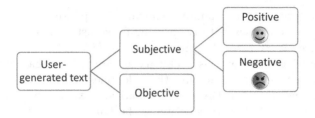

Fig. 1. Levels of sentiment classification.

Evaluation Metrics: The results are reported using two popular metrics: weighted F-score and accuracy.

Evaluations Methods: We use two methods for evaluating the performance of the trained models, namely cross-validation (CV) and independent test-set. CV relies on a fixed number of data proportions, i.e. folds. We also use our independent test-set account for the time-changing nature of the Twitter stream, following SemEval [25,33,34], that has not previously been considered for Arabic.

Statistical Tests: We employed two popular metrics, i.e. t-test and Chi-squared (χ^2) to provide evidence that variation among different classifiers is not caused by chance.

6   Experimental Results

This section displays the results of our empirical investigations.

6.1   Impact of Feature-Sets

First, we investigated the utility of a wide set of features (see Table 7) that has not previously been employed for SA on Arabic tweets. To assess the usefulness of the features, we conducted experiments on the only data-set available at that time. For that, we use the M&D data-set developed by Mourad and Darwish [23] (see class distribution in Fig. 2). The authors used SVM and experimented with CV setting. Table 8 displays the results of utilising our feature-sets on M&D data-set following similar experimental settings.

Subjectivity Classification (Polar vs. Neutral): The best performance is achieved with the morphological features at 66.25% accuracy. This is a 2.65% accuracy improvement compared to the top score originally reported by Mourad and Darwish [23] at 63.6% on this data-set. The addition of the morphological features has significantly improved performance over the stem n-grams baseline. Our morphological feature-set includes POS with 35 tags, as opposed to only five POS tags used by Mourad and Darwish [23]. We therefore concluded that a rich set of morphological features (e.g. gender, voice, aspect, among others) with an extended POS set is beneficial for Arabic SA.

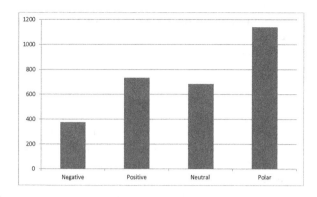

Fig. 2. Class distribution in M&D data-set.

Sentiment Classification (Positive vs. Negative): The average accuracy score is at 81.32%, which is 9.42% improvement as compared to 71.9% accuracy reported by Mourad and Darwish [23] on this task. The best performance is attained by the semantic features at 82.70% accuracy. For extracting the semantic features, Mourad and Darwish [23] used ArabSenti and a translated version of MPQA, which is similar to our work. However, they did not report on manually correcting/filtering the auto-translated entries of the MPQA in order to maintain its quality. We used a translated and manually filtered version of MPQA that

Table 8. Binary classification on M&D data-set: polar vs. neutral; positive vs. negative.

M&D data-set						
	Polar vs. neutral			Positive vs. negative		
	F	Acc.	SD	F	Acc.	SD
Majority baseline (B-mjr)	0.519	65.57	0.17	0.526	66.07	0.4
Stem n-grams[a]	0.620	65.13	2.81	0.818	<u>82.05</u>	2.64
Stem n-grams + Morph[a]	0.643	**66.25***	2.54	0.811	<u>81.18</u>	3.99
Stem n-grams + Semantic[a]	0.620	65.17	2.85	**0.827**	**82.70***	3.56
Stem n-grams + Affec-cues	0.624	65.27	2.87	0.816	<u>81.85</u>	2.93
Stem n-grams + Lang-style[a]	0.623	<u>63.12*</u>	3.51	0.776	<u>77.61*</u>	4.01
Stem n-grams + Twt-specific[a]	0.622	65.28	2.78	0.822	<u>82.38</u>	2.92
Comb. of all feat	**0.65**	66.14*	2.76	0.808	<u>80.78</u>	3.74
Average	0.628	65.19	2.88	0.812	81.32	3.54

Underline denotes a statistically-significant difference vs. majority baseline ($p < 0.05$).
*Denotes a statistically-significant difference vs. stem n-grams baseline ($p < 0.05$).
[a]Denotes that the feature-set or a subset of it has been used by Mourad and Darwish [23].

comprises 2.6k entries out of 8k in the original English MPQA. In addition, they automatically expanded the sentiment lexicon, which is likely to introduce more noise than benefit [36]. In our work, we utilised a new dialectal sentiment lexicon to adapt to the use of DAs in social media.

Use of M&D Data-Set in Other Studies: A recent study by Salameh et al. [35] on M&D data-set (positive vs. negative) with CV and an SVM classifier reported their best score at 74.62%. This still does not compete with our results on this data-set, with an average accuracy score of 81.32%. The performance variation can be attributed to the different feature-sets used. Salameh et al. [35] employed word-lemma n-grams and semantic features (leveraging manually and auto-generated sentiment lexica), while our system employs word-stem n-grams along with a wide set of semantic (manually created lexica) and a rich set of morphological features, among others.

In sum, our new, extended feature-sets have shown to outperform previous work on M&D data-set for both tasks: subjectivity (polar vs. neutral) and sentiment (positive vs. negative) classification.

6.2   Impact of Evaluation Method: CV vs. Independent Test-Set

To assess the impact of the time-changing nature of streaming data (e.g. Twitter stream) on the evaluation method employed, this section outlines experiments that compare the performance of classifiers when evaluated (1) using the standard CV and (2) using our independent test-set that was collected at different points in time than that of the training data (see Table 6). For that, we use a subset of 2.2k tweets of our manually annotated gold-standard (GS) data-set (see Table 5). Results of this set of experiments are displayed in Table 9.

For subjectivity classification (polar vs. neutral), we can observe a significant performance drop of 31.23% accuracy on average between CV and the results on independent test-set. This indicates that, despite the promising results with CV at an average accuracy of 95.49%, the classifiers do not generalise well to unseen topics.

For sentiment classification (positive vs. negative), again, testing on the independent test-set has resulted in an average performance drop of 17.03% in accuracy across all feature-sets compared to CV.

Conclusion: Unlike previous work, we re-evaluate our trained models on an independent, larger and more diverse test-set. We show that, despite very promising CV results, our models do not generalise well to data-sets collected at a later point in time, causing performance drops. The performance drop is likely to be caused by time-dependent topic-shifts issues in the Twitter stream and the prominent role of word n-gram features in our models [26, 36].

Table 9. Binary classification on subset of 2.2k tweets of GS data.

	10 fold CV			Ind. test-set	
	F	Acc.	SD	F	Acc.
Polar vs. neutral					
Majority baseline (B-mjr)	0.578	70.08	0.1	0.471	61.70
Stem n-grams	0.905	<u>91.01</u>	2.24	0.557	**65.26**
Comb. of all feat	**0.998**	**99.93***	0.23	**0.594**	63.14*
Average	0.952	95.49	1.86	0.577	64.26
Positive vs. negative					
Majority baseline (B-mjr)	0.335	50.16	0.25	0.531	66.51
Stem n-grams	0.736	<u>74.1</u>	3.71	0.586	<u>58.59</u>
Comb. of all feat	**0.908**	**90.77***	2.41	**0.702**	**69.68***
Average	0.80	80.24	3.29	0.635	63.21

Underline denotes a statistically-significant difference vs. majority baseline (p < 0.05).
*Denotes a statistically-significant difference vs. stem n-grams baseline (p < 0.05).

Since Twitter experiences topic-shifts over time, the vocabulary, especially the content words, are likely to change as well [13]. Investigating this hypothesis, we find that the word frequency distribution differs amongst the training/test data-sets: the overall overlap of unique tokens is only 12.21%. Next, we will address this issue by using a larger gold-standard training data-set and by using semi-supervised approaches to automatically obtain larger training data.

6.3 Impact of Size of Training Data

To assess the impact of increasing the size of the training data in reducing the performance gap encountered when using the independent test-set for evaluating our classifiers, we experimented with different sizes of the GS data. Table 10 shows the results of three sets of experiments, each with different training data size. Results show that the average performance gap has been reduced from 24.13% with 2.3k instances to 7.63% with 6.8k instances, reaching only 4.9% with 9k instances.[9] This indicates a utility for expanding the training set on the classifiers' ability to attain better scores. Next, we examine the possibilities of further expanding training by exploiting existing clues (e.g. emoticons) to *automatically* obtain sentiment labels.

---

[9] The performance gap here is the average across subjectivity and sentiment classification.

Table 10. Summary of GS results on various sizes of training data.

Data-set (size)	Average acc.	Performance gap (CV - ind. test-set)
GS (2.3k)	63.74	24.13
GS (6.8k)	72.96	07.63
GS (9k)	74.10	04.93

6.4   Impact of Annotation Method: Manually vs. Automatically

To assess the utility of employing automatic means for obtaining larger anno-tated data as opposed to standard manually-based ones, we follow previous work by Go et al. [16] in using distant supervision (DS) approaches. DS approaches have been successfully used for SA in English (e.g. [8,16]. However, we are not aware of existing studies with investigation of DS for SA in Arabic.[10] As such, we collected and automatically labelled emoticon-based and hashtag-based DS data-sets (see Table 5). Table 11 shows that the best average accuracy perfor-mance is attained when combining emoticon- and hashtag-based data-sets (with 1.2M instances) at 62.22%. However, it is interesting to note that this score is still below the average accuracy score attained by the manually-annotated GS data-set (9k instances) at 75.91% (Fig. 3).

Table 11. Binary classification positive vs. negative on the emoticon and hashtag-based data-sets.

Positive vs. negative						
	Emo		Hash		Emo+Hash	
	F	Acc.	F	Acc.	F	Acc.
Majority baseline (B-mjr)	0.531	66.51	0.531	66.51	0.531	66.51
Stem n-grams	0.537	52.77	**0.674**	69.22	**0.621**	62.81
Comb. of all feat	0.531	64.41*	0.258	36.97*	0.565	62.53
Average	0.544	56.23	0.531	56.53	0.60	62.22

Underline denotes a statistically-significant difference vs. majority baseline ($p < 0.05$).
*Denotes a statistically-significant difference vs. stem n-grams baseline ($p < 0.05$).

As for the stem n-grams baseline, it can be seen that hashtag-based data-set (Hash) outperforms the emoticon-based data-set (Emo). This is interesting, considering that Emo is about 8.6 times larger than Hash. To clarify this, we

---

[10] Since the vast majority of previous work has used DS only with binary sentiment classification positive vs. negative (e.g. [8,16]) and due to the controversy in the existing means for automatic collection of neutral instances [23], we report the results in this section for the binary sentiment classification.

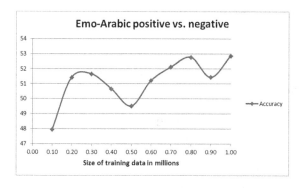

Fig. 3. Learning curve on a 1M Arabic emoticon-based data-set.

conducted an error analysis on a random sample of Emo data-set, in which we manually annotated a set of 303 tweets. We found that only in 34.32% of cases does the manual label match the automatically assigned label, i.e. using emoticons. Whereas, in 36.63% of the cases manual labels and automatically assigned labels do not match. This raises questions about the quality of automatically assigned labels using emoticons. A closer look at the sample reveals cases wherein emoticon-based labels do not match the emotion conveyed in the accompanying text, either due to sarcasm, as in example 1, or because of mistakenly interchanged parenthesis as a result of the right-to-left typing nature of Arabic, as presumably is the case in example 2.

جميل يَا اهلي :(1
great job Ahli :(- referring to a famous football team.

البقَاء لّه :(اللّهم ارحمهم 2
Condolences :) May Allah shower their souls with mercy

7 SAAT: A System for Sentiment Analysis in Arabic Tweets

In this section we present SAAT, a java-based system we developed to automatically classify sentiments conveyed in Arabic tweets, utilising our best trained classifiers. The system will receive a query from systems users about entities, e.g. *'Trump'*. The query will then be sent to retrieve tweets containing the query text from the Twitter live stream. The retrieved tweets will pass through the pre-processing steps described earlier. Next, the trained subjectivity classifier will decide if the tweet is neutral or subjective. Finally, subjective tweets will be classified by the sentiment model as positive or negative (see Table 12).[11]

---

[11] Codes are available at: goo.gl/qNLIZ2.

Table 12. Examples of tweets about *'Trump'* auto-labelled via SAAT.

1	
لو ساندرز عمل معجزه وقَابل ترَامب، فَاالأمر محسوم لهيلَاري	
If Sanders gets to the final with Trump, then things will be working really well for Hillary.	positive
2	
انونيموس تعلن حربًا شَامله علي دونَالد ترَامب	
Anonymous hackers declare total war on Donald Trump.	negative
3	
هل دونَالد ترَامب جورج وَاليس الجديد؟	
Is Donald Trump the George Wallace of this time?	neutral

8 Conclusion

In sum, DS-based approach using emoticons for SA in Arabic seem to be less useful as compared to English. The results indicate a tendency of a hashtag-based DS approach to be less noisy, attaining an accuracy score close to that achieved by manually annotated gold-standard (GS) data. As such, hashtag-based DS approach has the potential to obtain sentiment labels automatically and at the same time maintain quality levels close to GS, with the difference in performance as a trade off for the laborious effort required to obtain GS labels.

References

1. Abbasi, A., Chen, H., Salem, A.: Sentiment analysis in muliple languages: feature selection for opinion classification in web forums. ACM Trans. Inf. Syst. (TOIS) **26**, 1–34 (2008)
2. Abdul-Mageed, M.: Subjectivity and sentiment analysis of Arabic as a morophologically-rich language. Ph.D. thesis, The School of Informatics and Computing, Indiana University, Bloomington, Indiana, USA (2015)
3. Abdul-Mageed, M., Diab, M., Kübler, S.: SAMAR: subjectivity and sentiment analysis for Arabic social media. Comput. Speech Lang. **28**(1), 20–37 (2014)
4. Abdul-Mageed, M., Diab, M.T., Korayem, M.: Subjectivity and sentiment analysis of modern standard Arabic. In: Proceedings of the 49th Annual Meeting of the Association for Computational Linguistics: Human Language Technologies: Short Papers, HLT 2011, Stroudsburg, PA, USA, vol. 2, pp. 587–591. Association for Computational Linguistics (2011)
5. Ahmed, S., Pasquier, M., Qadah, G.: Key issues in conducting sentiment analysis on Arabic social media text. In: IIT, pp. 72–77. IEEE (2013)
6. Al-Twairesh, N., Al-Khalifa, H., Al-Salman, A.: Subjectivity and sentiment analysis of Arabic: trends and challenges. In: IEEE/ACS 11th International Conference on Computer Systems and Applications (AICCSA), pp. 148–155. IEEE (2014)
7. Banea, C., Mihalcea, R., Wiebe, J., Hassan, S.: Multilingual subjectivity analysis using machine translation. In: Proceedings of the Conference on Empirical Methods in Natural Language Processing, pp. 127–135. Association for Computational Linguistics (2008)

8. Bifet, A., Frank, E.: Sentiment knowledge discovery in Twitter streaming data. In: Pfahringer, B., Holmes, G., Hoffmann, A. (eds.) DS 2010. LNCS, vol. 6332, pp. 1–15. Springer, Heidelberg (2010). doi:10.1007/978-3-642-16184-1_1

9. Cohen, J.: A coefficient of agreement for nominal scales. Educ. Psychol. Meas. **20**(1), 37–46 (1960)

10. Cotterell, R., Callison-Burch, C.: A multi-dialect, multi-genre corpus of informal written Arabic. In: LREC 2014, Reykjavik, Iceland. ELRA, May 2014

11. Dodds, P.S., Clark, E.M., Desu, S., Frank, M.R., Reagan, A.J., Williams, J.R., Mitchell, L., Harris, K.D., Kloumann, I.M., Bagrow, J.P., Megerdoomian, K., McMahon, M.T., Tivnan, B.F., Danforth, C.M.: Human language reveals a universal positivity bias. Proc. Natl. Acad. Sci. **112**(8), 2389–2394 (2015)

12. Duwairi, R., Marji, R., Sha'ban, N., Rushaidat, S.: Sentiment analysis in Arabic tweets. In: ICICS, pp. 1–6, April 2014

13. Eisenstein, J.: What to do about bad language on the internet. In: Proceedings of NAACL-HLT, pp. 359–369 (2013)

14. Elfardy, H., Al-Badrashiny, M., Diab, M.: AIDA: identifying code switching in informal Arabic text. In: EMNLP 2014, p. 94 (2014)

15. Farra, N., Challita, E., Assi, R.A., Hajj, H.: Sentence-level and document-level sentiment mining for Arabic texts. In: IEEE ICDMW 2010, pp. 1114–1119. IEEE (2010)

16. Go, A., Bhayani, R., Huang, L.: Twitter sentiment classification using distant supervision. CS224N Project Report, Stanford, pp. 1–12 (2009)

17. Habash, N.: Introduction to Arabic natural language processing. Synth. Lect. Hum. Lang. Technol. **3**, 1–189 (2010). Morgan & Claypool Publishers

18. Hong, L., Convertino, G., Chi, E.H.: Language matters in twitter: a large scale study. In: ICWSM (2011)

19. Hsu, C.-W., Chang, C.-C., Lin, C.-J.: A practical guide to support vector classification. National Taiwan University, Taipei, Taiwan (2003)

20. Ibrahim, H., Abdou, S., Gheith, M.: MIKA: a tagged corpus for modern standard Arabic and colloquial sentiment analysis. In: IEEE ReTIS, pp. 353–358, July 2015

21. Joachims, T.: Text categorization with support vector machines: learning with many relevant features. In: Nédellec, C., Rouveirol, C. (eds.) ECML 1998. LNCS, vol. 1398, pp. 137–142. Springer, Heidelberg (1998). doi:10.1007/BFb0026683

22. Liu, B.: Sentiment analysis and opinion mining. Synth. Lect. Hum. Lang. Technol. **5**, 1–167 (2012). Morgan & Claypool Publishers

23. Mourad, A., Darwish, K.: Subjectivity and sentiment analysis of modern standard Arabic and Arabic microblogs. In: WASSA 2013, p. 55 (2013)

24. Nabil, M., Aly, M., Atiya, A.: ASTD: Arabic sentiment tweets dataset. In: Proceedings of EMNLP 2015, Lisbon, Portugal, pp. 2515–2519. ACL, September 2015

25. Nakov, P., Kozareva, Z., Ritter, A., Rosenthal, S., Stoyanov, V., Wilson, T.: Semeval-2013 task 2: sentiment analysis in Twitter. In: *SEM, Atlanta, Georgia, USA, pp. 312–320. ACL, June 2013

26. Pang, B., Lee, L.: Opinion mining and sentiment analysis. Found. Trends Inf. Retr. **2**(1–2), 1–135 (2008)

27. Pang, B., Lee, L., Vaithyanathan, S.: Thumbs up?: sentiment classification using machine learning techniques. In: Proceedings of EMNLP, pp. 79–86. ACL, 2002

28. Pasha, A., Al-Badrashiny, M., Diab, M., Kholy, A.E., Eskander, R., Habash, N., Pooleery, M., Rambow, O., Roth, R.: MADAMIRA: a fast, comprehensive tool for morphological analysis and disambiguation of Arabic. In: Proceedings of LREC 2014, Reykjavik, Iceland. ELRA, May 2014

29. Ptaszynski, M., Rzepka, R., Araki, K., Momouchi, Y.: Automatically annotating a five-billion-word corpus of Japanese blogs for sentiment and affect analysis. Comput. Speech Lang. **28**(1), 38–55 (2014)
30. Purver, M., Battersby, S.: Experimenting with distant supervision for emotion classification. In: Proceedings of EACL, Avignon, France, pp. 482–491. ACL, April 2012
31. Refaee, E., Rieser, V.: An Arabic Twitter Corpus for subjectivity and sentiment analysis. In: LREC 2014 (2014)
32. Refaee, E.A.: Sentiment analysis for micro-blogging platforms in Arabic. Ph.D. thesis, The School of Mathematical and Computer Sciences, Heriot-Watt University, Edinburgh, UK (2016)
33. Rosenthal, S., Nakov, P., Kiritchenko, S., Mohammad, S., Ritter, A., Stoyanov, V.: SemEval-2015 task 10: sentiment analysis in Twitter. In: Proceedings of SemEval 201), pp. 451–463, Denver, Colorado. ACL, June 2015
34. Rosenthal, S., Ritter, A., Nakov, P., Stoyanov, V.: SemEval-2014 task 9: sentiment analysis in Twitter. In: SemEval, pp. 73–80, Dublin, Ireland. ACL, August 2014
35. Salameh, M., Mohammad, S., Kiritchenko, S.: Sentiment after translation: a case-study on Arabic social media posts. In: NAACL, Denver, Colorado, pp. 767–777. ACL, May–June 2015
36. Taboada, M., Brooke, J., Tofiloski, M., Voll, K., Stede, M.: Lexicon-based methods for sentiment analysis. Comput. Linguist. **37**(2), 267–307 (2011)
37. Zaidan, O.F., Callison-Burch, C.: Arabic dialect identification. Comput. Linguist. **40**(1), 171–202 (2014)

Automatic Tweets Classification Under an Intelligent Agents Framework

Sebastián Rodríguez[1], Rodrigo Alfaro[1,2(✉)], Héctor Allende-Cid[1], and Claudio Cubillos[1]

[1] Pontificia Universidad Católica de Valparaíso, Valparaíso, Chile
sebastian.rodriguez.o@mail.pucv.cl,
{rodrigo.alfaro,hector.allende,claudio.cubillos}@pucv.cl
[2] Universidad Técnica Federico Santa María, Valparaíso, Chile

Abstract. Twitter is a microblogging platform that allows users to share opinions with a restricted amount of characters. Given the social characteristic of Twitter, it is a potential source for sentiment analysis. For this reason, opinions of certain subjects such as people or brands can change in short periods of time. A traditional approach of a sentiment classifier implementation performs poorly since it depends on how it is trained. We propose a novel method for tackling this problem, with the implementation of a multi-agent system for classifying and corpus analysis mechanism for retraining the classifier. This mechanism consists of a critic agent which compares the trained corpus of the classifier agent with new collections of documents from future time steps, using primarily two methods: hypothesis test analysis and histogram differences. A Naïve-Bayes based classifier was implemented with this mechanism with multiple configurations. The results of experimental data show that the mechanism boosts its performance, when compared to a pure Naïve Bayes classifier.

Keywords: Mobile social computing and social media · Text classification

1 Introduction

Since the use of social networks has been constantly increasing in recent years, social platforms like Twitter, Facebook and LinkedIn among others have been a potential source of information, since users write and share opinions, personal experiences and communication messages among groups of people. The selected platform for the development of this research is Twitter, where users write messages with a 140 character limit; these messages are called "tweets", and on average, 58 millions tweets are emitted daily [1].

It is because of this, that sentiment analysis may be a powerful tool for companies to assess their brand, as well as various campaigns that they may conduct, and thus being able to make decisions regarding them. For this purpose, automated text classification may be used, which corresponds to the process of

© Springer International Publishing AG 2017
G. Meiselwitz (Ed.): SCSM 2017, Part II, LNCS 10283, pp. 295–311, 2017.
DOI: 10.1007/978-3-319-58562-8_23

labeling texts in predefined thematic categories, given certain characteristics. Therefore, the automated text classification has been a subject of research that proposes, as it names implies, the automation of the tasks involved in the classification of manual texts. It has been used in several applications as well, such as filtering emails and organizing information.

The traditional approach of the automation of this process, is focused primarily on the use of supervised learning algorithms for text classification [13]. Supervised learning in the context of text classification uses pre-labeled data as an input for an algorithm, that then learns the patterns of the training set by probabilistic means (Naive Bayes) or decision rules (Decision Trees), among other mechanisms.

One of the not so well studied characteristics of sentiment analysis is the potential change of opinion concerning the topic that users are discussing. With a traditional approach of automated text classification this presents a problem, in that once the algorithm is trained, it only learned from a particular time frame. It is for this reason that we propose a novel method, by means of techniques based on artificial intelligence proposed by [12], where the implementation of a framework based on intelligent agents provides the classifier a method and a criterion for its retraining, as required. The use and implementation of this framework is justified due to the lack of studies oriented at the use of intelligent agents on tweet classification, more specifically, sentiment analysis. For this reason, it is expected that this research will supply significant knowledge for both areas.

This study is structured as follows: the next section presents the State of the Art. Section 3 presents a more detailed description of the problem and the dataset used in this study. Later, Sect. 4 shows the proposed methodology with a detail of the agents that compose the multi-agent system. The experimental results are showed in Sect. 5 and in the last section, a brief discussion of the results is presented with some insight into possible future work.

2   State of the Art

The baseline of this paper is inspired in the survey by [13] where the text classification problem is discussed thoroughly. In this work we explain the following: the subset of problems that derive from text classification, diverse methods for preprocessing the texts, supervised machine learning, algorithms for automating the process and the performance metrics used for the evaluation of these algorithms. In terms of intelligent agents, Russel and Norvig [12] provided a solid guideline defining the baseline for different types of agents. For this paper, we used the learning agent as an inspiration for implementing the intelligent agent framework.

In the context of the Twitter platform, the use of intelligent agents is more linked to information retrieval [5], simulation of user behavior facing rumors [14] and online influencing simulation [10]. However, as for the use of intelligent agents for text classification, studies out of the scope of sentiment analysis were found. Particularly, how to implement collaborative learning systems [11] and how to train the agents in game oriented environments [2].

Regarding the current state of the studies on text classification and sentiment analysis on Twitter using machine learning techniques, there is a larger body of literature. There are studies oriented to testing several supervised machine learning algorithms [9], the application of distant supervised machine learning approach [7], and the use of several text representation techniques applied to tweets [3].

3   Problem and Data Used

3.1   Problem Definition

In the subject of sentiment analysis of Twitter, with the massification of the use of social networks, companies can use Twitter for directing marketing campaigns for certain products, or for analyzing the opinion of the clients about the brand; these actions can be done in order to make beneficial decisions. In conjunction with this, another less explored aspect of sentiment analysis, corresponds to a possible change in the sentiment/opinions of the users with regard to the topic which is under analysis. This is an interesting point, because in a traditional work flow with machine learning algorithms, a model trained with this approach will perform poorly in the detection of those changes in opinions. The main cause of this is that the model is only trained once, and traditionally with a large enough dataset as to introduce as many possible cases to train the classifier.

For this very reason, it is crucial for the development of this study, to create a mechanism which can detect important differences between sets of tweets, in order to be able to use re-training techniques for the classifier. This mechanism can be useful not only in the context of detecting changes in opinions, it can also be used to see and learn from sets with words that have never been seen before in the training set.

3.2   Data

The dataset used in this project, is the original dataset used by [3], which corresponds to a collection of tweets emitted by people in relation to two Chilean retail companies. This dataset was obtained between the years 2013 and 2014, the tweets were labeled manually by a group of five people, and were granted by the company Analitic S.A. for the development of this study.

The main difference with the first use of this dataset, is that in this study, 3000 were used in total, with 1000 for each label available in the dataset: positive, negative and neutral tweets. The distribution of these tweets in terms of each retail company, was made evenly across each possible label.

It is worth noting that preprocessing techniques for the texts were applied before the training/testing process of the classification algorithm. The preprocessing consisted in the elimination of stopwords, symbols, numbers, hyperlinks and the term "RT". The latter was removed because it is a convention term used in Twitter for replicating a message emitted by another user, and a possible way to add commentaries given the 140 characters limitation.

In this way the final dataset is built, which will be used as a document pool for interacting with the distributor agent. This agent and all the intelligent agent framework will be described in the following section.

4   Methodology

4.1   Multi-agent Architecture

To address the problem described in the previous section, a multi-agent system composed by three agents was chosen. These agents are: the distributor agent, the critic agent and the classifier agent. In the literature related to these

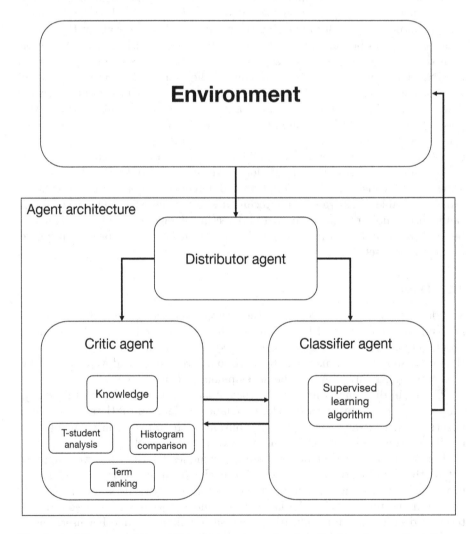

Fig. 1. Architecture of the multi-agent system, showing the 3 main agents and how the communication flow is directed

Setup

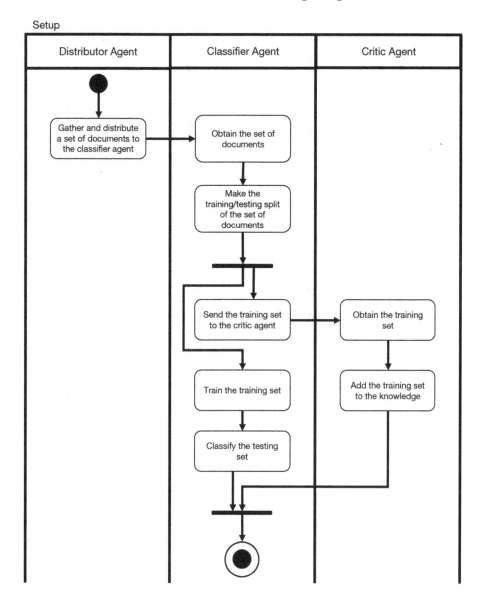

Fig. 2. Activity diagram depicting the setup phase for the three agents

systems [16], various methods are proposed on how the agents interact with the environment and with each other. In this sense, an approach focused on a hybrid layer placement of the agents (combining both vertical and horizontal stacking) has been taken into account. This means that not all the agents interact with the environment, in particular, the critic agent only interacts with the distributor and classifier agent.

N Iteration run

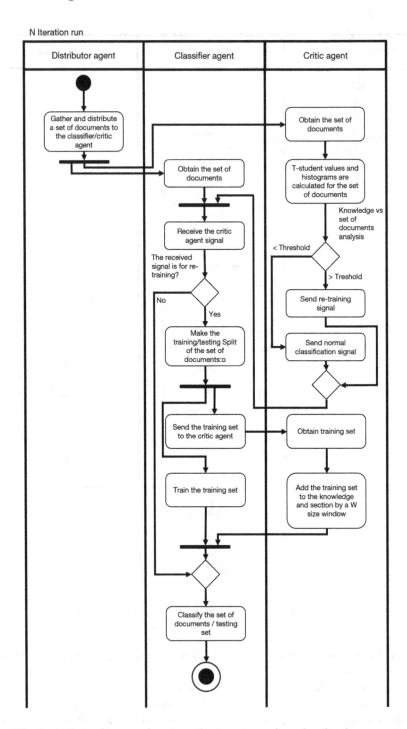

Fig. 3. Activity diagram depicting the iterations phase for the three agents

The positioning of the agents on the hybrid layer is as follows: in a first layer is the distributor agent, which interacts with the environment (document pool), then this agent collects a number of tweets from the pool and afterwards sends this set to both classifier and critic agent.

The critic agent is equipped with four elements: the knowledge of the critic/classifier (the set of tweets with which the classifier agent was trained), the mechanism for detecting the difference between a set of tweets and the knowledge (t-student analysis and histogram comparison) and finally a dimensionality reduction mechanism for the knowledge analysis (term ranking).

Finally, the classifier agent implements a supervised learning algorithm for the core mechanism of the classifier. The existing interaction between the classifier and the critic agent, corresponds to communication messages concerning certain behaviors of the agents, for example, coordination messages regarding their shared knowledge. It should be noted that the output of the classifier agent is the classification of the set of tweets sent by the distributor agent.

Next, in the Fig. 1 a diagram depicting the multi-agent system architecture is presented.

Interaction Between Agents. Next, in the Figs. 2 and 3, an activity diagram between the agents is displayed. Mainly the Fig. 2 represents the first iteration when the first set of documents arrives to both agents and there is no previous knowledge to make a comparison. The Fig. 3 shows the process of the multi-agent system through all iterations after the setup phase.

In the next subsections, the functionality of each agent will be further elaborated.

4.2 Distributor Agent

Main Functionality. The distributor agent has the purpose of reading n tweets out of a document pool (environment), and distributing those to both critic and classifier agents. For the test implementations, the process of obtaining the n tweets of the document pool is the feature that adds the temporal aspect to the tests, simulating tweets batches, that the agent picks for making the iterations. However, in a real world application, this agent has to pick the tweets in real time and create the batches of n size for later distribution.

For the implementation of the test, the distributor agent also knows beforehand the true classes of the tweets. This allows the re-training process of the classification agent, and evaluate its performance; but in a commercial application, this agent can use an approach based in [7] for the automatic labeling of a Twitter live feed. On the contrary, if this technique is not applied, the distributor agent should storage that set of tweets in the case that a re-training message is triggered, for later labeling by a human expert and the re-training process.

4.3   Classifier Agent

Main Functionality. The purpose of the classifier agent, as its name suggest, is to classify the tweets sent by the distributor agent. The algorithm of choice for the classification core of the agent is the Naïve Bayes algorithm [12,13], specifically the multinomial Naïve Bayes represented by the following equation:

$$P(c_j|d) = \ln P(c_j) + \sum_{i=1}^{M} \ln P(t_i|c_j) \tag{1}$$

where c_j corresponds to a j class, d to any document (or tweet for the scope of this study) and t_i to a term i present in the document d.

The multinomial Naïve Bayes was used in that is one of the best models that fits the feature vector used for the bag of words representation [8]. Also, this model can handle underflow errors, when handling low value probabilities caused by low term frequency in the trained corpus.

Re-training of the Classifier Model. This agent includes a re-training mechanism, triggered by a message given by the critic agent. This mechanism consists on adding a subset of the new feature vectors to the trained model; these subsets are generated by splitting a percentage of the set of tweets sent by the distributor agent randomly. For re-training purposes, this agent asks the distributor agent to obtain the true classes.

4.4   Critic Agent

Main Functionality. The main functionality of the critic agent lies in its knowledge. Using different statistical measures to the knowledge in a similar manner like [15], relevant information is obtained. These metrics are: T-student test, Histogram comparison test and the use of term ranking.

The main purpose of applying those analyses to the classifier agent knowledge, is to see if there are differences with another tweet corpus. Formally, given a document corpus D and two subsets A_t and A_{t+1}, both belonging to D, the hypothesis $(A_t - A_{t+1} \sim N(0,1))$ must be proved. An example for a representation of D is presented in the Fig. 4.

		t1	t2	t3	t4	t5	t6	t7
At	d1	0	2	1	5	3	4	1
	d2	2	4	2	0	1	0	3
	d3	0	0	0	5	0	1	2
	d4	0	1	0	2	0	3	0
At+1	d5	1	0	0	4	6	0	2
	d6	4	5	6	0	0	1	2

Fig. 4. A matrix representation of two set of documents A_t and A_{t+1}, with d_i representing each document of a set, and t_j representing as a term j for a document

Another important point for the development of the critic agent in this study, is the existence of two assumptions: first, that the subset A_t is independent and identically distributed (*i.i.d*); this implies that the documents that belongs to the subset A_t are *i.i.d.*, and the words of those documents also are *i.i.d.*. The second supposition is that both subsets A_t and A_{t+1} are temporal data fluxes (in time steps t), and this enables the subset statistical analysis in such a way that, if the subset A_t is normally distributed, then there should not exist a significant difference between future temporal subsets. If the opposite happens and there is a significant difference given a certain threshold, then the critic agent sends a message to the classifier agent, indicating that A_{t+1} has to be retrained. When this retraining process is repeated with future subsets $(A_{t+2}, A_{t+3}, ..., A_{t+n})$. It is expected that there should be a smaller difference for each re-training iteration, decreasing the possibilities of finding significant differences with future subsets, and therefore, reducing the retraining instances.

Knowledge Limit. Another mechanism added to the critic agent, is the restriction of the amount of tweets (or documents) that are handled in the bag of words representation (knowledge). The main reason for the use of this mechanism has to do with the scope of the sentiment analysis data used in this study. Here, forgetting old tweets can be useful for the classifier to learn possible changes in opinions and trends for each iteration of the tweets.

To establish the knowledge limit, for each iteration wherein the classifier agent receives a re-training message from the critic agent, a verification is made to monitor if the trained tweets plus the new quantity of tweets to re-train does not exceed a certain limit. If it does not exceed the limit, the new tweets are added to the knowledge by updating the bag of words representation. Otherwise, a *num* variable is calculated, indicating the quantity of how many documents need to be removed to avoid surpassing the limit. Then the first *num* tweets are removed from the knowledge and the new tweets are added to the bag of words representation. Finally, a new instance of the Naive Bayes algorithm is trained with the new bag of words representation.

Next the statistical methods used by the critic agent are explained:

T-Student Test. T-student test is part of hypothesis-contrast tests, wherein given a certain hypothesis, if the null hypothesis is not rejected, the test shows no statistical difference between both distributions. For this, the mean values and the variances of these sets are used, along with two statistical hypotheses: on the one hand, the null hypothesis, which assumes that the means of both distributions are equal; and the other, the alternative hypothesis which indicates that they are different. The above is represented in the equation

$$H_0 : \mu_a = \mu_b \tag{2}$$

$$H_1 : \mu_a \neq \mu_b \tag{3}$$

In order to reject the null hypothesis it is necessary to calculate the result of the t-test and contrast it with a critical value. If the test result is bigger than the critical value, the null hypothesis is rejected and the means of both sets of data are said to be different. In the case that the result is smaller than the critical value, the null hypothesis is not rejected, however it can not be guaranteed that the means of both sets are equal.

The result of the t-test t is calculated using two formulas: Tests with equal variances and different size of the samples (Eq. 4) and tests with different variances and different size of the samples (Eq. 5).

$$ t = \frac{\bar{X}_1 - \bar{X}_2}{S_{x_1 x_2}\sqrt{\frac{1}{n_1} + \frac{1}{n_2}}} \, , S_{x_1 x_2} = \sqrt{\frac{(n_1 - 1)S_1^2 + (n_2 - 1)s_2^2}{n_1 + n_2 - 2}} \tag{4} $$

$$ t = \frac{\bar{X}_1 - \bar{X}_2}{\sqrt{\frac{(S_1)^2}{n_1} + \frac{(S_2)^2}{n_2}}} \tag{5} $$

Since it can not be assumed that for these samples the variances are equal, a F-test is performed to check the sameness of the two variances. The result of this test is calculated using the following equation

$$ F = \frac{(S_1)^2}{(S_2)^2} \tag{6} $$

This result indicates that the more deviated is the proportion from 1, the stronger is the evidence that these are different. As for the t-test, two hypotheses are contrasted: the null hypothesis that the variances are equal for both sets, and the alternative hypothesis, which assumes that both variances are different. This value F is contrasted with its critical values, and if these are exceeded, it can be said that both variances are different.

Histogram Comparison. A histogram is the representation of the underlying frequency distribution of a set of continuous data. In the analysis of histogram differences, we take two sets of data A and B, with their corresponding histograms $H(A)$ and $H(B)$, and probability density functions P and Q respectively, and proceed to calculate the distances between each element of the density functions. For this, a Sorensen distance [6] is used, which is calculated by:

$$ d_{sor} = \frac{\sum_{i=1}^{D} |P_i - Q_i|}{\sum_{i=1}^{D} (P_i + Q_i)} \tag{7} $$

On the one hand, when the value of this distance is close to 0, it implies that distribution of both sets of data A and B are similar. Conversely, if the value tends to move farther from 0, the data sets are said to be different.

Term Ranking. In a corpus, the number of words within this scale increases rapidly both by the number of texts and by the nature of the texts. In the case that the texts are represented in a corpus as in Fig. 4, a two-dimensional matrix DxT, where D corresponds to the documents and T to the terms that exist within the documents. In order to reduce the size of this matrix, it is possible to perform feature selection operations which will filter unwanted words, since they provide information that is not relevant to the model.

Once the dimensionality is reduced, these terms can be grouped by the number of total occurrences in the corpus in descending order, generating a histogram for that new matrix. The ranking of terms for this project was carried out in two ways: performing the ranking for n terms from highest to lowest according to their frequencies, and applying the $tf - idf$ representation, which calculates the frequency of a term and multiplies it by the inverse document frequency where this word appears. Once these weights are applied to each word of the matrix DxT, the words with lower $tf - idf$ values are eliminated, to afterwards make a ranking of n terms according to their $tf - idf$ values for this new matrix.

4.5   Implementation

The implementation of the project was carried out on Julia [4], which meets the characteristics of being a high level language, oriented to the dynamic programming of high performance, and being relatively simple for the realization of prototypes. Although Julia offers a wide set of tools for the mathematical or statistical calculation used mainly by the critical agent, at the date of creation of this report, there is no framework for the creation and simple implementation of software agents and multi-agent systems. For this reason a basic implementation was made using the network protocols provided by Julia: each agent is a server, and the communication is done by sending messages through the tcp/ip protocol.

5   Experimentation

5.1   Test Configurations

First, two control tests were carried out, which consisted on designing a classifier that was trained only on the first instance, and a classifier that was trained in each instance in which the tweets arrive. These control tests will serve to compare the results obtained in the following experiments. A total of ten instances were carried out for each configuration of the test, and the results were averaged to obtain the performance measures.

T-Student Approach. The tests of the critic agent implementing t-student as a measure of comparison between texts entailed different configurations. In order to observe its effects on the performance of the classifier given its configuration. The different iterations involved the implementation of the agents with the following possible configurations:

- **Knowledge limit:** $[500, 1000, 1500, 2000]$
- **Number of document sent by iteration:** $[100, 150, 300]$
- **Term ranking:** $[0, 100, 500, 1000]$
- **Split value for re-training:** $[50\%, 70\%, 90\%]$
- **Critic threshold value:** $[0.15, 0.2, 0.25, 0.3]$
- **Tf-idf use:** $[True, False]$

The amount of possible results that can be obtained by combining all the configurations described above corresponds to 576 tests, which were repeated 10 times each in order to obtain the average for each configuration. After obtaining the averages, we proceeded to eliminate all the results which were not re-trained, and those that re-trained in each iteration. This is done because they present similar behaviour to that of the control tests 1 and 2 respectively. This filtering process left a total of 147 configurations that meet the criteria described above. That is, in 74.48% of configuration instances, one of the two filtering criteria was fulfilled (re-training all instances and not re-training any) leaving the rest for the result analysis.

Histogram Comparison Approach. For the tests of the critic agent implementing the difference of histograms as a measure for text comparison, similar configurations to the tests of the t-student approach were used, and others were also carried out with different parameters to see the effects of these configurations. The tests were:

- **Knowledge limit:** $[1000, 2000]$
- **Number of document sent by iteration:** $[150, 300]$
- **Term ranking:** $[0]$
- **Split value for re-training:** $[50\%, 70\%, 90\%]$
- **Critic threshold value:** $[0.5, 0.1, 0.15]$
- **Tf-idf use:** $[False]$

The number of possible results that can be obtained by combining these configurations corresponds to a total of 36 tests; these, as well as the tests of the t-student approach, were repeated 10 times, obtaining the average time for each configuration. The filtering process was then performed to eliminate the re-trained instances which presented the same behaviour that the control tests 1 and 2, which resulted in a reduction of 36 to 26 configuration instances corresponding to an elimination of 27.78% of configuration instances according to filtering criteria.

5.2   Evaluation Metrics

Regarding the evaluation of the performance of text classification algorithms, different methods have been established. The relevant literature [13] proposes that the accuracy and the F_1-score of the classifier should be analyzed, and in

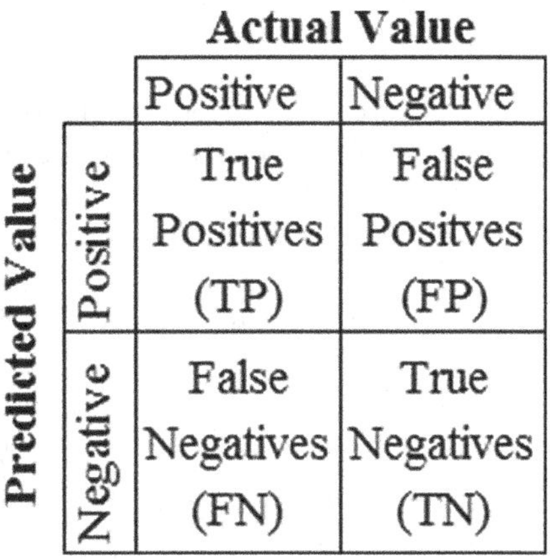

Actual Value

		Positive	Negative
Predicted Value	**Positive**	True Positives (TP)	False Positves (FP)
	Negative	False Negatives (FN)	True Negatives (TN)

Fig. 5. Representation of confusion matrix in a binary classification problem.

order to carry out these analyzes, the possible results of the classification of a document must be determined. These can be represented in a confusion matrix.

Figure 5 presents the confusion matrix according to the possible classification results of a document, which correspond to: true positive (TP) if a document was correctly classified in the category that it belongs to, false positives (FP) if a document was incorrectly classified in a class where it does not belong; false negatives (FN) if a document is not classified in a category where it should be, and true negative (TN) if a document was not classified in a category that does not match.

Accuracy: Accuracy (A) is the measure related of how the classifier predicted instances correctly through the whole sample. It is defined as:

$$A = \frac{TP + TN}{TP + TN + FP + FN} \tag{8}$$

F_1**-Score:** The F_1 score is another way to measure performance, and considers the precision (π) and recall (ρ). The F_1-value can range between $[0, 1]$, with higher values indicating a good performance of the classifier. It is defined as:

$$F_1 = \frac{2\pi\rho}{\pi + \rho} \tag{9}$$

where π and ρ are defined respectively as:

$$\pi = \frac{TP}{TP + FP} \tag{10}$$

$$\rho = \frac{TP}{TP + FN} \tag{11}$$

6   Results

The 10 best results of the tests given the various configurations described above are reported. The configurations of this tests are listed in the Table 1.

Table 1. Configurations for the 10 best test performances

N	Critic function	Tf-idf	Knowledge limit	Documents per iteration	Term ranking	Split percentage	Critic threshold
1	t-student	False	2000	100	0	90%	15%
2	t-student	False	2000	100	0	50%	15%
3	t-student	False	1500	100	0	50%	15%
4	t-student	False	1500	100	0	90%	15%
5	t-student	False	2000	100	0	50%	15%
6	t-student	False	2000	150	0	90%	15%
7	t-student	True	1500	150	0	70%	15%
8	t-student	False	2000	150	5000	70%	15%
9	t-student	False	2000	150	0	70%	15%
10	t-student	False	1000	150	500	70%	15%

As a summary, Table 2 is presented, detailing the best accuracy for all the iterations, average accuracy through all the iterations together with the best F_1-score for all iterations, and the F_1-score average. Test number 6 obtained the best accuracy score and the F_1-score, through all iterations, while test number 8 obtained the best average accuracy and average F_1-score. The test with less variation of the F_1-score, corresponds to test number 10.

Table 2. Performance metrics for both control and best tests.

Test N	Best accuracy	Average accuracy	Best F_1-score	Average F_1-score
Control 1	0.525	$0.516 \pm \mathbf{0.004}$	0.547	0.547 ± 0.005
Control 2	0.665	0.615 ± 0.062	0.656	0.632 ± 0.049
1	0.791	0.665 ± 0.074	0.742	0.649 ± 0.084
2	0.676	0.628 ± 0.082	0.733	0.643 ± 0.072
3	0.686	0.639 ± 0.075	0.733	0.653 ± 0.060
4	0.778	$\mathbf{0.677} \pm 0.076$	0.732	0.673 ± 0.084
5	0.725	0.639 ± 0.078	0.731	0.654 ± 0.064
6	$\mathbf{0.799}$	$\mathbf{0.677} \pm 0.076$	$\mathbf{0.757}$	0.6759 ± 0.088
7	0.741	0.667 ± 0.070	0.744	0.674 ± 0.065
8	0.742	$\mathbf{0.677} \pm 0.059$	0.734	$\mathbf{0.679} \pm 0.059$
9	0.751	0.668 ± 0.073	0.730	0.677 ± 0.061
10	0.738	0.655 ± 0.057	0.718	$0.665 \pm \mathbf{0.0524}$

Next, a summary of the re-training statistic for the top 10 tests is shown in Table 3. The best average re-training was obtained by test 8 and 9 (the lower the value, the better).

Table 3. Retraining metrics for both control and best tests.

Test N	Total iterations	Average re-training ↓	Re-training ratio ↓
Control 1	10	0	0.00%
Control 2	10	9	100.00%
1	30	27	93.10%
2	30	25	86.21%
3	30	24	82.76%
4	30	25	86.21%
5	30	27	93.10%
6	20	17	89.47%
7	20	18	94.74%
8	20	15	**78.95%**
9	20	15	**78.95%**
10	20	16	84.21%

6.1 Significance Test

In conjunction with the results showed above, two-tailed t-student tests were performed through all 12 tests (including control tests) in order to see if the improvements were statistically significant. Table 4 shows the results, displaying in numerical value all the tests that show a statistically significant difference; if there is no significant difference, NSS (No statistical significance) will be displayed. In the case of control test 1 and 2, all results correspond to improvements

Table 4. Two-tailed t-student test results for both control and best tests.

	Control 2	Test 1	Test 2	Test 3	Test 4	Test 5	Test 6	Test 7	Test 8	Test 9	Test 10
Control 1	9.63	-2.35	-6.03	-4.67	-1.86	-4.50	-2.76	-3.80	-4.62	-5.68	-2.86
Control 2		-5.50	-12.95	-10.48	-4.36	-10.42	-6.02	-8.56	-10.48	-12.23	-8.16
Test 1			NSS	NSS	NSS	NSS	NSS	NSS	NSS	NSS	NSS
Test 2				NSS	NSS	NSS	NSS	NSS	NSS	NSS	NSS
Test 3					NSS	NSS	NSS	NSS	NSS	NSS	NSS
Test 4						NSS	NSS	NSS	NSS	NSS	NSS
Test 5							NSS	NSS	NSS	NSS	NSS
Test 6								NSS	NSS	NSS	NSS
Test 7									NSS	NSS	NSS
Test 8										NSS	NSS
Test 9											NSS

when compared with all other tests. The other result exhibited with this table shows that there is no significant difference when comparing the tests. This could indicate that in terms of an implementation of this method to retrain the classifiers, one could choose the most cost effective method in terms of score performance F_1-score, versus re-training ration of the classifiers.

7   Conclusions

In this work an Intelligent Agents Framework for automatic tweets classification was proposed. The framework consists mainly of three types of agents: critic, classifier and distributor. For the critic agent two approaches were implemented. The first one is based on hypothesis tests (t-student test), which takes into account if there are statistical differences in the distribution of terms, and decides if it is necessary to retrain. The second approach, makes an analysis of the difference of histograms to make the same decision.

The experiments suggest that the implementation of the critic agent with all the mechanisms, improved the performance of the classifier agent. In addition, it was shown that a classifier that retrains in all iterations is not the optimal approach to solve the problem, as can be seen in the results.

It should be noted that the best classifier in terms of performance for all tests was obtained in the test configuration 6 in terms of accuracy and F_1-score. Furthermore, when analyzing the configuration that obtained the least amount of re-training for all the tests selected, it was found that the best classification was in test configuration 8.

As future work, the modification of the critical agent will be addressed, either by implementing other statistical tests for comparison, or by improving the same tests already implemented and possible actions to be performed. Regarding the classifier agent, it is possible to make improvements either by implementing different classifiers (support vector machines, decision trees, etc.), or by focusing on re-training, by creating an ensemble of classifiers that predicts cooperatively the set of tweets.

References

1. Statistic brain "twitter statistic". http://www.statisticbrain.com/twitter-statistics/. Accessed 21 Jan 2017
2. Multiagent learning using a variable learning rate. Artif. Intell. **136**(2), 215–250 (2002). http://dx.doi.org/10.1016/S0004-3702(02)00121-2
3. Alfaro, R., Oliva, F.: Clasificación automática del sentido de los mensajes en twitter: Comparando entrenamiento específico y contextual. WOPATEC (Workshop de Procesamiento Automatizado de Textos y Corpus) (2014)
4. Bezanson, J., Karpinski, S., Shah, V.B., Edelman, A.: Julia: a fast dynamic language for technical computing. CoRR abs/1209.5145 (2012). http://arxiv.org/abs/1209.5145

5. Bizid, I., Boursier, P., Morcos, J., Faiz, S.: MASIR: a multi-agent system for real-time information retrieval from microblogs during unexpected events. In: Jezic, G., Howlett, R.J., Jain, L.C. (eds.) Agent and Multi-Agent Systems: Technologies and Applications. SIST, vol. 38, pp. 3–13. Springer, Cham (2015). doi:10.1007/978-3-319-19728-9_1

6. Cha, S.H.: Comprehensive survey on distance/similarity measures between probability density functions (2007)

7. Go, A., Bhayani, R., Huang, L.: Twitter sentiment classification using distant supervision. Technical report, Stanford University. https://sites.google.com/site/twittersentimenthelp/home

8. Kibriya, A.M., Frank, E., Pfahringer, B., Holmes, G.: Multinomial Naive Bayes for text categorization revisited. In: Webb, G.I., Yu, X. (eds.) AI 2004. LNCS, vol. 3339, pp. 488–499. Springer, Heidelberg (2004). doi:10.1007/978-3-540-30549-1_43

9. Le, B., Nguyen, H.: Twitter sentiment analysis using machine learning techniques. In: Le Thi, H.A., Nguyen, N.T., Do, T.V. (eds.) Advanced Computational Methods for Knowledge Engineering. AISC, vol. 358, pp. 279–289. Springer, Cham (2015). doi:10.1007/978-3-319-17996-4_25

10. van Maanen, P.P., van der Vecht, B.: An agent-based approach to modeling online social influence. In: Proceedings of the 2013 IEEE/ACM International Conference on Advances in Social Networks Analysis and Mining, ASONAM 2013, pp. 600–607. ACM, New York (2013). http://doi.acm.org/10.1145/2492517.2492564

11. Panait, L., Luke, S.: Cooperative multi-agent learning: the state of the art. Auton. Agents Multi-Agent Syst. **11**(3), 387–434 (2005). http://dx.doi.org/10.1007/s10458-005-2631-2

12. Russell, S.J., Norvig, P.: Artificial Intelligence: A Modern Approach, 2 edn. Pearson Education, New Jersey (2003)

13. Sebastiani, F.: Machine learning in automated text categorization. ACM Comput. Surv. **34**(1), 1–47 (2002). http://doi.acm.org/10.1145/505282.505283

14. Serrano, E., Iglesias, C.A., Garijo, M.: A novel agent-based rumor spreading model in twitter. In: Proceedings of the 24th International Conference on World Wide Web, WWW 2015 Companion, pp. 811–814. ACM. New York (2015). http://doi.acm.org/10.1145/2740908.2742466

15. Wang, D., Zhang, H., Liu, R., Lv, W., Wang, D.: t-test feature selection approach based on term frequency for text categorization. Pattern Recogn. Lett. **45**, 1–10 (2014). http://www.sciencedirect.com/science/article/pii/S0167865514000543

16. Weiss, G. (ed.): Multiagent Systems: A Modern Approach to Distributed Artificial Intelligence. MIT Press, Cambridge (1999)

User Experiences Around Sentiment Analyses, Facilitating Workplace Learning

Christian Voigt[⊠], Barbara Kieslinger, and Teresa Schäfer

Zentrum Fuer Soziale Innovation, Technology and Knowledge, Vienna, Austria
{voigt,kieslinger,schaefer}@zsi.at

Abstract. User acceptance is key for the adoption of a new technology. In this work we experiment with a novel service for tutors in workplace learning settings. Sentiment analysis is a way to extract feelings and emotions from a text. In a learning setting such a sentiment analysis can be part of learning analytics. It has the potential to foster the understanding of emotions in shared discussions in learning environments, detect group dynamics as well as the impact of certain topics on learners' sentiments. However, sentiment analysis presents some challenges too, as lived experiences, expectations and ultimately acceptance of this technology varies greatly and can become barriers to adoption. In order to design a system for learning analytics accepted by tutors we experimented with proof-of-concept prototypes and received valuable feedback from tutors regarding the usefulness of the overall sentiment analysis as well as certain features. The qualitative feedback confirms the overall interest of tutors in sentiment analysis and gives important hints towards more detailed analytical elements.

Keywords: Sentiment analysis · Learning analytics · User experience

1 Introduction

The user experience of a product is the lived and felt interaction with that product, be it a web site, a tangible object or an administrative process [1]. These days, it is not enough that new products and services offer clear gains in terms of efficiency or effectiveness, they also need to provide a memorable experience. This argument can also be applied to introducing new services such as sentiment analyses in support of workplace learning. Adoption of new technologies cannot be reduced to an argument about functional benefits or user interface aesthetics. User experiences such as engagement, absorption, education or joy become ever more important if users are expected to stick with a new technology [2].

A second key concept of this paper is sentiment analysis, generally understood as a natural language processing task with the aim to extract feelings, affects, emotions or opinions in a text [3] opposed to the extraction of facts, e.g. characteristics such as weights or prices. Outputs generated by sentiment analyses can be very diverse including simple dichotomies (positive versus negative expressions), scoring approaches from −5 (very negative) to +5 (very positive) [4], or categorical approaches such as distinguishing basic emotions such as joy, trust or anger [5]. Although sentiment is

© Springer International Publishing AG 2017
G. Meiselwitz (Ed.): SCSM 2017, Part II, LNCS 10283, pp. 312–324, 2017.
DOI: 10.1007/978-3-319-58562-8_24

already widely applied for analysing texts included in product or movie reviews, political discourse analysis or spam detection, sentiment analysis is in its infancy so that completeness, accuracy and predictive powers of analytical results are far from prefect and also the degree of automation or human intervention needed differs depending on the analytical methods used [6].

Sentiment analyses can be presented in a variety of formats, with differing levels of details and explanations. In this article the primarily intended user group are course tutors facilitating online course for adult learners in large public employment service centres. The underlying assumption is that tutors' flow experiences, when exploring increasing levels of analytical details, is impacted by conceptual decisions such as the unit of analysis for sentiment detection (e.g. words, n-grams of two or more words, sentences or larger text units) or the sequence of analytical results (e.g. hot-spots in discussions and the respective context in terms of surrounding texts as well as how pervasive a sentiment is in relation to a group of learners). Also the analysis itself can follow a number of different approaches, which are often grouped into dictionary based approaches and methods based on machine learning, which itself can deploy supervised or unsupervised algorithms, depending on whether the system can be trained or not [7].

Moreover, user experience is not subject to systems design alone; e.g. the possibility that sentiment analyses could be misused for performance evaluations rather than for supporting course management is a serious concern for learners and tutors alike. Knowing about what data is used, for what purpose and by whom becomes part of the user experience.

2 State of the Art and Research Objectives

Sentiment analysis for training and education purposes is still very much discussed as part of the learning analytics debate. Learning analytics is analysis of data generated from and about the activities of learners with the aim to better understand learners and optimize their learning experiences [8]. Learning analytics can, for example, use data from social networks, learners' textual contributions, their activities within virtual learning environments and their navigational paths. These learner centric data can then be combined with tutor and lecturer inputs and other circumstantial data such as group sizes, frequency of off-line activities or learner profiles of course participants. Increasingly the explosion of available data as well as their innumerable combinations raises concerns about learning analytics' pedagogical values [9]. After all, training and education are also economic activities, hence using learning analytics to optimize the use of scarce resources, is an objective that has an increasing appeal to providers of education and training. The dual purposes of learning analytics are also reflected in related products where dashboards show developments over time, allowing for comparisons of courses based on their performance metrics, learner drop-outs or materials used. Adopting a business logic, the upward trending graph is seen as a sign of success, neglecting the need to integrate the computational aspects of data analytics with the methodological aspects of learning [10]. A good example where this integration has happened is [11], where clustering of learners based on their activities has been related to learner motivation such as Herzberg's theory.

There is a wide range of possible learning analytics technologies that can be used as listed in [9], including:

- *Predictive modeling*, based on mathematical techniques such as factor analysis and logistic regression;
- *Social network analysis*, identifying interaction patterns such as subgroups within a larger course or courses which are more teacher/tutor centric;
- *Analysis of usage data*, often including the tracking of clicks or time spend on certain learning activities;
- *Text analysis*, e.g. identifying the conceptual richness of a learner's contributions or, as done in this paper, estimating the sentiments and emotions within online discussions.

An area where learning analytics shows a lot of potential are MOOCs (Massive Open Online Courses). On the one side, student numbers in the hundreds and thousands generate large and rich data to make meaningful use of algorithms depending on the size of datasets. On the other side, depending on the number of participants, tutors can not read every posting and monitor the activities of every learner in order to anticipate a conflict or identifying the learners who would need additional support [11]. However, there is a danger that we measure and use what is there rather than what we need. Or put differently, given that we concentrate on learners' behavioral data, there is a risk that we go back to behaviorism as the dominating conceptualization of learning [8].

Hence this paper moves towards including sentiments within learners' expressions as an estimate for a group's wellbeing, e.g. a group's ability to accommodating a variety of opinions and empowering all members of a group to participate in collaborative learning activities [cf. 12]. A first step in that direction is the provision of related analytics to tutors and trainers. For this information we generated a number of visualizations (proof-of-concept prototypes), which were presented in a connected way, meaning that a given visualization (e.g. displaying an overly negative tone in week 2 of an online course) could trigger another visualization (e.g. showing the keywords of the debate, related co-word analyses or relevant text snippets). Eventually, we aim to shed light on the added values of sentiment analyses to the facilitation of online workplace trainings, whereas we wanted to avoid a purely cost - benefit driven evaluation. We aim to include the user experience as a method to extract the added values of sentiment analyses as seen by practitioners, placing the technology in the context of their daily workflows [13].

Our expectations are that trainers benefit from better understanding the emotional ups and downs during their courses. Learning for career and labour market transitions can be seen as occurring across four domains: relational development; cognitive development; practical development; emotional development [14]. Thus understanding which emotions are expressed during the learning process can improve trainers' options to facilitate the development of personal qualities, not only in dealing with others, but in dealing with one's own emotional and practical development.

3   Method

Our method included two steps: (a) the generation of proof-of-concept prototypes based on the data of an actual workplace-training course and (b) exploratory interviews with tutors and human development experts.

3.1   Proof-of-Concept Prototypes and Scenarios

The purpose of the proof-of-concept prototypes was to demonstrate possible applications and visualization of data analyses, in order to specify future requirements, tell a story about the expected benefits and, generally, have an open dialogue about the conditions under which learning analytics would be useful or maybe even be harmful [cf. 15].

In this paper we use a specific branch of sentiment analysis, based on dictionaries, which were developed to extract the most likely polarity (pos. or neg.) of a sequence of words (sentences, postings, tweets etc.). The full gamut of techniques is shown in the figure below (Fig. 1).

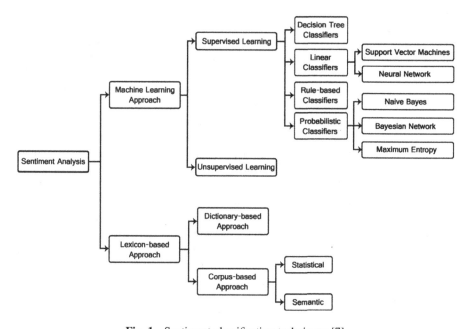

Fig. 1. Sentiment classification techniques [7]

Our sentiment analyses were based on text materials (n = 1,1170 postings) from 68 participants in an online workplace training course. The participants of this course were all employees of public employment services (Work Coaches) and aimed to learn about the challenges of a fast changing labour market. Learning objectives included developing a set of skills and competences in areas like coaching or providing labour market information, as well as the use of digital tools.

3.2   A Dialogical Evaluation of Prototypes

Bussolon [16] highlights the fact that despite 30 years of UX design, few publications explicate their understanding of 'experiences'. What follows are often UX definitions containing a loose collection of concepts rather than a systematic organisation of what influences 'experiences'. Research on user experience highlights the need for an interpretative, iterative and, most importantly, dialogical approach to understanding and evaluating user experiences [1].

Or as argued in [17], each technology includes both, a response to a problem and a hypothesis about how this problem will be solved. Hence the dialogue between user and designer can enable

(a) the *subtlety* needed to capture even minor divergences from what was intended by the design and
(b) the *empathy* needed to see users as the full persons they are, with needs going beyond efficiency and effectiveness [18].

The work with prototypes builds a bridge between the developers' design alternatives of a future system or feature and the users' needs by offering an intermediate presentation which is technically feasible and affords practical interpretation [19]. In our case we used low-fidelity prototypes [20, 21] in the form of paper-mock ups, as the hand-made appearance should focus the attention of the interviewees on the content and the functionalities of the proposed sentiment analysis rather than the appearance. We presented these prototypes along narrative descriptions derived from the data of the specific online workplace training course to facilitators exploring the goals they would like to reach when consulting the sentiment analysis [22].

We conducted five exploratory interviews, presenting the scenarios and prototypes. The interviewees were all facilitators of workplace learning interventions. Two interviewees were facilitators in the course that provided the pilot data for the sentiment analysis tool design and was structured along topics such as cultural change, impact of the digital, coaching, labour market information and sectorial knowledge, reflection on experience and learning. One of these course facilitators is part of the learning and development team within the organization, the other one is working for an academic institution advising the public organization on human development aspects. The third interviewee facilitated previously a very similar course in the same organization and was involved in the development of the new course.

Given the fact that the data in the low-fi prototypes were based on the real comments and discussions of this online course, the research team had the opportunity to anchor the feedback of those three interviewees in their concrete experiences with the course and the sentiments they witnessed from course participants.

The other two interviewees are employees and learning providers of a public employment service in another country. While they facilitated an online course, which had another training focus, both facilitators are familiar with the course setting providing the testing data for the sentiment analysis. The feedback from these two provided to enrich feedback with experiences from another context.

4   Conceptual Framework

The paper is based on a modular process for designing the user experience of sentiment analyses in the context of supporting large scale online training courses. Figure 2 presents a chain of decisions included in the design of sentiment analyses. The details in the boxes are not meant to be complete depiction of all possibilities. For example, sentiments can be extracted from a number of information sources including social interaction graphs, log files of system usage or even facial expressions and body postures. The same logic applies to the number of use contexts, which can be expanded in accordance to the needs of a trainer.

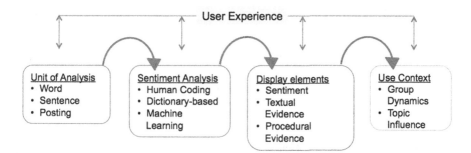

Fig. 2. Decisions determining the user experience

For now we envision the potential of sentiment analyses in supporting trainers' understanding of

- group dynamics [23],
- the way certain topics can impact on learners' sentiments [24], or
- the role of logistics and administrative elements that can impact on learners' sentiments too [25].

5   Discussion of Scenarios

Each interview started with a short presentation of the main rational for doing a sentiment analysis, followed by the scenario and the prototypes of different visualisions, such as shown in Figs. 3 and 4. Based on these visualizations for future interfaces and an interview guideline defined the main feedback questions of the interview.

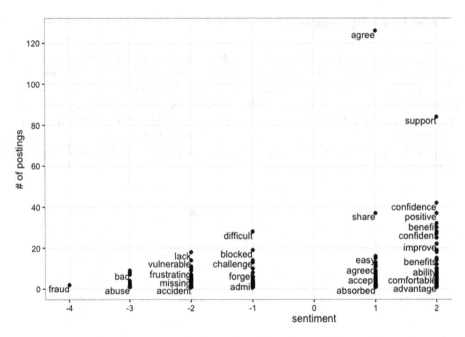

Fig. 3. Number of postings containing words, which determined a positive of negative sentiment

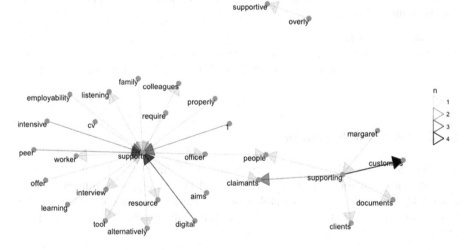

Fig. 4. Words and co-words: words that are in direct relation to another word

5.1   Usefulness of 'Sentiment Analysis'

The overall relevance of sentiment analysis was confirmed by the interviewees. In accordance with previous studies [25, 26], the facilitators reinforce that emotions are an important part of learning, independently whether they are considered positive or negative by a system, a tutor or a peer learner. As interviewee A. puts it *"when you express emotions there are greater chances of learning"*. The sentiment analysis was recognized as a tool that provides facilitators with a quick overview of what is going on in the course in terms of emotions and thus helps to identify those discussions where the presence and moderation of the facilitator might be required, or become aware of individual learners who might need support in their learning.

More than that, all interviewees related sentiment analysis to the overall course evaluation, for which they think it could be a very useful element. A sentiment analysis could help the tutors gain relevant insights into the emotional stages of the course and contribute to improving future courses.

When asked whether the sentiment analysis should also be visible for learners the interviewees expressed some concerns. While none of the tutors strongly objected to the possibility of providing the information not only to tutors but also to learners, tutors were concerned that the right interpretation of the data would be lacking, leading to some wrong conclusions or actions. The interviewees agreed that this needed very careful treatment and explanations of how to interpret the data. One suggestion was that the tutor would present an overview of sentiments and decide on what to show and what to take out from the data being displayed to all participants. One tutor was especially careful with very strong words, while another tutor found some value in showing negative sentiments in order to alert the learners and maybe trigger some changing behaviour within the course.

5.2   Unit of Analysis

The presented unit of analysis is on a word and co-word level as shown in Figs. 4 and 5. There was a common agreement amongst the interviewees that a word and co-word analysis can provide a good first overview for a tutor. It provides quick and manageable insights into current emotions of the course and is therefore a suitable unit of analysis

When it comes to the process of defining the value of words in terms of positive and negative meaning all interviewees expressed certain reservations towards the automatic classification by sentiment dictionaries. To get this feedback, we presented the results obtained from a dictionary-based classification algorithm. For example Fig. 3 shows words used most often in expressing positive sentiments (agree, support, confidence, etc.) or negative sentiments (difficult, blocked, lack), whereas Fig. 5 shows the percentage of positive or negative words during the six course weeks. To a trainer who knows his or her course, these single words might already mean something, however, the interviewees confirmed that a further link to an exemplary set of postings expressing a sentiment or a co-word analysis [27] to contextualize the sentiment analysis is needed.

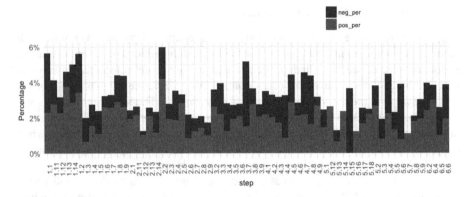

Fig. 5. Percentage of positive or negative words indicating positive and negative sentiments per learning step

All tutors agreed that a more detailed analysis of the context in which the words were used was perceived as being indispensable for facilitating the course, as none of the interviewed facilitators would solely rely on this analysis. Thus the first level of analysis needs to provide a quick access to the deeper and specific context in which the words are used, e.g. the posting within the course. Also, all interviewees stressed that they would go back to the learner in their analysis of emotions, read through the comments shared and get their own picture of emotions within the course. Automatically created sentiment analysis does not replace this need to dive into the context.

One interviewee perceived the word and co-word analysis as sufficient, not for tutoring the course, but for certain reporting tasks that are related to the evaluation and collection of formative feedback to the course

5.3   Valuable and Less Valuable Features

All interviewees could image the sentiment analysis tool offering some sentiment tracking features, or trend spotting. They also expressed their interest in an alert function as suggested by [28] in order to be made aware in real time about issues coming up in the course. Thus, when asked about whether they preferred a push or pull mechanism for obtaining results from the system, all favored a mix of both options.

In addition, one interviewee described a scenario where he could envision using the sentiment analysis in order to regulate the visibility of comments. As the visibility of comments tends to decrease with the number of participants, an emotion alert could be used to point to specific comments dealing with emotions, complementary to the commonly used "like" function.

Other display elements voiced during the interview are: a timeline view to see if emotions change of the course; or the recognition of patterns in use of negative/positive words.

Most importantly and shortly mentioned above, when it comes to displaying the words facilitators want to be able to see the words in context. The presented co-word

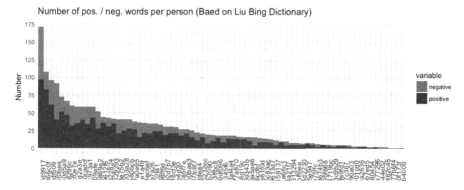

Fig. 6. Tracing back the number of positive and negative words to individual learners

analysis is perceived as being a good first step, but interviewees would also like to be able to dive directly in the context of the word and see where and how it has been used. The "individual learner view", where a user could see the emotional posting behaviour of individual learners, is rated less important by all five facilitators. They rather stress the importance of seeing an emotion expressed in context rather than assigning it to an individual learner (Fig. 6).

5.4 Training the Future System

A common agreement amongst the facilitators seems to be the fact that they need tools for regulating emotions [25]. However, the efforts they would put into training and adjusting such a tool differs across participants, with the answers being mainly driven by their institutional role. The idea behind this training is that sentiments of a course are once tagged manually in order to create a basis, which is then used to train the system and thus improve the validity of identified emotions in a learning intervention.

Especially the informant from the learning and development department in a very large public organization does not see a lot of value for training a sentiment analysis tool. Sentiment analysis is not considered of high importance within his specific organization and thus he states that the organization would not be willing to invest resources in such an activity. In the interviewee's opinion the training of the system would not outweigh the costs and therefore lack cost-effectiveness. This belief is expressed by a second interviewee who confirms that the specific public organization does not want to go into learning analytics as part of its approach to improve the experiences of learners. Rather there is a stronger focus on evaluation and that's why sentiments analysis could be seen as a tool that supports formative and summative evaluation of online courses too. .

6 Outlook

The first evaluation using low fidelity prototypes based on real data provided the research team with insights into usefulness and user experience of sentiments analysis in a work place learning context. It helped to prioritize features that would support facilitators of online courses in understanding the emotional dynamics amongst their professional training participants. The limitations of this work are in the small number of tutors giving feedback to a first set of proof-of-concept prototypes. However, important aspects have been addressed. As a next step we plan to work closely with a set of tutors to build further on the prototypes and develop an interface that allows the contextual view as requested by the interviewees. After several user-development loops we will try to implement a high fidelity prototype of the sentiment monitoring tool in a real course scenario and obtain further feedback, aiming to collecting detailed experiences from this usage with regard to applicability and impact.

New features will be integrated as low-fidelity prototype in this functional prototype for further conception and initial testing. First ideas are for instance using benchmarks, and observe how comparisons between groups and individuals affect personal motivation, e.g. comparisons with group averages can be counterproductive if an individual's set goal or previous performance had been better than the average.

7 Conclusions

Based on a set of initial decisions guiding the generation and presentation of a sentiment analysis, the paper discussed a number of options how to present the process as well as the results of such an analysis in different ways. A dialogical evaluation format is used to discuss these options under pragmatic and emotional aspects. Having this type of evaluation at a prototyping stage enables designers to prioritize developments for a final, productive system where some of these options can be combined according to trainers' preferences.

Overall, the qualitative feedback obtained with a limited number of trainers from the public sector confirmed the interest by tutors in the sentiments of their course participants. Sentiments analysis is understood as one way to support this need, especially when it comes to courses with high numbers of participants, where the human efforts of the tutor are not enough to follow all activities. Sentiment analysis can form part of a suite of learning analytic tools that serves the tutor as a monitoring tool. It is valued as a tool that provides a quick and manageable overview of sentiments in online courses in order to detect those situations, where the input from facilitators might be needed: to moderate discussions, manage group dynamics or support individual learners. It is understood as a tool that helps to quickly dive into the context where positive or negative words are used, but cannot replace the individual tutors' interpretation of words and expressions in context.

Learning is messy and simplistic models won't work [8], at least not when they stand alone. They can provide first orientation but cannot replace the complex processes that facilitators apply to interpret and regulate emotions in online courses. The simplistic and automated analysis of sentiments in learning can be used as an approach to provide an overview of dynamics and patterns of emotions, as a contribution to the evaluation and further improving of training interventions. In times where resources are scarce, workplace-learning interventions are driven by the need for efficiency and investments in this type of learning analytics are small. Thus this approach has to bridge the gap between the complexity of emotions in learning and the need for easy to use and efficient support tools.

Robust learning analytics requires investments which depend on regulatory frameworks that see added value in learning analytics [29] and thus require for the inclusion of management. On the other hand, the inclusion of management might bring the risk that sentiment analysis is used not to enrich the learning experience but to assess online training interventions. The latter could lead to 'teaching for the test versus teaching to improve understanding' [10], which requires organizations to develop cultures and policies around the appropriate use of sentiment analyses.

Acknowledgments. This work is part of the EmployID project, which has received funding from the European Union's Seventh Framework Programme for research, technological development an demonstration under grant agreement no. 619619.

References

1. Wright, P., McCarthy, J.: Experience-centered design: designers, users, and communities in dialogue. Synth. Lect. Hum. Centered Inf. **3**, 1–123 (2010)
2. Pine, B.J., Gilmore, J.H.: Welcome to the experience economy. Harvard Bus. Rev. **76**, 97–105 (1998)
3. Liu, B.: Sentiment analysis and opinion mining. Synthesis lectures on human language technologies. **5**, 1–167 (2012)
4. Nielsen, F.Å.: A new ANEW: evaluation of a word list for sentiment analysis in microblogs. arXiv preprint arXiv:1103.2903 (2011)
5. Plutchik, R., Kellerman, H.: The Measurement of Emotions. Academic Press, San Diego (2013)
6. Ravi, K., Ravi, V.: A survey on opinion mining and sentiment analysis: tasks, approaches and applications. Knowl. Based Syst. **89**, 14–46 (2015)
7. Medhat, W., Hassan, A., Korashy, H.: Sentiment analysis algorithms and applications: a survey. Ain Shams Eng. J. **5**, 1093–1113 (2014)
8. Siemens, G., Long, P.: Penetrating the fog: analytics in learning and education. EDUCAUSE Rev. **46**, 30 (2011)
9. Clow, D.: An overview of learning analytics. Teach. High. Educ. **18**, 683–695 (2013)
10. Gašević, D., Dawson, S., Siemens, G.: Let's not forget: Learning analytics are about learning. TechTrends. **59**, 64–71 (2015)
11. Khalil, M., Kastl, C., Ebner, M.: Portraying MOOCs learners: a clustering experience using learning analytics. In: The European Stakeholder Summit on Experiences and Best Practices in and Around MOOCs (EMOOCS 2016), Graz, Austria, pp. 265–278 (2016)
12. Voigt, C., Swatman, P.M.C.: Online case discussions – tensions in activity systems. In: Presented at the 6th IEEE International Conference on Advanced Learning Technologies (ICALT), 5–7 July (2006)

13. Sproll, S., Peissner, M., Sturm, C.: From product concept to user experience: exploring UX potentials at early product stages. In: Proceedings of the 6th Nordic Conference on Human-Computer Interaction: Extending Boundaries, pp. 473–482. ACM (2010)

14. Brown, A.: A dynamic model of occupational identity formation. In: Brown, A. (Ed.) Promoting Vocational Education and Training: European Perspectives. pp. 59–67. University of Tampere Press, Tampere (1997)

15. Rudd, J., Stern, K., Isensee, S.: Low vs. high-fidelity prototyping debate. Interactions **3**, 76–85 (1996)

16. Bussolon, S.: The X factor. In: Marcus, A. (ed.) DUXU 2016. LNCS, vol. 9746, pp. 15–24. Springer, Cham (2016). doi:10.1007/978-3-319-40409-7_2

17. Carroll, J.M.: Making Use: Scenario-Based Design of Human-Computer Interactions. MIT Press, Cambridge (2000)

18. Hassenzahl, M.: Experience design: technology for all the right reasons. Synth. Lect. Hum. Centered Inf. **3**, 1–95 (2010)

19. Asaro, P.M.: Transforming society by transforming technology: the science and politics of participatory design. Account. Manage. Inf. Technol. **10**, 257–290 (2000)

20. Rettig, M.: Prototyping for tiny fingers. Commun. ACM **37**, 21–27 (1994)

21. Kankainen, A.: UCPCD: user-centered product concept design. In: Proceedings of the 2003 Conference on Designing for User Experiences, pp. 1–13. ACM (2003)

22. Carroll, J.M., Chin, G., Rosson, M.B., Neale, D.C.: The development of cooperation: five years of participatory design in the virtual school. In: Proceedings of the 3rd Conference on Designing Interactive Systems: Processes, Practices, Methods, and Techniques, pp. 239–251. ACM (2000)

23. Soller, A., Ogata, H., Hesse, F.: Design, modeling, and analysis of collaborative learning. In: The Role of Technology in CSCL, pp. 13–20 (2007)

24. Plass, J.L., Kaplan, U.: Emotional design in digital media for learning. In: Emotions, Technology, Design, and Learning, pp. 131–162 (2015)

25. Regan, K., Evmenova, A., Baker, P., Jerome, M.K., Spencer, V., Lawson, H., Werner, T.: Experiences of instructors in online learning environments: Identifying and regulating emotions. Internet High. Educ. **15**, 204–212 (2012)

26. Plutchik, R.: Emotions: a general psychoevolutionary theory. Approaches Emot. **1984**, 197–219 (1984)

27. Callon, M., Courtial, J.-P., Turner, W.A., Bauin, S.: From translations to problematic networks: an introduction to co-word analysis. Soc. Sci. Inf. **22**, 191–235 (1983)

28. Suero Montero, C., Suhonen, J.: Emotion analysis meets learning analytics: online learner profiling beyond numerical data. In: Proceedings of the 14th Koli Calling International Conference on Computing Education Research, pp. 165–169. ACM (2014)

29. Ferguson, R., Brasher, A., Clow, D., Griffiths, D., Drachsler, H.: Learning analytics: visions of the future. In: 6th International Learning Analytics and Knowledge (LAK) Conference, April 25–29 , Edinburgh, Scotland (2016)

Social Data and Analytics

Visual Exploration of Urban Data: A Study of Riyadh Taxi Data

Aljoharah Alfayez[(✉)] and Salma Aldawood

Center for Complex Engineering Systems (CCES) at KACST and MIT,
King Abdulaziz City for Science and Technology, Riyadh, Saudi Arabia
{a.alfayez, s.aldawood}@cces-kacst-mit.org

Abstract. In this paper, we describe one approach of land classification through linking taxi drop-off cost to traffic analysis zones (TAZs). We visually explore the number and costs of taxi drop-off points in the city of Riyadh, Saudi Arabia, to identify social dynamics and urban behavioral patterns. After analyzing the data with regard to gender, we identify some expected gender biases in the data set for taxi traces of trips since female mobility is constrained in Saudi Arabia and public transportation options are limited. We present a series of case studies of gendered mobility analysis that show how our model enables domain experts to visually explore data sets that were previously unattainable for them. Finally, we visualize the number and cost of drop-offs per TAZ for males and females and identify potential areas for future research in visual analytics for taxi traces.

Keywords: Taxi traces · Taxi drop-off · Social dynamics · Taxi cost · Land classification

1 Introduction

Visual analytics and data visualizations provide users with new modes of interaction to explore data sets and aid in the discovery of trends in mobility. Understanding mobility patterns is an integral part of urban planning. It allows planners to explore how city inhabitants vary in land use and urban behavior. Researchers have explored many themes using mobility data. In this paper, we expand on taxi data specifically. We describe one approach of land classification through analyzing the cost of travel to different traffic analysis zones (TAZs) in Riyadh, Saudi Arabia. By analyzing drop-off cost distribution using taxi data, we can identify the median, minimum and maximum cost of travel to different parts of the city. Given that the mobility data provided is in the context of Riyadh, Saudi Arabia, a city where female mobility is prohibited, we have also visualized drop-off cost distribution for both genders, which allows us to examine TAZs that men and women spend more to travel to. These observations may help urban planners identify the demand on the city's transportation infrastructure and possibly improve the allocation of services targeted towards specific demographics.

The paper is structured as follows. Section 2 describes some previous work linking taxi data with social dynamics. Section 3 presents a land analysis based on taxi trip

© Springer International Publishing AG 2017
G. Meiselwitz (Ed.): SCSM 2017, Part II, LNCS 10283, pp. 327–337, 2017.
DOI: 10.1007/978-3-319-58562-8_25

drop-off cost. The discussion and lines for future work are included in Sect. 4. We conclude in Sect. 5.

2   Background

According to Zhang et al. "Traces of taxi GPS routes have been used for city-scale social event detection and analytics." [1]. Taxi data can be used to understand many different aspects of city life, from economic activity and human behavior to mobility patterns. In the literature, taxi data is frequently used to find and understand social patterns. In [2], the authors found drops in taxi activity in New York during August 2011 and October 2012, which they linked to hurricanes. Similarly, they identified a lack of trips along certain roads, which suggested traffic was blocked in those areas. Additionally, in [3], the authors identified a method to optimize linking taxi drivers to passengers, thereby reducing gas emissions. In [4], the authors utilized taxi origin and destination data to understand urban mobility. They relied on taxi data as opposed to other public transit mobility data because it gave greater accuracy.

An exhaustive survey of the work on mining taxi traces identified three categories of work on this data: social dynamics, traffic dynamics and operational dynamics [5]. The authors define social dynamics as "the study of the collective behavior of a city's population, based on their observed movements." Thus, understanding social dynamics is essential for the management, design, maintenance and advancement of a city's infrastructure [6]. Section 2.1 will expand on work in social dynamics linking taxi data to land use and Sect. 2.2 will describe some visualization work on taxi data that facilitates understanding the underlying social dynamics.

2.1   Using Taxi Data to Understand Land Use

Urban planning policies affect the world in different ways, from influencing the amount of energy consumption by controlling urban sprawl to the preservation of agricultural land [7]. One major factor that influences urban policies is transportation and mobility behavior. Understanding mobility patterns is crucial for measuring and characterizing urban form and urban policymaking [7, 8]. In [9], the author identified approaches for understanding the relationship between urban form and travel behavior. One method is to look at travel patterns.

With the emergence of new technologies, the transportation industry has revolutionized access to its services. New taxi companies have started disrupting the traditional models of transportation service [10], and through these new models, valuable urban data are captured. Researchers used these data to explore different areas in urban behavior, from traffic patterns to land classification.

Researchers in [11] concluded that data on land use is difficult to obtain, so they observed the social function of urban land by using taxi traces. Their classification technique aimed at identifying land-use classes of regions achieved a recognition accuracy of 95%. From taxi data, they found that pickup/drop-off locations "exhibited clear patterns corresponding to the land-use classes of these regions."

In [12], the authors attempted to identify land use types (commercial, industrial, residential, institutional and recreational) using seven-day taxi trajectory data in Shanghai. They believe that increasing availability of human mobility data "is valuable for urban planners and policy makers in mitigating traffic, planning for public services and resources, and other purposes."

2.2 Visual Representation of Transportation Data

Visually exploring data is the first step toward understanding emerging patterns and trends. There are many layers that can be explored in taxi transportation data, from GPS trajectories to rider demographics to trip cost evaluation. In [13], Hubcab creators created a visual platform that allows users to explore how to reduce the social and environmental costs embedded in transportation systems.

Additionally, in [14], a platform was developed to visualize the number of taxis operating during a specific date (chosen by the user) in Singapore. The developers used a heatmap representation to visually describe areas of taxi concentration throughout the city. Another example of applying visual analytics on taxi trajectory data appears in [15], where a graph was created to store and manifest real traffic information recorded by taxi trajectories over city streets.

Similarly, the authors in [16] analyzed taxi GPS traces collected in Lisbon, Portugal, and visualized the spatiotemporal variation of taxi services. They explored relationships between pickup and drop-off locations, and analyzed the behavior in downtime (between the previous drop-off and the following pickup). They also carried out the analysis of the predictability of taxi trips for the next pickup area type given history of taxi flow in time and space.

3 Taxi Trip Cost Analysis

3.1 Data Set

We used taxi drop-off data to examine trip cost distribution within the city of Riyadh. Data was acquired from a taxi booking service through which clients can request a car from their phone or through a website. We received the data separated into several files according to month, from May 2014 until December of 2016, with more than 122,000 finished trips in Riyadh since the service launched in Saudi Arabia. We used a gender annotation algorithm based on names [17] to find the gender of the trip requester. The spatial scale used for mapping costs to parts of the city was based on traffic analysis zones (TAZs), which are the official segmentation used in transportation planning. Segmenting the city into TAZs was based on census block information, such as population per hour, where zones tend to be smaller in denser areas and larger in areas of low density, creating 1,492 TAZs in Riyadh [18].

There are some biases in the data set that must be mentioned. First, we noticed there were considerably more female trips than male trips. This bias is expected because in

Saudi Arabia, women are prohibited from driving, and limited public transportation is available. Figure 1 shows a snapshot of the gender of riders between May 2015 and December 2016. We were able to gender-annotate approximately 80% of all trips in the data set. Additionally, 86% of all gender-annotated rides in our data set were female. Around July 2016 onward, female trips drop significantly, we have no data to explain this drop yet, but it is reflected in the overall trip count of those months. The dramatic drop in December's ridership is because we only have data on part of that month. Another important note is that our gender inference strategy relied on name annotation, and given that rider user names are self-reported, there is a possibility that they do not accurately reflect their gender. Finally, there is also no way of identifying whether the requester of the ride is the one taking it.

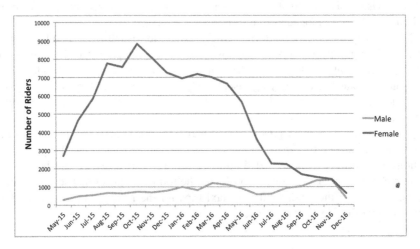

Fig. 1. Snapshot of male and female riders in the taxi data set between May 2015 and December 2016

3.2   Data Preparation

To produce the visualizations in Sect. 3.3, we began by annotating all trips with gender. To complete this step, we ran a method [17] that gender annotates the first name of the taxi customer using some Arabic-language-specific features. A data cleaning step was applied to remove all incomplete trips (where the cost was zero or null). Afterward, we linked drop-off points and cost with their associated TAZs (Fig. 2). We used TAZs because they allow us to explore the data in higher resolution than the larger defined neighborhood districts. Finally, we calculated minimum, maximum, average and median cost per TAZ. These are the scores we used to evaluate the TAZs.

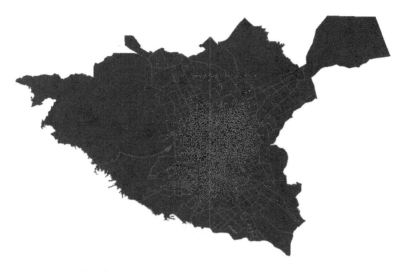

Fig. 2. Representation of drop-off points in Riyadh

3.3   Visualizations and Observations

In this section, we show the spatial distribution of Riyadh's taxi drop-offs in relation to TAZs and then explore the cost of drop-offs by TAZ. The trips cover 1,330 out of 1,492 TAZs. For all the choropleth maps in this section, the following description holds:

1. Areas that have no drop-off points are not colored.
2. Colors range from red to yellow, representing high to low values respectively.
3. Outlined in blue are twenty TAZs with the highest values.

To observe patterns of trips, we began by visualizing TAZs and their associated total number of drop-offs (Fig. 3). This step can identify areas in the city where people often go.

Figure 3 indicates that there is a relatively high number of trips toward the center of the city. This area is considerably high in commercial amenities, which could be a reason why there is a higher trip count. Figure 4 shows four choropleth maps linking the cost of trips to TAZs. After applying the steps mentioned in 3.2, we generated a choropleth map for every TAZ's median, average, maximum and minimum trip cost.

The median cost map (Fig. 4a) and average cost map (Fig. 4b) produced similar results; sixteen out of twenty of the highest value TAZs in these figures overlap. The figures indicate that most TAZs with higher average and median values appear around the edges of the city. This could be because there is a higher population concentration in the center of the city, and traveling to TAZs farther from the center is relatively expensive. However, this needs further analysis to prove. Figure 4c and d show the minimum and maximum cost distribution of TAZs. The purpose of these maps is to explore extreme values in the data set.

Fig. 3. Number of drop-off points per TAZ

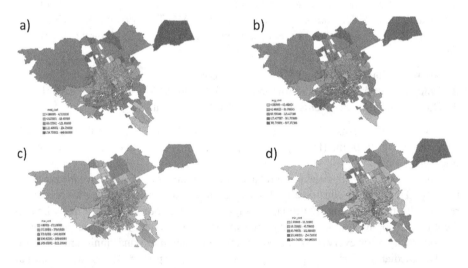

Fig. 4. Choropleth maps describing (a) median (b) average (c) maximum and (d) minimum trip cost in SAR per TAZ

Gendered Spatial Distribution of Drop-off Costs. We were interested in exploring differences in gendered drop off costs, to spatially explore cost distribution based on gender. First, we observed gendered trip distributions by number of drop-off points per TAZ in Figs. 5 and 6. We found that six out of the 20 highest value TAZs overlap.

Fig. 5. Distribution of female trips per TAZ

Fig. 6. Distribution of male trips per TAZ

As a second step, we applied the same methodology previously described to visualize female and male drop-off costs (Fig. 7).

One main pattern we noticed when looking at Fig. 7 is that women spend more money than men on taxis in this data set. In [19], Loukaitou-Sideris explains that although women predominate as users of mass transit around the globe, they may be reluctant to use taxis because they are more expensive. However, this observation

Female   Male

Fig. 7. Choropleth map describing the median (a, b), maximum (c, d), and minimum (e, f) trip cost in SAR per TAZ by gender.

contradicts our data set, as we clearly see a high number of female riders in our sample. We expect this is due to the limited availability of public transit options and the ban on driving placed on women in Riyadh.

4   Discussion

After computing the statistical distribution of different cost scores, we found that the average drop-off fare in our data set is around 13 dollars (approximately 50 SAR), the minimum fare is around 3 dollars (approximately 10 SAR) and the maximum fare is approximately 40 dollars (around 50 SAR). Finally, we were interested in examining the relationships between TAZs that attract trips with a relatively higher median cost and have a higher number of drop-off points.

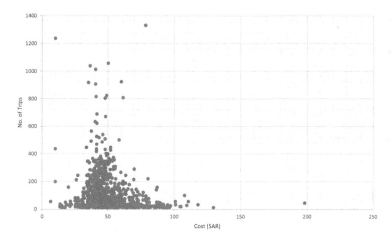

Fig. 8. Median cost and number of trips per TAZ

We chose to explore median values as opposed to average, minimum and maximum values, because median numbers avoid extreme values, which act as noise in the data. Figure 8 shows a scatterplot that represents TAZs based on their median cost and total trip count. We filtered out TAZs with fewer than 11 trips and TAZs with a median cost over 300 SAR (80 dollars). Each point on the plot represents one TAZ. After applying the filtration step, 896 TAZs (plot points) are represented.

Figure 8 shows that most TAZs with a higher number of drop-offs fall near the average taxi fare range. More analysis is needed to identify possible causes for this. Another observation from Figs. 3 and 4a, is that TAZs that have a higher number of drop-off points are mainly concentrated around the center of the city, whereas TAZs with a relatively high median cost are around the peripheral of the city. Additional work on pickup locations, TAZ population size and point of interest distribution can provide more insight.

This association can be useful in many domains since it can be improved to help identify areas in the city people are willing to pay more to go to. When linking this information with amenity and businesses distribution in the city, business owners can observe whether TAZs that have a higher aggregated cost or a higher trip count are associated with more amenities, allowing them to identify a link between amenity saturation and taxi visits or drop-off cost. Additionally, urban planners can use this information to identify how much different demographics pay to get to different parts of the city, which can be useful in service distribution.

5   Conclusion

Linking taxi drop-off cost to different parts of the city can be used to understand social dynamics and urban behavior. Utilizing 122,000 finished trips in Riyadh, mostly gender annotated, we observed social and urban patterns that result from linking taxi drop-off points to TAZs. We included gendered drop-off and total drop-off visualizations and then recorded general observations from those visualizations. The outcome of this research is intended to explore an approach for land classification that may be useful for urban planners and business owners.

Acknowledgment. The authors would like to thank Zeyad Alawwad for his help on this paper, and Dr. Anas Alfaris for his insightful feedback on this research study. The authors would also like thank the High Commission for Riyadh Development Authority (ADA) and the Taxi call center for providing the data used in this paper. This work was supported by a grant from King Abdulaziz City for Science and Technology.

References

1. Zhang, W., et al.: City-scale social event detection and evaluation with taxi traces. ACM Trans. Intell. Syst. Technol. (TIST) **6**(3), 40 (2015)
2. Ferreira, N., et al.: Visual exploration of big spatio-temporal urban data: a study of New York city taxi trips. IEEE Trans. Vis. Comput. Graph. **19**(12), 2149–2158 (2013)
3. Ge, Y., et al.: An energy-efficient mobile recommender system. In: Proceedings of the 16th ACM SIGKDD International Conference on Knowledge Discovery and Data Mining. ACM (2010)
4. Veloso, M., et al.: Exploratory study of urban flow using taxi traces. In: First Workshop on Pervasive Urban Applications (PURBA) in Conjunction with Pervasive Computing, San Francisco, California, USA (2011)
5. Castro, P.S., et al.: From taxi GPS traces to social and community dynamics: a survey. ACM Comput. Surv. (CSUR) **46**(2), 17 (2013)
6. Giannotti, F., et al.: Unveiling the complexity of human mobility by querying and mining massive trajectory data. VLDB J. Int. J. Very Large Data Bases **20**(5), 695–719 (2011)
7. Schwanen, T., Dijst, M., Dieleman, F.M.: Policies for urban form and their impact on travel: the Netherlands experience. Urban Stud. **41**(3), 579–603 (2004)
8. Lowry, J.H., Lowry, M.B.: Comparing spatial metrics that quantify urban form. Comput. Environ. Urban Syst. **44**, 59–67 (2014)
9. Handy, S.: Methodologies for exploring the link between urban form and travel behavior. Transp. Res. Part D: Trans. Environ. **1**(2), 151–165 (1996)
10. Deloitte: Transport in the Digital Age Disruptive Trends for Smart Mobility (2015). https://www2.deloitte.com/content/dam/Deloitte/tr/Documents/public-sector/transport-digital-age.pdf/. Accessed 5 Mar 2017
11. Pan, G., et al.: Land-use classification using taxi GPS traces. IEEE Trans. Intell. Transp. Syst. **14**(1), 113–123 (2013)
12. Liu, Y., et al.: Urban land uses and traffic 'source-sink areas': evidence from GPS-enabled taxi data in Shanghai. Landscape Urban Plan. **106**(1), 73–87 (2012)
13. Szell, M., Groß, B.: Hubcab–exploring the benefits of shared taxi services. In: Decoding the City How Big Data Can Change Urbanism (2014)
14. Singapore taxis data viewer developed by U-Zyn Chua. Singapore Taxis. https://uzyn.github.io/taxisg/. Accessed 5 Mar 2017
15. Huang, X., et al.: TrajGraph: a graph-based visual analytics approach to studying urban network centralities using taxi trajectory data. IEEE Trans. Vis. Comput. Graph. **22**(1), 160–169 (2016)

16. Veloso, M., Phithakkitnukoon, S., Bento, C.: Urban mobility study using taxi traces. In: Proceedings of the 2011 International Workshop on Trajectory Data Mining and Analysis. ACM (2011)
17. Alfayez, A., et al.: Understanding Gendered Spaces Using Social Media Data. Manuscript submitted for publication (2017)
18. Alhazzani, M., et al.: Urban Attractors: discovering patterns in regions of attraction in cities. arXiv preprint arXiv:1701.08696 (2016)
19. CityLab: More Women Ride Mass Transit Than Men. Shouldn't Transit Agencies Be Catering to Them? (2015). http://www.citylab.com/commute/2015/01/more-women-ride-mass-transit-than-men-shouldnt-transit-agencies-be-catering-to-them/385012/ Accessed 5 Mar 2017

Understanding Gendered Spaces
Using Social Media Data

Aljoharah Alfayez[1,2(✉)], Zeyad Awwad[1,2(✉)], Cortni Kerr[3(✉)],
Najat Alrashed[1,2(✉)], Sarah Williams[3(✉)], and Areej Al-Wabil[1,2(✉)]

[1] Center for Complex Engineering Systems (CCES),
King Abdulaziz City for Science and Technology (KACST),
Riyadh, Saudi Arabia
{a.alfayez,z.alawwad,n.alrashed}@cces-kacst-mit.org,
areej@mit.edu
[2] MIT, Cambridge, USA
[3] Civic Data Design Lab, MIT, Cambridge, MA, USA
{chkerr,sew}@mit.edu

Abstract. In Saudi Arabia, gender shapes cities in a way that is not commonly found in other cities due to Saudi Arabia's imposed gender segregation. This segregation policy drives both genders to different areas of the city in different ways, influencing the emergence of gendered spaces. In this paper, we utilize social media data to better understand gendered spaces throughout the city of Riyadh. For our analysis, we developed an algorithm to perform gender annotation based on users' first names. The method, optimized for English and Arabic language names, was applied to a sample of over 120,000 geotagged tweets between November 2016 and January 2017. The customer demographics of Foursquare venues were estimated based on the gender ratio of reviewers. Areas with a high degree of gender concentration in these datasets were used to identify gendered spaces. The correlation between gendered space identified from tweets and Foursquare venues was used to examine the link between amenities and gender-specific mobility habits in Riyadh. Throughout our analysis, we aim to identify ways in which government policies and the organization of businesses and services with similar customer demographics impact the mobility patterns of women and men and lead to the emergence of gendered spaces in Riyadh.

Keywords: Gendered spaces · Gender annotation · Gender segregation · Social media · Foursquare · Twitter · Urban planning

1 Introduction

In this work, our objective is to explore how gender information in social media can be used to understand the effects of gender segregation and mobility restriction on women in Riyadh, Saudi Arabia. Gender based variations of mobility is an established phenomenon across the world [1]. However, the depth of understanding this phenomenon in Saudi Arabia is inadequate [2]. By identifying and comparing gendered spaces from geotagged tweets and Foursquare venue reviews, we examine how female dominant

© Springer International Publishing AG 2017
G. Meiselwitz (Ed.): SCSM 2017, Part II, LNCS 10283, pp. 338–356, 2017.
DOI: 10.1007/978-3-319-58562-8_26

spaces differ from male dominant spaces and record general observations of where they tend to cluster most. To infer the gender of geotagged tweets in Saudi Arabia, we have developed an algorithm that relies heavily on Arabic specific language features to boost performance. We have also used Foursquare reviews and check-ins to understand the customer demographics of Foursquare venues.

Additionally, we describe a method we used to identify gendered spaces in the city. As a final step, we overlap female gendered spaces emerging from geotagged tweets and from our Foursquare demographic results to find patterns that emerge from those two data sets. We replicate this process with male spaces. Finally, we compare female patterns to male patterns. This work can be used as a first step to identify the innate differences between mobility patterns of men and women along with the implications of female mobility restrictions and segregation on the socio-spatial patterns of Riyadh.

2 Background

2.1 Gender Sensitivity in Urban Planning

The role of gender in urban planning theory and practice increased significantly toward the end of the 20th century, leading to the development of the concepts such as gendered spaces and gendered mobility [3–6]. This evolution in theory and practice occurred in response to rising awareness that women experience cities in different ways than men. The term "gendered spaces" is used here to refer to the spatial segregation of men and women at both the architectural and geographic scales [4, 7]. For example, a house may have specific women's and men's spaces and different parts of the city can be used differentially by men and women, whether it is a predominately male athletic stadium or a market frequented mostly by women. Spain (1993) argues that "Women's position within society, whether measured as power, prestige, economic position, or social rank, is related to spatial segregation insofar as existing physical arrangements facilitate or inhibit the exchange of knowledge between those with greater and those with lesser status" [4].

Gendered spaces have developed across many different contexts and cultures [4]. Despite a burgeoning literature on gendered spaces in U.S. and European contexts, limited work has been published that explores gender and space in Saudi Arabia at the city scale. Saudi Arabia is unique when it comes to gendered spaces. There is a national policy of gender segregation in public spaces dictating where and with whom women may occupy urban space. For example, restaurants and cafes have separate seating sections for men only and for women and families. Likewise, most schools and universities are gender segregated and athletic stadiums are primarily for men only. Moreover, women are prohibited from driving in Saudi Arabia, limiting their mobility options and potentially influencing the emergence of gendered spaces.

2.2 Gender and Mobility

Evidence shows that women and men travel within cities differently. Identifying gendered spaces in Riyadh is the first step in understanding gendered mobility in the city. According to Law (1999), "Daily mobility incorporates a range of issues central to human geography, including the use of (unequally distributed) resources, the experience of social interactions in transport-related settings and participation in a system of cultural beliefs and practices." [10] Gendered differences in travel patterns hold across the Global North and Global South contexts [8]. Much of the quantitative work on gendered mobility converges around the conclusion that women have shorter commute times than men [5, 8, 9]. However, context dictates whether this a positive or negative finding, when taking into consideration differential costs of travel. Moreover, this quantitative work is confined largely to national-scale, home-to-work commuting population surveys [11]. This type of data does not reflect non-work mobility and is also unavailable in Saudi Arabia. As an alternative, social media data is an opportunity to understand the spatial distribution of gendered spaces and mobility at the city scale.

2.3   Gender in Social Media

Social media are defined as tools for communication, where users can create and share their content with others through social networks. These web-based tools generate vast amounts of readily available data about populations around the world, triggering researchers to explore them. In Saudi Arabia, social media has become a major source of data. In 2016, it was reported that Saudi Arabia had the highest penetration rate of Twitter users in the world [12], A 2012 study reported that the number of registered twitter users in Saudi Arabia grew over 93% in six months, reaching 2.9 M. Additionally, Riyadh, Saudi Arabia's capital city, was described as the tenth most active city by number of posted tweets worldwide [13]. However, as informative as social media data is, it lacks some basic demographic information that can be highly useful in different domains. For this reason, many researchers have focused their efforts on finding ways of inferring some of this missing information.

Identifying user demographics from social media data is valuable and applicable in many domains, from business marketing to sociolinguistic analysis to behavior analysis. Several methods have been employed to infer data from social media. Most methods rely on using classification and regression techniques on certain characteristics found in a user's profile, such as names and language. From these characteristics, researchers have developed techniques to predict different demographic information, such as ethnicity, gender and political preference [16, 17, 19]. In particular, gender annotation using names has been a well explored theme, specifically in the context of social media [17–21]. The use of gender-name associations to label social media data is generally regarded as the most reliable gender inference method, specifically with tweets [17]. Gender inference accuracy is reported between 80 and 85% for English language names [16].

In the literature, gender inference from social data was used for understanding the Twitter population. A study of commuting patterns in Toronto, Canada found compelling evidence that Twitter data could be used to detect the demographic compositions of communities [14]. In a 2011 study, researchers utilized the U.S. Social Security Administration's database of birth records to classify the gender of 71% of the 3.2 million Twitter users in their study [19]. A 2016 study found that pairing web traffic demographic data with Twitter data in a non-fully-supervised regression model produced highly accurate gender classification, with moderately accurate ethnicity and political classification [18].

However, despite the growth of Twitter around world and across several language contexts, there is limited material on non-English gender inference. However, retraining the methods used for English-language names and incorporating language-specific identifiers has been shown to produce successful results [16]. This has yet to be applied in a significant manner to Arabic, which is the 6th most commonly used language on the platform [13]. In the next section, we shall describe our Arabic-optimized method of inferring the gender of geotagged tweets and Foursquare venue reviews in Riyadh.

3   Gender Annotation

3.1   Datasets

The analysis of this paper was applied on two datasets: 123,977 geotagged tweets collected from November 2016 to January 2017 using the Twitter API and 73,747 Foursquare venues collected from the Foursquare website in November 2016. With both data sets, only locations within a bounding box of 24.25° to 25.25° latitude and 46.25° to 47.25° longitude were considered in this study. After applying the name-based gender annotation methodology described in Sect. 3.2, a total of 18,302 tweets were classified as female and 32,839 were classified as male. The methodology described for Foursquare venues identified 1,057 male-oriented venues and 483 female-oriented venues

Both datasets contain implicit biases that should be kept into consideration. Since Foursquare data is crowdsourced, it relies on businesses' staff and customers to add venues to the database. Businesses that attract different demographics may not be equally represented in their data. Furthermore, the Foursquare data includes private reviews which do not publicly display the user's gender. With the Twitter data set, the user's name is self-reported so there is a possibility that it does not accurately reflect their gender [22, 23]. Due to a combination of sampling bias and potential limitations of the annotation method, both datasets have a significantly greater proportion of male users than female users.

3.2   Gender Annotation

As previously mentioned, the collected Foursquare data of Riyadh's amenities include a gender attribute in the reviews. Thus, the data set did not require the use of the name gender annotation algorithm described below. However, we applied a set of filters to determine if a venue was oriented toward a single gender. First, we removed venues that did not have at least 10 reviews with a gender attribute. This step reduced the number of venues to 2,915. Although this filtration step removed the majority of venues from our data set, venues with fewer reviews might not provide representative samples of their customer's demographics. For the remaining venues, we looked at the gender distribution of reviewers; If over 70% of reviewers were male or female, then the venue would be annotated with its respective dominant gender. After applying this step, 1,057 venues were labeled as male and 483 venues were labeled as female. The total number of gender annotated venues we have generated was 1,540 from a total of over 73,000 venues.

We have relied on a three-step method to gender annotate mainly Arabic names from geotagged tweets. Here is a description of our method:

(1) Preprocessing: Initial cleaning to prepare names for annotation.
   (a) Replace specific characters with a simpler variant (see Table 1).

Table 1. Replaced characters

Replaced characters	آ إ أ	ؤ و	ئ	ة	_ -/.
Replacement character	ا		و ي	ه	(space)

   (b) Remove any characters not in the basic English and Arabic alphabets.
(2) Annotation: Determines the gender of a name if a set of tests return exactly one unique gender (excluding null results).
   (a) Split the name by spaces and check the database for a match, beginning with the first substring and adding more substrings if a match is not found.
   (b) Check if the first name begins with certain prefixes (Table 2).

Table 2. Sample of prefixes

Arabic	ابو	عبد
English	Abu (Father of)	Abd

   (c) Check the name for certain keywords that indicate gender (Table 3).

Table 3. Sample of keywords

Arabic	سيد	سيدة	ام	بنت	بن
English	Mr	Mrs	Om (Mother of)	Bint (Daughter of)	Bin (Son of)

(3) Refinement: After running the annotation, names that were not annotated were exported and the most frequent 10–15% were manually labelled and added to the database.

Although this method can be applied to annotate any name in the database regardless of its language, it also leverages identifiers that are unique to Arabic since language-specific features can significantly improve the rate of annotation [16]. The database of names was initially populated from a list of over 1000 gender-annotated Arabic names with both Arabic and English spelling variants retrieved from the website Behind the Name [24]. Using the initial database, the method could identify the gender of approximately 34% of geotagged tweets, almost 75% of which were male. Although the database was further expanded by including names from various sources such as university registries, we found that the refinement step was the fastest way to increase our method's performance.

After applying the refinement step, the method could annotate 41% of tweets primarily by identifying a larger number of female tweets. Although the gender balance was improved, female users still represented only 35% of all geotagged tweets. Previous studies have estimated that Twitter is more female biased [20, 25] but due to cultural norms, we suspect that women in Saudi Arabia are more likely to have private accounts. As a result, users of social media platforms are unlikely to be representative of the population.

To reduce the rate of false positives in our results, gender-ambiguous names were removed from the database whenever they were identified. These included names that apply to both men and women (e.g. 'Sam'), or names that become indistinguishable when written in English (e.g. 'Alaa', which can refer to both the male علاء or the female آلاء). The quality of the results relies on the accuracy of self-declared names entered by Twitter users. Although this source of error is difficult to control for due to the nature of social media data, we checked the profiles of a random sample of annotated tweets to manually identify the user's gender (for example by looking at profile pictures and Arabic pronouns they use) and found the names generally appeared to be a reliable indication of the user's gender and rarely produced false positives.

4   Gendered Spaces

Prior literature has proposed that "all space is already gendered: we live, experience and in some cases have reinforced for us, our gendered identities in particular built environments which assume certain things already about codes of gender" [26]. In the context of Riyadh, such gender norms and characteristics are often enforced. The following section will explore how gender annotated data from Twitter and Foursquare can be used to identify Riyadh's gendered spaces and investigate regions of overlap between the results of the two datasets.

4.1   Spatial Distribution of Tweets and Foursquare Data

Method. To accurately reflect the raw data with minimal processing, we initially visualized the gender balance of Twitter and Foursquare data using grid-based heatmaps. The visualizations were displayed using Leaflet, an open-source JavaScript library commonly used to integrate geospatial data with interactive maps. The data points were aggregated using grid cells with side lengths of 0.01° by 0.01° (approximately 1 × 1 km) to determine the spatial distributions of genders based on Twitter (Fig. 1) and Foursquare data (Fig. 2). Using a higher resolution grid is generally preferred to reveal differences in gender balance but since the data is sparse, we found that using significantly smaller cells led to frequent gaps in the heatmap and a high sensitivity to outliers.

Fig. 1. Spatial distribution of gender annotated geotagged tweets (Color figure online)

The gender balance of cells in Figs. 1 and 2 is reflected in the color scale which ranging from red (female) to blue (male) with intermediate ratios shown in purple tones. The opacity of a cell varies based on the number of geotagged tweets or check-ins within that cell. In Fig. 1, the color intensity increases proportionally to the number of geotagged tweets up to a maximum of 250 tweets per cell. Since the number of reviews is not necessarily proportional to the number of visits, our analysis of Foursquare data used reviews only to determine the gender ratio. The ratio was used to distribute the check-ins between male and female users, resulting in a total of nearly 713,000 and 1,915,000 check-ins for women and men respectively. In Fig. 2, the color intensity increases proportionally to the number of check-ins up to a maximum of 20,000 check-ins per cell.

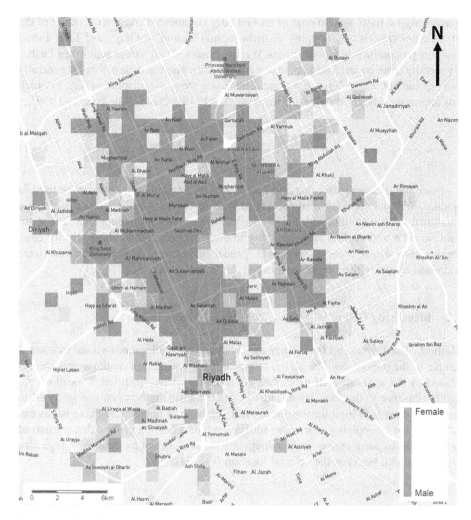

Fig. 2. Spatial distribution of gender-oriented venues weighted by check-ins (Color figure online)

Results. A few trends are apparent from the raw data visualization in Figs. 1 and 2. Since Twitter and Foursquare activity appears to correlate with population density, activity drops off in the more sparsely populated northern zone and southeastern zones. Additionally, a large gap in the middle of the city corresponds to a military air base with very little commercial and residential activity nearby. The level of social media activity in certain areas may also be affected by demographic factors such as age, nationality and socioeconomic status or a lack of amenities that tend to appear on Foursquare.

In addition, major segregated landmarks reflect their imposed gender segregation. For example, the grid cells in the northeast quadrant that cover the female-only Princess Noura University appear prominently in red. Likewise, the King Fahad stadium and the male campus of King Saud University were identified as male spaces. Furthermore, areas of high activity tend to emerge around busy commercial areas in the center of the city. Commonly visited shopping districts located around Al-Olaya and King Fahad roads are predominantly female spaces. We also observed that female activity on Twitter is generally more concentrated in the center of the city whereas male activity is generally more spread out. The difference was measured using the spatial dispersion (Eq. 1) which was approximately 20% higher for male tweets (0.119°) than female tweets (0.099°).

$$\sqrt{\frac{\sum_{i=1}^{N}(x_i - x_{centroid})^2 - (y_i - y_{centroid})^2}{N}} \tag{1}$$

Since the data is sparse, this approach limits in the resolution that can be used in practice. Without applying a smoothing method to the data, outliers can easily cause individual cells to conflict with the gender balance of the surrounding area. The sharp transitions between values and sensitivity to outliers make it difficult to identify large regions that demonstrate a consistent gender imbalance. These limitations were addressed by using the smoothing method described in Sect. 4.2.

4.2   Identifying Gendered Spaces from Social Media Data

Method. The Twitter and Foursquare data both capture the locations visited by a small sample of the population. The ability to perform high-resolution spatial aggregation is limited by the sparseness of these datasets since the values at different locations are highly sensitive to outliers. This results in sharp transitions between one grid cell to another and tends to limit the resolutions that can be used in practice. These issues can be minimized by applying a Gaussian filter to each data point, a method that consists of defining values for a region surrounding each tweet or venue by defining a Gaussian distribution that peaks at the original location (Fig. 3a).

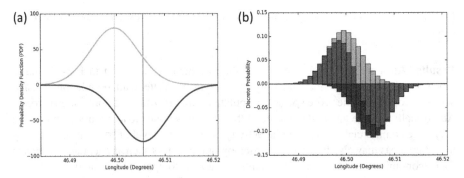

Fig. 3. (a) The results of a Gaussian filter applied to a female (red) and male (blue) location along the x axis with the exact location represented by thin vertical lines. (b) The discrete probability distribution of the same female (red) and male (blue) locations along with the distribution of the sum of all distributions (purple) (Color figure online)

The results were rasterized by discretizing the two spatial dimensions to cells with fixed widths that determine the resolution of the raster. The area under the curve of the probability density function was used to define a discrete probability value for each cell (Fig. 3b) along each dimension. The Gaussian filter is applied to each dimension independently and the value of each 2D grid cell is the product of the corresponding x and y values. This process is applied to each gender-annotated tweet and Foursquare venue to generate a raster using a sum of all the discrete probability distributions. The sum of the distributions were initially generated separately for males and females to produce a pair of aggregate distributions for both Twitter and Foursquare users. This methodology was used to define smooth gender distributions using the gender balance over a large area.

For the Twitter data, we generated an additional raster to represent the difference in gender concentration throughout the city. This was performed by using opposite signs

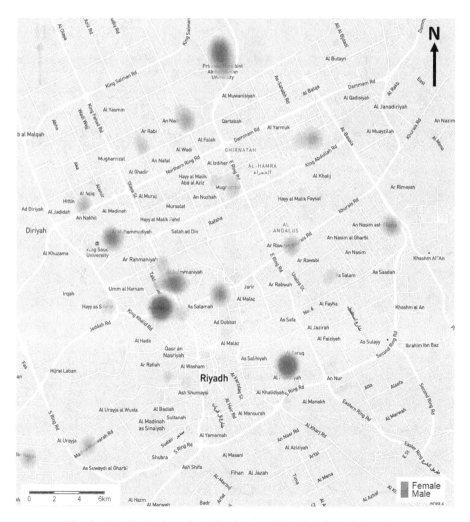

Fig. 4. The distribution of gendered spaces identified from Twitter data

for the genders and taking the sum of the distributions (Fig. 3b). This approach was used to distinguish areas with a high gender imbalance from areas that have a large number of tweets from both genders. This approach was not used with the Foursquare data since female-oriented venues accounted for less than 3.2% of all gender-oriented venues and the combined distribution was always dominated by male-oriented venues. As a result, our analysis was applied to each gender separately to identify areas of high concentration for male- and female-oriented venues.

Results. In Fig. 4, gender-annotated tweets were used to identify areas with a high gender imbalance. A cell width of 0.001 (approximately 0.1 km) was used for both axes to produce a rasterized distribution with a 2D spatial resolution of approximately 0.01 km^2. A threshold of ± 0.5 was used to isolate areas with a high gender imbalance.

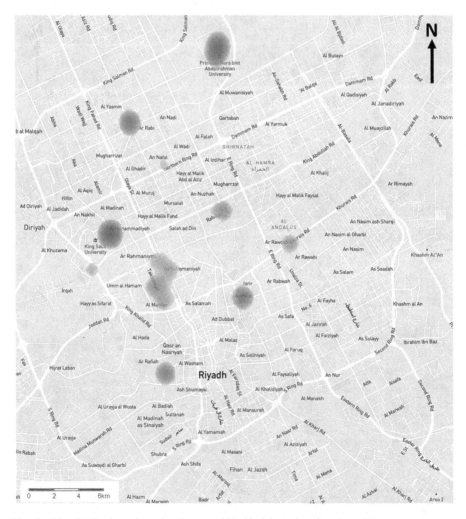

Fig. 5. The distribution of gendered spaces identified from female-oriented Foursquare venues

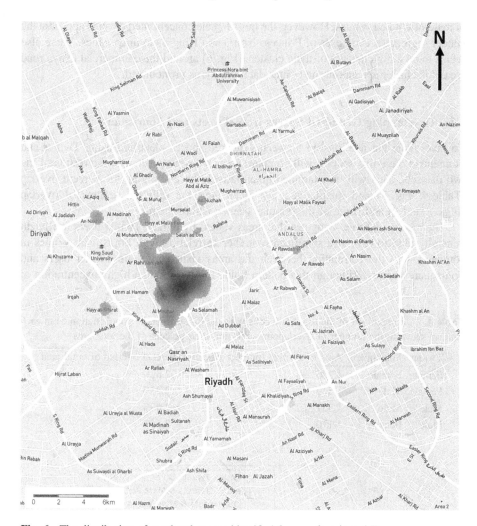

Fig. 6. The distribution of gendered spaces identified from male-oriented Foursquare venues

The smoothing process reveals more distinctive gendered spaces in the city, with some of the patterns from the raw data emerging still. First, as shown in Fig. 4, there is a distinct female cluster around the women's only Princess Noura University. Likewise, a female cluster appears on the female campus of King Saud University and a male cluster on the male campus of King Saud University. Female spaces also emerge in the previously mentioned Olaya commercial district and King Fahad road's shopping areas. A distinct male space emerges in the industrial Alfaruq and Alfaisaliyah areas. There are several factories located here that primarily employ men. Overall, it appears that male spaces are spread across a larger span of the city, whereas female spaces are located more closely to one another, Fig. 4.

Figures 5 and 6 reveal the highly-concentrated areas of gendered venues on Foursquare. Female-oriented venues (Fig. 5) appear more dispersed than the concentrations of male-orientated venues. However, the most female concentrated clusters appear at the gender segregated campuses of Princess Noura and King Saud universities. There also seems to be a high density of male clusters (Fig. 6) around the commercial Olaya road area, this cluster appears in the twitter data but not as pronounced.

4.3   Overlapping Gendered Spaces from Tweets and Foursquare

To investigate the relationship between gendered spaces identified using Twitter and Foursquare data, this section will compare areas of overlap between the results of the two datasets. This will be examined quantitatively by computing the percent overlap (Table 4, Fig. 7) and qualitatively by identifying the different regions of overlap (Figs. 8 and 9) and some of the popular venues within them.

The results in Table 4 suggest that areas visited by female Twitter users in Riyadh generally tend to exhibit a significantly higher correlation with Foursquare venues in comparison to the correlation between the areas visited by male Twitter users and Foursquare venues. Although this pattern holds for areas with a high concentration of

Table 4. A comparison of the top 2,500 cells with the highest gender concentration from each data set showing the number of overlapping cells and their percent of the total area

Twitter	Foursquare	Area of overlap (number of cells)	Percent overlap of yotal area
Female	Female	1,230	32.63%
Female	Male	549	12.33%
Male	Male	331	7.09%
Male	Female	170	3.52%

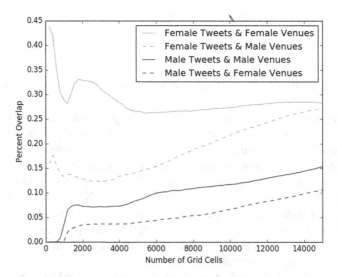

Fig. 7. The percent overlap of gendered spaces for Twitter and Foursquare data when different numbers of grid cells are used to define regions with the highest concentration

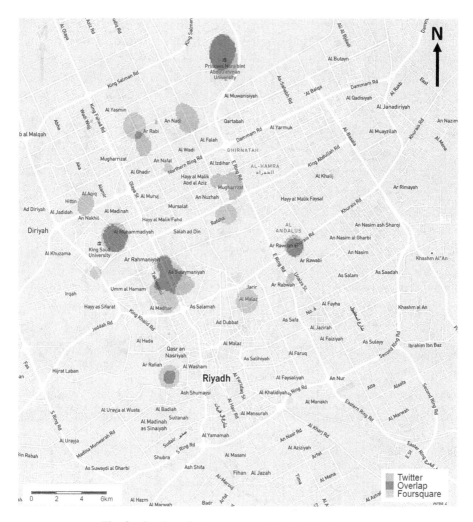

Fig. 8. Overlap of Foursquare and Twitter female spaces

venues regardless of the venues' targeted gender, areas with a high concentration of female tweets tend to overlap more with female venues and areas with a high concentration of male tweets tend to overlap more with male venues.

The findings in Table 4 and Fig. 7 suggest that gendered spaces for women in Riyadh tend to form in highly clustered venue spaces. Female tweets are most strongly correlated with areas containing a high concentration of female-oriented venues but they also exhibit a significant correlation with male-related venues. By contrast, areas with a high concentration of male tweets exhibit a much lower rate of overlap with venues regardless of gender. This suggests that areas of male activity in Riyadh are less likely to be driven by the density of venues. Since women in Riyadh are not allowed to drive and do not have any currently available public transportation options, it is

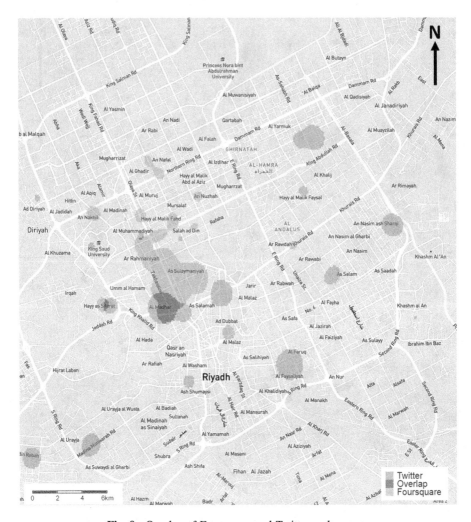

Fig. 9. Overlap of Foursquare and Twitter male spaces

possible that constraints on female mobility could lead women to prefer co-located venues and encourage venues that target women to form clusters.

The percent overlap between the areas of highest concentration changes depending on the coverage of the city, measured by the number of grid cells considered. However, the order of the results remains consistent across a broad range of coverage values. The overlap between female tweets and female venues is greatest when only the top 2,000 grid cells are included and stabilizes at approximately 30% as additional cells are added. The rate of overlap for female tweets and male venues gradually increases with the number of cells and converges with the overlap of female venues when the top 15,000 cells are considered. The percent overlap of male tweets and venues of either gender also increases but remains significantly lower regardless of the degree of coverage.

For consistency, the following results in Figs. 8 and 9 are based on the top 2,500 grid cells for each data set.

Application of this method resulted in six areas of overlap for females (Fig. 8). Overlap emerges at three female university campuses: Princess Noura University and King Saud University's primary and preparatory campuses. Both data sets also identified a high concentration of women at a commercial area along Khurais Road that includes popular stores, cafes and an all-women's gym. One of the largest areas of overlap was found along King Fahad Road and Olaya Street in the city's primary commercial hub which contains several shopping malls, popular restaurants and cafes. A small area of overlap was also found on King Abdulaziz Road in an area containing schools, restaurants and a private tertiary care center (the Kingdom Hospital).

A correlation between male space identified by Twitter and male-oriented Foursquare venues was only observed at two locations (Fig. 9). The first was the Al-Madhar area near the city's commercial hub, a region with substantial number of popular restaurants and coffee shops. A small area of overlap was observed in the Diplomatic Quarter (Hayy As-Sifarat). This neighborhood is home primarily to foreign embassies along with popular parks where sporting activities and social events are held.

5 Discussion

When applied to data from social media platforms, the methodology described above can help identify the impacts of Saudi Arabia's unique gender segregation policy on Riyadh's built environment and urban dynamics. The initial heatmap visualizations of the raw Twitter and Foursquare datasets displayed regions of gender imbalance throughout the city but didn't identify broad gendered spaces. A Gaussian filter was used to identify agglomerations with smooth transitions between values to identify gendered spaces from both Twitter activity and Foursquare venues. This analysis accurately picked up some of Riyadh's gendered landmarks such as male and female university campuses, male-only sporting venues, male- and female-oriented commercial areas and male-oriented industrial areas.

Furthermore, a comparison of the two datasets revealed the extent to which Twitter gendered spaces are correlated with single-gender oriented Foursquare venues. Areas with a high concentration of female tweets were more correlated with female-oriented venues than concentrations of male tweets were correlated with male-orientated venues. For female spaces, the overlap between the two datasets was 33%, whereas for males the overlap was less than 10%. This finding is potentially an indication that limits on women's mobility in Riyadh encourages the clustering of venues that cater specifically to them. Further testing of this hypothesis is necessary and might be explored using additional data sets that could identify the relationship between gendered spaces and mobility patterns.

The contributions of this study for future research are twofold: improvements to gender annotation for Arabic names and a new methodology to identify gendered spaces from social media data. This methodology could be combined with the advances in Arabic sentiment analysis [25] to analyze tweet content as a barometer for public opinion on key social or policy issues. There is also potential for utilizing gender annotated social media data in a comparative study with other Saudi Arabian cities and neighboring Gulf countries which share a similar culture but do not impose the same gender segregation policies as Saudi Arabia. Comparing the gendered spaces results with other results could give more insight on the implications of mobility limitation on women and gender segregation.

Due to the unique cultural context in Saudi Arabia, there is a high degree of spatial segregation between the destinations of females and males in Riyadh. Understanding the distribution of Riyadh's gendered spaces is meaningful for city planning, and specifically for the transit planning associated with the ongoing development of Riyadh's first public transit system. The system, which will include rail and bus, is expected to be the largest mass-transit system built from scratch when it opens in late 2018 [25].

Currently, Riyadh faces serious traffic congestion challenges [29]. The new metro system could alleviate congestion and lessen the dependence of the city's 6 million residents on fuel consuming vehicles. The metro also has the potential to alter women's dependence on male drivers and taxi services. Given Saudi Arabia's policy that prohibits women from driving, women are expected to be a significant user population of the metro [30–33]. By identifying gendered spaces, this paper takes the first step toward a nuanced analysis of gendered mobility in Riyadh. Future work could assess the impact of the metro system on women's transit to these places or design bus routes specifically for women based on the distribution of gendered spaces.

6 Conclusion

The varying roles and division of labor between genders appear at various scales in urban planning and design - individual buildings, neighborhoods, cities, and regions - and in the different domains of city design, such as housing, public facilities, transportation, streets and open space, employment and commercial/services areas. In this paper, we presented an overview of an innovative use of social media data to identify gendered spaces in the city of Riyadh. Utilizing 51,000 of geotagged tweets that were then gender annotated, we identified gendered spaces in Riyadh and opportunities for future research on gendered spaces and mobility in Riyadh and other cities, especially where social media users are Arabic speakers. The outcomes of this research are intended to allow researchers in urban design and city planning to understand how Saudi Arabia's social policies shape urban dynamics.

References

1. Uteng, T.: Gender and mobility in the developing world. World development report, 7778105-1299699968583 (2012)
2. Aldalbahi, M., Walker, G.: Riyadh transportation history and developing vision. Procedia-Soc. Behav. Sci. **216**, 163–171 (2016)
3. Sandercock, L., Forsyth, A.: A gender agenda: new directions for planning theory. J. Am. Plann. Assoc. **58**(1), 49–59 (1992). doi:10.1080/01944369208975534

4. Spain, D.: Gendered spaces and women's status. Sociol. Theor. **11**(2), 137 (1993). doi:10. 2307/202139
5. Hanson, S.: Gender and mobility: new approaches for informing sustainability. Gend. Place Cult. **17**(1), 5–23 (2010)
6. McDowell, L.: Towards an understanding of the gender division of urban space. Environ. Plann. D Soc. Space **1**(1), 59–72 (1983)
7. Spain, D.: Gendered Spaces. University of North Carolina Press, Chapel Hill (1992)
8. Loukaitou-Sideris, A.: A gendered view of mobility and transport: next steps and future directions. Town Plann. Rev. **87**(5), 547–565 (2016)
9. Crane, R.: Is there a quiet revolution in women's travel? Revisiting the gender gap in commuting. J. Am. Plann. Assoc. **73**(3), 298–316 (2007)
10. Law, R.: Beyond "women and transport": towards new geographies of gender and daily mobility. Prog. Hum. Geogr. **23**(4), 567–588 (1999)
11. Cresswell, T., Uteng, T.P.: Gendered mobilities: towards an holistic understanding. Gendered Mobilities, pp. 1–12. Aldershot, England (2008)
12. Globalmediainsight.com: Saudi Arabia social media statistics 2016 - official GMI blog (2017). http://www.globalmediainsight.com/blog/saudi-arabia-social-media-statistics/.   Accessed 27 Feb 2017
13. Semiocast: Semiocast—Geolocation of Twitter users, July 2012. http://semiocast.com/en/ publications/2012_07_30_Twitter_reaches_half_a_billion_accounts_140m_in_the_US. Accessed 27 Feb 2017
14. Liu, W., Al Zamal, F., Ruths, D.: Using social media to infer gender composition of commuter populations. In: Proceedings of the When the City Meets the Citizen Workshop, The International Conference on Weblogs and Social Media, May 2012
15. Bergsma, S., Dredze, M., Van Durme, B., Wilson, T., Yarowsky, D.: Broadly improving user classification via communication-based name and location clustering on Twitter. In: HLT-NAACL, pp. 1010–1019 (2013)
16. Ciot, M., Sonderegger, M., Ruths, D.: Gender inference of Twitter users in non-english contexts. In: EMNLP, pp. 1136–1145, October 2013
17. Al Zamal, F., Liu, W., Ruths, D.: Homophily and latent attribute inference: inferring latent attributes of Twitter users from neighbors. In: ICWSM, p. 270 (2012)
18. Culotta, A., Kumar, N.R., Cutler, J.: Predicting Twitter user demographics using distant supervision from website traffic data. J. Artif. Intell. Res. (JAIR) **55**, 389–408 (2016)
19. Mislove, A., Lehmann, S., Ahn, Y.Y., Onnela, J.P., Rosenquist, J.N.: Understanding the demographics of Twitter users. In: ICWSM, vol. 11, p. 5 (2011)
20. Burger, J.D., Henderson, J., Kim, G., Zarrella, G.: Discriminating gender on Twitter. In: Proceedings of the Conference on Empirical Methods in Natural Language Processing, Association for Computational Linguistics, pp. 1301–1309, July 2011
21. Liu, W., Ruths, D.: What's in a name? Using first names as features for gender inference in Twitter. In: AAAI Spring Symposium: Analyzing Microtext, vol. 13, p. 1, March 2013
22. Zafarani, R., Tang, L., Liu, H.: User identification across social media. ACM Trans. Knowl. Discov. Data (TKDD) **10**(2), 16 (2015)
23. Novak, J., Raghavan, P., Tomkins, A.: Anti-aliasing on the web. In: Proceedings of the 13th International Conference on World Wide Web, pp. 30–39. ACM, May 2004
24. Campbell, M.: Behind the name: meaning of names, baby name meanings (2017). Behindthename.com. http://www.behindthename.com/. Accessed 27 Feb 2017
25. Heil, B., Piskorski, M.: New Twitter research: men follow men and nobody tweets. Harvard Bus. Rev. **1**, 2009 (2009)

26. Long, J.: 'There's no place like home'?: domestic life, gendered space and online access. In: Proceedings of the International Symposium on Women and ICT: Creating Global Transformation, p. 12. ACM, June 2005

27. alOwisheq, A., alHumoud, S., alTwairesh, N., alBuhairi, T.: Arabic sentiment analysis resources: a survey. In: Meiselwitz, G. (ed.) SCSM 2016. LNCS, vol. 9742, pp. 267–278. Springer, Cham (2016). doi:10.1007/978-3-319-39910-2_25

28. Varinksy, D.: Saudi Arabia's Riyadh metro will be largest urban-transit system ever built from scratch. http://www.businessinsider.com/saudi-arabias-riyadh-metro-will-be-the-largest-urban-transit-system-ever-built-from-scratch-2016-5. Accessed 20 Feb 2017, 20 May 2016

29. Chodrow, P.S., Al-Awwad, Z., Jiang, S., González, M.C.: Demand and congestion in multiplex transportation networks. PLoS ONE 11(9), e0161738 (2016). doi:10.1371/journal.pone.0161738

30. Beasley, K.: For Saudi women, new subway will mean more than a cool ride. http://www.npr.org/sections/parallels/2013/07/30/207077269/for-saudi-women-new-subway-will-mean-more-than-a-cool-ride. Accessed 20 Feb 2017, (n.d.)

31. Kirk, M.: What a new metro in Saudi Arabia will mean for women. http://www.citylab.com/commute/2017/02/what-riyadhs-new-metro-will-mean-for-women/515859/. Accessed 20 Feb 2017, 7 Feb 2017

32. Winter, C.: For women, saudi arabia's new metro may mean greater mobility. Bloomberg.com. https://www.bloomberg.com/news/articles/2013-08-16/for-women-saudi-arabias-new-metro-may-mean-greater-mobility. Accessed 16 Aug 2013

33. Asmahan Alghamdi: المترو»..المرأة تنتظره لأسبابها الخاصة. http://www.alriyadh.com/854435. Accessed 24 July 2013

Visual Exploration Patterns in Information Visualizations: Insights from Eye Tracking

Jumana Almahmoud[1,2(✉)], Saleh Albeaik[1,2], Tarfah Alrashed[1,2], and Almaha Almalki[1,2]

[1] Center for Complex Engineering Systems (CCES),
King Abdulaziz City for Science and Technology (KACST), Riyadh, Saudi Arabia
{jalmahmoud,salbeaik,talrashed,aasalmalki}@kacst.edu.sa
[2] MIT, Cambridge, USA

Abstract. One of the common problems associated with measuring the usability of information visualizations is understanding human factors of visual perception and cognitive processing in interacting with dynamic data graphs that are commonly used in social computing applications. In this paper, we investigate the cognitive and perceptual processes in the visual exploration process of information visualizations. Increasing interest in recent years has been focused on the development of performance-based usability metrics, (such as accuracy, speed and visual scanning strategies captured from session logs) to address this problem. However, the growing number of new terminology related to eye tracking metrics have caused considerable confusion to the information visualization community, consequently making the comparison of these metrics and the generalization of empirical results from eye tracking studies of data visualizations increasingly difficult. This paper proposes a framework of eye tracking metrics related to interacting with information visualizations which demonstrate the underlying relationships between human factors in gaze metrics and information visualization design factors. Design implications and issues relating to the investigation of these metrics are also discussed.

Keywords: Information visualization · Recognition · Recall · Eye-tracking · Human-computer interaction · HCI

1 Introduction

The field of social computing has evolved in recent years and many technologies emerged in this field to facilitate the communication and interaction with social data [1]. In order to create more efficient mediums to support social computing applications, information visualizations were used to enhance the cognitive process [2, 3]. On the other hand, the growing interest in the application of eye tracking methodology for measuring the usability of information visualizations in recent years can be attributed to the need for objective measures that lead to insights in user interactions with information visualizations, which would be considerably more difficult to uncover with other usability testing methods. For the transfer and creation of knowledge, information

© Springer International Publishing AG 2017
G. Meiselwitz (Ed.): SCSM 2017, Part II, LNCS 10283, pp. 357–366, 2017.
DOI: 10.1007/978-3-319-58562-8_27

visualizations help make abstract concepts accessible to users, help to reduce complexity, amplify cognition, describe and explain causal relationships, segment and structure information. Novel approaches for information visualization are emerging that allow to illustrate higher complexity to embed factors such as social and cultural factors in knowledge-intense processes of interaction. To transfer knowledge, interactive information visualizations often (1) fascinate users whether they are interacting individually or in collaborative settings that are co-located or remotely linked, enabling interactive collaborations across time and space, and (2) facilitate interactions for representing and exploring complex scenarios or creating new insights. Increasing interest in recent years has been focused on measuring the usability of information visualizations and developing objective metrics, such as accuracy, speed and visual scanning strategies captured from session logs, to address this problem. Goldberg [4] provided an early discussion of applying eye tracking to information visualization. He considered the linear and radial visualizations to address variations in visual attention distribution and comprehension. However, the growing number of new terminology related to eye tracking metrics have caused considerable confusion to the information visualization community, consequently making the comparison of these metrics and the generalization of empirical results from eye tracking studies of data visualizations increasingly difficult. Our research goals are to understand the perceptual and cognitive processes in visual communication of information. Specifically, we proposes a framework of eye tracking metrics related to interacting with information visualizations which can describe the underlying relationships between human factors in gaze metrics and information visualization design factors.

2 Related Work

Kindly assure Interaction design for dynamic information visualizations is a multidisciplinary field. Usability research of information visualizations intersects visual design, human-computer interaction (HCI) studies, cognitive psychology, and computer science. Prior research has often focused on each of the above separately and from a specific point of view [5]. In this section, we provide an overview of those different perspectives. We present an overview of eye tracking studies in information visualizations, followed by the perceptual and cognitive processes that have been found to be relevant to the design of interactive information visualizations. Eye tracking research in knowledge and information visualization often aims to understand the perceptual and cognitive processes in visual communication of information [6]. Specifically, eye tracking methods are applied to investigate which visual elements do people actually pay attention to, when do they pay attention to these elements in the interaction, and for how long [4, 7]. Authors in [4] examined the visual scanning strategies of users in reading specific types of graphs (radial and line graph). A taxonomy of tasks and abstract data types was presented by Shneiderman in 1996 that was proposed to understand the cognitive processes involved in interacting with information visualization [8] are acceptable.

3 Exploratory Eye-Tracking Study

Inspired by research methodologies originally developed for analyzing graphic visualizations, we explore eye-tracking methods that measure various static and dynamic aspects of visual perception, and their relations to an underlying cognitive processes. The eye fixations and visual scanning patterns allow us to analyze and quantify what information visualization elements viewers encode, retrieve, and recall from memory. In this exploratory study, we look at the different ways in which we can analyze people's eye-movements and responses as they interact with information visualizations.

3.1 Participants

A total of 23 participants (8 females, 15 males) participated in the experimental study. All of the participants were recruited from the local communities in Riyadh, Saudi Arabia with an average age of 28.09 years (SD = 5.18 years). All participants had bachelor's degree or higher. The participants had normal color vision. Table 1 shows the demographics of participants in the study's sample.

Table 1. The demographics of the participants

Age group	Female	Males	All
21–30	6	11	18
31–40	2	3	5
All ages	8	14	23

3.2 Apparatus

For the eye-tracking study of our experiment, we used a Tobii X120 stand-alone eye-tracking system with participants seated approximately 60 cm from a 23 in. monitor (resolution: 1920 × 1080 pixels). Tobii studio V 3.4 was used for recording and analysis. Sessions were conducted in an office setting where noise was reduced compared to the usual setting within the space. The process of establishing the framework of mapping gaze metrics involved merging taxonomy with the taxonomy of gaze metrics. Table 1 describes the metrics.

3.3 Procedure

A single session of the experiment took between 15 to 20 min for each participant. At the beginning of an experimental session, participants were introduced to the session by giving them an overview of what eye-tracking is and the nature of the tasks they will be performing. When the session starts for each user, we conducted a randomized 5-point calibration procedure to establish the 3D coordinates of the eyes. At regular intervals, a drift check was performed and, if necessary, recalibration took place, and optional breaks were offered to participants. This exploratory study involved two sections; the first one prompts the user to perform informational tasks in which there were asked a set of questions and were asked to look for the answer using the stimuli they were exposed to. The second one involved a navigational task in which the users were asked to explore a webpage from the visualization platform.

For this exploratory study we used the data visualizations from the Observatory of Economic Complexity by MIT. The informational task exposed the user with two visualization patterns; stacked graph and a treemap. The theme of the informational questions was selected to test the findability and comparability of the visualization pattern. And to insure consistency and in the same time reduce the effect of learnability, the same set of questions were asked for each visualization pattern but for a different country. For the navigational task, the users were prompted by looking and using the mouse, and then asked to give their feedback at the end of the session as shown. Figure 1 illustrates the set of questions that were asked to the user.

Fig. 1. The two set of tasks in the exploratory study (Informational Navigational)

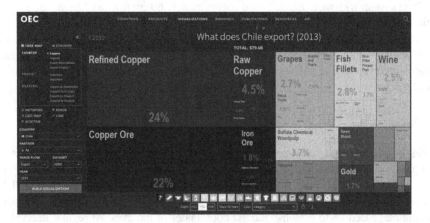

Fig. 2. The first visual trigger displayed to the user in the form of a treemap visualizing the exports of Egypt

Two research methods were applied in this study; observation and retrospective think aloud (RTA). The study was audio recorded to capture users' comments as they performed the tasks. At the end of the session, we wrapped up by replaying the recorded eye tracking session to the user and asked the participant to explain if there were some clear patterns or unusual behavior using RTA (Figs. 2 and 3).

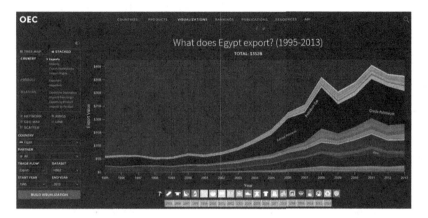

Fig. 3. The second visual trigger displayed to the user in the form of a stacked graph visualizing the exports of Egypt.

4 Framework

The process of establishing the framework of mapping gaze metrics involved merging taxonomy of gaze metrics in [9] with task by data type taxonomy in [8]. The table in Fig. 4 describes the framework we are proposing of eye tracking metrics related to interacting with information visualizations.

4.1 Visual Exploration Patterns in Information Visualization

For this study we analyzed the eye movements of 23 participants examining visualizations to determine which graphic elements of a data visualization attract people's attention, and patterns of visual exploration. The mapping of gaze metrics to design factors was verified by reflecting on the experimental results of our exploratory study. While the proposed framework for eye tracking research (described in the Framework section), can empirically support conventional design guidelines for information visualization, patterns in visual exploration that are aligned with the shape, form and function of data visualizations can provide a taxonomy for visual orientation and exploration for data visualization.

The findings demonstrate that there is a marked difference between the fixation patterns and their corresponding spatial distribution in different visualizations as

Eye Metrics	Design/Visual Factor	Human Factor	Task [13]
Fixation			
Time to first fixation on target	Salience: attracts attention (short), less attractive (long).	Background Curiosity Interest	Overview
Fixation spatial density	Focused based on the characteristics/content of visualization/area of interest or beyond area of interest	Background Interest Confusion	Overview Zoom Filter Relate
Fixation duration, Fixation length	Complexity of the information embedded in the visual element.	Background Interest Cognitive	Overview Zoom Relate
Fixations on target divided by total number of fixations	Relevance High: the visualization "target" attracts attention. Low: other elements distract attention from the target. "Layout"	Background Recognition	Zoom Filter Extract Relate
Percentage of participants fixating on area of interest	Salience: More noticeable (high), less noticeable (low).	Recognition	Extract
Number of fixations overall until task achieved	High or low based on if the visualization is meaningful or not.	Recognition	Relate Zoom
Repeat fixations (after first fixation on target)	High or low based on meaningfulness or visibility of target	Recognition	Zoom Filter Relate
Fixations per area of interest	High or low based on if the AOI is important or noticeable.	Background Recognition	Zoom Details-on-demand Filter
Fixations per area of interest adjusted for text length (or area size)	High or low based on elements identifiability	Background Recognition	
Scanpath			
Longer scanpath duration	Long if the layout of the focal points is overwhelming, shorter otherwise.	Interest Confusion	Overview Filter Details-on-demand
Scanpath direction	Directed if layout is optimal. Otherwise, scanpath direction is scattered.	Background Confusion	Overview Filter Relate
Longer scanpath length	Long or short based on the efficiency of the layout.	Cognitive	Zoom Filter
Spatial density of scanpath	Small if the group of elements in the area of interest is coherent and contain needed information. Otherwise, spatial density increases.	Background Confusion	Overview Relate Details-on-demand
Scanpath regularity	Consistent use of familiar layout and visualization elements.	Recognition Confusion	Relate Details-on-demand
Transition matrix (back and forth between areas)	Inefficient grouping of elements led to higher number of transitions.	Recognition	Filter Relate Details-on-demand
Transition probability between AOIs	Probability increases if existing elements are familiar and in their expected arrangement.	Recognition	Relate Details-on-demand

Fig. 4. The framework.

expected; however, our understanding of which visual elements in the information visualization contribute to this difference in fixation patterns, and which human factors help explain the usability issues or the overall user experience is inadequate.

These are areas for further investigation that can be guided by the proposed framework described in the Framework section.

More illustrative examples include mean fixation duration of gaze within elements in an information visualization and across different information visualizations. In examining the mean fixation duration (i.e. the average duration a user fixated inside a specific area of the information visualization), we assume the intended target in visualization would contain the gist of information the user would need to direct his/her attention and process. This information, being the target, would be the hardest to comprehend, or the most interesting in the visualization explains the anticipated high mean fixation duration, which is proportional to said factors. A competing target would as well contain important information, yet less important than that contained in the target. The mean fixation duration over this area is therefore anticipated to be shorter. The mean fixation duration over the remaining areas of the visualization is anticipated to be shortest of the three (Fig. 5).

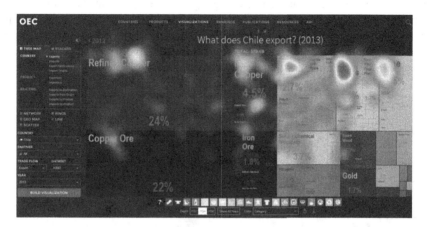

Fig. 5. Gaze heat map of orientation phase for the stacks visualization pattern.

Our measured mean fixation duration over all users reflects the anticipated order of duration lengths. As per the discussion in the Exploratory Eye Tracking Study section, the users were presented with two different visualization patterns and were asked to find the largest of two values. In this case, the target area becomes the area in the visualization that encodes information about the correct answer, or the item with largest value.

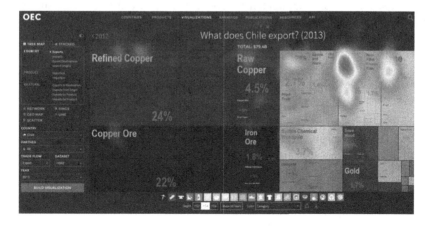

Fig. 6. Gaze heat map of convergence phase for the treemap visualization pattern.

Likewise the competing target is the area where the user would find information about the item with smallest value. Across the two different visualization patterns that we presented to our participants, mean fixation durations were consistent with our predictions. The results of this experiment shows that mean fixation duration is sensitive and thus a candidate to measure cognitive processing or mental effort spent during the exposure to information visualizations (Fig. 6).

Another example is aggregate visual attention that were captured in heat maps. Animated gaze heat maps show users' aggregate fixation locations over time. In this section, we are to elaborate on two interesting segments of the animated heat maps: orientation phase, and convergence phase. In the orientation phase (i.e. the first few seconds of users exposure to the visualization when they search for elements to help them identify key information such as units, scale, and search for their target), the animated heat maps of this phase showed an interesting distribution of gaze areas (Fig. 7).

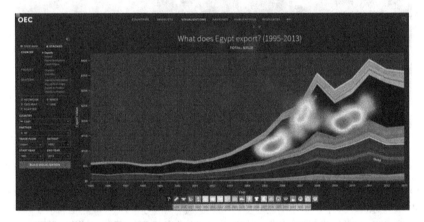

Fig. 7. Gaze heat map of convergence phase for the stacks visualization pattern.

In the treemap pattern, most gaze areas correspond to labels possibly indicating that users were searching for their target. In the convergence phase, the treemap visualization pattern presented to our participants showed gravitation of eye gaze towards the targets, and the competing target. More specifically, users aggregate eye gaze accumulated at labels of the target and the competing target (Tables 2 and 3).

Table 2. Mean fixation durations for treemap pattern (fish vs. wine exports)

	Target area	Competing target area	Remaining area
Fixation length	2.824 s	1.035 s	2.809 s
Fixation count	8.043	3.652	12.130
Mean	0.350 s	0.283 s	0.231 s

Table 3. Mean fixation durations for treemap pattern (crude vs. refined oil exports)

	Target area	Competing target area	Remaining area
Fixation length	2.424 s	2.434 s	2.078 s
Fixation count	7.304	7.435	7.043
Mean	0.330 s	0.324 s	0.295 s

Similar patterns appeared in the stacks visualization pattern. Users' aggregate eye gaze were gravitated towards targets. However, in this case, visual elements that encode information users were expected to compare had low color contrast. In this heat map, eye gazes were attracted to labels of actual target and competing target, and as well attracted to a label of another area similar in visual properties (similar background color) with target and competing target, and attracted to the separating line between the three areas.

5   Conclusion

In this paper, we have introduced a framework for incorporating eye tracking in the usability/ux toolkit for information visualization. An exploratory user study has shown that designers and analysts can use the framework to map metrics from eye tracking research to the process of usability and user experience evaluations of dynamic information visualizations. Based on the eye tracking results presented in the preceding sections, we summarize in this section the key observations from our study. This work presents an outline of mapping eye-tracking metrics to usability metrics for investigating interactive information visualizations. The emphasis was on the dimensions of design factors, human factors of perception and cognition, and task. In addition, we characterize visualization design considerations that are related to individual and aggregate gaze metrics, including fixations, saccades and scan paths. Based on insights from our exploratory eye tracking study and previous research, we are able to offer framework to support usability evaluations based on existing conventional visualization design guidelines.

Acknowledgment. This research was supported by the King Abdulaziz City for Science and Technology (KACST) as part of the research under the Center for Complex Engineering Systems (CCES). We thank our colleagues in CCES who provided insight and expertise that greatly assisted the research, and special thanks for the director of the center, Anas Alfaris.

References

1. Erickson, T.: Designing visualizations of social activity: six claims. In: Extended Abstracts on Human Factors in Computing Systems, CHI 2003. ACM (2003)
2. Chen, C.: Information visualization. Wiley Interdisc. Rev. Comput. Stat. 2(4), 387–403 (2010)
3. Wang, F.-Y., et al.: Social computing: from social informatics to social intelligence. IEEE Intell. Syst. 22(2), 79–83 (2007)

4. Goldberg, J.H., Helfman, J.I.: Comparing information graphics: a critical look at eye shop: beyond time and errors: novel evaluation methods for information visualization, pp. 71–78. ACM (2010)
5. Card, S.K., Mackinlay, J.D., Shneiderman, B.: Information Visualization: Using Vision to Think. Morgan Kaufmann, San Francisco (1999)
6. Keller, T., Tergan, S.-O.: Knowledge and Information Visualization. Springer, New York (2005)
7. Goldberg, J., Helfman, J.: Eye tracking for visualization evaluation: reading values on linear versus radial graphs. Inf. Vis. (2011). doi:10.1177/1473871611406623
8. Shneiderman, B.: The eyes have it: a task by data type taxonomy for information visualizations. In: Proceedings of IEEE Symposium on Visual Languages, 1996, pp. 336–343. IEEE (1996)
9. Ehmke, C., Wilson, S.: Identifying web usability problems from eye-tracking data. In: Proceedings of the 21st British HCI Group Annual Conference on People and Computers: HCI... but not as we know it, vol. 1, pp. 119–128. British Computer Society (2007)

The Rise of Hackathon-Led Innovation in the MENA Region: Visualizing Spatial and Temporal Dynamics of Time-Bounded Events

Sitah Almishari[1(✉)], Nora Salamah[1], Maram Alwan[1],
Nada Alkhalifa[1], and Areej Al-Wabil[1,2,3]

[1] King Abdulaziz City for Science and Technology (KACST),
Riyadh, Saudi Arabia
{salmishari,nsalamah,malwan,
nalkhalifa}@kacst.edu.sa
[2] Center for Complex Engineering Systems (CCES),
KACST, Riyadh, Saudi Arabia
[3] MIT, Cambridge, USA
areej@mit.edu

Abstract. Hackathons are poised to accelerate technological progress and redefine the technology innovation lifecycle. Time-bounded events have spawned a raw form of creativity that is rarely seen elsewhere in the digital innovation landscape. Efficient monitoring and analysis of data emerging from time-bounded events - and trends in the technology innovation process that emerge from encouraging developers, designers and entrepreneurs to go from the drawing board to a working demo - is of interest to both professional analysts and the general public. This research identifies the distinguishing characteristics of hackathons in the MENA region. It also introduces a visual analytics platform for uniquely identifying the technical, socio-cultural and contextual differences that define hackathon practices and the emerging hacking communities in the MENA region. The benefit of such understanding not only supports the continued growth of such activities in these countries, it also helps to disambiguate hackathon activities from other productive practices for software development, entrepreneurship and computing education.

Keywords: Hackathon · Software engineering · CSCW · Time-bounded events · Information visualization · Knowledge engineering

1 Introduction

As increasing volumes of data for time-bounded events are captured and become available, new opportunities arise for data-driven analysis that can lead to insights for researchers interested in the social dynamics and computer supported collaborative work in time-bounded events such as hackathons. The term hackathon was coined in 1999 [1]. Over the years, variants of hackathons have emerged across disciplines as a means of channeling creativity toward a common goal, contribution or theme.

© Springer International Publishing AG 2017
G. Meiselwitz (Ed.): SCSM 2017, Part II, LNCS 10283, pp. 367–377, 2017.
DOI: 10.1007/978-3-319-58562-8_28

In recent years, a growing momentum of events for leveraging the power of hackers to deliver an accelerated digital product has emerged to redefine the technology innovation lifecycle. The contributions of these time-bounded events vary across a spectrum of deliverables ranging from prototypes of digital products, to capacity building and the creation of a community with a stronger collective technical domain knowledge, which is demonstrated and expressed through sustained collaborations and completed technical projects after the event. In the past two decades, the rise of the hackathon culture in the global context was fast and utilitarian [1, 2]. Time-bounded events began in the early 2000s as a collaborative effort towards pooling computing resources collectively to stress-test new software in advance of launch. They evolved to digital and tangible hacking contexts, and engaged people from across a wide range of disciplines [e.g. 3–6]. Hackathons often have the format of being decentralized and involve distributed development. The typical characteristics of hackathons are simple; participants engage in a focused, typically thematic effort that is resource-limited and goal-oriented. The typical resource limitations are time and expertise [1, 7]. The goals are often prescribed but the prescription may be as general as thematic notions, business goals or concepts.

In the Middle East and North Africa (MENA) region, the emergence of time-bounded events that are typically focused on the creation of a software application or hardware prototype development was slower than the global trend. Sustained growth in the past decade has been supported by an increasing appreciation of the contributions of time-bounded event towards innovation, community building, and accelerated technology development. However, our understanding of the trends and challenges in organizing time-bounded events in the MENA region is inadequate for the burgeoning analytics-driven strategic planning and decision making that is taking place in innovation-oriented organizations in these countries. As researchers in Human-Computer Interaction (HCI), we are often situated at the intersection of technology sectors from both industry and academia, and have the exposure to the multiple approaches, motivations, modes of engagement and characterizing features of time-bounded events. We anticipate that data-driven insights might be used as a heuristic or benchmark to align the communities that are (a) involved in organizing these time-bounded events in the MENA region and/or (b) engaged in researching these computer-supported collaborative work contexts.

This article is organized as follows. In Sect. 2, we begin by providing an overview of time-bounded events, along with the interactive platforms and tools used to find and visually explore data related to time-bounded events. In Sect. 3, we review the work on categorization of hackathons and describe some examples from the MENA region aligned with the categorizations and typologies of time-bounded events; in Sect. 4, we describe the interactive MENA Hackathon platform that we developed for data-driven analytics for the region; we conclude the paper in Sect. 5 with reflections on the review of time-bounded events, and future directions for research on insights from visual exploration of time-bounded events in the region.

2 Background and Related Work

Hackathons are gaining popularity and fast becoming a recognized approach for technological progress and innovation [2]. Accelerated development often occurs in contexts that provide rapid collocation of individuals who have diverse expertise in the problem domain, and the space (i.e. physical spaces and virtual spaces) for them to collaborate in tackling complex problems [2]. The popularity of such events started in the early 2000s, as they were sponsored by companies or investment entities in the tech industry for facilitating rapid development of software technologies along with exploring new avenues of funding and innovation [1]. Although hackathons started in technical domains, their popularity spread to other fields such as education, bioinformatics, marketing, healthcare, big data analytics, and dance composition [7]. Datathons are often aligned with the format of hackathons, but focus on crowdsourcing content or open-sourcing models to foster innovation and connect communities across various disciplines [4]. Motivations for organizing and participating in hackathons vary across a wide spectrum of intrinsic and extrinsic dimensions. Briscoe and Mulligan have highlighted that learning and networking are among the most cited motivations for participating in hackathons [1]. The concept of crowdsourcing in problem solving is not unique to hackathons. Boudreau and Kakhani [9] have outlined four models of crowdsourcing that are aligned with the typologies of hackathons. These include crowd contests (e.g., hackathons), crowd community collaborations such as those found in civic time-bounded events, crowd complementors in which developers build extensions or services linked to existing products, and crowd labor markets in which third party intermediaries match buyers and sellers [9].

Data-driven visualizations are becoming more abundant in the visual experience of online hackathon communities and the general public. Interactive information visualization take advantage of the relatively broad bandwidth between a human's eyes and the mind which helps users to not only see and visually explore, but also understand information in large amounts, all at once. Information visualization has been shown to be an effective tool for spatial and temporal exploration of dynamics datasets. Aligned with the emerging hackathon phenomenon, the need arises for interactive information visualizations to aid in the processing, comprehension, tracking, and retention of data on time-bounded events in static, animated, dynamic and interactive visuals. In recent years, interactive platforms for promoting and participating in hackathons have been introduced such as hackathon.io; where hackathons are featured and interactive tools provide event-related information (e.g. scope, schedules, rules, prizes and judging criteria) as well as computer-mediated communication tools for team formation and community building prior to the event and after the events as shown in Fig. 1.

In the context of an ongoing data-driven research study on social dynamics in time-bounded events for the MENA region, existing web platforms such as hackathon.com and hackathon.io and the extracted data sets were not sufficient for analysis-driven recommendations (an example of data extracted via the hackathon.com web site is depicted in Fig. 2). Sophisticated tools were needed for analysts, policy

Fig. 1. Features and functionality of the Hackathon.io website

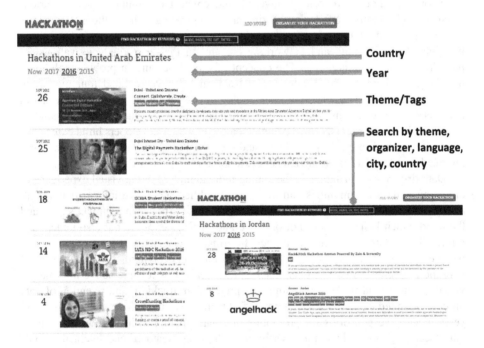

Fig. 2. Example of online hackathon platforms (Source: Hackathon.com)

makers and researchers to track, process, and communicate data about the phenomenon of hackathons and time-bounded events and how they contribute toward innovation eco-systems in the region. This motivated us to develop an interactive platform, described in Sect. 4, to visualize the phenomenon of hackathons in the MENA region and to provide the capability to visually explore the crowdsourced data sets (a) spatially by zooming in and out of regions and countries, and (b) temporally by exploring the data sets across different time frames.

3 Typology of Hackathons in the MENA Region

In this section, we outline a preliminary categorization of time-bounded events in the MENA region, referencing some of the events we have observed and their digital traces on the web. The categorization is aligned with Briscoe and Mulligan's high level classification of the type of hackathons, technology-centric and focus-centric groups [1]. Our observations have centered on time-bounded events in the MENA region that have emerged in the overlapping domains of academia, technology industry, government and civic organizations.

The technology-centric classification of hackathons focus on software development for specific technologies or applications [1]. Single application hackathons, such as the IBM Bluemix hackathons in Saudi Arabia in 2015 and 2016, the Blockchain hackathon in the UAE and the 2017 Blockchain Hackathon in Riyadh, Saudi Arabia focus on a specific technology platform. Application-type hackathons, which focus on a specific genre of applications (e.g. mobile apps), have also been observed in the MENA region. Examples include Microsoft's AppinAction hackathon in Riyadh, Saudi Arabia and the DevAppLB hackathon in Beirut, Lebanon for mobile platforms using the touch Cloud BaaS Backend-as-a-Service Baas; both hackathons were held in 2013. Similar application-type hackathons, sponsored by telecom companies in the region include the Zain Hackathon in Kuwait for telecom mobile applications, held in 2013 and the Vodafone hackathon in Doha at the Carnegie Mellon Qatar University in 2014[1].

Focus-centric hackathons, as noted by Briscoe and Mulligan [1] as well as Frey and Luks [2] target software development that addresses civic or social issues. These time-bounded events aim to spark civic engagement, bring together software designers, developers, and community organizers to solve their society's needs, and to tackle complex problems with technology-oriented solutions [8–13]. Johnson and Robinson [13] have shown that civic hackathons have spurred innovative use of open data which consequently led to the creation of applications and services for citizens and improved civic engagement. Examples of focus-centric hackathons in the MENA region include the NYU Abu Dhabi annual Hackathons for Social Good which started in 2011 [11], the Saudi Computer Society's Hackathon for Social Good in 2015, and the Misk Hackathon for health applications. Briscoe and Mulligan categorize focus-centric hackathons further into socially-oriented, demographic specific, and company-oriented time-bounded events. Socially-oriented hackathons aim to contribute to issues of social concerns by exploring innovative solutions for challenges in providing public services or crisis management. Examples include the Techfugees hackathon in Jordan in 2016, in which Techfugees partnered with "Startup Weekend Amman" and UNICEF Jordan to organize a 52-hour hackathon to tackle refugee challenges; and the 2014 MyUNHCR 3-day hackathon in Jordan, organized by United Nations High Commissioner for Refugees (UNHCR) to develop applications in the context of the Syrian refugee crisis[2].

---

[1] https://webext.qatar.cmu.edu//news/view/1353.

[2] http://unhcr.github.io/hackathon/.

Demographic-specific hackathons are motivated by perceived or recognized disparity between specific demographic groups in society such as women, students or people with disabilities [1]. Hackathons are often open to people with diverse backgrounds and skill sets– not just people who know code [2, 13]. Some demographic-specific hackathons focus on bridging the gender gap in technology such as the "She Develops" hackathon Lebanon in 2015, The Meera Kaul Foundation's "Women in STEM Smart City Hackathon" in Dubai, UAE in 2016, the "Lady Problems" Hackathon (http://ladyproblemshackathon.com/) in Gaza in 2016, and the "Girls in Tech" hackathons in Kuwait. Student-focused hackathons include Elm hackathons for college students, held in Riyadh, Saudi Arabia; the student-led TechBench Hackathons organized by a tech community run by students at King Fahd University of Petroleum and Minerals (KFUPM) in Dhahran, Saudi Arabia and the Dubai Electricity and Water Authority (DEWA) Student Hackathon for UAE college students, sponsored by DEWA and SquareCircle Tech and held in Dubai in 2016. Notably, there is also a growing Space Apps community in the MENA region, emerging from the annual hackathons supported by NASA's Open Innovation Initiative. The Space Apps hackathons have been held in Jordan, Egypt, and Morocco in the 2015-2016 time frame; and is expanding to several cities in Saudi Arabia in 2017[3].

Some events have elements of more than one category, such as the 'Startup Weekends' in Badir technology incubators that were held in three cities in Saudi Arabia, and the startup weekend hackathons in Amman, Jordan[4]. Moreover, new configurations of time-bounded events in the MENA region may form in this rapidly evolving space.

4   MENA Hackathon Platform

One of the best ways to explore and try to understand the large datasets of hackathons is with visualization [14]. Motivated by the data-driven insights gained from researching time-bounded events in the MENA region, we developed an interactive platform to visualize the phenomenon of hackathons in the geographically scope of the MENA region. The platform embeds an information visualization that can be explored spatially by zooming in and out of regions and countries, and temporally by exploring the data sets across a dynamic timeline using a slider to move from one time-frame to another as shown in Fig. 3.

The data visualizations serve the purpose of facilitating access to scattered information of hackathons in the MENA region, fostering the recognition of structures in abstract data about the hackathons across different regions, and supporting information retrieval and exploratory analytics of these events and trends related to the emerging phenomenon of hackathon-led innovation programs, strategies and initiatives. The spatio-temporal visualization of time-bounded events in the MENA region facilitates closely coupled human and machine analysis. A screenshot of the platform's frontend prototype is depicted in Figs. 3 and 4. Dynamic chart visualizations overlaid on the

---

[3] https://spaceappschallenge.org.
[4] http://startupweekend.org/.

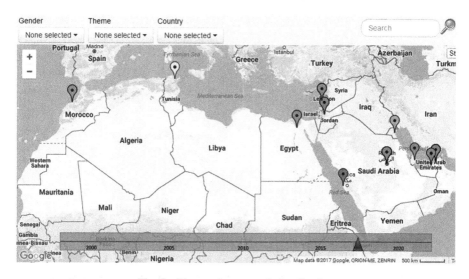

Fig. 3. The spatio-temporal visualization

spatial plots of events were designed to amplify viewers' cognitive capabilities by enhancing the recognition of patterns of when and where time-bounded events are held. When information on time-bounded events is organized in space by its time relationships, further analytics on the scale and scope of events can be explored. The use case scenario depicted in Fig. 4, and the interlinked dynamic charts, show how the visualizations support relatively easy perceptual inferences of relationships that are otherwise more difficult to induce. Zooming in the map provides a clear view of regional events when users click on a specific pin the map to visually explore spatial mapping of the related events along with detailed aggregate information about events as shown in Fig. 4.

Fig. 4. Layering event information with hover popup windows

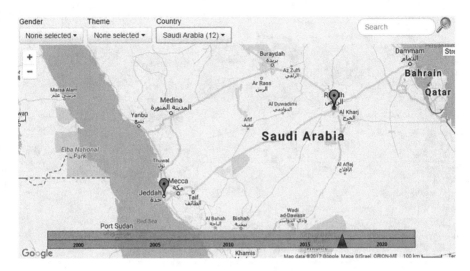

Fig. 5. Filtering the data-driven visualizations by location, time, theme, and demographics

The platform data visualization can be filtered across time by location, format (e.g. gender participation if it is a male-only, or female-only or an event open to both genders), and theme (e.g. health, humanitarian aid, sport). Filters are applied to explore subsets of datasets, as shown in the scenario captured in Fig. 5. When the user chooses Saudi Arabia as the first filter; the map will zoom into all time-bounded events in Saudi Arabia and all other filters will show the related data only. In addition, the platform supports search feature where we can type search keywords, for instance if the user type "Misk" in the search field the platform will open the pop-up description about "Misk" event as shown in Fig. 6.

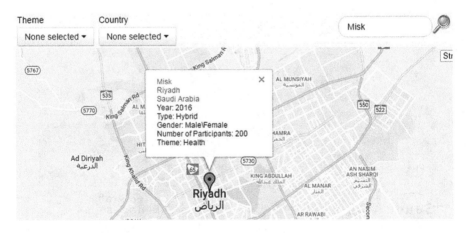

Fig. 6. Filtering the platform data by search keywords

While the volume of information is growing rapidly, opportunities to expand insights by combining data are accelerating. The spatial exploratory mode of interaction with the MENA Hackathon platform gives analysts and researchers more panoramic and more granular views of the typology of time-bounded events for selected regions. The platform encourages a more comprehensive look at time-bounded events' data by highlighting specific information about hackathon typologies, themes, and collocation as well as data on the scope and scale of the event. An example is depicted in Fig. 6. The platform also facilitates hypothesis-led modeling to generate insights and root models in practical data relationships that are more broadly understood by researchers interested in computer supported cooperative work (CSCW) and social dynamics that influence innovation eco-systems.

The visual representation of pins on the spatial map of the MENA region translates data gathered from the crowd into a visible form that highlights important features, including commonalities and anomalies for time-bounded events in time and space. These visual representations of time-bounded events make it easy for users to perceive salient aspects of regional distribution of events as well as the density of events across time. The visualizations augment the cognitive reasoning process with perceptual reasoning through color-coded visual representations of these time-bounded events.

The MENA Hackathon platform is an openly-editable website where users can contribute to the content of hackathon events in the MENA region. This content crowdsourcing approach was considered to facilitate a sustainable dynamic data set and to encourage users to contribute towards maintaining the accuracy and quality of data submitted through the platform's frontend, aligned with content crowdsourcing models such as Wikipedia [12]. In fact, the early motivation for users to participate in contributing to Wikipedia's content was reported to be mainly the desire to edit and/or correct articles posted by others, but with time, editors become Wikipedians and their motivation gradually shifted to participate in endeavors for improving the quality of the content and raising the level of awareness, participation and knowledge in the community [12]. The content crowdsourcing architecture of our hackathon platform, depicted in Fig. 7, is the bridge between the abstract goals of a crowdsourcing application and the final concrete resulting web platform. While the path from abstract to concrete can be complex, the block diagram in Fig. 7 embeds the set of structures needed to reason about the hackathon platform (i.e. software elements of location data and event-oriented data, the relations among them and the properties of both) and the flow of verification and validation of models for data-driven analytics.

Fig. 7. Content crowdsourcing in the MENA Hackathon platform

Charts and graphs have evolved into not just tools to detect patterns but also as vehicles to communicate ideas. In our MENA Hackathon platform, data graphics are used to enhance exploratory search scenarios with a different lens on the same dataset, whereas other times the graphics tell the entire story by expanding on details for a specific geographic region. For example, motivation for participation in hackathons is an important element in the innovation eco-system. Data from respondents to surveys on motivation for participants have revealed trends across the region with learning and networking being the top responses, followed by the motivation to connect with like-minded people in the technology sector and seek opportunities for meaningful contributions to digital innovation. Analytics-driven recommendations derived from these insights can help analysts, researchers and strategic decision makers.

5   Conclusion

The increasingly digitized, distributed and disintermediated future of the technology industry in the MENA region is predicted to have hackathons, hackers and potentially agile models of development embedded as a core part of its growth strategy. Overall, time-bounded events in this region appear to interest communities because of the opportunities for rapid collocation and the allotted time and space for working intensively with teams in modes that are not often supported in their day-to-day environments of work, leisure or study.

The contribution of this paper outlines the trends and issues relevant to hackathons in the MENA region and focuses on how insights can be sought by dynamically exploring information visualizations that are crowd-sourced from the community. This paper has shed light on insights that can be drawn from collaborative development of digital systems in a concentrated time period. Themes from technology-centric and social-centric hackathons are often aligned with global trends. Data-driven analytics from our MENA Hackathon platform suggest that time-bounded events in the MENA region contribute beyond producing digital artifacts, with building capacity and technical expertise, building community and expanding social networks, exposing participants to different modes of design thinking, and shaping cross-domain identities for the human capital in these regions. Future directions for research include reporting insights from the typology of hackathons in the region and the trends in spatial and temporal dynamics of these time-bounded events.

Acknowledgment. Sincere thanks to the hackathon researchers at King Abdulaziz City for Science and Technology (KACST), Dr. Amany Alshawi, Ghaliah Alrajban, Nour Alshaqha, Shurouq Aljadaan and Athari Alnassar. Authors also thank the HCII2017 reviewers for their help in improving the presentation of this work.

References

1. Briscoe, G., Mulligan, C.: Digital Innovation: The Hackathon Phenomenon. Creativeworks London, London (2014)
2. Frey, F.J., Luks, M.: The innovation-driven hackathon – one means for accelerating innovation. In: Proceedings of the 21st European Conference on Pattern Languages of Programs, EuroPLoP 2016 (2016)
3. Silver, J.K., Binder, D.S., Zubcevik, N., Zafonte, R.D.: Healthcare hackathons provide educational and innovation opportunities: a case study and best practice recommendations. J. Med. Syst. **40**, 177 (2016)
4. Anslow, C., Brosz, J., Maurer, F.: Datathons: an experience report of data hackathons for data science education. In: SIGCSE 2016, Memphis (2016)
5. Goggins, S., Winter, S., Wiggins, A., Butler, B.: OCData Hackathon @ CSCW 2014: online communities data hackathon, CSCW 2014, Baltimore (2014)
6. Katayama, T., et al.: BioHackathon series in 2011 and 2012: penetration of ontology and linked data in life sciences domains. J. Biomed. Semant. (2014)
7. Lara, M., Lockwood, K.: Hackathons as community-based learning: a case study. TechTrends **60**, 486–495 (2016)
8. Möller, S., Afgan, E., et al.: Community-driven development for computational biology at sprints, hackathons and codefests. BMC Bioinform. (2014)
9. Boudreau, K., Kakhani, K.: Using the crowd as an innovation partner. Harvard Bus. Rev. (2013)
10. Walker, A., Ko, N.: Bringing medicine to the digital age via hackathons and beyond. J. Med. Syst. (2016)
11. The Annual NYAD International Hackathon (n.d.). http://sites.nyuad.nyu.edu/hackathon/
12. Bryant, S.L., Forte, A., Bruckman, A.: Becoming Wikipedian: transformation of participation in a collaborative online encyclopedia. In: Proceedings of the 2005 International ACM SIGGROUP Conference on Supporting Group Work, pp. 1–10. ACM (2005)
13. Johnson, P., Robinson, P.: Civic hackathons: innovation, procurement, or civic engagement? Rev. Pol. Res. **31**, 349–357 (2014). doi:10.1111/ropr.12074
14. Shrinivasan, Y., van Wijk, J.: Supporting the analytical reasoning process in information visualization. In: Proceedings of the SIGCHI Conference on Human Factors in Computing Systems (CHI 2008), pp. 1237–1246. ACM, New York (2008). http://dx.doi.org/10.1145/1357054.1357247

How Visual Analytics Unlock Insights into Traffic Incidents in Urban Areas

Abdullah Alomar[1]([⊠]), Najat Alrashed[1], Isra Alturaiki[2],
and Hotham Altwaijry[1]

[1] Center for Complex Engineering Systems at KACST and MIT,
King Abdulaziz City for Science and Technology, Riyadh, Saudi Arabia
{aalomar,najat,htwaijry}@mit.edu
[2] College of Computer and Information Sciences, King Saud University,
Riyadh, Saudi Arabia
ialturaiki@ksu.edu.sa

Abstract. Nowadays, the way people observe mobility in their cities is significantly changing by the prevalence, accessibility, and abundance of large volume of traffic data. However, capturing perceptions from large and heterogeneous traffic datasets and providing them to people is a challenging task. A better understanding of how rhetorical design choices shape users' experience of traffic visualizations should help make interactive data visualizations more engaging and useful to audiences as they use data-driven analytics to make decisions in traffic contexts. In this paper, different visualization techniques for traffic data are explored and an investigation of what insights each visualization will yield is carried out using the traffic incidents in the city of Riyadh for the 2013 to 2015 timeframe.

Keywords: Information visualization · Traffic visualization · Visual analytics · Crash analytics

1 Introduction

In traffic modeling, researchers have been collecting, analyzing, and visualizing large datasets in the past two decades [19,22,25]. The volume, velocity, and variety of traffic data in urban areas are growing at an exponential rate and thus, understanding and capturing the semantics of traffic data is an increasingly complex challenge. Given the critical importance of the problem, many efforts, in both industry and academia, have explored systematic approaches to addressing the challenges of *data visualization*, which refers to the process of graphically representing data in order to illustrate the relationships within data and to uncover hidden patterns [24].

It is well-recognized that road safety in the Kingdom of Saudi Arabia is in an extremely dire state, where more than half a million accidents occur each year [8]. Moreover, a significant number of these accidents are severe, which

© Springer International Publishing AG 2017
G. Meiselwitz (Ed.): SCSM 2017, Part II, LNCS 10283, pp. 378–393, 2017.
DOI: 10.1007/978-3-319-58562-8_29

makes road traffic injuries the leading cause of death for young males between the age of 16 and 30 [20]. We believe that enhancing road safety is paramount to traffic regulators and understanding traffic accidents temporal and spatial patterns can help in achieving such a goal. Insights gained from visualizations of accidents' data demonstrate how valuable visual analytics can be to authorities and policy makers to better understand traffic, enhance future planning, and determine corrective actions.

Although the prevalence and accessibility of traffic data are changing the way people view mobility in their cities and roads, the task of retrieving such insights from huge and heterogeneous traffic datasets and presenting them to people is very challenging. In this paper, we aim to aid people understand the mobility patterns of their cities by exploring different visualization techniques for traffic data and investigate what insights each visualization technique yields. In particular, we aim to contribute to improving road safety in the Kingdom of Saudi Arabia by capturing insights from an *Accidents Dataset* collected from the General Directorate of Traffic (GDT) in Riyadh [5] and providing those perceptions through an interactive visualization platform to the policy makers in the GDT. Due to the characteristics of traffic data, its multivariate nature, and the importance of its spatial and temporal properties, the visualization techniques we explore are: spatial visualizations, temporal visualizations, spatio-temporal visualizations, and multivariate visualizations [14].

The remainder of this paper is organized as follows. Section 2 provides a brief background about data visualization in general, with an emphasis on traffic data visualization. A description of our visualization platform is presented in Sect. 3. Section 4 presents the visualizations of traffic accidents in the city of Riyadh as a case study. Finally, conclusions are drawn in Sect. 5.

2 Related Work

We start this section by discussing data visualization in Sect. 2.1. Then, we present the process of visual analytics in Sect. 2.2. Finally, we cover traffic data visualization in Sect. 2.3.

2.1 Data Visualization

Data visualization refers to the process of graphically representing data in order to illustrate the relationships within data and to reveal hidden patterns and structures [24]. Different types of data visualizations including *Information Visualization* and *Visual Analytics* are used to help people in understanding and exploring their data [18]. One the one hand, information visualization relies on visual computing in order to help humans acquire abstract information [13]. On the other hand, visual analytics is not only graphical representation of the data – it is an integrated approach that combines data analysis, data visualization, and human interventions. Note that the human interventions (e.g. interaction, collaboration, cognition, perception, etc.) in visual analytics plays an important role in the decision making process [18]. The main objective of visual analytics is not to only allow users in detecting expected patterns, but to enable them in identifying unexpected patterns and relationships to observe the hidden insights and relationships.

2.2   Visual Analytics Process

The process of visual analytics consists of: information gathering, data preprocessing, data analysis, data visualization, interaction and decision making. Figure 1 shows an abstract overview of the visual analytics process, where ovals represent different stages and arrows represent transitions.

In general, heterogeneous data sources need to be integrated before analyzing or visualizing the data itself. Therefore, the first step after integrating the raw data is often preprocessing and transforming it to derive different representations for further explorations. Other typical preprocessing tasks include data transformation, data cleaning, and/or integration of heterogeneous data sources [17].

After data preprocessing, analysts have the option to choose between visualizing the data directly or applying several analysis methods. If they choose to analyze the data first, data query and machine learning methods are applied. Visualizing the data whether at the beginning or after the analysis allows the users to interact with the resulted visuals by modifying different parameters. One of the characteristics of visual analytics is the ability to alternate between visualizations and analysis methods, which leads to a continuous refinement and validation of initial results. To conclude, knowledge from the visual analytics process can be gained from analysis methods, visualization, as well as human-computer interactions [15].

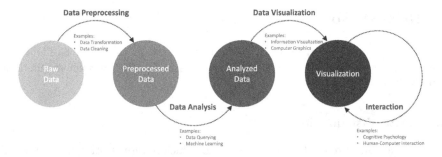

Fig. 1. Visual analytics process

2.3   Traffic Data Visualization

Information visualization and visual analytics are becoming an integral part of many recent traffic systems. They help in understanding traffic behavior and uncovering spatial and temporal patterns in traffic information [4,21]. In traffic data visualization, the different kinds of visualization usually incorporate the data's spatial and temporal properties, due to the significance of these properties in the context of traffic.

A number of tools have been developed for traffic incidents visualization. For example, Incident Cluster Explorer (ICE) is a web-based visual analytics tool for traffic accidents dataset [21]. This tool provides interactive spatial visualizations, which include (i) an icon mode to show every incident on the map and (ii) a heat-map mode to aggregate the incidents into grids. The ICE tool also provides other types of visualization such as: histograms and scatter plots.

A second example is the CrashMap web-based tool, which visualizes traffic crashes that occurred on British roads [4]. This tool compiles the accidents data into an easy-to-use format showing each incident on a map. In addition, it provides detailed information regarding each accident, e.g., when did the accident happen?, at what time of day?, how serious was the incident?, etc.

Traffic Origins [11] is another visualization tool that highlights the effect of traffic incidents on congestion. This tool uses historical accidents and traffic flow data, and allow the user to investigate the effect of these accidents on traffic flow. This is facilitated by visualizing traffic conditions within an expanding circle that surrounds the accident's location 15 min before it occurs till it clears out.

3   System Framework

Riyadh is among the fastest growing cities in the Kingdom of Saudi Arabia and the world: the city is seeing an increase in vehicular trips at a rate of 9% per year, and population growth of 3.9% annually [12]. Using data generated from the crash records, call details records (CDRs), and other datasets (e.g., Riyadh road network) an interactive visualization platform called SaudiTraffic [7] was developed.

In addition to presenting complex information with innovative statistical analyses and computational algorithms, SaudiTraffic presents that information in an interactive and intuitive way, while making it accessible to both policy makers and users to aid them in exploring, analyzing, and understanding mobility dynamics. To facilitate the process of capturing the data's semantics, the platform provides different types of visualizations including: basic data visualization and analysis-based visualization.

The SaudiTraffic platform presents interactive visualizations of real traffic accidents that occurred in Riyadh. Different visualizations are created for the four categories of visualization techniques (i.e., spatial visualizations, temporal visualizations, spatio-temporal visualizations, and multivariate visualizations) with an emphasis on analytics. By using these techniques, the SaudiTraffic platform invites users to explore, interact, and discover patterns in traffic incidents on the roads of Riyadh. This platform also aims to bring together machine intelligence with human intelligence through visual analytics. The interaction with SaudiTraffic platform can act as a decision support system allowing stakeholders to explore the impact of traffic accidents on social and economic progress. This provides a valuable lens to explore how to enhance road safety in the Kingdom.

In this web-based platform, different libraries are used to produce the interactive visualizations. Leaflet [6], a commonly used open-source JavaScript library, is utilized to visualize geospatial data. Its interactive maps and support for mobile and desktop platforms, makes it one of the most popular libraries when it comes to geospatial mapping. Chart.js [3] and ZingChart [10] are used in SaudiTraffic as well. They are JavaScript libraries that create different types of responsive and interactive charts including line plots, bar charts, radar plots, and pie charts. The goal of these libraries is to overcome the scalability and flexibility issues in JavaScript and develop a flexible, fast, and modern way to create charts.

4 Case Study: Visualization of Traffic Accidents in Riyadh

Given the characteristics of traffic data, visualization techniques for traffic analysis are often aligned with four aspects of design guidelines; namely, spatial, temporal, spatio-temporal, and multivariate. In this section, we present examples from a case study of traffic incidents in Riyadh for these four aspects with an emphasis on analytics to shed light on the insights gained from these visualization techniques.

4.1 Datasets

The data used in this paper is the records of crashes that occurred in the period from January 2013 to October 2015, provided by the GDT [5]. This dataset consists of three tables: accidents, parties, and vehicles. The *accidents* table contains almost 250,000 accidents records, each record with 23 attributes such as: exact location, time, severity, and type of the accident. The *parties* table contains information about all parties involved in the accident, such as their role in the accident, health status, gender, and nationality. The *vehicles* table provides details about all vehicles involved in the accident, including the car make and model, its color, and its registration type.

Other datasets are used in this paper as well. The Riyadh road network dataset, obtained from Arriyadh Development Authority (ADA) [2], is used to map accidents to the roads where they have occurred. In addition, CDRs were used to identify how people move across the urban landscape by extracting the origin-destination matrix, and then estimate the congestion on each road segment in the city.

4.2 Visualization of Spatial Properties

Understanding mobility dynamics and identifying accidents hotspots are some of many insights that can be obtained from the spatial properties of traffic data. The level of aggregation plays an important role in capturing these insights. Therefore, spatial visualization can be categorized based on the aggregation level into three categories: Dot-based visualizations, Heat-map visualizations, and Region-based visualizations.

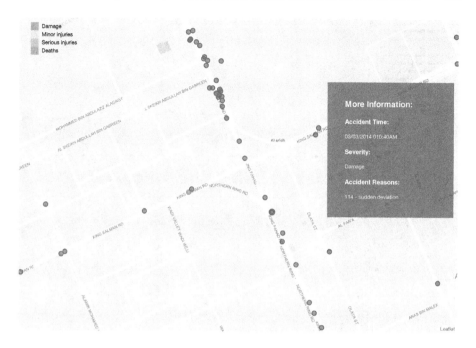

Fig. 2. Dot-based visualization (Color figure online)

Dot-Based Visualizations. In dot-based visualizations, the location of each record in the dataset is represented by a dot without any aggregation. Since no aggregation is done, this approach allows for providing details for each record, which are often indicated using the color and the size of the dot.

We utilized this approach to visualize each accident from the accidents dataset, where each accident is represented by a dot, whose color corresponds to the severity of the accident, as shown in Fig. 2.

The dot-based approach is not only an intuitive way to visualize traffic incidents spatially, it can also provide users and stakeholders many insights regarding the location of accidents hotspots in the city, and which road segments are more dangerous to commuters.

The visualization in Fig. 2 allows the user to interact with each incident by hovering over it to obtain more information regarding the accident such as the reason behind the accident, when did it happen?, and its severity. It also allows for zooming in and out, which helps when having hundreds of accidents clustered in a certain region.

Heat-Map Based Visualizations. Heat-map visualizations are suitable for large-scale data where huge and complex information can be mapped in a clear and intuitive way like the dataset we are dealing with [14]. Research has shown that heat-maps are suitable for generating patterns of dots. In addition, heat-maps are useful when dealing with thousands of dots that may overlap.

Greater than or equal 10
Greater than or equal 9
Greater than or equal 8
Greater than or equal 7
Greater than or equal 6
Greater than or equal 5
Greater than or equal 4
Greater than or equal 3
Greater than or equal 2
Greater than or equal 1
Greater than or equal 0

Diriyah

Riyadh

Leaflet

Fig. 3. Heat-map visualization (Color figure online)

The heat-map visualization in Fig. 3 helps in presenting the distinction between areas with many accidents versus areas with few ones. In particular, this visualization is used to represent the number of run over accidents in Riyadh, where warmer colors (i.e., orange and red) indicate a larger number of run overs; and colder colors (i.e., yellow and green) indicate a smaller number of accidents or no accidents at all.

Using the aforementioned heat-map can help in identifying where run over accidents clusters. This information should direct the authorities' attention to these locations, with the hope that it will lead eventually to safer roads for pedestrians as well as commuters.

In heat-maps, unlike the dot-based approach, the observation process on each object is not applicable. However, heat-maps are much easier to perceive the density of points, e.g., number of run over accidents.

Region-Based Visualizations. In region-based visualizations, data points are aggregated into predetermined regions, which in contrast to dot-based visualizations, are more suitable for capturing macro patterns in large datasets.

In SaudiTraffic, the aggregated number of accidents in each district in Riyadh is visualized, demonstrating the contrast in the number of accidents between different districts. The size of the district along with its boundaries were determined using the districts' shapefiles obtained from the ADA. Afterwards, accidents were

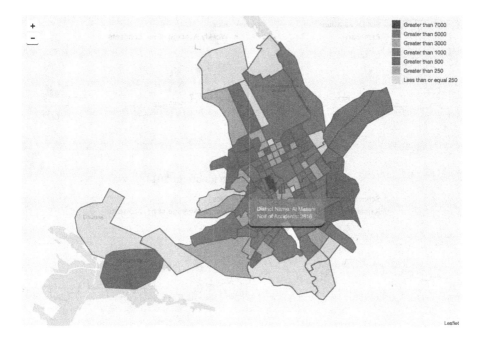

Fig. 4. Region-based visualization

mapped to districts according to these boundaries. As a result, accidents located outside the city are discarded.

Aggregating the number of accidents in each district can help in many ways. For example, the map in Fig. 4 helps in presenting which districts are more vulnerable to accidents, in the hope that those districts can be made safer for commuters. It can also help insurance companies in determining the impact a driver's home district should have on the evaluation of his vehicle insurance price. Note that this map allows hovering over any district to get the name and the number of accidents in the aforementioned period.

4.3   Visualization of Temporal Properties

Time-oriented visualizations facilitate the exploration and discovery of trends, periodicity, and abnormality of traffic data along the time dimension. As noted by Chen et al. [14], visualizations designed solely on the time axis are often categorized into: linear-time information visualizations and periodic-time information visualizations.

Linear Temporal Visualizations. In linear temporal visualizations, time is represented as a linear field with a start and an end points. This visualization technique is often used to detect trends and patterns of another variable's temporal behavior, and is very easy to comprehend. It is however less capable

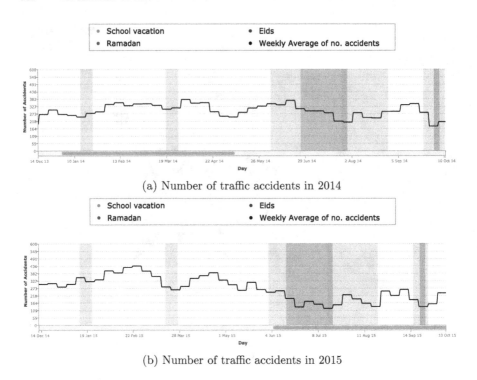

(a) Number of traffic accidents in 2014

(b) Number of traffic accidents in 2015

Fig. 5. Linear temporal visualization

of detecting periodic patterns in discrete timeframes, and of showing multiple variables, because of the clutter problem [14].

In this case study, linear temporal visualization was utilized to investigate the correlation between school calendar and significant events and the number of accidents. The daily average of the number of accidents in a week is shown with the school vacations, Islamic holidays (i.e., Eid Al-Fitr and Eid Al-Adha), and the holy month of Ramadan. The daily average in each week was used to eliminate the significant variation between working days and weekends. The school vacation dates were taken from the Ministry of Education in Saudi Arabia [1], whereas the month of Ramadan and the Islamic holidays dates are based on Umm Al-Qura calendar (viz., the official Hijri calendar used in Saudi Arabia) [9].

The visualizations, shown in Fig. 5, have shown that the number of accidents drops during both the school vacations and the Islamic holidays. This drop is quite significant during the summer vacation, and it decreases further during the holy month of Ramadan. The drop during school vacations might be attributed to the decreased traffic flow in that period. These patterns are repeated throughout 2014 and 2015, as shown in Figs. 5a and b respectively. This indicates that there is a consistent pattern with the number of accidents in specific events.

The interactivity in this visualization allows for the exploration of a longer timeframe without losing any details, where the user can scroll through the years to discover patterns in different years.

These findings about the correlation between these events and the number of accidents will help traffic departments with the management and allocation of their resources.

Periodic Temporal Visualizations. Periodic temporal visualizations help in emphasizing the contrast between discrete timeframes such as weekends and weekdays or months of seasons. Although they are known for their low spatial

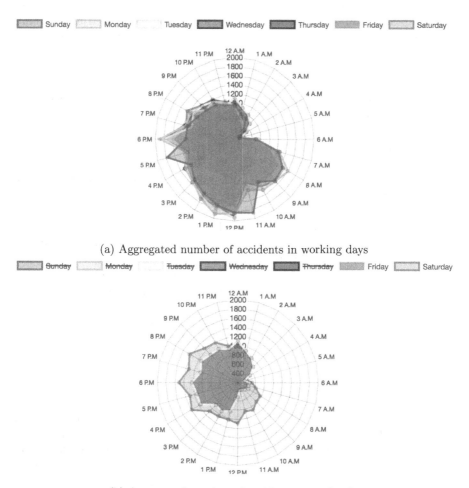

(a) Aggregated number of accidents in working days

(b) Aggregated number of accidents in weekends

Fig. 6. Periodic temporal visualization

efficiency, they excel in communicating patterns visually to decision makers to elicit an understanding of contrasts related to time.

To understand and identify these patterns, an interactive radar visualization for the number of accidents for each day of the week was used. This visualization has shown a consistent pattern for the working days, where peaks coincide with the traffic rush hours in a typical working day, as Fig. 6a shows. However, in weekends, these peaks disappear, and a slight increase around midnight is apparent, as Fig. 6b illustrates. Out of these seven days, Friday has the most distinct pattern, where the number of accidents decrease dramatically in the morning hours, as shown in Fig. 6b. The reason for this dramatic decrease can be attributed to Friday prayer, since most stores do not open on Friday before the prayer, and the residents of Riyadh tend to postpone their commutes till after the prayer. The interactivity in this visualization has helped in obtaining these findings, since it allows the user to select which weekday(s) to show.

4.4   Spatio-Temporal Visualizations

The two main attributes in the crash records dataset are accident location and time. Spatio-temporal visualizations utilize both attributes to discover hidden temporal patterns that might appear for a given location [23]. In other words, they allow the users to compare data in different timeframes and observe the changes, if any.

To investigate the safety of each road segment in the city, each accident was mapped to the nearest segment in the road network dataset obtained from the ADA. Moreover, the temporal dimension is added, where each month can be investigated separately using the scroll bar. The road segments are then visualized, where the number of accidents that occurred on each segment in the selected month is indicated by its color.

Adding both the spatial and the temporal dimensions enables the user to identify the temporal variations in the number of accidents in each segment. For example, Figs. 7a and b show a spot where accidents have occurred sporadically, with more than 15 accidents in November 2014, and a notable decrease in the following month. On the other hand, Figs. 8a and b show a consistency in the number of accidents on Khurais road in the months of August and October 2014.

4.5   Multivariate Visualizations

Traffic dataset contains different types of attributes besides location and time. Multivariate data visualization is used when the purpose of the visualization is to find the correlations between many attributes of interest. In this visualization type, attributes are not limited to temporal and spatial, but can also include other attributes such as: numerical, categorical, and textual [26].

In this case study, the traffic data is layered over the crash data to investigate the interrelationships between these layers. The grid heat-map shown in Fig. 9 represents traffic accidents in the city between 7 to 10 in the morning in the month of December, whereas the road heat-map represents volume of traffic in

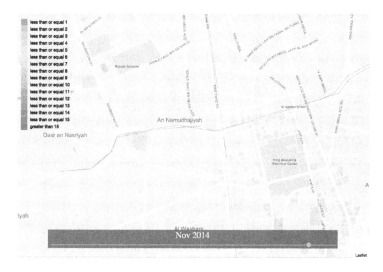

(a) King Fahad road in November 2014

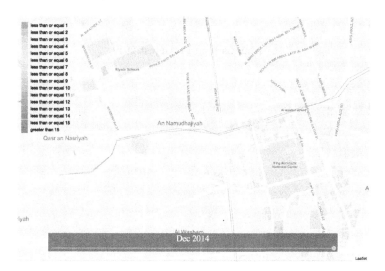

(b) King Fahad road in December 2014

Fig. 7. Spatio-temporal visualization: number of accidents on King Fahad road

the same period. Figure 9 shows traffic accidents are concentrated in regions where traffic volume is higher. This correlation would help the GDT in the placement of traffic monitoring sites.

Despite the advantages of multivariate visualizations, layering several layers in the representations may confuse the users [26]. Moreover, the ordering of

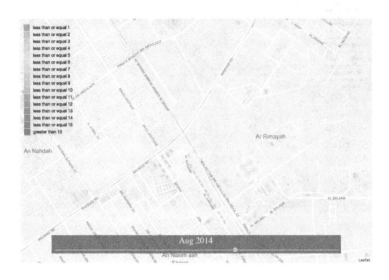

(a) Khurais road in August 2014

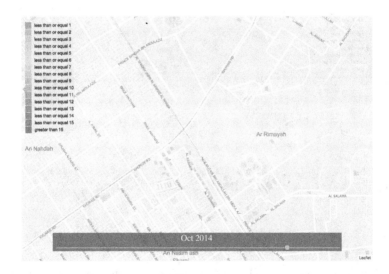

(b) Khurais road in October 2014

Fig. 8. Spatio-temporal visualization: number of accidents on Khurais road

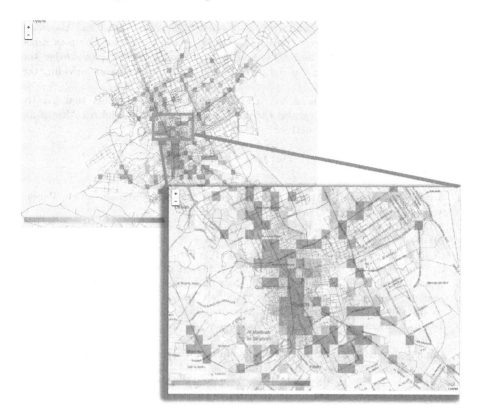

Fig. 9. Multivariate visualization

layers has a major impact on the expressiveness of visualization [16]. Different orders infer different conclusions to be drawn, but no arrangement principle is established so far [26].

5   Conclusions

In this paper, different visualization techniques for traffic data are explored and utilized to gain insights about traffic accidents in Riyadh. These insights include how the number of accidents changes throughout the day and how it varies within the weekdays, how the number of pedestrians fatalities is distributed spatially, and what is the correlation between the number of accidents and significant events throughout the year.

As the case study demonstrates, the interactive visual analytics in SaudiTraffic platform can help users answer questions related to integrated transit system in general, and traffic accidents specifically. It also helps in understanding the semantics of complex and multivariate data, giving the user the ability to control different variables to uncover hidden pattern and subtle insights.

Acknowledgments. This research was supported by a grant from King Abdulaziz City for Science and Technology (KACST) awarded to the Center for Complex Engineering Systems at KACST and MIT. The authors would like to acknowledge the General Directorate of Traffic and Arriyadh Development Authority for providing the datasets used in this paper.

Authors extend their thanks to Areej Alwabil for her comments that greatly improved the manuscript. They also thank Zeyad Alawwad and Aljohara Alfayez for their help with some of the visualizations.

References

1. Academic calendar. http://www.moe.gov.sa/ar/PublicEducation/Gov/Pages/ AcademicCalendar.aspx. Accessed 7 Dec 2016
2. Arriyadh development authority. http://www.ada.gov.sa/ada_e. Accessed 28 Feb 2017
3. Chart.js. http://www.chartjs.org/. Accessed 28 Feb 2017
4. Crashmap. http://www.crashmap.co.uk/. Accessed 19 Feb 2017
5. General department of traffic. https://www.moi.gov.sa. Accessed 18 Dec 2016
6. Leaflet. http://leafletjs.com/. Accessed 28 Feb 2017
7. Sauditraffic. http://SaudiTraffic.net. Accessed 28 Feb 2017
8. Traffic accidents by region. https://www.stats.gov.sa/en/3465. Accessed 20 Dec 2016
9. Ummulqura calendar. http://www.ummulqura.org.sa. Accessed 17 Dec 2016
10. Zingchart. http://ZingChart.com/. Accessed 28 Feb 2017
11. Anwar, A., Nagel, T., Ratti, C.: Traffic origins: a simple visualization technique to support traffic incident analysis. In: 2014 IEEE Pacific Visualization Symposium (PacificVis), pp. 316–319. IEEE (2014)
12. Ashwan, M.S.A., Salam, A.A., Mouselhy, M.A.: Population growth, structure and distribution in Saudi Arabia. Humanit. Soc. Sci. Rev. **1**, 33–46 (2012)
13. Card, S.K., Mackinlay, J.D., Shneiderman, B.: Readings in Information Visualization: Using Vision to Think. Morgan Kaufmann, San Francisco (1999)
14. Chen, W., Guo, F., Wang, F.-Y.: A survey of traffic data visualization. IEEE Trans. Intell. Transp. Syst. **16**(6), 2970–2984 (2015)
15. Keim, D., Andrienko, G., Fekete, J.-D., Görg, C., Kohlhammer, J., Melançon, G.: Visual analytics: definition, process, and challenges. In: Kerren, A., Stasko, J.T., Fekete, J.-D., North, C. (eds.) Information Visualization. LNCS, vol. 4950, pp. 154–175. Springer, Heidelberg (2008). doi:10.1007/978-3-540-70956-5_7
16. Keim, D.A.: Designing pixel-oriented visualization techniques: theory and applications. IEEE Trans. Visual. Comput. Graphics **6**(1), 59–78 (2000)
17. Keim, D.A., Mansmann, F., Schneidewind, J., Thomas, J., Ziegler, H.: Visual analytics: scope and challenges. In: Simoff, S.J., Böhlen, M.H., Mazeika, A. (eds.) Visual Data Mining. LNCS, vol. 4404, pp. 76–90. Springer, Heidelberg (2008). doi:10.1007/978-3-540-71080-6_6
18. Keim, D.A., Mansmann, F., Schneidewind, J., Ziegler, H.: Challenges in visual data analysis. In: Tenth International Conference on Information Visualization, IV 2006, pp. 9–16. IEEE (2006)
19. Kim, S., Jeong, S., An, S.U., Yoo, J.S., Han, S.M., Yeon, H., Yoo, S., Jang, Y.: Big data visual analytics system for disease pattern analysis. In: Proceedings of the 2015 International Conference on Big Data Applications and Services, pp. 175–179. ACM (2015)

20. Mansuri, F., Al-Zalabani, A., Zalat, M., Qabshawi, R.: Road safety and road traffic accidents in Saudi Arabia. A systematic review of existing evidence. Saudi Med. J. **36**(4), 418–424 (2015)
21. Pack, M.L., Wongsuphasawat, K., VanDaniker, M., Filippova, D.: Ice-visual analytics for transportation incident datasets. In: IEEE International Conference on Information Reuse and Integration, IRI 2009, pp. 200–205. IEEE (2009)
22. Schreck, T., Keim, D.: Visual analysis of social media data. Computer **46**(5), 68–75 (2013)
23. Shrestha, A.: Visualizing spatio-temporal data (2014)
24. Viégas, F.B., Wattenberg, M.: Artistic data visualization: beyond visual analytics. In: Schuler, D. (ed.) OCSC 2007. LNCS, vol. 4564, pp. 182–191. Springer, Heidelberg (2007). doi:10.1007/978-3-540-73257-0_21
25. Yi, J.S., Kang, Y.-A., Stasko, J.T., Jacko, J.A.: Understanding and characterizing insights: how do people gain insights using information visualization? In: Proceedings of the 2008 Workshop on BEyond Time and Errors: Novel EvaLuation Methods for Information Visualization, p. 4. ACM (2008)
26. yi Chan, W.W.: A survey on multivariate data visualization (2006)

SparQs: Visual Analytics for Sparking Creativity in Social Media Exploration

Nan-Chen Chen[✉], Michael Brooks, Rafal Kocielnik, Sungsoo (Ray) Hong, Jeff Smith, Sanny Lin, Zening Qu, and Cecilia Aragon

University of Washington, Seattle, WA 98195, USA
nanchen@uw.edu
https://depts.washington.edu/hdsl

Abstract. Social media has become a fruitful platform on which to study human behavior and social phenomena. However, social media data are usually messy, disorganized, and noisy, which makes finding patterns in such data a challenging task. Visualization can help with the exploration of such massive data. Researchers studying social media often begin by reviewing related research. In this paper, we consider the idea that information from related research can be incorporated into social media visualization tools in order to spark creativity and guide exploration. To develop an effective overview of social media research with which to seed our tool, we conducted a content analysis of social media related papers and designed *SparQs*, a visual analytics tool to spark creativity in social media exploration. We conducted a pilot evaluation with three social media researchers as well as a participatory design workshop to explore further directions.

Keywords: Visualization · Visual analytics · Social media · Exploratory analysis · Research questions · Social science

1 Introduction

In the past decade, social media has become a useful platform on which to study human behavior and social phenomena. Many fields, among them sociology, communication, and epidemiology, leverage the richness of social media to investigate how different dimensions and elements (e.g., time, hashtags, and network connectivity) relate to their subjects of interest. However, social media data are usually messy, disorganized, and full of noise, which makes finding patterns within the data a challenging task. Visualization can be useful for the exploration of such massive data. Although numerous tools have utilized visualization to study social media data, few systems have focused on giving users an overview of the research field itself and on helping the users generate ideas for exploring the data.

Research is typically informed by or based on previous work. Researchers often begin their studies with a review of related work, so developing visualizations based on an overview of existing research may be able to spark creativity

© Springer International Publishing AG 2017
G. Meiselwitz (Ed.): SCSM 2017, Part II, LNCS 10283, pp. 394–405, 2017.
DOI: 10.1007/978-3-319-58562-8_30

and guide exploration. To develop an effective overview of social media research with which to seed our tool to inform such guidance, we conducted a content analysis of social media related papers. We collected 75 papers related to social media research and manually extracted research questions, dimensions, visualization type, analysis methods, data sources and scale. Based on the results from content analysis, we designed *SparQs* to present research questions along with the visualization of data distributions of tweets over user-specified dimensions. We then conducted a pilot evaluation with three social media researchers and a participatory design workshop to explore further directions of improvement for SparQs.

The contributions of this paper are three-fold: First, the results from content analysis on social media papers provide an overview of recent progress in social media research. Specifically, the extracted research questions, dimensions, and other properties can inform future system design to support social media research. Second, we present SparQs, a visual analytics tool that incorporates visualization with research questions for exploratory analysis. Last but not least, the outcomes from the pilot evaluation and participatory design indicate many potential research directions that extend the use of research questions in visual exploratory analysis.

2   Related Work

Visual analytics is "the science of analytical reasoning facilitated by interactive visual interfaces" [12]. The goal of visual analytics is to leverage visual channels to deliver synthesized information as a way to support analytical tasks [7]. As visualization is commonly used in exploratory data analysis (EDA) [13], visual analytics can further facilitate exploratory processes through carefully designed support for analytical tasks (e.g., automatically extracting potential points of interest, explicitly displaying commonly-used analysis functions).

Past research has attempted to use visual analytics for studying social media data. For example, Diakopoulos et al. created *Vox Civitas* for journalists to explore topics, sentiment, and keywords among tweets of an event [4], and Marcus et al. built *twitInfo* to automatically detect peaks of stream tweets and highlight important text to use in labeling these peaks [8]. Brooks et al. developed *Agave* for collaborative sentiment analysis among tweets of a specific event [1]. Chae et al. designed a location-based visual analysis system for disaster events using geo-location tweet information [2]. These examples all utilize visualization to display results and information about the analysis targets, but they explore only limited dimensions. Furthermore, none of these works consider social media literature as a medium that can inform design and guide the exploratory process.

To support exploration in early stages, when the dimensions of interests have not yet been decided, SparQs focuses on incorporating dimensions and research questions from previous social media literature. The goals are to discover unknown aspects of a dataset, and to spark creative ideas when examining the dataset.

3   Content Analysis on Social Media Papers

3.1   Process

To understand what research questions and dimensions are interesting to social scientists, we collected 75 papers from university library databases by searching on social media-related keywords (e.g., twitter, social media, social network) and filtered them to focus on social science-related papers only. We collectively conducted content analysis on a web interface (Fig. 1) where a paper's PDF file and analysis questions were shown on the interface. The analysis questions included the source and scale of the dataset(s), the research questions explored, variables, as well as the visualization and methods used in the papers.

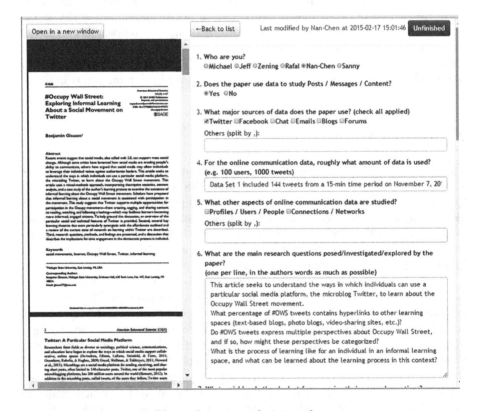

Fig. 1. Content analysis interface

Full list of questions used:

1. Does the paper use data to study Posts/Messages/Content? [Yes/No]
2. What major sources of data does the paper use? (check all that apply) [Twitter/Facebook/Chat/Emails/Blogs/Forums]

3. For online communication data, roughly what amount of data is used?
4. What other aspects of online communication data are studied? [Profiles/Users/People Connections/Networks/Others]
5. What are the main research questions posed/investigated/explored by the paper?
6. What variables do they look at to answer their research questions?
7. Is the paper *primarily* concerned with: (social phenomena includes individual, group, interactional, or otherwise human-related phenomena) [Offline social phenomena/Online social phenomena/Computational data processing technique/Research methodology]
8. In the authors' own words, what methods of analysis are applied to the online communication data? (e.g. manual/auto content analysis, machine learning, some type of modeling, close reading, qualitative analysis, etc.)
9. In your words, what methods of analysis are used? [Modeling (e.g. machine learning models, topic models...)/Statistical analysis (e.g. descriptive statistics, comparing two subgroups)/Social network analysis (e.g. centrality)/Human interpretation (e.g. qualitative coding, close reading)]
10. How are the results presented? [Simple charts and graphs/More complex visualizations/Tables/Quotations or excerpts/Statistical results/Narrative accounts]
11. Should we look at the visualizations? [Yes/No]
12. For each visualization in the paper, what is the primary question they answer?

We not only looked for explicit statements of research questions, typically in the introduction or methods sections, but also uncovered and collected implicit questions indicated in other sections. Dimensions of interest were sometimes explicitly referenced in research questions, but in many cases they also came from sections describing analysis, charts, and visualizations, as well as tables of results.

3.2 Results

About 350 dimensions, 250 research questions, and 140 visualizations were extracted. Selected examples of research questions and dimensions are shown in Table 1. We printed out the dimensions and research questions and sorted them into groups in a collaborative affinity diagramming activity. As a result, we created the dimension topology shown in Table 2. This topology is an effort to organize the dimensions into a structured form, so that we can create visualizations based on these dimensions. Furthermore, two of the authors further analyzed 56 questions in detail to rewrite them in a form less connected to the particular past research. They also extracted words representing specific dimensions of interest explored in the questions. These were later used to link the questions to the dimensions in the visualization. The full set of results can be found on https://github.com/hds-lab/sparqs-data.

Table 1. Example dimensions extracted from the research questions

Social science research question	Dimensions
How do Twitter users communicate their involvement with Haiti relief efforts? [10]	Qualitative labels (e.g. connecting, promoting, personalizing)
How do professional athletes use Twitter to communicate with fans and other players? [6]	Qualitative labels (e.g. interactivity, diversion, sharing, promotional, fan-ship)
To what extent does distance determine the informal communication of users from different nations? [5]	RT network, country, external data about countries

Table 2. Dimension topology

High-level category	Dimension	Open/closed	Variable type	Subtype	Range	Twitter-specific
Time	Time	Open	Quantitative	Time		
Time	Timezone	Closed	Nominal	-		
Contents	Topic (from topic model)	Open	Nominal	-		
Contents	Specific words in the message	Open	Nominal	-		
Contents	Specific hashtags in the message	Open	Nominal	-		
Contents	Contains a hashtag	Closed	Nominal	Boolean	Yes, no	
Contents	Contains a photo	Closed	Nominal	Boolean	Yes, no	
Contents	URL domain	Open	Nominal	-		
Contents	Contains URL	Closed	Nominal	Boolean	Yes, no	
Meta	Language (of a tweet)	Closed	Nominal	-		
Meta	Sentiment	Closed	Nominal	Small set	Positive, neutral, negative	
Interaction	Message type	Closed	Nominal	Small set	Original, retweet, reply	Yes
Interaction	Number of replies	Open	Quantitative	Frequency		
Interaction	Number of shares	Open	Quantitative	Frequency		Yes
Interaction	People mentioned in message (name)	Open	Nominal	People		
Author	Language (of an author's profile)	Closed	Nominal	-		
Author	Author of message (name)	Open	Nominal	People		
Author	Number of messages authored	Open	Quantitative	Frequency		
Author	Number of friends	Open	Quantitative	Count		Yes
Author	Number of followers	Open	Quantitative	Count		Yes
Author	Number of times replied to	Open	Quantitative	Frequency		
Author	Number of times mentioned	Open	Quantitative	Frequency		
Author	Number of times retweeted	Open	Quantitative	Frequency		Yes

4   SparQs

In this section, we describe SparQs, a visual analytics tool to support exploratory analysis on social media data and suggest creative research questions. SparQs leverages the dimension typology and research questions we extracted from the content analysis. The key idea is to enable users to explore the common dimensions and their combinations quickly through visualization, and also to display potentially relevant research questions along these same dimensions.

4.1   Visualizing Dimensions

The SparQs interface is shown in Fig. 2. The left panel lists 20 dimensions which are grouped into five high-level categories. Users drag and drop these dimensions to the rounded rectangle boxes in the middle panel to create visualizations (The red color indicates the primary dimension, whereas the blue is a secondary dimension). The visualization types with regard to dimension compositions are shown in Table 3. Users also filter on any of the dimensions by opening the filtering box at each dimension (Fig. 3). For time-series plots, a focus+context view [3] is displayed in the middle panel where users brush to focus on a specific range of the quantitative dimensions. When mousing over a data point, a tooltip shows its corresponding values. Example tweets sampled based on the dimension compositions are displayed on the right panel. When clicking on the data points, the list of tweets is updated to tweets that belong to the corresponding

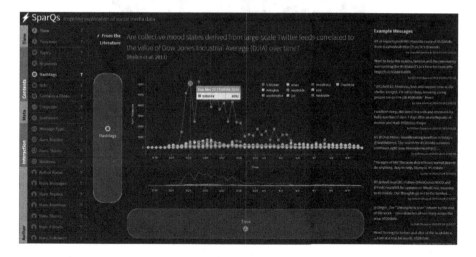

Fig. 2. SparQs. The left panel allows users to filter a list of dimensions from the typology. Visualizations are created and displayed in the middle panel. Users drag and drop variables or dimensions in the red and blue rounded rectangle boxes. The area above the visualization depicts a research question relevant to the current set of filters. Example tweets are displayed on the right. (Color figure online)

Table 3. Visualization types with regard to dimension topology

Secondary dimension	Primary dimension				
	Time	Open quant	Open nominal	Closed nominal	Boolean
Nothing	Time series	Time series	Bar chart	Bar chart	Bar chart
Open quant	Time series	Scatter-plot	Bar chart	Bar chart	Bar chart
Open nominal	Multi-series line chart	Multi-series line chart	Grouped bar chart	Grouped bar chart	Grouped bar chart
Closed nominal	Multi-series line chart	Multi-series line chart	Grouped bar chart	Grouped bar chart	Grouped bar chart
Boolean	Multi-series line chart	Multi-series line chart	Grouped bar chart	Grouped bar chart	Grouped bar chart

Fig. 3. SparQs filters. The view shows the filter on Hashtag.

point. For the sake of simplicity, SparQs only shows 10 levels of a categorical dimension in the visualization at a time (as in the dimension Hashtag in Fig. 2, which displays only the top 10 most frequent hashtags). Other levels are shown by filtering. For dimension "Topics", we modeled topics using Gensim [9] using the top keywords as topic names; for dimension "Sentiment", we used TextBlob [11] to label sentiments as positive, negative, or neutral.

4.2 Displaying Research Questions

When a user creates a visualization with dimensions in SparQs, a research question shows up in the top of the middle panel. The research question is randomly sampled from the set of research questions that examines the same dimension(s). The words corresponding to the dimension(s) are highlighted in the same color as the matching dimension(s). When users hover over the citation text, the details of the reference are displayed. In order to make the research questions understandable, two of the authors rewrote the questions based on their original text

Fig. 4. Example research question for dimension "Time" and "Hashtag"

in the papers. For example, the original text for the research question in Fig. 4 is "we study how information spreads through the social network by measuring how the number of in-network votes a story receives, i.e., votes from fans of the submitter or previous voters, changes in time".

5   Pilot User Testing

5.1   Study Procedure

To evaluate SparQs, we conducted a pilot user test with three social media researchers. We loaded the tool with a Twitter dataset containing 685,311 tweets about the 2014 Oso mudslide in Washington State, USA. All the social media researchers for the study were familiar with the dataset. We invited them to test SparQs individually in one-hour sessions. We first introduced the interface and then let them use the tool to come up with potential research questions while seeking for interesting or unexpected insights regarding the dataset. All the participants were asked to think aloud during their sessions. The study moderators took notes and audio and screen recordings of the sessions.

5.2   Results

Listed dimensions helped users explore aspects they had not considered. All the participants tried to look at all the dimensions SparQs provided, and they were able to discover a few patterns that they did not notice before. One participant raised a question to further look into what types of accounts receive more positive sentiment. Another participant was wondering how hashtags were used between different groups of accounts. The participants liked the ability to combine dimensions to create plots, but two mentioned it would be more useful if they could create customized groups.

Research questions were not directly useful. We noticed most participants did not spend much time reading the research questions; according to their explanations, the research questions seemed irrelevant to the dataset. Some questions were not even from the same discipline as theirs, and thus they did not see why those questions were important.

The need to incorporate prior knowledge. During the sessions we found that all the participants looked for something that came from their prior knowledge. For example, since the Oso dataset was about a disaster, they wanted to look at specific types of accounts such as governments or non-government organizations. They also wanted to compare the tweeting behavior among people who were or were not victims of the disaster. These inquiries all went beyond dimensions that we could directly derive from the dataset; this indicates the need to enhance our tool to incorporate prior knowledge and other sources of information.

6   Participatory Design Workshop for Future Directions

In order to explore ways to improve the use of the research questions and SparQs, we held a participatory design workshop with four social media researchers to explore potential extensions of the tool. One of the researchers participated in the pilot user test, but the other three were new to SparQs.

6.1   Process and Materials

We invited the four participants to a conference room in our department building, explained the background and goals of the workshop to them, and provided each of them with a stack of ideation resource printouts, including tweets from the Oso mudslide dataset as well as visualizations, titles, abstracts, and research questions from papers. We asked them to use these materials to brainstorm questions and directions that they would want to investigate further. To structure the brainstorming session, we proceeded in 5-minute sprints, and after each sprint we asked them to briefly describe their ideas, and then continue the brainstorming. We ended up running four sprints with a brief discussion after each sprint. The whole brainstorming session continued for about 40 min, after which we asked them to reflect on the experience and describe what they found useful during the session. Figure 5 shows an example set of sketches and notes along with the materials provided from the workshop.

6.2   Results

Use and comments on the provided materials. During the brainstorming session, the four participants approached the materials with very different strategies. One participant primarily focused on reading research questions and sometimes the tweets, whereas another participant used many tweets and only some research questions. One other participant only flipped through the provided materials, and he later explained that he was very familiar with the tweets and he was thinking about some directions on his own. Other findings include that the abstracts were not used much due to limited time, and tweets with photos got more attention where the participants described them as "attractive". Based on the comments, we found it is important to let users of exploration tools like SparQs directly read the text and images during exploration.

Fig. 5. A photo of the sketches and notes from the participatory design workshop

Integration with qualitative coding and other types of analysis. Two of the participants mentioned the desire to do qualitative coding. From their perspectives, qualitative coding is a common task for them during the exploration stage. Some of the research questions we provided had manually coded categories as targeted research dimensions, and our participants pointed out that they were also interested in categories that were not standard and emerged from the data. Another participant with experience in network analysis suggested an interface which combined tweets, a follower-followee network, and code (bottom-right sketch in Fig. 5). As a result, incorporating both qualitative coding and other types of analysis with SparQs is a valuable direction for future research.

Diverse context. In the final reflection section, the four participants agreed that the research questions were not very helpful because they were high-level and not exactly relevant to disaster-related research. However, one participant pointed out that some of the research questions were necessary to examine because they were basic. Another participant commented that it was still fascinating to read these research questions that came from very different research contexts. These points indicated that research questions may be useful during exploration, but we need better ways to draw research questions that are closer to the user's research context. Therefore, we suggest that future research should focus on building a system that can automatically identify research questions that are relevant to a user's research interest, and adaptively take into account exploration logs for better recommendations.

7 Conclusion

In this paper, we presented SparQs, a visual analytic tool for exploratory analysis on social media data which lays out research dimensions and questions from social media literature. We conducted a pilot user test as well as a participatory design workshop to examine the tool. The results showed that incorporating information from literature can be valuable, but more study is required to effectively use extracted questions from past research. Future work should explore in-depth automatic analysis on structuring the information and incorporation with other methods such as qualitative coding and network analysis. Additionally, the dimension topology we constructed from the literature can be useful to inform the design of exploratory tools for social media.

Acknowledgments. We would like to thank everyone who participated in the user testing and the participatory design workshop, as well as the research group who shared the Twitter dataset with us for testing the tool.

References

1. Brooks, M., Robinson, J.J., Torkildson, M.K., Hong, S.R., Aragon, C.R.: Collaborative visual analysis of sentiment in Twitter events. In: Luo, Y. (ed.) CDVE 2014. LNCS, vol. 8683, pp. 1–8. Springer, Cham (2014). doi:10.1007/978-3-319-10831-5_1
2. Chae, J., Thom, D., Jang, Y., Kim, S., Ertl, T., Ebert, D.S.: Public behavior response analysis in disaster events utilizing visual analytics of microblog data. Comput. Graph. **38**, 51–60 (2014)
3. Cockburn, A., Karlson, A., Bederson, B.B.: A review of overview+ detail, zooming, and focus+ context interfaces. ACM Comput. Surv. (CSUR) **41**(1), 2 (2009)
4. Diakopoulos, N., Naaman, M., Kivran-Swaine, F.: Diamonds in the rough: social media visual analytics for journalistic inquiry. In: 2010 IEEE Symposium on Visual Analytics Science and Technology (VAST), pp. 115–122. IEEE (2010)
5. García-Gavilanes, R., Mejova, Y., Quercia, D.: Twitter ain't without frontiers: economic, social, and cultural boundaries in international communication. In: Proceedings of the 17th ACM Conference on Computer Supported Cooperative Work and Social Computing, pp. 1511–1522. ACM (2014)
6. Hambrick, M.E., Simmons, J.M., Greenhalgh, G.P., Greenwell, T.C.: Understanding professional athletes use of Twitter: a content analysis of athlete tweets. Int. J. Sport Commun. **3**(4), 454–471 (2010)
7. Keim, D., Andrienko, G., Fekete, J.-D., Görg, C., Kohlhammer, J., Melançon, G.: Visual analytics: definition, process, and challenges. In: Kerren, A., Stasko, J.T., Fekete, J.-D., North, C. (eds.) Information Visualization. LNCS, vol. 4950, pp. 154–175. Springer, Heidelberg (2008). doi:10.1007/978-3-540-70956-5_7

8. Marcus, A., Bernstein, M.S., Badar, O., Karger, D.R., Madden, S., Miller, R.C.: Twitinfo: aggregating and visualizing microblogs for event exploration. In: Proceedings of the SIGCHI Conference on Human Factors in Computing Systems, CHI 2011, New York, USA, pp. 227–236 (2011). http://doi.acm.org.offcampus.lib.washington.edu/10.1145/1978942.1978975

9. Řehůřek, R., Sojka, P.: Software framework for topic modelling with large corpora. In: Proceedings of the LREC 2010 Workshop on New Challenges for NLP Frameworks, pp. 45–50. ELRA, Valletta (2010). http://is.muni.cz/publication/884893/en

10. Smith, B.G.: Socially distributing public relations: Twitter, Haiti, and interactivity in social media. Public Relat. Rev. **36**(4), 329–335 (2010)

11. Textblob (2016). https://github.com/sloria/TextBlob

12. Thomas, J.J.: Illuminating the path: the research and development agenda for visual analytics. IEEE Computer Society (2005)

13. Tukey, J.W.: Exploratory Data Analysis. Addison-Wesley, Reading (1977)

Social Networks Serendipity for Educational Learning by Surprise from Big and Small Data Analysis

Niki Lambropoulos[1]([⊠]), Habib M. Fardoun[2], and Daniyal M. Alghazzawi[2]

[1] London South Bank University (LSBU), 103 Borough Road, London SE1 0AA, UK
nikilambropoulos@gmail.com
[2] King Abdulaziz University of Saudi Arabia, Jeddah 21589, Kingdom of Saudi Arabia
{hfardoun, dghazzawi}@kau.edu.sa

Abstract. This paper follows our stream of research on Serendipity Engineering for series events connected in time and space. Occurring by rather hidden and unexpected connections Serendipity Engineering is also related to the bipolar decision making process: hesitate before taking the risk, accept and engage in serendipity or deny it. Although research exists within the Global Systems Science field for serendipity identification and engineering, the results are not encouraging as such research now fails in predictions. Massive global research and apparent impact is evident and reachable in social media such as Twitter, Facebook, Instagram etc. Furthermore, utilising a range of tools, methodologies and techniques, it may be possible to identify activities and hidden connections in both big and small data and predict, aid or even interfere in the decision making process. Such interference based on prediction can actually alter the future decision making users' domino of events and items selected and orchestrate series of events that may have possible utility in psychology, marketing, serendipity systems design and engineering design or other influential disciplines. Our research main aim is the identification, collection and analysis of both big and small data in order to shed light in serendipity connections in chrono-spatial intelligence and even engineer it, called Chrono-Spatial Intelligence for Serendipity Engineering (CSISE). A second aim is to identify tools, methodologies and evaluation techniques to facilitate such deep understanding via Chrono-Spatial Intelligence Analytics. Here, we propose a serendipity engineering model for learning insights anchored in big and small data methods, tools and learning analytics.

Keywords: Social networks · Semantic latent analysis · Sentiment analysis · Serendipity engineering

© Springer International Publishing AG 2017
G. Meiselwitz (Ed.): SCSM 2017, Part II, LNCS 10283, pp. 406–415, 2017.
DOI: 10.1007/978-3-319-58562-8_31

1 Online Bipolar Decision Making: The Brain Hesitation Gap

This paper follows our stream of research on Serendipity Engineering. Although research exists within the Global Systems Science field and social networks in particular, serendipity identification and engineering is rather a new field. Instead of being lost into massive amounts of data, our aim is to find meaning into both and small and mass data so to discover hidden connections appearing as unexpected and pleasant serendipity surprising events. However, chance favours the prepared. Based on underpinned connections and the ways a user acts upon decision making, our proposition is related to the bipolar decision making process. As such, discrepancies in the research are still to be solved and the results are not encouraging as such research now fails in predictions.

The research aims and objectives here refer to the massive global impact of different predicted serendipity events engineered so the users get involved into a predicted decision making process in social media such as Twitter, Facebook, Instagram etc. Furthermore, manufacturing serendipity involves research on initially identifying positive and negative actions and hidden connections between clicks in both big and small data. As such, there can be possibilities to strategically engage users into predicted processes, aid or even interfere into the decision making process. Our research main aim is the identification, collection and analysis of both big and small data in order to shed light in serendipity connections in chrono-spatial intelligence and even engineer it, called Chrono-Spatial Intelligence for Serendipity Engineering (CSISE). A second aim is to identify tools, methodologies and evaluation techniques to facilitate such deep understanding via Chrono-Spatial Intelligence Learning Analytics. Here, we propose a serendipity engineering model for learning insights anchored in big and small data methods, tools and learning analytics.

Choice is the act of hesitation that we make before making a decision. In this mind gap and when online, we decide click or not to click. Every user is battling with mass amount of information on social media; however, such scanning instead of reading, only does attract the attention to a few postings. Furthermore, the user decides on clicking on even fewer. Such initial hesitation, second thought and then, immediate action before changing his mind involves identifying serendipity and taking the risk, accept, and engage into the serendipity flow or deny it.

Stanford researchers [1] observe the moment when a mind is changed. A new algorithm enables a moment-by-moment analysis of brain activity each time a laboratory monkey reaches this way or that during an experiment. It's like reading the monkey's mind. This prediction is possible by calculating the average results from different repeated trials. However, average calculation misses the ways the brain functions requiring moment-by-moment research o small data. The authors agree with the San Francisco neuroscientist Benjamin Libet, who conducted an experiment in the 80 s to assess the nature of free will via an electroencephalogram (EEG). Libet's experiments showed that distinctive brain activity began, on average, several seconds before subjects became aware that they planned to move. Libet concluded that the desire to move arose unconsciously; 'free will' could only come in the form of a conscious veto: what he called 'free won't.'

A user decides to click or not to click or even changing his mind on the way. If a series of events are engineered towards the happiness and euphoria produced in serendipity, it is rather possible to imply the demise of the free will. However, the change of mind may also imply a change into a new string of possible events and items to click. As the Internet is a connecting ecosystem, the users decide on the social networks to use, creating the background of their own communication space. As such, interoperability between social networks allows the researchers to study the connections and further-more, to orchestrate actions so the users create the social media buzz on demand.

2   Serendipity Through Macro and Micro Data Perspectives and Analysis

There is no wide research to shed light and understand the magical serendipity expe-rience, which in social networks used for learning is a user-learner experience. As such, serendipity implications for user/learner-centred design processes are very limited or even missing.

In this research proposal, our main research aim is the identification, collection and analysis of both big and small data in order to shed light in serendipity connections in chrono-spatial intelligence and even engineer it. A second aim is to identify tools, methodologies and evaluation techniques to facilitate such deep understanding via Chrono-Spatial Intelligence Analytics [2] in order to manipulate bipolar decision making and change the user's future clicks or even preferences. These were never certain in the first place, unless the user knows exactly his purpose. Hence, in this paper, we take advantage of such knowledge of the bipolar decision making and hesitation brain indecision in order to propose a serendipity engineering model for learning insights anchored in big and small data methods, tools and analytics in regard to informal learning via social media.

Serendipity is a tendency for making fortunate discoveries while looking for something unrelated; therefore, there is a surprise element attached to it that differs it from the novelty feature. Iquinta and colleagues [3] suggested that there are some context in which user requires unsearched but still useful items or pieces of informa-tion. He proposed serendipity heuristics in order to mitigate the overspecialization and accuracy problem with the surprise suggestion.

Changing the mind in a changing environment requires both a time-series research approach for predicting the average user responses as well as qualitative case study to shed light into the process itself. Even though there is mass data analysis at the moment, there is no evidence of improvement into the decision making processes other than improving the systems usability that enable users to reach their targets in a few clicks. 'Big data', data so large and complex that processing them by conventional data processing applications isn't possible or even conventional data collection and analysis, convey information that for some reason is numerical and thus limited. As for edu-cation, there was no effort to improve Education significantly. Both 'Big and small data' collection and analysis are required to identify suitable and appropriate indicators about bipolar decision making connected to teaching and learning processes, student levels, even social trends.

Education policymakers around the world are now reforming their education systems through correlations based on Big Data from their own national and international education data bases without adequately understanding the details that make a difference in learning paths and processes. Both big data and small data analysis can improve teaching and learning and also indicate or even manipulate trends in education or any other area one desires. Users also act as learners as they need to make decisions under uncertainty or conflicting evidence. Serendipity sequences fill the structural holes in indecision and bipolar decision making, and therefore, aid in proactive decision making and even change of opinion. This is possible via Big and small data analysis, integration and visualisation, cascading and escalating effects in social networks and media [2].

Social Media provide the advantage that are dynamic user generated context, social reactors and mimic groups or even critical masses. In such informal learning environments, causal collisions indicators can serve as predictors for future behaviours. When utilising Chrono-Spatial Intelligent analytics the user can reflect his process on a meta-cognitive level and thus, expand the hesitation gap in order to make better decisions or change initial decisions.

Learning Analytics (LA) is an emerging fast growing area, according to which Learning analytics is the measurement, collection, analysis and reporting of data about learners and their contexts, for purposes of understanding and optimising learning and the environments in which it occurs. Analytics as data mining can be used for teaching, learning and assessing student progress; in this proposition, combining it with chrono-spatial intelligence analytics so to reveal serendipity events for the purpose of learning. Kohavi and Provost [4] suggest five desiderata for success in data mining applications:

- data rich with descriptions to enable search for patterns beyond simple correlations
- large volume of data to allow for building reliable models
- controlled and reliable (automated) data collection
- the ability to evaluate results
- ease of integration with existing processes to build systems that can effectively take advantage of the mined knowledge.

There are several LA tools that meet such desiderata, such as: Mixpanel analytics, which offers real-time data visualization documenting how users are engaging with material on a website; Userfly for usability testing and analysis; Gephi is open source for interactive visualization and exploration platform for exploratory data analysis; Socrato for diagnostic and performance reports; SNAPP (Social Networks Adapting Pedagogical Practice) for Learning Management Systems (LMS) data and analysis that visualizes how students interact with discussion forum posts, giving significance to the socio-constructivist activities of students. LA toolkits also already exist, such as the Java-Script InfoVis Toolkit, (http://thejit.org/demos/), Prefuse Visualization Toolkit (http://prefuse.org/) or the learning analytics tool LOCO-Analyst (Liaqat Ali et al. 2012).

Other studies are related to temporal serendipity heuristics and temporal novelty for dynamic features of recommender systems [5], shuffling algorithms [6], through ambient intelligence and interactive datamining [7]. Rana's research on serendipity for recommender systems focuses on techniques that could predict user interest and assist user's interaction in finding and following relevant information. Rana is also anchored in making sense past data to accurately predict in future choices. As such, novelty and serendipity refers to the search of finding something new by a user, in our case while searching social media for learning purposes. In order to keep the tricky combination of both accuracy and serendipity novelty, novelty was defined as providing something new which the user have not accesses before but similar in taste while serendipity is a chance discovery that could be really beneficial for a user at certain times and specific purposes. Rana also anchored his research and methodology based on temporal parameters to include the novelty and serendipity in a recommender system. Real-time dynamics is an essential element and play an important role in today's fast paced life where choices of users depend on many factors susceptible to change anytime [8].

As before, Leong and colleagues [6] conducted a research study analysing online data about the shuffle experience. The results revealed a range of rich and unusual user-experiences and serendipity in particular. Although serendipity is often imbued with 'magic' or regarded as a product of chance and luck, its effects can be inspirational and transformative.

Our research on Chrono-Spatial Intelligence and Serendipity contexts [2] are based on global events, people, time and locations can generate visible pathways and connections via Chrono-Spatial Intelligence Analytics. These are: Chrono-Spatial Intelligence Analytics design methodologies as with time-series design; quantitative and qualitative mainstream methods, focus groups and interviews; data analysis via sequential analysis, Natural Language Processing and Social Network Analysis. Indicated Chrono-Spatial Intelligence Analytics Design Methodologies is real-Time series design with streaming data real-time visualisation. Big and small data analysis, therefore, derives from diverse tools, methods and techniques; triangulation is not enough. The suggested research methodologies categories are the following: (a) Spatial Analysis (space – locations); Sequential Data Analysis (events – contexts); Social Network Analysis; and Natural Language Processing. Relationships between big and small data information, events, people, time, locations can be identified by Chrono-Spatial Intelligence Analytics. Context-aware computing can now integrate the suggested methods and techniques in social media platforms translating theories into tools. Time-series real-time streaming data visualisations are set for predefined patterns and peak point identifications, abnormalities identification, and decision making identification points.

Context-aware time is also related to presence tools integration into social media. A user's presence information includes audio and visual cues for the following factors: self-presentation, distance, location, activity, feeling, form of expression, availability, willingness and readiness for communication, current device or application on which he can be communicated (cell-phone, home & work-hub landline phone, IM client), motivation and enjoyment, prediction. Presence brings this important information to the social network incorporating sets of different types of information that enables better communication and range of feelings. Deep presence and copresence enable embodied communication and immersion with user's situation (feeling and activity of the user, buddies, friends and broader networks) that possibly influences the main user to act or silent accordingly. Presence is also a critical element is serendipity engineering related to bipolar decision making on increasing awareness regarding the learner learning paths. Time-based coordination examines the nature of decision, clicking or not clicking on the suggested information item: (a) the form of the effect (the level, slop, variance and cyclicity); (b) its permanence (continuous or discontinuous) and (c) its immediacy (immediate or delayed). The research question now is revolved around the ways such serendipity events can be integrated into a learning system. This is discussed next.

3 To Click or not to Click? Brain Hesitation and Randomness

People use social media from different education levels, cultural backgrounds, and ages can provide us with the underpinned structures, relations, activities, scale and impact of such networks and human relationships [9]. Therefore, we may create a model to identify and measure cues as well as users' behaviour for learning purposes, as for example user's levels of engagement in serendipity events and the way they learn to change their decision for greater learning impact. In this way, we may possibly predict serendipity as happy accidental surprises or even engineer it. Data can be extracted and analysed via specific and valid methods, tools and techniques mainly focusing on users' preferences, experiences and satisfaction. Another serendipity element is the attached value and importance to the related person; a serendipity event may be important with emotional arousal, capture of attention and immediate response to engage and click for one person and completely insignificant and seemingly unimportant for another. Taking this concept further, a person or/and application has to be proactive for such serendipity events to occur. This may be a behavioristic approach in education; however, utilising the creative euphoria for learning is not only for marketing purposes but for enhancing educational behaviours as well via repetitive reinforcement towards the educational target.

Experiencing serendipity is a pleasant surprise and such it conveys intrinsic satisfaction of being lucky. Perceiving serendipity is also a decision making challenge as the same information may appear relevant or irrelevant to the user. As such, we argue, that the levels of emotional achievement and satisfaction may aid in changing serendipity perception and insightful creative thinking via social media. Understanding the way that people think and make associations among their own interests, resources and other people can encourage serendipity with even more communication and collaboration towards serendipity.

Randomness is an occurrence with no definite aim or guidance in a particular direction and without any method or conscious choice (adapted from the Oxford English Dictionary on 'random'). In systems design, a large number of alternatives can be randomly generated, which are then reduced to a smaller set by a non-random selection process. A number of creative ideas can randomly be triggered and then assimilated into a pre-existing system of beliefs in order to sustain its consistency and integrity, which is a non-random process of reinforcement [11].

Unexpected associations are influenced by in situ chrono-special intelligence i.e. they are context-aware relations [2]. Such relations indicate information organisational convergence, coordination and sequencing. Coordinating and sequencing learning activities in social media is of major importance and contradicts educational material fixation. The degree of coercion and tackling unpredictability is a delicate design choice [10]. Therefore, predicting and assists such learning sequences can scaffold students' social and learning interactions in such a way so to be taken by learning surprise and achieve peak performance based on excitement and creativity. Prediction of specific linear and non-linear sequences online for preferable activities and resources as well as repetition of such actions and clicks with minor variations can be used. Traversion and rotation are two modes to be used. The first is the repetition of the same educational material in the same order looped through as extracted from learning analytics, with only one element being in use at a time; the second is rotates the elements in a given set towards the same direction.

Randomness in this sense can be used as an innovative learning serendipity design as a resource for supporting rich and novel user experiences when navigating in social media. Leong and his colleagues [6] assert that encounters with serendipity are more likely to arise when the random selection is unconstrained (i.e., when the shuffle algorithm picks tracks randomly and freely from people's entire music or photo library instead of being constrained to only subsets of the library).

4 Discussion: Taking Learning by Surprise via Serendipity Engineering in Social Networks

In our research proposition, social and emotional needs in design refer to safety, social and esteem needs that can trigger the click i.e. engagement and actualisation. The research design follows our previous research on Chrono-Spatial Intelligence Analytics [2] for (a) Spatial Analysis (space – locations); Sequential Data Analysis (events – contexts); Social Network Analysis; and Natural Language Processing. Other researchers such as Rana and colleagues [4, 7] conducted studies on web personalization, customizing recommendations towards the needs of each specific user or set of users, and taking advantage of the knowledge acquired through the analysis of the user's navigational behavior. Profiling [2] and data analysis integration updating the learner's profile can alleviate the information overload problem so social media can be friendlier and more easy to use. As each user has also the learner personal on social media and the Internet in general, experiences serendipity differently, profiling and personalisation can solve several usability and pedagogical usability overloading problems. Such challenge for social media designers requires involving serendipity engineering into the initial systems design so to include learning analytics together with business analytics for both past analysis and future prediction. In other words, analytics can also be used for learning purposes not just marketing and business.

Novelty and serendipity has been investigated together to support human-centered discovery of knowledge; however, shuffling novelty in general and new learning suffers due to lack of related research. Social media mining for learning purposes needs to be optimised towards serendipity and novelty in learning using temporal dimension. Serendipity Engineering in social media builds upon randomness and interaction, relaying on user's bipolar decision making processes and hesitation before each click, so to embrace innovative learning in favour of the user as learner. In this way, serendipity and unintended outcomes can be manipulated to orchestrate pleasant learning surprising experiences.

Hidden and unexpected connections for Serendipity Engineering related to the bipolar decision making process and randomness can work within the decision making hesitation gap existing before taking the risk on a click. Further action depicts the user's acceptance and engagement in serendipity or even denial to participate. The proposed serendipity engineering model based on both engineered learning insights and random learning items and events are anchored in big and small data methods, tools and learning analytics.

5   Concluding Remarks and Future Work

This paper discussed the possibility of including learning analytics together with business analytics in social media in order to support serendipity in a user's learning path. This notion is supported by the ways the human brain works during the decision making processes. When shuffling online for information items or else, there is a hesitation gap before entering an action such as a click so to engage in a series of events, hopefully ending in a pleasant and magical surprise and experience. Such magical immersive experience has enormous learning gains if taken advance effectively by the user. The user in online and social networks acts also as a learner.

Fortunate and unfortunate series of events can lead the user by preference or avoidance to act with a click. Such underpinned matrix can be investigated to reveal hidden connections base upon Chrono-Spatial Intelligence for Serendipity Engineering (CSISE). Digital CSISE depends on the effectiveness for past behaviour analytics combined with user profiling and preferences between human or machine generated data. Social media data in correlations with other data formats can provide information for real-time political impact related to political decision making, as for example quality in education. Social media also provide by definition important temporal information related to user's presence and rich context interactions.

In this paper, only the individual approach for Chrono-Spatial Intelligence for Serendipity Engineering (CSISE) for learning purposes in social media was discussed. Groups and community usage and collaborative human factors were not the proposition target. Nonetheless, social interactions for group activities can provide a mass moving serendipity effect which is not the purpose of this paper. Serendipity in learning engages the user as learner in 3 ways: (a) behavioural engagement with involvement and participation; (b) emotional engagement, regarding positive feelings and surprise as a pleasant experience used in learning in general; and (c) cognitive engagement, as conscious efforts for excelling in acquiring comprehensive knowledge and skills when in social media.

In regard to technological factors, CSISE for learning purposes can aid users as learners to reach a meta-cognitive awareness on past actions in order to enrich their preferences and online engagement in suitable and appropriate learning paths for achieving excellence. Furthermore, users as learners can also be aware of their constraints and disadvantages and build upon reversing difficulties. Traditional tools and models of learning engagement are more teacher-oriented and are designed based on complete scripting of the learning behaviours and educational material, omitting the serendipity element.

Lastly, in regard to research methodologies and suggested CSISE learning analytics for social media as such, both quantitative and qualitative results as well as other sources of data visualisation and utilisation need to be converged for a high level of engagement in predicted serendipity events, resulting in high level of learning and understanding of online information. Utilising a range of tools, methodologies and techniques, can create intervention and interference based on prediction can actually alter the future decision making users' domino of events and items selected and orchestrate time-based series of events that may have possible utility in psychology, marketing, learning and business analytics, serendipity systems design and engineering design or other influential disciplines.

To conclude, the random presentation of objects can engage or intrigue people; however, in combination with serendipity past activities research can aid people to attract their attention and drawing them into the serendipity flow. A change of mind may also imply a change into a new string of possible events and items to click. There is only commitment and determination that diminish the hesitation moment [12]. Such drawing of attention can also be part of a thought suspension process or defamiliarization; introducing a slightly strange item or a gap can also heighten attention Serendipity based on randomness and unpredictability is an important and exciting element and social media systems feature for users' immersive experience for to inform CSISE subsequent design and application.

In our future research, sentiment text analysis for positive, negative or neutral attitudes including the indecision hesitation gaps follows our research stream on Chrono-Spatial Intelligence for Serendipity Engineering (CSISE) for learning purposes. Revealing any interaction patterns utilising past data, in fact reveals learning attitudes and behaviours for the future. Changing a deterministic and fixed future may be of interest for anyone involved in learning and human excellence.

References

1. Rae-Dupree, J., Abate, T.: Stanford researchers observe the moment when a mind is changed. Stanford News (2015). http://news.stanford.edu/2015/05/05/decisions-monkey-mind-050515/
2. Lambropoulos, N., Fardoun, H., Alghazzawi, D.M.: Chrono-spatial intelligence in global systems science and social media: predictions for proactive political decision making. In: The Proceedings of the Serendipity Engineering via Creative Context-Aware Learning in Social Media, the 8th International Conference in Social Computing and Social Media, HCI International 2016, Toronto, Canada, 17–22 July 2016. The Westin Harbour Castle Hotel (2016)
3. Iaquinta, L., Gemmis, M., Lops, P., Semeraro, G., Molino, P.: Can a recommender system induce serendipitous encounters? In: Kang, K. (ed.) E-Commerce, pp. 229–246. IN-TECH, Vienna (2010)
4. Kohavi, R., Provost, F.: Applications of data mining to electronic commerce. Data Min. Knowl. Disc. 5(1–2), 5–10 (2001)
5. Rana, C.: New dimensions of temporal serendipity and temporal novelty in recommender system. Adv. Appl. Sci. Res. 4(1), 151–157 (2013)

6. Leong, T.W., Harper, R., Regan, T.: Nudging towards serendipity: a case with personal digital photos. In: Proceedings of BCS Conference on HCI, pp. 385–394 (2011)
7. Beale, R.: Supporting serendipity: using ambient intelligence to augment user exploration for data mining and web browsing. Int. J. Hum.-Comput. Stud. **65**(5), 421–433 (2007)
8. Rana, C., Jain, S.: A study of the dynamic features of recommender systems. Artif. Intell. Rev. **43**(1), 141–153 (2012)
9. Kefalidou, G., Sharples, S.: Encouraging serendipity in research: designing technologies to support connection-making. Int. J. Hum.-Comput. Stud. **89**, 1–23 (2016)
10. Dillenbourg, P., Tchounikine, P.: Flexibility in macro-scripts for CSCL. J. Comput. Assist. Learn. **23**, 1–13 (2007)
11. Scaruffi, P.: Gregory Bateson: Mind and Nature (1979) (2012). http://www.scaruffi.com/mind/bateson.html
12. Lewis, T.L., Amini, F., Lannon, R.: A General Theory of Love. Random House, New York (2000)

What People Do on Yik Yak: Analyzing Anonymous Microblogging User Behaviors

Joon-Suk Lee[1], Seungwon Yang[2(✉)], Amanda L. Munson[2], and Lusene Donzo[1]

[1] Virginia State University, 1 Hayden Street, Petersburg, VA 23806, USA
[2] Louisiana State University, Baton Rouge, LA 70803, USA
seungwonyang@lsu.edu

Abstract. In recent years, online microblogging services such as Yik Yak—an anonymous microblogging platform—have gained popularity. Yet these anonymous platforms spurred concerns and uneasiness among educators and parents. To many people anonymous online blogging equates to cyber-bullying, hate crimes, sex and drugs. In this study, we explore Yik Yak users' blogging behaviors. From March 2016 to July 2016, we collected 5,437 message postings on Yik Yak. This research reports on the findings that we gained from conducting content and structural analyses on Yik Yak data. Our findings show that even though postings exist that can be categorized as hate-speech and criminal activity related, the numbers are minuscule. We report different Yik Yak usage patterns, and analyze Yik Yak posts' thread structures.

1 Introduction

In recent years microblogging platforms such as Twitter have gained popularities. Features that are supported by the microblogging platforms such as message posts, replies, comments, retweets, and hashtags are known to explicitly define potential user interactions on these platforms. While such interaction-defining features have a direct and immediate impact on the user behaviors, different microblogging platforms also support features that are less visible, but that still confine and shape user interactions. Such features include character limitations for posting a message (e.g., Twitter), supports for anonymity (e.g., Kik and Yik Yak), and the use of geo-data (e.g., NearbyFeed and Yik Yak). Yet not enough studies have investigated how these different features do indeed impact user interactions. In this work, we explore microblogging user behaviors on an anonymous social networking platform, *Yik Yak*[1].

Yik Yak is a location-based, anonymous social media platform which is serviced primarily on smartphones. It was first introduced in November 2013, and gained an instant popularity amongst college students [9]. Yik Yak groups users based on their geographical proximities. While Yik Yak mobile users are allowed to 'peek' into different locations (colleges and cities) to view Yik Yak posts, the platform allows only the users belonging to the same local messaging group to

---

[1] http://www.yikyak.com.

© Springer International Publishing AG 2017
G. Meiselwitz (Ed.): SCSM 2017, Part II, LNCS 10283, pp. 416–428, 2017.
DOI: 10.1007/978-3-319-58562-8_32

post anonymous messages, *"yaks"* on the local messaging board. Yik Yak users can post yaks, leave replies to the specific yak postings, and either up-vote or down-vote yaks and replies.

In recent years, Yik Yak, an anonymous microblogging/social networking platform has instigated concerns for cyber-bullying and hate crimes, and sometimes caused spontaneous repulsions from educators and parents (e.g., [1,7,12]). Citing several anonymous threats including a mass shooting threat made on Yik Yak, for instance, Alblow rightfully raises his concerns and states that "Yik Yak is most dangerous app" he has ever seen [1]. Threats of sex and hate crimes have been reported numerous times. Racist, xenophobic, homophobic and misogynist yaks have created controversy at many US-based colleges [5].

Compared to a large body of research done on Twitter, another online social networking platform created in 2006, only a handful of research works done on Yik Yak exist. McKenzie et al. conducted a thematic difference analysis using a latent Dirichlet allocation (LDA) technique to compare Twitter and Yik Yak datasets [6]. Results of qualitative analyses on yak data have been reported also [2,8,11]. Saveski et al. investigated the usage patterns of vulgarity, and reported that yaks containing offensive and vulgar terms are more likely to be down-voted [11]. Black et al. developed a coding scheme which consists of 11 codes to conduct a thematic analysis on over 4000 yaks, and reported that most postings were benign, arguing "whether Yik Yak creates and promulgates a negative culture remains debatable [2]."

In this research, we aim to learn how Yik Yak users communicate on the platform, understand the role of *anonymity* in computer-mediated communication, and inform future communication-technology designs.

2   Methods

2.1   Data Collection

During Spring Semester 2016, we collected *yaks* from two US-based Universities (Virginia State University and Louisiana State University) using a web-based yak scraping tool developed in-house. We used *Selenium*[2], a web automation framework to create a data collection tool specifically designed to extract yaks from the Yik Yak website, and used the tool to collect the yak data periodically for 4 months. Since, unlike Twitter, Yik Yak has yet to provide users its own application programming interface (API) sets for automated yak data extraction, we decided to use the Web automation solution to mimic manual data scraping to collect yaks as well as replies/comments added to the original posts.

Unlike Black et al. [2] who collected the yak data by manually peeking into different locations and then screen-capturing iOS Yik Yak application screens, we chose to automate the data collection process. However, as a consequence, we had to restrict the data collection locations to Virginia State University and Louisiana State University because the Yik Yak web interface did not support

---

[2] http://www.seleniumhq.org.

"peeking", and our yak scraping tool only worked on PCs and Macs, but not on mobile devices.

During the time of data collection, Yik Yak changed their web document object model (DOM) more than once, and we had to update our tool to reflect the changes made on the Yik Yak website.

Our yak scraping tool collected 100 yaks, the maximum number of yaks displayed on the Yik Yak website at any given moment, per each run, and stored yak posts, replies, up-vote and down-vote numbers for both yaks and replies into a text file. During the four-month period, we used the tool to generate 150 daily yak collection files:

- LSU yak collection dates: 3/28/2016–7/27/2016 (4 months): 137 text files
- VSU yak collection dates: 3/18/2016–4/19/2016 (13 days): 13 text files

We then merged these files from each university into a single collection file, removing empty lines, duplicated yaks and replies using Python scripts. We kept emoticons and picture links. The final merged LSU yak file contained 4,670 yak threads, and the merged VSU yak file held 767 yak threads.

Our findings in this paper draw from both the qualitative analysis and the thread structure analysis conducted on the yak dataset we collected over a four-month period at two locations.

2.2   Coding: Two-Layered Hierarchical Coding Scheme

The data analysis was done in multiple iterations. During the initial analysis, the third author randomly selected 200 yaks from each location (400 yaks in total) and used the dataset to develop an initial coding scheme. The third author went through the posted messages and conducted open coding [3,10] to categorize various kinds of messages posted on the platform. Our initial coding scheme was built on the yak coding scheme developed by Black et al. [2], but we further refined the coding scheme as we analyzed our yak data.

After developing the first round coding scheme, the first and fourth authors again refined the coding categories and finalized the coding scheme by conducting open and axial coding [3,10] on the 200 most up-voted and the 200 most down-voted yaks from each data collection site (800 yaks in total). Then the researchers revisited the dataset and annotated the collected yaks with the finalized thematic codes to develop fuller understandings of various kinds of message posting behaviors. While many yaks were expressed in social networking lingo and slangs foreign to the first author, the fourth author who is a 24-year old undergraduate student was able to translate most of the yaks into common English.

The final coding scheme consisted of 20 top-level categories and 51 second-level categories. The authors used *affinity diagramming* [4] to organize and visualize the coded data.

2.3   Thread Structure Analysis

For clarification, we first define the terms used in the analysis:

- Yak: a social media message posted on Yik Yak
- Thread: a combined group of messages containing an original yak post and the replies to it
- Thread Length: number of replies +1 (original yak post)
- Frequency: a count of threads that have the same length

As a means to understand the yak posting behaviors of users, we analyzed the structures of yak threads (Fig. 1). The first step was to examine the frequency of threads by grouping them based on their lengths, and then counting the number of threads in each length group. It provided us a general idea of the size of communications in the Yik Yak community. The second step was to identify the number of unique participants in the threads. Understanding the average number of unique participants in threads, which have different lengths between 1 (i.e., the original poster—OP—only posted a single yak) and 102 (i.e., many communications by multiple participants), may give us insights into whether a thread was dominated by just a handful of participating users, or by many. Based on this analysis, we have developed a metric, *Participant Diversity*, as shown below:

Participant Diversity = number of unique participants in a thread/thread length

This metric is an indicator which shows how many diverse users are participating in a thread relative to the number of yak communications occurring in the thread (Fig. 1(c)).

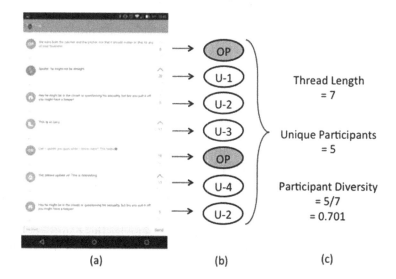

Fig. 1. Yik Yak thread: (a) an example Yik Yak thread on a smartphone GUI; (b) extracted users of posted yaks and replies; and (c) metrics for thread structures.

3   Findings

3.1   Primary Codes

This section describes 20 primary codes, lists our rationales for creating the codes, and presents illustrative examples. In addition, by providing and discussing sample yaks, we highlight Yik Yak usage patterns that weren't previously reported.

Sex. Black et al. used "dating/sex/sexuality" to code posts that "explicitly mention sex, sexual fantasies/urges, and romantic relationships with a partner [2]." However, while analyzing our yak data, we noticed that many yaks mention friendships and relationships without showing clear romantic intent. For that reason, we dedicated "sex" to denote posts that either explicitly mention sex and sexual intent or at least show unequivocal sexual innuendo. For instance, the fourth author identified *"any ladies want their cat ate?"* not as "consuming cat meat", but as "finding casual sex partners." Fourteen percent of our yak data belonged to this category.

Friendship/Partnership/Dating. There were as many yaks that mentioned relationships without direct reference to sex as there were yaks that mentioned sexual relationships. For instance, we coded *"I want company while i do homework...ugh"* and *"I need to find some people to play online with on the Xbox one because I have no friends"* under this category. Sometimes the distinction between this category and **Sex** wasn't as clear. We thought, for example, *"Roommate's leaving this weekend, any ladies want to come through later"* could possibly be implying sex. Yet when we did not see any direct evidence to put yaks under **Sex**, we put them under this category.

Threats/Crimes. Even though threats of sex and hate crimes made on Yik Yak including a mass shooting threat and revenge pornography circulations have been previously reported [9], Black et al.'s coding scheme did not include a code for categorizing such crimes. We devised this category and a **Hate Speech** category to mark posts that show intent to inflict harm on others or posts that mention illegal/criminal activities with the exception of drug consumption. Drug related posts were coded under **Drug**. Although we did not expect/hope to see any posts coded under this category in our dataset, we had to create this code because we believed that even one criminal activity related post was too critical to overlook.

In our dataset, we ended up coding three posts under this category. The first post described a rape incident or a possible rape attempt. A user posted *"I liked this guy and thought he was so cool until he forced me to have sex"* and received three down-votes. Another post mentioned bartering sex for homework. The last one stated, *"If I was a serial killer I'd pretend to be willing to suck dick on yik yak and then shoot you when we meet up. Or I'd just give you my AIDS."*

While! we hoped this statement was a hypothetical one which was meant to warn users not to engage in certain activities, we coded the post under this category.

Hate Speech. We used this code to categorize posts that include racist, sexist, and xenophobic statements or comments. While some number of yaks that we collected from Virginia State University, an HBCU (Historically Black College and University), contained variations of an ethnic slur directed at African Americans, the fourth author who is himself African American mentioned that the use of this term in some of the posts should not be seen as racist. For instance, we coded *"Thou Shall Not Throw Shade If Thou Can Not Throw Hands .. - Niggalations 17:38"* under **Humor/Joke/Rapping** instead of **Hate speech**.

Drug. This category includes posts that reference illegal drugs. Unlike Black et al. [2] who used "Drug/Alcohol" to code both illegal drugs and legal intoxicants such as alcohol. We dedicated this category to identify posts that mention illegal drugs such as marijuana, and coded posts that mention alcohol consumption under *Food, Sports and Life*.

Profanity/Obscenity. Some posts included obscenities and profanities. However, most yaks that contained generally considered offensive and vulgar terms such as 'fuck' and 'shit' used these terms to decorate sentences and convey nuances instead of communicate literal meanings of the words. In such cases, we coded these posts under other categories that are contextually more appropriate. For instance, the post *"When you're new to Yik Yak and are wondering what the fuck you've gotten yourself into..."* was coded under *Yik Yak Related* instead of *Profanity/Obscenity*, while "Yall bitches aint shit !" got coded under this category.

Information Sharing. To the authors' surprise, a good number of yak posts contained informational contents. For instance, a yak collected on 03/18/2016 at VSU was used to announce an official school-wide event (*Town Hall meeting at 3:30 in Foster*), and a yak collected at LSU on 4/11/2016 was used to inform the availability of exam grades (*PSA: Hopkins exam 3 grades are posted*). Although we do not have direct evidence to show why users decided to use Yik Yak to post such messages instead of using non-anonymous platforms (e.g., Twitter or Facebook), nor do we know if users posted the same messages on multiple platforms including non-anonymous ones, it would be plausible to conjecture that this kind of yak posting behavior is motivated by the location-based posting mechanism Yik Yak provides. The platform is both anonymous and location-based, and the location-based postings might be a convenient way to guarantee that the messages would be seen by the target community regardless of the anonymity. In such cases, Yik Yak is not so different from the traditional flyer boards that can be easily found on most US University campuses.

Information Seeking. While analyzing our data, we also found that a greater number of yaks was used to query information (9%) rather than announce or broadcast informational messages (2%). This category included posts such as *"What time cookout close?"* or *"need a job that pays well :(the struggle is real. If y'all know anything that's hiring please let me know."*

As we just mentioned, questions such as *"is there a good hair salon for natural hair around here?"* can be viewed as a post is motivated by location-based nature of Yik Yak rather than by its anonymity. However, we also think that there were questions that users might deem more appropriate to ask anonymously. While the question, *"Easiest art gen ed for engineer majors?"* is very location relevant, users might not want to ask such question on non-anonymous platforms since it might give other people an impression about the message poster being a person who only wants to take the easiest class, and therefore academically less motivated.

Identity Sharing. A common perception about using other people's names on anonymous sites, whether names are real or fictitious, is that the use of these names is to bully other people as Black et al. previously noted [2]. Yet, while coding our data, we noticed that some Yik Yak users chose to reveal their own identities or left trails that could lead someone to identify them. Many yaks included either inquiries about other users' online IDs for different social media platforms/instant messengers, or included statements (either in yaks or in replies) revealing their own online IDs. Multiple yaks asked other users' Kik[3] IDs, and users voluntarily shared what seemed to be their Kik IDs on Yik Yak. For instance, as a response to a post, *"GF applications? Kik me! (Kik inside)"* one user replied *"My kik is ******"*—the actual ID used in this reply is anonymized by the researchers. We have no way of knowing if what looked like a Kik ID in this reply was one's own, somebody else's, real or fake. We have no way of knowing whether the original poster of the yak had actually intended to solicit other users Kik IDs or just posted the yak as a joke. However, the fact that some Yik Yak users do mention and/or are willing to share what look like online IDs, on Yik Yak, an anonymous platform, is noteworthy.

Seeing users of one anonymous platform (Yik Yak) sharing their online identities from another, more or less anonymous platform was quite unexpected. And realizing that the IDs shared on Yik Yak were mostly for one-on-one chat/video chat applications such as Snap Chat, Glide and Kik was even more surprising. While any social media platform accounts can be created with pseudo-identities, users sharing non-anonymous platform IDs on an anonymous platform is a type of behavior that warrants further investigation.

In addition, based on the evidences we saw on multiple yaks, we think it is safe to assume that at least some number of Yik Yak users do use the application to connect to others online, and possibly, in some cases, to meet with other

---

[3] Kik is a mobile instant messenger application which can be used anonymously since the application does not require users to associate their actual phone numbers to the accounts.

users offline. Since Yik Yak users are all located in close proximity, it is more possible for Yik Yak users, as compared to other online platform users, to take online interactions offline, and meet with other users in person. This is also a type of behavior that requires further exploration.

Personal Experience. We coded posts that describe personal experiences or tell personal stories under this category.

Expressing Emotion. Posts that express one's current state of mind and feelings such as anger, loneliness, stress, boredom, despair, and gratitude were coded under this category.

Campus Life. This is another code that we borrowed from Black et al. [2]. Black et al. used this code to denote school-related postings. However, unlike Black et al. who used to the code, **Greek** to mark fraternity/sorority related postings, we included course-related, grade-related, and campus-life related postings as well as fraternity/sorority related postings under this category.

Food, Sports and Life. We used this category to capture postings that mention events, objects and sentiments related to everyday lives except school-related ones.

Pop Culture. Posts that mention issues, events, products, or ideas related to pop culture.

Humor, Joke and Rapping. This category included explicit jokes and funny stories. We had a post that sounded very much like "rapping." The post said *"We living two to a dorm, ain't out of the norm, got noodles and oddles, AKAs and Poodles, swipes at the door, but wait there's more ... ,"* and we decided to categorize the post under this category. Hence we named this category **Humor, Joke & Rapping**.

Yik Yak Related. Some number of posts directly mentioned Yik Yak. Soliciting up-votes was the most common in this Yik Yak related. For instance, we coded posts such as *"Story time! 10 upvotes and I'll post story #4!!"* under this category.

Religious Statements. Biblical and religious posts were coded under this category.

Political Statements. Yaks that include political statements or references to any political issues and events were put under this code. Activists' statements such as anti-racism, anti-sexism, feminist, anti-drug and remarks that showed political consciousness were also coded under this category.

Announcement. We borrowed this category from Black et al. They defined this category to include "posts that are making a statement or imparting information or wisdom. This category included posts that were not able to be contextually understood or otherwise categorized [2]".

Not Codeable. Some yaks were not at all decipherable. Whenever we could not understand the meanings of yaks, we put them under this category instead of **Announcement**.

As shown in Fig. 2, **Announcement** was the largest code covering 21% of collected yaks, followed by **Sex** (14%), **Expressing Emotion** (13%), **Friendship/Partnership/Dating** (12%), **Information Seeking** (9%), **Campus Life** (8%) and **Trading** (5%). The remaining 14 categories consisted of less than 20% of the data. (1.5% of yaks belonged to **Drug**, **Threats/Crimes** and **Hate Speech** were 0.75 % and 0.25% respectively.)

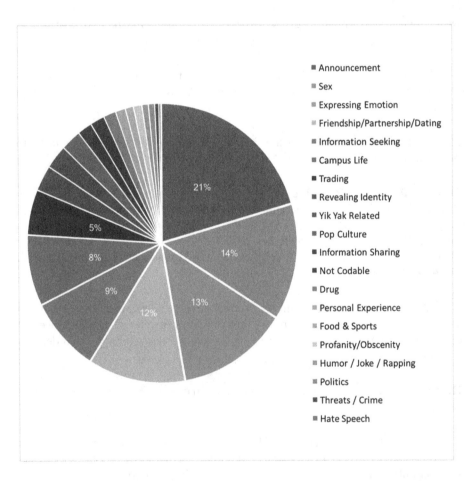

Fig. 2. Relative frequency of primary codes

3.2   Thread Structure Analysis

Figure 3 illustrates the Power-Law distribution between lengths of threads and their frequencies, which is not unusual in any online communities. For example, there were 1,915 cases of threads that had length = 1 in our dataset, which means that only the original poster (OP) posted a yak and did not receive any replies. However, there were only 2 threads which had a large length of 102.

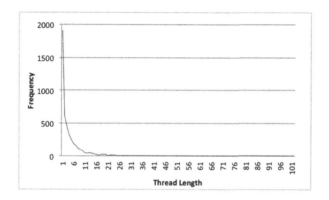

Fig. 3. Frequency of threads by thread lengths

In social media platforms and online communities, having diverse participants in discussion threads might be essential for the sustainability of the community, considering that new ideas and information can be shared in the community from contributions of different people with a broad range of ideas. To understand such user participation behavior in Yik Yak threads, we computed the average number of unique participants, who had been identified from threads with varying lengths as shown in Fig. 4. On average, there were 4.52 unique participants in discussion threads, and the standard deviation was 1.14. In the case of missing values (e.g., there were no threads with length 63), we simply used a mean value between existing values (i.e., average participants in threads with lengths 62 and 64) to connect the graph line.

Figure 5 illustrates average Participant Relevant Diversity by lengths of threads. It conveys how many unique participants contributed in a yak thread relative to the number of yaks and replies in the thread (See Sect. 2.3). The 'elbow' of the graph is found around Thread Length = 13, and the graph is continuously decreasing except for slight ripples around Thread Lengths 45 and 49. In a sense, this graph is another interpretation showing that the number of unique participants in yak threads is not increasing as much as the length of threads increases. Thus, the finding is that long yak threads are the results of frequent communication among a small group of participants in the thread in general.

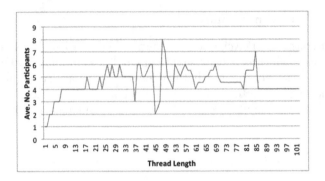

Fig. 4. Average number of participants by thread lengths

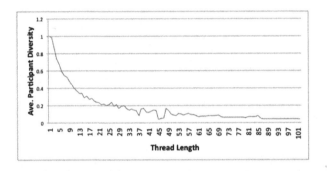

Fig. 5. Average Participant Relevant Diversity by thread lengths

4   Discussion and Conclusion

A few points stood out when we analyzed our dataset. **"Sex"** and **"Friendship /Partnership/Dating,"** two codes that we used to mark yaks that mention relationships, both sexual or non-sexual, made up more than one quarter of our yak data. Some users posted yaks that included very private, sexual statements. Some posted yaks to seek such relationships. Some posted yaks to find people to just hang around with. Another 13% of the yaks were marked as **Expressing Emotion**, under which yaks that expressed and revealed very personal feelings and emotions were coded. Some even shared their own personal stories (i.e., **Personal Experience**). By looking at these yaks, we could not help but think that maybe these users, college students, are in need of connecting to other people, *real people*.

Conforming to common preconception, there existed yaks that included offensive and vulgar language as well as the ones that mention and describe criminal activities. Yet these were only a fraction of the yaks we analyzed. We do not despise the invention of paper even though paper has been used to print pornographic materials. Following the same logic, we believe that misusage of Yik Yak should not be the reason to stigmatize the platform nor the users. As we have seen in our dataset, many yaks were used to deliver informational contents, and in some cases, users might feel more comfortable posting their messages anonymously regardless of the language used in the post.

From the point of structural analysis, we found that 4.52 participants on average contributed to threads that had lengths between 1 and 102. This tells us that even for long threads (e.g., length = 102), only a handful of people (e.g., 4) participated in the thread by communicating with each other using multiple yaks and replies. Although the idea might be far-fetched, we surmise that this phenomenon might be telling us that the most effective size of a voluntary and interest-based online gathering, where its members can communicate with each other comfortably, is approximately 4–5.

Limitations in this study include the following factors:

- (1) The data collection was conducted only from two locations—VSU and LSU. Although we collected yak data over a four-month period, and gathered over 5,000 yaks, we cannot say our dataset represents the entire Yik Yak community. This limits us from building a general understanding of user behaviors occurring in the broader Yik Yak community.
- (2) In addition to (1), we ended up coding only a small portion of the collected data (800 coded vs. 5,437 collected). This further limits our ability to understand overall Yik Yak users' behaviors.
- (3) In some cases, we had to try to infer the meanings of the postings. Many yak messages included slang, emoticons and pictures. Some of these yaks were not easily understood by the authors. In order to code such texts, we consulted just one undergraduate student, the fourth author of this paper. Therefore our coding depended on one person's interpretation of the yaks, and we weren't able to measure inter-rater reliability (There was only one rater).
- (4) Each code was applied to yaks in a mutually exclusive manner. That is, when we assigned a code to one yak, we were not able to add second and third codes. However, in many cases, putting a yak into just one category seemed limiting. If we had chosen to allow applying multiple codes to a single yak—as if we are to assigning tags to yaks instead of acting as if we were putting yaks into different folders—the results might have been drastically different.

References

1. Ablow, K.: Psychiatrist's view: Yik Yak is most dangerous app. I've ever seen, May 2014. http://www.foxnews.com/opinion/2014/05/09/psychiatrist-view-yik-yak-is-most-dangerous-app-ive-ever-seen.html
2. Black, E.W., Mezzina, K., Thompson, L.A.: Anonymous social media - understanding the content and context of Yik Yak. Comput. Hum. Behav. **57**(C), 17–22 (2016)
3. Corbin, J., Strauss, A.: Basics of Qualitative Research: Techniques and Procedures for Developing Grounded Theory. Sage Publications Inc., Thousand Oaks (2008)

4. Hanington, B., Martin, B.: Universal Methods of Design: 100 Ways to Research Complex Problems, Develop Innovative Ideas, and Design Effective Solution. Rockport Publishers, Beverly (2012)
5. Mahler, J.: Who spewed that abuse? anonymous Yik Yak App. Isn't telling, March 2015. https://www.nytimes.com/2015/03/09/technology/popular-yik-yak-app-confers-anonymity-and-delivers-abuse.html
6. McKenzie, G., Adams, B., Janowicz, K.: Of oxen and birds: is Yik Yak a useful new data source in the geosocial zoo or just another Twitter? In: Proceedings of the 8th ACM SIGSPATIAL International Workshop on Location-Based Social Networks, LBSN 2015, pp. 4:1–4:4, NY, USA (2015). http://doi.acm.org/10.1145/2830657.2830659
7. Miller, J.R.: Messaging app. Yik Yak causing bullying concerns at some schools (April 2014). http://www.foxnews.com/tech/2014/04/28/messaging-app-yik-yak-causing-bullying-concerns-at-some-schools.html
8. Northcut, K.M.: Dark side or insight? Yik Yak and culture on campus. In: Proceedings of Professional Communication Conference (IPCC), IEEE International (2015)
9. Parkinson, H.J.: Yik Yak: the anonymous app. Taking US college campuses by storm, October 2014. https://www.theguardian.com/technology/2014/oct/21/yik-yak-anonymous-app-college-campus-whisper-secret
10. Saldana, J.: The Coding Manual for Qualitative Researchers, 3rd edn. SAGE Publications Ltd., London (2015)
11. Saveski, M., Chou, S., Roy, D.: Tracking the Yak: an empirical study of Yik Yak. In: Proceedings of the 10th International AAAI Conference on Web and Social Media (ICWSM 2016) (2015)
12. Wagstaff, K.: What Is Yik Yak, and Why do college students love it so much?, November 2015. http://www.nbcnews.com/tech/mobile/what-yik-yak-why-do-college-students-love-it-so-n461471

BLE-Based Children's Social Behavior Analysis System for Crime Prevention

Shuta Nakamae$^{(\boxtimes)}$, Shumpei Kataoka, Can Tang, Yue Pu, Simona Vasilache, Satoshi Saga, Buntarou Shizuki, and Shin Takahashi

University of Tsukuba, Tsukuba, Japan
{nakamae,shizuki}@iplab.cs.tsukuba.ac.jp, kataoka@adapt.cs.tsukuba.ac.jp, tangcan@padc.cs.tsukuba.ac.jp, pu@cavelab.cs.tsukuba.ac.jp, {simona,saga,shin}@cs.tsukuba.ac.jp

Abstract. We propose an IoT-based children's behavior analysis system for crime prevention, aimed at infants and elementary school students. The system logs children's behavior with accelerometers and Bluetooth low energy (BLE). We conducted a preliminary experiment with a test application to examine whether BLE-based ID logs can be used to analyze daily social behaviors, such as how a child spent the day with his or her friends. The results suggest that the history of behavior with a child's friends was acquired accurately. Furthermore, the system could detect the period when the user (that is, a child) was with friends or not, and what kind of activity (for example, walking or staying in one place) the user was involved in.

Keywords: Bluetooth low energy · Activity log · Crime prevention · Wireless communication · Wearable device · Data visualization

1 Introduction

In Japan, most kidnappings of infants and elementary school students occur when the children are alone [9]. To address this issue, numerous tools and systems have been developed by companies for crime prevention. However, these methods exhibit various problems, such as battery consumption and large device size. For example, a crime preventing tool "Amber Alert GPS Locator" developed by "Amber Alert" [1] can track the children and can send emergency alerts to their parents. However, the system can only run for 40 h, because it acquires a global positioning system (GPS) signal and this drains the battery.

To solve these problems, we propose an IoT-based children's behavior analysis system for crime prevention, aimed at infants and elementary school students. The system logs children's behavior with accelerometers and Bluetooth low energy (BLE). The use of accelerometer logs allows the user (for example, parents) to analyze the child's behavior in a single device scenario. Furthermore, it allows the user to analyze children's social behavior, such as, whether the child' friends are nearby or not in a multiple device scenario, which enhances

© Springer International Publishing AG 2017
G. Meiselwitz (Ed.): SCSM 2017, Part II, LNCS 10283, pp. 429–439, 2017.
DOI: 10.1007/978-3-319-58562-8_33

analysis. Our system uses BLE instead of GPS; therefore, it has effective battery conservation and can be used both indoors and outdoors. Moreover, the size of the battery and thus the system can be reduced when necessary. In addition, our system does not require special operation by the child.

In the following sections, we first explain the design of our system, which consists of the child's device, the parents' application, and an analysis server. Next, we describe the two experiments conducted in support of our research. We developed and executed a test application to examine whether BLE-based ID logs can be used to analyze daily social behaviors, such as how a child spent the day with his or her friends. We then implemented the system and conducted another experiment to demonstrate its capabilities in terms of detecting friends nearby the user (a child) and activity recognition. Finally, we present our future work and conclusions.

2   Related Work

Local governments and various companies have worked on the prevention of incidents such as kidnapping. Local governments employ police and volunteers to keep children secure when going to school and returning home. In addition, companies have developed various crime prevention tools, one such major tool being a personal alarm. IoT-based crime-prevention tools have been increasingly used for protecting children; for example, GPS [1], classic Bluetooth [3,12], and other communication channel-based tools have been developed.

Several systems have been developed that record the user's activities for analysis. Tsubouchi et al. [10] proposed a system that uses step information acquired from a pedometer to detect working relationships, and which can automatically write organization profiles at a low cost. Ellis et al. [4] presented a health log system for adults based on physical activity recognition using multiple wearable sensors. Zeni et al. [11] developed a method to collect the user's personal information from smartphone-integrated sensors and wearable devices. While these systems focus mainly on adults, our system focuses on children.

Various works have also focused on the location of the user. Zheng et al. [13] proposed an approach based on supervised learning to infer people's motion from their GPS logs. Their method uses common-sense constraints of the real world and typical user behavior in addition to GPS logs. Mizuno et al. [7] presented a system that tracks the user's position, which is considered to be related to the user's activity. Our system uses BLE information rather than the specific position.

In addition to GPS, which is a specialized system for position tracking, Bluetooth has attracted attention as a method of behavior tracking and activity logs; thus, many attempts at using only Bluetooth have also been undertaken. For example, Chang et al. [2] proposed a system that uses Bluetooth tags and beacons to reconstruct the user's route and uses the information to improve the user's experience.

Nishide et al. [8] used the detection history of classic Bluetooth devices to analyze a single user's behavior. Katevas et al. [6] presented a system that is able to detect dynamic groups by combining the estimated distance between people using Bluetooth data with motion activity classification. In particular, this method can estimate the stationary versus moving status of each user to detect the group's state.

Many studies in this field have been conducted using BLE, a new standard of Bluetooth with the feature of high battery conservation, in contrast to classic Bluetooth with its high energy consumption. In crowd-sensing applications, using smartphones as the main source of sensor data is difficult because of the need for downloading and installing applications, and the added burden of energy consumption. Jamil et al. [5] proposed a novel hybrid participatory sensing approach to capture large group dynamics by distributing a large number of BLE tags and smartphones to the group members. They performed a large experimental deployment with 600 tags and 10 smartphones, which was conducted during the Hajj, to prove that the approach was effective. Our approach makes use of BLE for the detection history of Bluetooth devices and their social relation, in order to analyze the child's and his or her friends' behavior.

3 System Description

Our system, as shown in Fig. 1, consists of small BLE devices for children (child's device), a smartphone application for the parents (parent's application), and an analysis server.

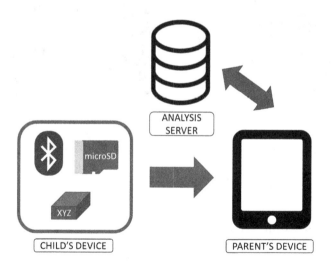

Fig. 1. System components

3.1   Child's Device

The child's device (Fig. 2) continuously reads and sends IDs via BLE. We designed the device in such a way that a child is able to carry it in his or her bag. It consists of a microcontroller (Switch Science mbed TY51822r3), an SD card as internal storage, a 3 dimensional accelerometer (Analog Devices ADXL345), and an LED. The size of the device is $4.8 \times 4.5 \times 1.4$ cm and it weighs approximately 24 g, without the battery. Various batteries can be connected to the child's device (we used two AA batteries in our experiments). The case of the device is printed using a fused deposition modeling 3D printer. The device reads IDs sent by other Bluetooth devices, including those of the child's friends. The IDs and acceleration are stored as a log in the internal storage of the device. The device also sends out its own ID to be received by other children's devices. The IDs and relationships are registered to our system's server beforehand, and the values obtained are saved to the internal storage. The LED is used for indicating the operation status of the device.

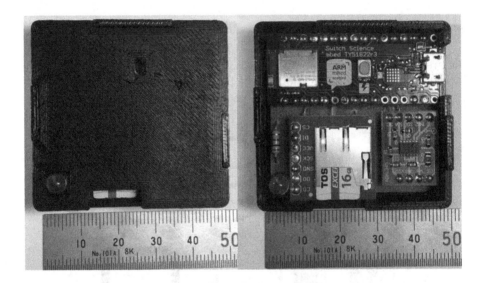

Fig. 2. Child's device (left) and inside of child's device (right)

3.2   Parent's Application

When a child returns home with their device, his or her parents connect the SD card of the device to their smartphone or tablet, and transfer the saved log to the parent's application. The parent's application has functions for visualizing the periods when the child was alone (alone periods), and for communication with the analysis server for the visualization.

In order to reduce the operational burden of checking the child's alone period, we implemented two functions in the application. The first function, namely the

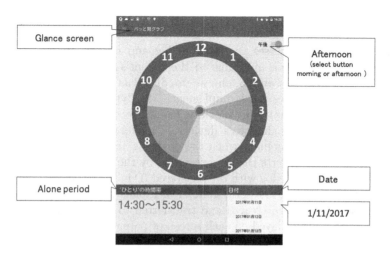

Fig. 3. Screenshot of glance screen

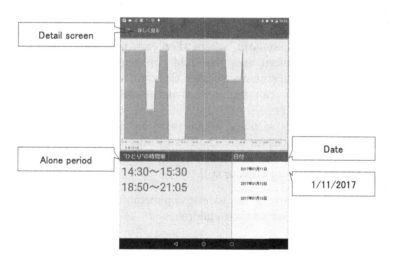

Fig. 4. Screenshot of detail screen

glance screen, displays the alone period in a simple manner (Fig. 3), where the user can check the alone period in hourly units. The purpose of this screen is to enable the parent to easily understand the alone period and reduce the burden of the parent's operation. The second function, namely the detail screen, displays the number of friends nearby in detail (Fig. 4). In each function, the user can select the item of the date they wish to view from the date column.

3.3 Analysis Server

The analysis server processes the received log and returns the total number of nearby friends per time unit time to the parent's application. The process operates as a daemon on CentOS, and we use SFTP as the transferring protocol. The following data processing is implemented in Python. Because the child's device does not have a hardware clock, it cannot record the global time when the device detects other children's devices. Therefore, the device records the time, starting with the moment when the device is activated. When the server receives the data, it converts the data recorded by the child's device into global time. Thereafter, only the log with the registered ID in the friend list is extracted as data from the log, and the total number of friends is collected for each time unit. The daily results are created and transferred to the parent's application, and the data can be displayed on each screen of parent's application.

3.4 System Scenario

Our system can be used in two scenarios: a single and multiple device scenario, as shown in Fig. 5.

- In the single device scenario, where there are no child's friends' devices in proximity, the system uses the child's movement, as analyzed by the accelerometer log, to estimate whether the child was walking or not. From these logs, the parents can determine that the child was alone, and walking or staying in one place.
- In the multiple device scenario, where there are one or more of the child's friends' devices, the system uses the IDs to estimate whether the child was near his or her friends, and also uses the child's movement to estimate whether the child was walking or staying still.

By using the system, parents can identify opportunities to provide crime prevention behavior education to their children.

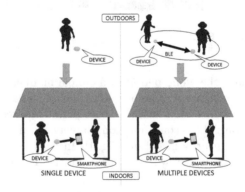

Fig. 5. Single device scenario (left) and multiple device scenario (right)

4   Preliminary Experiment

Before developing the system described in Sect. 3, we conducted a preliminary experiment to determine whether BLE-based ID logs can be used to analyze daily social behaviors, such as how a child spent the day with his or her friends. To do this, we developed a test application for an Android smartphone or tablet, which simultaneously sends and receives a BLE signal as a service, as long as the device is powered on. A total of 24 volunteers from our university, who formed teams of four to five members per team, participated in the experiment. We explained informed consent (based on the ethical guidelines of the University of Tsukuba) to all subjects and obtained their consent. We requested them to use the devices for two weeks during their school days.

Figure 6 shows the number of IDs detected by a participant's device according to time. Participants performed group work throughout the two weeks. By observing the number of IDs, we could estimate that the group work started at approximately 09:30 and ended at approximately 19:00. We could also determine that the participants had lunch with their team at approximately 13:30, because at this time there were no other friends nearby apart from members of the same team. We could furthermore observe that the participants were alone before and after the group work. In summary, the results show that by analyzing the logs of relations between people using BLE, it is possible to understand the user's activity to an extent.

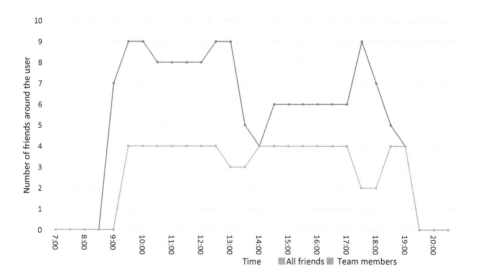

Fig. 6. Log of a day, which represents friends detected by the device of a participant

5   Experiment

As mentioned previously, the results of our preliminary experiment show that a user's activity can be estimated from the log acquired by analyzing the Bluetooth IDs near the user. However, in the experiment, the system was implemented on an Android device (smartphone or tablet); thus, it was not suitable to be held by children. For this reason, we developed the child's device which is described in Sect. 3.1, achieving downsizing and hardware robustness.

We conducted a three-day experiment using the developed device. The participants in this experiment were four male graduate students, 22 to 25 years old. They all carried a child's device during the experiment and went about their usual daily life. Since these participants were in the same research group, they spent most of their time together. After returning home, they checked the results with the parent's application. Furthermore, during the experiment, each participant recorded the names of all their friends (participants in the experiment) who were nearby in their notes every time the number of friends changed.

As an example of the results, Fig. 7 shows the number of friends nearby participant P0, which includes the number as determined by the analysis server and that recorded by the participant himself. As shown in the graph, these numbers agree. This result suggests that the system can correctly detect the period when the user is with friends or alone.

Figure 8 shows a graph representing the average acceleration per minute of P0. The graph also shows the number of friends analyzed by the system (the same data as shown in Fig. 7). We found three characteristic sections (1, 2, and 3) in Fig. 8, and interviewed P0 regarding his activities on the given day to examine the three findings.

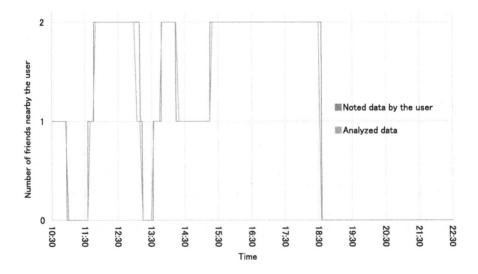

Fig. 7. Friends nearby P0 in a day

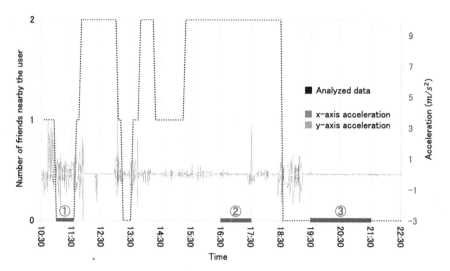

Fig. 8. Graph of the analyzed data and average acceleration per minute

1. P0 was alone between 10:50 and 11:30. However, during this period, the acceleration changed rapidly; therefore, we estimated that he was walking or running alone. P0's comments support this, as he stated that he was walking alone during this time.
2. P0 was not alone between 16:30 and 17:30. We can see there is no significant movement; therefore, we estimated that P0 was not moving. P0 confirmed this by stating that he was working at a desk with his friends during this time.
3. P0 was alone between 19:30 and 21:30. We can see that there is no significant change in the recorded acceleration; therefore, we estimated that P0 was not moving. P0 stated that he was studying alone.

We observe that we can estimate the type of activity the user was involved in by using the Bluetooth IDs and accelerometer logs. Moreover, if we simultaneously log the activity of the accelerometer, we can estimate the user's activity more precisely.

6   Future Work

We observed several problems during the experiments. In our current implementation, the user has to remove the SD card from the child's device each time they wish to transfer the saved log from the device to the parent's application, which is time consuming and troublesome. In future, we plan to enable the system to transfer data wirelessly. Moreover, because our experiment was conducted with graduate students, the logs of their daily lives show different activities to the usual activity of children. In the near future, we plan to conduct an experiment with families who have children. This will allow us to collect various data (including questionnaires) and present the log data to the parents in order to examine our design of the parent's application. Based on this new data, we plan to implement improvements to system.

7   Conclusions

In this paper, we have presented a system employing BLE and an accelerometer to analyze the social behavior of children in order to prevent crimes such as kidnapping. The results of our preliminary experiment show that using a BLE log enabled us to determine how the participant spent the day with his friends. Therefore, we implemented a child's device with BLE and an accelerometer. We conducted an experiment using our prototype of the child's device, and it was found that behavior history with the user's friends was obtained accurately. Furthermore, the system could detect periods when the user was with friends or alone, as well as what type of activity (for example, walking or standing still) he or she was involved in. The system could recognize multiple activities in both the single device and multiple device scenario. In the future, we plan to enable the system transfer data wirelessly. In addition, we plan to conduct an experiment using actual families with children.

Acknowledgement. This work was supported in part by JSPS KAKENHI, grant numbers 16K00265 (Grant-in-Aid for Scientific Research (C)) and 16H02853 (Grant-in-Aid for Scientific Research (B)).

References

1. Amber Alert: Amber Alert GPS Locator. http://www.amberalertgps.com/. Accessed 21 Oct 2016
2. Chang, C.M., Li, S.C., Huang, Y.: Crowdsensing route reconstruction using portable bluetooth beacon-based two-way network. In: Proceedings of the 2016 ACM International Joint Conference on Pervasive and Ubiquitous Computing: Adjunct, UbiComp 2016, pp. 265–268. ACM, New York (2016). http://doi.acm.org/10.1145/2968219.2971361
3. Chen, Z., Chen, Y., Hu, L., Wang, S., Jiang, X., Ma, X., Lane, N.D., Campbell, A.T.: ContextSense: unobtrusive discovery of incremental social context using dynamic Bluetooth data. In: Proceedings of the 2014 ACM International Joint Conference on Pervasive and Ubiquitous Computing: Adjunct Publication, UbiComp 2014 Adjunct, pp. 23–26. ACM, New York (2014). http://doi.acm.org/10.1145/2638728.2638801
4. Ellis, K., Kerr, J., Godbole, S., Lanckriet, G.: Multi-sensor physical activity recognition in free-living. In: Proceedings of the 2014 ACM International Joint Conference on Pervasive and Ubiquitous Computing: Adjunct Publication, UbiComp 2014 Adjunct, pp. 431–440. ACM, New York (2014). http://doi.acm.org/10.1145/2638728.2641673
5. Jamil, S., Basalamah, A., Lbath, A., Youssef, M.: Hybrid participatory sensing for analyzing group dynamics in the largest annual religious gathering. In: Proceedings of the 2015 ACM International Joint Conference on Pervasive and Ubiquitous Computing, UbiComp 2015, pp. 547–558. ACM, New York (2015). http://doi.acm.org/10.1145/2750858.2807548

6. Katevas, K., Haddadi, H., Tokarchuk, L., Clegg, R.G.: Detecting group formations using iBeacon technology. In: Proceedings of the 2016 ACM International Joint Conference on Pervasive and Ubiquitous Computing: Adjunct, UbiComp 2016, pp. 742–752, ACM, New York (2016). http://doi.acm.org/10.1145/2968219.2968281

7. Mizuno, H., Sasaki, K., Hosaka, H.: Indoor-outdoor positioning and lifelog experiment with mobile phones. In: Proceedings of the 2007 Workshop on Multimodal Interfaces in Semantic Interaction, WMISI 2007, pp. 55–57. ACM, New York (2007). http://doi.acm.org/10.1145/1330572.1330582

8. Nishide, R., Ushiokoshi, T., Nakamura, S., Kono, Y.: Detecting social contexts from Bluetooth device logs. In: Supplemental Proceedings of Ubicomp, pp. 228–230 (2009)

9. Saitama Prefectural Police: Approaching incidents to children bysuspiciousperson (2016). (In Japanese). https://www.police.pref.saitama.lg.jp/c0020/kurashi/documents/koekakeh27cyu.pdf, https://www.police.pref.saitama.lg.jp/. Accessed 28 Oct 2016

10. Tsubouchi, K., Kawajiri, R., Shimosaka, M.: Working-relationship detection from fitbit sensor data. In: Proceedings of the 2013 ACM Conference on Pervasive and Ubiquitous Computing Adjunct Publication, UbiComp 2013 Adjunct, pp. 115–118. ACM, New York (2013). http://doi.acm.org/10.1145/2494091.2494123

11. Zeni, M., Zaihrayeu, I., Giunchiglia, F.: Multi-device activity logging. In: Proceedings of the 2014 ACM International Joint Conference on Pervasive and Ubiquitous Computing: Adjunct Publication, UbiComp 2014 Adjunct, pp. 299–302. ACM, New York (2014). http://doi.acm.org/10.1145/2638728.2638756

12. Zhang, Y., Martikainen, O., Pulli, P., Naumov, V.: Real-time process data acquisition with Bluetooth. In: Proceedings of the 4th International Symposium on Applied Sciences in Biomedical and Communication Technologies, ISABEL 2011, pp. 21:1–21:5. ACM, New York (2011). http://doi.acm.org/10.1145/2093698.2093719

13. Zheng, Y., Li, Q., Chen, Y., Xie, X., Ma, W.Y.: Understanding mobility based on GPS data. In: Proceedings of the 10th International Conference on Ubiquitous Computing, UbiComp 2008, pp. 312–321. ACM, New York (2008). http://doi.acm.org/10.1145/1409635.1409677

Unified Structured Framework for mHealth Analytics: Building an Open and Collaborative Community

Hoang D. Nguyen[(✉)] and Danny Chiang Choon Poo

Department of Information Systems,
National University of Singapore, Singapore, Singapore
{hoangnguyen, dpoo}@comp.nus.edu.sg

Abstract. Mobile health (mHealth) is going through a massive growth spurt that would promisingly transform healthcare delivery for a huge number of patients. The key to unlocking the full potential of mHealth is data analytics which is capable of revealing insights for personalised and just-in-time health interventions. Analysis of mHealth data is uniquely distinguished from conventional health analytics. Hence, this study proposes a Unified Structured Framework for mHealth Analytics (USF-mHA) as an open process model that can be adopted in mHealth apps. With the consideration of data and knowledge management, it provides a standardised guideline for mHealth developers to integrate analytics components with open standards for various stakeholders. Besides, the paper discusses a USF-mHA platform for building an open and collaborative community amongst patients, caregivers, and researchers. The study contributes to the cumulative theoretical development of mHealth analytics and standard methodologies.

Keywords: Mobile health (mHealth) · Data sensors · Data fusion · Health analytics

1 Introduction

The rapid proliferation of mobile and sensing technologies is reshaping healthcare for patients and communities towards improved health outcomes, higher quality of care, and reduced costs of healthcare delivery [1]. Integrated with ubiquitous and versatile wearable devices, mobile health (mHealth) is capable of generating a big amount of real-time, high-frequency, high-volume, and multi-dimensional data to support patients' daily life decisions and activities [2]. mHealth analytics, therefore, is an emerging key to unlocking the full potential of mHealth by translating such data into actionable information and knowledge for timely health interventions [3, 4].

There are over 60,000 mHealth apps in Apple AppStore and Google Play which continually contribute to the health ecosystems [5]. However, the development of mHealth apps has been witnessed as fragmented and siloed hampering healthcare innovations by impeding non-standardised data collection and sharing [6, 7]. Open initiatives in mHealth, hence, have been established to ease the friction among caregivers, patients, and app developers [8]. mHealth data can be collected and exchanged

© Springer International Publishing AG 2017
G. Meiselwitz (Ed.): SCSM 2017, Part II, LNCS 10283, pp. 440–450, 2017.
DOI: 10.1007/978-3-319-58562-8_34

using publicly available and open interfaces for better scientific efficiency and inter-operability; however, there is a dearth of a process model for mHealth analytics in conjunction with the existing standards that can be embedded in the development of mHealth platforms.

In this research, patients are put at the centre of an open and collaborative community where they are connoisseurs about their own health observations; while clinicians and researchers are experts about disease knowledge and sense-making on patients' health data [9]. This paper, therefore, aims to understand the uniqueness of data analytics on mHealth data to provide a principled and practical guidance for mHealth developers. A Unified Structured Framework for mHealth Analytics (USF-mHA) is proposed to translate the complex analytical process into easy-to-follow methodological steps for active and fruitful involvement from patients, caregivers, and researchers. It also encompasses data management and knowledge management as well as various relevant data modelling techniques.

The study contributes to the cumulative theoretical development of mHealth, data analytics and open standards. It has also drawn out some implications for both academic bodies and mHealth developers.

The structure of the paper is as follows. Firstly, we describe the literature review of our study in the next section. Secondly, we highlight the challenges of mobile analytics. And then, the paper presents our proposed framework with detailed methodological steps. Fourthly, building an open and collaborative community to promote the utilisation of mHealth data analytics is discussed. Lastly, we conclude our paper with findings and contributions of the research in the final section.

2   Literature Review

2.1   Mobile Health (mHealth) and Open Initiatives

Today, mobile devices, because of their ubiquitous and dynamic nature, are capable of creating extensive smart care systems to support various medical and public health practice [4, 10]. This is broadly defined as mobile health (mHealth) [11] which employs both mobile and wearable technologies to deliver healthcare to a huge number of people as well as enormous communities. By removing geographical and temporal constraints, mHealth apps have been widely integrated into a variety of healthcare practices such as disease management and prevention [12–14], care surveillance [15–17] and instructional interventions [14, 18].

In 2014, there are 47,883 apps in Apple AppStore and 12,272 apps in Google Play which have been listed under either health & fitness or medical categories [5]. With the significant advantages of usability and mobility [19, 20], mHealth apps are promising to empower patients to take control of their own health observations anytime anywhere. The data from mHealth apps are immensely important for patient-centred care; however, the dissonance of mHealth data across multiple health apps and devices is hindering the full potential of healthcare delivery over mobile phones. Open initiatives, hence, have been established to offer a resourceful approach standardised and agreed upon through collaboration among care providers, and mHealth developers [8]. mHealth data can be collected and exchanged using publicly available and open standards for better scientific efficiency and interoperability.

Contributing to the open initiatives in mHealth, the study is seeking for a process model in conjunction with open mHealth standards that can be embedded in mHealth apps for health analytics.

2.2   Health Analytics

Data mining has been long recognised as a creative process in which the result of the process heavily depends on the right combination of experts and proper tools [21]. Standard approaches such as CRISP-DM (Cross Industry Standard Process for Data Mining) [22] and SEMMA (sample, explore, modify, model, assess) by SAS [23, 24], hence, were proposed to aid stakeholders to achieve the successful outcome of data mining tasks [25]. In healthcare, data mining is used extensively [26] and is an integral part of health analytics. To address the ontological complexity and constraints in medical domain [27], some studies have extended CRISP-DM and SEMMA to systematise the process of health analytics.

A six-step data mining knowledge discovery (DMKD) process model was developed as an extension to CRISP-DM considering the uniqueness of medical data mining [27, 28]. It is a semi-automated process from problem specification to application of the discovered knowledge that requires user inputs throughout the process.

Catley et al. [29] suggested the integration of time series data and data analytics when modelling clinical systems. CRISP-TDM considering temporal data mining (TDM), hence, was presented to conduct dynamic health analytics. Storage of raw data and temporal abstractions was recommended to be referenced in multiple stages of the process model.

A pioneering health analytics (HA) methodology was introduced by Raghupathi and Raghupathi [3] which is known as a manual on "how to do things" in a health analytics project. It encompasses four stages: (i) concept design, (ii) proposal, (iii) methodology, and (iv) presentation and evaluation.

Nonetheless, these DMKD, CRISP-TDM, and HA methodology are prone to common methodological issues. Structured procedural steps, clear objectives and systematical communication strategies on knowledge, data, methods, and results vitally constitute to the success of a health analytics project [30]. Therefore, Ahangama and Poo [31] proposed a novel framework which defines a standardised process model to transform data into actions through systematic analytics and well-structured insights. It emphasises on the completeness, ease of use, consistency and relative advantages of health analytics; thus, is capable of managing and iterating conventional health analytics process as well as eliminating repeating mistakes in well-organized steps. The analytical process on continuous and rapid mobile sensing data, however, is uniquely distinguished from conventional data sources. The data involved in mHealth are typically vital signs or medical stream data which prompt for the needs of a new health analytics process model on continuous, high-frequency, high-volume, and multi-dimensional data streams [29, 32].

The next chapter highlights the uniqueness of mHealth analytics.

3 Challenges of mHealth Analytics

As the ubiquity of sensing and mobile technologies for patient-centred care increase, mHealth analytics is supported by these technologies in health care systems for effective decision making, planning and administration of healthcare and related activities [33]. In the early development of mHealth analytics, we have identified several major challenges of the field as follows.

- **Big Data:** mHealth technologies are capable of continuously and simultaneously collecting diverse individual and environmental data signals to support health decisions [1]. A variety of sensors and their capabilities have been discussed in recent research [34–40]. Unlike conventional data sources such as laboratory data, physician's notes, or interviews [41], mobile sensing data are not only captured at very high sampling rates (e.g., ECG has a sampling rate of 128 Kbps) [42], but also are high-density, high-volume, and multi-dimensional data streams [29]. Besides, aggregating and combining the sensed data from multiple sensors in conjunction with medical and related data stored in dispersed locations (e.g., EMR, paper-based medical reports, etc.) are imperative for better outcomes of mHealth analytics. For the data to be useful, various aspects of big data challenges including volume, velocity and variety need to be addressed.
- **Reliability:** The success of mHealth analytics is susceptible to various data validity issues of mobile sensing technologies [33]. For example, wearable sensors could be slip away or detached due to patient's movements; thus, the measurement data might be interrupted or distorted. In many other scenarios such as excessive thermal effect, bad signal attenuation, low battery life, or conflicts in data/packet delivery [43], the quality of mobile sensing data might be unexpectedly degraded which might lead to inaccurate health recommendations.
- **Real-Time Processing and Analytics:** Data collection in mHealth analytics can happen in real time without the patients having to participate in regular measurement visits [33]. The major challenge is to process and analyse the data in a timely manner, sometimes in real time; therefore, different types of deliverables need to be clearly defined focusing on the process rather than the product of various analytics tasks. The dynamic nature of big data streams prompts for the use of dynamic data processing and data analytics techniques. Furthermore, deployment and reporting of health analytics on mobile streaming data should also be reshaped into a mobile representation for mobility and promptly decision making.
- **Security and Privacy:** In the context of mHealth, privacy, security and confidentiality concerns exist as highly personal information are being transmitted wirelessly [44]. For example, the sensitive location information and physical movements of sensor data (e.g., GPS, accelerometers), which are shared with the analytics team to evaluate and improve physical activity levels, can be exposed by sophisticated reverse-engineering algorithms [45]. It is crucial to conceal personal identifiable information when sharing and allow only involved parties to access them. Incorporation of privacy standards such as HIPPA (Health Insurance Portability and Accountability Act) is an essential requirement in mHealth analytics.

4   Unified Structured Framework for mHealth Analytics

This paper proposes a Unified Structured Framework for mHealth Analytics (USF-mHA) to address various issues of health analytics on mHeath data. The framework provides a 'unified' representation of the analytics process, and a 'structured' procedure of the tasks involved which can be ingrained in mHealth platforms.

The USF-mHA is an iterative-incremental life cycle model that comprises of 6 steps. Figure 1 shows the organisation of these steps in a flexible structure compatible with open mHealth architecture which permits the possibility of transiting back and forth between the sub-cycles (data and model) and the steps. The important key to a successful mHealth analytics is to achieve enough confidence on both data and model sub-cycles before delivering the actionable information and knowledge. Besides, the aspects of data management and knowledge management are fully considered in the USF-mHA process model.

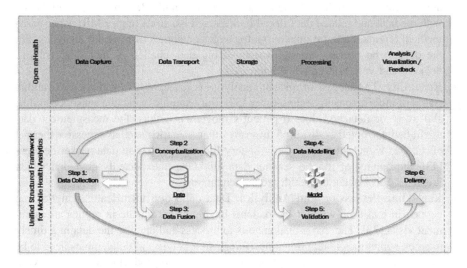

Fig. 1. A Unified Structured Framework for mHealth Analytics in conjunction with open mHealth architecture

Step 1. Data Collection: This step involves data collection and familiarising with the data. A wide range of wearable and sensing devices are readily available for continuous health monitoring of vital signs such as heart rates, blood pressure levels, and blood sugar levels. In mHealth, such devices can be easily purchased by patients at will or can be recommended by healthcare professionals. While patients play a central role in data collection, mHealth developers can adopt open standards for integrating data from disparate multi-dimensional streams. As mobile sensing data are typically real-time and high-speed, establishing the process of data collection and data quality is essential for subsequent steps.

For example, in mHealth apps for patients with Type 2 Diabetes Mellitus (DM), blood glucose self-monitoring is highly encouraged for patients to have good diabetes management. A Bluetooth-enabled glucose meter and test strips, hence, can be used to capture the blood glucose measurements at different times of the day. The collected mHealth data will be useful to patients, clinicians and mHealth developers in later stages.

Step 2. Conceptualization: Mobile technologies can support, enable and initiate changes, but they are only through understanding and addressing real-world healthcare situations [11]. The conceptualization step involves the considerations of disease-specific knowledge and the collected data (e.g., types, variables, properties, etc.). A number of questions can be drawn based on the nature of the domain and the data. In this step, analytical hypotheses should be clearly defined for each and every question that have been concerned with patients, doctors, or communities.

In the example of diabetes management, "how good is your glucose control?" or "what is your risk of having hyperglycemia?" are typical questions can be asked by either patients or clinicians. mHealth developers would take further initiatives by recommending analytical hypotheses based on the meta information of the collected data.

Step 3. Data fusion: This step employs diverse data fusion strategies to eliminate uncertainty and reliability issues in mobile health data. The process of data fusion integrates multiple data sources into a robust, accurate and consistent representation to be used in the modelling step [42]. It involves many data processing techniques such as aggregation, data selection, feature selection, cleaning, construction, and formatting. For example, Lee et al. [43] suggested a hierarchical decomposing method to handle the data at three different levels: raw sensor data fusion, feature level fusion, and decision level fusion. For instance, the fusion of blood glucose data into a patient-day model appears to the most trustworthy for analysing the quality of glycemic control in healthcare settings [46]. The detailed process of data fusion should be clearly considered based on the conceptualization of the data, especially on integrating real-time and continuous streaming data. The transport and storage of mHealth data, therefore, are heavily dependent on this step.

Step 4. Data modelling: This is the core step of the analytics process that includes a selection of modelling techniques, application of data modelling, and assessing the data models built in the process. Examples of modelling techniques are association, clustering, classification, and estimation [47]. Nevertheless, real-time streaming data require simultaneous storage and modelling methods that are not commonly used in conventional health analytics. To find the best analytic strategy, iterative tests and well-structured process are required on both individual-level and population-level data streams. For example, machine learning techniques can be applied to blood glucose readings identify trends of short-complications for personalised care. Data and analytical models should be stored for the re-use of health data and knowledge services.

Step 5. Validation: The developed data models in step 4 will be thoroughly evaluated against the hypotheses in step 2. There are several possible validation strategies such as bootstrap, holdout, k-fold cross validation, and leave one out. An evaluation metrics (e.g., accuracy, speed, and flexibility) should be clearly considered together with the selection of validation strategies. Once the models attain high confidence based on evaluation metrics, it will be ready for the delivery step.

Step 6. Delivery: Mobile health analytics aims to gain insights for making informed health-related decisions supported by mobile technologies. Storage of the models, results, and interpretations should also be established for future references. This final step also underlines packaging the results into actionable information and knowledge, and delivering them in an effective way. Furthermore, mobile technologies enable the possibility of contemporary health analytics tasks such as co-mining, action-based recommendation, mobile monitoring and real-time alerting. The deliverables of this step are shareable health analysis, visualisation and feedback. The model-based inference process for the re-use of mHealth analytics products should also be considered by mHealth developers.

5   Building an Open and Collaborative Community for mHealth Analytics

mHealth analytics is an emerging field in which achieving successful outcomes requires a systematic process model, and notably good supporting tools. Therefore, the manifestation of USF-mHA has been investigated in this study to demonstrate its capability of building an open and collaborative community. As there is a drought of software packages/mobile apps on mHealth analytics, a mobile platform is designed which consists of a cloud-based backend system for USF-mHA engine, and interfaces for various stakeholders involved in health analytics (Fig. 2).

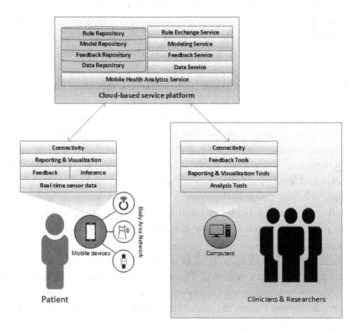

Fig. 2. A platform for USF-MHA

The proposed platform employs a distributed computation architecture for con-tinuous and rapid sensing data; thus, mobile phones in the USF-mHA process are mobile analytics agent in which data are captured simultaneously and compute capa-bilities are ready for data understanding and data preparation/data fusion. A rule engine plays a revolutionary role for recording and automation of these steps. Subsequent steps of USF-mHA are also well-integrated into the platform. Figure 3 demonstrates the distributed computation architecture of the platform.

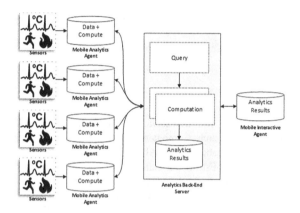

Fig. 3. Distributed computation architecture in USF-MHA

6 Conclusion

nHealth analytics is promising to shape patients' journey with clinicians and researchers. Our study proposes a unified structured framework which transforms mHealth analytics into an iterative-incremental process to gain insights for making better and fact-based health-related decisions. The framework is organised in 6 steps from data collection to delivery of the analytical outcomes. In conjunction with open mHealth standards, the process model can be integrated into mHealth apps for data analytics. An agenda of a USF-mHA platform is introduced to demonstrate the usage of the process model for building an open and collaborative community for health analytics.

Our study considerably contributes to the cumulative theoretical development of process models for mHealth analytics. The uniqueness of mHealth data analytics is evidently highlighted to shed light on the needs for an open framework compatible with existing data standards. The extended artefact allows reusability and applicability in various mobile health scenarios. Besides, there are several implications for practitioners. First, the USF-mHA provides meaningful guidelines on the development of mHealth apps for health analytics. Second, the proposed model promotes continuous collabo-ration among patients, caregivers, and developers with concrete objectives and deliv-erable for better outcomes. Last but not least, as opposed to conventional data sources, storage and process techniques of mHealth data are underlined for practitioners.

This paper is not an end, but rather a beginning of forthcoming research. It is important to note that mobile health data can be high-dimensional, high-density and high-frequency which prompt for a new camp of dynamic data process techniques, modelling techniques and model representations. This also hints to a great opportunity for automation of the proposed process model in which rule engines play a critical role in various steps such as data fusion, data modelling, validation, and delivery. Besides, we are in progress to carry out an ex-ante evaluation to demonstrate the effectiveness of USF-mHA in healthcare settings.

Acknowledgements. This study is funded by a grant from Singapore Ministry of Education (grant number: T1 251RES1410).

References

1. Kumar, S., Nilsen, W., Pavel, M., Srivastava, M.: Mobile health: revolutionizing healthcare through transdisciplinary research. Computer (Long. Beach. Calif.) **46**, 28–35 (2013)
2. Kumar, S., Abowd, G.D., Abraham, W.T., Al'Absi, M., Gayle Beck, J., Chau, D.H., Condie, T., Conroy, D.E., Ertin, E., Estrin, D., Ganesan, D., Lam, C., Marlin, B., Marsh, C.B., Murphy, S.A., Nahum-Shani, I., Patrick, K., Rehg, J.M., Sharmin, M., Shetty, V., Sim, I., Spring, B., Srivastava, M., Wetter, D.W.: Center of excellence for mobile sensor data-to-knowledge (MD2K). J. Am. Med. Inform. Assoc. **22**, 1137–1142 (2015)
3. Raghupathi, V., Raghupathi, W.: An overview of health analytics. J. Heal. Med. Inform. **4** (2013)
4. Anta, R., El-Wahab, S., Giuffrida, A.: Mobile Health: The potential of mobile telephony to bring health care to the majority. Inter-American Dev. Bank. **32** (2009)
5. Xu, W., Liu, Y.: mHealthApps: a repository and database of mobile health apps. JMIR Mhealth Uhealth **3**, e28 (2015)
6. Kleinke, J.D.: Dot-Gov: Market failure and the creation of a national health information technology system. Health Aff. **24**, 1246–1262 (2005)
7. Chen, C., Haddad, D., Selsky, J., Hoffman, J.E., Kravitz, R.L., Estrin, D.E., Sim, I.: Making sense of mobile health data: an open architecture to improve individual- and population-level health. J. Med. Internet Res. **14**, 1–10 (2012)
8. Estrin, D., Sim, I.: Open mHealth architecture: an engine for health care innovation. Science (80-) **330**, 759–760 (2010)
9. Bodenheimer, T.: Patient self-management of chronic disease in primary care. JAMA **288**, 2469 (2002)
10. Kahn, J.G., Yang, J.S., Kahn, J.S.: "Mobile" health needs and opportunities in developing countries. Health Aff. (Millwood) **29**, 252–258 (2010)
11. van Heerden, A., Tomlinson, M., Swartz, L.: Point of care in your pocket: a research agenda for the field of m-health. Bull. World Health Organ. **90**, 393–394 (2012)
12. Hervás, R., Fontecha, J., Ausín, D., Castanedo, F., Bravo, J., López-de-Ipiña, D.: Mobile monitoring and reasoning methods to prevent cardiovascular diseases. Sensors (Basel) **13**, 6524–6541 (2013)
13. Walton, R., DeRenzi, B.: Value-sensitive design and health care in Africa. IEEE Trans. Prof. Commun. **52**, 346–358 (2009)
14. Van Woensel, W., Roy, P.C., Abidi, S.S.: A mobile & intelligent patient diary for chronic disease self-management. In: MEDINFO 2015 eHealth-enabled Heal, pp. 118–122 (2015)

15. Prociow, P.A., Crowe, J.A.: Towards personalised ambient monitoring of mental health via mobile technologies. Technol. Health Care **18**, 275–284 (2010)
16. Magill, E., Blum, J.M.: Personalised ambient monitoring: supporting mental health at home. In: Advances in Home Care Technologies: Results of the Match Project, pp. 67–85 (2012)
17. Paoli, R., Fernández-Luque, F.J., Doménech, G., Martínez, F., Zapata, J., Ruiz, R.: A system for ubiquitous fall monitoring at home via a wireless sensor network and a wearable mote. Expert Syst. Appl. **39**, 5566–5575 (2012)
18. Junglas, I., Abraham, C., Ives, B.: Mobile technology at the frontlines of patient care: understanding fit and human drives in utilization decisions and performance. Decis. Support Syst. **46**, 634–647 (2009)
19. Carroll, A.E., Marrero, D.G., Downs, S.M.: The HealthPia GlucoPack diabetes phone: a usability study. Diabetes Technol. Ther. **9**, 158–164 (2007)
20. Istepanian, R.S.H., Zitouni, K., Harry, D., Moutosammy, N., Sungoor, A., Tang, B., Earle, K.A.: Evaluation of a mobile phone telemonitoring system for glycaemic control in patients with diabetes. J. Telemed. Telecare. **15**, 125–128 (2009)
21. Wirth, R.: CRISP-DM: towards a standard process model for data mining. In: Proceedings of the Fourth International Conference on the Practical Applications of Knowledge Discovery and Data Mining, pp. 29–39 (2000)
22. Chapman, P., Clinton, J., Kerber, R., Khabaza, T., Reinartz, T., Shearer, C., Wirth, R.: CRISP-DM 1.0: Step-by-step Data Mining Guide (2000)
23. SAS: SAS Enterprise Miner: SEMMA. http://www.sas.com/technologies/analytics/datamining/miner/semma.html
24. Matignon, R.: Data Mining Using SAS Enterprise Miner. Wiley, Hoboken (2007)
25. Azevedo, A., Santos, M.F.: KDD, SEMMA and CRISP-DM: a parallel overview. In: IADIS European Conference Data Mining, pp. 182–185 (2008)
26. Raghupathi, W.: Data mining in health care. In: Healthcare Informatics: Improving Efficiency and Productivity, pp. 211–223 (2010)
27. Cios, K.J., Moore, G.W.: Uniqueness of medical data mining. J. Artif. Intell. Med. **26**(1), 1–24 (2002)
28. Eggebraaten, T.J., Tenner, J.W., Dubbels, J.C.: A health-care data model based on the HL7 reference information model. IBM Syst. J. **46**, 5–18 (2007)
29. Catley, C., Smith, K., Mcgregor, C., Tracy, M.: Extending CRISP-DM to incorporate temporal data mining of multi- dimensional medical data streams: a neonatal intensive care unit case study. Comput. Med. Syst. **1**, 1–5 (2009)
30. Bellazzi, R., Zupan, B.: Predictive data mining in clinical medicine: current issues and guidelines. Int. J. Med. Inform. **77**, 81–97 (2008)
31. Ahangama, S., Poo, D.C.C.: Unified structured process for health analytics. Int. J. Medical, Heal. Biomed. Bioeng Pharm. Eng. **8**, 768–776 (2014)
32. Benselim, M.S., Seridi-Bouchelaghem, H.: Extended UML for the development of context-aware applications. In: 4th International Conference on Networked Digital Technology NDT 2012. 293 PART 1, pp. 33–43 (2012)
33. Kumar, S., Nilsen, W.J., Abernethy, A., Atienza, A., Patrick, K., Pavel, M., Riley, W.T., Shar, A., Spring, B., Spruijt-Metz, D., Hedeker, D., Honavar, V., Kravitz, R., Craig Lefebvre, R., Mohr, D.C., Murphy, S.A., Quinn, C., Shusterman, V., Swendeman, D.: Mobile health technology evaluation. Am. J. Prev. Med. **45**, 228–236 (2013)
34. Abidoye, A.P.: Using wearable sensors for remote healthcare monitoring system. J. Sens. Technol. **1**, 22–28 (2011)
35. Bonato, P.: Wearable sensors and systems. IEEE Eng. Med. Biol. Mag. **29**, 25–36 (2010)

36. Allet, L., Knols, R.H., Shirato, K., de Bruin, E.D.: Wearable systems for monitoring mobility-related activities in chronic disease: a systematic review. Sensors (Switzerland) **10**, 9026–9052 (2010)
37. Bonato, P.: Advances in wearable technology and its medical applications. In: Annual International Conference of the IEEE Engineering in Medicine and Biology Society EMBC 2010, pp. 2021–2024 (2010)
38. Lane, N.D., Miluzzo, E., Lu, H., Peebles, D., Choudhury, T., Campbell, A.T.: A survey of mobile phone sensing. IEEE Commun. Mag. **48**, 140–150 (2010)
39. Chan, M., Estève, D., Fourniols, J.-Y., Escriba, C., Campo, E.: Smart wearable systems: current status and future challenges. Artif. Intell. Med. **56**, 137–156 (2012)
40. Mukherjee, A., Pal, A., Misra, P.: Data analytics in ubiquitous sensor-based health information systems. In: Proceedings of the - 6th International Conference on Next Generation Mobile Applications, Services and Technologies NGMAST 2012, pp. 193–198 (2012)
41. Raghupathi, V.V., Raghupathi, W.W.: Exploring the relationship between ICTs and public health at country level: a health analytics approach. Int. J. Healthc. Inf. Syst. Inform. **8**, 1–22 (2013)
42. Touati, F., Tabish, R.: U-Healthcare system: state-of-the-art review and challenges. J. Med. Syst. **37**, 9949 (2013)
43. Lee, H., Park, K., Lee, B., Choi, J., Elmasri, R.: Issues in data fusion for healthcare monitoring. In: Proceedings of the 1st ACM International Conference on Pervasive Technologies Related to Assistive Environments - PETRA 2008, p. 1 (2008)
44. Raij, A., Ghosh, A., Kumar, S., Srivastava, M.: Privacy risks emerging from the adoption of innocuous wearable sensors in the mobile environment. In: Proceedings of 2011 Annual Conference on Human Factors in Computing Systems - CHI 2011, p. 11 (2011)
45. Guha, S., Plarre, K., Lissner, D., Mitra, S.: Autowitness: locating and tracking stolen property while tolerating GPS and radio outages. In: ACM Transactions, pp. 29–42 (2012)
46. Goldberg, P., Bozzo, J.: "Glucometrics"-assessing the quality of inpatient glucose management. Diabetes Technol. Ther. **8**, 560–571 (2006)
47. Koh, H.C., Tan, G.: Data mining applications in healthcare. J. Healthc. Inf. Manag. **19**, 64–72 (2005)

Discovering Subway Design Opportunities Using Social Network Data: The Image-Need-Design Opportunity Model

Tianjiao Zhao[1(✉)], Kin Wai Michael Siu[2], and Han Sun[1]

[1] Tianjin University, Tianjin, China
zhaotianjiao@tju.edu.cn
[2] The Hong Kong Polytechnic University, Kowloon, Hong Kong

Abstract. Online social networks have permeated into people's daily lives. An increasing number of people from diverse backgrounds have expressed their viewpoints, feelings, and needs through the internet. Data from social network is widely used in every kind of academic social science. This study aims to apply data from online social networks into subway design work and promote a new way to discover design chance. By considering the Hong Kong, Shenzhen, and Tokyo subways as case studies, this study attempts to capture the images of subways. Through comparing the data from social network with users' needs level, an updated Image-Need-Design Opportunity model with a cyclical process is created at theoretical level. This research provides an insightful reference for future design work and aims to evoke in researchers a desire to excavate potential design information from online social networks.

Keywords: Case study · Design model · Design opportunity · Design research · Social network service · Subway

1 Introduction

Currently, social media is widely used by people of different education levels, cultural backgrounds, and ages to facilitate communications within social networks. A social network is a social structure comprising of persons or organizations with social relations (Yu and Kak 2012). Social media is the sister of social networks; it comprises platforms that help users to create and exchange content, it is also widely called consumer-generated media (CGM). (Loader 2008; Reynolds et al. 2010; Romero et al. 2011). Online social networking services (SNSs) are a subset of social media (Yu and Kak 2012). There are currently no reliable data regarding how many people use SNSs, but many people have integrated these sites into their daily practices (Ellison 2008). Since there are many users sharing their opinions and experiences via social media and SNS, there exists therein an aggregation of personal wisdom and different viewpoints (Yu and Kak 2012). The data available via social media can give us insights into the scale and extent of social networks and societies. This digital media can transcend the boundaries of geography to facilitate the study of human relationships (Lauw et al. 2010) and help measure popular social and political sentiments without the use of

© Springer International Publishing AG 2017
G. Meiselwitz (Ed.): SCSM 2017, Part II, LNCS 10283, pp. 451–466, 2017.
DOI: 10.1007/978-3-319-58562-8_35

explicit surveys (Kumar et al. 2009; Ritterman et al. 2009; Ulicny et al. 2010). Thus, social network data is widely researched by scholars from disparate fields to understand the practices, implications, cultures, and meanings of the sites, as well as the users' engagement with them (Bothos et al. 2010). According to Yu and Kak (2012), network data can also be used to predict some human related events if the data is extracted and analysed properly. Nowadays, data from social networks are used to predict movie box-office results, disease, equity market, tourism, and more (Asur and Huberman 2010; Tse and Zhang 2013). In Mayer Schoenberger and Cukier's (2013) book *Big Data: A Revolution That Will Transform How We Live, Work, and Think*, it is written that analysing "big data" from the internet would bring an unprecedented revolution of our future life. Many decisions could be made based on big data mining from the online social networks. The fact that participation on social network sites leaves online records offers unprecedented opportunities for researchers.

Considering the character of online social network data, we try to apply the data from the network to design work. In order to develop user centred design principles, we must discover design opportunities according to the users' opinions. Designers must recognize that they should not, and cannot, make decisions for users about their requirement and use method. This means that they should not impose their value judgments on users (Siu 2003). Currently, there are a great many methods to obtain design opportunities. In his book Design Investigation, Li (2007) mentioned that there are 11 methods used to discover design requirements, including interview, observation, questionnaire, users' psychological experiments and so on. All these methods require direct communication with users. They are niche targeting and accurate methods, but they require a good deal of time and labour to perform.

This research hopes to predict users' needs for subway life design and find design opportunities by analysing big data. If big data can be applied to the design work, this will help to reduce costs associated with the labour and time required by the other discovery methods. As Yu and Kak (2012) identified, automatic prediction with machines has a much lower cost than human labour; furthermore, this method could process greater amounts of data and provide answers more quickly (Barbier and Liu 2011).

In this research, by considering the Hong Kong, Shenzhen, and Tokyo subways as case studies, this paper attempts to capture the image and needs of subways. By comparing the data from social network with users' needs level, an updated Image-Need-Design Opportunity model with a cyclical process is created at the theoretical level. This model defined the subway images through the observation in the three case stations, by analysing the relationship between image and needs, the design opportunities are found. This research attempts to provide an insightful reference for future design work and aims to evoke in researchers a desire to excavate potential design information from online social networks.

2   Research Method

This study focuses on the city subway. City subway is the public transport which is shared and used by all the citizens. Almost every person has the experience of using a subway. There are two reasons of choosing the Subway as the research object. Firstly, the background of the users is rich. Public facilities are widely used by the citizens and the images from the users are colourful and representative. It is also easy to collect the users' images through internet. Secondly, it is easy to capture the images in the public environment. When people have the experience in the environment, they would obtain direct images and feelings in it. We don't need to arrange special usage scenario. By analysing the subway environment, we try to see how the design opportunity model is constructed.

As the object of this study is to determine the relationship between subway image and users' needs and develop a new method of discovering design opportunities, the research assesses the interaction between users and environment. A case study approach is adopted. Data are collected primarily through observation and interviews.

2.1   Case Study

Martyn (1998) stated that a case study research focuses on one instance (or a few instances) of a particular phenomenon with the goal of providing an in-depth account of events, relationships, experiences, or processes occurring in that particular instance. The purpose is to arrive at a comprehensive understanding of the groups under study. Siu (2001) mentions that case study has many advantages in urban research, particularly for the qualitative investigation of human behaviour. Some typical cities in Asia (Tokyo, Hong Kong, and Shenzhen) are selected as the cases studied in this research; observation and interviews are conducted in these city subways.

The Tokyo metro typifies what is meant by metro in a global context. As the first subway in Asia, it has an 86-year history. With the development of Tokyo's society and economy, the Tokyo metro experienced a complicated history of development. The abundant use of the Tokyo subway and the historical element of the subway's story endow the Tokyo metro with a unique but representative character.

Hong Kong's Mass Transit Railway (MTR) is also selected as a case. The city of Hong Kong is known for its combination of Eastern and Western culture through its accommodation of people from all over the world. Hong Kong MTR is the most important transport means in this city. It carries an average of 4 million passengers each day (MTR 2012). It is famous worldwide for its security, stability, high quality of service, and use by other cities for subway research.

Shenzhen metro is the third selected case. As a Special Zone in China, Shenzhen is filled with young people from different provinces. It is a lively, multicultural city. Shenzhen Metro was constructed in 1999, which is very recent compared to Tokyo and Hong Kong. The different social environment and era of its production have created a modern subway that has benefited from the experiences of past metros and developed a unique style.

We conducted observations and interviews in typical cities and organized the results to obtain a comprehensive list of subway needs. The research results from these cities are comprehensive, as the Tokyo, Hong Kong, and Shenzhen city subways have very different cultural aspects. Besides this, these subways were constructed in different times and were developed at diverse prosperity levels. The subway images in these cities are typical and interesting.

2.2   Unstructured Interview

The image of the subway is not the subway itself but a subway that is experienced by its users. To obtain accurate images of the subways, the study combines observation with unstructured interviews conducted among its users. Citizens' experience in the subway is very realizable and valuable for this research. We have interviewed several citizens from each city who have abundant subway experience, as well as persons who have experience using all three subways. We asked open ended questions that asked users to describe the city subway or their feelings when the city subway is mentioned. By analysing their feelings, we try to define different categories of subway image and determine how subway image corresponds to subway needs.

2.3   Observation

Observation of subjects can be performed to obtain a better understanding about people's behaviour in the environment as it is a method of looking at action between people and their environment and the result from observation is always reliable (Siu 2007; Sanoff 1992). In this research, cameras are used to record information about peoples' behaviours in the metro. This study observes two elements of the subway: (a) the static subway space and its facilities and (b) the dynamic subway life that occurs when the space is filled with people. These are the primary aspects affecting subway image.

3   Classification of Subway Images

Through interviews with 90 persons in Hong Kong, Shenzhen, and Tokyo about their subway impressions of these cities, we have obtained some key words which are provided in Table 1. The descriptions of subway image were organized into the categories described below.

Table 1. Description of each city subway

Subway image	
Tokyo metro	Silent, humanity, historical, fast rhythm, accessible, detailed, can buy food, enough toilets, old, indifferent, deep, convenient
Hong Kong metro	Clean, low temperature, safe, convenient, frequency, punctual, chaos, orderly, flourishing, crowded, high priced, fast, humanized, civilized, global, multi-elements, callosity, MTR shop, unacquainted, flexible, artistic
Shenzhen metro	New, reasonable price, crowd, chaos, fancy, emotional, clean, comfortable waiting environment, airtight, modernized, alive, novelty, unclear information, spacious

3.1 Function of the Railway

As one of the most basic forms of city transportation, the current functioning of the railway impressed people the most in all these three cities. Safe, frequency, punctual, and accessible were words used to describe the railways' functions. No matter whether the city subway is well-functioning or ill-functioning, functional feature is an obvious image. Although it cannot become a special label of the city subway, the functioning of the subway is the image that leaves the greatest impression. Figure 1 shows the map of Tokyo and Shenzhen subways to demonstrate the feature (image) of well-accessible and ill-accessible subways in these two cities.

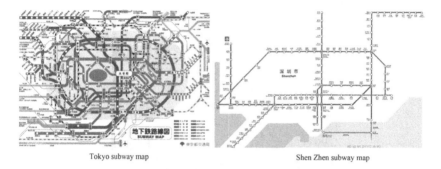

Tokyo subway map   Shen Zhen subway map

Fig. 1. Tokyo subway map and Shenzhen subway map

3.2 Intuitive Feelings of the Environment

When people walk into a subway they immediately obtain an intuitive feeling about the environment. "New", "Historical", "Crowded", "Quick rhythm", "Capacious", and "Cleanness" were all representative words used to express the participants' images of the subways. Figure 2 shows the fast rhythm that is widely felt by passengers of the Tokyo subway.

Fig. 2. People walk fast in the Tokyo subway

3.3   Stimulates Emotional Feelings and Sense of Being Respected

One of the most important feelings for passengers in the subway environment is a sense that they are respected and heard. "Humanity", "comfortable", and "kind" were all words used to describe passengers' sense that they were respected. Some passengers also perceived emotion images such as "emotional", "indifference", and "no communication". These emotion descriptions show users emotional needs in the subway. As Ho and Siu (2012) state, emotional design was not only communicated through the style of design, function, form and usability, but also built up experience for the user on their needs and demands. Figure 3 is an example that demonstrates the factor of humanity in the Tokyo metro. They provide compartment for women use only. Hong Kong MTR and Shen Zhen metro do not provide this service.

Fig. 3. Women-only compartment

3.4   Self Identity

A few of the interviewees mentioned that the subway included some special image of the city, such as a city card or reflection of city culture. In his book, *The Image of the City*, Lynch (1960) mentioned that clearly portraying a city image is one of the standards of an excellent city. A readable city may arouse citizens' senses of security, comfort, and freedom. The identity of a place can make it special and can create in users a feeling of self-actualization. Much like a city, the subway should portray a distinct identity to make it special and impressive. Figures 4 and 5 shows some special design elements in Hong Kong and Tokyo subways that reflect the features of these subways' identities.

Fig. 4. Distinctive design in the Hong Kong MTR station

Fig. 5. The station seal for passengers in the Tokyo subway

Among all the images, there are two main elements constructing these elements: the static environment (facilities, etc.) and the dynamic people (behaviour towards and interactions with the environment).

When assessing participant responses, one must consider that passengers are both observers and the observed-target. Furthermore, their images of the subway will differ according to their backgrounds.

4   From Subway Images to Subway Needs

Based on the classification of the subway images provided by participants, we aim to gain insight into people's images of the subway and thereby ascertain users' needs inside the subway space, which will be divided into diverse categories. As images of the subway are the first-hand impressions of the users, they can reflect users' needs. We aim to discover the process that occurs inside the black box (Fig. 6) as we move from collecting the image to determining the subway needs.

Fig. 6. The first black box

Many scholars have discussed the needs of design. According to Maslow's hierarchy of needs (1943), these needs can be assigned to five different levels, hierarchically organized as follows: physiological needs are on the bottom of the hierarchy, followed by safety needs, social needs, and esteem needs. The bottom four (physiological needs safety needs, social needs, and esteem needs) are deficiency needs (D-Needs). The top level self-actualization, also known as growth needs (G-Needs) (Maslow 1943). In the consumer marketing field, Maslow's hierarchy of needs corresponds to different requirements. These are needs of function, of the user's body, of social image, of the user's symbolic needs, and individual brand needs (in order from low level to high level needs) (Wu 2001).

As the subway is a special functional transport system in the city and is an independent underground facility, users' needs towards the subway space may not perfectly line up with Maslow's identified needs. But it is no doubt that the subway's needs are hierarchical in nature.

Based on the interview, these images will be divided into different levels by comparing the subway images with the Maslow needs theory. Figure 7 shows the five levels of subway image categories, which are: function, sensory aspects, sense of being respected, emotional response, and identity. These images correspond to Maslow's needs. The highest image level, identity image, can be divided into three sub levels. The first level is the identity of the subway. Like the city in which it runs, a subway should possess its own special image. This image is not achieved by fulfilling the low level needs but by constructing a specific character to stimulate users' senses, memories, and souls. This identity is the visiting card of the subway. The second identity is that the city identity (culture, character, and image) should be reflected in subway. As an important element of the city, the subway plays the role of defining the city's borders, landmarks, and nodes, which are all elements of city image (Lynch 1960). The third and highest level of the subway identity is its ability to express its users' identity. The subway experience should promote its users self-actualization and give them some inspiration about life. In this way, the role of the subway in people's lives becomes much more meaningful. These images correspond to their needs. Figure 7 shows the process of the analysis used to determine the levels of subway needs. Like Maslow's hierarchy of needs, the subway needs are also hierarchically organized.

Based on the interviews, the functional images emerged most frequently while the identity image emerged least often. Within the hierarchy, it is more difficult to realize higher levels than lower. But the higher need satisfaction of the majority in a society, the greater the quality of life (QoL) of that society is (Sirgy 1986). In each case, according to the result of the questionnaire, the research found that images from different levels exist together. The basic image does not disappear when the high level positive image emerges. This is congruent with Maslow's theory (1943), which notes that every person has needs. When the low level needs are fulfilled, the high level needs emerge. For each individual, when different needs exist together, the most basic levels of needs must be met before the individual will strongly desire (or focus motivation upon) the secondary or higher level needs. Needs in different levels depend on each other—low level needs do not disappear once they are fulfilled. Different people have diverse feelings towards the subway, which is why people's evaluations of the subway differ. For instance, we can see people describe Hong Kong MTR with both functional image (safe) and subway identity image (artistic). Some people are more sensitive to high level needs than others. Images can be both negative and positive; no matter what they are, they correspond to the same needs.

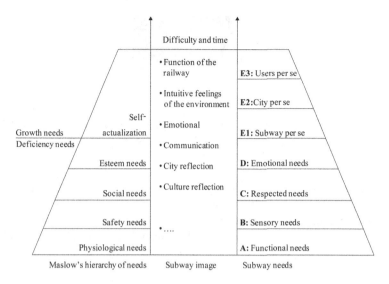

Fig. 7. The categorization of subway needs

As our research aim is to find a method for discovering design opportunities using the context of subways. In order to achieve this, a comprehensive understanding of subway needs should be generated. Our current subway needs pyramid combines all the images provided by subway users and distils the subway needs from these images. The elements of each level of needs and even the levels themselves will change with the development of technology and time. This subway needs level should be used in specific design contexts in future research.

5   The Application of an Online Social Network System

After setting up an integral subway needs hierarchy, we try to construct the connection between design opportunity and subway needs. As mentioned before, needs emerge and are fulfilled from low level to high level. We should first identify what the needs are and then see what need levels have already been fulfilled. According to Maslow's theory (1943), when people's low level needs (such as function and sensory needs) are fulfilled, they pursue and focus on high level needs. Users' descriptions about the subway focus on high level needs, and the data available on social network systems provides an effective testing method for such needs. There are thousands of information points available from online social networks. In information driven design, the designer tries to define the design problem as strictly as possible (Kruger and Cross 2006). The information from the users is quite valuable to this end. The big data from internet should be used appropriately. Figure 8 depicts another black box of this process: the transition that occurs from retrieving social network data to determining subway needs.

Fig. 8. The second black box

In order to open this black box, we set Micro Blog and Hong Kong MTR as an example. When the big data from Micro Blog was obtained from the internet, content with the key words: "HK MTR", "Hong Kong Subway", and "subway life" was extracted from the large amount of Micro Blog data. By data mining towards these extracted descriptions, some high-frequency words (emerged frequently in the extracted data) were gained with sequence. The amount determining what makes a word considered high-frequency depends on the amount of the basic data.

Most of these high frequency words can be categorized in the subway needs levels. Based on these high frequency words, the subway needs pyramid for Hong Kong MTR is as shown below.

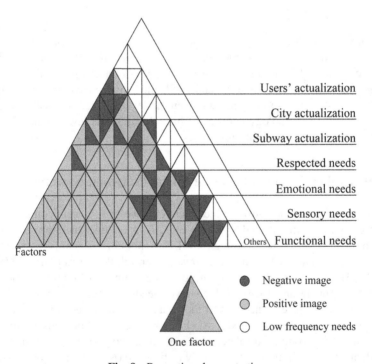

Fig. 9. Proportion demonstration

Some aspects were described with both negative and positive images. Such as punctual and unpunctual. We then counted the scale of each part. The black part depicted in Fig. 9 represents the negative evaluations while the gray part represents the positive ones. The white part represents images that are just barely high-frequency words. For instance, "indifference" is one of the subway images that emerged only several times - it is sensed only by a few sensitive users. However, it could also be a key design need in the future. By analysing the context of the needs pyramid, including place and time, some design needs can be discovered. In the proportion demonstration shown in Fig. 9, the section in gray colour represents aspects of the subway that should not be paid attention to, the section in black colour represents aspects that should be improved, and the section in white represents potential design opportunities. Figure 9 not only demonstrates the current evaluation of the subway's needs but also includes information about design direction. Based on the above discussion, the whole process that occurs within the black box is shown in Fig. 10.

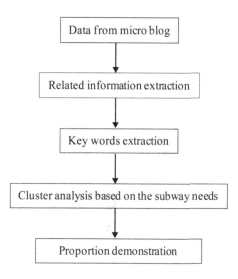

Fig. 10. Process of data analysis

6   An Update System

The result of data mining demonstrates users' current evaluations of and future needs for the subway. As data from online social networks is dynamic and unending, this method can be designed as an updated system that is sensitive and seasonable. This circulation system, with the name image-need-design opportunity model, is depicted in Fig. 11. The process described in Fig. 11 starts from design opportunity, at the top. The designer and policy maker design the current subway space according to the initial design requirements. When users interact with the completed subway design, they have their own image about the subway. Through interviews and questionnaires, the subway's needs can be obtained by assessing and categorizing images of the subway and extrapolating needs. This step can be designed according to the requirements of the specific location and time in which it occurs.

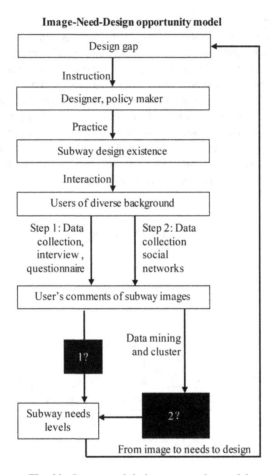

Fig. 11. Image-need-design opportunity model

In Fig. 11, black box 1 contains the process of transforming images to needs, as explained in the above discussion. Black box 2 (data mining) represents the transition that occurs from retrieving social network data to determining subway needs. The subway images retrieved from the social network can be used both to evaluate the current design and to reflect future design needs.

When social network users' subway descriptions and subway images are organized in the needs pyramid, we find the users' current focus and design opportunities. The new emerged requirements can then be used to instruct design work, and the cycle begins again from the top.

Figure 12 illustrates the predicted changing of subway needs as the process is implemented again and again, and shows how new design opportunities emerge in the updated system. At the beginning, most of the subway image is about the function and sensory needs. Only a few people can sense the high level image of the subway. When most of these low level needs are fulfilled, people are anticipated to begin to focus on higher level needs. White areas, which represent low frequency key words or newly emerged words, become green over time as design opportunities are fulfilled. Meanwhile, to avoid the confusion that current words of gray part became low frequency words in the future, once some of the factors emerged with almost full gray situation, it can be ignored in the future evaluation. The data analysis finds new needs and higher level needs as time passes.

Like described in Hauffe's design and society model (1998), design is changing from function-focused to consumer-focused to human-focused. Currently, design is no longer just a tool for the development of functional, innovative consumer products: it is increasingly seen as a process for radical change—for developing services, systems, and environments that support more sustainable lifestyles and consumption habits (Bjögvinsson et al. 2012). For example, since the emergence of the smart phone, we seldom see people focused on the quality of connection during phone calls. When asking people their impressions about their mobile phones, they currently focus on the brand, interaction, or even the appearance instead of the basic functions. Sometimes, people also mention how the mobile phone affects their lifestyle. Users' needs of mobile phone are changing from low level to high level. The subway would also experience this process in the future. The development would always bring some surprises. There still thousands of subway needs to be excavated in the future.

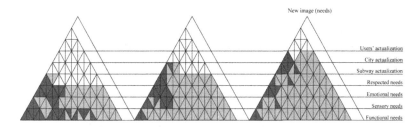

Fig. 12. Predicted change in subway needs

7 Problem Predictions

Until now, we have promoted a new method of applying social network data into design work at the theoretical level. More research is needed to supply and test this model with practice. Some of the difficulties and problems with this method can be predicted in the current stage, and future research should address these potential issues as described below.

We are far from knowing everything about social media. During data mining, it is difficult to avoid unpredictable problems, such as errors in semantic analysis (Yu and Kak 2012). We don't know whether the selected data with the key words includes some unnecessary message (such as an advertisement) or even interference information. For example, Face book has a limit of 420 characters for status updates and Twitter has a 140-character limit. The shortness of the content affects the reliability of data analysis

(Saif et al. 2011). What's more, users tend to use a large variety of short forms and irregular words, which also increases the difficulty of data analysis. These problems are common problems in the field of data mining, and the quality of the data mining directly affects the result of design instruction.

The subway needs obtained using the qualitative method change across different cities and eras. When applying this method to diverse cities, the subway needs should be designed accordingly. Targeted needs can help to find more suitable design opportunities.

Currently, we are just at the first step of data collection. Some detailed difficulties would be found in the practice. This model provides a basic frame for discovering design opportunities; this frame should be improved and supplemented in practice.

8   Conclusions

Big data from online social networking sites is widely used in diverse fields. The application of online social network data is an inexorable trend in the field of prediction and could bring great benefit to the future world. This paper has proposed a conceptual model for discovering design opportunities. This study utilizes a qualitative research method to hierarchically categorize subway images into five levels, and then constructs a subway needs pyramid to connect the subway image with design opportunities. This study also promoted an Image-Need-Design Opportunity model to evaluate the subway environment and discover subway needs by filling the subway needs pyramid with data from online social network. Compared with the traditional, interview method of determining design opportunities, this model provides a creative way to collect, extract, and utilize the wisdom of crowds in an objective manner with low costs and high efficiency. This method is also advanced in that it shows the updated dynamic result by time and location. It could not only be used to predict updated design needs but also bring a new era for the design process. It can be applied not only in subway space design but also in product design, city planning, policy formulation, urban design, and other design fields that conduct human-centred design work. The exploration and utilization of online social network data would begin a new stage for the design field and demonstrates unlimited potential in future research.

Now that the theoretical framework has been constructed, more practical work is needed. Relevant research should construct systematic correlations between object image and design needs, extract valuable design information from online social networks, and perform detailed data mining for design.

Acknowledgements. We thank The Hong Kong Polytechnic University for the research grants. We would also like to acknowledge Massachusetts Institute of Technology for Visiting Professor/Scholar support for the final analysis of the data and preparation of the paper.

References

Asur, S., Huberman, B.A.: Predicting the future with social media. In: Proceedings of 2010 IEEE/WIC/ACM International Conference on Web Intelligence and Intelligent Agent Technology (WI-IAT), Toronto, Canada, 31 August–3 September 2010 (2010). http:// ieeexplore.ieee.org/stamp/stamp.jsp?tp=&arnumber=5616710. Accessed 20 May 2013

Barbier, G., Liu, H.: Data mining in social media. In: Aggarwal, C.C. (ed.) Social Network Data Analytics, pp. 327–352. Springer, New York (2011)

Bjögvinsson, E., Ehn, P., Hillgren, P.A.: Design things and design thinking: contemporary participatory design challenges'. Des. Issues **28**(3), 101–116 (2012)

Bothos, E., Apostolou, D., Mentzas, G.: Using social media to predict future events with agent-based markets. IEEE Intell. Syst. **25**, 50–58 (2010)

Ellison, N.B.: Social network sites: definition, history, and scholarship. J. Comput. Mediated Commun. **13**(1), 210–230 (2007)

Hauffe, T.: Design: A concise history. Laurence King, London (1998)

Ho, A.G., Siu, K.W.M.: Emotion design, emotional design, emotionalize design: a review on their relationships from a new perspective. Des. J. **15**(1), 9–32 (2012)

Kruger, C., Cross, N.: Solution driven versus problem driven design: strategies and outcomes. Des. Stud. **27**(5), 527–548 (2006)

Kumar, S., Agarwal, N., Lim, M., Liu, H.: Mapping socio-cultural dynamics in Indonesian blogosphere. In: Proceedings of the 3rd International Conference on Computational Cultural Dynamics, Washington, USA, 7–8 December 2009 (2009). http://www.aaai.org/ocs/index. php/ICCCD/ICCCD09/paper/viewFile/1019/3317/. Accessed 30 May 2013

Lauw, H., Shafer, J.C., Agrawal, R., Ntoulas, A.: Homophily in the digital world: a LiveJournal case study. IEEE Internet Comput. **14**(2), 15–23 (2010)

Li, L.S.: Design Investigation, Chinese edn. China Building Bookshop, Beijing (2007)

Loader, B.D.: Social movements and new media. Sociol. Compass **2**(6), 1920–1933 (2008)

Lynch, K.: The Image of the City. The MIT Press, Cambridge (1960)

Martyn, D.: Good Research Guide. Open University Press, London (1998)

Maslow, A.H.: A theory of human motivation. Psychol. Rev. **50**(4), 370 (1943)

Mayer Schoenberger, V., Cukier, K.N.: Big Data: A Revolution that will Transform How We Live, Work and Think. Houghton Mifflin Harcourt Publishing, New York (2013)

MTR (Mass Transit Railway): Our pledge for service 2012. Mass transit railway.com (2012). http://www.mtr.com.hk/chi/publications/images/MTR_Pledge.pdf. Accessed 30 May 2013

Reynolds, W.N., Weber, M.S., Farber, R.M., Corley, C., Cowell, A.J., Gregory, M.: Social media and social reality. In: 2010 IEEE International Conference on Proceedings of the Intelligence and Security Informatics (ISI), Vancouver, Canada, 23–26 May 2010. http://ieeexplore.ieee. org/stamp/stamp.jsp?tp=&arnumber=5484733. Accessed 30 May 2013

Ritterman, J., Osborne, M., Klein. E.: Using prediction markets and twitter to predict swine flu pandemic. In: Carrero, F.M., Gomez, J.M., Monsalve, B., Puertas, P., Cortizo, J.C.A. (eds.) Proceedings of the 1st International Workshop on Mining Social Media, pp. 1–7. ACM, NY (2009)

Saif, H., He, Y., Alani, H.: Semantic smoothing for twitter sentiment analysis. In: Proceeding of the 10th International Semantic Web Conference (ISWC), Bonn, Germany, October 23–27 2011 (2011). http://dosen.narotama.ac.id/wp-content/uploads/2012/03/Semantic-Smoothing-for-Twitter-Sentiment-Analysis.pdf. Accessed 30 May 2013

Sanoff, H.: Integrating programming, evaluation and participation in design: a theory Z approach. Ashgate, Hants (1992)

Sirgy, M.J.: A quality-of-life theory derived from Maslow's developmental perspective: 'Quality' is related to progressive satisfaction of a hierarchy of needs, lower order and higher. Am. J. Econ. Sociol. **45**(3), 329–342 (1986)

Siu, K.W.M.: The practice of everyday space: The reception of planned open space in Hong Kong. In: Doctoral dissertation, Hong Kong Polytechnic University (2001)

Siu, K.W.M.: Users' creative responses and designers' roles. Des. Issues **19**(2), 64–73 (2003)

Siu, K.W.M.: Guerrilla wars in everyday public spaces: reflections and inspirations for designers. Int. J. Des. **1**(1), 37–56 (2007)

Tse, T.S., Zhang, E.Y.: Analysis of blogs and microblogs: a case study of Chinese bloggers sharing their Hong Kong travel experiences. Asia Pac. J. Tourism Res. **18**(4), 314–329 (2013)

Ulicny, B., Kokar, M.M., Matheus, C.J.: Metrics for monitoring a social-political blogosphere: a Malaysian case study. IEEE Internet Comput. **14**(2), 34–44 (2010)

Wu, Z.Y.: Marketing. Economy & Management Publishing House, Beijing (2001)

Yu, S., Kak, S.: A survey of prediction using social media. arXiv preprint arXiv:1203.1647 (2012)

Author Index

Abdul Aziz Bin Husainan, Lamia I-3
Abdullah, Malak II-191
Achalakul, Tiranee I-71
Aciar, Gabriela II-203
Aciar, Silvana II-203
Afonso, Orlando II-3
Agredo Delgado, Vanessa II-20
Albeaik, Saleh II-357
Aldawood, Salma II-327
Alfaro, Rodrigo II-258, II-295
Alfayez, Aljoharah II-327, II-338
Alghazzawi, Daniyal M. II-406
Alhaidary, Reham I-13
Alhassan, Amal II-32
Alhassan, Sarah II-32
Alhumaisan, Alaa I-22
Alhumoud, Sarah II-215, II-226, II-236
Ali AL-Shehri, Hanan I-3
Alkhalifa, Nada II-367
Allende-Cid, Héctor II-258, II-295
Almahmoud, Jumana II-357
Almalki, Almaha II-357
AlMansour, Nora II-226
Almishari, Sitah II-367
Almuhrij, Alreem II-32
Almuqren, Latifah II-215
Alnasser, Ahad II-236
AlNegheimish, Hadeel II-226
Al-Nufaisi, Muneera II-236
Alomar, Abdullah II-378
Alomar, Noura I-22
Alotaibi, Shahad II-215
Alowisheq, Areeb II-236
Alrajebah, Nora II-236
Alrajhi, Wafa II-32
Alrashed, Najat II-338, II-378
Alrashed, Tarfah II-357
Al-Razgan, Muna I-3
Alrumikhani, Asma II-236
Al-Shamrani, Ghadeer II-236
Alshobaili, Jowharah II-226
Altammami, Shatha I-13
Alturaiki, Isra II-378
Altwaijry, Hotham II-378

AlTwairesh, Nora II-226
Álvarez Rodríguez, Fco. Javier II-110
Al-Wabil, Areej II-338, II-367
Alwan, Maram II-367
Alzammam, Arwa II-215
Anacleto, Junia C. I-289
Aragon, Cecilia II-394
Arroyo, Yoel II-44
Awada, Hachem II-161
Awwad, Zeyad II-338

Baranauskas, M. Cecília C. II-91
Berthelé, Davina I-379
Bhandari, Upasna I-32
Bin Shiha, Rawan II-226
Brachten, Florian I-379
Braman, James II-55
Brooks, Michael II-394
Bueno, Andre O. I-289

Cano, Sandra II-148
Cao, Shiya I-94
Cappelli, Claudia II-125
Caraman Hudea, Oana Simona I-139
Chang, Klarissa I-32
Charoenpit, Saromporn I-71
Chen, Nan-Chen II-394
Clendenon, Kyle I-337
Cockcroft, Sophie I-159
Collazos, César A. I-117, II-20
Coman, Adela I-139
Coto, Mayela II-65
Cristea, Alexandra II-215
Cruz, Lívia A. II-246
Cubillos, Claudio II-295

Dai, Yafei I-274
de O. Melo, Claudia I-103
Donzo, Lusene II-416
dos Reis, Julio Cesar II-91
Duarte, Emanuel Felipe II-91
Dudley, Alfreda I-307, II-55
Duque, Jaime II-148

Fardoun, Habib M.   II-20, II-138, II-161, II-406
Fernández Robin, Cristóbal   II-82
Fietkiewicz, Kaja J.   I-317
Fuentes, Jennifer   II-65

Gallud, Jose A.   II-138
Gonçalves, Fabrício Matheus   II-91
Grigore, Ana-Maria   I-139
Gros, Daniel   I-44
Guzmán, Daniel   I-200
Guzmán Mendoza, José Eder   II-110

Hackenholt, Anna   I-44
Hadzikadic, Mirsad   II-191
Hashimoto, Ko   I-177
Hayashi, Yuki   II-178
Heales, Jon   I-159
Hong, Sungsoo (Ray)   II-394
Huang, Hung-Hsuan   II-178
Huang, Li-Ting   I-58
Hüper, Nick   I-362

Ilhan, Aylin   I-317
Intapong, Ploypailin   I-71
Iwasaki, Sachiko   I-177

Johnson, Davian   I-307
Johnson, Nathan   I-337
Jones, Brian M.   I-337

Kataoka, Shumpei   II-429
Kerr, Cortni   II-338
Kieslinger, Barbara   II-312
Kimura, Seiya   II-178
Knautz, Kathrin   I-44
Kocielnik, Rafal   II-394
Kuwabara, Kazuhiro   II-178

Lacave, María del Carmen   II-44
Lambropoulos, Niki   II-406
Lee, Joon-Suk   II-416
Lei, Tian   I-84
Lima, Afonso M.S.   II-246
Lin, Sanny   II-394
Linde, Claudia   I-350
Lizano, Fulvio   II-65
Loiacono, Eleanor T.   I-94, I-234
Lu, Ming-Yang   I-58

Maciel, Cristiano   II-125
McCoy, Scott   I-94, II-82
Mendes, Marilia S.   II-246
Molina, Ana I.   II-44
Mora, Sonia   II-65
Muñoz Arteaga, Jaime   II-110
Muñoz, Patricia   I-127
Munson, Amanda L.   II-416

Nakamae, Shuta   II-429
Nakano, Yukiko   II-178
Namatame, Takashi   I-177, I-210, I-223, I-244
Nguyen, Hoang D.   II-440

O. Bertholdo, Ana Paula   I-103
Ohkura, Michiko   I-71
Ohta, Naoki   II-178
Okada, Shogo   II-178
Opresnik, Marc Oliver   I-190
Ortega Cantero, Manuel   II-44
Ortega Cordovilla, Manuel   II-44
Otake, Kohei   I-177, I-210, I-223, I-244

Pérez-Vera, Sebastián   II-258
Pinheiro, Alexandre   II-125
Poo, Danny Chiang Choon   II-440
Pu, Yue   II-429

Qu, Zening   II-394
Quiñones, Daniela   I-117, I-127, I-200

Redondo, Miguel A.   II-44
Refaee, Eshrag   II-275
Ren, Huimin   I-234
Rodríguez, Sebastián   II-295
Roncagliolo, Silvana   I-117, I-127, I-200
Rusu, Cristian   I-117, I-127, I-200
Rusu, Virginia Zaraza   I-127
Rusu, Virginica   I-117, I-127, I-200

S. Rozestraten, Artur   I-103
Safa, Nehme   II-20
Saga, Satoshi   II-429
Saijo, Naoya   I-210
Salamah, Nora   II-367
Salgado, Luciana   II-3
Santaolaya Salgado, René   II-110
Sato, Yusuke   I-223

Schäfer, Teresa   II-312
Scheiner, Christian W.   I-362
Schlaus, Mira   I-379
Sebastián, Gabriel   II-138
Shaabi, Maha   II-236
Shah, Purvi   I-234
Shizuki, Buntarou   II-429
Silva, Paloma B.S.   II-246
Siu, Kin Wai Michael   II-451
Smith, Jeff   II-394
Solano, Andrés   II-148
Sotelo, Julián   II-148
Stieglitz, Stefan   I-379
Sun, Han   II-451

Takahashi, Shin   II-429
Takase, Yutaka   II-178
Tang, Can   II-429
Tesoriero, Ricardo   II-138, II-161
Trieu, Van-Hau   I-159

Usami, Syun   I-244

van der Vyver, Abraham G.   I-396
Vasilache, Simona   II-429
Venetopoulou, Chrissoula   I-379
Veutgen, Daniel   I-379
Vincenti, Giovanni   II-55
Viterbo, José   II-3
Voigt, Christian   II-312

Wagner, Timm F.   I-256
Wanner, Brigitta   I-44
Williams, Sarah   II-338

Yáñez, Diego   II-82
Yang, Seungwon   II-416
Yang, Zhi   I-274

Zawadzki, Piotr   I-44
Zhang, Qi   II-178
Zhang, Sijia   I-84
Zhao, Tianjiao   II-451
Zhu, Zhenhui   I-274

Printed in the United States
By Bookmasters